Union Pacific

Union Pacific

The Reconfiguration:
America's Greatest Railroad
from 1969 to the Present

MAURY KLEIN

OXFORD
UNIVERSITY PRESS

OXFORD
UNIVERSITY PRESS

Oxford University Press, Inc., publishes works that further
Oxford University's objective of excellence
in research, scholarship, and education.

Oxford   New York

Auckland   Cape Town   Dar es Salaam   Hong Kong   Karachi
Kuala Lumpur   Madrid   Melbourne   Mexico City   Nairobi
New Delhi   Shanghai   Taipei   Toronto

With offices in

Argentina   Austria   Brazil   Chile   Czech Republic   France   Greece
Guatemala   Hungary   Italy   Japan   Poland   Portugal   Singapore
South Korea   Switzerland   Thailand   Turkey   Ukraine   Vietnam

Published by Oxford University Press, Inc.
198 Madison Avenue, New York, NY 10016

www.oup.com

Oxford is a registered trademark of Oxford University Press

Library of Congress Cataloging-in-Publication Data
Klein, Maury, 1939–
Union Pacific : the reconfiguration / Maury Klein.
p.   cm.
Includes bibliographical references and index.
ISBN 978-0-19-536989-2
1. Union Pacific Railroad Company—History.
2. Railroads—United States—History. I. Title.
TF25.U5K532   2011
385.06′573—dc22
2010027471

1 3 5 7 9 8 6 4 2

Printed in the United States of America
on acid-free paper

This book is dedicated to John C. Kenefick,
the founding father of the modern Union Pacific

CONTENTS

ACKNOWLEDGMENTS

As was the case with my two previous volumes of Union Pacific history, this book was made possible by support from the company. This support went beyond financial to include access to company materials, use of company facilities, visits to company sites such as the Harriman Dispatching Center and Powder River Basin, and the complete cooperation of its employees, past and present, from the presidents on down the ranks. Their input gave me information and insights that would not otherwise been available. For this support and encouragement on so many levels I thank the Union Pacific Railroad.

Histories that have been underwritten by a company tend to be regarded as little more than public relations efforts. Anyone who has read the first two volumes of my Union Pacific history should be convinced that they hardly fit this description. So too with this third volume, which does not hesitate to be critical or frank. As with the previous volumes, the company had no editorial input and made no editorial demands other than desiring a sound and honest history. Only one officer read the manuscript to offer suggestions or corrections. Mike Hemmer, the vice president of law, with whom I have had a long and pleasant association, not only read the chapters but also saw to it that his department did its due diligence without obstructing necessary research. On more than one occasion he pointed me toward and smoothed my path to source materials. For his help, suggestions, and encouragement I am deeply grateful.

One other individual deserves special mention. Brenda Mainwaring, currently the public affairs director for Iowa and Nebraska, shares with Hemmer a passion for and curiosity about the railroad's history, and has supported this project from its very inception. No one did more to bring about its realization. As my primary liaison with the company she fielded every request, answered every inquiry, and remained a staunch and enthusiastic advocate of the work. From our many conversations came both insights and potential leads for information.

If all working relationships were as pleasant and productive as mine has been with Hemmer and Mainwaring, life would be a joy.

The same might be said about the contribution of others as well. At the Union Pacific Museum John Bromley, whom I first met in 1983 on my tour of the Union Pacific System, promptly answered my steady stream of questions and made available the materials housed at the museum, including a complete set of the invaluable company magazine. At company headquarters two individuals, Wayne Huddleston and Jan Fedrizzi, went the extra mile in digging out and bringing to me hundreds of boxes of records stored at the company's off-site facility. The vast majority of these boxes did not have their contents marked or inventoried. Some had vague descriptions; most had none at all. Researching them amounted to a kind of crap shoot that was made easier by Wayne and Jan's willingness to keep bringing them to the headquarters building in quantity. I hope the final product makes their efforts worthwhile. These materials are indicated in the endnotes as coming from Union Pacific Records (UPR).

The book would not have been possible without the contribution of thirty-six individuals who granted me interviews, and in several cases patiently fielded my e-mails seeking more detail or clarification of specific points. They are the strength of this book as they were of the railroad itself, and I thank them for making my work so enjoyable and enlightening. They are listed here in alphabetical order: Merill Bryan, Paul Conley, Dick Davidson, Jerry Davis, John Deasey, Jim Dolan, Dennis Duffy, Charley Eisele, Ike Evans, Jim Evans, Ebby Gerry, John Gray, Dick Grove, Mike Hemmer, Dennis Jacobson, John Jorgensen, John Kenefick, Brad King, Rob Knight, Jack Koraleski, John Marchant, White Matthews, Mary McAuliffe, Joe McCartney, Stan McLaughlin, Dick Peterson, John Rebensdorf, Lou Anne Rinn, Barry Schaefer, Gary Schuster, Art Shoener, Gary Stuart, Carl von Bernuth, Linda Waller, Tom Watts, Beth Whitted, and Jim Young.

Several of these interviewees also contributed materials, documents, maps, and photographs, and cheerfully answered a host of e-mail inquiries on specific issues long after their interview. In particular I want to thank Merill Bryan, Dennis Duffy, Charley Eisele, Dennis Jacobson, John Jorgensen, Jack Koraleski, John Marchant, White Matthews, Stan McLaughlin, John Rebensdorf, Barry Schaefer, Art Shoener, and Jim Young. Rollin D. Bredenberg of BNSF, formerly of SP, provided helpful information on the service crisis era. Cameron Scott introduced me to the North Platte yard complex, and Steve Barkley to the Harriman Dispatching Center. A number of people guided me through the Powder River mines and facilities.

At the University of Rhode Island library Emily Greene, Sandy Sheldon, Mary Anne Sumner, and Eileen Tierney were their usual extremely helpful selves in obtaining needed materials for me. Greg Ames expedited my research at the Mercantile Library in St. Louis, and Matt Hull did a mountain of copying there.

At Oxford University Press my editor, Tim Bent, provided extensive and useful counsel along with his good cheer and encouragement. His assistant editor, Dayne Poshusta, did yeoman service going over the draft of the manuscript and offering suggestions.

My agent, Marian Young, sustained this project, as she has many others, with sage advice and the support of a good friend. Last but hardly least, my wife, Kim, offered not only encouragement but help with a variety of tasks while enduring more hours alone than I care to count. For that I am ever grateful.

Without these people this book could not have been written. For any errors that remain, I alone am responsible.

Maury Klein
Saunderstown, RI

Union Pacific

Introduction

The story of the Union Pacific Railroad since 1969 has been an odyssey through American railroad history. From that journey it emerged as the largest and strongest railroad in the world. It also happened to be one with a storied history deeply woven into the westward movement. As one half of the first transcontinental railroad, the Union Pacific opened the West to settlement and exploitation. The driving of the golden spike to complete the first connection to the West Coast became enshrined as a great national myth, one that symbolized American greatness. In its time it was our first conquest of unknown space.

Railroads developed and dominated American life in the nineteenth century. By routinizing the shipment of goods, materials, and people, they orchestrated the growth of the economy. The locomotive became the symbol of the age, enchanting starry-eyed dreamers and hard-nosed businessmen alike. Its sheer power reflected the restless energy of a people forever on the move. For rural folk the cry of its whistle or clang of its bell evoked images of distant places to which the train might someday carry them. For urban dwellers the train station became the gateway to their city, the hub of its commercial life.

For a century railroads dominated overland transportation. The frenzy of construction and expansion reached its peak in the 1880s, when more than 70,000 miles of new track were laid. The competition spawned by this frenetic growth sent numerous major railroads, including the Union Pacific, into bankruptcy during the depression of 1893–97. From that nadir UP rebounded to become one of the nation's strongest rail systems under the guiding hand of the nation's foremost rail entrepreneur, E. H. Harriman. After his death in 1909 members of his family, along with members of the family of his close associate Robert S. Lovett, dominated the company for most of the twentieth century.

Through war and peace, good times and bad, UP remained a prosperous company even in an industry growing steadily weaker. By 1969 newer forms of transportation—the automobile, truck, airplane—had seized center stage in American life while railroads faded steadily into the background. Americans no longer rode the railroad, and it slipped from their consciousness and became a relic from another age even though it remained a crucial part of the freight transport system.

Nevertheless, while other landmark companies in many industries vanished as their time passed, UP not only endured but increased in size and strength through mergers. Long a prisoner of tradition in a hidebound industry, it reinvented itself between 1969 and 2004, a period during which more changes occurred in railroads than in all their previous history. Of the four major American rail systems today, the UP alone retains its original name and history. It remains a unique company that has left an indelible imprint on American history.

This book tells the story of how UP managed to reconfigure itself in an age of rapid change without losing touch with its roots. Many people feared the railroad industry would be gone by 2000; hardly anyone, including myself, expected to find it a thriving industry still performing vital services to the nation. In a 1975 article I wrote, "The golden age of the locomotive was over. Ahead loomed the challenges of the automobile, the bus, the truck, and the airplane. No longer the dominant form of land transportation, the iron horse faced in the coming years a difficult struggle for survival. Unlike many other historical romances, the ending did not promise to be a happy one."[1]

But the ending has proven far happier than anyone dared hope. The past four decades have witnessed an almost complete restructuring of the railroad industry and its operations. Galvanized by new technologies and techniques, it has regained much of its original vitality and preeminence in the field of transportation. Those who wish to understand this transformation would do well to begin with the story of the Union Pacific.

Prologue

The Celebration

They came again as their forebears had a century earlier to that parched, remote pocket of Utah. The landscape looked much the same—a windswept flatland pocked with sagebrush—but the setting could not have been more different. In the past it could hardly have been reached except by the train just completed. The tracks had long since moved to a new and more efficient location, and the small town that sprang up there soon withered away. In place of the rails came State Highway 83, which accommodated any visitors to the site where history was made.

The place seemed as remote and uninviting for the celebration as it had been for the original ceremony in 1869. Promontory was a mountainous peninsula that jutted like a stubby finger into the north shore of the Great Salt Lake. It housed a narrow valley, perhaps a mile wide, flanked on both sides by rounded humps of mountain still wearing snow in May, its bleak floor broken only by the patches of scruffy sagebrush and pools of water glazed with ice. Yet it was there that American history recorded one of its greatest moments: the joining of rails for the first transcontinental railroad. When the Union Pacific and Central Pacific railroads came together on May 10, 1869, it became possible for Americans to travel from one end of the continent to the other by rail. The distant West Coast had at last been directly connected to the rest of the nation.[1]

From that event, burnished and enhanced by constant retelling down through the decades, evolved the great national myth of the Golden Spike. Symbol of the industrial might that would transform the nation into an economic giant, it was the harbinger of a new era of progress. New lands would be opened for settlement; the mountains would yield their treasure trove of ores, and a pathway would be forged to the Far East with its storehouse of wealth. By far the longest railroad yet built, it promised to thrust the United States to the forefront of a new and exciting world.

The joining of the rails was to that generation of Americans what the landing on the moon became to a later one. They were reaching out toward a larger world, confident of making it smaller through familiarity and conquest. A frontier of immense possibilities had been breached, and over the next century opportunities were realized of a scale and scope that dwarfed the vision even of the most expansive dreamers of an earlier time.

During that century the UP struggled to survive in a world of rapid economic change. Wracked by inept management and tarnished by the Credit Mobilier scandal, it skirted the edge of bankruptcy before Jay Gould took hold of it in 1874 and shored up both its finances and strategic position. After Gould's departure the UP, like other western roads, engaged in perpetual rate and expansion wars with its rivals until the onset of depression sank it into bankruptcy in 1893. For five years it languished in receivership. Then, in 1898, a syndicate that included E. H. Harriman devised a plan that succeeded in reorganizing the road on a new basis.[2]

Over the next decade Harriman transformed the UP into the strongest and most efficient railroad in the West. In the process he pushed the rail industry into a new era with a host of innovations. The most brilliant and imaginative railroad executive of the era, Harriman made the once poor UP a cash cow that paid steady dividends for decades. Although he died in 1909, his legacy endured not only in the standards of efficiency and performance that he demanded but also in the management itself. For the next seventy years his sons and disciples would dominate the company.

While the UP struggled to survive, the Central Pacific became part of the Southern Pacific, which emerged as the largest transportation company in the world. In 1901 Harriman acquired the SP system and reunited the two Pacific roads only to have the Justice Department separate them in 1912. Since then the two roads had engaged in competition that was alternately fierce and friendly. Both companies clung tightly to their heritage as the first transcontinental railroad and were not about to let the centennial pass without a fitting commemoration of the golden spike.

Neither was the federal government or the state of Utah. In 1965 President Lyndon Johnson declared Promontory a National Historic Site. Plans went forward to build a visitors' center at the site where the rails met, complete with replicas of the two locomotives that had met symbolically in 1869, UP No. 119 and Central Pacific's Jupiter. New track would have to be laid for them; the original rails had been taken up in 1942 to provide scrap iron for the war effort. Utah created its own Golden Spike Centennial Commission to plan an extensive program of celebration including a reenactment of the original joining of the rails.[3]

In April 1965 UP's public relations people met to consider what should be done. A laundry list of ideas was drawn up and forwarded to Reginald M. Sutton, the company's chief financial officer. The first important anniversary—the laying of the first rail on July 10, 1865—was coming up in only three months, followed by a succession of centennial celebrations along the route by individual communities, many of which had been created by the coming of the railroad. The grand climax would be a celebration of the Golden Spike ceremony at Promontory on May 10. "Naturally," concluded the memo, "a campaign of such duration and intensity will depend in whole or in part upon a budget or step-by-step authorization of expenditures." The question was raised "as to what extent management wishes to become involved in this program." Management did not leap at the opportunity. Sutton asked the question most pertinent to him: "Are centennials worth the money?"[4]

More than a year later C. R. Rockwell in Salt Lake City reminded his colleagues of the need for action. The federal government had moved ahead with work on the visitors' site and had a superintendent for the project living in Brigham City. "It is almost inevitable that questions will be asked very soon about what UP is planning to do," Rockwell stressed in a memorandum. Rockwell urged the company to approach roads that had held centennial celebrations to pick up new ideas and learn what to avoid. The two old locomotives used by Paramount Pictures for Cecil B. DeMille's classic 1939 film *Union Pacific* were stored in the company's east yard at Los Angeles; they might be restored and fitted out as power for display trains.[5]

Rockwell outlined an ambitious marketing campaign, and nearly all his suggestions were adopted. Letterheads, place mats, napkins, ashtrays, and other memorabilia were adorned with centennial artwork. A leading plastic model-kit company expressed interest in producing a large-scale kit of both No. 119 and the Jupiter. SP agreed to provide enough light rail and ties to build a half mile of track on either side of the meeting point. Artist Howard Fogg was commissioned to do a series of oil paintings showing the development of the original line. A documentary film called *Tracks of the Iron Horse* was produced, and a commemorative medal authorized by President Johnson was struck.[6]

At a ceremony outside the visitor's center the original joining of the rails would be reenacted, using the replica locomotives and costumed actors. It would be performed twice on May 10 and then repeated daily throughout the summer at exactly 1:47 P.M. In collaboration with artists and technicians from the Nebraska State Historical Society, the UP outfitted a museum train to tour its routes the entire summer. It contained displays of artifacts from the company's history, the most curious of which was the scalp of UP telegrapher William Thompson, who lost it to a Cheyenne raiding party in August 1867. Thompson had managed not only to survive but to retrieve his scalp, which later found its way to the Omaha Public Library. The train also featured a fifty-seat theater car to show *Tracks of the Iron Horse* as well as flatcars carrying an old wooden coach, a boxcar, a crane car, and a blacksmith car complete with forge.[7]

Despite some setbacks, the preparations grew more elaborate. Stanford University loaned the original golden spike, a companion silver spike, and a silver maul for the ceremony. Western Union helped create a telegraph connection to reproduce the sending of the original messages nationwide in 1869. Towns, libraries, and historical societies eagerly devised activities and displays for the week leading to the great day.[8]

In March the UP shops began work on the borrowed locomotive to transform it into a replica of No. 119. On April 3 the Centennial Expo museum train began its tour of the Pacific Northwest before heading eastward to its appearance in Ogden on May 9. A week later *Tracks of the Iron Horse* made its debut in Salt Lake City. An exhibit by California artists displayed a hundred paintings dealing chiefly with the building of the Central Pacific. On May 6 and 7 the University of Utah hosted a Golden Spike Railroad Symposium featuring talks by several prominent rail executives.[9]

Everywhere the mood was festive and expansive, especially aboard the special trains created to bring people to the weeklong celebration. Five such trains were created. The High Iron Company underwrote one that left New York on May 3, its vintage 2-8-4 Nickel Plate Berkshire locomotive pulling fourteen cars that included a B&O dome car and a Canadian Pacific scenic car. At Kansas City the steam locomotive gave way to a massive UP Centennial diesel for the trip to Salt Lake City. The SP ran specials from Oakland and Los Angeles to Ogden for the ceremony. UP's train, pulled by its last remaining steam locomotive, No. 8444, made daily excursion trips from Salt Lake City to Ogden every day from May 10 to 14. At Ogden, the nearest railhead to Promontory, everyone boarded buses for the trip to Promontory. The replica locomotives fared no better; they had to be hauled to the site on flatbed trucks—an irony that railroad executives preferred not to contemplate.[10]

A week of special events in Salt Lake City culminated early on the morning of May 10 with the departure of a special train filled with dignitaries. Powered by a UP Centennial diesel, it carried the special guests to Ogden, where the UP and SP had arranged their shiniest and most modern diesels nose to nose in a tribute to the joining of the rails. The mayor presented Edd Bailey of the UP and Ben Biaggini of the SP, as well as Thomas Goodfellow, president of the Association of American Railroads, with keys to the city. Afterward the officials, members of the centennial commission, some eight hundred guests of the railroads, and 350 members of the press boarded a caravan of eighty buses for the ride to Brigham City, where keys to the city were again tendered. Their ranks included Secretary of Transportation John A. Volpe, actor John Wayne, and railroad executives from other lines. A train buff, Wayne had ridden the High Iron special to Salt Lake City, where a special premiere of his new film, *True Grit*, had been shown, and then stayed on for the week's celebration.

The scene awaiting the bus caravan at Promontory was impressive. A crowd of twelve thousand people had made its way to that forlorn stretch of desert and milled around in anticipation of the ceremony. The actors stood in place along with a military band dressed in period uniforms. An elderly telegrapher waited to transmit the original message to a waiting nation. The Mormon Tabernacle Choir was poised to sing its hosannas to the great moment. Some eighty dignitaries climbed onto the platform for the opening of the ceremonies. *"Fantastique!"* murmured French television director Claude Fayard, who scrambled with his light and sound crews to record the event. "I wouldn't have missed it for anything," marveled an executive for Reynolds Metals. "I don't know why every railroader and every railroad supplier didn't come here today." A little boy, who had slipped into the press section while the crowd cheered and waved flags, said with wide eyes, "This is going to be a famous day."

Shortly after noon, beneath a cloudless sky, the band struck up a medley of patriotic airs. They were followed by a local high school band, after which the Mormon Tabernacle Choir raised its voices in song. As part of the ceremony the new visitors' center was dedicated and Promontory officially proclaimed a National Historic Site. Goodfellow stepped forward to give an upbeat and encouraging welcome. "Just because we're old doesn't mean we're through," declared Goodfellow, who stressed the railroads' "intent to meet the challenges of the future." A jet plane streaked overhead as he predicted that "in the future there'll be no railroads, truck lines or airlines as we know them today. All modes of transport will be fully integrated into a transportation system."[11]

Secretary Volpe emphasized the same theme. Earlier he had toured the SP operation in San Francisco and come away impressed by the technology at work. "The use of computers, video tape, microwave links and other sophisticated devices," he declared, "is resulting in genuine 21st century railroading." Rejecting the view that the railroad industry was outmoded, he declared, "I personally view the railroad not as an anachronism, but as a growth industry. I am convinced that it will give birth to even more new ideas, and will transform itself steadily and progressively in response to new technology and new opportunity. So in honoring the pioneers of the past, we also acknowledge the promise of tomorrow."

Then it was time to honor the past. The actors stepped forward to reenact the laying of the last rail in place and the driving of the golden spike. That done, the locomotives were rolled forward to touch noses. Since they had no power, they were pushed by blue-blazered High Iron members. The telegrapher promptly sent the same message to President Richard M. Nixon that had been dispatched a century earlier to President Ulysses S. Grant: "Sir, we have the honor to report the last rail laid and the last spike driven. The Pacific Railroad is finished." Afterward Volpe, Bailey, and Biaggini obliged photographers by driving and redriving the spike. That night commemorative banquets were held in Salt Lake City, Los Angeles, San Francisco, and elsewhere.

All of this served to burnish the myth of the Golden Spike, which remained firmly in place along with a welter of contradictions that surrounded the centennial ceremony no less than they had the original event. In the first volume of this history I described the celebration in 1869 as one "in which the wrong people came to the wrong place for the wrong reason." To some extent the same held true in 1969. Neither President Nixon nor Vice President Spiro Agnew bothered to attend; nor did California governor Ronald Reagan. While national enthusiasm for the railroads' past remained high—the High Iron special included a display car that attracted an estimated 50,000 visitors at every one of its stops—the train itself lost between $35,000 and $45,000. *Trains* magazine castigated the industry for its "soft sell" of the centennial and for bungling a "vast and nonrecurring opportunity to erase a backlog of public indifference or hostility toward the rails."[12]

In particular the industry had failed to get a commemorative stamp, a television special on the reenactment, a spread in *Life* magazine, a railroad fair built around Promontory, or even a reissue of *Union Pacific*. The cardinal error, charged *Trains*, was in choosing "Past as Prologue" as the theme for the celebration: "This obsession of the rails with soft-pedaling the past ignores the demonstrable fact that the one sure hold the industry has upon the public at large is the romance of the past. That public looks to Cape Kennedy for its Space Age news, not to Promontory."[13]

Unquestionably the rail industry had its eye more on the future than on the past, if only because it feared the present. Its executives desperately wanted the public to view the railroads as engines of progress rather than relics of a bygone era. Some of them hammered home this message during the week of events leading to the reenactment. No one was more pointed than John C. Kenefick, vice president of operations for UP. At the University of Utah symposium he delivered a speech entitled "Railroading into Another Century." Kenefick offered his listeners a stunning vision of the railroad of the future. Within two decades, he predicted, freight schedules of 90 miles an hour would be commonplace over a network of strengthened and improved main lines. Trackside signals would give way to cab signals and automatic controls sophisticated enough to handle individual operating units with the engineer serving merely as monitor.[14]

A system of key terminals associated with market areas would organize traffic flow. Computerized waybills would calculate charges and bill shippers automatically. Equipment would undergo radical changes in design. "Motive power will also see the effect of change," Kenefick added. "Because of high speed and control necessary, electrification holds the greatest promise of the future." A second speaker, L. E. Hoyt of the SP, emphasized that "our railroads must be allowed to change, at a faster pace than in the past, into uninhibited transportation companies."[15]

The same theme infused a glossy UP centennial brochure aimed at shippers that announced, "Power, Car Fleet, Technological Advances Demonstrate Dynamic U.P. Service for Second Century." Every picture of equipment, facilities, and yards delivered the same message: "Union Pacific Service Keeps Pace with the Times." The UP was hardly alone in emphasizing this theme. The harsh truth was that in 1969 *all* American railroads faced the same intractable dilemma. For nearly a century they had been by far the biggest business in the nation and pioneers in most key areas of business organization. After 1920, however, they came increasingly to be prisoners of their past. Besieged by new forms of transportation that drained business from them, hamstrung by archaic government regulation and suffocating work rules that left them little room to maneuver, they struggled to adapt to a world in which change had become a way of life and seemed to come ever faster.[16]

That rapidly changing world threatened to relegate railroads to mere anachronisms. They were by far the most complex technology of their era, which made it difficult for them to adjust to change. Every attempt to improve their operation or equipment had to be balanced against the intricacies of their systems. As Steven W. Usselman observed, they increased productivity not through stunning new technologies but "precisely *because* they restricted the realm of technical possibilities and pursued one grand objective with single-minded purpose . . . laying down clear ground rules about operations and shunning innovations that threatened to disrupt those rules."[17]

For generations railroading had been a family affair, an occupation passed proudly from father to sons to grandsons. Tradition governed nearly every aspect of the industry, making it one of the most ingrown—some said hidebound—businesses in the nation. It was not only an occupation but a way of life, one that imposed harsh demands outsiders seldom understood. The hours were long, the work hard and often dangerous. Railroaders lived largely in their own world, resistant and often immune to outside influences. They prized routine because it kept the trains running and simplified their lives. They followed orders because the boss was the boss whether right or wrong. On the job they did what they did in the way they did it because it had always been done that way. And they kept doing it that way, unless told otherwise by the boss, for thirty, forty, or fifty years until they retired and let someone else do it that way.

For more than a century railroaders marched through the same daily rituals in good times and bad, war and peace, summer heat and winter snow, mostly oblivious to the changes occurring around them. Even the alarms seemed familiar enough. The railroads were struggling financially, but they had been there before.

New technologies intruded on their routine but were gradually absorbed after a period of grumbling and discomfort. By the mid-twentieth century, however, the alarms had become too incessant to ignore. New forms of transportation were gouging large portions of the railroads' core traffic. In little over a decade the diesel locomotive rendered extinct not only steam locomotives but the firemen who manned them. The ranks of the railroaders were thinning at a rate never before seen as the overbuilt American rail system tried to trim itself down to a size that could be sustained.

Change was in the wind, more of it than ever before at a faster pace than ever before. In railroading, as in other areas of American life during the late 1960s, the spectacle was one that had been captured so beautifully many years before by the English poet Matthew Arnold: "Wandering between two worlds, one dead, the other powerless to be born." Many people wondered whether the railroads could survive in that emerging world. In that sense the celebration at Promontory, for all its brave rhetoric, did more than honor the joining of the rails. To some ears it sang a requiem to the once dominant place held by the railroad in American life. In this emerging new world, what was the most appropriate ceremony for the railroad industry: a celebration or a wake?[18]

PART ONE

THE KENEFICK ERA, 1970–1985

1

The Industry

A family portrait of the railroad industry in 1969 would have captured a group in distress facing an uncertain future. Many of its members were sickly, and some had already faded into the limbo of mergers and bankruptcy. Once the largest and most powerful sector of the nation's economy, it had been losing health and vitality for half a century. For many decades the railroads had dominated the American economy as well as its financial markets; now they seemed on their way to becoming dinosaurs.

In many ways the railroads had created modern America. During the nineteenth century they opened new areas for settlement, created new markets, and developed old ones. Unlike riverboats they could travel almost anywhere, in a straighter line at faster speeds and in nearly any kind of weather. They ran on regular schedules using equipment that could be tailored to their customers' needs. They fostered the rise of new towns and cities and turned sleepy villages into thriving economic centers. In the process they banished much of the isolation that dominated American life on so vast a continent by bringing the outside world to remote towns.

As the nation's first big business, the railroads became the arteries of the emerging industrial economy. Their construction and operation fed the growth of nascent industries, most notably iron and steel, coal, lumber, heavy machinery, and construction. Railroads also provided the template for organizing large enterprises. The first companies to do business across entire regions, they created new methods of finance, accounting, and organization. As the first industry with a large and scattered labor force, the railroads pioneered in labor relations. As private corporations providing a public service, they became the first industry to experience the complexities of competition and to undergo state and federal regulation. In all these areas the railroads set precedents later followed by giant industrial corporations.[1]

Wall Street sprang to life once a flood of railroad securities energized its activities. European capital poured into New York to underwrite the construction of

American railroads, making it the nation's financial center and capital market. For more than half a century railroad securities dominated the New York Stock Exchange, along with such related industries as the telegraph and express companies. A new breed of professional speculator learned to operate on an unprecedented scale.

During the nineteenth century most American businesses were still run by their owners. Railroad operations required a more sophisticated form of administration for which the only precedent even remotely relevant was that of the military. Army officers understood such things as administrative structure, hierarchical command, internal communication, and staff/line divisions of authority. The Civil War created a large supply of military officers, many of whom later found work in the management of the burgeoning rail network. They became the nation's first corps of professional managers and often had to create systems where none existed as the structure of their companies grew larger and more complex.[2]

These managers devised systems for operations, maintenance, equipment, scheduling, accounting, billing, traffic, repairs, and rates. The railroad industry dwarfed any earlier business in terms of its diversity of functions. No other enterprise approached the complexity of its logistics. A railroad had to orchestrate the flow of goods and people on a preset schedule. In most cases its trains ran in opposite directions on a single track, which required careful planning and execution. A company had to keep track of trains, crews, workers, shipments, and equipment coming and going from its line. Inspections and maintenance had to be performed daily on everything from equipment to track and bridges. Men, equipment, and facilities had to be in the right place at the right time. Large sums of money gathered in many places by many hands had to be accounted for, and payments made to an army of vendors and employees for a wide variety of goods and services.

Systems and new forms of measurement had to be created for keeping track of the flood of paperwork generated by these activities, for figuring out whether the road was making or losing money, and for determining how much it should charge for a given service. Some way had to be found for calculating costs. Reports of all kinds had to be generated, read, and culled for important data on every aspect of the road's operation. Facilities ranging from shops to roundhouses to fueling and water stops had to be kept in order. Railroads even needed a foreign policy to handle relations with connecting and competing roads. To manage these complex matters required a hierarchical structure with clear lines of authority and efficient internal communication.

By the mid-nineteenth century railroads had become the dominant form of transportation in the United States. They held this position unchallenged for another half century, during which time they competed less with other modes of travel than with themselves. From these intramural wars flowed a rapid expansion of the rail system to the point where it became seriously overbuilt. By 1916 the nation boasted 254,251 miles of track—enough to circle the globe ten times. The depression of 1893–97 swept a quarter of American railroad mileage into receivership and hastened the industry's reorganization around large systems. Thus began a trend toward consolidation that gained even greater momentum in the twentieth century.[3]

As the nation's first big business, railroads aroused mixed feelings among the American people. Controversies erupted over nearly every aspect of their operation, particularly over the rates they charged. Railroads were an anomaly, something new under the sun that did not fit existing law and custom. They were private companies offering a public service, which thrust them into the political arena. Their activities crossed state lines and thereby subjected them to mixed jurisdictions. A railroad passing through four states needed a charter from each of those states, and the terms of those charters might vary widely. The conflicts that arose from the peculiar nature of the railroads led to their being regulated first by state governments and then by the federal government.

No issue aroused more vehement debate than the question of how much to charge for transportation. The sheer complexity of the matter compounded the controversy from the beginning. Here, too, the railroad was unlike any other business. Foremost among its characteristics was the fact that it discriminated. Other industries did so as well, but the railroad had more types of discrimination that affected more people in more direct ways. Three distinct forms arose early: geographic, classification, and individual. The first was inherent in the very nature of the railroad, as it is with any form of transportation. The second was a logical response to difficult pricing problems, while the third resulted largely from pressures brought to bear by shippers and the railroad's own fierce scramble for traffic.[4]

These discriminations provoked most of the public wrath against carriers that led to their regulation. This wrath in turn derived largely from confusion over another characteristic of railroads: No one knew how to calculate costs in a manner that made them a meaningful basis for rates. Without a sound cost basis, rate structures evolved from experience, trial and error, and a witches' brew of internal needs and external pressures. They were called tariffs for a good reason; if there was a model for how rates were made, it was the tariff system, where logic took a back seat to expediency, pressure, and self-interest. The result was a common carrier lacking rational means to calculate either its costs or its pricing structure, which made public defense of them lame and unconvincing. By contrast shippers took a marvelously simple approach to these matters. They simply wished to pay as little as possible or what they could afford to pay, whether or not it covered the railroad's costs.

The confusion over rates was further compounded by the emergence of two different rate structures, one based on "local" or noncompetitive traffic, the other on "through" or competitive rates. Railroads enjoyed monopoly power over the first type but were at the mercy of competitive forces in the second type. From this duality arose vast confusion over whether the "railroad question," as it was known in the nineteenth century, was one of monopoly or excess competition. To befuddle matters even more, there was a tendency to lump two very different conditions under the heading of "monopoly." One involved the domination of whole traffic routes by merging systems; the other referred to the domination of a railroad over the captive shippers on its line.

The public attack on railroads denounced monopoly, excessive competition, and all forms of discrimination with equal vehemence. The bitter expansion wars of the 1880s sent rates inexorably downward despite dogged efforts by the carriers to stop the bloodletting through agreements. The public outcry over these battles led to government intervention, first at the state level during the 1870s and then by the federal government, which passed the landmark Interstate Commerce Act of 1887. The first attempt by Washington to regulate an industry, it served as a template for later federal regulation.

From the start the attempt to regulate the railroads bogged down in a welter of conflicting interests and misunderstandings. Foremost among them was the inherent contradiction in the purpose of government regulation. Some viewed federal intervention as a remedy to curb excessive competition; others saw it as a device to prevent monopoly. Thus did the Interstate Commerce Commission (ICC) begin life with several missions that were incompatible with each other. It tried both to prevent monopoly by enforcing competition and to outlaw discrimination. However, any policy designed to preserve competition also perpetuated discrimination. As early as 1870 Charles Francis Adams, president of the UP from 1884 to 1890, got to the heart of the matter. The gist of the whole transportation problem, he observed, was that *"competition and the cheapest possible transportation are wholly incompatible."*[5]

In characteristic fashion Americans wanted both. They harbored a long and deep hatred of monopoly, whether in royal, public, or private hands. The result was a policy gridlock rooted deep in the national culture. The law banned discrimination but hedged its definition of the various forms and how they related to competition. It barred pools but left other forms of collective rate-making in legal limbo. If the object was to stabilize or cartelize the industry, banning the most popular vehicle for carrier collusion seemed an odd way to go about it. Not surprisingly, this remedy proved ineffective. The competitive wars grew steadily worse until the depression after 1893 swallowed many of the major roads in receivership. Once the depression lifted, a new generation of rail giants led by E. H. Harriman caught the rising tide of prosperity by overhauling the railroads into efficient modern systems on a scale never before witnessed.

Clearly a new era in railroad history had dawned. Determined not to repeat past mistakes, these leaders tried to rationalize competition in a variety of ways ranging from private understandings to mergers on a grand scale to interlocking directorates. Ironically, the systems forged by Harriman and others in the 1900s bore a striking resemblance to the railroad map that emerged in the 1970s, but Americans could not let go of the belief that competition in the rail industry was essential. The new systems were denounced as bald attempts at monopoly. The Supreme Court broke up two key mergers, the UP-SP and the Northern Securities Company (Great Northern, Northern Pacific, and Chicago Burlington & Quincy), to restore competition among the roads.

By 1898 the ICC had come to share the views uttered by Adams nearly thirty years earlier. "The benefits supposed to result from railroad competition," observed former chairman Martin Knapp, "I believe to be greatly exaggerated." The agency echoed the complaint of rail executives that competition was wasteful, yet in the next breath it warned against the threat posed by vast rail combinations forming to suppress competition. Its members could not shake free of the contradiction inherent in the belief that both combination and competition were dangerous. While the Supreme Court upheld the banner of competition, the ICC gradually gained new powers from Congress until by 1910 it exerted full control over rates and therefore over much of competition. Between 1903 and 1916 power drained steadily from the railroads to the regulatory agencies.[6]

Then the unexpected happened: American entry into World War I led to government takeover of the railroads. Once responsible for the roads' performance, the government could not help but view their problems in a more sympathetic light. The war's end forced Americans to confront directly the question of what should be done with the carriers. By then the country had undergone a radical shift in mood. The wartime experience had demonstrated advantages in a rail policy emphasizing cooperation under government supervision. From this experience emerged a sharp and fateful reversal of regulatory policy in the form of the Transportation Act of 1920.

Instead of enforcing competition, the new approach sought to create a protected cartel under tight regulation. It allowed pooling of traffic and earnings. Mergers that had been denounced only a few years earlier were now actively encouraged so long as they conformed to a master plan designed to combine strong roads with weak ones. The goal was to create a limited number of systems of equal strength that might compete in healthy ways. As historians Ari and Olive Hoogenboom noted, "Consolidation became the panacea competition had been in the decades surrounding the turn of the century." Machinery was devised to guarantee the roads a minimum return, and the ICC received power to fix minimum rates, decide questions of line extensions and abandonments, and oversee the issuing of new securities. The result was to make railroads the most tightly regulated industry in the nation.[7]

In one stroke national policy reversed itself from unbridled competition to regulated monopoly. Many rail leaders welcomed the new structure of things, if only because they craved stability no less than the public did. With the ICC possessing absolute control over rates, competition among railroads shifted from rates to service. Belatedly rail managers learned that this brand of head butting could be very expensive and wasteful in its own fashion. They were even slower to grasp the unpleasant truth that the Transportation Act of 1920 came a generation too late and was fatally flawed. It decreed in effect that there should be competition without losers.

"A major purpose of the transportation act," declared the ICC in a 1929 decision, was to preserve "substantially the whole transportation system . . . through a union of weak with strong lines" to ensure the survival of all. In effect strong roads would be rewarded for their efficiency by being saddled with weak roads.[8]

It seems not to have occurred to the architects of this policy that strong roads were strong and weak ones weak for reasons that went beyond hard luck or a bad horoscope. If rail managers had learned one lesson from the bitter expansion wars of the 1880s, it was the folly of eliminating unprofitable competitors by absorbing them. Predictably, strong systems resisted the plan until it collapsed in failure after a decade of futile attempts to impose it. However, the act of 1920 contained another poison pill in the form of a provision giving the ICC sweeping authority to approve line extensions and abandonments. It even allowed the commission to compel carriers to construct new mileage in certain circumstances.

No one could have predicted that in the long run the railroads would suffer more grievously from being forced to maintain service (i.e., not abandon mileage) than from being told when and where they could (or must) lay down new track. But history played yet another cruel trick on the carriers. The act of 1920 bound them in a straitjacket of regulation at precisely the time when they fell victim to an onrush of new competition. For seventy years railroads had dominated land transportation because no new forms had risen to challenge them. After 1920, however, several new modes appeared as the automobile, truck, bus, and airplane all utilized the internal combustion engine and new lightweight alloys to gain competitive advantages over the railroad. Within a few years a vicious contest for business among different modes of transport ensued.

Two events symbolized the arrival of this new era of intermodal competition. In the spring of 1936 American Airlines began regular passenger service between

New York and Chicago. It utilized the Douglas DC-3, the first plane large enough to turn a profit carrying only passengers. Within a few years World War II would demonstrate the superiority of aircraft and greatly accelerate their development, all of it underwritten by the government. In October 1938 the Public Works Administration, a New Deal agency, started work on what would prove a landmark highway, the Pennsylvania Turnpike.[9]

The irony could not have been more crushing. Suddenly the ground rules of regulation required a complete overhaul. After enduring largely unchanged for a century, the structure of competition in the transport industry was revolutionized within a decade. Once the Great Depression intensified the scramble for a dwindling traffic, the nation found itself in the grip of yet another transportation crisis. Two broad policy alternatives existed. Congress could loosen the regulatory straitjacket binding railroads, or it could try to fit the other modes with straitjackets of their own.

Some railroads were eager to compete, not only by cutting rates but by diversifying into other forms of transportation. The obstacle was always whether the regulators would permit it. However, the times were all wrong for this strategy. The Depression cast business in an unflattering light, and to many people the proposed transportation companies raised the old specter of monopoly. Moreover, the New Deal administration, grappling with huge problems of deflation and unemployment, showed no interest in forms of competition that threatened to drive rates even lower, incur higher deficits, and ruin more firms.

Coordination and control were the buzzwords of the new era. Some way had to be found for all modes to coexist under federal supervision. After the usual exhaustive public debate, the transportation jumble was rationalized on familiar terms by placing the new modes under regulatory strictures similar to those already in force for the railroads. A series of acts beginning with the Motor Carrier Act of 1935 and culminating with the Reed-Bulwinkle Act in 1948 applied to the new modes the old formula of regulatory cartels that suppressed competition and stabilized rates.

The Transportation Act of 1940 became the cornerstone of this effort. It added a preamble to the Interstate Commerce Act defining the national transportation policy as the "fair and impartial regulation of all modes of transportation . . . to recognize and preserve the inherent advantages of each." The ICC was directed to formulate policies that created a transport system adequate to the needs of commerce, defense, the postal system, and "sound economic conditions" among the carriers. As part of this tall order it had to protect each mode from competition in the form of rate cuts by the others. Where the act of 1920 eliminated intramural rate competition among railroads, the new directive sought to ban it from intermodal competition. The object became not only coordination but perpetuation of services as well.[10]

The problem was that almost nothing in the rail model fit the other types of transport. All railroads were regulated, but private automobiles, most trucks, and 90 percent of inland water carriers were exempt. The harsh truth was that the competitive environment had changed radically in ways that hurt railroads the most. This became painfully clear when the avalanche of traffic from World War II ended. Rail traffic suffered a precipitous fall that was all the more shocking for having occurred during a period of relative prosperity. Trucks swept away most of the high-value freight traffic, airplanes were fast scooping up the long-haul passenger business, and the automobile and bus had long since claimed short-haul passengers. Even long-haul freight, the staple of rail earnings, was being nibbled away on several fronts.

The loss of traffic appalled even cynics. Less-than-carload traffic (LCL) shriveled from 13 million carloads in 1928 to 1.8 million in 1960, nearly all of it claimed by trucks. Raw petroleum moved to pipelines, leaving railroads with less than 1 percent of it in 1960. Livestock dwindled as well; by 1958 only 12 percent of it went by rail. Trucks also muscled into the Florida fresh fruit market, hauling 45 percent of it in 1950 and 72 percent in 1963. Finished manufactured goods shifted to trucks that provided faster service and gentler handling. Trains simply could not compete with the door-to-door service of motor vehicles.[11]

Performance statistics underscored the distress of the industry. Class I railroad cargoes increased from nearly 597 billion ton-miles in 1950 to 780 billion ton-miles in 1969, yet their share of total ton-mileage traffic dropped from 56 percent to 41 percent. Their operating revenues rose from $9.4 billion to $11.7 billion, but their rate of return shrank from an already low 4.3 percent to a mere 2.36 percent. The number of employees declined from 1.2 million to 578,300, but their average hourly wage more than doubled, going from $1.58 to $3.79. The problem was as obvious as the solution was elusive: One of the most capital-intensive industries around, the railroads were not coming even close to earning their cost of capital.[12]

The railroads were bereft not only of money but of ideas as well. They lacked unity and stood ready to ignite a turf war over any major disagreement. Shippers demanded that the carriers be kept under tight regulation, labor fought any action that might result in lost jobs, and states and towns resisted any effort to eliminate service regardless of the losses incurred by the company. The railroads bitterly resented the government's aid to other modes of transport, most notably the building of highways and airports, yet they feared direct aid to themselves because it would give the government an enlarged role in their affairs. While opposing the proposals of others, they had no clear program of their own around which to rally.[13]

New technologies such as the diesel locomotive held great promise for improving the efficiency of railroads but they took time to develop and cost a lot of money, which most rail companies did not have. Mergers offered another possible route to profitability. The Transportation Act of 1940 freed the railroads to plan mergers on their own provided they were consistent with the public interest. Terminals could be combined and duplicate mileage eliminated, reducing the nation's excess track to more manageable dimensions. Nearly everyone agreed that such mergers made sense, but only a few had been put together since 1935. Despite all the rhetoric that infused the Transportation Act of 1920, the railroad map had changed little in thirty years.[14]

Labor stoutly opposed mergers and technological innovation as a threat to jobs. Already a long and bitter fight had been joined over the requirement that diesel locomotives, which had no fires to tend, nonetheless carry firemen as part of their crew. In 1936 the unions negotiated the Washington Agreement in which the railroads guaranteed a ninety-day notification of job termination and a severance package of 60 percent of salary for five years. The act of 1940 contained an amendment that provided workers with 100 percent protection for four years after a merger. Not until 1952 did the ICC reconcile these conflicting terms by enacting the so-called New Orleans Conditions, which gave labor the four years of 100 percent coverage from the date of a merger along with anything more that might accrue under the Washington Agreement. In return the unions agreed not to block a merger by striking after they had said their piece on the issue.[15]

During the 1960s the railroads continued their downward spiral at an accelerating pace. For many roads, especially those with marginal business, the effect of a bad earnings year was cumulative and sometimes fatal. Historian Richard Saunders Jr. has succinctly described the downward cycle after revenue declines:

> The decision is made to temporarily cut back on maintenance. Like a good highway, the railroad will remain sound for a while, but then low spots develop here and there, the result of normal rain wash and pounding trains. Speed over those sections is reduced to, say 40 mph. In railroad lingo that is called a "slow order." Elsewhere, rotted crossties require more slow orders, and the first spots get worse. Speed has to be reduced to 30 or even 20 mph. The productivity of train crews, locomotives, and cars falls because trains are taking too long to complete their journeys and deliver their goods. Labor costs rise. Connecting roads complain. Shippers complain. Shippers begin to divert traffic, and revenue falls further. As revenue falls, the company defers more maintenance, and the trouble spreads. All of a sudden, there is a cataclysmic downward spiral as costs rise, service deteriorates, shippers desert, and revenue plummets.[16]

The eastern roads were in the worst shape, largely because of their shorter hauls and greater dependence on passenger traffic. Railroads had a long history of bankruptcies, but most earlier versions resulted from excessive debt. Once reorganized with a leaner capital structure, they usually stayed solvent unless beset by another national financial or economic crisis. In 1961, however, the New Haven fell into bankruptcy despite a robust national economy—the first railroad to fail since the Great Depression. Six years later the Central Railroad of New Jersey followed suit.[17]

The Midwest also had a surplus of roads for the available traffic. In the golden age of railroads the core systems of the so-called Granger roads—the Burlington, the Chicago & North Western, the Chicago, Rock Island & Pacific, and the Chicago, Milwaukee, St. Paul & Pacific—had spread a spider's web of lines through the territory west of the Mississippi River. Although the overall volume of business continued to grow, the stiff competition for it squeezed these and other Midwestern roads into a deadly game of musical chairs that threatened to eliminate one or more of them.

A growing number of roads had begun to approach what Saunders called the "point of no return . . . when a railroad can no longer hope to restore itself with its own resources." By 1967 the RI had 500 miles of track under slow orders; three years later the figure had swollen to 2,300 miles, 1,800 of it on main lines. Even its troubles paled before the financial difficulties of both the Pennsylvania and New York Central railroads. They had been the crown jewels of the industry; the Pennsylvania boasted of being the "standard railroad" of America and had paid dividends since 1847. Yet both systems were facing insolvency.[18]

Two of the industry's most intractable problems, labor productivity and the passenger malaise, only grew worse during the 1960s. In November 1959 the railroads served notice of their intent to eliminate firemen on diesels. Four years later, after a fierce battle, a federal arbitration board ordered the position of fireman phased out with generous severance packages. Within two years 55 percent of the firemen's posts had been vacated; then the union secured a freeze on any further eliminations, leaving 45 percent of trains still carrying firemen. Some states still had "full crew" laws requiring trains to carry six or even seven members, a crew size that had not been necessary for more than forty years.[19]

Work rules constituted another problem. Operating people still got paid by mileage rather than hours at the rate of a hundred miles equaling a day's pay. The diesel locomotive and other innovations made a mockery of this rate, yet it persisted. In addition, rigid walls separated road work from yard work and hampered the road's ability to expedite shipments to a customer's loading dock. One crew had to do the switching or set-outs inside a yard; then a different crew had to deliver cars to a siding even if it was only a few feet outside the yard. As wages and the cost of benefits increased, the burden of paying workers who did little useful work grew heavier. To the railroad's complaints that it could not afford such waste the unions turned a deaf ear.[20]

The rail industry had its own blind spots, especially when it came to dealing with the federal government. Rail executives complained incessantly about the straitjacket of regulation but seldom offered constructive alternatives or solutions. Instead they continued to adopt an imperious attitude toward outsiders and each other, and to battle over issues large and small. Above all, they dreaded the word that must not be spoken: nationalization. Their worst nightmare was what might happen if major roads sank into bankruptcy and could not be revived through reorganization. If their service was too important to let die, the only options would be to carve them up into pieces for other roads to absorb or have the government take them over. National railroads were a fact of life virtually everywhere else in the world, but to American rail executives the concept was anathema.

During the 1960s the railroad industry faced an inescapable dilemma: It wished to be freed from regulation (or at least much of it), yet it needed the government. Above all, it desperately needed capital, fresh ideas, and executives whose minds were not held prisoner by the past. One such figure emerged in the form of D. William "Bill" Brosnan, who rose to power on the Southern Railway, the largest road in the poorest section of the nation. Brosnan was a tough, autocratic, brutal personality who treated people like dirt and was his own worst enemy. He was also a genius in railroading. No man did more to shove the industry into the twentieth century.[21]

As early as 1946, when he was made chief engineer, Brosnan saw the need to replace men with machines if the railroad was to survive. Few rail executives cared to face this unpleasant truth, and the unions stonewalled it entirely. Once named vice president in 1952, Brosnan confronted the problem head-on. "The Southern is on the rocks," he told his officers bluntly. "We have to replace people, I mean people by the thousands, replace them with machinery and more efficient methods. . . . There is no other way."[22]

Brosnan's rise to vice president of operations coincided with the Southern's outstanding record as innovator. It was the first major road to dieselize fully (1953), and it opened the first automated yard, the John Sevier in Knoxville, two years earlier. New automated yards were installed in Birmingham and Chattanooga; then, in 1957, the grandest of them all, the Inman Yard in Atlanta, opened. It became the "centerpiece and crowning achievement of the automated yard program."[23]

Brosnan saw early that track maintenance was the most crucial and also the most labor-intensive kind of railroad work. He attacked the problem with a slew of innovations. He created and improved a machine known as Gravel Gertie that sucked up ballast, cleaned it, and spewed it back on the track. He devised the

Matissa Tamper, which firmly tamped the ballast automatically, and a machine that could unspike an old crosstie, lay a new one, and spike it in place. Brosnan also conceived the idea of creating pre-assembled, pre-spiked track in sections that could be carried to a site and laid. As early as 1958–59 he pioneered in laying welded rail in mile-long sections.[24]

Two other Brosnan innovations had a profound impact on the national economy as well as the railroad industry. When piggyback service started to become popular, Brosnan saw that existing equipment was inadequate and the system not yet economical. One day he saw a gantry crane that could hoist a trailer or any detachable container and set it on a flatcar. Brosnan saw at once that the crane held the key to the piggyback problem. He designed his own version, a giant four-legged crane that became the source for a universal model manufactured by several companies. It made intermodal shipping cheap and fast enough to give it a clear advantage over through shipping by truck alone.[25]

The second innovation came in the form of Big John, a revolutionary 100-ton-capacity covered hopper car created by Brosnan for hauling grain. Prior to Big John, grain moved in 40-foot boxcars that held only 25 tons of grain, were awkward to load and unload, and leaked badly en route. So efficient was Big John that the Southern cut its grain rates 60 percent, which enabled grain to move to the South cheaply enough to nurture thriving cattle, pork, and chicken industries fed on western food. This lowered the price of these meats and helped make chicken a staple of the American diet.[26]

Brosnan's restless mind knew no bounds. He invented and patented the SPOT car repair system, which brought cars to repair crews instead of sending them to the cars. This innovation cut repair costs by more than half. As early as 1956 he pioneered in microwave communication and then used that knowledge to develop the first hotbox detector. First installed experimentally in 1960, this device simplified and improved one of the most important maintenance tasks: catching an overheated wheel bearing (hotbox) before it caused a wreck. Communications became an interest bordering on obsession with Brosnan. He saw early the value of radio and began installing a microwave system on the Southern in 1956. By 1964 the company had a 19,000-mile microwave network, the largest private system in the United States.[27]

Brosnan's keen interest in communication led him to his next pioneering step. The expensive microwave system could transmit vast amounts of data to Atlanta from hundreds of outlying offices and yards, but some way had to be found to sort and harness this mass of information. The logical answer was computers. In 1956 Brosnan decided to computerize the Southern as fully as existing technology would permit. The idea germinating in his fertile mind was the creation of a central command and control headquarters patterned after the Strategic Air Command model.[28]

The technology for this vision did not yet exist. Computers were only as good as the data fed into them; processing data still relied on punch cards, which required far too many clerks. By 1962 Brosnan was also seeking ways to operate locomotives by remote control. His views on railroading startled his peers. "A railroad is nothing more than an assembly line," he told *Forbes*. ". . . We're just manufacturing transportation, just as GM manufactures cars."[29]

In challenging the conventional wisdom of the industry Brosnan took on fights that other executives had long shirked. The Big John car provoked a war that caught even Brosnan by surprise. Although the forerunner of a whole generation of jumbo cars, at the time it aroused a storm of protest from those unable to compete with it. In 1961 the ICC rewarded Brosnan for his innovation by rejecting his proposed reduction in grain rates, saying it would give the Southern an unfair advantage.[30]

Brosnan was furious. "Of what conceivable advantage is it to our country," he growled, ". . . for railroads to generate low-cost transportation and then have their efforts nullified by government regulation that keeps them from lowering their prices?" He fought the ICC all the way to the Supreme Court, which finally decided in his favor in 1965. Brosnan relished his victory. "We are boring holes," he said, "through mountains of traditional thinking about how rates should be made." In retrospect the fight marked a historic turning point. For the first time the ICC saw its ruling countermanded; later some observers thought it the first step toward its eventual demise.[31]

So too did Brosnan battle the unions, which he despised. His clashes with labor were legendary and often embarrassing to the company. Disgusted with the national bargaining over firemen in diesels, he pulled the Southern out of the negotiations. Since the company was not party to the settlement that followed, Brosnan had to keep firemen on his locomotives. To show his contempt for having to use unneeded workers, Brosnan hired some two hundred elderly black men with no railroad experience to fill the jobs. One of them, a retired Atlanta garbageman, told a reporter that the company just showed him where to sit and where to pee.[32]

At the same time, Brosnan fought to overturn the traditional structure of his own company. "Railroads had almost forgotten that they were in the competitive business of furnishing—and selling—transportation," he said in 1962. "They were lost in a meaningless and nonproductive petrified forest of stereotyped practices of the cuspidor age. Competition from other modes of transportation . . . requires innovation of services, inventiveness of means, and changes in pricing. Some railroads are still slow to make these changes, which all too often are greeted with suspicion or turndown by the ICC."[33]

In particular Brosnan worked to tear down the traditional wall between the operating and traffic departments. On every railroad the attitudes were the same:

Operations dismissed the traffic people as lightweights whose idea of heavy lifting was wining and dining customers. Traffic repaid the compliment by complaining that they worked like hell to get the business that paid everyone's salaries only to have the operating dolts lose or damage it or get it there late. Brosnan brushed these cobwebs aside and forced the two groups to talk to each other, drink with each other, and thrash out mutual problems. The railroad began working with shippers on rates and on the design and acquisition of equipment. In this work he launched a marketing revolution that would not reach fruition for many years.[34]

Amid these fights Brosnan did not hesitate to chide his fellow rail executives for their timidity and lack of foresight. "Unregulated competition is the music we must dance to if we are going to dance at all," he insisted, "and we choose to dance. . . . I think the railroads are a growth industry and we're going to prove it." After the mid-1960s Brosnan's attention to the Southern waned sharply. He retired in 1967 but lived until 1985, long enough to see most of his innovations come to full flower.[35]

Years, sometimes decades, later, nearly every one of Brosnan's innovations became gospel in the new era of railroading. "Bill Brosnan . . . literally dragged the railroad industry kicking and screaming into the Twentieth Century—some fifty odd years late," declared Robert B. Claytor, the chairman and CEO of Norfolk Southern. "If the industry hadn't adopted the Brosnan approach to railroad operations, I think we would now all be part of a nationalized system." At the time only a few rail executives understood the importance of Brosnan's reforms. One of them was Al Perlman of the NYC, who passed these ideas along to his large stable of protégés. One of them, John C. Kenefick, would in turn bring this thinking to the UP.[36]

While Brosnan was unleashing his torrent of change on the industry during the 1950s and 1960s, most railroads were looking in quite another direction. Many still viewed mergers as their road to salvation. Between 1955 and 1966 the ICC received no fewer than fifty merger applications from Class I railroads. Included among them were two combinations of staggering proportions. One proposed to join the two eastern giants, the Pennsylvania and NYC; the other hoped to reunite the western roads separated in the Northern Securities case of 1904, the Northern Pacific, Great Northern, and Burlington.[37]

A rash of combinations followed. In 1957 the Louisville & Nashville absorbed the Nashville, Chattanooga & St. Louis, which it had long controlled. In 1960 the Canadian Pacific merged its three midwestern lines—the Soo Line, Wisconsin Central, and Duluth, South Shore & Atlantic—into the Soo Line, and the Chicago & North Western acquired the Minneapolis & St. Louis. That same year the ICC approved the merger of the Erie Railroad and the Delaware,

Lackawanna & Western into the new Erie Lackawanna, and the Chesapeake & Ohio gained control of the Baltimore & Ohio. The Norfolk & Western finalized plans to acquire the Nickel Plate and leased the Wabash Railroad from the Pennsylvania, which announced plans to acquire the Lehigh Valley. By 1962 nearly all these deals had won approval from the ICC.[38]

Suddenly the railroad map, which had remained stable for decades, seemed on the verge of being redrawn. Western roads could hardly ignore the pattern developing east of the Mississippi River. The Granger roads realized that some of them would not survive and scrambled desperately to find partners. West of the Missouri River the transcontinental roads also viewed the shifting railroad map uneasily. On one hand, they hesitated to disturb long-standing traffic relationships by choosing a partner at the expense of alienating other roads; on the other hand, they feared that sitting still might leave them out in the cold.

Mergers shrank the number of roads, and with them the options for connections. No company, however prosperous, was immune to the possible loss of vital connecting roads or the creation through merger of alternate routes that might redirect traffic away from it. The malaise of the industry in general pushed roads even faster toward mergers as a solution to their financial woes.

Other major roads were also rushing to the altar. The Southern swallowed the Central of Georgia, the Missouri Pacific absorbed the Chicago & Eastern Illinois, the Illinois Central joined with the Gulf, Mobile & Ohio, the Louisville & Nashville gained control of the Monon, the North Western bought the Chicago Great Western, and the Atlantic Coast Line merged with the Seaboard Air Line to form the Seaboard Coast Line. The UP decided to cast its lot with the RI in what became the most prolonged and notorious merger attempt of the era.[39]

Not since the 1880s had the railroad map seemed so fluid or the industry so unsettled. Already the merger mania had created a procession of once proud railroad names and emblems going to their final rest in the corporate graveyard of a larger company. Many more would soon follow. Eastern roads were petitioning to shed their passenger business; so were roads elsewhere, but they did not carry the volume of people that rode the eastern lines. State governments could not stand by and allow this huge mass of riders to be deprived of transportation. They would have to intervene somehow to preserve the trains. The federal government, too, found itself being drawn ever more into the tangled web of the railroad industry's decline. The creation of Penn Central in February 1968 looked at first to be a reprieve from disaster but soon turned into the catalyst for disaster of even greater dimensions. In this unsettled and rapidly changing environment, every railroad had no choice but to rethink its strategy and its place in the industry.

2

The Fat Old Lady

In 1969 the UP was a fine railroad with a proud heritage and a fatter bottom line than most of its rivals. During the years after World War II, Wall Street and the railroad industry alike regarded it as a sleeping giant, rich in assets and slow to maximize its use of them. Some called it a gold-plated railroad; others sneered at it as the fat old lady with a bag of candy that might one day be snatched from her.[1]

During the postwar years the fat old lady got fatter. In 1947 the dividend returned to its pre-Depression level of $10 a share. In ten years, thanks to splits, a holder of UP stock owned ten shares for every original one, had collected $65.75 in dividends per share, and had seen the stock's market value soar about 245 percent. For decades the company had bolstered earnings with nonrail income. Between 1946 and 1960 these activities added nearly $35 million a year to the rail earnings. By 1960 they provided nine times the sum needed to pay all interest charges.

The railroad itself did very well. It owned the longest average haul (588 miles) of any railroad, carried a smaller burden of passenger traffic than most, and served a region that was growing at a phenomenal rate. The UP originated more than 60 percent of its freight tonnage, and nearly 56 percent of its freight traffic terminated on its own line. In 1968 the company earned $639 million gross and $71.7 million net. Of the net $50.1 million came from the railroad, $11.8 million from the natural resources division, $3.5 million from the land division, and $5.5 million from other sources.[2]

By any external measure the UP looked to be a sound, conservative, well-managed operation. In some respects it was exactly that. Compared to most railroads, the UP was doing splendidly; however, compared to its own potential, it had barely scratched the surface of possibilities.

The UP was a linear railroad with a main line that ran from Omaha, Nebraska, to Ogden, Utah, where it handed off traffic to the SP. At both Ogden and Granger,

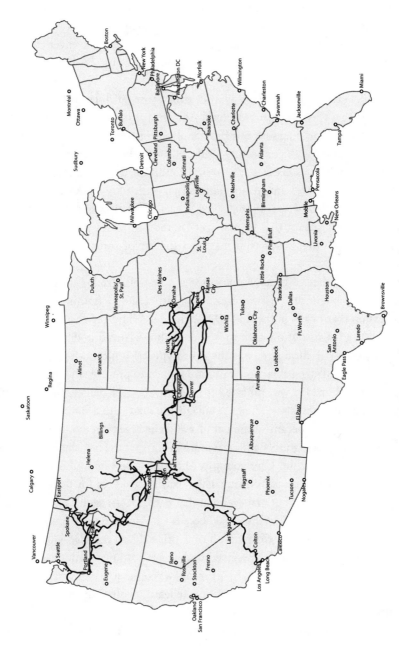

LINEAR RAILROAD. The Union Pacific Railroad in 1969.

Wyoming, it owned lines that ran north to Pocatello, Idaho. From there lines ran north to Butte and West Yellowstone, Montana, and west to Portland, Seattle, and Spokane. Another branch traveled southwest from Ogden through Salt Lake City to Las Vegas, a city created by the railroad, and Los Angeles. Farther east two lines met at Topeka, Kansas, and continued into Kansas City, Kansas. One of these lines went from Laramie, Wyoming, through Denver and Salina, Kansas; the other left the main line at Gibbon, Nebraska. A third branch ran directly from Omaha to Topeka.

This relatively straightforward layout over a vast territory enabled the UP to get the longest possible haul for itself. As a bridge carrier—receiving traffic at one terminus and handing it off at another—it depended on maintaining friendly relations with connecting roads. Historically the company was known to keep its main lines in excellent physical condition, a legacy that traced back to Harriman's influence. Unlike most railroads, it could afford to keep roadway and equipment in peak shape. In that sense it was a first-class operation. However, prosperity also meant that its managers never had to learn the ways of their colleagues on other roads who mastered the art of running their lines on a shoestring.

As a result the UP became notorious as a first-class railroad without a first-class management. Its postwar presidents perpetuated a tradition of mediocre leadership that began in the mid-1930s. George Ashby, the first postwar president, was a bright but misanthropic drunk who departed in disgrace. His successor, Arthur E. Stoddard, was the prototype UP officer who had come up through the ranks, relished his climb, and looked to preserve the traditions that had shaped him. He was followed in 1965 by Edd H. Bailey, the last of the up-through-the-ranks presidents. A tall, affable man with a simple manner and ready smile, Bailey became more popular and effective than Stoddard.[3]

For all his good nature, Bailey was still a product of the old school that always promoted from within. One young yardmaster called him "this god that we spoke to through clouds of dust." Bailey had a weakness for flattery and still embraced the old style of management that used special agents as secret police and planted informants in the ranks. Like his predecessors, he presided over a shadow organization in which an officer's title seldom revealed what he really did or what power he really possessed, and where nothing was done without the president's approval. An old dog set in his ways, he at least managed to learn some new tricks. One lesson he was slow to learn involved the handling of UP's nonrail assets.[4]

The company's nonrail assets traced back to its original land grant, which provided not only an enormous amount of acreage but a host of minerals including coal, oil, trona (soda ash), and uranium. Despite their great value, the railroad could not exploit them directly. The Hepburn Act of 1906 forbade railroads from engaging in any other business. It also prohibited them from carrying any article (except timber and its manufactured products) that was mined, manufactured, or produced by them or in which they had an interest.[5]

A second problem arose from the deepening crisis of American railroads during the 1960s, which led to demands that the government simply take them over. If that occurred, the government would also acquire the nonrail assets belonging to any railroad. Something had to be done to preserve them for the stockholders. In addition, the UP's unusual management structure complicated its handling of nonrail assets. The management team in Omaha operated the railroad, but broader policies and financial decisions were made by executives in New York City, to whom the railroad's president reported. This division of authority had existed from the beginning of the UP.

As a general rule New York gave the Omaha officers free rein to run the railroad but kept tight rein over financial and policy matters. The nonrail assets posed a special problem in that their development remained in the hands of railroad officers who had little skill and less interest in dealing with them. Moreover, Omaha had over the years insulated itself from New York, which had grown ineffective and even timid in dealing with the western headquarters. In many ways the New York office resembled the Land That Time Forgot.

For decades after Harriman's death in 1909 the New York office continued to do things in the same old way and often with the same old people. The company still occupied the same office at 120 Broadway that it did when Harriman presided over it. The furniture was old and worn. When Dick Grove arrived at the office to become assistant secretary, he was given an ancient rolltop desk with the top removed and a large patch of linoleum covering a hole in its back. The boardroom's magnificent wooden table had grown too small for the number of directors. "Would you buy a new board table under those circumstances?" Grove recalled. "No. You buy two cheap tables and face one at each end like a caboose and an engine."[6]

Through depression and wars the office plodded along its well-worn path. Officers grappled with such weighty problems as ice for the office coolers, turning off lights at the day's end, the quality of the towel supply, and Omaha's too profligate use of cipher in telegrams. The same pallid faces hunched over the same well-thumbed files, dutifully adding new sheets to the swollen pile of yellowing documents held together by large adjustable fasteners. "It was not a live-wire office," deadpanned James P. Coughlin, who went to work there in 1949 and ultimately became office manager.[7]

Automation was an unknown word. Each department still did its own payroll and paid people in cash, taking back receipts for every outlay. Even the directors got paid in cash. Everything was done by hand much the same way it had been for half a century. "They were always great on precedent," sighed Coughlin. "If

you did it the way it was done the last time, it has to be right this time." The executive committee members used a separate entrance and dealt only with the officers, who themselves rarely made personal appearances in the general offices.

The office had no receptionist because it seldom got visitors. The lone telephone operator was tucked away in her own cubbyhole. Anyone entering the office was greeted by an elderly black man who had been the chef on Judge Robert S. Lovett's railroad car. Another black employee, Ira Williams, who had started with the company in Harriman's time, toted a gun because his task was to carry bank deposits and securities.

"These guys were kind of at the end of the line," observed John L. Jorgensen, one of the youngsters brought in by Reginald M. Sutton in 1961 to help modernize the payroll process. "I mean, vests, watch fobs, the whole bit, spittoons.... I'm the kid coming in trying to automate all of this, and they were all drunks... go to lunch, knock off a couple of martinis... then the afternoon was shot." Once apprised of the situation, Sutton took charge. "Boy, he just brought down an iron fist," marveled Jorgensen, "and from then on it was an Omaha lunch."[8]

The office was preserved in a time warp because Roland Harriman liked it that way. "It was just a historic museum to [E. H.] Harriman," said Grove. The office was also isolated from the outside world. All communication with the railroad president's office flowed through the chairman of the board; other officers never picked up the phone to talk with their opposite number in Omaha. "There was no [direct] communication between anybody in the office and the western office," confirmed Coughlin. "It was all done either by telegram or by letter.... I never spoke to a person in Omaha."[9]

This striking degree of insularity does much to explain why New York knew so little about what actually went on in Omaha, and why information for New York could be packaged however the president desired. Neither office had learned to use modern communications as a management tool. Nor had they adopted a host of other tools available to them. The company lacked a capital budget, an income budget, or even a cash-flow statement. Capital budgets got made by an ad hoc process in which Omaha proposed and New York disposed. "The company more or less ran itself, you know," observed Coughlin. "There didn't seem to be any big decisions being made here."[10]

As a result, Omaha went its way and New York followed. The system worked only because the company was strong and prosperous enough to survive its internal lethargy. Paying attention and showing up every day on time remained the criteria for keeping a job, and people were very anxious about job security. The people in the Land That Time Forgot creaked dutifully through their rounds, knew their place, and hoped to keep it forever.

The UP was unique in still another respect: For the first seventy years of the twentieth century it had been dominated by two families, the Harrimans and the Lovetts. When Harriman died in 1909, he was succeeded by his close friend and advisor, Judge Robert S. Lovett. The judge also became a surrogate father to the Harriman boys, Averell and Roland, who were the closest of friends with the judge's own son, Robert. Judge Lovett served as chairman of the UP board until his death in 1931 and was succeeded by Averell Harriman. The company remained a family affair with both Roland Harriman and Bob Lovett serving on the board as well. These ties also reflected the close relationship between UP and the private banking firm of Brown Brothers Harriman in which all three men were partners. Another partner at the banking house was Elbridge T. Gerry, who had married one of Harriman's daughters.[11]

Averell managed the UP through the tumultuous years of the Great Depression. During that time he tried valiantly to revitalize the dying passenger traffic through two splashy innovations, the streamliner and the opening of a posh resort at Sun Valley. In 1940 Averell was posted to London as the start of what became a distinguished career in diplomacy and politics; he never again played a significant role in management. That same year Bob Lovett went to Washington as assistant to the secretary of war and was lost to UP for most of the decade. This left Roland to manage the company.

Unlike his brother, who possessed the fierce, unquenchable drive of his father, Roland was quiet and uncombative and preferred the background. Their nicknames told the tale; Roland had always been called "Bunny," while Averell became the "Crocodile." Like a dutiful English cleric, Roland was content with the ancient verities of class and family and never let his ambitions stray beyond them. His character had the sweetness and the simplicity of one who wore his heart on his sleeve. There was nothing self-righteous about him; to everyone he was gracious, accommodating, and forever pleasant.[12]

Roland gave the UP competent and well-meaning but unforceful leadership, which is what enabled Omaha to assert its independence. The soul of tact and discretion, he preferred management by consensus. "Roland Harriman," said Gerry, "was never one to give an order." However, sometimes orders had to be given and feathers ruffled. Roland had his own style of dealing with difficult situations. "He didn't like controversy," said Reginald Sutton, who became the company's controller. ". . . If anybody was getting in trouble, just ease [him] out and don't make an issue of it."[13]

For all his good qualities, Roland was hardly the man to initiate change in a time of turbulence. For that he needed his alter ego, Bob Lovett, the astute, urbane power broker who had gone on to become undersecretary of state, then undersecretary, deputy secretary, and finally secretary of defense. In January 1953 Lovett let Roland know that he was leaving government and could return to the railroad. Four months later Roland made him chairman of the executive committee. Two years earlier Joe Mann, the eastern general counsel, had died and was replaced by Frank E. Barnett of Mann's old firm, Clark, Carr & Ellis. Without realizing it, Roland had put into place the two men who became the architects of change.

Roland and Lovett made a smooth team because they thought so much alike yet complemented each other well. But no one doubted which person mattered most. "Mr. Lovett was the boss," said Barnett, "no question about that." Roland was a man with good common sense and some shrewd insights. "But he didn't ever want to be a person who was running something," observed James H. Evans, who became a director in 1965, "so Lovett was the man who ran it." Barnett considered Lovett to be a genius; Sutton called him "the finest executive that I have ever worked for. He had a way of inspiring you."[14]

Lovett's remarkable self-control served him well at UP, as it had in government, but it also exacted a steep price. A dozen years in Washington had cost him most of his stomach in a series of operations for bleeding ulcers. Although something of a hypochondriac, he bore the ordeal of what he called his "glass insides" with typical good humor. After one operation he told Sutton cheerfully that he was through with hospitals because he had nothing left to take out. When later he had to get a pacemaker installed, Lovett observed that another corner had been turned; the doctors were starting to put stuff back in.[15]

By 1953 Lovett was a tired, unwell man who probably didn't want the chairman's job. But he was only fifty-eight and could not turn down Roland's insistence that he take it. He stayed at the post for fourteen years, investing it with grace and style as well as a genius for grasping the essentials of a problem. "Lovett was a real doer," added Evans, ". . . but always recognizing that in the background we had the Harriman family as the owners and chairman of the Board." The Harriman family owned 6 percent of UP's stock, a large stake; even more, they represented its historical legacy.[16]

Lovett, said Evans, "was our patron saint. Roland maybe should have been, but the guy you went to in the final clutches was Lovett." From his government duties Lovett brought an appreciation for the importance of staff work, a virtue sorely lacking at UP. In 1956 he brought the dean of Columbia's Graduate School of Business onto the UP board. A year later the board was enlarged from fifteen to nineteen. Three of the new directors came from the West; the fourth was Elbridge Gerry, from Brown Brothers Harriman. For another half century the board would always include a member of that firm. These moves signaled the beginning of much deeper changes.[17]

In November 1958 a brokerage firm concluded its analysis of the UP by observing that "a greater separation of [its] natural resources from the railroad operations, looking towards their commercialization to a far greater degree than now exists, would be a desirable objective for Union Pacific stockholders."[18]

Lovett had long since come to that conclusion. "Our problem," he explained, "was to get out of the iron maiden that we were in . . . the past construction of the law which prohibited a railroad from doing anything other than operating a railroad." The iron maiden took many forms, including both federal and state statutes. The Mineral Leasing Act barred the railroad from holding coal leases on the federal lands checkerboarded with its own land grant. The commodities clause of the Hepburn Act prevented the railroad from developing its own natural resources; the UP could not engage in any business in which it hauled the commodity produced. As a result, the railroad found itself in the position of owning valuable assets that could not be developed.[19]

One solution was to create a holding company that spun off the nonrail assets into separate firms outside the reach of the ICC. Sometime around 1959 Lovett penned a memorandum that became the blueprint for what followed. "It took a little persuading," Lovett conceded in his gracious way, "because of course everybody has a slightly different approach to things." Once Roland came around, no one else's opinion mattered; the executive committee was never even involved until the final plan was presented for approval. In 1960 the process of reorganizing the company got under way.[20]

The first step was to find the right people to execute the plan. An obvious choice was Barnett, one of the brightest corporate lawyers around. He shared Lovett's view of the UP as a prosperous railroad in a failing industry. Lovett also needed a good finance man. In July 1960 he brought in as controller Reg Sutton, the vice president and general auditor in Omaha. An affable, energetic man with a homespun manner, Sutton imported several people from Omaha to reinvigorate the New York office. He had started his own career at UP in 1915 as an office boy and managed to climb through the ranks without becoming fossilized like so many others.[21]

When Sutton arrived at 120 Broadway in July, he and Barnett were told they had six months to devise a plan for separating out the nonrail assets. "When people talk about splitting up companies in terms of function," observed Barnett, "they normally think about creating a corporation. That is a lot of BS because it doesn't do any good to create a new corporation if you don't have anybody to run it. And we didn't have anybody to run it or run different divisions at that time. So I suggested to Messrs. Lovett and Harriman that we create divisions, get the divisions started, and then go to the corporate reorganization."[22]

The result was a reorganization around three divisions: transportation, natural resources, and land. The key provision called for the head of each division to report directly to New York, not Omaha. "There was a lot of yelling and screaming from Omaha," admitted Gerry. "It didn't do them any good. . . . When they ceased to report to Stoddard and began to report to Lovett in New York, well, that's when things began to move." The new plan went into effect on January 1, 1961.[23]

Creation of the divisions marked a major step forward, but they were merely a halfway house. Lovett and Barnett envisioned a four-stage process: create the divisions, find managers for them, convert the divisions into corporations, and fold them into a holding company. By 1962 the way seemed clear to proceed to stage three. Unfortunately, unexpected pitfalls and detours delayed the process for seven years.[24]

In April 1962 President John F. Kennedy gave a speech calling for far-reaching changes in the "chaotic patchwork of inconsistent and often obsolete legislation and regulation" affecting transportation. No one knew what this meant, but given the fragile state of the railroad industry, many feared it might lead to nationalization. Other railroads besides UP were moving to protect their nonrail assets in separate companies, and the growing merger mania, coupled with the specter of bankruptcies, threatened the most drastic overhaul of American railroads in history.[25]

Aware that a bridge road like UP, however prosperous, could not afford to sit idle, Lovett and Barnett decided to reverse its most historic policy and acquire lines east of the Missouri River. The problem was how to pursue both a merger and the formation of a holding company at the same time. The latter required a new capital structure that would complicate any tender offer for another railroad. A merger would confuse matters by intertwining its capital structure needs with those of the holding company.

Under Barnett's scheme a new holding company would own the railroad, natural resources, and land subsidiaries, while the merged road would be owned by the railroad. Going beyond the Missouri River was necessary, he argued, because truck and plane competition kept speeding up schedules, and connecting roads with poor earnings could not keep their track in good enough condition to meet these faster times. As a bridge carrier the UP could not control its schedules beyond its own lines. Every physical improvement only put it another step ahead of its connector lines. The company had always envied the ability of the Atchison, Topeka & Santa Fe to control its own line from Chicago to California, which allowed it to introduce new schedules without regard to what competitors thought or connections would permit.[26]

Two other issues pushed the UP toward a change of policy. Since 1923 the courts had required the SP to solicit a maximum amount of freight traffic for the Ogden gateway, the historic junction between the Central Pacific and the UP. In September 1960, however, an ICC examiner recommended that this stipulation be dropped. The commission rejected his recommendation, but the Rio Grande took it to court, and the outcome remained uncertain. Eliminating the provision could have a devastating effect on the flow of traffic through the Ogden gateway.

The transcontinental division cases posed an even greater threat. In 1953 some eastern and Midwestern roads asked the ICC for a larger share of the rates on transcontinental traffic. These requests launched a fight that dragged on for fifteen years. If granted, the gains would come at the expense of western roads, including the UP, which derived 57 percent of its freight revenues from this traffic.[27]

For all these reasons Lovett set in motion the search for a suitable partner east of the Missouri River. A study done by vice president of traffic J. R. McAnally in Omaha confirmed that the best partner for UP would be one that reached Chicago and also went from Kansas City to St. Louis. The RI fit this profile. Its capital structure promised a cheaper, less complicated takeover than most other roads. Although in poor physical shape, the RI offered the best access to the vital Chicago and St. Louis gateways. In March 1962 the decision was made to go after the RI.[28]

Thus began UP's quest to make its first major acquisition since 1901, when Harriman bought the SP. The experience bore an uncanny resemblance to the Vietnam War. The company's best and brightest minds plunged into an intensive effort to make the right decision in the right way based on mountains of data and endless hours of discussion. Despite all the expertise it could muster, however, the company found itself bogged down in a morass that outlasted even the Vietnam War and was no less filled with perils, pitfalls, and well-intended decisions that backfired. The story of that tortuous journey has been told in the previous volume of this history.[29]

By 1969, the year of the centennial celebration, UP had already spent a decade—10 percent of its entire history—on the RI merger with the end nowhere in sight. The ordeal had become a meat grinder chewing up company resources badly needed elsewhere. "Our practically total energies . . . [were] on this thing and the hearings," lamented Reg Sutton. Meanwhile, the holding company concept languished in limbo. In July 1966 Bailey objected to the divisions being independent and urged that they be placed back under his direction. Lovett rebuffed this attempt with a reminder that the ultimate objective was a holding company, and that "any backward step" was to be avoided until that goal was reached. Bailey retreated, but only to await another day.[30]

By the mid-1960s Lovett and Barnett were painfully aware that UP had to modernize both its organization and management techniques, but where to get the managers? The ranks were barren in both New York and Omaha. Lovett and Harriman were nearing retirement; Barnett was younger, but his health was questionable. The board had some capable members, but their average age was in the sixties and some were doddering. None of the division heads impressed Lovett as being aggressive, imaginative leaders. As a first step two new directors were recruited. James H. Evans, president of the Seamen's Bank, and William D. Grant, head of a Kansas City insurance firm, became—at forty-five and forty-eight respectively—the spearhead of a youth movement. Barnett told them frankly that they were there to lower the average age of the board.[31]

Lee Osborne of the natural resources division lacked vision but showed some capacity for growth. The head of the land division, John W. Godfrey, "was a pretty good go-getter," said Sutton wryly. "He got us into quite a lot of things that later we didn't like very much." Lovett and Sutton pressed them both and Bailey for real capital budgets instead of the traditional wish lists. Early in 1966 A. O. Mercer, the general auditor, introduced responsibility accounting, or Management Cost Control, as UP called it. Unlike the ICC-mandated accounting system, this approach allowed the railroad to pinpoint responsibility for expenditures and make useful budget projections. The Pennsylvania and CNW already used the system with excellent results.[32]

One key to improved performance lay in finding and keeping good officers. The old system of promoting from within rewarded endurance rather than talent and often amounted to a process of attrition. Its value diminished steadily as railroads grew more dependent on new technologies that made traditional experience more an obstacle than an asset. In 1965 UP began developing formal systems for recruiting new talent from outside and identifying promising officers within the ranks.

Bailey polled his fellow rail presidents and found that here, as elsewhere, the UP lagged well behind its neighbors. The SF had been sponsoring a six-week course at the University of Southern California for its managers since 1952, and also sent promising officers to programs at Harvard, Columbia, Northwestern, and MIT. Bailey remained skeptical about sending managers to school. "During our busy season," he wrote Lovett, "the absence of Operating and Traffic officers for a protracted period of time from four to six weeks would not seem to be in the best interests of the Company." Lovett thought otherwise, and within a year college recruitment and management training programs were well along in their development. A tuition aid program for all employees with at least two years' experience went into effect in September 1967, and the following April Omaha sent its first student to the Program for Management Development at the Harvard Business School.

However, it would take years to develop a new generation of managers, and the UP was running out of time. Lovett retired at the end of 1966; as a favor to Roland he remained a director and consultant. The committee of directors appointed to choose his successor quickly discovered that the only suitable inside candidate was Barnett, who still divided his time between UP and Clark, Carr & Ellis. Harriman and Lovett asked him to take the job full-time. Mentioning the image of UP as the fat old lady with a bag of candy, Barnett said, "This to me is a very exciting assignment. I'll be glad to take it on one condition . . . that you two men back me up when I kick the old lady in the ass." Lovett and Roland agreed to do it.[33]

Barnett became chairman of the executive committee, and Sutton was promoted to vice president of finance. Their elevation revealed how thin the ranks were behind them. "Until we could get competent people in there," said Gerry, "Barnett was the whole thing." By 1967 two different forces were converging to spur the recruitment of fresh executive talent. First, someone was needed to back up Barnett if anything happened to him. "Frank was a diabetic," said Evans. ". . . He was supposed to never drink alcoholic beverages . . . but he did." The second was Barnett's desire to push ahead with the long-delayed holding company, which required able managers to head the new corporations. To help design the new organization he hired the Cambridge Research Institute (CRI) as consultants; to find new talent he enlisted the headhunting firm of Ward Howell.[34]

The relationship with CRI proved crucial to Barnett's modernization efforts. In July 1967 Barnett met with its two key principles, Professor Edmund P. Learned and Gerald A. Simon. "I have so many problems, I don't know where to begin," he told them. He needed fresh blood at both the corporate and division levels, especially at the railroad. In particular he thought the railroad needed more college graduates. Later, Lovett emphasized the need to improve the railroad's marketing operation. Bailey agreed that marketing was the chief problem in his organization.[35]

That fall the Cambridge team invaded Omaha, asking questions and conducting interviews until Bailey and his officers began to feel like the last dinosaurs. They were right to worry. Barnett wanted CRI to redefine every department in all three divisions along with the job descriptions of its top managers. His goal was to create a thoroughly modern organization capable of handling diversified activities with maximum efficiency. For this he needed a new breed of officers attuned to modern techniques and management tools.[36]

The traffic department underwent an intense examination. Privately a CRI team member reported that the department had a plethora of problems. It lacked profit orientation. "All they talk about," he reported, "is carloads and revenue. Return on investment appears to be a foreign concept to them." They had no grasp of customer needs or how service could be tailored to those needs. They ignored reports and other data generated for their use. "As a result," he added, "the solicitors seek carloads and revenue with little or no conception of the profitability of the traffic." They made no attempt to use forecasts as a tool to motivate the sales force or measure its performance.[37]

CRI found five basic flaws that needed correction. The railroad had not adapted to a rapidly changing external environment. It still relied on "the tradition of an operation-oriented philosophy ... in an age when a much stronger marketing orientation is required." It lacked long-range economic and policy planning as well as "rigorous organizational planning." For promotion it still relied on seniority to the exclusion of other factors. CRI also noted the presence of racial unrest in Omaha and pointed out that UP headquarters did not have a single black person in any position of authority.[38]

Armed with the CRI findings, Barnett presented Bailey with an agenda of changes to create systems that supported profit-oriented management decisions not only at the railroad but in the other divisions and New York as well. He wanted a seminar program to train railroad personnel to make full use of the new marketing information system being developed. Conceding that traffic personnel were paid lower than their counterparts in other industries, Barnett wanted to redefine job descriptions, salary levels, and evaluation methods. Finally, he wanted an outside review of the railroad's advertising to see whether it reflected changes being made within the company.[39]

Bailey tried to respond positively to the list. In a memo dated the same day as Barnett's, he chided his officers, in words taken directly from Barnett, that "in our reporting system we need to be more concerned with profit than with volume," and complained that "we have too many of certain types of reports and not enough of others." To rectify that problem, he reconstituted the Marketing Information System Steering Committee with fresh members. But he balked at changing the name from traffic to marketing.[40]

More generally Bailey took exception to "the academic approach to railroad traffic functions" because it "largely ignores or discounts the fact that we are a regulated industry, especially in the areas of rates and charges." He urged Barnett to "retain and preserve those elements which have been effective in the past while we are developing experience with newer techniques which are as yet unproven in railroad application." He complained, too, about an organizational chart proposed by CRI in which "the theoreticians are placed in charge of the practical people, who have performed so well for Union Pacific through the years, and [which] could only result in a demoralizing effect on the latter." To that end he strongly urged that J. R. McAnally, the current vice president of traffic, be promoted to senior vice president.[41]

Simon tactfully incorporated Bailey's suggestions into the agenda of a meeting on May 17 to thrash out the marketing issues. In setting up the seminar for UP personnel, Simon reminded Bailey that "the essence of this marketing mission lies in *identifying and solving shippers' transportation problems at a profit to the Railroad.*" By the spring of 1968 CRI had also produced job descriptions for several new positions on the railroad. Recruiting began for an executive vice president, vice presidents of finance and marketing, and a director of advertising and public relations.[42]

Although CRI developed a list of six candidates for executive vice president, Barnett knew exactly who he wanted. John C. Kenefick was a protégé of Al Perlman. Kenefick had begun his railroad career with UP in 1947 but left after five years. In the spring of 1968 he was vice president of transportation at the newly merged Penn Central; Barnett invited him to lunch and offered him the same position at UP. Leaving the Penn Central for UP was for Kenefick an easy choice. The merger had made painfully obvious the wide disparity in styles between the NYC and the Pennsylvania. "The Pennsylvania was shit," Kenefick said bluntly. "They were just totally different from us in style and everything else."[43]

Lunch told the tale in Kenefick's mind. The NYC had a dining room at the Biltmore for officers, who simply came over alone or in groups and ordered off a simple menu. The Pennsylvania had a private catered dining room on the top floor of its building. The officers gathered outside the door and waited until 12:45, at which point the senior officer present led the others into the room. Everyone sat down and stayed seated until the senior officer got up and left. Kenefick also thought the blueblood Pennsylvania resented Perlman for being Jewish. As for himself, he was asked by his opposite number on the Pennsylvania, "Is it true there are a lot of Catholics in the New York Central?" Kenefick eyed him quizzically and replied, "Well, not too many of us."[44]

Kenefick also found a difference in work ethic. On the NYC he and other officers were constantly out on the line in their business cars. "We spent more nights on the business car month after month than we did at home because we shuttled around," he said. "Pennsylvania, they used business cars, it seemed to me, primarily to go to New York for the theater or a dinner." Convinced that the NYC style was not going to survive the merger, Kenefick had no hesitation in accepting Barnett's offer.[45]

Even before their meeting Barnett called Perlman and told him he was having lunch with Kenefick. "Al," he said, "unless it would be embarrassing to you or there is some reason that the timing is wrong, I'm going to offer him a job today." Barnett remembered that "he went silent on the telephone, which is extraordinary for Al Perlman. He's usually yak, yak, yak." When Perlman regained his voice, he said, "If I were ten years younger I'd be down in your office trying to beat him out of a job." Brushing aside the CRI plan, Barnett made Kenefick the vice president of operations.[46]

Bailey watched uneasily at what he deemed a concerted effort to shrink his base of power. Although Kenefick had once worked for the UP, the old guard still considered him an outsider. "I was the bastard calf," Kenefick recalled with a smile. "I think Bailey would have loved it if I had suddenly got hit by a car or something." That May Bailey warned that bringing in another outsider as vice president of marketing would "create a pattern and result in an extremely serious morale problem affecting all departments." When he submitted a list of inside candidates to fill the new post, Barnett let him have his way for the moment.[47]

New York had leadership issues as well. Roland planned to retire once the holding company was in place, which meant a new chairman of the board would be needed. Barnett decided to take the position himself and also serve as CEO of the new corporation. As both Harriman and Lovett reminded him, he desperately needed a second in command. Barnett recruited Jim Evans, who had been on the board since 1965, to be president of the holding company and vice chairman of the board.[48]

Evans's special task was to find able people to staff the new corporation. This prospect troubled Roland, the keeper of the grail of tradition in New York. "I don't want a palace guard," he insisted. To fill his old position as chairman of the executive committee, Barnett chose Elbridge Gerry. "Absolutely the last thing I thought of," Gerry admitted, but he agreed to do it.[49]

With Sutton also nearing retirement, a vice president of finance was also needed. A friend at General Electric pointed Evans toward Bill Cook, who had left GE after fourteen years to go to the Pennsylvania Railroad in 1962. After the Penn Central merger Cook stayed on as vice president and controller for only two months before taking a job with Ebasco Industries. Sutton knew Cook from his Pennsylvania days and agreed that he was the right man. By April 1969 Cook had agreed to terms, and Sutton moved up to executive vice president. Two other GE and Penn Central alumni, Ed Hill and Bruce J. Relyea, joined Cook at UP. When a few other GE refugees also came to the company, a bemused Gerry thought that "the place looked like we were a subsidiary of General Electric for awhile."[50]

Earlier, in September 1968, Barnett had recruited another key player by luring William J. McDonald from Clark, Carr & Ellis to be chief counsel for the new company. A bright, demanding, scrupulously honest lawyer, McDonald was also difficult to work with. Nevertheless, Barnett liked him and enjoyed talking cases with him. The addition of McDonald gave Barnett what he considered a capable team. A few years later, Gerry recalled, Barnett "liked to look around the room at some of these guys and say, 'All my boys.' He is pretty near right."[51]

By the fall of 1968 Barnett had enough of his boys in place to proceed with the holding company. In November he informed the heads of the three divisions that the time had come to create that entity. It was, he said, merely an "extension of the reorganization plan announced by Mr. Harriman in 1960." Management's commitment to the railroad would in no way be diminished; the object was more flexibility to develop its resources and take advantage of other growth opportunities. However, Barnett stressed that under the reorganization "the headquarters in New York will be expanded and will assume a greater overall leadership."[52]

Barnett also emphasized that "we do not expect to become a conglomerate corporation that invests in a wide-ranging group of unrelated industries. Rather, we intend to grow *from* our present base." In the future all divisions and subsidiaries would have to compete for capital, manpower, and other assets, which would be allocated by the holding company. The main criteria would be the best return on investment in relation to risk. The principal theme of the new organization, he added, was "central direction and control from the General Office in New York, combined with top-quality general management direction and control at the operating level of divisions or subsidiary corporations."[53]

True to his word, Barnett pushed the project forward. On January 30, 1969, five months before the centennial celebration, the new Union Pacific Corporation (UPC) was born through an exchange of stock with the railroad's holders. "The new company," said Barnett in the press release, "will better enable us to meet the challenge of . . . changing circumstances, eliminating as it does the restriction on diversification imposed on an interstate carrier by rail."[54]

The transition did not come easily. The ICC frowned on the new enterprise. That summer it issued a policy report declaring that "the conglomerate restructuring of the railroad industry could pose a threat to the public's interest in an adequate rail transportation system and complicate the Commission's regulatory and enforcement problems." The RI case complicated and delayed the process. Since the UPC was created through an exchange of stock with the railroad's stockholders, its stock had to be used in working out an exchange ratio of stock between the UP and the RI. Obviously the company did not want to include the nonrail assets in the exchange; the problem was how to shield them for the UP's own stockholders. It took until 1971 to complete these legal and financial maneuvers, and even longer to sort out and secure new titles for the landholdings.[55]

The management did not wait for the outcome of these events before bringing the new corporation to life. In 1970 it abandoned the historic offices at 120 Broadway and took over two floors of an imposing glass skyscraper at 345 Park Avenue. The change could not have been more symbolic: The UP was moving uptown in every sense.

3

The New Approach

It was one thing to create a new company, quite another to chart its course. The corporate office in New York had to devise new lines of authority and systems for itself as well as for the former divisions that became separate entities. Staffs had to be put in place, policies formulated, procedures outlined, and acquisitions sought for the nonrail companies.

While the UPC put itself together, the disarray within the industry was fast reaching a crisis point. The RI merger dragged on with no end in sight, leaving western and midwestern railroads in limbo about possible mergers. Then, in June 1970, the floundering Penn Central collapsed into bankruptcy. The largest failure in American business history, it sent shock waves through the industry and Washington alike. Suddenly the future of rail transport in an entire section of the country was in doubt. No longer could Congress ignore the plight of the railroads.

In November 1970 *Business Week* published a report advocating a drastic overhaul of the transportation sector. It began by announcing that "the common carrier principle, backbone of the regulated transportation system, is a wreck." Under that principle transportation companies were required to carry people and goods at published fares on set schedules. They also had to serve both profitable and unprofitable areas on the principle that high-profit markets would subsidize losses elsewhere. In recent years, however, the principle had caused major financial damage to airlines, trucks, and especially railroads. A rising tide of inflation aggravated the problem.[1]

Immediate action was needed because the eastern railroads were on the verge of implosion. The Jersey Central was already in bankruptcy. The Boston & Maine went down six weeks before the Penn Central, the Lehigh Valley in July, and the Reading in November 1971. Major roads elsewhere, most notably the RI and the Milwaukee, also teetered on the edge of collapse. Salvaging rail service in the East would likely require some form of government aid. The fear of nationalization hung like a sword over the railroads' heads. Apart from the United States, only Canada still had one major privately owned rail system. Every other major industrial state owned and subsidized its railroads.

By 1972 thirteen railroads besides UP responded to the threat of nationalization by forming holding companies. Some were content to preserve assets they already owned; others became conglomerates by acquiring entirely different businesses. Suspicions arose that some rail executives were diversifying not only to protect nonrail assets but to get out of the railroad business altogether. Barnett took pains to reject this charge. "The railroad industry, in fact, is one of the great growth industries in the country today," he said ". . . Costs are what are going to determine the ball game." The UP had plenty of room for growth, he added. "Our present plant is only about 60% utilized now. . . . You have all sorts of things which you can do on a railroad which . . . will produce a 15% or 20% return."[2]

What the railroads needed, Barnett insisted, was for the government to relax its regulatory stranglehold on them. "All we are permitted is to furnish rail transportation," he stressed. "There is no legal reason why United Airlines could not come in tomorrow and acquire control of the UP. And yet we are not allowed to participate in any ownership in the air industry, not even an air freight business. These rules *have* to work both ways."[3]

Gradually Barnett emerged as the industry's most forceful voice against nationalization or even partial government ownership. In 1971 he had the company prepare and publish a booklet showing how the railroads of all other industrialized countries were nationalized, ran at a loss, and survived only through heavy government subsidies. The privately owned American lines and the CP were the only ones whose income exceeded expenses.[4]

Barnett did not object to the federal government involving itself in one aspect of the industry. For most of the postwar era, the railroads had struggled to divest themselves of the unprofitable passenger business. The passenger train died a slow, agonizing death during the 1960s as railroads cut service to the bone and tried to get rid of it entirely. Relief finally came in 1970 when Congress passed the Rail Passenger Service Act, creating the public corporation that became known as Amtrak. When the new company started operation in 1971, the railroads bid farewell to the business.[5]

Another turning point in railroad history had been reached. The transfer of passenger business to Amtrak removed the railroads from the consciousness of most Americans, who no longer experienced them except at a grade crossing or from a distance. For all practical purposes they became an invisible industry except to their own people and shippers. Amtrak did not include the busy commuter lines in the Northeast. The collapse of Penn Central and other lines forced the states of New York, Connecticut, New Jersey, and Massachusetts to take over this vital service with their own transit authorities.

Meanwhile, the national debate continued over what to do with the failed northeastern railroads. Nearly everyone agreed on what the key problems were. The American rail system had receded from its peak of 259,000 miles in 1916 to 207,000 miles in 1970, but far too much unprofitable mileage remained. The railroads also had a surplus of workers operating under outmoded work rules. Both problems were politically explosive. Abandoning unprofitable routes meant depriving innumerable small towns and shippers of their railroad, while getting rid of unproductive labor meant eliminating jobs. The long-running fight over firemen demonstrated the difficulty of attempting reforms, and the northeastern crisis led many rail unions to view nationalization as their best hope.

In February 1972 the Penn Central trustees, still struggling to find a way out of bankruptcy, issued a stunning reorganization plan that called for discarding no less than half its mileage and 12.5 percent, or 9,800, of its workers. After a year of floundering, the presiding judge in March 1973 ordered the trustees to come up with a workable reorganization plan by June 30; otherwise, he would order the railroad liquidated on July 2. Liquidation meant that the vast Penn Central system would be broken up and sold piecemeal to whoever made the best offer. With the clock ticking, an intense debate developed over what should be done.[6]

Into the breach stepped Barnett, who recognized that the UP delivered 27 percent of its business to Eastern Territory roads. Together with chief counsel Bill McDonald, Barnett crafted a plan that became the basis for the Regional Rail Reorganization Act of 1973. Montana representative Dick Shoup agreed to sponsor the bill even though it came from the largest corporation in his district, saying, "I don't give a damn who wrote it if it will work."

The act went into effect January 2, 1974, and created a federal corporation later called the United States Railway Association (USRA) empowered to issue loans and loan guarantees to railroads from public funds without being subject to the national debt ceiling. Once in full operation, it would form a new railroad out of the Penn Central debris that would eventually be privatized. The new railroad would be called the Consolidated Rail Corporation, or Conrail. The act set aside $1.5 billion to rehabilitate and modernize its facilities and brought labor on board with generous payout provisions. For his role in its creation Barnett was named Man of the Year by *Modern Railroads*.[7]

Like most compromises, the 3R Act pleased no one entirely, but it bought time and offered a concrete plan for unraveling the northeastern tangle. Still, the drawn-out ordeal left many executives and observers alike apprehensive about the industry's future. Amid this uncertainty Barnett charted a careful course. The oil business received special attention during the UPC's first year of 1969. Early in September Barnett closed a deal with the Celanese Corporation to buy the Champlin Oil Company and the Pontiac Refining Corporation for $240 million.

"Wall Street at that time said, gee you really paid through the nose for Champlin," Barnett snorted. "The hell I did."[8]

Prior to the acquisition UP owned oil and fields and a pipeline, Calnev, but no other facilities. The new companies added another 30,000 barrels daily to its production in nine states and three Canadian provinces. They provided refining capacity of 91,000 barrels, and Champlin owned 1,400 service stations in twelve midwestern states. For the first time UP could compete in the oil business from the field to the gas pump. It formed a Canadian subsidiary to partner in exploration leases on the Alaskan North Slope. At the same time, the natural resources division joined with other oil companies to explore for oil southeast of Denver and across the entire seven million acres of the UP land grant. The division's scientists also discovered commercial-grade uranium in the Powder River Basin of Wyoming. Upland, the new land company, bought large parcels along the line and unveiled an ambitious development program that included a hotel in Las Vegas, residential subdivisions, and a commercial center in Portland, Oregon.[9]

To help pay for the oil exploration, Barnett employed a clever device. The UP had bond ratings of AAA on its equipment trusts and AA on its bonds. To get funds for drilling at the cheapest possible rate, the railroad paid cash for its locomotives, then borrowed money on them under equipment trusts and loaned it to the oil subsidiary. Each subsidiary kept its own books and paid its own bills as well as its share of the corporation's income tax. The corporation served as bank and auditor, and any subsidiary borrowing from another one had to pay interest on the loan. This new arrangement enabled the corporation to use the railroad's excellent credit to funnel developmental funds to the other divisions. It marked the beginning of the railroad's role as cash cow for the UPC.[10]

Gradually the relationship of the corporation to its subsidiaries took shape. Pontiac Refining was merged into Champlin, which became the core oil company. Originally the corporation had two mining subsidiaries: Rocky Mountain Energy, which handled coal, and the Union Pacific Mining Corporation, which took care of trona, uranium, and other minerals. In 1974 Barnett merged the Mining Corporation into Rocky Mountain Energy to put all mining activity under one roof. Lovett's vision had at last been realized. UPC served as a hub for four distinct enterprises: the railroad, Champlin Oil, Rocky Mountain Energy, and Upland. All of them were related directly to the railroad and its historical assets.[11]

Barnett had what he wanted, and wanted to add nothing else to the mix. Shortly after the corporation was formed he emphasized two points: "First, you will not find us buying a department store. . . . We will not enter any fields that will compete with our large shippers. Second, our diversification doesn't in any way imply a lesser commitment to the transportation business." His goal was to develop the synergies among the four subsidiaries and also to put the nonrail businesses on the same plane of profitability as the railroad. At one of the first board meetings of UPC Barnett observed that the railroad produced about two-thirds of the corporation's net income. His goal was to have the railroad produce no more than half of its net.[12]

Everyone got the point. The railroad was carrying the load for the corporation, and no one knew how long this would continue given the uncertainties surrounding the industry. It was imperative that the nonrail assets be developed as rapidly as possible. "They were serious about this, and as far as I know in quite a proper way," recalled Kenefick. "They didn't want all their eggs in one basket."[13]

One uncertainty continued to dangle like a loose thread. On December 3, 1974, the ICC finally approved the RI merger subject to a host of conditions, including the sale of the RI's Tucumcari line to the SP. However, the railroad world had changed radically in the eleven years since the original offer. The UP needed time to study the three-hundred-page report, reconsider the exchange terms, and decide whether the merger still made sense. More litigation might ensue, which meant that "neither the ultimate resolution of this matter nor the effective date can be forecast." By 1974 that phrase had become a mantra in UP annual reports.[14]

To outward eyes the fat old lady was doing just fine, and her bag of candy seemed to be growing ever larger. In May 1969 *Modern Railroads* paid homage to the railroad's centennial with an extended profile of what it called "The Modern Union Pacific." It described the road in glowing terms and concluded that "Union Pacific is probably today's nearest equivalent of the true 'super-railroad.'"[15]

Since 1964 the company had invested $750 million for new equipment, including twenty-five new 6,600-horsepower Centennial diesels, the largest ever built. Its fleet was one of the youngest in the industry. It budgeted $70 million to $75 million a year to maintain and upgrade track as well as straighten curves. Automatic block signals governed 3,348 miles of the line, and Centralized Train Control (CTC) took charge of 2,188 miles. Although several modern machines were employed along the line for track maintenance, the UP still utilized section gangs to inspect the track and keep it in good shape. "We are convinced that we get a higher quality of track inspection and maintenance with these small stationary gangs," said chief engineer Bob Brown.[16]

The giant new $12.5 million Bailey Yard at North Platte opened in the fall of 1968 to supplement an older yard built twenty years earlier. Together they provided modern, fast blocking for both the UP and other roads. Computers classified and controlled cars at the hump yards, prompting Kenefick to observe, "We're a wholesale railroad." Freight trains ran at speeds as high as 70 miles per hour on the main line. No stretch of track was more important to UP than that between North Platte and Granger, Wyoming; it boasted the highest density of freight traffic of any western railroad, about twenty trains a day in each direction.[17]

To move the trains faster, the company eliminated short stretches of twisting track, cut back station sheds at Cheyenne to let freights use the main line, and installed a modern fueling station at Rawlins. Experimental radio-controlled diesels were put in the middle of trains, increasing top speed by 5 percent and allowing brakes to be set and released seven times faster. Better utilization of both cars and locomotives was pursued on several fronts. "A 5 percent improvement in utilization," observed Jack Bowen, the general superintendent of transportation, "would be equivalent to over 3000 cars representing $50 million to $60 million in investment."[18]

Computerization and microwave communication lay at the core of the UP's modernization. Two men, Glenn R. Van Eaton and C. Otis Jett, ushered the company's communication system into the modern era from its roots in the telegraph, telephone, and teleprinter. During the 1960s Jett installed a microwave system to supplement the two-way radios in diesel switch engines despite the qualms of engineers. "When radio first came on," said former public relations director E. C. Shafer, "I think they had to pay three bucks to have every engineer just use the radio in the cab. Today you can't get a crew out if their radio doesn't work."[19]

The communications system did more than send voices. Its ability to transmit data revolutionized the way railroads did all kinds of things. The industry had always been buried in paper, and forever grappled with handling huge flows of information on everything from car movements to billing to inventories to payrolls. During the 1950s the computer made its debut, and Bill Brosnan was already showing how useful it could be to railroads. For UP the pivotal moment came in 1954 when Art Stoddard joined Otis Jett on the elevator and asked, "Mr. Jett, what's a computer? I hear that we could use one profitably."

While pushing the development of communications, Sutton also worked to bring the newfangled computer to the company. Behind his owlish appearance and folksy demeanor lay a shrewd mind that recognized what the new machines could do for the railroad. Sutton created the Electronic Data Processing Machines Committee (EDPM), a six-person group. From it flowed much of the progress that followed.[20]

Gradually the needs of several departments converged. Jett wanted faster data transmission with greater capacity, Sutton wanted to automate the payroll, and others hoped to do the same for the yards and store supplies. In 1954 the first machines went into yard offices at Council Bluffs, North Platte, and Cheyenne. The yard people expressed their feelings by not showing up for work the first day the new system was to operate. Superintendents also fought them. One at Kansas

City insisted he could eliminate thirteen jobs without the computers. The machines were promptly removed. Next day the superintendent requested ten new people; a week later he asked sheepishly that the computers be returned. "All of a sudden," Sutton observed, "they discovered what we'd been trying to tell them in the first place."[21]

A major breakthrough came in 1958 when UP leased a new IBM Type 705 computer. Sutton went to Stoddard with the request, saying he'd need twenty-three men to train. Years later Sutton shook his head at the memory. "I didn't know about all my marbles either," he admitted. "... From then on it was just one great expansion. It wasn't too long after that we had 400 people working."[22]

A monster machine powered by vacuum tubes, the 705 forced the company to build a five-story addition to the Omaha headquarters to provide the rigid temperature, humidity, and dust controls needed. In 1962 the 705 gave way to the IBM 7080, which was bigger and faster and ran on solid-state transistors. As Sutton hoped, these first- and second-generation machines performed accounting functions for payroll, revenue, and inventory control.[23]

John Jorgensen typified a new breed coming to the railroad. He had started college at the University of Nebraska and in 1955 began working for the UP during summer vacation. One day a man came around with aptitude tests to see whether anyone had the talent to learn programming for the new computers. Jorgensen did well on the test and a few months later was one of thirty employees invited to attend a thirty-day class. He left college after only one year to work for the railroad.[24]

Jorgensen did well enough to become the second manager of the computer center in 1964 at the age of twenty-eight. He found himself present at the creation of an ongoing cycle of upgrade and expanding functions. But change did not come easy to a company encrusted with tradition. No one yet grasped the impact computers would have on the railroad. Jorgensen and the others who passed the tests were put on temporary assignments. "I was on a temporary job for ten years," he said, "because ... they thought we were just going to program this computer, do accounting, payroll, inventory control, and go back to our other jobs."[25]

But the computer proved to have a more enduring life. It was like nothing they had experienced before. Dennis Jacobson got his first taste of computers after he entered the management training program in 1975. The first time he visited a site with a regional computer he walked into the room, admired the big machine in front of him, and told the technician how impressive it looked. The technician smiled and told him it was the air-conditioning unit. He pointed to a much less impressive box that was the computer.[26]

A new generation of computers arrived in the mid-1960s with the IBM 360, which made it possible to devise systems for online interactive processing using the microwave communication network. The 360 series was used to implement the new Complete Operating Information (COIN) system. Its creation took two years of relentless work and another addition to the office building to provide the right climate-controlled setting. By 1975 the UP was installing the rail industry's first interactive graphics design system for producing, storing, and retrieving engineering drawings.[27]

Other railroads were struggling up the same hill in different ways. The SP hired 150 IBM people and a consulting firm to create its Total Operations Processing System (TOPS). It proved to be expensive, cumbersome, and faulty in its data reporting, but it became a useful prototype. The UP management decided to develop its own system based on IBM's QTAM software.[28]

Prior to 1967 the computers handled a dozen or so operations that consisted mostly of historical information. "Railroad officers need to know about events *as they occur*," explained a rail official. ". . . Real-time reporting is what the operating men need." To make that happen, a group was formed in October 1965 to develop COIN. In January 1967 the first interim phase of COIN went into operation utilizing an IBM 1460 computer linking the general superintendent of transportation in Omaha with traffic department officers in San Francisco and Los Angeles.[29]

COIN marked a bold venture into interactive communication. UP had long used its punch-card system to transmit advance train consists from yard to yard. Under COIN the consists moved first through the Omaha computer center on their way to the next yard. The COIN computer also received other car movement data, such as car receipt and delivery, load origins, and the placing of cars on repair, industry, shop, hold, and cleaning tracks. In August 1968 conversion of yard offices to the final COIN procedures got under way. By the year's end all yards had been converted and the final COIN file went into full use.[30]

Teams of programmers, themselves recruited from the company's clerical force through an arrangement with the unions, went to the yards to monitor the system in operation. As the installation gained momentum, the number of programmers increased. Success of the system depended entirely on two key factors: accuracy of data input and prompt reporting of it. On October 30, 1969, Bailey announced that the first phase of COIN was fully operational. "We've stepped into the 21st century overnight," he proclaimed.[31]

The "temporary" jobs had become more permanent than anyone dared imagine. On April 1, 1969, the company established the new department of management information services (MIS) with Jorgensen as director. Within months its electronic data processing (EDP) division had a workforce of fifty running an average of three hundred projects every day seven days a week. Another eighty-six programmers and analysts, recruited from the company's rapidly shrinking clerical force, toiled at designing, writing, and updating the programs requested by other departments. From this work emerged a huge and growing library of some fifteen thousand computer-tape reels that had to be kept clean and well organized. One sign of the growing importance of the MIS operation came when it was the first department to move into the new $5.5 million addition to the headquarters building on Dodge Street.[32]

The computers led to the creation of another new department, FLOCON, an acronym for "flow control." Using data provided by COIN, the system made decisions on the handling of empty freight cars. Its inventory also supplied traffic officers and shippers with information on car location and movement. The computers supplied waybill data on any desired car as well as its last move. "With this improved system of movement and tracking," said C. H. May, FLOCON's director, "the 19-day turnaround we have on each car should be reduced. If it can be reduced by 24 hours, that is equivalent to adding 3000 cars to our fleet." Another new department, operation control, pulled data to help it distribute locomotives more efficiently. In 1976 Jorgensen achieved an impressive first by linking COIN to the SP's TOPS system. It was the first time the computers of two different railroads talked to each other.[33]

By 1969 the communication network had also expanded dramatically. UP boasted a microwave network totaling 3,400 miles. It also had 4,574 miles of open-wire pole lines along with a VHF radio system and a telephone system on which any phone could dial directly any station on the line. The VHF system supported four thousand mobile phones through two hundred base stations; they were installed in every locomotive and caboose as well as hyrail and business cars.[34]

In 1969 the UP looked to be a pillar of strength in an industry that was fast crumbling. Where other roads struggled to master the art of survival in lean circumstances, the fat old lady relished her superiority with a smug satisfaction that to many rivals smacked of arrogance. Few observers realized that she had had her own struggles of a very different kind. The veneer of modernization did not extend deeply into her inner workings.

Despite its progressive rhetoric, the Omaha management, especially operations, remained a stronghold of the old militaristic hierarchy that had dominated its executives and officers since the advent of Bill Jeffers in the 1930s. Even under Bailey things had not changed that much. "If he was going through town in a business car . . . in the middle of the night," recalled Jorgensen, "and he wasn't even going to stop at a major terminal, a division superintendent, the general manager, all the top officers had to be standing on the platform when that train went by with their hats on."[35]

For all UP's accomplishments and technological advances, the old railroad with its crabbed ways and closed minds still lived in many of its corners. In July 1970 Frank Barnett received a summary report from CRI detailing what had been accomplished during the past three years and what remained to be done. It proved an eye-opener in many respects.[36]

The chief task, emphasized CRI, was for the railroad to build an organization that would allow it to adapt to the new conditions it faced. To that end it was essential that "the thinking of the New York Headquarters be allowed to permeate the Transportation Division organization to a greater extent than is now permitted." Tradition still inhibited efforts at control, planning, and personnel change on the railroad. Its departments "still tend too much to be individual fiefdoms pursuing their own ends." Planning still amounted to little more than a form of budgeting. The traffic department still focused on promoting volume instead of serving customer needs and still ignored the concept of tailoring services to individual customers. It also refused to adopt new budgeting techniques such as the responsibility accounting system.[37]

Changes in the social environment had compelled businesses to pay more attention to problems in that area. "The Union Pacific Railroad has its share of social problems," CRI noted, "but practically no one in authority is worrying about them." These problems ranged from physical plant security to minority hiring and advancement, pollution, and safety issues. All these issues, CRI concluded, boiled down to one fundamental shortcoming: a crisis of management at the top.[38]

Barnett had already come to this last conclusion. He also recognized that the management's relationship to New York had to be redefined. That could only be done by bringing in someone from outside the railroad's own cloistered culture. He hoped fervently that John Kenefick was the right man to meet the formidable challenge that awaited him in Omaha.

Few railroad executives offered a more varied and puzzling résumé than John C. Kenefick. Born in 1921, a native of Buffalo, he went to Princeton at the insistence of his father, who had never gone to college. While there he majored in mechanical engineering because he thought he might go into railroading. Two days after his graduation in 1943 he began officer training in the navy. After earning a commission he went to a sub-chaser submarine warfare school in Miami and then to a destroyer escort plying the waters between New York and Ireland. "Miserable as hell going across the Atlantic in a destroyer escort in the wintertime," he said. "It rolled thirty degrees." But it also gave him ten days off in New York every five weeks.[39]

Later Kenefick was made chief engineer on a transport in the Pacific. His ship went to Ulithi, Guam, and other islands as they were secured, hauling troops and their gear, delivering mail and other supplies. After three years Kenefick left the navy and went home to Buffalo. His father had died during the war, and he told his mother of his intention to go into railroading. He got a job at the NYC as an apprentice in the mechanical department but quit after a year and headed west to seek work. "I was single, I didn't have anything else to do," he said later. On the train west he decided on a whim to try UP first. "I didn't know much about any of the railroads," he admitted. "... I wanted to go into railroading but other than that I didn't know how to go about it."

In Omaha Kenefick walked into the office of Perry J. Lynch, the vice president of operations, and asked for a job. He got a place in the mechanical department but quit and became a brakeman to "figure out how the hell trains run." A few months later Perry Lynch asked why he had quit his first post. "Well," Kenefick replied, "maybe I can learn a little more about the business." Two weeks later Lynch promoted him to assistant trainmaster at Topeka.

Kenefick spent five years with the UP, then left in 1952 to work for the Rio Grande, then headed by Al Perlman, who had rescued it from bankruptcy. Perlman was fast becoming a legendary figure in railroading, a maverick with unconventional ideas and a managerial style that attracted talented underlings and gave them free rein to show their stuff. His mane of white hair crowned a head with stunning blue eyes that twinkled when he was pleased and bored in mercilessly when angered.[40]

Perlman demanded the best from his people and usually got it. He was hard to please, yet men loved working for him because they knew exactly where they stood. He believed in a culture of competence and, unlike other railroad executives, actually fired incompetents rather than move them to another position. Before retiring in 1976 he would salvage two more railroads from the edge of failure, the ill-fated NYC and the Western Pacific. In the process he tutored an entire generation of future railroad leaders. Given the quality of its officers from the top down, Kenefick could not have come to a better place than the Rio Grande to learn railroading and show what he could do.

"They were more professional than the UP was," Kenefick thought. "... They were running things, and UP was just keep ahead of the boss as best you could." Perlman liked his boys to get experience with track work, so Kenefick found himself put on an extra gang as assistant foreman. The superintendent was Gus Aydelott, who later became president of the road. When part of a double track washed out and a work train was struggling to go around, Aydelott put Kenefick in charge of getting food and other supplies for the work train. Kenefick came up with what he later called a "scathingly brilliant idea." Instead of hauling meals from a nearby beanery, he ordered a load of groceries and had the conductor, who was a good cook, prepare meals on the caboose so the crews could rotate and eat on the spot.[41]

An impressed Aydelott promoted him to roadmaster and trainmaster at Steamboat Springs. Phippsburg was the terminal, and every day it received a full-sized train of coal cars hauled by a four-unit diesel. It sat there all day and was loaded with coal at night for the return trip to Denver. The grade west of Phippsburg was so stiff that locals required two crews, one to push and another to pull. To avoid using the extra crew, Kenefick "borrowed" the four-unit diesel sitting at Phippsburg. The dispatchers went ballistic when they found out what he had done. Kenefick soon received a visit from the general manager, K. L. Moriarty, who came out to Kenefick's house, chatted a bit, then said, "I understand you're swiping locomotives."

"Not really," replied Kenefick, "but it saves a crew."

Nothing more was said. Three weeks later Kenefick was promoted to assistant superintendent at Alamosa, where he again called attention to himself by converting some flatcars to carry other loads without any authority to do so. "Moriarty loved it," Kenefick said. ". . . He just loved that we took a chance and did something that worked out." Kenefick was promoted again, this time to Salt Lake City. Once a day the Rio Grande had to run a train from Ogden down to Salt Lake City with cargoes that didn't go all the way to Grand Junction. Kenefick hatched another idea. If he had a crossover, he could put the local cars on the through train, stop at the crossover, cut the engine off, remove the local cars, and put the engine back on—all in fifteen minutes. But where to get a crossover?

Since the advent of ICC bookkeeping in 1920, railroads had been divided into evaluation sections. It was important that the book value of each section match its actual assets. Unmoved by this need, Kenefick located a rarely used crossover in Salt Lake City. Without authority he had it pulled up and installed on the main line. Halfway through the work Moriarty showed up and asked what was going on. Kenefick explained the situation and added that, "what I told the chief engineer, I said that we had been looking over the property and it seemed that the crossover on the map here was really over here, and if they didn't believe it, they could come out and look."

Moriarty gave him a flicker of a smile. "Try to remember," he said, "that you're not on a narrow gauge still."

Years later Kenefick still treasured this memory. "It was a pleasure to work with a guy like that," he said. "He loved it when we cut through the red tape." He became good friends with Moriarty and considered him one of the best operating men he had ever known. One night he sat with Moriarty and his wife discussing a Provo trainmaster who was pleasant but ineffective. Mrs. Moriarty listened quietly, then said suddenly, "I've known that young man since he was a baby, and he's one of the nicest young men I've ever known." Then she turned to Kenefick and said sweetly, "But I always say to my husband, K. L., you can't switch boxcars with bullshit." It was a maxim that stuck with Kenefick all his life.

In 1954 Perlman went to the NYC. Although he promised not to take the Rio Grande's best people, several key officers found their way to New York. One of them was Moriarty, whose promising career flamed out in a haze of alcohol.

Another was Kenefick, who rose steadily through the ranks to become vice president of operations in 1966.[42]

His education continued at the NYC, where Perlman was introducing massive changes and had decided to build new yards at Buffalo and Elkhart. Kenefick
was sent to Buffalo to help with the work. In the middle of the operation Perlman
showed up with his good friend Bill Brosnan, who knew a thing or two about
designing yards. He saw that Buffalo was laid out poorly but too far along to be
corrected. However, work at Elkhart had only just begun.[43]

At a meeting Brosnan put up a large drawing to show the flaws in the Elkhart
design, but NYC's officers resisted his suggestions. Undecided, Perlman sent
Kenefick to look over the Southern's yards. He spent a week touring three iden-
tical yards. "I had never seen anything work like that did before," he recalled.
"They had figured every angle, how to make them move fast and how to do it
cheap. Well, it was quite a show. And this was all Brosnan."

The show impressed itself deeply on Kenefick. Asked to build a new yard at
Indianapolis, he told the engineers to start with a map of the Southern yard. "If
you can show me how you can improve on it," he added, "let me know." The yard
became a duplicate of the Southern model, as did the NYC's big new Selkirk
Yard near Albany. Still later its influence would be found in two UP yards, including the huge west yard at North Platte. In these projects and others, Kenefick
carried the legacies of both Brosnan and Perlman in his professional DNA.

By the time Kenefick moved to UP as VPO he was widely regarded as one of
the top operating men in the nation. No one doubted that Barnett intended for
Kenefick to succeed Bailey when the latter turned sixty-five in September 1969.
The board mollified Bailey by extending his contract for one year, but circumstances forced Barnett's hand in the summer of 1970 when Kenefick was
offered the presidency of the bankrupt Penn Central. "You don't turn down the
presidency of the biggest railroad in the world very lightly," Kenefick said later.
Barnett realized that; the problem was how to keep Kenefick until Bailey's term
expired.[44]

Ever the good lawyer, Barnett found a solution in the bylaws he had drafted
for UPC. Under their provisions power flowed not to the president but to the
position of CEO of transportation, just as in the other divisions. In August 1970
he induced Kenefick to remain with UP by giving him this position and with it
the real power over the railroad. Bailey kept the title of president until September 1971 but little else. "When we got back here that night," Kenefick said of this
move, "Bailey didn't have the authority to fire his secretary."[45]

Barnett handled the transition with a masterful touch. He genuinely liked
Bailey and had no desire to wound his feelings. Having already extended Bailey's
contract one year, he added another year with a salary increase from $110,000 to
$125,000, or $25,000 more than Kenefick made. Bailey was allowed to stay on

the board of the Association of American Railroads (AAR) for another year, and on the boards of UP and its subsidiaries through 1975 if he wished. In September 1971 Kenefick helped arrange a gala retirement party for Bailey in Omaha.[46]

A fitting tribute to a loyal company man, it came not a moment too soon. Three months later the *Wall Street Journal* broke the story of what became known as the "Edd and Tedd" scandal. The affair involved favoritism in land deals and kickbacks from suppliers shown by Bailey toward his son-in-law, Tedd Richardson, who denied all charges in unconvincing fashion. The land he bought in North Platte from the UP, he claimed, was low and wet. However, eleven months later he unloaded it for ten times the purchase price. The UP conducted its own investigation and, although the evidence was damning, the board's audit committee reported in July 1972 that it found nothing amiss with this or other transactions. The scandal tarnished Bailey's name even though his role never became clear.[47]

John Deasey, who assisted in the internal investigation, concluded that Richardson was the culprit. "Edd Bailey didn't have a thing to do with it," he said, "except poor judgment and accommodating his son-in-law. . . . I never for one moment had any reason to question Edd Bailey's integrity . . . but it caused us a lot of embarrassment."[48]

The "Edd and Tedd" scandal provided a sad coda to the end of the old regime on the UP. Bailey was the last of the dinosaurs—managers who were neither incompetent nor dishonest but simply products of another era. To Barnett and Evans, he was as much about the past as Kenefick was about the future. With his departure Kenefick became, as he liked to say, the MFICC—the Mother Fucker in Complete Charge.[49]

4

The Godfather

Barnett thought Kenefick was the best operating man in America. He was impressed by the fact that Kenefick was the only man he knew who had ever gone directly into railroad service from Princeton. Evans considered him "the superior, the best single railroad man in the nation." Tall, courtly, and reserved, Kenefick was a commanding presence. He did not have to shout to make his point; his steely gaze and superior intelligence were enough to fix the toughest railroader in his place. His shrewd, appraising eyes seemed to notice everything, and he asked questions that had never even occurred to his officers. His silences could be more unnerving than the rants of past presidents.[1]

The UP had never had an outsider as president, let alone a college graduate. Although Kenefick knew the UP by reputation and from past experience, he was still surprised by much of what he found on his arrival in May 1968. He expected a traditional railroad with heavy emphasis on the boss's authority, but the extent of that authority shocked him. "There was almost no crossing of knowledge or management between the various departments," he noted, "and *that* is rather unusual for a railroad of this size, particularly that the senior officers are that way." John Marchant, who arrived a year later, described it as "very, very top-down structure, very siloed. . . . You didn't go to another department unless it was very informal. . . . There was a lot of turf war and jealousy . . . between the departments, and some resentment. . . . It was . . . in some ways a living history museum."[2]

No one did anything without checking first with the president, who had long adopted the practice of giving his favorites de facto power while stripping officers in charge of their authority. At the NYC Kenefick was accustomed to delegating authority and expecting results. Instead he found one guy who took care of some things and another who ran around making notes and directing train operations even though he was not the general superintendent of transportation. Learning who actually did what became Kenefick's first and most annoying task.[3]

Kenefick set out to dismantle the vise-like grip of the authoritarian system and the scourge of office politics. He chose a new VPO in a manner that ignored tradition. "Everything was so political then," declared Jerry Davis, who later became president of the company. ". . . If you weren't from the eastern district of the UP, you'd never be the VPO." Kenefick appointed Bill Fox, who had come up through the south central district. Old-timers grumbled that he hadn't come from the main line and so didn't know anything. An engaging blend of hard-ass officer and free spirit, Fox became one of Kenefick's most invaluable assets. "One of those kind of two-fisted railroaders, and could drink and everything," said John Marchant, "but he was . . . intelligent and funny."[4]

Fox helped steer Kenefick through the peculiar UP way of doing things. "He knew the people and everything else," marveled Kenefick, "and so that made a big difference." With Fox as his guide, Kenefick set out to reform the operations department. Its members were surprised to find themselves with a VPO that actually made decisions instead of running first to the president.[5]

One small incident exemplified the problem for Kenefick. Normal signaling was three aspect—red, yellow, and green. The UP main line used four aspects (adding a flashing yellow) because the passenger trains ran at such high speeds they needed extra time to stop. At Laramie, however, a town ordinance restricted trains to 40 miles an hour, so speed was not an issue.[6]

"Why do we need four-aspect signaling there?" Kenefick asked the engineer who had put in an order for the installation.

"Because that's our standard," came the reply. "We always put it in."

"Whether we need it or not?"

"Whether we need it or not." The engineer paused, then said, "Nobody ever asks me questions like that."

"Well, you might as well get used to it," retorted Kenefick. "I'm going to ask you questions like that."

After the engineer left, Kenefick called the chief engineer and asked, "How much longer does that son-of-a-bitch go to his pension?"

Kenefick began hacking away at the "we've always done it this way" attitude on several fronts, but he was careful not to change things for the sake of making changes. He discovered that the UP was one of the few railroads that still used section men—several trackmen with a foreman—every ten or fifteen miles. This seemed like a good place to make cuts, but before taking action he ordered a study to find out how much the practice actually cost the railroad. Using ICC data, he compared the results to those of several other major roads.[7]

The results surprised him. "We weren't at the bottom," he found, "but we were in the lower half and we had arguably the best railroad, the best maintained. . . . So I didn't . . . cut off all the section men." The reason for the good showing, he concluded, was that having the gangs enabled the company to find and fix bad spots before they became more serious and costly.

One of these fixes took place on what was then the fourth subdivision, the line from Gibbon, Nebraska, to Kansas City. The UP's largest interchange gateway, Kansas City handled the most traffic with other roads. Jerry Davis, then a dispatcher, described the line as "nothing but a turkey trail" with a couple of sidings too short for a big freight train. When two trains met, Davis said, "we had to head up the old LK&W to Omega to get him off the main line." Westbounds coming out of Marysville needed helpers to get over Brayman Hill, and eastbounds used helpers all day long. The problem had been there for years, but no one did anything about it until Kenefick came along.

"How did these other general officers miss this?" Davis asked Kenefick.

"They never come down here, Jerry," replied Kenefick. "They always rode their business car on a passenger train and they never came down through here."[8]

Twice a year Kenefick conducted an end-to-end inspection of the road in a manner that soon became legendary. As the train carrying his business car rumbled over the track, Kenefick sat at the rear on the right side facing forward. Directly opposite him sat the superintendent of the district, with other officers in the remaining seats. When the train hit a bad spot, Kenefick jotted down the milepost number and handed it to the superintendent. Next morning a section gang would fix the problem. Kenefick looked at everything and seemed to miss nothing. He peppered the officers with questions, and they learned two rules very quickly: know the answer and never, ever, pretend you know it when you don't. "I realized quickly in my career never to say anything to Kenefick in idle chatter," said Paul Conley, then a young company lawyer, "because he would bore right in on something if he didn't think you knew what you were talking about."[9]

Another young officer, Dennis Duffy, who later became VPO, was more blunt. "You didn't bullshit him," he said. "You better just tell him like it is . . . and then be prepared to discuss the issue with him." Other officers shared this view. "He was unbelievable," said Jorgensen. "He would get right down to the nitty-gritty on every damn thing going on." Everyone learned the danger sign. When Kenefick got angry, which wasn't often, his bald head would turn red and he'd start to rub it. Out came what Duffy called his "Irish temper" to blast whatever victim had uncaged it. However, Kenefick's outbursts passed quickly, and he never held a grudge. His way of smoothing things over was not to apologize but to call the victim up and tell him a joke or suggest they have lunch.[10]

One up-and-coming marketing officer failed to grasp the Kenefick style and paid the price. Denny Robinson was on an inspection trip to look at a new steel mill that had gone up at Brigham City, Utah. The UP had built a line to the plant, and Kenefick wanted to see what the company was getting for its investment.

When the train arrived, Kenefick looked out his car window at the steel mill. He noticed a big truck stop being constructed on the other side of the track and trucks rumbling across the track to the steel plant. "I don't understand that," he said to Robinson. "We spent the money, rebuilt the line, got these guys to build this facility, and it doesn't look like we're getting any business out of here."[11]

Robinson looked at Kenefick and said coolly, "Well, Mr. Kenefick, you just don't understand railroad marketing."

Kenefick stared at him in cold silence and moved on. Later one of the officers present told a colleague, "Denny Robinson's dead meat," and he was. His career went downhill from that day.

Even the best employees got the Kenefick needle occasionally. Because of all the traffic that passed through Marysville, Kenefick wanted the company to buy any house or building near the right-of-way that came up for sale. An old hotel was acquired and torn down. When Kenefick arrived there during an inspection trip, he saw a signal case sitting right in the middle of the lot where the hotel had been. He asked Emil Krause, the signal officer, what it was doing there. "Well," Krause answered, "we had to put these new crossing signals in and I didn't have any place to put it."

"Well, tell me this, Emil," said Kenefick. "If we hadn't bought that hotel, what would you do? Rent a goddamn room to put that signal case in?"[12]

On the inspection trips Kenefick imposed a style and discipline that kept officers scrambling. "He was holding court," said Duffy. "He wanted to know everything . . . about the particular territory he was on . . . about the customers and the flows and train consists and . . . when's the last time you did the tie program here? How are the train engines running? . . . He was just . . . very, very thorough."[13]

As a young officer Duffy was summoned to Kenefick's office to discuss a project to install CTC through the Blue Mountains in Oregon. Nobody else was in the office to answer Kenefick's questions. "I thought I was a doomed man," said Duffy. When he arrived, Kenefick pulled out a slide rule and they started making calculations. Kenefick wanted details on the benefits, the return on investment (ROI), every aspect of the financial calculations. "He wanted to do the project," Duffy said. "He knew it was the right thing to do, but the superintendent couldn't quite make the economics of it come together, but Kenefick could. And . . . we did the project and it made a hell of a difference in the Blue Mountains. It actually changed the whole scheme of things we were doing."[14]

Some officers grew adept at improvising. During one inspection trip the train arrived in Nampa, Idaho, on a beautiful, crisp fall morning. Kenefick got out to inspect the facilities and came upon a huge metal structure that was padlocked. He ordered the lock cut off. The door was opened to reveal a pile of unidentifiable detritus from past decades, stacked to the ceiling. Even Kenefick couldn't figure out what most of the stuff was. "Get rid of all that crap," he barked and moved on to other stops.[15]

The following year Kenefick stopped again at Nampa and found the building completely empty. "Tear it down," Kenefick ordered and moved on. John Jorgensen noticed an odd triangular-shaped patch of ground that looked to be freshly sodded. "I hope they don't ever drop a bomb there," the division superintendent told him quietly, "because they're going to find all that stuff that was in that barn." His men had just buried it all and also sprayed with aluminum paint the handrails, trash barrels—everything in sight. Jorgensen peeked into a trash barrel and found that even the trash had been spray-painted.

Jorgensen was there because Kenefick made it a point to take young officers as well as all the department heads on his inspection trips. For those willing to observe and learn, the trip became a classroom. Officers set in their ways found it a painful ordeal. The pressure of being under the gun intimidated many officers. Kenefick had a regal air about him, born partly of his Princeton background and partly of his superior knowledge of railroad operation. Although he was very approachable, his formal manner discouraged familiarity. No one called him John; it was always Mr. Kenefick.[16]

Another classroom for officers emerged with the new budgeting process implemented by Kenefick. Once a year in the ballroom of a local hotel Kenefick, Fox, and Bob Brown presided from a raised platform over a budget summit that lasted all day and sometimes into the next one. Every department head had to submit his budget and justify every authority for expenditure needed. "You got questioned on everything," said Stan McLaughlin, "and you'd better have your homework done." The scene reminded Dennis Jacobson of a king holding court; for others it felt more like the grand inquisition.[17]

Supplicants who tried to puff up their argument got nowhere with Kenefick. One request asked for funds to "inhibit the expulsion of incandescent carbon particles." Kenefick looked at the man and said, "You mean sparks?" For those not on the hot seat the spectacle could be entertaining, but it was also deadly serious. Kenefick wanted every manager to know his budget and his projects well enough to explain them to others. Equally important, he wanted officers from departments long insulated from each other to gain some insight into what went on elsewhere.[18]

No one felt the budgetary pressure more than Jorgensen. "I think I had the toughest job in the place," Jorgensen said, "'cause he hated computers." Yet he thought it a good thing that Kenefick pressed him hard. "He made me cost-justify everything," Jorgensen added, "which was excellent because the railroad was so capital intensive and everything with computers became capital intensive."[19]

Kenefick admitted to being illiterate about computers and made little if any effort to educate himself in them. To him IBM stood for "It's Better Manually."

At meetings and cocktail parties he referred to Jorgensen as the guy in charge of "computer shit." Jorgensen thought a bad experience with IBM on the NYC had jaundiced Kenefick's view of computers. As late as 1976 Kenefick warned of two hazards associated with them: "One, the generation of a multitude of reports and paperwork, more than is needed or can be digested; two, dependency on an intricate system operable only by a couple of wizards and a wand with no simple emergency backup arrangement."[20]

However, Kenefick never let his personal dislike blind him to what computers could do for the railroad. For all the grief heaped on him, Jorgensen seldom got turned down when he asked for more equipment. But it was seldom easy. In those days IBM required an eighteen-month lead time on orders for its latest machines. When Jorgensen asked Kenefick for $1.5 million to acquire the newest version, he was turned down cold. On his own initiative Jorgensen sent IBM a letter of intent, which got him in line for the machine. He hoped to win Kenefick over by the time it was built.[21]

Every two weeks for months Jorgensen sent a request to Kenefick only to have them ignored. As the shipping date neared, a frantic Jorgensen went to Kenefick's office to plead his case and was thrown out with some "very unkind words." Jorgensen believed his operation would crash within six months if he didn't get the new computer. In desperation he left a note with Kenefick's secretary saying that if he did not get the new computer his entire operation would collapse. After two agonizing days of worrying that he would be fired, Jorgensen received a phone call from John Deasey, the controller. "What the hell's this goddamn computer you want to buy?" asked Deasey. "He told me to give you a million and a half bucks."[22]

A few days later Kenefick invited Jorgensen to lunch. As they walked past the back loading dock to the garage, Kenefick noticed a Global Van Lines truck unloading some big IBM boxes. "What the hell is that?" he asked Jorgensen.

"That's that computer you authorized," replied Jorgensen.

"Well, Jesus Christ, that was fast," said Kenefick.

"Yeah, IBM's very responsive these days."[23]

Unlike Jorgensen, who always felt like a stranger in a strange land, most of the operating people loved Kenefick because of his ability to size up a situation at a glance and see what was needed. "He was the consummate operating guy," said Duffy. "He could . . . take you down to the quick, the very basics about what had to happen to make the railroad function." Kenefick constantly stressed the need for capacity, the ability to get the most out of the road's resources, and he made his point in terms anyone could understand. Not having capacity, he said, was like running a whorehouse without whores.[24]

A picture of E. H. Harriman adorned the wall behind Kenefick's desk in his office. It reflected not only his love of history but also his grasp of what Harriman had brought to the railroad. "He had the philosophy that Mr. Harriman had of running the railroad," said Davis, "reducing operating costs, keeping trains moving, customer satisfaction. Every year that he was president . . . we made a line change to improve the flow of the railroad."[25]

Davis was a rare type among UP officers—an old-line railroader who didn't act like one and who had a capacity for growth. Convinced that the road suffered from hardening of the arteries, Kenefick made it a priority to infuse fresh blood into the ranks. Barnett also understood the railroad's resistance to change and the need to break down the old boys' network. He had chosen Kenefick because he seemed the perfect man to recruit bright young men to fill the company with fresh ideas. Aware that the railroad could not be run from New York, Barnett wanted Kenefick to take charge of Omaha and leave the New York office free to run the corporation.[26]

This approach suited Kenefick just fine. He recruited new people for every department. In July 1970 John P. Deasey was brought in to be controller; his only railroad experience had been five years with the Pennsylvania. Walter "Pat" Barrett began his career as a UP stenographer but graduated from the executive program at Carnegie Mellon. In 1971 he replaced the vice president of traffic, who was an alcoholic, and worked closely with Kenefick.[27]

A year later Kenefick hired Thomas B. Graves Jr., whom he had known at the NYC, to work under Barrett. "I just want you to come out here," Kenefick told Graves candidly, "and try to help me figure out how we make money." Graves got the message. The first step was to create a marketing department to join the sales, pricing, and rate departments inside the traffic department. Young Dick Peterson became manager of service planning. "We worked with the operating people," he said, "to have the liaison between marketing and operating to develop new train services."[28]

Even the law department got an overhaul. Kenefick thought it stodgy and poorly led. He wanted someone bright and experienced enough to deal with legal and legislative issues that were growing ever more complex. It was a sensitive time for the railroad; there was still fallout from the "Edd and Tedd" scandal. McDonald needed someone who would be independent of the operating department, which dominated the company culture in Omaha. A search firm turned up several candidates, but none wanted the job. Finally McDonald and Kenefick agreed to give the job to C. Barry Schaefer, who was then only thirty-two years old and untested as a manager.[29]

Schaefer had credentials that went beyond impressive. A native of New Jersey, he had graduated from Princeton in 1961 with an engineering degree, picked up a master's degree in engineering from Penn, then earned a law degree from Columbia and an MBA from NYU. After law school he landed a job at Clark, Carr & Ellis. There he worked for McDonald, who brought him to the new UPC as assistant general counsel in July 1969 when McDonald became general counsel. A bear on ethical and moral issues, McDonald wanted someone in Omaha to repair the damage done by the scandal. Kenefick simply wanted someone who could modernize the law department and keep out of his way.[30]

Schaefer flew to Omaha in April 1972 and walked into Omaha's version of the Land That Time Forgot. His office contained a small washbasin, a coat rack, and a large desk with enunciator buttons. Schaefer pressed one of them. "In comes a thin, bald guy in a J. C. Penney black suit with a steno pad," he recalled. The man introduced himself as the secretary. Schaefer pushed another button and was greeted by the chief clerk, who handled his mail and files. The mail was still kept in thick volumes that went back to the 1880s.[31]

Eager to call a staff meeting, Schaefer dictated a four-sentence memo to the elderly secretary. Three hours later he was still waiting for it. He stepped into the back room and found the man laboring mightily over an ancient typewriter, struggling to type over a word he had erased clean through the paper. No one had heard of electric typewriters; copies still came from carbon paper. The filing system was as antiquated as the clerks, many of whom were refugees from the mail cars. Some of the department lawyers were smart and able, but no women or minorities were to be found.[32]

Gradually Schaefer modernized the department. He ordered good equipment and trained the staff to use it. To spruce up the place, he brought in his own oriental rugs and artwork to hang on the walls. He sought out women lawyers that other companies were reluctant to hire. The first of them, Valerie Scott, joined the company in 1973. "This was just unheard of," recalled Marchant, "and it really shook the place up." As the older male secretaries retired, Schaefer hired women to replace them. By the time Lou Anne Rinn joined the staff in the spring of 1981, all the secretaries and many of the lawyers were women. At the same time, Schaefer tried to instill in everyone a higher professional standard, which meant that for a while he found himself rewriting a lot of their work.[33]

His style contrasted sharply with the department's traditional way of doing things. Formality went out the window; he insisted that everyone call him Barry. He put no chairs in front of his desk, so that anyone coming to see him had to stand there. "You felt like a school kid," said Marchant, "and it obviously was by design." He was demanding, did not tolerate incompetence, and, as Tom Watts noted, "didn't want you to take an hour to tell him five minutes worth of stuff." He rewarded hard workers and good performance. Lazy staff members he labeled country club lawyers and rode them hard.[34]

No one knew quite what to make of Schaefer. He liked to talk in euphemisms. He was brilliant and did not hesitate to let other people know it. While placing great value on pedigree, he tolerated, even encouraged, differences among people. He made no secret of his determination to break the railroad mold. He wanted more lawyers like himself—young, ambitious, aggressive, and hard-working. Those who produced would advance; it was as simple as that. Some resented his style and left, which is what Schaefer had in mind. Those who stayed usually held him in high esteem.[35]

At the same time, Schaefer did things that amazed his people. If someone had a broken electrical outlet at his house, Schaefer cheerfully came over and fixed it. Every year he hosted a department Christmas party at his own expense with a little band to play carols and a Santa Claus with gifts for the kids. To build team spirit he held annual staff meetings at Sun Valley that combined serious departmental business with recreation. He did not discard the older male secretaries but tried when possible to turn them into paralegals.[36]

One aspect of Schaefer's approach did not sit well with Kenefick. The railroad's culture expected officers to come in on Saturdays in case Kenefick wanted to call them. Schaefer didn't mind working on weekends, but he wasn't about to sit around waiting for the phone to ring. Brashly he gave Kenefick his home phone number and said, Call me if you need me; otherwise I'll be at home with my family. "Well," said Schaefer, "he never forgave me for that." However, Kenefick was smart enough to recognize Schaefer's talent even if the lawyer didn't kowtow to the culture of the operations department.[37]

Both Kenefick and Barnett wanted more officers with college degrees or at least extra education. Every year they sent several of them to advanced management programs at the Harvard Business School, Stanford, Northwestern, or Columbia. In 1972 Kenefick introduced one-week seminars in management development for middle managers and two-week programs for executive development. At lower levels switchmen and others had access to two-week courses introducing them to operating procedures. These programs ensured that education on the railroad no longer consisted simply of on-the-job training.[38]

Kenefick realized that education alone could not dismantle UP's inbred authoritarian culture. He had to break down the walls between departments as well as the one-way flow of information. In 1972 he did something unheard of on the railroad; he ordered a broad survey of employee opinion. More than six thousand individuals responded with confidential views about their jobs, working conditions, and the company in general. Lack of communication ranked high as a complaint; 83 percent said that they first heard about important developments through the grapevine, which was often inaccurate. Glen Farr, the vice president of labor relations, set about devising new channels of communication.[39]

During 1972 Kenefick also moved to deal with one of the company's oldest and most persistent problems: alcohol. Under Rule G, which prohibited drinking, employees could be fired simply for being seen leaving a bar. Labor agreements tempered dismissals; men who were fired seldom left permanently but could be reinstated after several months. But neither Rule G nor any other company rule provided help to those with serious alcohol or other personal problems. Although alcohol—and later drugs—posed a major threat to railroad operations, most companies winked at the problem as a price paid for the hard life of a railroader. The issue went beyond operations. "We had some alcoholic people in the sales department," Kenefick acknowledged. "We were known for that."[40]

Instead of ducking the issue, Kenefick launched an employee assistance program. Only one other railroad, the Great Northern, had attempted such a thing. A puzzled John Reed of the SF asked Kenefick, "You mean you're taking care of drunks?" Kenefick initiated a program that invited those with a problem to seek counseling and improve their impaired job performance. Within three years the program expanded to deal with drugs and with marital, financial, and family problems.[41]

Kenefick's vision extended beyond day-to-day issues to a realm neglected by many railroads: planning and analysis (P&A). He differed from most old-line railroaders in demanding as much data as he could get from as many sources as possible. The advent of computers opened new realms of possibilities, but UP had nothing that resembled planning or analysis. In developing that capability one man proved indispensable.

John Rebensdorf was like no one who had ever worked for the company. A native of Lincoln, Nebraska, he developed early an unquenchable love of railroads through his family, many of whom worked for the Burlington except for a lone UP man. At the tender age of twelve Rebensdorf used passes from his father to ride the trains throughout Burlington territory, often staying overnight. After graduating from high school in 1961 he worked for the Burlington and the RI while attending the University of Nebraska. In January 1966 he earned a degree in civil engineering, then spent two years obtaining an MBA at the Harvard Business School.[42]

Three of his Harvard professors happened to be part of CRI, the firm Barnett had hired to help set up UPC. Aware of Rebensdorf's passion for railroads, they recommended him to Barnett, who hired him sight unseen. Worried that the UP's antiquated culture would frustrate Rebensdorf, Barnett kept him on the UP payroll but had him work at CRI's office in Cambridge.[43]

Two years later Barnett asked Rebensdorf to come to New York. Rebensdorf refused; he wanted to work for the railroad in Omaha. During his work for CRI he had come to know Kenefick, who he thought "could lead the UP in a totally new direction." He had also met Jorgensen and wanted to work in his department but had no computer experience. Instead Jorgensen recommended him to Deasey, who offered him a job in the accounting department.[44]

Before accepting, Rebensdorf went to Omaha to seek Kenefick's advice. How were things different now, he asked. "The difference is," replied Kenefick, "right now I'm the MFICC." That was good enough for Rebensdorf, who started the job in May 1971.[45]

His job title was manager of budget research. Charged with implementing a new responsibility accounting system, he set up cost centers and codes to learn what expenses were incurred by location and types of expense throughout the system. From this data Rebensdorf built a financial and information reporting system. On weekends he secured passes and rode freight trains to learn the entire system firsthand. It was the ultimate busman's holiday, but for Rebensdorf it was also serious business.

In his spare time Rebensdorf started doing what he called "operations planning work." At the time UP had no analytical planning capability. He looked at power assignments and found that shortages occurred because power was assigned without reason. A North Platte local, for example, got three high-horsepower units even though only one was needed for the tonnage hauled. The same pattern existed all over the system. Gradually Rebensdorf made himself the point man on cost and profitability analysis.[46]

Like Jorgensen, Rebensdorf was considered an oddball. An intense, serious perfectionist, he demanded as much of others as he did of himself. He took great pride in his work and could be difficult to deal with. "He's so live-or-die of the railroad," said Jack Koraleski. ". . . He's got his vision. He . . . wants you to go get it done for him. But at the same time, he gives you the freedom and the where-withal to . . . do the stuff." Jim Young, who also worked for Rebensdorf, regarded it as a great learning experience. "There was no BS in terms of getting to a point," he said. "He's a very, very smart man . . . didn't always trust the numbers but [in] a lot of cases [relied on] kind of gut instinct, and that was something I learned from."[47]

Koraleski was another of the new breed coming to the UP. A native of Omaha, he graduated from the University of Nebraska at Omaha in 1972 and went right to work for the railroad. Like his father, Koraleski was a finance guy. He had no railroad background and no traditions to unlearn. He started in the traffic department but within a year moved to the newly created Business Planning and Analysis Group headed by Rebensdorf. The new group reflected Kenefick's desire to centralize P&A in one cohesive group, making it available to every department.[48]

This influx of new faces gave Kenefick some of the personnel he needed to reorient the railroad. Unfettered by the past and eager to make their own mark, they recognized that everything around them was changing—the industry, the political environment, the culture, and especially the technology. Kenefick understood the challenge. "If I had one single, major worry in my job," he said in a 1971 interview, "it would be in . . . keeping the executive pipeline filled." As early as 1966 UP began an officer training program for introductory supervisory and managerial jobs. The program exposed students to every district on the railroad and all the major departments before capping their work with a major project assignment.[49]

One basic dilemma perplexed Kenefick. "University graduates can be rather easily blended into an organization in marketing areas, finance, law, accounting," he observed, "but the operating side is the big one. How you become a good superintendent without having been a trainmaster, or how you become a good general manager without having been a superintendent."[50]

Finding a solution mattered greatly to Kenefick because he was an operating man at heart. All of the changes he introduced had one goal: making UP the most efficient railroad in the nation. In his mind the operating department was still the sun around which all other departments orbited. It was also the one most resistant to change, especially in hiring practices. By 1971 the Civil Rights Act had been on the books for seven years. As a government contractor UP was required to recruit minorities and women. As the company's top field compliance officer, Marchant decided that the time had come to hire the first female fireman as a first step to making her an engineer.[51]

Marchant made the arrangement through an officer in Kansas City. He didn't bother telling his boss because he wasn't sure how he would react. Somehow Fox got wind of the hire and summoned Marchant to explain the legislation. They argued back and forth before Fox roared, "The overriding consideration is, I don't want a woman fireman." A week later Fox had cooled down and even joked about the episode. Marchant, he said, was just trying to put the romance back into railroading.[52]

Changes came slowly but they did come. More women and minorities appeared on the payroll, more information was shared among departments, and the workplace grew more open and relaxed. Some changes were small but visible, such as men no longer being required to wear hats.[53]

Time was on Kenefick's side in dealing with the older heads. Bob Brown, the chief engineer, was first-rate in his field. He respected Kenefick for his expertise, but he was also a tough, hard-headed old railroader who insisted on doing things his way. "How did you ever get that son-of-a-bitch to do what you wanted him to do?" Davis once asked Kenefick. "Jerry, I didn't," came the reply. "He'll be retired one of these days." Kenefick could live with headstrong so long as it was accompanied by competence and dedication. He understood that, like himself, Brown only wanted what was best for the railroad.[54]

5

The Shifting Landscape

All the new approaches, fresh faces, and glittering technologies meant nothing unless the railroad performed. Kenefick's job was to see that it did, and he did it very well during a turbulent decade that saw the economy gyrate like a yo-yo. Inflation unleashed by the Vietnam War averaged 12.2 percent between 1974 and 1979. The Arab oil embargo of 1973 forced Americans to confront their growing dependence on foreign oil. Unemployment averaged 6.7 percent even as the Consumer Price Index climbed from 49.3 in 1974 to 72.6 in 1979. The age of "stagflation" had dawned.[1]

During the 1970s Americans staggered through one national crisis after another: the oil embargo, the withdrawal from Vietnam, Watergate, the emergence of OPEC, the Iranian revolution, Three Mile Island, and the bailout of Chrysler, among others. Fuel prices soared as OPEC transformed oil into a diplomatic weapon as well as a source of wealth. Between 1972 and 1977 the combined yearly earnings of petroleum exporters soared from $23 billion to $140 billion. As historian Daniel Yergin observed, "Oil prices were at the heart of world commerce, and those who seemed to control oil prices were regarded as the new masters of the global economy." Although their power over prices waxed and waned over the next three decades, its presence remained a force of instability throughout the American and global economies.[2]

The surging price of oil hit railroads especially hard in the cost of fuel for diesel locomotives. In 1974 alone the price jumped 95 percent to twenty-six cents a gallon, which cost the UP an extra $37 million. By 1980 it had leaped to eighty-three cents. As the cost of everything rose during the 1970s, the railroads could not recover the extra expense quickly because they could not raise rates without ICC approval. This cost/price squeeze steadily worsened during the decade as inflation soared and the economy soured. By one estimate the rate of return for all railroads between 1975 and 1979 averaged a pitiful 1.71 percent, lower even than during the Great Depression years of 1931–35.[3]

Against this gloomy economic backdrop the UP continued to flourish. Between 1970 and 1979 the road's earnings increased from $638 million to $1.8 billion. Kenefick's skillful management kept the operating ratio (the ratio of operating expenses to income) around 75 percent, one of the lowest among major lines. Revenue ton-miles rose every year from a record 60.9 billion in 1977 to 79.2 billion in 1980. Between 1973 and 1979 net earnings averaged nearly $156 million.[4]

These results were even more impressive given Kenefick's policy of maintaining the railroad in peak condition. During the 1970s the UP invested just under $2 billion in capital expenditures, or nearly $198 million a year. Of that amount, $138.3 million went for new equipment—932 locomotives and 31,319 cars in all. This policy gave the UP one of the youngest fleets in the industry. By the end of 1980 the company's 1,725 locomotives had an average age of 9.9 years and its 66,835 freight cars 12.4 years.[5]

Yards also got close attention from Kenefick. In 1977 a modernized yard at Hinkle, Oregon, featured an unusual layout that enabled operators to view the entire process from a single tower at the crest of the hump. Two separate computer systems ruled the yard; the entire classification process was automated. The new yard reflected Hinkle's importance as a hub for traffic moving from Pacific Coast ports to the Midwest.[6]

North Platte remained the crown jewel of the UP system. Located at the center of an hourglass configuration of lines moving westward to Oregon in the Northwest or Los Angeles in the Southwest, and eastward to Chicago or Kansas City, it became the busiest railroad route in the world during the 1970s.[7]

The west retarder yard at North Platte opened in November 1948 and soon found itself hard-pressed to handle the traffic load. Between 1966 and 1970 the much larger eastbound hump yard was constructed and named Bailey Yard. It handled eastbound traffic while the original yard confined itself to westbound movements. The new facility also included a major diesel repair and servicing shop. Spread over 156 acres, the L-shaped 140,000-square-foot shop housed eleven tracks to handle everything from ICC inspections to spot repairs to complete overhauls. Two years later it was joined by a new "one-spot" car repair facility.[8]

Impressive as the new complex was, it too struggled to keep pace with growing traffic demands. Between 1968 and 1978 tonnage on the UP increased 65 percent, most of which moved through North Platte. Aware that the old westbound yard lacked the capacity to handle this load, Kenefick decided to replace it. In June 1978 construction began on a new $38.5 million westbound facility. The eastbound yard had sixty-four classification tracks; the new westbound plant had fifty with additional capacity for twenty more along with ten departure and eight receiving tracks. Even before the new west yard opened,

North Platte emerged as a beehive of activity. The yards and the shops ran 24/7 with an intensity that made it either a launching pad or graveyard for ambitious superintendents.[9]

Elsewhere Kenefick pushed for similar projects to improve service. A new classification yard helped expedite flow through Los Angeles, as did a doubling of capacity at the East Los Angeles intermodal terminal. The Omaha shops got a $1.6 million facelift with two new buildings and new equipment to modernize the locomotive repair shop. New one-spot freight car repair shops were installed at Council Bluffs, Iowa; Kansas City; Pocatello, Idaho; and Albina, Oregon. In March 1972 Pocatello opened a new locomotive service and repair facility; in November 1973 it welcomed a new heavy car repair shop alongside an older facility that had been modernized. By March 1974 the company had seven mechanized car repair shops along the system.[10]

For all the attention given to new facilities and equipment, the line itself proved even more crucial in Kenefick's program to upgrade service while reducing costs. Large sums went into maintaining the roadway, adding and upgrading sidings, and projects to reduce curvature. The UP had a reputation for being an operating man's railroad that ran big, heavy trains. Kenefick defended the practice but emphasized that it applied only to routes that warranted big trains. "If we were in the airline business," he said, "we'd be buying 747s. But for some reason, in the railroad business it seems to be a sin to want to run freight trains like the airlines run 747s. Certainly, the bigger the train you run, the lower the cost. But you don't see the airlines putting a 747 on every run, and we don't do everything on the big-train scale."[11]

In this area he had little choice but to rely on the expertise of his imperious chief engineer, Bob Brown, whose unconventional views had earned him a widespread reputation in the industry as a curmudgeon. Tall and burly with craggy features, large eyeglasses, and an omnipresent pipe, Brown was a native of Pocatello. One grandfather had been a UP conductor, the other a telegraph superintendent. His father had been UP's youngest division engineer until Brown himself came along. "I was raised on the Union Pacific," Brown said proudly. After earning a degree in engineering in 1941, he started with the UP as an instrument man and reached the coveted position of chief engineer in 1965 at the age of forty-seven.[12]

Brown took enormous pride in the UP's reputation of having one of the highest track and roadbed maintenance standards in the industry at a cost consistently lower than that of most other major roads. He had watched railroads let their physical condition deteriorate in the late 1940s and 1950s and then scramble frantically to upgrade their maintenance of way (MOW) programs. At professional meetings engineers held earnest discussions about mechanization, productivity, cycle maintenance, and unit costs. "The term that seems to have lost much prominence in these discussions during recent years," Brown said bluntly, "is the word 'quality.'"[13]

The word was to assume vast importance at UP in future decades, and it already mattered deeply to Brown in the 1970s. He did more than simply perpetuate a heritage; he rationalized and implemented quality maintenance on a scale that dwarfed previous efforts. In doing so he viewed even the most basic elements of the business in ways that often departed from the conventional wisdom.[14]

These departures came not only from his own experience but also from extensive homework. Charts in his office dating back to 1958 compared the UP's MOW expenses with those of six other major roads. Between 1968 and 1973 UP's average MOW costs ran about $1,650 per million gross ton-miles while that of the other roads varied from $1,735 to $2,350. The primary reason for the UP's superiority, Brown believed, sprang directly from continuous maintenance using the section gangs. Even as he neared retirement, Brown affirmed his belief in the gangs as the key to superior maintenance.[15]

Like the office force, the track gangs got help from new technologies. One sophisticated gadget, the EC-1 track geometry car, could roam the track at 40 or 50 miles an hour and measure eleven dynamic parameters within the tolerances specified by new Federal Railroad Administration (FRA) track standards. Built in 1975 to UP specifications, its array of electronic gear was a harbinger of what became a procession of complex equipment designed to replace manual labor with faster and cheaper automated work. In that sense it followed the path blazed by Bill Brosnan two decades earlier.[16]

MOW work fell into two broad categories. "Spot" work consisted of ordinary day-to-day tasks performed without disrupting train movements. "Out-of-face" work involved major projects using large gangs of workers that sometimes interrupted train schedules. The trick was to complete these quickly. Brown had definite ideas on the best way to get this done.[17]

Other railroads tried to save money by reducing their labor force and using roving gangs to perform not only out-of-face but also spot work on cyclical schedules. Over a period of fifteen years the UP had experimented with several different approaches to cyclical spot maintenance, and none of them had worked. "In each instance our track went to pot," Brown admitted, "and our costs went up to bring it back to acceptable standards." His answer was to deploy lots of section gangs equipped mostly with hand tools to monitor the track and fix problems before they grew. The heavy machines that required track time were largely reserved for out-of-face projects.[18]

Brown also discarded the cyclical approach in out-of-face projects because it could not take into account such factors as uneven traffic loads and weather conditions. "We don't have any set period of time to run a tie gang over a particular territory," he said. ". . . We determine our program strictly in accordance with the track conditions as they exist." The heavy use of section gangs kept a close watch on those conditions.[19]

Brown relished his reputation. Once a reporter asked him to what he attributed his long tenure at the UP, given that most other chief engineers had relatively short terms. "To the fact," he answered, "that I am the meanest son of a bitch on the railroad." But he was no dinosaur. Under his direction the UP was one of the first roads to deploy a track geometry car. Brown was also one of the first to enlist suppliers in developing specific equipment for his road. He welcomed innovations but insisted on their being practical and applicable to the UP's peculiar needs.[20]

Laying new rail constituted the single most expensive item in Brown's budget, and he took special pains to see that it was done right. Predictably, Brown deviated from conventional wisdom in his approach. "We are almost fanatic in our effort to install rail with the precision necessary to insure low cost, trouble-free maintenance, and maximum service life," he declared. In 1969 UP began laying strings of continuous-welded rail. The key lay in paying especially close attention to requirements for heating or cooling the strings to expand or contract them to a predetermined length before spiking. Brown had charts created to determine specific rail-laying temperatures for every territory. Every rail's temperature was measured before laying and had to be within three degrees of an established standard. This approach all but eliminated sun kinks in hot weather and pull-aparts caused by extreme cold.[21]

The same close attention went to ties and tie plates. Brown decreed the practice of adzing and creosote-treating the ties within the tie plate to be "absolutely essential" even though many railroads ignored these steps. He also believed in using one of the biggest tie plates available with a different cant than that used by most other roads, and in using high-carbon steel spikes exclusively. Among other things the larger plates helped eliminate shelling on the outer rail of curves.[22]

Tie replacement was the second most costly item on Brown's agenda. Overall the UP had about 37.3 million ties in its system. From 1966 to 1976 the company replaced some 600,000 of them annually, though during that period it had been coasting on the tail end of an extensive program between 1934 and 1944 that replaced more than two million ties every year. This cushion was nearly gone, and the need to step up the pace prompted Brown to study the whole problem closely. Again he departed from the conventional wisdom. Unlike most rail engineers, he rejected the notion that weather was the chief factor in tie wear or that hardwoods made the most durable ties. The life of a tie, he argued, depended on a host of factors including its size, quality of preservative treatment, plate size, type and quality of ballast, traffic flow, and maintenance practices. He preferred softwoods because they allowed deeper penetration of wood preservatives.[23]

The demands on track kept growing at a rapid pace. More trains with heavier power and larger cars were running at faster speeds. When the 125-ton hopper became popular, Brown persuaded the traffic and operating departments not to use them because they overstressed the track at speeds above 45–50 miles an hour. In 1976 he won the argument and the oversized cars were restricted. He thought that the existing track composition of carbon steel could accommodate only about a 70-ton car at a speed of 70 miles an hour. The solution lay in improving rail metallurgy, and Brown took an active role in the effort to research and rewrite rail specifications.[24]

In all this work Brown kept his eye on the prize. "Our basic objective," he declared, "is to maintain a suitable track and roadbed structure to handle the ever-increasing demands of our traffic requirements—and to do this at the lowest possible cost." He took great pride in his ability to reach these goals. In August 1979 he said in his usual blunt fashion, "I believe Union Pacific's track system is second to none in the industry." Many observers agreed with him. In 1978 *Modern Railroading* named Brown its Railroad Man of the Year.[25]

The industry's landscape continued to shift rapidly during the 1970s. The new USRA, created by the 3R Act, struggled toward completion of its mandate to reorganize the bankrupt eastern roads into a new entity. In June 1975 it released its Final System Plan. The most important provision gave the Northeast Corridor line—a combination of the former Pennsylvania Railroad route between Washington and New York, and the New Haven route between Boston and New York—to Amtrak. This move made Amtrak an operating railroad charged with taking care of its own track and dispatching its own trains. The core system that remained became Conrail. Parts of the bankrupt eastern roads were sold off to surviving roads; other mileage was simply abandoned. The railroad map of the East was radically redrawn.[26]

Meanwhile, the problem continued to spread beyond the East. The RI clung desperately to the fast-fading hope that the merger with the UP would finally be completed. The Milwaukee tried frantically to attach itself to any solvent road that would have it. By contrast the CNW resorted to an innovative solution. Under the leadership of Larry Provo a deal was struck in 1970 to sell the railroad to its employees for $19 million and assumption of $340 million in debt. The new Chicago and North Western Transportation Company made its debut in June 1972 but still faced an uncertain figure.[27]

By 1975 the crisis had reached a boiling point. The 58 Class I railroads earned only $351 million net income on revenues of $16.4 billion. Their return on net income averaged a scrawny 1.2 percent. A study by the Senate Commerce Committee predicted that the industry would suffer a cash shortfall of $5 billion over the next decade. "There is no way," concluded an analyst, "the number of railroads that exist today can continue to operate, pay dividends, repay interest obligations and maturing debt, and maintain its fixed plant at the current level of utility."[28]

Congress was finally forced to act. In February 1976 it passed the Railroad Revitalization and Regulatory Reform Act, better known as the 4R Act. In the short term the act provided $1.6 billion in emergency funds to get Conrail and Amtrak's Northeast Corridor line off the ground. In broader terms it tried to formulate a plan for determining what rail services were most needed and how best to provide for them. The FRA was to study the entire industry, not just the Northeast, and its technology.[29]

More important, the 4R Act began a movement toward deregulation of the railroads. Mindful of the UP-RI merger fiasco, it stipulated that the ICC must complete merger investigations within two years and render a decision within 180 days after that. It also loosened the ICC's hold over rates by declaring that for seven years all railroads would be free to price their service up or down within a range of 7 percent provided they did not control more than 70 percent of the traffic in question. These provisions reflected a growing consensus that regulation was a major cause of the rail industry's problems, and that the ICC itself was, as a Ralph Nader report put it, "an elephants' graveyard of political hacks." In May 1975 President Gerald Ford urged that the ICC be restructured.[30]

On Conveyance Day, April 1, 1976, Amtrak acquired its own lines, and Conrail took over the remains of the once mighty Penn Central, Erie Lackawanna, Lehigh Valley, Reading, Jersey Central, and Lehigh & Hudson Valley. The new government-fostered entity was enormous. Conrail possessed 25,000 miles of track (but would operate only 17,000 of them), 95,000 employees, 5,000 locomotives, and 162,000 freight cars. Its gross revenues exceeded that of any other railroad, as did its ton-miles of freight. While pundits debated whether government could operate a for-profit enterprise, Conrail got off to a shaky start and seemed for a time likely to go the way of its predecessor roads.[31]

Amid this bleak landscape even solvent railroads viewed the future with alarm. The traditional strategy based on high volume, low rates, and minimal service was fast becoming obsolete even though traffic managers clung doggedly to it. The old-fashioned railroad was dying; its replacement would have to be leaner, more productive, and more reliant on technology. It would also have to rethink every aspect of its operation, particularly marketing. To survive, the new railroad would have to be bigger, better, more efficient, and more attuned to what markets it could hold and which ones were forever lost to rival modes. Finally, it would have to find ways around the work rules that remained the biggest single obstacle to productivity.[32]

One technology held intriguing possibilities for the railroads. Piggyback hauling made its debut as early as 1936 but was slow to take off until the advent of the giant rolling gantry crane in 1961. The trailer itself was another problem in that the process amounted to putting one wheeled vehicle on top of another, creating too much extra weight and a high center of gravity. In the 1950s some railroads adapted standardized containers from the ocean shipping lines. These could be loaded and unloaded quickly and easily and hoisted onto a ship, flatcar, or truck. Longer flatcars capable of handling two containers reduced tare weight and burned less fuel in transport. Later the empty-well flatcar capable of carrying "doublestacks" made the process even more efficient.[33]

Delivery posed another serious problem. At first most roads put loading ramps as close to their customers as possible to lengthen the haul. But this practice resulted in excess switching and waiting in yards for delivery to each ramp. Shippers wanted their goods on time; manufacturers were moving to just-in-time delivery schedules to reduce inventories. To compete with trucks, railroads had to meet this demand. Gradually a solution emerged in the form of the container terminal, which became the hub for the business, and a revitalized concept known as the unit train.[34]

The concept involved creation of a single-purpose train with cars that were permanently coupled and carried a single commodity from point of origin to destination with no switching of cars. It could be applied to containers as well as bulk commodities like coal or grain. It eliminated the need for branch lines because trucks did all the local hauling of the containers. Each mode did what it did best. However, this approach required a state-of-the-art roadbed, special equipment, and a mechanized terminal, all of which meant large capital investment. This last demand alone placed the concept beyond the reach of many railroads.

But not the UP. As a bridge road devoted to procuring the longest possible haul, the UP had long experimented with prototype versions of the unit train. However, the major impetus for the innovation occurred elsewhere, most notably with the Southern, the SF, and the SP. The high cost of rolling stock coupled with the relatively low usage of it on most railroads remained a stumbling block. Although freight cars represented 30 percent of a railroad's investment in physical plant by 1976, the average car made only eighteen revenue trips a year with an average length of 53 miles, traveled a meager 1,500 ton-miles a day, and spent only 6 percent of its time actually moving under load. The rest of the time it sat idle in a terminal, in a yard, or on a customer's siding.[35]

The reasons were several. Customers liked to use cars as free storage units. Back hauls usually ran as empties because no cargo could be found for them before they were needed at another location. Long delays often occurred in interchange yards, the most frustrating delay of all. A railroad might speed delivery of freight to an interchange point only to have it languish there for days. In 1974 an exasperated Graham Claytor of the Southern voiced this warning:

Large shippers . . . do not show much interest in how *one* railroad performed in an interline movement if the total service didn't come up to
par. With some 50 percent of rail freight movements involving more
than one railroad, this gives us another clear indication that we are all in
this together.[36]

One obvious way to eliminate an interchange problem was to merge with the
connecting road. The 4R Act gave mergers fresh impetus even though many
earlier ones had not realized large improvements. For all its positive effects,
however, the act could not solve the fundamental problem that continued to
plague the industry: too many railroads with too much underperforming
mileage.[37]

The Midwest exemplified the problem. Seven railroads ran between Chicago
and Kansas City and five between Chicago and Omaha. They all fought for
traffic that could barely support half their number. Around their routes lay
thickets of branch lines built to haul grain to them in the days when it came by
wagon to rail-side elevators. Everyone sensed that most of this excess mileage
had to go, but no one seemed to know how to address the issue. The politics of
expansion was always much easier than the politics of contraction.

The first mergers of the 1970s got off to rocky starts. The biggest of them created the Burlington Northern in 1970. The new company struggled at first,
partly because of the large investment it was making at the same time in developing a delivery system for coal in the Powder River Basin of Wyoming. The
joining of the parallel IC and Gulf, Mobile & Ohio into the Illinois Central Gulf
(1971) turned out poorly. The failing Milwaukee had tried desperately but in
vain to be included in the BN merger and stood grimly at the brink of bankruptcy. Then there was the sad-sack RI, playing out the final episodes in what
had become the longest-running soap opera in railroad history.[38]

In 1969 the Justice Department had finally filed its approval of the merger
with the ICC after hedging it with several conditions. RI president Jervis Lang-
don Jr. pleaded with the commission to act before all the participants died of old
age. In July 1970 Nathan Klitenic, the ICC examiner, recommended that the
merger be approved on condition that the SP be granted the Tucumcari line.
However, in December Klitenic suffered a heart attack before he could issue his
final report, the final installment of which did not appear until February 1973. In
it Klitenic urged that the merger be made subject to a broader restructuring of
western railroads into four systems built around the UP, SP, BN, and SF.[39]

Predictably the railroads denounced the plan, and the examiner had no power
to compel anyone to do anything. The commission dropped the Klitenic plan
and in November 1974 finally approved the merger subject to several conditions. "It has been suggested that due process may, in the eyes of some, seem like

undue process," said ICC chairman George M. Stafford, "but that is often the price our legal system imposes in litigation of this enormous magnitude."[40]

Evidently Stafford forgot one of the oldest of legal maxims: that justice delayed is justice denied. During its eleven-year odyssey the case had devoured 200,000 pages of transcripts and exhibits, required sixteen proceedings, and kept more than three hundred lawyers gainfully employed. The total cost has never been calculated.

An analysis of the RI by Bruce Relyea in June 1973 revealed its finances to be in worse shape than expected. Barnett and UP were unhappy with the decision and asked for more time to study it. Much had changed in eleven years, including the relative value of the securities of the two companies. Moreover, UP had ·expected to get the entire RI, not chunks of it, and the parts themselves were in far worse condition than when the process began.[41]

David P. Morgan of *Trains* magazine got straight to the heart of the decision's weakness: "What essentially flaws the outcome . . . is the commission's failure to address itself to the malady that caused its deliberations in the first place: There is too much track between Chicago and Colorado and between the Twin Cities and Texas. The commission has, in effect, ordered the participants in the case to play musical chairs without the removal of any seats before the piano stops."[42]

On March 17, 1975, less than four months after the ICC issued its decision, the hapless RI filed for bankruptcy. Ten days later UP formally terminated the merger agreement and asked the ICC for an order denying the application. The ICC complied in January 1976, putting an end to the saga. The RI became the first major American railroad to be liquidated, its parts sold to whoever wanted them.[43]

In December 1977 the Milwaukee followed the RI into bankruptcy and eventual liquidation. Two of the once proud Granger roads had been swept into oblivion. In February 1977 the BN opened merger talks with the Frisco, while the parent holding company of the Seaboard Coast Line and Louisville & Nashville began negotiations with the Chesapeake & Ohio that led to the formation of a new holding company, CSX Corporation, in November 1978. Both mergers had received ICC approval in 1980.[44]

As Kenefick plotted his course through this fast-shifting landscape, one fact became increasingly clear to him: Like it or not, UP as it had existed since its separation from the SP in 1912 would soon be rendered obsolete. Bridge carriers were fast becoming either larger systems or parts of other systems. Kenefick had no doubt about which role UP should play. Well before the RI fiasco ended he had begun exploring other possibilities on both ends of the line. For this work he needed something UP did not yet have: a group dedicated to P&A.

In the past the UP had outsourced most of its P&A on strategic questions to firms like Wyer, Dick. In his new hires Kenefick did not seek out planners directly, but he acquired bright young men who recognized that planning was important and had the skills to undertake it. Foremost among them were Schaefer, Rebensdorf, and Jorgensen. All three were considered eggheads by railroad standards, and they dwelled in separate corners of the company. A curious chain of developments brought them together.

Rebensdorf had known Jorgensen since 1968, when he was working in Cambridge. Schaefer's keen interest in upgrading technology naturally brought him to Jorgensen. "I loved Barry," Jorgensen said later. ". . . He was just so smart and lucid and articulate, and he didn't take prisoners." When interest in mergers began to develop, the two of them began discussing the subject. Jorgensen suggested that they add a third voice to the conversation and brought in Rebensdorf.[45]

Deasey saw at once that Rebensdorf was no ordinary employee. His intense interest in operations made him a natural to do work for that department. The quality of his work soon drew the attention of Fox and his assistant vice president of operations, Bob Richmond. "They became very sophisticated very quickly," said Jorgensen. As early as January 1972 Fox arranged a meeting for the planners to show their projects to operating officers. Shortly afterward Rebensdorf was brash enough to ask for permission to hire thirteen new people at a time when business was poor and adding people was anathema. To his surprise, Kenefick approved the request. Rebensdorf hired only five people, but four of them boasted MBA degrees. He put his little group to work studying a host of problems dealing with costs and profitability. The results found their way to Kenefick, who liked what he saw.[46]

Rebensdorf was never bounded by a job description and relished that freedom. The combination of analytical training and knowledge of the railroad business enabled him to come up with insights that old-time railroaders sensed but couldn't articulate. He resembled Bach in his ability to take a theme or topic and tease out every possible variation on it. "I was able to come in," he said, "go through the data, put it together in such a way that they could see what was happening. And once they saw that, they could take the appropriate action."[47]

By 1974 the value of his work had been amply demonstrated. Deasey asked him to design an organization devoted to planning. On December 1, 1975, the UP formally established the P&A group with Rebensdorf as its head. The few planners already in the traffic department became part of Rebensdorf's operation; the move brought Jack Koraleski under Rebensdorf's wing.[48]

The new group contained people of varied backgrounds in business, economics, and other fields. "We had people that understood the rail industry," said Koraleski. "We affectionately referred to them as foamers. . . . And then we had analytical types, statistical types. . . . We had all these disciplines in research operations, finance, computer modeling, research and development." Presided over by Rebensdorf, they managed to establish a rapport with the operating department.[49]

P&A came into existence because Kenefick saw the urgent need for such a group. "I do not recall that we were ever turned down on a request for resources, particularly staff," said Rebensdorf. "I believe that was because we were giving him the work product that he wanted." However, some requests did not meet a gracious reception. When the personal computer made its appearance, P&A was eager to be the first group to get one on everyone's desk. Rebensdorf took the request to Kenefick, who received it with his usual skepticism about computers. When Rebensdorf tried to explain the value of having a PC on each desk, Kenefick growled, "Well, for God's sake, everyone uses the shithouse but we're not going to build one on everyone's desk." Nevertheless, he soon relented and approved the request.[50]

P&A remained part of the finance department but served the entire company as it took on more roles and developed a capacity for strategic planning. Rebensdorf still reported to Deasey but saw Kenefick often, thanks to P&A's growing role in the capital budget process. Kenefick liked him for his brains, his vision, his honesty, and his utter dedication. He became one of the few people who knew how to disagree with the boss and tell him so without getting run out of the office.[51]

The emergence of P&A as a formal process within UP occurred at a fortuitous time. By 1975 the RI ordeal was finally over and talk of mergers was widespread. Given the crucial decisions that lay ahead, nothing was more crucial to the company than the capacity for broad strategic analysis. A new path for UP's future had to be forged, and wrong choices could bring it to an abrupt and unhappy end. Finding the right choices was the task Kenefick assigned to Rebensdorf and Schaefer.

‖ 6 ‖

The Corporate Relationship

During the 1970s UP, like the railroad industry, found itself moving into uncharted territory. The worlds of the corporate boardroom and the railroad's management were each insular in its own way and largely separate until the most profound transformation of the industry in history pushed them toward convergence. By 1970 the structure of their relationship had been formalized in the form of UPC. Each of its operating companies had its own management team and ran its own operation except for treasury and tax functions, which remained with the corporate staff. The railroad was no longer *the* entity; it was one among several within the corporate umbrella.

The assets spun off from the railroad were impressive. Champlin, which had been acquired for $240 million, included among its reserves lands in the Overthrust Belt that had been part of the UP's original land grant as well as the Calnev pipeline. Upland's inventory of land contained 17,000 prime industrial development acres, 872,000 land grant acres, and 46,000 acres formerly belonging to the old UP Coal Company. Rocky Mountain Energy inherited coal reserves estimated at 10 billion to 15 billion tons of good-quality, low-sulfur coal in Wyoming, Colorado, and Utah. It also owned a coking coal reserve, one of the largest reserves of trona (soda ash) in the world, and sand, gravel, and limestone holdings. Like Champlin, Rocky Mountain received royalty income from other companies that leased its lands; it also owned 49 percent of Stauffer Chemical Company, which produced soda ash in Wyoming. Finally, it held mineral rights for some 7.85 million acres of the land grant for all the minerals mentioned along with uranium.[1]

The corporate management team set up shop in its bright, modern offices at 345 Park Avenue. Although Lovett and Roland Harriman still sat on the board, Barnett as CEO and chairman of the board, Evans as president, and Gerry as chairman of the executive committee formed the ruling troika. The subsidiary presidents reported to Barnett, who had by 1970 put together a young and able staff. Bill Cook as vice president of finance brought to the company the disciplined and sophisticated accounting methods he had learned so well at GE. Bill McDonald, the general counsel, and Chuck Olsen, the secretary, were no less meticulous in their work.

Part of their task involved UPC's need to create its own identity. Its first report in 1969 defined its objective as providing "a vehicle for sound diversification with special emphasis on growth areas that have some relationship to the existing businesses of Union Pacific." Three years later the report outlined two major long-range objectives. The first was to "operate the Railroad in the utmost faith that we will stay in the business and stay as the best." To that end more than a billion dollars had been invested in the road during the past eight years. The second and equally important goal was to "raise the earnings of UP's nontransportation businesses to match the continually increasing income of our Railroad."[2]

An inherent tension existed between these objectives. Growing the other businesses required capital as well as management expertise. The railroad far outstripped the other subsidiaries in both respects. It had one of the nation's top managers, and it provided most of the income for the corporation. Between 1969 and 1974 nearly 79 percent of UPC's net income came from the railroad. The problem was how to maintain the high level of capital investment in the railroad while allocating money for development programs in the other companies. The nonrail enterprises also had to establish their own identities and define their relationships with each other.

Barnett had hired Kenefick to manage the railroad in a manner that required little attention from New York. During the first few years Barnett let him do just that. The railroad still had a full staff covering all departments except the treasury. Two functions, cash management and income taxes, were consolidated in New York under Cook's financial staff. UPC acted as bank for all the companies. The railroad, for example, forwarded excess cash to New York as an advance and was credited with interest on it. If the railroad needed cash, the transaction was reversed. To raise capital, the corporation took advantage of the railroad's strong cash flow and AAA credit rating. The railroad borrowed against new equipment and advanced the money to UPC, which used it to provide capital for the other companies. In that way, along with its strong earnings, the railroad served as cash cow for the corporation.[3]

Cook succeeded in building a strong financial staff in New York. His objective was to strengthen it to the point where it could exert control over the subsidiaries as well. In addition to Bruce Relyea and William F. Surette, he brought in Charles E. Billingsley as assistant controller. Only thirty-six when he was hired in October 1969, Billingsley came from Ebasco Industries but had earlier worked for both GE and the Pennsylvania Railroad. He took charge of all auditing functions for the railroad with headquarters in Omaha. There he built up an audit staff that later provided the company with some of its best officers.[4]

Cook wanted to centralize the audit function in New York as a means of imposing controls on the subsidiaries. However, Kenefick wanted his own audit staff. "He seemed to have a distrust of Bruce and Charlie Billingsley," said John Deasey. It was the GE connection that bothered Kenefick, who did not want key railroad functions swept up to the corporation in the GE manner.[5]

The budget process soon emerged as the main item of business between UPC and the subsidiaries. In September the presidents of each company submitted preliminary budgets to Barnett. The controller's staff analyzed the submissions and sent their findings along to Barnett for a review to establish final income and capital budget targets. The presidents came to New York for that exercise. In November these procedures were repeated to finalize budgets for the coming year. Later the corporate officers used the review process as the occasion for an annual visit to Omaha.[6]

Predictably, UPC's attempt to impose its will on the subsidiaries met with resistance from both the railroad and Champlin. Bill Surette became the point man for the corporation, especially in the area of capital spending. Rebensdorf dismissed Surette as the consummate bean counter who had difficulty seeing the big picture. Kenefick enjoyed taking positions that infuriated Surette, and he normally prevailed with the corporation. Surette could only retaliate by making life miserable for the railroad finance staff. The result was constant tension between the railroad and corporate finance groups.[7]

Every year produced its own mini-drama during budget season. Forecasting proved fiendishly difficult in an era wracked by rampant inflation, high interest rates, costly labor contracts, shifting traffic patterns, and a volatile political environment. Capital became a sore point because of soaring interest rates. In July 1974 Evans informed the four presidents that "the current high cost of financing has caused us to deter long-term financing and this situation is not likely to abate in the near future." Barnett warned that "the nation will undergo a strenuous test in the next 12–18 months, and each of your operating plans should be concerned with the problems inherent in high inflation rates, depressed residential construction, generally sluggish consumer buying, and continued high interest rates."[8]

Barnett proved a good prophet. In February 1975 Kenefick alerted him to a drastic decline of 20 percent in freight volume with little hope of an upturn during the coming months. In response Kenefick slashed all maintenance programs and furloughed three thousand employees, about 13 percent of the workforce. Although the economic skies brightened somewhat in the spring, the outlook remained uncertain. In November Barnett asked Kenefick for a five-year forecast even though it was difficult to predict what was going to happen in the next month.[9]

"It was kind of a game," Kenefick said of what he deemed the GE style introduced by Cook and his cohorts. Every fall Kenefick went dutifully to New York for the budget review. Barnett sat across from him and asked questions. On one occasion he mentioned that Kenefick's revenue figure for the automobile business differed from that in the national forecasts. Kenefick replied that he had never seen the national forecasts. Surprised, Barnett asked where he got his figures. "We asked General Motors, Ford, and Chrysler how much business they thought they'd be giving us next year," Kenefick replied.[10]

When the corporate staff came to Omaha for the annual budget review, Kenefick had moles inside UPC that leaked to him the figures the corporation set for the coming year. Kenefick would come up with his own realistic set of figures and then give Barnett a forecast below that amount. "They would come out here and argue with us," he said, "and finally we would reluctantly increase it some, and sometimes we would increase it to something below what we thought we could make ourselves. And the last year that we did this, after some argument, I offered them a figure that was exactly in their forecast, and Cook woke up to what had been going on."[11]

A game it might be, but it was a serious one, especially when dealing with capital projects. Kenefick had to persuade Barnett to invest large sums in his projects, and Barnett had to convince the board to approve the requests. Cook did his due diligence in the GE style, which meant he expected to see the financial benefits directly associated with a given project. Kenefick had to educate him on the fact that the value of some projects could not be measured by numbers alone. The Aspen tunnel provided a classic example. The original was built in 1901 by Harriman through the Wasatch Mountains. Since it held only a single track, the company constructed a second tunnel in the 1950s to create a double track. But rolling stock got steadily larger. Some roads went to the Plate C boxcar, which wouldn't fit in either Aspen tunnel. Any train bearing just one oversized car had to be sent another route.[12]

To Kenefick the solution was obvious but expensive: enlarge the tunnels. He sent the request to Cook, who warned that he'd have a tough time getting it past the board. At the board meeting Kenefick explained the problem and admitted there was no way to put a reliable estimate of return on the project. "I just think we have to do it," he emphasized. "If you're going to run trains, you gotta have tunnels big enough for them to go through."

A long pause ensued. Then Bob Lovett moved approval of the request, Roland Harriman seconded it, and the motion passed unanimously. "But that was Lovett," said Kenefick. "I mean, he just saw the point. You could fiddle all day long, but you just really needed to do it, that's all." The project cost $7 million and took eighteen months to complete. When the enlarged tunnel opened in

1975, nearly all UP trains could use the double-track main line straight through from Omaha to Odgen.[13]

The economy improved during the late 1970s, and the railroad performed well, as did the other companies. However, it soon became clear to New York that the nonrail subsidiary in which they had the highest hopes for development was by far the most volatile and unpredictable. UPC was scarcely four years old when the oil crisis of 1973 and the emergence of OPEC drastically changed the world of energy. Oil became the hottest business sector.

Champlin's three refineries ran near full capacity during 1973, and the company poured large sums into joint-venture exploration programs in Wyoming, the North Sea, the Gulf Coast, Indonesia, the Philippines, and Peru. Capacity expansion was as costly as that on the railroad; by one estimate a new medium-sized refinery required more than $350 million and two or three years to complete. Coal production, too, increased steadily as the price of oil rose. Rocky Mountain Energy had one of the nation's largest reserves of recoverable coal. In 1973 it mined nearly four million tons, 27 percent more than the previous year, and its royalties from leases nearly doubled. Although the railroad's earnings continued to increase, the future looked even rosier for the energy companies.[14]

However, the corporate managers soon learned that the energy sector was as fickle as it was promising. The huge sums invested into Champlin's exploration ventures resembled casino bets. Some paid off handsomely; others, like the Gulf Coast, Indonesia, the Philippines, and Peru, came up empty. UPC set aside a $60 million reserve against possible losses in 1974 and another $60.8 million the following year. In 1975 Champlin's net income dropped more than $13 million thanks to repeal of the depletion allowance for oil production and related tax adjustments for drilling costs. Undaunted, Champlin invested $250 million to expand its Corpus Christi refinery and joined a $630 million venture to build an ethylene complex near the refinery.[15]

The oil business was a high-stakes, high-risk game. Unlike the railroad, it was also a game new to UPC's managers, who continued to believe that it held the key to future success. The corporation's 1977 budget projected that for the first time nonrail ventures would provide 50 percent of the corporation's net income and allocated 55 percent of capital expenditures to energy-related businesses. In fact, the nonrail companies managed only 48 percent of UPC's net that year. The following year they were projected to provide 52 percent of the total net income and received 61 percent of a record capital budget totaling $585 million. In that budget the railroad's capital allocation increased a mere 3 percent while Champlin's rose 42 percent and Rocky Mountain Energy's 36 percent.[16]

During 1978 the nonrail companies again fell short, managing only 47 percent of UPC's net, but the gap was closing. Between 1979 and 1982 the railroad's contribution to corporate net income averaged only 38.3 percent. For the first time the nonrail subsidiaries provided more than half of the net income. Doubts began to circulate at corporate headquarters as to whether the railroad had a future comparable to that of the other companies. For all its innovations railroading was a tired old industry struggling to survive in a world of wondrous new technologies. Barnett never lost his faith in the railroad's importance, but he was about to retire. As the first generation of corporate leaders began leaving the company, they gave way to successors who did not all share the same commitment to the railroad.

Through the 1970s the corporate staff expanded enough to occupy two floors at 345 Park Avenue. "We never have had over 110 or 120 people over in the New York headquarters," said Evans. In 1973 Cook was elevated to the newly created post of executive vice president and McDonald to the new position of senior vice president–law. Cook's promotion signaled that he was being groomed for a top management post.[17]

In 1974 Cook went onto the board along with James Robinson III, the executive vice president of American Express. Time was running out on Barnett. As the strain of the job took its toll, he began to drink more. "We'd go to the Racquet Club for lunch," said Schaefer, "and he couldn't wait to get his martini." The drinking aggravated his diabetes, but he didn't stop. In July 1977 Barnett turned sixty-five, the mandatory retirement age. Reluctantly he stepped down on August 1 but stayed on the board. Evans moved up to chairman of the board, and Cook replaced him as president. Seven months later Roland Harriman died, depriving the company of its symbolic link to the past. Lovett had always said he would remain on the board only as long as Roland; true to his word, he resigned less than a month after Roland's death.[18]

The founding fathers of UPC had departed the scene, leaving Elbridge Gerry as the sole surviving link to the Harriman and Lovett families. No one had done more than Lovett and Barnett to create UPC. In separating the nonrail assets from the fat old lady, they never lost sight of the primacy of the railroad and the need to keep it in excellent shape. The three old lions had been the keepers of a proud tradition with an imposing financial legacy. Since 1898, when it was reorganized out of bankruptcy, UP had paid dividends every year.

To replace Lovett and Harriman on the board, Evans recruited two men on whom he knew he could rely. E. Virgil Conway was the current president of Seamen's Bank, Evans's old institution, and became one of the youngest directors at forty-nine. John R. Meyer was Professor of Transportation, Logistics, and Distribution at the Harvard Business School and a noted scholar. At fifty-one he too helped lower the age of the board. By 1978 the corporate officer corps had grown to fourteen with the addition of vice presidents John P. Halan in employee relations, Richard W. Anthony in corporate relations, Charles L. Eaton in strategic planning, Chester A. Rose as controller, John R. Mendenhall in taxes, and Richard N. Little, who handled company business in Washington. The board was an unwieldy group of twenty-two, not one known for being proactive or likely to challenge most management policies.[19]

Evans and Cook seemed an ideal management team in the ways they complemented each other. Evans thrived as "Mr. Outside," the congenial, gracious glad-hand who became the public face of the corporation. He knew everybody, did interviews freely, charmed the investment community, joined other boards, and graced important functions. However, he was not a hands-on manager. "He liked being the big shot," said Kenefick, but he understood that his role was to modernize a stodgy company. It was Evans who found the space at 345 Park and jumped at the opportunity. "That was Jim's platform," said Barry Schaefer, "because he was right in the center of Manhattan and he had a lot of relationships he was developing . . . to change UP's image in the investment community from a staid railroad company to a diversified, growing enterprise."[20]

The son of a Baptist minister, Evans had always been a climber in the best sense of the word. Born in Lansing, Michigan, in 1920, he moved to Louisville, Kentucky, at age eleven. He graduated from Male High School in 1938, having helped support his schooling with a paper route. The family had little money for college, but a fortuitous connection enabled him to go to Centre College in Danville. After graduating in 1942 he served in the Naval Reserve and used the GI Bill to attend the University of Chicago Law School. He got his JD degree in 1948 and started work with a Chicago bank. From there he went to the Reuben H. Donnelley Corporation and Dun & Bradstreet before becoming president of Seamen's Bank in October 1965. Through his work in the Red Cross he became friends with Roland Harriman, his link to UP.[21]

"I was there to concentrate on the nonrail side," Evans said of his role at UPC. He liked a first-class life, and he wanted UP to be a first-class operation. "Jim tried to bring a whole new style to this," said Schaefer. "He bought a corporate aircraft, and officers were permitted to fly on business. Union Pacific adopted a stock option plan for managers and executives, and the price of the company stock became an important focus. . . . Jim was good in attracting attention to the stock." Evans knew how to charm analysts and how to present the company's performance in the best possible light. An excellent speaker, he gave talks to a wide variety of audiences.[22]

Cook could not have been more different. He was the quintessential "Mr. Inside," the numbers man who was as introverted as Evans was sociable. Two years younger than Evans, a native of Duluth, Minnesota, he joined the army in 1943 as a private and left three years later as a captain. After graduating from the University of Minnesota in 1948, he began a fourteen-year career at GE. In 1962 he became comptroller of the Pennsylvania Railroad, and then vice president and comptroller of the Penn Central. He did not linger long after the merger but jumped to Ebasco Industries. Sutton knew him from the Pennsylvania and regarded him highly. On his advice Barnett and Evans recruited Cook explicitly to succeed Sutton, who was nearing retirement.[23]

A trim figure at five feet eight and 150 pounds, he was quiet of manner and dress. Where Evans exuded warmth and good cheer, Cook remained cool and somewhat distant. "Bill was a great guy, actually," said Schaefer, "... great with the numbers. Very ill at ease in terms of making public speeches ... very honest guy, thoughtful, kind of abrupt.... He wasn't a leader of men." Cook was also a good judge of talent. The people he brought in, such as Relyea, Surette, Hill, and Billingsley, shared his desire to impose sound, honest, centralized accounting procedures on the companies.[24]

Kenefick noticed one immediate change of style in the new leadership. "When Frank Barnett was there," he observed, "he was the old school. If he wanted to know anything about the railroad, and it wasn't very often he did, he'd call me." Evans and Cook would have a vice president call Kenefick and say New York needed such-and-such information. "So I'd call Cook myself," Kenefick said, "and say, 'Hey Bill, you were asking about this,' and he wouldn't know anything about it, see? He played these games."[25]

During the late 1970s UPC reveled in record earnings. The subsidiaries seemed at last to be fulfilling the role of matching the railroad in income. In 1978 revenues rose 17 percent to nearly $3 billion and net income 19 percent to $264.1 million. "The past decade," crowed the annual report, "has seen the attainment of the goals set in 1969, accompanied by a strong growth of all of our businesses." The dividend was hiked from 50 cents to 57.5 cents a share. The railroad carried a record volume of freight and earned a record net income for the third straight year. Champlin produced record earnings, Rocky Mountain Energy did well, and even Upland had a banner year.[26]

Even this impressive record paled before the performance of 1979. Revenues soared 35 percent to $4.03 billion and net an astounding 45 percent to $382.5 million, prompting the board to raise the dividend an unprecedented 22 percent to seventy cents a share. The return on stockholder's equity reached a new high of 15.8 percent, three times what it had been in 1969. Although the railroad continued to do well, the other subsidiaries provided 61 percent of the total earnings, the first time they had even matched the railroad. Champlin's net income soared to $182 million, a 91 percent increase over 1978; the railroad managed only a respectable 8 percent gain.[27]

These results were exactly what Evans and Cook hoped to achieve. They justified not only their own policies but the rationale for creating the corporation in the first place. For the coming year the corporation allocated nearly a billion dollars for capital expenditures, 62 percent of which went to energy and natural resources. "We intend to invest heavily in the Railroad and maintain it as the best in the country, because it is profitable and a good generator of cash," Surette told analysts, "but in terms of growth and return on investment it will probably not be as big a contributor to future earnings as our nonrail business. . . . More money is going into the nonrail side because there are, frankly, more opportunities for greater returns in that area."[28]

For Kenefick the view from his corner office on the twelfth floor of the UP office building was neither as sunny nor as cloudless as that from corporate headquarters. A new round of consolidations could produce either a few big regional systems or even fewer giant transcontinental systems. Kenefick realized that the company could not stand idle while other roads redirected the routing of traffic with new combinations. To ensure its connections the UP had to acquire other roads, but where and which lines?

Through the early 1970s the UP watched the BN complete its merger and the SP continue to divert traffic from the Utah gateway to the Cotton Belt line, which it acquired in 1932. Bad blood had been brewing on the western front for some time. The SP still wanted the RI's 966-mile line from Tucumcari to Kansas City and St. Louis, which would shorten its route by 400 miles and enable it to divert still more traffic from the Utah gateway.[29]

The Utah gateway had been a thorny problem for decades. Ogden became the meeting point for the UP and the Central Pacific. By 1882 the SP had opened a southern transcontinental route by connecting with the Santa Fe at Deming, New Mexico, and with the Texas & Pacific at El Paso, Texas. A year later it owned a single-line system from San Francisco to New Orleans. Collis P. Huntington then formed the Southern Pacific Company in 1884 and had it lease the SP and Central Pacific railroads for ninety-nine years. Since then the temptation existed for the SP to divert traffic from the Utah gateway to its southern route until Harriman bought control of the SP in 1901 and merged it with the UP.[30]

Harmony reigned until the federal government dissolved the combination in 1912. By then the SP owned the Central Pacific outright. The UP tried first to acquire the Central Pacific, then moved to separate it from the SP. After prolonged legal maneuvering the SP was allowed to keep the Central Pacific provided that it accept five conditions imposed by the ICC.[31]

Among other things the Southern Pacific Conditions, as they became known, committed the SP to keeping the Utah gateway open. In May 1924 the UP and SP agreed to accept the same preferential routing requirements, but their agreement was never tested before the ICC. Then the SP acquired the Cotton Belt line, which gave it an even longer haul than through the El Paso or Tucumcari gateways. Commissioner Joseph Eastman warned that "if the application is granted, it is inevitable that the Southern Pacific will endeavor to put its eggs in the Cotton Belt basket just as far as it can," but the ICC approved the merger anyway.[32]

There matters rested until June 1957 when the Rio Grande challenged one of the 1924 UP-SP agreement conditions. The ICC ruled that changed circumstances made this one condition "no longer just and reasonable" and ordered the agreement canceled or modified to fit the original Southern Pacific Conditions. In June 1968 both the 1924 agreement and a Memorandum of Understanding reached in December 1947 were canceled. While this struggle went on, the SP absorbed the Central Pacific in June 1959. A year later it applied for permission to control the WP as well, touching off a battle with the SF over the road. In January 1965 the commission denied both applications.

During these years the SP searched tirelessly for ways to funnel more traffic onto its southern route. On an inspection trip in 1971 Kenefick observed that "the Southern Pacific is really going all out to solicit against us for other than perishable traffic, favoring the southern route. There is nothing new about this." Between 1960 and 1975 the number of eastbound carloads delivered to the UP at Ogden plummeted 49.4 percent from 244,553 to 123,648. During that same span UP westbound deliveries to the SP dropped only 2.9 percent. If the SP bought the Tucumcari line, more traffic might be diverted from the Utah gateway. Tensions also existed between the UP and the SP over Pacific Fruit Express (PFE), the jointly owned subsidiary that provided refrigerator cars for hauling unit trains of produce from California.[33]

In many ways PFE encapsulated the deteriorating relationship between its co-owners. Founded in 1906 by Harriman when he controlled both the UP and the SP, PFE opened the continent to California perishables with trainload after trainload of eastbound fruits and vegetables. A highly profitable company until perishables began moving to trucks after the interstate highway system opened, PFE began running a deficit in 1971. In April 1978 the partnership was dissolved. SP kept the original PFE title for its refrigerator car subsidiary, while UP's company became Union Pacific Fruit Express.[34]

The situation on the eastern front was no less fluid and volatile. As late as 1968 six railroads interchanged business with the UP at the Omaha gateway. The traditional UP policy of not extending beyond the Missouri River evolved from its ability to exchange traffic with so many roads. During the 1960s and early 1970s, however, the relationship between UP and the Iowa roads underwent a profound shift. The Burlington became part of another major system and an important coal carrier, which strained its capacity and lessened its need for UP traffic. The failing RI and Milwaukee roads could no longer provide reliable service, especially for time-sensitive goods. The Illinois Central Gulf remained primarily a north-south road, and its share of UP traffic dropped steadily.[35]

That left the CNW, long the UP's favorite partner because it owned the shortest and best route to Chicago. By 1975 it handled 59 percent of the UP traffic delivered to the Iowa lines. Physically it was in better shape than any of the others except the Burlington and enjoyed more favorable grade and curvature profiles. For run-through and time-sensitive traffic, which was gaining steadily in importance, no other road offered the UP a better connection to Chicago. However, the CNW had problems of its own, and some doubted it could remain an independent road. Clearly the UP could not afford to lose it as a connector; the question was how best to go about ensuring that it remained in friendly hands.[36]

Kenefick understood that these issues could not be left dangling for very long. In October 1974 he sent Barnett a report on the state of the railroad. "We are deeply concerned about the deteriorating condition of some of our connecting railroads," he said. "We are all well aware too of the Northeast rail crisis and its possible effect on the UP, for example. We continue to believe that we must protect our position through the Chicago and St. Louis gateways: if this cannot be done by merger, then we must work out other alternatives to give us control over pricing and service standards. We need to strengthen our connections to the East, Southeast and West if we are to develop fully our bridge traffic over the central route."[37]

The crucial issue was where potential mergers fit into this need. A year earlier Kenefick had asked Schaefer to develop a plan on where the UP might fit in any rail restructuring. Schaefer pulled in Rebensdorf, and together they created what Schaefer called "Project Manhattan" because he thought it was "the big bomb."[38]

By the end of 1975 the strategic puzzle had grown incredibly tangled. The economic recession that year hit railroads hard. Both the RI and the Milwaukee were up for grabs, the one in bankruptcy and the other headed there. The Katy was floundering, and many other roads, including the CNW, were deferring maintenance to save money. Ben Biaggini of SP began running longer, heavier trains and skimping on upkeep, commencing a downhill slide of service on that system. Rumors of impending mergers filled the air.

There was so much to sort out, and it had to be done carefully. Kenefick wanted no missteps or false steps. He needed a clear picture of the options, and who better to put one together than the bright young men in P&A? Before he even assembled his team, however, the telephone rang.

The Return of Humpty Dumpty

Ben Biaggini was not a favorite of Kenefick, who admitted, "We just never really meshed." He was a good railroad man, congenial, and a fine speaker, but he was also imperious with a manner that struck many people as arrogant. "Biaggini had an extremely autocratic style," said Schaefer, "and everybody was petrified. . . . Anybody who worked for him was simply a foil." He was tough and so was Kenefick, which helps explain why they never got along until both of them had retired.[1]

Early in 1976, however, Biaggini surprised Kenefick by calling him to say that the two systems should work together more closely. They had been drifting farther apart and had already agreed to dissolve their partnership in PFE. Kenefick had already told him the UP was not going to buy the RI, calling it a "bag of bones," and friction remained over the shrinking interchange at the Utah gateway. To resolve their differences, Biaggini produced a thirteen-point memo on ways the two roads might work together. Then he said that the SP and UP should come together, adding that he could be either the buyer or the seller, though it was clear he preferred the latter.[2]

Kenefick notified New York of the offer and directed Rebensdorf to study whether the SP was worth acquiring. Rebensdorf joined with Ed Hill, who did P&A at the corporation, to compile a detailed analysis. They got more data on the road from Biaggini and were dismayed at what they found. Schaefer compared ICC annual reports for both roads and concluded that while Kenefick had been building up the UP, Biaggini was running the SP into the ground. "It was a pretty sad situation," he said. "They had an enormous amount of deferred maintenance in California. . . . Their traffic base was not particularly good. . . . [Their] freight car fleet had been allowed to deteriorate."

Rebensdorf and Hill came to similar conclusions in more detail. The SP's operating margin on transportation revenues was only about half that of the UP's. In recent years its operating ratio had consistently run three or four points higher, and its bad-order ratio continued to worsen even though it spent large sums on equipment repairs. Nearly 65 percent of its main line consisted of rail weighing less than 130 pounds, compared to only 33 percent on the UP. Its traffic mix had changed little in recent years and showed no signs of future growth or diversity. The report concluded that "Southern Pacific cannot remain a vital operating railroad without making significant adjustments to its operation and its ways of doing business."[3]

What Kenefick later called a "super-secret meeting" was arranged. Kenefick, Barnett, Evans, and Schaefer traveled to Palm Springs to inform Biaggini that they weren't interested in a merger with the SP. "We thought the bloom was off SP's rose," Kenefick recalled. "Its big business . . . was disappearing. The fruits and vegetables went to trucks; automobile plants were shut down one by one; and the transcontinental lumber market declined due to competition from Canadian and southeastern sources."[4]

"Biaggini was crushed," Schaefer said. "That was his take out, so he didn't know what to do." Neither did Kenefick. He ordered Rebensdorf to assemble a team and produce an in-depth study of the entire merger scene and its possibilities. From this effort emerged the massive "Merger Planning Study 1976," consisting of thirteen formidable volumes that analyzed in detail every conceivable combination among western railroads and their connectors. It was an imposing achievement, one not duplicated by any other railroad. Drawing on his knowledge of history as well as his sense of whimsy, Kenefick dubbed it "Project XYZ."[5]

The project pulled in more than thirty people divided into teams. Schaefer and Tom Graves, the marketing vice president, also got heavily involved, and Jorgensen supplied MIS support. The teams identified every possible combination and generated for each one detailed marketing assessments, traffic diversion studies, operating analyses, and financial pro formas. Altogether the project consumed more than three months. Although the volumes gather dust today, they proved to be a landmark influence in UP's history.[6]

In March 1976 Graves's marketing department delivered its first study on the UP and other western roads. It assumed that "the western railroad environment will not remain static in terms of merger developments, and the Union Pacific cannot continue to operate effectively in such a dynamic environment without significant increase in size." It also assumed that the federal government would insist that competition be reduced on routes where too many roads operated, and that virtually all western roads would be included in the restructuring process. The basic premise was as clear as it was stark: The Humpty Dumpty that was the current railroad map was about to have a great fall, and nothing could put it back together again.[7]

"The studies clearly demonstrated," Kenefick explained later, "that the most attractive alternative for Union Pacific was to preserve the status quo for as long as possible. As the leader of the industry, it was clearly a disadvantage for us to acquire any other railroad." UPC did not want a merger. It would upset the balance between its rail and nonrail assets and inhibit the latter's development by consuming needed capital. Nor would the financial markets look favorably on such a move.[8]

But the status quo grew ever harder to maintain. At the Omaha gateway UP's relationship with CNW grew tighter. It had become strained during the 1960s when Ben Heineman fought his brilliant guerrilla campaign against the RI merger. Once Heineman sold out to the employees in 1970, however, the mood in Chicago changed dramatically. Larry Provo, who became president in 1967 at the age of 40, improved CNW by eliminating low-density branch mileage and putting money into the main line to Omaha and Fremont, Nebraska—the latter being a more efficient connection with UP.[9]

Provo had a clear-eyed vision of the road's future. Soon after taking office he reminded Kenefick that the old war hawks—the people who caused all the animosity of the sixties—were gone. "There are four railroads across Iowa and they really only need one," he added. "My strategy is to have the CNW be the survivor, and I think the survivor is going to be the one that's got the most support from the UP." Kenefick thought this was a fine idea and went to Chicago to see Provo. "And so we kind of had an extramarital affair, if you will, with the North Western from that point on," Kenefick said. Provo did his part by redeploying offline traffic and sales offices to coincide with those of the UP. In several cases they moved into the same building that housed the UP's offices.[10]

From this effort developed a warm relationship between the presidents and their railroads. "It was not quite the same as single-line service," observed Kenefick, "but it was the next best thing." Unfortunately Provo did not live to see the fruit of his efforts. A heavy smoker, he developed lung cancer and died on October 19, 1976, at the age of forty-nine. UP officers, including Kenefick and his wife, filled two pews at his funeral. Six weeks before his death the CNW's board had named James Wolfe president and chief operating officer. An abrasive, outspoken but capable manager, Wolfe moved seamlessly into a good relationship with Kenefick. "Jim Wolfe was an energizer and a modern thinker," Kenefick observed. "Fortunately, while many railroad presidents 'preside' over their railroads, Mr. Provo ran his—and so, later, did Jim Wolfe."[11]

While relations on the eastern front warmed, those on the western end grew chillier. Thwarted in his overtures to UP, Biaggini searched elsewhere for a new partner. Meanwhile, Kenefick got wind of another potential threat from Schaefer, whose father-in-law sat on the board of the Missouri Pacific. The news went public in April 1976 that the Southern had approached the MP to discuss a possible merger. "The two railroads are among the best managed, best maintained, and most consistently profitable in the industry," declared *Business Week*. "A combination of the two would be a powerhouse."[12]

If consummated, the merger would create a 22,135-mile system that combined strength with strength, in contrast to the old philosophy of having strong roads absorb weaker ones. For half a century the dilemma had been how to shrink the number of railroads and their track mileage equitably. Sentiment was growing to discard past policy and let railroads find their own combinations; those unable to find suitable partners, like the RI and Milwaukee, would have to go down.[13]

Barnett and Kenefick got this message. Kenefick had Project XYZ under way. The corporation produced a white paper in May on western railroad mergers; a month later Bill McDonald outlined some alternative systems to those in the paper. "It seems clear at this time," Barnett concluded on July 9, "that there will be a restructuring of the railroads west of the Missouri and Mississippi (and perhaps to the east)." He appointed Cook, Evans, Kenefick, McDonald, and Surette as a task force; Kenefick put Schaefer and Graves to work on regulatory and competitive issues as well as traffic distribution.[14]

The pressure eased somewhat in September 1976 when the MP and the Southern broke off merger talks, saying only that they could not agree on terms. Privately some MP officers thought the Southern's arrogance too overbearing. "They're a good railroad," said one, "but they're not that good." This gave UP a few months of breathing room. In December Biaggini informed Kenefick that SP was going after the Tucumcari route. Two months later the BN announced that it was holding talks with the Frisco.[15]

This combination posed a formidable threat. The Frisco was a good lean operation that connected St. Louis and Kansas City with Memphis, Birmingham, and the Gulf Coast east of the Mississippi River and Arkansas, Texas, and Oklahoma west of it. Parts of it served the territory coveted by the BN for its growing coal traffic out of the Powder River Basin. "The Frisco," said Kenefick, ". . . was our principal way of getting . . . to the Southeast. . . . The Mop now became the only way we could get a friendly connection to the Southeast."[16]

By October 1976 the XYZ teams had completed most of their work. From their mountains of text and data emerged some intriguing conclusions. They began with the assumption that western railroads would reorganize around four core systems: the UP, BN, SF, and SP. From that base they analyzed every possible combination. They assumed, too, that in the 1980s at least 75 percent of rail traffic would continue to move interregionally and that competition from other modes, especially trucks and barges, would continue to eat into the railroads' share of total freight traffic. During the 1920s the railroads had carried 80 percent of all freight; the figure dropped below 50 percent by 1954 and below 40 percent by 1970.[17]

Traffic flows were projected to increase during the next decade, especially in bulk commodities and manufactured goods. However, changes in control at the

Ogden, Omaha, and Kansas City gateways could upset all calculations. To emphasize this point, the first XYZ volume analyzed what might happen if UP stood still and other roads merged around it. It concluded that "continuation of the close relationship between the UP and a viable Chicago and North Western is critical to maintenance of Union Pacific's East-West traffic base." Any threat to that relationship, whether from another road or from faltering management or financial weakness within the CNW, had to be deflected. The UP no longer had any other worthwhile routes to Chicago. "Union Pacific's need for control," concluded the summary report, "either via a strong working relationship as presently exists with the CNW, or through acquisition, cannot be overstated."[18]

Having examined the threat posed by other mergers, the study turned to an analysis of possible combinations by the UP with other roads. The Utah gateway offered few appealing prospects. The SP had already been dismissed as a merger partner. California had emerged as a major manufacturing center, and the SP dominated the northern part of the state as well as southern Oregon. Neither the Rio Grande nor the WP offered a challenge to that domination. The WP reached northern California but had a weak traffic base and required major capital investment to be competitive. However, if the UP did not acquire it, the road might fall into the hands of the SF or BN. In the end, conceded the study, "it seems likely that the SP will always be the dominant carrier in Northern California and Southern Oregon."[19]

The situation looked far more promising—and complex—on the eastern front. An exhaustive analysis of the CNW led the team to conclude that it would make an excellent merger partner. Besides the obvious advantage of creating single-line service to Chicago, it possessed some significant north-south traffic flow that would enhance connections to the South and Southwest. Moreover, its western lines offered an intriguing possibility in the form of access to the promising Powder River Basin coal fields. BN was already exploiting these fields. The CNW could gain entry if it came up with half the cost of building a new 98-mile line from a point east of Douglas, Wyoming, to the coal deposits. It had until December 1977 to raise the money; otherwise the line reverted to BN.[20]

The team viewed a merger with the CNW as a defensive one. It looked next at adding the MP to this combination and found the result attractive. The MP offered access to the St. Louis and Memphis gateways as well as to Gulf Coast ports and power plants requiring heavy low-sulfur coal. It featured a strong and growing north-south flow of traffic that balanced the UP's east-west flow.[21]

The combined system would cover about 31,500 miles, have more than 60,000 employees, and generate some $3 billion in freight revenues. The MP was the largest carrier of chemicals in the West and moved large quantities of grain through its Gulf outlets. It handled a rich variety of traffic and had a much more complex route structure than the UP. It was well maintained, and its progressive management had enhanced the system by acquiring the C&EI road. Overall it looked to be a good partner, especially in tandem with the CNW.[22]

None of the other possible combinations looked appealing. To clarify comparisons, the XYZ team compiled a detailed route analysis listing the mileage, level of maintenance, maximum freight speed limit, physical characteristics, and line capacity for every major segment of the companies under study. The eighty-three-page outline in small print of every major western service corridor was a tour de force.[23]

Once completed, the XYZ volumes were shipped off to New York, where Surette took charge of the analysis. On December 6, 1976, he sent to Omaha the results of the New York team's review. McDonald and Surette doubted the feasibility of a merger with either the CNW or the MP, especially from a financial perspective. Rebensdorf responded with a ten-page critique of New York's argument. McDonald arranged for both the New York and Omaha teams to meet in New York on January 14, 1977, to thrash out the question of merging with the CNW alone, the MP alone, or both roads.[24]

Meanwhile, Kenefick was again trying to reach agreement with Biaggini over a number of issues. The SP wanted to get into Kansas City and needed trackage rights over the UP between Topeka and there. The two companies also had differences over the division of Oregon traffic. Kenefick voiced his concerns over the Utah gateway and suggested a traffic protection agreement. The Utah gateway was a matter of divisions, Biaggini said, and could be worked out. "Give me five points," he added, "and I'll give you more traffic than you can handle." Then he grew emotional, declaring that the Kansas City and Utah issues were not related, that the UP had stolen the SP's Los Angeles traffic, and that the Oregon dispute should never had gone to court.[25]

On December 29 Kenefick and Schaefer met with officers of the SP and the RI. Biaggini outlined three alternatives he had presented to Kenefick earlier for reaching Kansas City. He would buy the Tucumcari line to Topeka and use UP trackage to Kansas City; failing that, he would acquire the RI lines in and east of Kansas City to St. Louis and Trenton, Missouri, and inherit that company's right to use the UP line from Topeka to Kansas City; or SP might buy the entire RI line. After the meeting broke up, Biaggini asked Kenefick to be reasonable about the trackage rights.[26]

The next afternoon, December 30, Kenefick called Biaggini in Palm Springs and said he thought something could be worked out, but he wanted assurances that any UP losses in southern California from the new SP route would be offset by gains at the Utah gateway. He followed the call with a letter that drew a swift reply from Biaggini, who accused UP of breaking the agreement on gateway traffic and contending in a lawsuit against SP that no such agreement existed.[27]

Warming to his task, Biaggini denounced the attempt to keep SP out of Kansas City as "an anti-competitive effort which, if not illegal, is certainly not in the public interest and not worthy of a great company like Union Pacific." From this exchange Kenefick concluded that SP desperately wanted entrance into Kansas City, and that it might be willing to link the Utah gateway to trackage rights if necessary. For the moment, however, the western front looked to be stalemated.[28]

This round of diplomacy proved a fitting prelude for the January 14 meeting in New York, which focused on the eastern front. Seated around the conference table were Evans, Cook, Kenefick, McDonald, and Surette, Gerry, Ed Hill, Paul Coughlin, Schaefer, Graves, and two outside consultants, Charles J. Meyer of Wyer, Dick and Richard Barber. Kenefick opened the proceedings by giving his overall views of the XYZ studies. Yes, they were prolix and extended, he conceded, but they provided new and valuable insights into the railroad. In particular they had shown him how important the east-west traffic was to UP. The studies convinced him that MP would be an attractive merger partner, that CNW was vitally important to UP, and that the Utah gateway problem defied easy solution.[29]

Surette followed by observing that UPC had asked its longtime consultant, First Boston, to examine Hill's financial analysis of possible mergers. The First Boston analysts agreed with Hill that any merger between UP and MP, UP and CNW, or all three roads would have an adverse effect on UPC's credit ratings and the market value of its securities. To offset any erosion of railroad earnings caused by maintaining the status quo, First Boston suggested acquisition of some nontransportation company "to further the oft-stated UP Corporate goal to achieve and maintain a proper balancing of our non-transportation and transportation businesses."

The potential for conflict between UPC's objectives and those of the railroad had existed since its creation. For the first few years such conflicts dwelled mostly in the background; at this crucial meeting they took center stage. Hill jumped in to say that he recognized the importance of CNW to the railroad, and added that the corporation's "financial clout" in the money market depended heavily on the railroad, and anything that eroded its asset base would reduce UPC's access to capital markets.

Barber agreed that a merger with MP would be more offensive than defensive and raised again his argument about the lack of affinity between the two roads. Meyer called the XYZ studies "adequate to a negative strategic decision, but not adequate with respect to an affirmative decision to merge." He suggested instead that UP seek a half interest in the RI line from Kansas City to St. Louis. The two consultants left the meeting along with Graves, leaving the others to grope their way to some decisions. Talk turned to alternative ways for acquiring CNW.

Kenefick was asked for his minimum requirements in regard to CNW. He replied that he needed to control that road's rates and standard of service, which meant in effect that UP had to control its management. The group decided not to pursue a merger with MP. Secondly, it would explore further "possible 'acquisition' of the CNW, with particular reference to the alternative forms for acquisition and the implications" for both the railroad and UPC. Omaha need not do any further studies on the subject. The New York team would determine if a merger was feasible on terms that would meet Kenefick's needs, not damage UPC's credit rating and stock price, and gain ICC approval. A time frame of four to six weeks was set.

From this meeting clear lines of differences emerged. Evans tended to follow rather than lead in these kinds of decisions. Cook and Surette exemplified the GE emphasis on financial results. McDonald was skeptical of any merger and agreed that none should be undertaken without complete understanding of all its ramifications. Kenefick and Schaefer tried with only partial success to get them to appreciate the broader strategic picture. For the corporate staff, the larger picture was the overall mix of businesses, not the railroad by itself. Important as the meeting was, it produced no conclusive results beyond more delay and inaction.

New York came up with five alternative ways to acquire CNW, and Omaha provided six more; a meeting on February 11 added another two. Schaefer analyzed the entire list and informed McDonald that "from the operating point of view, alternative 10, i.e. outright acquisition of all the outstanding securities of the CNW, would certainly appear the most desirable." Surette asked Hill to produce a strategic overview of the project from a financial perspective and recommend a course of action. Hill obliged with an analysis that became the basis for another meeting on March 31.

While conceding that major realignments of western roads were taking place, Hill argued that they would "require large sums of capital and another two or three years of time. It appears, therefore, that UP would not be adversely affected by potential realignments much before the year 1982." Of all possible merger partners, CNW offered the best protection for the investment required, but it carried a heavy debt load relative to its earning capacity and had too much excess capacity. In his view UP would be hurt more than helped by immediate acquisition of CNW. Even though it would increase the cost, Hill insisted that it would be "in the Union Pacific's best interest to delay, as long as possible, acquisition of the C&NW."[30]

Kenefick and Schaefer were appalled. They saw time as working against them. Schaefer wrote a detailed rebuttal that demolished much of Hill's argument, while Kenefick stressed yet again the critical importance of CNW to UP. They modified their position by urging McDonald to acquire at least a minority stake of 25 percent to 40 percent in CNW as soon as possible. McDonald thanked him for the critique but replied, "Speaking for myself, I am not personally persuaded that the acquisition of a minority interest in the CNW 'preserves maximum flexibility' to us."[31]

Nor could Kenefick interest McDonald in the MP. In the spring of 1978 he had received a phone call from Downing Jenks, the head man at MP. Earlier, in mid-1977, Jenks had sounded Kenefick on his interest in a possible merger and was told the timing was not right for UP. Now he wanted to know if UP was ready to talk merger. He and Kenefick had great respect for one another, and the two companies got along well. Kenefick was receptive to the idea and told Jenks he would talk to the corporate people. Cook agreed to go to St. Louis with Kenefick to meet with Jenks and Thomas H. O'Leary, president of the Missouri Pacific Corporation. They arrived on May 22 and were greeted by Jenks, who handed them sheets of data on MP during their ride from the airport.[32]

Jenks stressed that he wanted to merge with another strong carrier and that he preferred UP. However, he was engaged in a drawn-out recapitalization struggle with some minority stockholders and couldn't undertake serious discussions until it was resolved. Cook confided that UPC had been studying possible mergers intensely for some time, and that MP was an attractive partner despite its high debt/equity ratio. Any disclosure of talks, however, would adversely affect UP's price/earnings ratio. For that reason, Cook did not want to go public or bring in outside consultants to determine an exchange ratio for the stocks.

A sticking point soon emerged. Jenks thought MP stockholders should get a premium for their shares, as was customary in an acquisition. Cook was adamant that the exchange ratio be tied to market values because UP had superior earnings, better growth prospects, and higher credit ranking. Six days later, in New York, O'Leary handed Cook and Surette his own ten-year projections and reiterated the need for a substantial premium. Cook disagreed. Since nothing could be done until the ICC decided the recapitalization fight, they agreed to adjourn until then.

The weeks dragged on. In September 1977 the FRA agreed to provide CNW with $24.6 million to upgrade its lines to Fremont and Milwaukee. In December Biaggini opened merger talks with the Seaboard Coast Line, thereby creating the possibility of the first real transcontinental railroad. A CNW spokesman said, "We aren't interested in merger at this time." However, CNW was very much interested in maintaining its partnership with UP for reasons that went beyond their traffic interchange. A new element had entered the equation: the Powder River Basin.[33]

For centuries the vast coal fields in the Powder River Basin of Wyoming lay unnoticed and untapped. Many people, especially geologists, knew the coal was there, but no one showed interest in claiming it from the remote grasslands that barely concealed it. Where a good coal seam in Pennsylvania might be seven feet thick, some in Powder River ran a hundred feet, and the deposits seemed to run on forever. They also lay close to the surface and could be mined cheaply. The lack of interest in them had mostly to do with the fact that in terms of BTUs Powder River coal produced 30 percent less heat than the bituminous coal carved out of Appalachia. But it had five times less sulfur in it—a fact that seemed unimportant until passage of the Clean Air Act in 1970 required power plants to install scrubbers to cleanse the coal they burned of sulfur or burn coal containing less sulfur. Powder River coal fit the act's requirements.[34]

No one could have imagined that a seminal piece of legislation, one often praised as the foundation of the environmental movement, also gave birth to the development of the greatest coal field on the planet. American use of electricity was growing, and the oil embargo of 1973 had dampened the switch from coal to oil as an energy source. Suddenly Powder River looked to be a bonanza if its endless beds of coal could be tapped. In 1973 CNW sent Gene Lewis, a civil engineer, to explore the area and develop traffic projections. He reported that the potential for coal revenues was "unbelievable."[35]

The problem was getting to it. The CNW's Cowboy line from Norfolk, Nebraska, to Lander, Wyoming, ran only 75 miles south of the deposits but was in poor shape. It would have to be rebuilt and a new line constructed to reach the coal fields. The BN also had a keen interest in the deposits. Early in 1973 it had applied for permission to build a 113-mile extension from Gillette, Wyoming, to Orin, Wyoming. In May CNW filed its own application to construct track northward from its Lander line. Two months later it suggested to BN that the two companies consolidate their applications. BN said no thanks, arguing that the basin was "exclusively Burlington Northern territory." It didn't want CNW horning in on its potential bonanza, and, as one of its officers admitted, "we could not see how the North Western could finance even half a line."[36]

Undaunted, CNW asked the ICC to consolidate the applications. Grudgingly BN agreed in December to build a 106-mile line jointly but CNW's triumph was short-lived. It had to come up with the money for both its share of the joint line and upgrading the Lander line to handle heavy unit trains of coal. The economy was sluggish, capital markets languished, and CNW's credit was poor. In June 1976 the two companies signed a supplemental agreement stipulating that BN would move ahead with the joint project and CNW would pay its share of the cost by November 30, 1977. CNW found itself in a quandary. Apart from paying its share of the joint line, it needed an estimated $530 million to improve the Cowboy line. This urgent need for funding brought it to a possible source: the UP.[37]

Kenefick first got wind of BN's intentions as early as October 1972 from an article in the *Wall Street Journal*. In May 1976 he joined a group of BN officers and directors on a tour that reached Gillette. What he saw impressed him deeply. "I knew that coal was big for the Burlington," he wrote Barnett, "but I do not think I really appreciated its proportions until I saw some of their statistics and visited two of the mines."[38]

That same spring Kenefick received a phone call from Larry Provo, who wanted UP to help finance the joint line and build a connector between their two roads from Node, Wyoming, to Joyce, Nebraska. Kenefick needed little prodding; he already sensed the immense potential of Powder River coal for both roads. Louis Menk contemptuously referred to UP's growing interest in the region as the "Yellow Peril," which may have led the bemused Kenefick to designate UP's study of the region as "Project Yellow."[39]

Discussions between the two companies continued into the fall of 1976 despite Provo's death. Equally intent on building a good relationship with Kenefick, Wolfe formed his own Project Yellow team to work on the project and applied to the FRA for a loan guarantee of $350 million to fund its share of the joint line. Coming as they did during the period when UP was struggling to reach decisions on the options posed by Project XYZ, the Powder River negotiations soon got intertwined with those deliberations.[40]

During the spring of 1978 Rebensdorf and his crew produced another detailed merger study, this time factoring in the potential impact of a Powder River connection. Using projections for the period 1977–90, the study spun out a series of scenarios. "The key issue," it declared, ". . . is whether the Corporation is willing to significantly increase its commitment to the railroad industry at this time. The Corporation must therefore give consideration to some sacrifice in short-term financial performance in order to assure the long-term strength and continued financial contribution of the Railroad to the Corporation." Nothing could get done if UPC rejected any outlay of capital that affected its finances adversely in the short term. "The long-term risk of such a strategy is immense," warned the study, "and the prospect of stagnation in a major business segment of the Corporation a very real possibility."[41]

Having emphasized that the status quo was not a viable option, the study then departed from some earlier XYZ conclusions. Affiliation with the CNW would have an unfavorable financial impact on the UP. The Powder River connection improved the impact, but not for a five- to eight-year period. Merger with the MP would have a favorable financial impact, but only in five to seven years. A three-way affiliation without Powder River would be unfavorable because of the negative impact of the CNW. It became more favorable with the Powder River connection, but not for five to eight years. In short, none of these mergers could be undertaken without an adverse short-term financial impact.[42]

However, if the CNW remained friendly and the UP undertook a joint venture for the Powder River line, "Union Pacific's best option would appear to be aggressive pursuit of the Missouri Pacific... to maximize the return from Project Yellow and to protect and expand its commercial presence in the growing markets of the south and southwest." This strategy offered two striking benefits. The MP provided access to the major markets for Powder River coal, and it reduced "the risk and adverse impact associated with the west-end problem by expansion into new markets." In any scenario, gaining access to Powder River coal was an investment worth making.

On this point the corporate staff agreed. In December 1978 the railroad closed an agreement with the CNW to build a joint 80-mile line from the Powder River Basin to points on both railroads. Coal traffic would flow southward along the connector to a point on the UP main line near Torrington, Wyoming, and from there to the CNW at Fremont. The CNW also agreed to obtain financing to preserve its half interest in the 106-mile joint line with the BN. The latter extended the deadline for the funds two years to 1979 while CNW sought money from the FRA to underwrite the construction.[43]

Still UPC balked at acquiring other lines. In May 1978 Cook told security analysts in San Francisco that UP had no interest whatever in creating a transcontinental line. "I'm not sure anyone wants to get into the Northeast," he said. "... Certainly we don't." Kenefick went one step further. He saw the railroad map of the future as having not two or three transcontinental lines but rather two or so systems in every region. Early in October Schaefer drafted a presentation for the New York officers on "the major reshaping of the industry which appears to be underway."[44]

Schaefer itemized the forces driving the reconfiguration. A recent Task Force on Rail Productivity stressed how the number of Class I railroads competing in some markets while depending on connections in others had created a schizophrenia in the industry that reduced intermodal competition and supported an industry-wide pricing structure. This protected less efficient routes and hampered the railroads' ability to compete effectively against trucks. To counter this "balkanization" of the industry, the report urged a restructuring through mergers into a handful of transcontinental systems capable of offering single-line service.[45]

The debate over competition prompted the Justice Department to renew its attack on railroad rate bureaus. The Reed-Bulwinkle Act of 1948 had legalized the rate bureaus, which were basically cartels enabling the carriers to present united rates to the ICC for approval. The bureaus prevented railroads from cutting rates to compete against one another, which also prevented them from cutting rates to compete against trucks. The passage of the 4R Act in 1976 seemed to produce more flexibility by requiring the ICC to review all rate bureau agreements. The commission took several steps that together looked to unravel the collective rate-making process and place "a much greater reliance on independent action by individual railroads."[46]

If this happened, Schaefer warned, UP would become more vulnerable to traffic diversions. As the rate bureau process eroded, competitors able to quote single-line rates would gain an enormous advantage. Moreover, the 4R Act contained a provision to deregulate some rates on a selective basis. While this might help some railroads, it also threatened "the prospective elimination of gateway protections on affected commodities." Congress was also considering amendments to the Federal Bankruptcy Act that would lessen the ICC's role in evaluating mergers or sales of lines from bankrupt roads. This would enable stronger roads to acquire desirable parts of such lines more quickly—the Tucumcari line came obviously to mind—and create new market positions much faster.[47]

The implications were clear. "One result," Schaefer warned, ". . . will be to force more affected carriers into larger systems or into bankruptcy. An immediate consequence for Union Pacific will be to put additional pressures on its connecting lines and also reduce the extent to which Union Pacific can expect to protect its gateways through the imposition of traffic conditions."[48]

The realignment process had already begun. Merger talks were under way among several roads. "Regulatory, service, economic and political pressures favor rail consolidation," Schaefer concluded, "and other railroads are beginning to move in that direction." The process was moving faster, and carriers affected by it would be hard-pressed to protect existing markets and relationships as more companies sought single-line status. Railroads like the UP that depended on interline connections to major markets or gateways would be at a disadvantage in every respect.[49]

The timing of Schaefer's report proved fortuitous. By the fall of 1978 the railroad's profits were up 21 percent from the previous year. At the same time, the oil business suffered from even more volatility than usual, the mining industry was being slapped with environmental restrictions, and five lawsuits had been filed challenging UP's mineral rights on its landholdings acquired from the government. Evans chose that November to announce that UPC was putting $240 million toward equipment and track maintenance for the railroad and that UPC believed strongly in the industry's future. "The oil industry is no panacea," he added. "Government regulation and controls have hurt the oil and gas business. Now it's no more profitable than manufacturing."[50]

The industry had a lot going for it. Trains could haul certain cargoes, especially bulky loads, far more cheaply than any other mode. They were energy efficient and did less damage to the environment. In 1978 railroads grossed $22 billion, employed 490,000 workers, and carried 70 percent of the nation's coal, 60 percent of its grain, 77 percent of its auto products, and over 60 percent of its chemicals and primary metals. Yet the industry earned only about $265 million that year. Ten railroads had gone bankrupt since 1967, three remained in bankruptcy, and another road was heading there. It was something of a paradox: either a very healthy sick industry or a very sick healthy industry.[51]

The corporate officers still debated whether capital should be plowed back into the railroad or diverted to nonrail needs. McDonald still doubted the value of mergers, telling a group of editors they were no cure for the industry. In the Midwest corridors he saw "too many carriers, competing for too little business, over too many rail lines, with too much deferred maintenance." Instead of mergers he proposed joint use of track, market swaps, and abandonments to rationalize the national network. L. Stanley Crane of the Southern agreed with McDonald. "Merger is not a panacea or a substitute for good railroad management," he declared.[52]

Both the ICC and the Department of Transportation (DOT) had gone on record favoring mergers as one solution to the industry's woes. Four merger proposals were already before the ICC, and two or three others were rumored in the offing. The key question—the one raised by McDonald and Crane—was whether mergers would solve the underlying problems of the rail industry or simply create more Penn Central debacles. The toxic influence of that failure lingered. A 1972 Senate Commerce Committee report concluded that mergers were "more likely to be harmful than beneficial." Their justification rested almost entirely on cost savings, but "the alleged savings have generally failed to materialize or have been much smaller than was anticipated."[53]

However, the new merger wave differed from that of the sixties in several respects. Most obviously it featured end-to-end rather than parallel mergers. The chief rationale was not to cut costs but to provide single-line service that was more efficient and flexible for shippers. The main goal was to streamline service to compete better with trucks and barges. Transportation Secretary Brock Adams agreed that "our overall goal is to produce efficient through-service transportation companies that can effectively compete with the through service we have with trucks and barges now."[54]

James Cook, in a thoughtful *Forbes* article, pointed out that railroads competed mostly with each other, which meant the gains realized by most mergers would come out of the hides of other railroads. Even worse, they could not control their pricing. "The railroads could charge considerably more for [bulk] freight than they currently do and still retain their competitive advantage," he noted, "but they are prevented from doing so by the Interstate Commerce Commission which is responding to pressures from politicians, shippers, and consumers." Nor would mergers do much to reduce the excess capacity problem unless they were accompanied by a freer policy on abandonments. This too suffered from the pressure of politicians who did not want constituents to lose their rail depots.[55]

Every major road recognized the necessity of being ready to act once the next round of mergers began. "If Southern Pacific gets the Tucumcari line," said

Downing Jenks, "other midwestern railroads have their own merger maps to pull out of the drawer." Hays T. Watkins of the Chessie had on his office wall a huge map of the United States with overlays that let him put different railroads together and take them apart again. "I suspect every other president or chairman has one," he said. "And whenever somebody announces a merger or a merger study, all the other companies start looking around."[56]

Therein lay the dilemma for UP. Which way should it move? It had already been burned once by the RI attempt, and that bitter memory lingered. But Humpty Dumpty had had a great fall. The rail industry was in many respects smashed into pieces, and no one could restore its traditional form. The issue for UPC was whether to move aggressively to expand its position or play it safe by clinging to the status quo as long as possible. As the officers in Omaha well knew, the time for decisions had come.

8

The Year of Decisions

In July 1979 Andras R. Petery of Morgan Stanley did an in-depth analysis of UP and liked what he saw. He thought its diversity of businesses provided a "unique ability to withstand a recession, especially at this time." Its decentralized operating responsibility, coupled with centralized financial controls and planning, made it "one of the few transportation-based concerns with a truly integrated approach to management." The railroad's success lay in the "wholesale" nature of its business. It handled large volumes over long hauls and impressed him as "one of the country's finest examples of a modern, efficient freight rail system." UP had also "been able to control its costs about as well as any railroad in the industry."[1]

Petery lavished praise on the "forward-looking leadership of John Kenefick" that had made the road "an industry leader in strategic planning, marketing, and development of modern information systems." He also thought the railroad possessed "one of the most sophisticated marketing departments in the industry," a telling observation given the company's long struggle in that field. He found general agreement among rail executives that the UP was "in the best shape of any major railroad." He was impressed not only by the railroad's computer system but also by its link-up via microwave with the SP's computers.[2]

Although oil and gas had recently upstaged the railroad's earnings, Petery accepted UPC's stated goals of keeping the railroad "one of the best" while striving to "balance the earnings between railroad profits and nonrailroad sources." A recession was coming, the railroad strategic scene was again in flux, and UP's management seemed fully aware of the potential threats posed by other western railroads through mergers. Any expansion by a rival system would compel UP to do the same thing. "UP could make a defensive, large acquisition or consolidation with a financially strong end-to-end railroad," Petery concluded, "in view of unfolding competitive changes forced on the Line."[3]

As 1979 opened, planning continued to hold center stage at UP headquarters. The corporation demanded long-range plans from each of the subsidiaries—ten-year projections that seemed the height of fantasy at a time when the onward rush of events made hash of underlying assumptions. Kenefick regarded long-range strategic planning as more a staff exercise to satisfy New York than anything else, but he had by far the best planning team in the corporation. He also had an agenda to promote in the form of finding the best possible merger partners for the UP and then persuading UPC to pull the trigger on them. However, the planning process itself got into a tangle in Omaha, thanks to one of those bureaucratic snafus that infect even efficient organizations.[4]

It began innocuously enough. After Tom Graves was promoted to the new position of vice president of finance in 1977, he decided in 1978 to create a separate strategic planning group for his own operation and put Jim Farrell in charge. Within a short time Farrell enlarged the group to about twenty people; by contrast Rebensdorf's P&A cadre had only a few people because it drew on other departments for help on a given project. This arrangement promoted duplication of effort and wasted resources, but Rebensdorf could do little about it. He reported to Deasey, who reported to Graves, while Farrell reported directly to Graves. Nor did Graves talk to Rebensdorf about creating another group to do what his staff already did.[5]

In July 1978 Farrell was asked to evaluate what portions, if any, of the failing Milwaukee road the UP might want to acquire. D. Chandler "Chan" Lewis was assigned the project but fell ill with mononucleosis and handed responsibility over to young Charley Eisele, whom he had hired only two months earlier. Eisele had less than three weeks to prepare a briefing for Kenefick. On a Saturday morning he marched up to the twelfth floor for his first encounter with the boss. His basic conclusion was that the Milwaukee line and facilities between Seattle and Spokane were the only parts worth acquiring. Kenefick asked about the Montana lines; Eisele ticked off a list of reasons why they were not worth the investment. The more he explained, the more the redness crept up Kenefick's neck—a warning sign that Eisele did not yet know.[6]

"Bullshit!" exploded Kenefick at last. "Young man, don't tell me what I can or can't do with the railroad." He waved toward the door. "That's it, I don't want to hear any more. I know what I'm going to do. Get out of here." Eisele slunk back to his office and called his wife. "Honey," he said softly, "if there's any boxes you haven't yet opened, don't." After a miserable weekend he returned Monday morning to learn that Kenefick wanted to see him. He found Kenefick sitting with his back to the open door. "I'm thinking about what you said," Kenefick said. "You're right about the stuff in the Northwest, so make it happen."

Farrell's group completed their study of what they called "Project M" on December 18, 1978, more than four months after UP had begun negotiations with Stanley Hillman, the Milwaukee's trustee. Ten days later Kenefick offered Hillman $14.5 million for certain Milwaukee segments totaling 241 miles. In October 1979, after protracted negotiations, Hillman accepted a revised offer for only 91 miles of Milwaukee road, including 26 miles of jointly owned line in Washington state, at a price of $19 million. The purchase included trackage between Seattle and Tacoma along with the Milwaukee's yard and tracks in Spokane. It was the first time the UP had bought parts of a bankrupt railroad.[7]

To Rebensdorf's chagrin, Graves's cadre also took charge of producing the long-range plan. Kenefick wanted a participatory process that engaged all departments. In February 1979 more than a hundred upper and middle managers gathered in Omaha for a "dialogue session" to identify major issues and formulate long-range objectives and strategies. The managers divided into groups for free-ranging discussions, after which group leaders pulled together consensus statements. Every department then prepared a written assessment of business conditions and resource needs. The results were sent to New York in preparation for a meeting between Kenefick, Graves, and the corporate leaders on April 24.[8]

This process was remarkable in several respects. It revealed clearly how far UP had begun to move from the old way of formulating policy and making decisions. The object was to move people around enough to understand areas of work outside their own department. Graves thought the meetings achieved his primary objectives of "encouraging broad-based communication and participation in the analysis of long-term company issues" and "generating a sense of understanding and enthusiasm for the process of planning."[9]

From the dialogue sessions the senior officers extracted a final set of eleven objectives and the strategies needed to realize them. The overall study offered a revealing portrait of the railroad on the eve of what became its era of reconfiguration. Its role as a bridge carrier could be seen in the fact that less than a third of its tonnage and 20 percent of its revenues originated and terminated on the UP's own line. Its traffic fell into three broad categories: dry bulk, consumer-related goods, and other products. For most of the 1970s it had the lowest labor cost ratio of the nation's five largest railroads.[10]

Pricing remained a prisoner of the regulatory process. The study emphasized that "the most pervading issue is certainly that of regulation," a subject on which no one agreed. Late in 1978 the DOT had proposed sweeping changes in railroad regulation designed to loosen the regulatory shackles and inspire more price competition. In March 1979 the AAR countered with a more conservative fourteen-point proposal on deregulation, and the Carter administration followed with its own legislative proposal. The ICC's position, drawn largely from the recent deregulation of airline passenger fares, seemed contradictory. It took steps to loosen the regulatory bonds, yet its incredibly restrictive view of the 4R Act's regulatory provisions virtually nullified many of its reforms.[11]

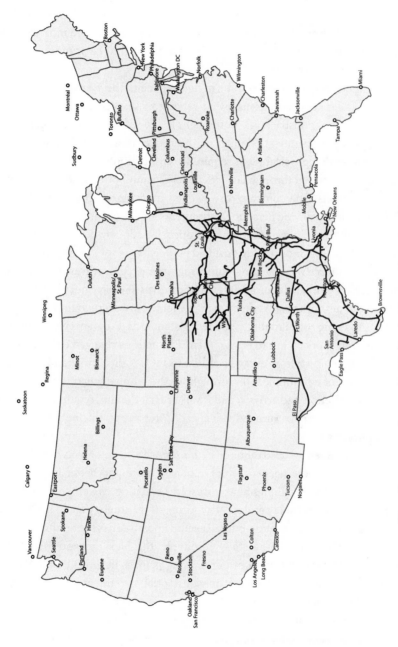

New Partner. The Missouri Pacific Railroad on the eve of the merger in 1982.

However, deregulation posed its own perils, including the possible resurgence of antitrust activity and state regulation as well as intensified competition both intramural and intermodal. Consideration also had to be given to the nation's energy and environmental policies. The former sought energy independence, which promised increased use of coal; the latter, enacted most recently in the 1977 amendments to the Clean Air Act, seemed to favor more use of low-sulfur coal such as that from Powder River.[12]

Competitively UP looked to be in fighting trim. The average age of its locomotives and freight cars was just over twelve years, and its bad-order ratio ranked well below the industry level. In the fight for speed-sensitive traffic, few other railroads could operate at 70 miles per hour over most of their main lines. But maintaining this physical plant required continued infusions of capital, which had to be generated through cost efficiencies, sound pricing, and development of new markets. The company also needed fresh blood. The study noted that "massive industry-wide personnel retirements will be occurring over the next 10 years. Union Pacific can maintain a competitive edge by developing the incentives to attract the most highly qualified people."[13]

The workforce was changing—growing younger, more diverse, and better educated. New workers required different incentives and were not likely to respond to the old authoritarian style of management. Turnover would likely increase thanks to rising social mobility and living standards. Programs were needed not only to train workers but to retrain them as functions changed or became obsolete. Leadership style at every level had to be less dictatorial and more open. Better lines of communication throughout the company had to be developed. Affirmative action had arrived, and it was crucial that its "requirements be handled positively to maximize individual and Company productivity and minimize disruption."[14]

Being competitive also required better service and new forms of it. More run-through trains were needed, which required more and better interroad automated data exchange. Equipment costs were escalating, as were shipper demands for faster, more reliable service. New forms of technology such as fiber-optics and satellite communication offered exciting possibilities for removing capacity restraints. However, as the study admitted, "the high demand for additional capacity and modernization of our existing plant is in direct conflict with the economic constraint imposed by our substantial investment in existing ground-line and microwave equipment."[15]

The new study impressed UPC, but not enough to move it toward a merger. Despite Kenefick's efforts, the summer of 1979 drifted by without a decision. Meanwhile, the CNW continued to impress observers with its resilience. Wolfe continued to pour most of his limited resources into the main line between Chicago and Fremont, the interchange point with the UP. By the summer of 1979 he

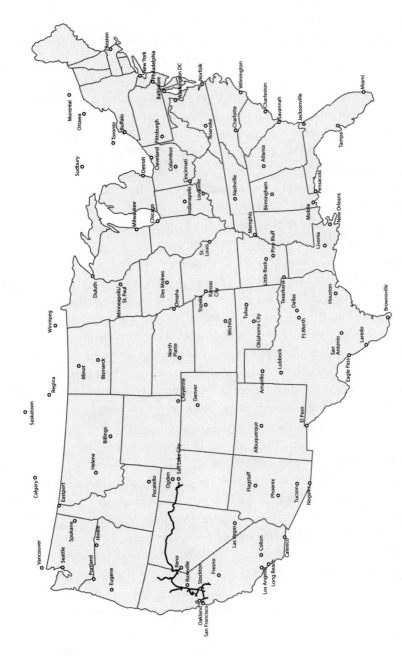

New Acquisition. The Western Pacific Railroad on the eve of its acquisition by the Union Pacific.

had cut two hours off the running time and had installed CTC at both ends of the route. However, it cost $300,000 a mile to upgrade the line from 30 to 70 miles per hour, and money remained in short supply. The FRA had already allotted the CNW $147.5 million to improve the line; the company applied for another $52 million to finish the CTC installation and $230 million for the extension into Powder River. The contractual deadline for the latter obligation was November 30, and no one expected BN to grant another extension.[16]

"It is widely assumed that the Union Pacific eventually will buy the North Western," observed one reporter, "ending the father-son relationship between the two that has existed for decades." But no sign was forthcoming. In October Kenefick submitted his strategic plan for 1979 to UPC. The corporation accepted the proposed "strategies, programs and financial targets" and agreed that the railroad's central mission was to preserve its "historic position as the leader in freight transportation." This would be accomplished through continued high levels of investment in physical plant and equipment, enhanced service performance, and selective growth of system capacity.

Evans praised Kenefick's plans to develop internal growth opportunities, "particularly your efforts to penetrate Power River Basin coal production regions via the Chicago and North Western connection—an excellent growth opportunity that should be aggressively pursued." But UPC would not go beyond this commitment. "We do not feel that an aggressive offensive pursuit of territorial market extensions through merger or acquisition activities should be undertaken at this time," Evans added. While conceding that at some point current strategies might have to be adjusted, he emphasized that "we found no reason to make any significant change in our basic corporate strategy that we have followed so successfully during the past decade."[17]

As late as October 1979, then, the corporate officers showed no interest in moving toward a merger with anyone. The CNW would impose too large a debt burden, and the MP would not solve the problem of the Chicago connection. Either partner would result in significant retaliatory traffic diversions. More important to UPC, any acquisition would increase the weight of the railroad in the overall business mix of the corporation, which would reduce its price/earnings ratio and stock price. While the corporation did not want to move away from the railroad industry, neither did it wish to increase its commitment. Yet in less than two months events forced UPC's officers into an almost complete about-face. The year of decisions, it turned out, was to be not 1979 but 1980.[18]

For nearly two years Rebensdorf stewed over the divided realm of strategic planning. He thought Farrell's group was floundering and had become something of a laughingstock. "John is a very smart guy," observed Eisele, "probably one of the smartest guys in the company, and I think John's always known he was a very smart guy." Rebensdorf was meticulous and a perfectionist, but no one ever accused him of untoward ambition or putting anything above his concern for the railroad. Late in 1979 he decided to resolve the issue that was tormenting him.[19]

One Saturday morning Rebensdorf told Graves bluntly that Farrell's strategic planning group accomplished little and was an embarrassment to both Graves and the finance department. Graves took the message well. On January 1, 1980, he combined the two strategic planning groups with Rebensdorf in charge as assistant vice president of P&A. The new group reported directly to Graves, as did Farrell, who confined his attention to Project Yellow. Deasey accepted the new arrangement. "I hated like hell to give up Rebensdorf," he admitted, "but I just thought that was a more solid organizational design."[20]

Graves had already given Kenefick his thoughts on the strategic scene in a November 2, 1979, memorandum. "The desire of the Corporation not to make additional investments in the rail industry is a restriction with which we will probably have to live," he conceded. "It behooves the UP to attempt to develop alternative ways of protecting its competitive position." Graves assumed that the western-end dilemma had no immediate solution, that the RI was nearing liquidation, and that the Rio Grande might seek to extend eastward through a merger. He recommended buying the WP and paying for it by selling to the Rio Grande the UP line between Topeka and Denver and granting it trackage rights from Topeka to Kansas City.[21]

WP posed an interesting problem. In April 1979 its parent company, Western Pacific Industries, spun off the railroad as a separate entity. UP owned 199,500 shares, or 6.9 percent, of the holding company's stock; it sold that stock and bought 9.9 percent of the WP Railroad's own stock to maintain its "historic" position. Three months later CNW acquired the same amount of WP stock, spurring rumors of a possible takeover. The WP's president, Robert G. "Mike" Flannery, another refugee from the NYC and Penn Central, was an old friend of Kenefick.[22]

In December Rebensdorf prepared financial forecasts for three potential merger candidates: CNW, MP, and WP. Kenefick already knew what he wanted to do. Appealing as CNW was, it did not offer the same potential rewards as MP. The fit was a good one. He and Jenks respected each other and got along well. Jenks saw where the industry was going and knew his company needed a merger to survive. He had long since concluded that UP was the best and strongest fit. Back in the 1960s he had made a formal proposal to UP for a merger but the timing was wrong. Now, he thought, the time was right if the obstacles could be overcome.[23]

Kenefick had come to the same conclusion. In deciding which way to turn, Powder River proved to be a crucial link between the options. The UP had already partnered with the CNW in that undertaking. The CNW created a new company, Western Railroad Properties, Inc. (WRPI), for that purpose. It had until November 30 to pony up $45 million to the BN for its half of the joint line or lose its right to share the route. The CNW had no way to raise the money internally and hoped to get it from the FRA. On November 2, however, the FRA dealt it a serious blow by dismissing the application. The BN planned to complete the 116-mile joint line by the year's end and made it clear that the CNW would not receive another extension.[24]

The entire project looked to be in limbo. The ICC had not yet even approved the joint ownership and operating agreement for the joint line. The Justice Department opposed approval, and Sun Energy Development Company had filed a $100 million lawsuit charging antitrust violations. The secretary of transportation reaffirmed his desire for competition in the Powder River Basin and talked of asking the ICC to set aside the November 30 deadline. The obvious and possibly only other alternative was for UP to provide the money. Chuck Eaton, another GE émigré who did strategic planning for UPC, outlined four possible options for Cook: direct purchase of CNW's franchise rights, financing in return for an ownership position in WRPI, financing in exchange for renegotiated revenue divisions on Powder River coal, or short-term interim financing.[25]

Kenefick knew that UPC wanted into the Powder River Basin as badly as he did, and that the November 30 deadline meant little until the ICC acted on the joint application. Lou Menk, BN's chairman, helped the cause by boasting to analysts how much money his railroad was going to make on Powder River coal. "This was okay to boost BN stock," said Schaefer, "but not a good idea when the competitive Powder River case was before the ICC." Schaefer was in the middle of the deal; he had devised the plan to join with the CNW after Kenefick asked him for the best way to get into the Powder River Basin. Menk went ballistic when he learned of the UP's involvement and never forgave Schaefer.[26]

Although the outcome was still pending, Kenefick figured that the Powder River deal bound the CNW even closer to the UP. Once into Powder River, another key question crossed his mind: Where would the coal go? The obvious answer was to power plants in the Southeast and Southwest, the territories served by the MP. More and more that system looked like the perfect fit for the UP. On a map the two systems meshed beautifully with hardly any overlap. The MP provided access to fast-growing regions of the South and the Gulf Coast as well as the St. Louis and Memphis gateways. It was in good physical shape, well managed, and progressive in its policies. Since Jenks wanted a merger, any negotiation should go smoothly.

Unbeknown to Kenefick, Jenks was thinking along similar lines but for a different reason. He had watched the same scenario unfold around his road that Kenefick had observed. The BN was swallowing the Frisco, the SP had taken a run at the Seaboard Coast Line, which instead got together with the Chessie. The SP was still searching for a new best friend and had already applied for the Tucumcari line. After the breakup of its talks with the MP, the Southern had wooed first the Illinois Central Gulf and then the N&W. Their flirtation lasted until November 1979, at which point the Southern reopened talks with the MP. This time Jenks was more receptive, but he still preferred the UP as a partner.[27]

"I would also like to be able to say that Jenks and I anticipated that the Staggers Act deregulation would wipe out the old, regulated network of through routes and rates, making mergers even more important," a bemused Kenefick said much later. "I did not see it coming, however, and if Jenks did he never mentioned it. It is often better to be lucky than smart."[28]

On a beautiful Sunday morning in late November or early December, Kenefick went up to the marketing department's offices on the eleventh floor. Pat Barrett was there, as were many of the senior officers. Kenefick had heard about the Southern-MP talks from two sources, including Schaefer's father-in-law. He and Barrett talked the situation over and agreed that the time had come to make a move. The MP might soon be the UP's only viable outlet to the South and Southeast. One other piece of the strategic puzzle at the western end remained loose: the WP. It would give the UP a foothold in northern California. Kenefick wanted to buy it but thought that if he did, "we'd have no chance of peace with the Southern Pacific." Barrett disagreed, saying that the SP had already done the most it could do to the UP. What was there to lose?[29]

Next morning Kenefick called Cook and afterward sent what became known as the "the jig is up" memorandum in which he argued forcefully that the time had come to go after the MP. The SP was very likely to get the Tucumcari line, and the MP might merge with the Southern. "If they go with the Southern," Kenefick warned, "we're dead." Cook told him to come to New York and make his case to the senior executives. Gerry saw the importance of the issue at once. Everyone agreed that the merger made sense and, given the length of the approval process, could not be put off any longer. While we are at it, Kenefick told Cook, we ought to buy the WP as well. It was a small road but would plant the UP squarely in the SP's backyard. Cook frowned. What, another railroad? he said. How much? About $18 million, replied Kenefick. "Oh hell," Cook snorted, "we can take that out of petty cash."[30]

Afterward a relieved Kenefick hastened to call Jenks and tell him the way was clear for a merger if he was still interested. Jenks replied that the call had come just in time. He was near an agreement with the Southern but was happy to inform them that he had a better deal even though he didn't yet know what it was. Terms were put together with blinding speed. Evans called Jenks to arrange a meeting. On January 4, 1980, Jenks came to New York to negotiate with the UPC people. Two days later they had a detailed agreement in principle, which

Evans, Cook, and Gerry took to the board. At the same time, the MP board, with data in hand on both the UP and the Southern, met to consider the agreement.[31]

"Currently a number of events have taken or are taking place which require us to reassess the future of our railroad," Evans told his directors. The first signs of deregulation had appeared, which meant that the industry might have to operate in a fully competitive environment. The industry itself was undergoing realignment, as was evident in the pending BN-Frisco merger.[32]

When Evans finished, Kenefick gave the board a more detailed picture of the deteriorating competitive scene. "At one time we had five good connections at our Omaha gateway for Chicago traffic," he said. "Today we have only one, Chicago & North Western." At Kansas City the RI was in bankruptcy and the Frisco was merging with the BN, leaving only the MP and the N&W as friendly connectors. To the west the SP, if it got the Tucumcari line, would do everything possible to route traffic away from the central corridor to its southern route. "I believe," he added, "Ben [Biaggini] fully intends to push from Kansas City on to Chicago which will give him a fully competitive route with the Santa Fe and with us. . . . Our estimates indicate that we could lose as much as 20% of our revenue base if we do not do something to protect our position." The WP was needed, he added, to ensure access to northern California.[33]

"I think we all agree with John," said Evans in summary, "that the MOPAC is our best rail merger candidate and that we have reached the point where the best defense is a strong offense." The board readily approved the merger. On January 8 news of the agreement went public and stunned the industry. It became popularly known as the "Mop-Up" merger; one observer likened it to "combining the Pittsburgh Steelers and the Dallas Cowboys." Two weeks later UP offered $20 a share for the 1.26 million shares of WP stock it did not already own.[34]

On a Sunday Kenefick called his officers together and outlined how things were going to work once the merger went through. For them the merger amounted to entry into a strange new world, one filled with as many uncertainties as opportunities. It was a more familiar world to Kenefick. In the back of his mind hovered memories of the Pennsylvania-NYC merger, and he vowed not to repeat the mistakes that destroyed those companies.[35]

Kenefick had one other important call to make. Just before the agreement went public he telephoned Biaggini to give him the news. Biaggini sputtered and denounced the merger as the most traitorous act since Benedict Arnold tried to sell West Point before slamming the phone down. Two weeks later Kenefick called again. "Ben, I've got a little surprise for you," he said. "We're going to acquire the Western Pacific." Biaggini called it "corporate treachery of the highest order" before calming down. "I don't understand it," he said. "Why wouldn't you acquire the Southern Pacific instead of the Western Pacific and the Missouri Pacific?"

"I don't want the Southern Pacific," Kenefick replied.[36]

Thus jilted, Biaggini mounted a vigorous campaign against the merger as "anticompetitive and otherwise contrary to the public interest" even as he scrambled to find yet another partner for the SP. The ICC approved the SP's acquisition of the Tucumcari line in June 1980. On May 15 Biaggini sprang another surprise: The SP and Santa Fe Industries signed a memorandum of intent to merge the SP with its historic rival, the SF. Clearly news of the Mop-Up merger provided the spark for another frantic round of musical chairs in the rail industry. Darius Gaskins, the incoming ICC chairman, lamented over "some of the best brains in the railroad industry playing around with the railroad map like kids with a Monopoly board when there were so many problems that went unresolved." For those seeking mergers, however, the point was precisely to solve some of those problems.[37]

It was one thing to agree on a merger and quite another to pull it off. Despite the reforms contained in the 4R Act, the MP and UP, which had reached agreement within weeks, took two and a half years to gain formal approval. The SP-SF courtship broke up within a few months, leaving both roads in search of other partners. Rumors of other possible alliances swirled in every direction; by September 1980 nine major railroads were involved in various stages of mergers. One wag predicted that within another decade "you could hold an AAR meeting in the corner booth of your favorite restaurant."[38]

For the next thirty months the UP poured much of its energy and resources into the merger process. During 1980, however, it had also to cement the second of its objectives, entry into the Powder River Basin. The case before the ICC to approve the joint line and provide authority for building a connector did not go well. The administrative law judge ordered CNW to pay its share of the joint line in full by February 25, 1980. An appeal delayed that date, but Schaefer worried that "the C&NW's financial credibility is, and will continue to be, a central issue in the entire case."[39]

If CNW could not convince the judge that it could raise the funds, the game would be lost for UP. No connector line would be needed because CNW would not be hauling any coal out of Powder River. It was imperative that UP come to some financial agreement with CNW to bolster the latter's financial credibility. Schaefer wanted UP to "take the initiative to force both the C&NW and the FRA to resolve the financial issue."[40]

Negotiations moved quickly enough for Tom Graves to testify before the ICC on March 10 that UP had reached a preliminary understanding with CNW to invest $60 million in building the connector and rehabilitating the CNW's line on both ends of it. UP would do this by acquiring an equity interest in a grantor trust formed for the purpose of owning and leasing the Powder River facilities. It would then lease these facilities to WRPI, a wholly owned subsidiary of CNW. WRPI would borrow most of the funds needed to pay for CNW's half interest in the joint line and own it outright along with the connector, related facilities, and improvements to CNW's existing line. UP would expand the capacity of its own facilities as part of the agreement.[41]

The agreement was signed on April 30. In June the UPC board approved the $60 million contribution toward the project. The ICC ruled that BN could not deny the CNW access to the joint line. However, the CNW's request for government funds to build the road got embedded in a much larger and even more controversial bill being thrashed out in Congress—one that threatened to produced the most far-reaching changes in the industry in a century. The year of decisions turned out to have one more major surprise in store.[42]

Some form of deregulation had been on the table for years. In 1967 Canada's National Transportation Act gave that nation's two major roads, the CN and CP, almost complete freedom to make rates and sign contracts with shippers. Four years later the Nixon administration put forth ambitious plans to free up land transportation only to run up against tough opposition from both the rail and trucking industries. "It has become apparent," noted *Business Week*, "that large segments of the industry are afraid that deregulation means a return to cutthroat competition." The railroads also feared that the freedom to make rates and contracts would come at another steep price: loss of their immunity from antitrust laws.[43]

For most of the century the railroads had lived in the secure if stifling cocoon of regulated rates. Their rate bureaus, which enjoyed antitrust immunity, made joint rates within limits imposed by the ICC. No road could raise or lower rates or offer a special rate without ICC approval, and all contracts had to be public. As public carriers they were obliged to carry whatever cargo shippers brought to them at a rate approved by the ICC. Under this system railroads could not compete by offering better rates; they could do so only by providing better or faster service. Marketing consisted of wining, dining, and playing golf with customers to maintain relationships. The only thing railroad salesmen had to sell was service, which was something they neither understood nor could control in any way.

This system produced a deep and unfortunate disconnect between the traffic and operating departments on most railroads. The two departments usually had thinly veiled contempt for each other. Operations always considered itself the heart of the railroad. To it the railroad existed to haul stuff from one place to another. What the stuff was, who the customers were, or what they wanted mattered little. The operations people had no contact with the customers and did not want any. Their job was to make the trains run efficiently and on time. Most traffic people knew little and cared less about operations. Once they procured the business, which came to them as much as they sought it out, they tossed the orders over the transom to operations and gave it no further thought.

This incredibly insular system persisted on most railroads deep into the twentieth century. However, the growing competition from other modes of transport forced railroads to rethink the relationship. On the UP Kenefick had brought in Barrett and Graves to breach the wall between marketing and operations. But reform pushed slowly against the dead weight of tradition. Deregulation could collapse the old system like a house of cards by enabling railroads to compete not only against other modes of transportation but against each other. For most railroad men, who tended to resist change, the consequences of so radical a transformation were too terrible to contemplate.

They were not alone in their fears. Shippers loved the regulated system because it protected them against what they considered unwarranted fluctuations in rates. Shippers and passengers had always demanded rates that fit their pocketbooks regardless of whether they covered the actual costs of transportation or not. This was especially true of captive shippers—those situated on a rail line with no access to a competing railroad. They liked to point to the bad old days of the nineteenth century when a host of purported railroad abuses—rebates, secret contracts, different rates for different customers or seasons—had led in 1887 to passage of the Interstate Commerce Act. But in those days railroads monopolized land transportation.

Nevertheless, shippers clung doggedly to a system that in effect compelled the railroads to subsidize their transportation costs. By the 1970s it had become painfully obvious that the railroads could no longer do so. As their return on investment shrank below 2 percent—it reached 1.24 percent in 1977—they could not earn even the cost of capital to maintain or improve their physical plant. To survive, most of them needed more money. It could come either from higher rates or from government aid. The latter amounted to a form of a subsidy for shippers by taxpayers; the former could be achieved by removing regulatory restraints and allowing railroads to price their service. Nearly every other nation had chosen the path of government subsidy, and in recent years the United States seemed headed in that direction.[44]

Few people wanted the government to be heavily involved in the railroads, yet fewer still wanted the roads to fail. The election of Ronald Reagan in 1980 signaled a retreat from heavy government involvement in business. Even before his election, however, the administration of Jimmy Carter had charted a course toward deregulation of the transportation industries. The first step came in 1978 with passage of the Airline Deregulation Act, which led to profound changes in the airline industry and resulted in the demise of the Civil Aeronautics Board six years later. Stage two occurred on July 1, 1980, with the Motor Carrier Act, which allowed trucks to solicit back hauls actively and to price this service below cost to secure business for otherwise empty return trips.[45]

Since the back-haul provision posed a direct threat to railroads, it became clear that rail rates would also have to be deregulated to some degree. In March 1979 Carter sent Congress a message urging deregulation to prevent the problems that had engulfed northeastern railroads from spreading elsewhere in the nation. He proposed giving railroads complete freedom to make rates after a transition period of five years in which rates could move no more than 7 percent in either direction without investigation. In return the rate bureaus would surrender their antitrust immunity and abide by all price-fixing laws. The railroads retained their common-carrier obligation but could quote a rate high enough to cover their costs. Rates became a contract between the railroad and shipper and did not have to be disclosed to other shippers.

Once introduced into Congress, the bill brought howls of protest from all sides. Captive shippers, represented by organizations such as the National Industrial Traffic League (NITL), complained that their rates would soar. Some rail leaders joined the chorus. John Fishwick of the N&W warned that deregulation would be an "unmitigated disaster" and a "blueprint for chaos." Farmers and elevator operators added their lamentations, along with some corporations. Since coal was a commodity captive to the railroads, the utilities joined the cry against deregulation. The bill languished into 1980. Meanwhile, in January 1980 the bankruptcy judge formally ordered the liquidation of the RI. The following month the Milwaukee ceased operations over much of its system. Two once great railroads had become ghosts, and no one knew which line was next.[46]

In September 1980 the ICC approved the merger of the Chessie and Seaboard Coast Line into a new system with the charmless name CSX. The Southern and the N&W were arranging their own merger. Five major systems—SP, SF, CSX, BN, and Conrail—dominated the newly emerging railroad map along with two as yet unfinished mergers, the MP-UP and the N&W-Southern. That autumn President Carter, anxious to get the deregulation bill passed before leaving office, brokered a compromise that put a ceiling on rates for captive shippers.[47]

Still another snag remained in the form of the provision for the loan guarantee enabling the CNW to fund its Powder River line. BN lobbied hard against the entire bill because of this one element, arguing that the real beneficiary was not the CNW but the UP. "I don't mind the competition," said Richard M. Bressler, BN's president, "but if the Union Pacific wants to build this road, let them do it with their own money and not the public's."[48]

Despite these obstacles, the Staggers bill—named for Representative Harley Staggers of West Virginia—finally passed Congress and was signed by President Carter on October 14. The railroads were now free to make their own rates and sign private contracts with shippers. They could cancel joint rates and their gateway agreements and impose premium rates for special services. General rate increases would be phased out by 1984. Railroads could use pricing as a competitive weapon against other transportation modes as well as each other, and they could start going after business that had long been beyond their reach. They could, in short, become creative in that most fossilized area of their activity, marketing. Rail managers would have to rethink not only their marketing but virtually every activity of their business. As Richard Saunders observed, "Staggers did change the economics of American railroading fundamentally and forever."[49]

The event received surprisingly little publicity. Ever since the demise of the passenger business, the railroads had passed from the general public's consciousness. Hardly anyone realized that Staggers betokened a new era in railroad history, and that not only the map but the very nature of railroads would never be the same again. To most observers, however, the future promised only uncertainty and dislocation as the newly emerging rail systems tried to understand and adjust to the act's provisions. Workers who had for so long relied on institutional memory to plot their course found that guide increasingly irrelevant to the realities confronting them. American railroads had begun the process of losing their unique character and becoming more like other businesses.

The battle over Powder River continued long after passage of the Staggers Act. The BN demonstrated its sobriquet, the "Big Nasty," in the fight that followed. "BN claims a virtual ancestral right to its present monopoly of railroad service in northeast Wyoming and southern Montana," wrote *Business Week*. The controversial provision in the Staggers Act called for the FRA to rule quickly on CNW's request for $310 million in loan guarantees. If granted, the loan would consume most of the FRA's program funds for a line that paralleled two existing roads owned by BN. But BN had refused to grant trackage rights over them to CNW lest the coal traffic be diverted to UP. This attitude prompted Wolfe to declare that "BN management has had the feeling that they own Wyoming, and that God gave it to them."[50]

Other parties agreed with Wolfe. An ICC staff member called BN "the most high-handed company around," and a rail executive said that the road's philosophy was "to get all you can, and then get some more." BN in turn charged that the loan was part of a deal set up to benefit UP. The proposed lease arrangement to WRPI would give UP upward of $150 million in tax write-offs for its $60 million investment along with title to both the improvements and CNW's share of the joint line. "To use the government's credit to give the Union Pacific all that tax shelter is an outrage," said a BN vice president indignantly, "especially when the UP could just write out a check for the whole project."[51]

Evans bridled at the charge. "All along we told the ICC," he insisted, "that, if they wanted us to be the competition in the Powder River, we'd go in and build a line without federal money." But the FRA thought that would further weaken CNW and create wasteful duplication of tracks. If BN refused to grant trackage rights, the government wanted CNW to build the connector. However, UP hesitated to advance funds for a line over which it had no control. In October 1980 Bressler offered to haul CNW's coal eastward to Iowa over its own tracks on a breakeven basis. "Sure, it was a self-serving offer," admitted Bressler. "But the effects on us of coal traffic diversion from the proposed UP-MoPac merger would be so devastating that I'd rather write out a check to the CNW. It's a question of which cannibal you want nibbling on your limbs."[52]

Kenefick and Wolfe agreed that meaningful competition in Powder River could happen only if CNW had its own service to the mines and could interchange traffic with UP at some point in western Nebraska. The new year opened with BN still hammering away at UP involvement and no end in sight for the dispute.[53]

The year of decisions drew to a close in a shroud of uncertainty. Although no one yet realized it, the economy had turned sour. Inflation still exceeded 10 percent a year, home mortgages cost 12 percent, and the cost of some borrowing approached 20 percent. The new Reagan administration, convinced that nothing could be done until inflation was curbed, pushed interest rates to their highest level in recent times. The result was the most severe recession since the 1930s, one that did not begin to ease until 1983. Unemployment shot past 10 percent in the fall of 1982, and railroad traffic crumbled. Even in their infancy the 1980s promised to be very different from the 1970s.[54]

9

The New Partners

The UP-MP-WP merger marked a milestone in Kenefick's career. It opened a new era in the UP's history, one that signaled the end of its historic role as a bridge carrier. In planning how to go about it, Kenefick could not help but keep in mind the merger fiasco that had nearly wrecked his own career. The Penn Central had been a textbook example of how not to integrate two large rail systems. Even while undergoing the long and tedious process of getting the merger approved, Kenefick began planning how best to put the two systems together.

It helped greatly that this was an end-to-end merger with little overlap or duplication of track. The UP ran primarily east-west, the MP north-south. One of the latter's two east-west arms ran to Pueblo, Colorado; the other reached El Paso, where it connected with the SP and SF. Although the two systems had several meeting points, the only major one was Kansas City. The MP was actually the larger of the two systems, with about 11,500 miles of track compared to 9,315 for the UP; the WP added another 1,436 miles. Their combined total created the third-largest system in the nation. Where the UP's mileage was split almost evenly between 4,848 miles of main and 4,467 miles of branch line, the MP had 7,900 miles of main and only 3,600 miles of branches.[1]

During 1979 the UP earned nearly $1.8 billion gross and $149 million net, while the MP took in $1.46 billion gross and $110 million net. By contrast the WP managed only $193 million gross and $4.7 million net. Their fleets were remarkably similar in size. The UP had about 1,500 locomotives, the MP 1,200; of that combined number 47 percent were less than a decade old. The MP had 20 percent fewer freight cars than the UP, and 39 percent of them were less than ten years old compared with 38 percent for the UP. Both systems believed ardently in strong maintenance programs. As of 1978 the MP had 110-pound or heavier rail on 71 percent of its main line compared to 74 percent on the UP. The WP required large expenditures to bring it up to UP standards, but the MP was in good shape.[2]

The formal application went to the ICC on September 15, 1980. The commission had to issue its ruling within thirty-one months. Predictably, nearly every railroad west of the Mississippi River challenged the merger on the grounds that it would harm competition. A Katy official complained that his company's best freight connection was merging with its biggest competitor. BN charged that the merger would drain $190 million worth of coal traffic annually from its lines and demanded trackage rights over the MP.[3]

Some state officials protested that ICC approval amounted to a willingness to eliminate its time-honored policy of requiring railroads to serve assigned territories in exchange for protection from intrusion by other roads. Captive shippers would become the first casualties of such a policy. One analyst, looking at the broader merger picture, predicted gloomily that "what the commission is doing is creating impregnable fortresses. My God, it would be easier for me to start an automobile company and compete with General Motors than a railroad to compete with what the commission is creating."[4]

Schaefer created a team of four to oversee the merger process: himself, Paul Conley, Charley Eisele, and Tom Watts. An army of lawyers descended on Washington to organize and present the case. "It was just an enormous undertaking," said Conley. "We actually had a merger office in Washington, D. C., where . . . if you were working on the case that would be headquarters. And we had four rooms at the guest quarters at 2500 Pennsylvania Avenue, which we used for a year. It was nuts."[5]

Schaefer spent two years working full-time on the merger case along with other lawyers from the company and from Covington & Burling. They compiled immense amounts of data, testimony, and endorsements from shippers who favored the merger. "Everybody was at us," said Schaefer. ". . . It was a real battle royal." The SP, SF, and BN attacked the merger vehemently while the KCS followed its usual practice of fishing in troubled waters for whatever it could catch. Despite the opposition, the outcome was seldom in doubt. The Justice Department and DOT gave their approval with some reservations, and in September 1982 the ICC voted 5–1 to approve the merger subject to some conditions granting trackage rights.[6]

By the time the ICC granted approval, it had long since sanctioned the other major merger proposals—BN's acquisition of the Frisco, the joining of the N&W and Southern into the Norfolk Southern, and the blending of the Chessie and Seaboard systems into CSX. BN emerged as the nation's largest system with 29,000 miles, followed by the CSX with 27,000 miles and the new UP-MP-WP system of 22,800 miles. Reginald Gilliam Jr., the ICC vice chairman, called the latter merger the "culmination of the first phase of a fundamental reordering and modernization of the railroad industry."[7]

A legal merger was one thing, physical integration quite another. Any merger poses difficult questions over how to blend a wide range of differences ranging from computer systems to operating rules to organizational structures to company cultures. Nor could the human element be overlooked. A large number of people would not be doing the same things in the same way at the same place. Many would not have jobs at all; others would find themselves working for strangers in a strange place. Employees at all three railroads asked the same two questions: Who are these people and what's going to happen to me?[8]

The WP had at least a management familiar to Kenefick. In August 1970 Howard Newman had summoned Perlman to rescue the floundering road. Newman had created Western Pacific Industries, a holding company that most rail experts expected to siphon cash from the railroad for nonrail investments. Perlman came to the WP from the dying Penn Central and brought with him Mike Flannery, another familiar figure to Kenefick. Both men took pay cuts to leave the largest railroad in the country for an obscure western road.[9]

The WP's history intersected that of the UP at points. It had been built by George Gould, the eldest son of Jay Gould, as the western link in his grandiose scheme to forge a true transcontinental system. Completed in 1909, it languished from the start. The road reached the Bay Area but had little business on its line and could not begin to compete with the SP. Gould had visions of competing with Harriman's system but was utterly unequal to the challenge.[10]

The WP fell into bankruptcy in 1915 and was bought by a group of bondholders. In 1926 Arthur Curtiss James, called by some the last rail entrepreneur, gained control and refurbished the line. Five years later the WP completed a link northward to the Great Northern at Bieber, California, but the Depression undermined the hope of increased business between the roads. In 1935 the WP again went into receivership. Using funds from the Reconstruction Finance Corporation, the company rehabilitated its line and entered World War II in sound condition. During the 1960s it fought a five-year legal battle against takeover attempts by the SP and the SF and remained independent until Newman's takeover in 1970.[11]

Flannery admitted he was "pleased and relieved" at UP's offer. "The Western Pacific . . . absolutely couldn't operate as an independent under deregulation," he said. "We were just too short of business. . . . In addition, we were directly competing with the much larger Southern Pacific. I was desperately trying to find a home for the Western Pacific." Apart from his relationship with Kenefick, what sold Flannery on UP was that company's willingness to upgrade the WP's line.[12]

The WP connected with the UP at Salt Lake City. It skirted the southern shore of the Great Salt Lake and ran across the salt flats of Nevada through the

Sierra Nevada Mountains of California to Oakland. Once into the mountains, the line endured endless curves, 894 of them totaling 182 miles, or 20 percent of the main line. Sixty-six of them exceeded 8°, all but three of which lay in the spectacular but treacherous Feather River Canyon. Assimilating the WP posed no problem; it simply became the fourth operating division of the UP. However, to handle more and heavier traffic it had to be overhauled. The merger application included a commitment to invest $90 million to bring the WP up to UP standards.[13]

The MP had even deeper roots in the Gould family than its new partners. In 1874 Jay Gould, the most controversial entrepreneur of his era, joined the UP board and turned that floundering road into a sound and growing enterprise. He put the road on sound financial footing but never managed to solve its most burdensome legacy, the government loan used to help construct it. Realizing that he could never fully control the company under this restriction, Gould essayed a series of lightning maneuvers in 1879–80 that took him out of the UP and into the creation of a new rail empire built around the MP.[14]

The MP began with transcontinental aspirations but got only from St. Louis to Kansas City. Gould acquired the road in 1879 and made it the nucleus of a new rail system. Conventional wisdom dictated that any major system be built around a significant trunk line. Gould defied that dictum. In short order he leased the Katy, acquired the St. Louis, Iron Mountain & Southern, and absorbed the International & Great Northern through an exchange of stock. From Tom Scott he bought the floundering Texas & Pacific, completed it to El Paso, and folded into it the New Orleans & Pacific. By 1881 the MP emerged as a major system. Gould then built an Omaha extension to tap traffic directly from the UP and gained control of the St. Louis Bridge Company.[15]

The MP remained part of the Gould business empire until 1911, when George surrendered the presidency and sold off the family's holdings. During the 1920s it fell into the hands of the quixotic Van Sweringen brothers, who fashioned a huge rail empire through the their holding company, the Alleghany Corporation. The Great Depression threw the MP into receivership as it did so many other roads. In 1933 the company became the first major railroad to file for bankruptcy under Section 77 of the Bankruptcy Act. Ironically, it became the last Depression-era road to emerge from bankruptcy, in 1956 after twenty-three contentious years. A syndicate that had acquired the Alleghany Corporation fought bitterly through these years to maintain control of the road.[16]

To complicate matters, MP emerged from bankruptcy still bearing a huge debt of $500 million, an amount equal to that of the Pennsylvania Railroad's but with revenues only a third as large to support it. The size of the debt gave pause to many investors but not to William Marbury, a lawyer who controlled a pipeline firm, Mississippi River Fuel Corporation of St. Louis (MRFC), and had joined the MP board in 1958. "That big debt doesn't scare me," Marbury declared. "I know it as a technician and it's the most beautiful debt structure I've ever seen."[17]

Marbury had MRFC buy enough MP stock to control the widely scattered issue, creating a bizarre situation in which a small $150 million pipeline company dominated a $1 billion major railroad. Marbury was a controversial figure in both Wall Street and St. Louis, a "very strong, very ruthless, very dynamic maverick type guy," as one analyst put it. He offended St. Louis elites by refusing to serve on local boards and by buying a 4,500-acre site on the Mississippi River complete with an antebellum plantation house named Selma Hall that became known as "Marbury's Castle." Marbury shrugged off the criticism. "The status quo is very important in Saint Louis," he said. ". . . I came in from the country and started stirring things up. This is a provincial town and they didn't like it."[18]

In September 1960 Marbury was made chairman of the MP board. He wanted a talented young man to run MP and found him in the presidency of the RI. Downing Jenks had reached that exalted office in 1956 at the unheard-of age of forty. A native of Portland, Oregon, Jenks had railroading in his blood. His grandfather had been a superintendent on the Great Northern of James J. Hill, and his father became vice president of operations for the same road. Determined to build on his family's legacy, Jenks earned a degree in engineering from Yale before launching his own railroad career as a chainman for the Spokane, Portland & Seattle.[19]

After a stint at the Pennsylvania, Jenks moved back to the Great Northern and rose quickly through the ranks. Like many other railroad men, he loved being superintendent most because it enabled him to capsule the rail experience within a single realm. "You've got to get out and see the property," he declared, "see what's going on, talk to people." Jenks developed a special feel for the railroad that only the best railroaders acquire. He would pass this gift on to a large stable of young officers.[20]

Historian Craig Miner described him astutely as "a fastidious person who was genuinely comfortable in a conservative suit and hat and who disliked long hair on his employees. He brooked no moral or ethical compromise and subscribed to a code much like that of the Boy Scouts, of which he later became national president. . . . He was not interested in making any adjustment in personal temperament to the modern age, although he was one of its most flexible innovators in management technique." Jenks did not like to socialize, partly because his wife was a recluse.[21]

In November 1960 Jenks came to St. Louis to discuss with Marbury the possibility of merging the RI with the MP. Marbury had no interest in the merger but was impressed with Jenks, who had grown unhappy at the RI. It seemed an unlikely partnership, the straitlaced Jenks and the boisterous, sometimes crude

Marbury. After a luncheon meeting in December, however, Marbury took Jenks to meet his family, and this glimpse into the maverick's domestic life convinced Jenks that he could not be all that bad.[22]

On this slender premise Jenks came to MP. In January 1961 Marbury resigned as chairman, Russell Dearmont moved up to that office, and Jenks became president and director. He told the board bluntly that the road was in poor shape and needed massive amounts of capital to operate efficiently; they responded with applause. Thus began one of the most impressive and influential presidencies in railroad history. During his first three months in office Jenks logged more than 30,000 miles inspecting the railroad. "The company was a little like a dowager," he said later, ". . . a little down at the heels."[23]

Jenks brought with him two key officers from the RI: John H. Lloyd as VPO and Frank Conrad as vice president of traffic. From the Great Northern he recruited John German to be chief mechanical officer, giving him a solid management core. Lloyd became the indispensable man, the practical anchor to Jenks's flights of fancy. "He's an impetuous fellow," Lloyd said of his boss, "and I get madder than hell at him." Lloyd was tough, astute, and frugal with the company's money.[24]

A young officer named Dick Davidson found this out early, as did most of his peers. For Davidson, Jenks was "the guy who always had the vision of wanting to get out and build things: build sidings, build shops, and get things done." When Mr. Jenks—and he was always "Mr." Jenks to the other officers—went over the road, Lloyd acted as governor. "You'd have a whole list of projects you'd want to talk him into," said Davidson, "and he'd always agree. Then lo and behold, here comes John Lloyd along behind and say, now what did the boss commit to here? And he'd cut off about 90 percent of it before you could get it done."[25]

But Jenks had a clear vision of what needed to be done, and Lloyd helped him do it. He shed branch lines, dumped passenger trains, rebuilt shops, upgraded the roadbed, and overhauled yards. Everywhere he cleaned out clutter, taking down 155 buildings in Sedalia alone. He reduced the road's fourteen divisions to four operating districts and decentralized the sales department into eleven districts. Jenks also excelled at speaking, lobbying, and enhancing the road's public image. Marbury supported his work. He got the MP into Chicago by acquiring the 862-mile C&EI in 1967 after a long and complicated fight. Although the road had to be rebuilt at a cost of $15 million, it proved invaluable for the huge flow of traffic through Chicago and St. Louis to the Gulf Coast.[26]

As Jenks upgraded MP, the major stumbling block continued to be the fight with Alleghany Corporation over a peculiarity in its capital structure. Apart from forcing management to watch its back constantly, it stood in the way of any merger or acquisition. Already it had greatly complicated the purchase of the C&EI. The more MP's earnings improved, the more imperative it became to recapitalize the road on a more rational basis. Thus began in 1963 a fight that raged for a decade.[27]

During the 1960s and early 1970s Marbury and Jenks cultivated a number of plans that dangled in limbo pending the outcome of the recapitalization fight. They did manage to buy some small Oklahoma roads known together as the Muskogee Lines, which totaled 767 miles, but other efforts failed. An attempt to absorb the Texas & Pacific was challenged by Alleghany and went all the way to the Supreme Court, where in 1967 Alleghany won a stunning 8–0 victory. The recapitalization fight dragged on.[28]

When Marbury died in July 1971, Jenks replaced him as chairman of the board, and Lloyd moved up to the presidency a year later. A year later the management came to terms with Alleghany. Not until December 1973 did the plan finally win ICC and court approval. By that time Jenks had introduced a host of impressive innovations. Two in particular exerted a profound influence: the management training program and the development of a computer system.[29]

Having become a railroad president at thirty-nine, Jenks preferred talented youth to veterans whose chief asset was time in the ranks. The unique culture of railroad experience, earned through years of apprenticeship under tough old warriors and handed down, was giving way to one in which younger workers had the advantage of having less to unlearn. The mystique was fading, replaced by new skill sets coupled with a willingness to learn new things. As railroading became more like other businesses, it could no longer be content merely to recruit from within.[30]

Jenks understood that the key to success lay in having a pool of good managers. He recruited young people from local colleges and universities, trained them for whatever jobs they filled, and rewarded them with good salaries and rapid promotion. "He loved youth," said Davidson, one of many officers who went through the training program. "He loved to challenge people. He told me time after time, don't be afraid to throw them out of the boat and see if they can swim. If they start to drown, pull them back in." Jenks launched a training program at MP soon after his arrival. By the time of the UP merger, nearly six hundred trainees had gone through it and more than half of them still worked for the railroad. Through this program Jenks educated the next generation of rail managers not only for MP but, as things turned out, for UP as well.[31]

Known formally as the Management Development Program, it began with the operating and traffic departments but soon spread to others. A key objective was to acquaint participants with every department on the railroad. This helped break down the traditional barriers between departments and gave trainees a taste of areas in which they might like to work. The program included both classroom and field experience. For a year trainees went through operations, traffic, mechanical, engineering, finance, and accounting, not only observing but doing work.[32]

Much of the trainee's time was spent in the field—riding trains, learning the ritual of yards, track gangs, and shops. Sometimes events overrode the lesson plan. Davidson's first day in the program in 1965 found him serving as a conductor (which he had been) during a wildcat strike on a freight train. When a flood in East Texas washed out part of the line, it threw a locomotive and several cars into the river. Jenks ordered all the trainees to the scene and put them with the crew of a work train. "When you have high water come up like that," said Davidson, "the railroad's the highest thing around, so all the snakes and the animals and everything come to the railroad to try and stay out of the water. It was a very dicey situation." Davidson had on a suit with no waders or boots. "I was wading out in the mud and the water trying to make myself useful. And lo and behold, here came Mr. Jenks and Mr. Lloyd down there, showing the flag more than anything. That's the first time I'd ever met them."[33]

The experience deeply impressed Davidson, as it did most other trainees. "You couldn't of staged a disaster like that if your life depended on it," he said, "and there you really were; you were thrown right in the middle of it." The program was rigorous, and it proved to be a striking success. Soon after his arrival in 1961 Jenks sent three of his top officers on an eight-week safari to colleges and universities in the railroad's territory to recruit potential trainees and promote the program.[34]

From the program emerged a solid corps of able managers, many with the potential to advance far up the hierarchy. "Missouri Pacific has the best management group I know of," wrote an analyst. "It is the only company I know where I don't know of any strategic or tactical mistakes." The men who went through the program cast a wide net in the railroad industry. Brad King, who entered it in 1970, recalled that he was one of fourteen candidates. "After ten years," he said, "I was the only one left." The rest had moved on to other railroads or companies in other industries.[35]

Although a diverse set of personalities, the best of them shared a common core of values. They were dedicated to their work, ambitious, savvy, and utterly loyal to Jenks, Lloyd, and the MP Railroad. Promotions came quickly to them along with opportunities to shine in more challenging positions. Davidson typified the breed. Starting with the MP as a brakeman at the age of eighteen, he was promoted to trainmaster at twenty-five, superintendent at twenty-nine, and assistant general manager at thirty. Three years later he moved to St. Louis as assistant to the vice president of operations. In 1976, at the age of thirty-four, Davidson became the vice president of operations. In that office he replaced the man widely considered as the heir to Jenks and Lloyd.[36]

James W. Gessner held a master's degree in civil engineering from Michigan. Quiet, cerebral, peering out from behind large horn-rimmed glasses, he resembled a professor more than a railroader. "You'd ask him a question," said Davidson. "he might not answer you for two or three minutes. You could see the wheels turning." Almost everybody liked Gessner and admired his intellect. He had spent three years in the army before joining the Southern Railway in 1955. There Gessner rose rapidly through the ranks while absorbing the harsh but sound lessons in the Brosnan school of railroading. He had risen to director of planning and development at the Southern when Jenks lured him to the MP in 1969 as assistant to the VPO.[37]

Within two years Gessner became a general manager; a year later he was put into a newly created position, general manager of transportation. In April 1974 he became VPO. Two years later he relinquished the position to Davidson and moved up to executive vice president, a clear signal that he was on track to succeed Lloyd when he retired. In May 1978 Lloyd became vice chairman of the board and turned the presidency over to Gessner. The line of succession seemed clear. Gessner would be the godfather for the next generation of MP officers following the retirement of Jenks and Lloyd.[38]

Jenks liked Gessner not only for his brains but for his adaptability. At the Southern Gessner had absorbed the primary lesson that change was both inevitable and desirable for the railroad, and that managers had to embrace rather than fear it. Those who thought he lacked personality or color were surprised to discover that he was a decent musician with a passion for Stan Kenton. He was also a splendid mentor to younger officers like Davidson, who admitted that Gessner taught him "it's better to really think things through thoroughly instead of getting your gun out and shooting before you aim." They also learned from Gessner the importance of technology to the railroad's future and the need to master every new generation of it.[39]

At the Southern Gessner had worked on that road's pioneering computer system. This too endeared him to Jenks, who had already begun the task of developing an advanced computer system on the MP. Nothing in Jenks's background even hinted at the role he would play in giving the MP arguably the most modern and efficient computerized control system in the industry. His predecessor, Russell Dearmont, bought the company's first computer in 1958 and then appointed a three-man committee to figure out how best to use it. The committee concluded that its most efficient use lay in solving materials and supplies problems. From this decision evolved a revolution in inventory control.[40]

Inventory control became the proving ground of the computer, and its influence spread quickly. Above all else, it promoted centralization and standardization, two virtues that had always been elusive on railroads because of their far-flung operations. The company closed four of its twelve warehouses and in

1965 built a centralized system supply warehouse at North Little Rock. Newer-model computers enabled the writing of more sophisticated programs and applications.[41]

Jenks sensed the vast possibilities of computers without knowing much about them. In 1965 he told a Texas audience, "These are the railroads' tools of competition which in the days ahead will be honed to an even finer edge." He created an ad hoc committee on computerization, gave it free rein to imagine and plan, and asked, "What would you do if you were creating a new railroad using computers?" The new technology was expensive, and Jenks was also committed to upgrading the physical plant and equipment, but he considered that work easy because it was familiar. The harder task was to find ways to apply computerization to operations with the awareness that doing so would change radically how almost everything was done.[42]

From the beginning Jenks sought more centralized control over operations, but the lack of current information above the yard level remained an insuperable obstacle. As one member of Jenks's ad hoc committee observed in 1966, when a car left the Dupo Yard near St. Louis for Little Rock, "effectively it was leaving the Dupo Pacific Railroad and going to the Little Rock Pacific Railroad." Every process done at Dupo had to be repeated at Little Rock as if the car had come from a foreign line. So too with car distribution; every yard acted autonomously, and it was impossible to keep track of what car was where on a real-time basis.[43]

The existing communication system was one in which contact with yard offices moved through a relay office in St. Louis via a "contention mode" in which parties waited patiently for an open line to transmit information that sometimes got garbled. The early computers began tracking cars using punch cards but at best showed only where a car had been twenty-four hours earlier. They provided history and statistics but not a tool for making decisions on the spot or in advance. Empties got shuttled between yards and often arrived too late to meet demand. Yardmasters hoarded cars while steadfastly denying the process, and no one was in position to see how the local flow of cars affected the entire system.[44]

The solution appeared in the form of the TOPS system developed by the SP, Stanford University, and IBM. Hailed as a successful management information system, it became the first major experiment with computers outside purchasing and accounting. TOPS became the foundation for the MP's program just as it had for COIN. It had relatively limited uses but served as a basis for the development of more sophisticated versions.[45]

TOPS was essentially a reporting system. As the committee's work progressed, it became increasingly clear that what it wanted was a system that not only provided information but enabled management to control the transportation process. "The critical part," said Merill Bryan, who worked on the system, "was, we were going to put all of the master files in the system . . . but we were also putting the operating plan in the computer." This would tell them what trains ran, what blocks of cars they handled, and how they were organized. As a result the name of the emerging system was changed that summer to Transportation Control System (TCS). No one yet suspected the profound influence it would ultimately exert.[46]

"That's a fundamental key thing with TCS," said Bryan. "We put the operating plan in the system. . . . If you were going to change the way we were going to switch and handle a bunch of cars or traffic, it might take a lot of wires to a lot of different places a week or two. . . . Well, here you can go in and change it in the computer, change the operating plan instantly. . . . Once you have that information, you can now produce a consist and work orders. . . . You can affect changes immediately and they're really following instructions instead of just reporting after the fact what they did."[47]

Jenks expedited the process by giving it a new and experienced leader. In 1969 he hired Guerdon Sines, the man who had overseen the development of TOPS at SP. Like so many other officers, Sines came from a railroad family. He graduated from West Point in 1951, saw action in Korea, and spent a dozen years at the SP, where between 1960 and 1966 he worked on the TOPS system before Perlman lured him to the NYC. Sines remained at Penn Central until coming to the MP. A year later he was made director of information and control systems.[48]

Sines could not have asked for a better situation to inherit. By 1968 Jenks's committee had sold management on the concept of TCS and begun designing the system, choosing equipment, and figuring out ways to implement it. Their hardest task was convincing skeptics that the railroad could function on a computer system without reams of paper as backup. Veteran railroaders did not take easily to electronic mediums. "We had to change people in some cases," recalled Davidson, "because they couldn't adapt to using computer technology to manage their operations with."[49]

In the end it was Jenks who made it clear to everyone that the project would go forward. "TCS," he said in the 1969 annual report, "may well be the most revolutionary development in railroading of this century." In its final form it would be "more complex than any commercial management information system now in existence." He was right on both counts.[50]

His committee had done its work well, but the members labored under one misconception. They assumed that the entire TCS system would be implemented in one fell swoop. Sines showed them the fallacy of this thinking. He told them that they had "designed a cow to be eaten in one bite and if we didn't break our jaws, sure to God our stomachs would have exploded." To ease acceptance, the implementation had to be done in small, easily digested bites that everyone could understand. This approach helped remove fears by allowing time for training in advance of each new step. The equipment chosen was first-rate; Sines's predecessor had committed to IBM's new 360 and 370 series.[51]

Phase 1 of TCS was a fundamental train movement reporting system. As it neared readiness, design and development of the remaining phases were broken into twelve detailed segments for later implementation. On November 16, 1970, a major milestone was reached when the Neff Yard in Kansas City became the first to use the TCS Car Movement Information Network. Once completed, the network would furnish the central computer in St. Louis with real-time data on car arrivals, departures, interchanges, bad-orders, and no-bills for all fifty thousand cars in the MP fleet. The system utilized a new telephone system installed two months earlier that reserved several circuits between all locations solely for data transmission.[52]

The revolution was under way. Prior to its coming, cars were tagged by hand with side cards that often got dirty and obscured. "The most vital piece of equipment," declared Dick Davidson, "was actually the nail gun where you'd put the side card on a car [saying] what the next destination was so the switchman would know what to do with it. And if that gun broke, you were dead." A clerk walked the train writing down the car numbers, and the conductor carried the waybills that told the car's route. Each car's destination was put on a list and handed to the yardmaster, who marked what track the car should go to. TCS eliminated all this slow, tedious, inefficient work along with the army of clerks needed to perform it.[53]

In July 1971 the Memphis Yard began using the new Yard and Terminal Subsystem (YATS), which transferred to a minicomputer thirty-three yard functions formerly handled by punch cards. The next step was to create a network of Customer Service Centers (CSCs) where shippers could get full information with just one telephone call. By 1974 some twenty-five centers were operating, with another twenty-five planned. Phase 2 of TCS called for upgrading the data on freight car movements fed to the central computer in St. Louis.[54]

The new system performed beyond expectations. TCS reduced car hire by $9.1 million in 1972, and the stay of foreign cars shrank by nearly two million days. In February 1973 the company established its new Transportation Control Center in St. Louis with Gessner in charge. On July 16 the center assumed full responsibility for the central coordination of all train and car movements.[55]

Phase 3 introduced autobilling—the production of waybills by computer—and installed CRT terminals in the CSCs to utilize the new system. Phase 4, which upgraded the entire system for complete reporting and car distribution, was cut in overnight on November 30, 1975, thanks to the most intensive training program the MP had ever attempted. The switchover involved training every dispatcher, conductor, and engine foreman on the MP system.[56]

YATS proved to be the most complicated of the TCS subsystems, and Sines was careful to choreograph its installation. The first phase, installed at Memphis and then Omaha, replaced the existing Yard Car Control with a sophisticated computer system that contained management reports and inquiry capabilities. The second phase linked the yard computer to the TCS central computer and could accommodate all of the TCS event-reporting requirements. The final phase computerized the Industry Card Control and completely disposed of all punch-card activities.[57]

Phases 5 and 6 focused on car scheduling, the most advanced feature of the system, and the generation of work orders. The FRA praised the MP for its pioneering work and awarded it a $5.5 million grant to help develop an automated car-scheduling system for the industry. The MP became the test case for a project intended to improve freight car utilization nationwide. Since the funds came from the federal government, any railroad would have access to the software once it was developed. It speaks volumes about the industry that no road took advantage of the offer.[58]

Nevertheless, the money was well spent; TCS-5 eventually accounted for 30 percent of the car hire savings attributed to the whole system. TCS-6 extended scheduling from the major yards to the rest of the railroad served by local trains. With it came a wholesale closing of small stations, with clerical savings estimated at $2 million a year. Two final phases concentrated on management issues. TCS-7 developed executive and middle-management controls, while TCS-8 dealt with accounting. Together they enabled much closer analysis of cost accounting on individual shipments.[59]

The response followed a predictable cycle. Veteran officers reacted with skepticism, fear, hesitation, and then delight as what seemed at first a fiendishly complicated system began to show what it could do for them. "I started railroading 31 years ago as a yard clerk," said a trainmaster at Texarkana, "and all we had was pencil and paper to prepare transportation documents. Ten years ago, I would not have believed we could get this much help from a computer." It was, he enthused, the greatest thing to happen to the MP since dieselization. A trainmaster at Omaha was no less thrilled. "YATS has taken all our yard car inventory records and placed them at our fingertips," he said.[60]

While the major phases were being implemented, some had been subdivided even more to create extra functions that proved invaluable. These included YATS, the autobill system, and the car-scheduling and -distribution capabilities, all of them rail industry firsts. An even more impressive first was the general inquiry feature, which allowed a manager to ask the computer almost anything he wanted about the railroad. Officers who had once resisted or doubted the TCS system were by the late 1970s besieging Sines with demands for more programs with different functions.[61]

Another advantage did not become clear until later: TCS had been created in modular form, making it possible to extend and expand it to ever larger systems. The database could also be expanded at will as the technology grew more sophisticated. As a complex system it required a steep learning curve, but once mastered it performed superbly.[62]

That same year Bill Hillebrandt, the assistant to the VPO, gave a speech that included a quotation about what railroads needed. The list featured the most effective use of motive power, regulation of speed to the lowest level consistent with business needs, effective control of rolling stock, the reduction of dead weight, and an increase in useful load. TCS accomplished all these things, he said, then added with a smile that the list came from a statement made by an officer of the Erie Railroad in 1854. When a reporter asked why he was so confident about the system, Hillebrandt replied, "It works. It has already paid for itself."[63]

Had Jenks done nothing more than develop the management training program and foster the creation of TCS, he would have solidified his reputation as a great railroad manager. But he did much more. To develop a more diverse traffic base, he pushed the traffic and operating departments to work together in promoting industrial development along the MP line and to come up with service innovations attractive to shippers. A strong believer in the future of intermodal traffic, Jenks expanded the company's role in piggyback and container business. He positioned MP as a "total transportation and distribution company" with its own truck operation, the MoPac Truck Lines. However, under ICC rules the MP trucks could solicit business only along routes that paralleled the rail line.[64]

In August 1972 the MP unveiled what it called the "Port of St. Louis by rail," a new 22-acre intermodal facility. Joseph Austin, the vice president of traffic, declared that the new facility would expand the city's role in world trade. "The link is the container," he said, "the giant, standardized shipping box that rides equally well in the belly of an airplane, on a truck chassis, in a ship's cargo hatch or on top of a railroad flatcar." That same year *Modern Railroads* named the MP its Railroad of the Year.[65]

Chemicals and grain formed the core of MP traffic. Unit trains carried both commodities and coal as well; by 1977 two 75- to 100-car trains of chemicals ran daily between Houston and St. Louis. To expedite their movement, Jenks overhauled major yards. In September 1971 the new Centennial Yard at Fort Worth opened. Fully automated, it could classify three thousand cars daily. Jenks also bought as much new equipment as his budget could stand; by 1974 the MP fleet included more than thirty types of freight cars. Mindful of the importance of chemicals, the company pioneered in the development of a computer-generated hazardous materials response system.[66]

Safety also mattered greatly to Jenks. During 1978–80 the MP earned three straight Harriman Safety Awards bronze medals, and followed them with a silver medal in 1981. The welfare of employees also concerned him. In December 1973, less than two years after Kenefick had done the same on the UP, the MP launched its social counseling program. Nearly 80 percent of those who sought help had alcohol problems; the others included drugs, family, and other personal issues. Only five other railroads had similar programs even though alcoholism had long been a rampant problem in the industry. "Our past experience," admitted a union leader, "is that nearly one employe [*sic*] per week . . . in the St. Louis area, lost his or her job because of alcoholism problems."⁶⁷

In October 1980 Jenks realized another ambition when the company announced that it would start construction on a huge $40 million locomotive shop at North Little Rock. It was the first American shop to be designed and built for locomotive heavy repair; the others had been converted from facilities used for steam locomotives. In this and other ways the MP made itself into the very model of a modern railroad. It had survived bankruptcy, fought the long recapitalization battle, and steadily improved the road on a lean purse. Shops and yards had been standardized, specialized, and centralized. The employee roster was steadily reduced as functions became more automated and computerized. Jenks and Lloyd had long since mastered the art of running a railroad with never enough money. In 1974, after the recapitalization fight ended, they finally absorbed the Texas & Pacific and C&EI roads into the parent company.⁶⁸

By the time of the merger MP had become not only a worthy but a formidable partner. Although Jenks and Kenefick were not at all alike as individuals, the methods they had used to modernize their railroads bore a striking resemblance. "Mr." Jenks and "Mr." Kenefick never became close buddies, but they enjoyed a bond of mutual respect. The overriding question, the one most on the mind of employees of both roads, was how their leaders would bring the two companies together.

10

The Coming Together

The merger of two major railroads is a complex task. Two different cultures are thrown together and must be made to accommodate one another. Departments have to be integrated; some employees will be promoted, others will lose their jobs. Two different sets of rules and procedures must be combined. Routes and possible abandonments must be determined along with traffic patterns over a much larger field of operation. For modern railroads a merger also means combining two separate computer systems on which operations depend.[1]

Although three railroads were involved in this merger, WP posed little problem. It was simply absorbed as the fourth division of UP. The only question was what role Mike Flannery would play in the new organization. MP was another matter. UP was the dominant partner and by far the richer of the two roads but MP was larger and had a solid management team as well as a very different culture. Putting the two companies together required careful thinking and delicate diplomacy.[2]

The key to a successful merger, Kenefick believed, was to go slow. He still recalled the horrors of the Penn Central merger, in which two incompatible cultures had been jammed together with disastrous results. The first decision, then, was *not* to merge the roads physically right away. "Missouri Pacific will operate as a sister railroad to Union Pacific," read the official declaration. "It will maintain its separate identity, but it will work closely with Union Pacific to coordinate single system operations."[3]

Earlier Jenks had given the same assurance. "We will keep two separate profit centers to avoid getting a railroad that is too big to handle," he said. "By keeping them separate, on merger day everyone will go to work as usual." But everyone knew this approach would last only a short time. The true savings and efficiencies would come only from integrating the two roads into one giant system. Managing so large a system posed a major challenge to whoever assumed the task.[4]

The top level posed no obvious problems. Kenefick would take charge of the combined roads; he was only sixty-one in 1982. Jenks turned sixty-seven that same year and was looking to retire; Kenefick thought that was one reason Jenks was so eager to find a safe haven for MP. Gessner was only fifty-one and seemed an ideal candidate to succeed Kenefick. However, on May 24, the evening before an important MP board meeting, he dropped dead of a heart attack. A stunned Jenks called Kenefick to suggest that Flannery replace Gessner. Kenefick thought it was a good idea, that it would make "one less guy we have to place when the merger occurs."[5]

Gessner had suffered an earlier heart attack, but the news still devastated the other MP officers. He had been their great hope in the integration to come; now no one knew what to expect. "I mean, we had no godfather," said White Matthews, the treasurer. Jenks sensed their uneasiness and called the senior people together. Davidson recalled the scene. "He said, 'Let me assure you of one thing. It may not happen the first day, but I will assure you the MP people will end up running the company.'" Matthews couldn't believe it. "I kind of rolled my eyes, like, hello," he said, but others took the message to heart. Privately Jenks told Davidson, "Dick, don't worry about how they put this management structure together. My guys, you guys, are going to end up running it."[6]

Jenks had taken the measure of the UP men. When UP held its annual senior staff meeting at Sun Valley, Kenefick invited Jenks and his top officers to join the party. On one occasion Jenks went up to Oregon and looked the UP system over. Davidson went along and got his introduction to UP as well. What Jenks found was a group of operating officers that were older and less talented than his own boys. Jim Dolan, who came to Omaha in December 1983 as vice president of law, saw the same thing. "Coming in from the outside," he said, "it became clear that Missouri Pacific people were a notch above the Union Pacific people. They probably had better educational backgrounds. They were trained much better."[7]

Knowingly or not, Jenks had found one of Kenefick's few weaknesses. He lacked a successor; and his management training program was not as developed as that of MP. Years before the merger Elbridge Gerry had prodded Kenefick on the subject of a successor. Suppose you drop dead? Gerry asked. In that case, Kenefick replied, go after Mike Flannery, who was four years younger. "I thought what they would probably do," said Kenefick, "was to put Flannery in there for about three years and spend that time finding, picking out a guy that would have a longer term." Gessner's untimely death had already elevated him to head of the Missouri Pacific.[8]

Jenks formally retired from the MP on January 31, 1983, but joined the UP board. A senior management team was formed to oversee the transition. Kenefick became chairman and CEO of what came to be known as the Union Pacific

System. Flannery moved to the presidency with Schaefer, Barrett, and George A. Craig, MP's senior vice president of marketing, as executive vice presidents. The logical first step was to integrate the marketing departments. "It would be ridiculous," said Kenefick, "to have two sales offices in the same damn city calling the same customer." Barrett became the top man, with Craig as his number two. Both were exceptionally able men who got along well. Kenefick told Barrett that for every trip Craig made to Omaha to do planning, Barrett should go twice to St. Louis to see him. Thanks to their competence and compatibility, this first layer of combination went smoothly. "Craig had as much influence, I think," said Kenefick, "running the marketing department . . . as I think Barrett did."[9]

As chairman of the UP System Kenefick took care to maintain offices in both Omaha and St. Louis. The locomotives became another source of subtle integration. Within a short time the WP engines disappeared into the Armour yellow paint and red trim the UP had used since 1934. Early in 1984 MP locomotives began surrendering their traditional blue luster to the UP's yellow and red coats although the lettering on them still read *MP*. As Kenefick observed with a smile, "They sure looked like a UP engine from a distance."[10]

Despite the slow pace of change and the care taken to avoid ruffling feathers, problems inevitably cropped up. Part of the reason lay in the differences between the two railroads. "They were very different," said Jerry Davis, who was then VPO for UP. "The Union Pacific . . . was more of a pipeline of trains. . . . I could move a car from New York state to the West Coast and only switch it one time. . . . On the Missouri Pacific, to get a car from Houston to Chicago you'd probably switch it three times at many more yards." Turn a map of the UP on end and the road looked like an hourglass with the North Platte yards as the neck through which traffic was funneled in both directions. The MP had a more complex set of routes with shorter hauls, more yards, and more local work.[11]

Davis liked the MP's ability to do more with less, and he especially admired the management training program. However, he also thought they lacked the sense of urgency in moving trains that characterized the UP. "When I was assistant VPO," he recalled, "I'd sit out at Cheyenne with the VPO at that time. If the train set there over three minutes, he was gnawing on my ass. Why hadn't I got moving? Move that train, get that train, move on. Move him!" This sense of urgency came in part from the UP's traditional hierarchy, which Kenefick had succeeded in dismantling only in part.[12]

Davidson, Davis's counterpart on the MP, was surprised to find how much more structured and formal UP was. "We weren't nearly as bound up by tradition," he said. ". . . We didn't really worry about hierarchy and management and that sort of thing. . . . People were a lot more informal and really didn't worry about reporting lines." When he went to Omaha, Davidson was shocked to discover that the senior managers all had their doors closed and saw people only by appointment. "We had an open door policy," he said. ". . . If a switchman wanted to come in and talk to me or anybody, you just felt free to walk in and talk." Reporting lines mattered greatly to UP men. The fastest way to get in trouble on the UP was to go around your boss with information. "It was so formal it was mind-boggling," said Davidson. ". . . It was almost impossible for something to percolate from the bottom all the way to the top without somebody being able to say no and stop it."[13]

"The two cultures did *not* at all immediately blend," said Brad King of MP. The biggest difference lay in their heritages. The UP was the gold-plated railroad that always seemed to have money for whatever it wanted to do. This good fortune bred a sense of confidence—some said arrogance—that the company could do anything it set out to do. Not by accident did "We Can Handle It" become its slogan of choice.[14]

The MP heritage could not have been more different. "The culture was one based on not wasting a single penny anywhere," admitted Davidson. "We rewarded frugality. In fact, I think some of the Union Pacific people described us as almost being anorexic about head count, and not wanting to hire personnel, and finding ways to do more with less. . . . While Kenefick wanted to run an efficient organization, to us it looked like they had an embarrassment of riches. . . . We wanted to get results and we didn't have a lot of extra people, and we didn't have staff to do a lot of research." By contrast Kenefick took pride in the fact that, for all the games he had to play with UPC, "in the end the railroad always got what it asked for."[15]

Gradually the different departments were put together. On the larger issues a task force was created to reach a consensus, but in many cases department heads made the final choices. "You had to get one decision," said Jacobson. "Of course, every time you would make that decision, somebody would feel like they lost . . . and you'd watch these two camps argue why theirs was best."[16]

No one argued more than the engineering and mechanical departments, where pride ran especially strong. Bob Brown and John German were both strong leaders with set ideas. They fought over standards such as what weight of rail was needed, but slowly the differences got resolved despite some hard feelings that the debate generated. Both departments looked to standardization as a means of simplifying inventories and saving money. "A lot of the standards fell to the UP side, practices to the MP side," said Charley Eisele, who was in the middle of the discussions.[17]

Standardization became the quest of every department, especially those with large inventories of parts and equipment. It produced impressive savings when combined with bulk purchasing. In 1983 Kenefick estimated that the road saved $20 million through bulk purchases of everything from fuel to spikes and looked to double that amount in the future. Elsewhere hackles rose over other technical issues. Schaefer put Eisele to work figuring out how to merge the finance, accounting, and law functions of the three roads.[18]

Schaefer harbored ambitions to move up to UPC but had first to find replacement vice presidents of law and finance. He went outside the company to fill both slots, bringing in James V. Dolan from the Washington law firm of Steptoe & Johnson and Richard Ames from Ford Motor Company. Dolan's acceptance surprised everyone. He was a hardcore Beltway type—born in Washington, schooled there through Georgetown University and Law School, and had spent twenty years at Steptoe. No one expected Dolan to leave D.C., but Schaefer impressed him deeply. After his interview Dolan came to Omaha and stayed nineteen years.[19]

Two areas in particular could not be meshed without a lot of friction and ill will: operations and the computer systems. In both cases there would be winners and losers. Whoever got the top job would likely impose the systems familiar to him, and those on the other road would have to change their ways. A brilliant operating man himself, Kenefick understood what would be involved and waited three years before integrating the two operating departments. However, the computer systems could not wait, and they could not be combined. Partly because computer technology had always been Kenefick's blind spot, he left the decision to others.

Kenefick had assured Jorgensen that the two systems would be kept separate and intact. That seemed plausible since the railroads were operated separately. "I was extremely naïve about the internecine politics and everything else," said Jorgensen. "I was a good soldier. The general tells you to do something, you do it." Jorgensen was also justifiably proud of what he had accomplished at UP despite what had been an uphill climb the whole way. He had built a strong MIS organization and in December 1978 was made vice president of management information services and communication.[20]

In his quiet, scholarly way Gessner might have approached the computer issue with greater care and dispassion. However, the ascendance of Flannery to the presidency first of the MP and then of the UP changed everything. Flannery knew both Kenefick and Guerdon Sines from their days at the NYC and Penn Central. A stranger to his new high positions, he gravitated naturally to whatever familiarities he could find. "When Flannery came to the MP," said Merill Bryan, who had come with Sines from the SP to the MP, "we immediately showed him all the systems . . . introduced him to TCS, what we had done with the computer systems. I think he was impressed."[21]

For Flannery the choice proved an easy one. He knew Sines and didn't know Jorgensen. He had seen the TCS system but knew little about COIN. One day that spring he called Jorgensen to his office and told him that he had decided to put Sines in charge. "You're both damned good," he added, "but I've known Guerdon a long time, and nobody said life was fair."[22]

Sines became vice president of information and communication services, while Jorgensen was made vice president of computer operations and communication systems. Bryan assumed the post of assistant vice president of systems development and implementation. In effect, Sines held the top spot in computer operations with Jorgensen overseeing communications. A stunned Jorgensen felt himself "laterally arabesqued" out of the systems design area that had been his forte for a quarter century. He understood Flannery's decision; what he didn't understand, and what rankled him deeply, was Kenefick's refusal to get involved in any way. Kenefick had put Flannery in charge of computer services along with several other departments, and he let the decision stand without comment.[23]

Ever the good soldier, Jorgensen tried to work with Sines in hopes of demonstrating the virtues of the COIN system. A joint task force was assembled to develop a comprehensive plan to, in Sines's words, "integrate the railroad industry's best computer departments." By the summer of 1983, however, Sines had decided to upgrade the WP to the TCS system. This project, he added, would enable him to "evaluate how successfully TCS meets the needs of both operating departments. We will then proceed with a feasibility study to determine if we go systemwide with TCS on the UP or develop an entirely new system for both railroads." No mention was made of COIN or any of the UP's own systems.[24]

In his own thinking Sines had no choice but to install TCS on the WP. The UP had already set dates to convert the WP to COIN. If TCS was to prevail, why waste time and money putting COIN on the WP? Sines ordered Bryan and others to formulate a plan for installing TCS in the same time frame scheduled for the COIN project. "That was a big, tall order," said Bryan, but they managed to get it done.[25]

The two systems had some common elements. Both had their roots in the base code of the SP's TOPS system. Both contained car information and processed it through yard systems to identify train blocks and tags for switching cars into trains. They also generated train lists or consists for crews and handled accounting functions. The major difference between them lay in the car-scheduling component of TCS, which COIN lacked. This subsystem detailed the handling plan for every car from the customer's loading to unloading dock by identifying the specific local and mainline trains handling it. Each car thus had a plan for the field operations to execute.[26]

COIN identified cars by block and tag but not by specific job. This left decisions on work to be done to local officers. Tracing a shipment on the UP could tell you what had happened so far but nothing about future movements. TCS detailed the entire handling plan, including future movements. As Jacobson explained, "UP's COIN ... provided very good data that you could use to know what happened and current status of today. MP's TCS system . . .

provided a framework to *control* the operation. You knew what happened yesterday, what should happen today and tomorrow." Bryan agreed that TCS "contained much more robust car cycle data as well as the scheduled trip plan."[27]

Both the UP and MP used IBM equipment and software for most of their systems, but they developed those system in different directions, partly because the UP had an advanced communications network with its extensive microwave and emerging fiber optics base. Since the MP had nothing comparable, Sines had developed a centralized system, while Jorgensen had taken the COIN system in the opposite direction. Where Sines sought consolidation, Jorgensen looked to remove "the single point of failure aspect of a totally centralized system," reduce the complexities of scale, and keep the system failure free. Given the railroad's growing dependence on computers, this last goal became paramount to Jorgensen. Recent problems with communications lines had slowed or shut down computers; an outage would affect only one territory instead of the entire system.[28]

Both TCS and COIN had good features. Since there were positives and negatives to both systems, comparing which was better was in the eye of the beholder. Like many of his peers, Jacobson viewed the process as a zero-sum game. "You had to get one decision," he said. "Of course, every time you would make that decision, somebody would feel like they lost. If you went with the MoPac computer system, then the UP guys think that they lost."[29]

Jorgensen had invested his career developing what he considered a superior system and believed passionately in its virtues. Sines had forged the TCS system with Jenks's enthusiastic support, while Jorgensen had created COIN despite Kenefick's lack of overt support beyond the resources needed. Nor did it help that their personalities clashed. Jorgensen was intense but usually reasonable. Having battled uphill his entire career at UP, his promotion to vice president in 1978 seemed to confirm that the fight had at last been won. Now he found himself in yet another battle on a different front with an adversary he came to despise.

Sines had a deliberate, militaristic, no-nonsense air worthy of his West Point background. On the wall behind his desk hung a picture of a wagon train with the caption "The cowards never started and the weak died along the way." Those words, thought Jacobson, "may be the best description you will find on Guerdon Sines." Although he did not suffer fools and could be aloof, Sines welcomed discussion of issues with those whose opinions he respected. "He was very fair," said Bryan, "but . . . would not tolerate somebody not pulling their weight."[30]

While most of the staff adapted to Sines's style and his often fearsome outbursts, Jorgensen found it increasingly hard to deal with him. "He never, ever, discussed the differences of our approaches," he said. "He simply didn't care. It was his way or the highway." It didn't help that Sines viewed the operations people as his valued clients while Jorgensen often regarded them as an obstacle to be overcome. Ultimately Jorgensen came to view Sines as a "backstabbing, underhanded, conniving eogmaniac."[31]

However, COIN had its drawbacks as well. Apart from the lack of centralized control and car-scheduling component, it had problems with response time. The special rooms that housed the equipment were expensive to build and maintain. A system based on distributive processing could not change boundaries easily. The MP had a comparable system in YATS but concluded it was not worth the cost and went to the centralized system. Nor was COIN all it was supposed to be, in King's opinion. "Their manual looked great," he said. "You said *oh wow*, but when you get in and try to use it . . . COIN had not been fully implemented. The manual said it had, but in reality it had not."[32]

In the winter of 1984 Sines made the decision to apply TCS to the entire system. When the decision was announced, Jacobson estimated that COIN performed about 75 percent of the functions done by TCS. A six-phase schedule for the cutover was created. To demonstrate the system's virtues, Sines had his staff stage a dog-and-pony show for anybody who wanted to attend. When it was done, one employee asked Sines where he got the authority to install TCS over the entire system. Sines paused a moment, then said that it would save millions of dollars. "It's going to save that much money," he emphasized, "and it's balls to the wall and I'm not stopping unless somebody comes out with a hook." Nobody knew what that phrase meant, but nobody asked another question.[33]

Like the original implementation of TCS, the cutover from COIN occurred in phases; the transition to autobilling, for example, took place in April 1985. Not until December 1, 1985, did the entire UP system begin operating with TCS. A trainmaster at North Platte, the busiest yard on the system, admitted he had been apprehensive over the change but said that under TCS "we have access to 10 times more information about trains and cars, which will save us a lot of time and telephone calls."[34]

"TCS was the superior system," said Jacobson. "The car scheduling module alone made it the right choice." But it was difficult to implement. Every clerk, trainman, yardmaster, and operating manager had to learn the new system. Employees made data errors as they struggled to master the system. It took between one and three months for employees to become comfortable with the new system and to clean up the control and data files. "Data incompatibility on the initial load," said Jacobson, "even at one percent can create hundreds or thousands of car records that move the car wrong or stop it altogether."[35]

While conceding that COIN had "some components and pieces that we thought were very good," Bryan insisted that TCS "was functionally richer and it had all those job benefits, all those savings. . . . I don't think John really understood TCS and what the power was, and what you could do with it." *Railway Age* described the TCS car-scheduling program as "the system which comes pretty close to the ultimate." Kenefick called it "a powerful marketing tool because it permits us to interchange very efficiently with other railroads and provides real-time information to shippers."[36]

The conflict between Jorgensen and Sines grew deeper and more personal. When Jorgensen was summoned to the New York office to work on a project with Schaefer, Sines had his belongings moved into an office in another building and installed the assistant vice president of communications in what had been Jorgensen's office. Jorgensen also thought Sines had pushed some good UP personnel out of the company, although others insisted this was not the case.[37]

Deasey, who liked both men but was especially close to Jorgensen, watched the struggle in dismay. "I thought John Jorgensen was probably one of the most able executives I've ever known," he said. Deasey himself had been shoved into what he deemed a meaningless position and left the company in 1986. "The thing that disappointed me," he said, "is Kenefick never bothered to say anything to me about it." He wrote Kenefick a note saying it had been an honor to serve under him and got no response.[38]

The good soldier also realized that his war was lost. Despite the pressure, Jorgensen hung on until 1986 to vest his retirement. Then he walked out. "I was fifty when I quit, and didn't get any benefits or anything else," he said. "I just said screw it and I just went out and started my own company." It especially rankled him that Kenefick never said a word of farewell. Eighteen years after his departure, Jorgensen wrote Kenefick a two-page letter of remonstrance. "Some things can't be forgotten nor forgiven, only accepted," he said in closing. "It is too bad that we could not have parted on more amicable terms. I will be forever saddened by that because I held you in such high regard."[39]

No reply was forthcoming.

Most of the other integrations went more smoothly. Purchasing was combined in March 1983, and public relations blended with little friction. "I just went down and took over there," said Joe McCartney, UP's director of public relations and advertising. One important function of the public relations department was integrated almost immediately: The publications of the three railroads were merged into one new magazine called *InfoNews*. In October 1984 the name was changed to *Info Magazine*, which no longer served the UP and MP railroads but rather the UP System. Although a small thing in itself, the change was a harbinger of a much larger shift to come.[40]

By the fall of 1985 Kenefick was ready to proceed with the final and most difficult piece of the merger. In November he informed Cook that "all other areas of the Company have now been fully consolidated and function without regard to previous corporate identities and we have concluded that it is time to consolidate Operations."[41]

In fact, Kenefick could wait no longer. The clock was ticking on his own retirement, which was scheduled for 1986 when he turned sixty-five. There was no possibility of his staying on beyond that age; he had long been an advocate of mandatory retirement. "When you have an arbitrary retirement age," he said, "there's no stigma to the fact that you're out. You walk out the door and the band is still playing." Kenefick also sensed changes coming in New York that would impact Omaha as well. He wanted to leave a strong and stable operation for whoever succeeded him. That person would have neither the clout with UPC that Kenefick had nor as much autonomy to run the railroad. Cook had made it clear that things were going to be a lot different after Kenefick retired.[42]

The first and most crucial step was deciding on department heads. Seniority was an obvious factor, and the UP operations men tended to be older. "Our operating guys," said John Marchant, "felt that because we were the acquiring railroad that we were going to just kind of coast in on this seniority system." The selection of a chief mechanical officer proved an easy one. John German of MP had retired in 1983, and Jack McDonough, who became chief mechanical officer of UP in 1980, got the position. Engineering posed a different problem. Brown retired in October 1983, and his successor, Herald Durrant, was an old-school type who did not cope well with change. He struggled with his new job, and the company retired him after only twenty-one months.[43]

To the surprise of many, he was replaced by Stan McLaughlin. Only thirty-seven when he became chief engineer in January 1986, McLaughlin was twenty years younger than Dean Barton, the chief engineer of MP, and had worked for him for the past two and a half years. On August 1, 1985, McLaughlin returned to Omaha to replace Durrant as UP's chief engineer. Five months later the consolidation of the operating departments began, and McLaughlin took charge of the combined roads. Fortunately, he and Barton got along well and liked each other. Although he was the chief engineer, McLaughlin received the title of assistant vice president. This enabled Barton to keep his title of chief engineer while working under McLaughlin.[44]

McLaughlin proved to be an inspired choice. "Stan was a good ambassador," said King. ". . . He was liked and also respected for his knowledge." A native of South Dakota with an engineering degree from the University of Nebraska, he had joined UP in 1971 and held a variety of engineering positions before earning a master of science degree at MIT. He returned just as the merger was getting under way and was assigned to MP. His approach differed strikingly from that of Brown. "Early on I decided my role was not to micromanage those people," he said. ". . . My job was to manage the engineering department, manage the budgets, manage the people that were my bosses, and basically let the people that worked for me do their jobs."[45]

Brown and Durrant had already thrashed out most of the thorny issues of standards. Future construction and roadway work would use the UP's 133-pound rail instead of the MP's 136-pound rail, and the UP's 9' ties instead of the 8'6" ties favored by MP. "The engineering implementations," McLaughlin thought, ". . . always went smoother than the transportation implementations. The engineering people tended to have more common backgrounds and shared goals, while the transportation people had more varied practices and ideas."[46]

Merging the operating departments traveled a bumpier road. Both railroads had what Kenefick regarded as superior top officers. Davidson was younger than the UP's Davis, but this time Kenefick did not favor youth. He made Davis the executive vice president, to whom four vice presidents reported. Davidson became the vice president in charge of operations; he would oversee all train operations and supervision with six general managers reporting directly to him. Chuck Dettmann, the vice president of transportation for MP, assumed that same role in the combined operation. McDonough and McLaughlin were the other two vice presidents reporting to Davis, who reported directly to Flannery.[47]

"I understand why they made him the senior vice president of operations," Davidson said later, "because he was a UP guy and Kenefick knew him and didn't know me all that well." At first he did not take the choice with grace. "It was painful for me," he admitted. He told Flannery that he and Kenefick had made the wrong choice. That's our decision, replied Flannery, and you need to tell me whether you're going to work or quit. "As long as I'm here drawing a paycheck, I'll work like hell," said Davidson. The arrangement set Davis and Davidson up as rivals for the next decade. "I know he was hurt over that," said Davis, "but he never showed that. . . . I don't know as Dick and I ever had a cross word in that relationship."[48]

Although they remained friends, some officers thought Davidson continued the battle behind the scenes. "There was never going to be anything but a rivalry," said Tom Watts, because they were both excellent operating men. However, King thought "they did a real good job of not letting conflict be seen by the troops." They had much in common. Both men grew up in tiny Kansas towns not far from the tracks of the railroad they would operate. Both had risen rapidly through the ranks and proven their mettle at every stage. They knew how to listen and how to make decisions, and they believed ardently in safety. Despite their deep roots in railroad tradition, both men realized the need to modernize the industry and accepted, even welcomed, innovation. Their personalities differed markedly. Where Davidson was cool and aloof, Davis was gregarious and easy with people. Davidson tended to be more authoritarian, Davis more the facilitator.[49]

At forty-seven, Davis was only four years older than Davidson. The son of a UP conductor, he started as a telegrapher after high school in 1957. In 1975, when he was a superintendent, UP sent him to the Sloan management program at MIT. Davis spent a year there before returning to Omaha as assistant superintendent of transportation. In 1978 he was made assistant VPO under Bob Richmond; two years later he replaced Richmond and introduced a radically different approach to management in operations. "I didn't want to be a tyrant," he said. "I worked for a tyrant."[50]

Despite being an old-line railroader, Davis brought a completely different style to the job. He had a temper but, like Kenefick, let it blow over quickly and never held a grudge. He was tough but affable, and he disarmed everyone with his sense of humor and ability to poke fun at himself as well as others. He treated union people with respect and took a genuine interest in his employees. "Everybody thought Jerry was their best friend," said Jacobson. ". . . He's just very gregarious and very fun to be around. . . . He really was the first of a new breed."[51]

Yet Davis pulled no punches. During the difficult days of the merger when jobs hung in the balance, he told union reps and employees alike what was likely to happen. This combination of honesty, good nature, and affability made him one of the most popular officers on the railroad. While sometimes slow to change, he understood its importance and adapted willingly to new ideas and practices. He never pretended to know more than he did, and made a distinction between mean and tough. Men like Richmond were both and made employees miserable for no reason. Kenefick was in Davis's eyes tough but not mean. Davis's own sunny personality reflected his major shortcoming: a deep distaste for conflict.[52]

In joining the operating departments, nothing frayed nerves more than sorting out who got what jobs. "I think there was probably as many ill feelings from Missouri Pacific managers as there was UP managers," said Davis. Although he tried earnestly to pick the better man regardless of their affiliation, the MP's operating officers were not only younger but more aggressive. The idea that the two departments would blend or coexist easily proved illusory. "There was this war within the operating department," said Marchant, "sort of an internecine conflict."[53]

The MP operating men were often more talented and better equipped, the products of Jenks's management training program. Some UP hands referred to them snidely as the "MOP Boys Club" and resented their rapid promotion. To get around this tension, it was decided to assign officers from each road to positions on the other road. The first operating officer to receive this transfer was Art Shoener, who was assigned to run UP's Northwest division. The surprised Shoener headed west, unaware that he was about to demonstrate to his new UP charges the true meaning of culture shock.[54]

11

The Right Stuff

"Well, you're the first," Davidson told Shoener.

"For what?" Shoener asked.

"Effective February 1, you're going to Portland, Oregon."

"Oh shit."

Shoener called his wife, Sharon. They were living in Little Rock and loved it there. As a railroader he had moved so often that he always gave her something she wanted as part of the bargain when they were being transferred. "Well," he said, "you wanted a new refrigerator. We're going to Portland, Oregon."

"Is that in the United States?" she asked.[1]

The Northwest was no random choice for this first fling at cross-pollination. Local traffic there was channeled in and out of the main corridor at several points. In that sense it resembled MP's system, what one analyst called "the kind of map that might be created if you threw a handful of spaghetti at a wall and it stuck."[2]

Davis rode to Portland with Shoener on a special. He was the first surprise for Shoener, insisting on being called Jerry instead of Mr. Davis. The second surprise was the railroad itself and the landscape it crossed. Where the MP had hills, the UP had mountains, lots of them. They were the major factor that separated the two locomotive fleets. West of North Platte the UP was basically a six-axle diesel operation, while the MP used four-axle units for its flatland system. Shoener got his first glimpse of helper engines and crews shoving big grain trains over the Blue Mountains. Everywhere along the way the scenery dazzled him.[3]

At Seattle Flannery joined the party for an inspection trip back down the line. Shoener had met Flannery on the latter's first trip across the MP when he assumed the presidency. He was a short man who combined business suits with cowboy boots and smoked enormous cigars that, said Brad King, "looked like a table leg." The inspection train struck Shoener as palatial compared to MP's business cars. Flannery had his own car, as did Brown and McDonough. The train included a theater car with rows of seats facing an all-glass rear so that everyone could watch the track. It had fifteen cars for the twenty-two riders, one more example of what Davidson called the UP's "embarrassment of riches."[4]

So too with the infrastructure. The track was in fine physical condition; most of the mileage had CTC and long sidings every ten or twelve miles. And it was double-tracked. "You could count the double-track places on the MoPac," said Shoener. "You wouldn't get past your hands." He couldn't believe the number of trains he saw—big intermodals, grain trains, long boxcar trains, more than he could count. Every time a boxcar train swooshed by, Davis would smile and say, "There goes another mortgage lifter." Shoener saw a hump yard at Pocatello and another one at Hinkle, only a few hundred miles away. This was railroading on a different scale.[5]

After the trip Shoener spent the next several weeks hyrailing across the Idaho division, trying to get a feel for the whole territory. He thought his new job might be easier with only two divisions to oversee compared to five at Little Rock, but he soon discovered that these were very large divisions. Every Friday was track inspection day; Brown might be retiring, but he still had the troops walking the track.[6]

While Shoener absorbed everything he could about his new territory, the UP officers tried to take his measure. At thirty-seven he was by far the youngest general manager they had ever seen. King, the first MP operating guy to go to Omaha, was about the same age and got a chilly reception at headquarters. "I'd get on an elevator here in the building," he said, "and everybody would quit talking." He was not impressed with most of the people he found at UP. "We didn't see the talent level on the UP side compared to Missouri Pacific," he said. "They thought we were hard-nosed, arrogant. They were probably right."[7]

No one told Shoener why he had been selected as the point man for exchanging positions. A native of Garrett, Indiana, he was a third-generation railroader who started part-time in the industry while going to Evansville University. Shoener earned an accounting degree because his family thought he would make good money in that occupation. The training came in handy when he had to deal with budgets and other financial matters. After graduating in 1968, he joined MP because it was close to Evansville and its management training program put graduates right into the field.[8]

Part of his training took place in Fort Worth, Texas, where Centennial Yard was being rebuilt. Davidson was a trainmaster there, and the two men became friends. After finishing the program, Shoener did six months' active duty in the military before starting his career as an assistant trainmaster in Sherman, Texas. From there he moved on to Pine Bluff, Arkansas, and Shreveport. Gessner brought him to St. Louis as one of the bright young men in the new transportation control center. Six months later Shoener went to Chester, Illinois, at twenty-six MP's youngest division superintendent ever.[9]

Shoener was on the fast track at MP because he had shown unmistakable talent. He was bright, quick, tough, unflappable, and a hard worker. He also revealed an uncanny knack for walking into a new situation and sizing it up. "Art Shoener," said Davis, "other than Mr. Kenefick, could understand a complex transportation problem quicker than anybody I was ever around." Shoener reckoned "the good Lord gave me a gift. . . . Certain people see things, and some don't." Those people didn't last long around him. He didn't tolerate fools and had a harsh, almost brutal style of dealing with people. Yet even his victims agreed that he was brilliant and knew his stuff.[10]

He had shown these talents from the start. At both Pine Bluff and Shreveport he cleaned up discipline problems in short order. At Shreveport he had to endure Bookie Joe Cranford, "a superintendent everybody told stories on because of his stupidity." Shoener lobbied for relief and got assigned to the control center, where he helped manage the road's locomotives as a fleet rather than lone wolves. Predictably he met resistance from dispatchers who resented the intrusion on their authority.[11]

At Chester he again imposed his zeal for order. The old C&EI ran five or six trains a day into Chicago, none of them preblocked. Chicago was a hellhole for switching; it worked a fleet of more than thirty switch engines, and the delays were interminable. Shoener remembered that Gessner had earlier cleaned up the Memphis Yard by preblocking trains entering there. He wondered why the same thing could not be done at Chicago. Bill Farrell, who was then in charge, dismissed the idea and told Shoener to worry about running his own division. Then Davidson replaced Farrell and listened to Shoener's idea. "By golly, Art, we need to do this," he said. He knew how bad the Chicago operation was and remembered what Gessner had done at Memphis.[12]

The problem at Chicago revolved around the intermodal, or piggyback, traffic, which was growing rapidly. Davidson and Shoener huddled for a week and came up with a plan. Within a short time Chicago went from about thirty-five switch engines to fifteen or sixteen, and the traffic flow improved dramatically. "It was just like the sun coming up over the mountain," said Davidson. "It just cleared up all that congestion overnight." The experience became one of two defining moments in Shoener's career; the other one was Houston.[13]

After two years at Chester, Shoener was moved to another major problem area, the Houston Belt & Terminal Railway. It was a joint operation. The MP owned half the company, the SF a quarter, and the RI and Burlington shared the other quarter. The third-largest switching terminal in the nation, it operated seventy-five switch engines in a busy loop around the east side of Houston and connected with the Port Terminal Railway. "Nobody wanted to go to the HB&T," Shoener said. "It was a dark hole. Most people came in and never came back out again." Its inefficiencies had cost MP a lot of money. The challenge was to make it not only better but actually profitable.[14]

Houston was plagued with the kind of problems that Shoener had developed a reputation for solving. It struggled with discipline problems—everything from people stealing televisions out of cars to drinking issues to crews telling customers they wouldn't get any service unless they ponied up Christmas presents first. Shoener had thirteen trainmasters; within three months two had been fired and nine more quit. He scrounged trainmasters from the defunct Milwaukee and RI, and the service improved. Only then did he have time to look at the overall operation and see what had to be done.[15]

Houston had three yards, including Settegast, the MP facility. Gessner had always pushed him to think outside the usual lines. Once Shoener looked closely at the yard, the solution seemed obvious: "Get your yard classified and keep it classified. Sort of basic now, but back then . . . the best job protection for a yardmaster was to have an unclassified yard." Settegast was actually three different classification yards, A, B, and C, with three leads on each end. It required six switch engines a shift to operate. "If you don't yard your trains right and depart them right," he said, "you're always passing cars back and forth for the classifications. And you had all the chemical business coming in and there wasn't a discipline of running trains on time." Shoener imposed the discipline and got his crews to keep their classification, and the yard became much more fluid.[16]

The Houston Belt was, he realized, an in-and-out railroad. It needed two yards instead of three. By expanding and coordinating the receiving and departure tracks he cut down on passing cars and reswitching. He had two Dowty retarders installed to help automate the process. The improvements paid for themselves in a short time and enhanced Shoener's reputation as a problem solver. George Graham, the general manager, promoted Shoener to be one of his two assistants in August 1977. In his new job Shoener oversaw the south end of the MP, which remained a mystery to many officers, while Leon Miller had the north end.[17]

The southern region generated 60 percent of the gross for the entire MP, thanks largely to the lucrative chemical business, but it never got the recognition or capital needed to improve it because Jenks had concentrated on upgrading the main lines from Little Rock north. "We used to joke," said Shoener, "on the old southern region . . . that we'll just secede from the rest of the company." Six chemical trains a day ran over track with 110-pound jointed rail in what was still ABS train order territory; the CTC went only to Spring, Texas. Capacity was strained and congestion was growing worse. When Davidson became VPO, he traveled to the Gulf Coast and saw the problems there.[18]

With Davidson's backing, Shoener worked on upgrading Settegast and the smaller yard at Spring. Settegast, with its small "bump" hump, was the first of its kind on the MP and became the model for later work on yards such as Livonia and Roseville. For Shoener the experience proved invaluable for the rest of his career. Between 1978 and 1982 MP poured $17 million into rehabilitating Settegast. Although Shoener was there for only part of that time, he left a deep imprint on both the Houston Belt and Settegast. Morale soared at the Belt, which earned six consecutive Harriman Safety Medals.[19]

In 1979 Shoener was sent off to the management program at the Harvard Business School. He returned just as business had started to boom on the MP. Within a few months he was made general manager at Little Rock. He was there when the call came from Davidson about the Northwest assignment.[20]

This was the firebrand that Davidson was about to unleash on UP's unsuspecting Northwest operation. "Art had only been there about a month," Davidson said later, "and they wanted to know if they could give him back to me. 'Cause he was walking tall out there, and Art was that way. He's shoot first and ask questions later.... He was very insightful and decisive and would get things done, but somebody had to kind of come along . . . behind him and put the pieces back together again. And the Union Pacific wasn't used to doing that."[21]

Shoener began his sweep across the territory. At the Hinkle Yard he wanted to know why they were only humping eight hundred to nine hundred cars a day when the right transportation plan could do twice that number. Told that Hinkle only blocked west, he demanded to know why, with forty-two blast tracks, it couldn't block east. He walked the track with Herald Durrant and observed that the north end needed more ties. "Now I've got both guys torqued at me," said Shoener. "The mechanical guys don't like it, and now the engineering guy's seeing I was walking track." Both were quick to complain to Thane Rogers, his predecessor, and Brown.[22]

The next clash came with a union chairman over some rules violations. He informed Shoener that Rogers used to put the violators back to work after only a short time. Not anymore, said Shoener. "Miss a stop signal, they're fired. Fired means six months." Neither insubordination nor violation of rules would be tolerated; discipline would be imposed.[23]

After examining the yards and transportation plans, Shoener decided that all the business from Seattle to Portland could be swept into Hinkle and humped east for a time, and then west. That way the yard could serve both directions. Several senior officers insisted that the old methods remain in place. Shoener took his case to Flannery and explained how his reforms were being undone. Flannery said, "I'll take care of that." The changes remained in place.[24]

In Idaho, UP had many more agents than it needed; the company had been letting them go, but only one at a time. Shoener served notice on the remaining thirty-six all at once and got eighteen dismissals. Within a couple of years he pared the number down to five or six. Buildings became a favorite target for Shoener, as they had been for Kenefick. Shoener went down the track asking what every building was for. In many cases he dismissed the answer and ordered the structure torn down. So too with workers. What do these people do? Well, came the answer, we might need them to do such and such. "We don't need people we might need," snapped Shoener. "Let's get rid of them."[25]

Shoener accomplished more in less time than any other officer, but he was brutal to people. Marchant called it a reign of terror: "He'd have these morning calls and morning meetings, and he'd get on them and just raise holy hell with people . . . cuss and swear . . . totally lose his temper." One of his men liked to refer to these sessions as "Art having another attack of Tourette's." Some resentful workers printed up T-shirts and signs that said, "Will Rogers never met Art Shoener."[26]

Part of what made Shoener difficult was his decisiveness. Once he got a notion in his head, he went full bore to make it work, and woe to the person who suggested it might not be a good idea. "If it didn't work out so good," said McLaughlin, "why, then Art might back off. But one thing that you absolutely couldn't do with Art Shoener is say, 'Art, that just won't work.'"[27]

Yet Shoener also forged some good working relationships. Lavonne Nelson was a tough union leader, a table pounder used to getting his way. He butted heads with Shoener, whose goal was to cut as many people as possible, yet the two men managed to work together on several key projects. They reached agreements that enabled the running of a slingshot intermodal train between Seattle and Portland and also on some container business. Together they brought Red Block, a pioneering voluntary drug and alcohol program initiated on the MP in 1983, to the Northwest. Within a year the program began spreading to other railroads as well. Shoener also listened to Nelson. "We put some people back that some other people might not have taken a chance on, based on his word," he said, "and to his credit he stood behind it."[28]

Davis admired Shoener's work in the Northwest even though he sometimes cringed at his methods. "People hated him," he said; "I mean the way he managed them. He wouldn't pull any punches. . . . He was the grim reaper. He's just ruthless. He'd walk into a yard office and say, 'What are all these assholes doing sitting around here?'" Davis tried to get Shoener to understand that he had to be patient with people who didn't grasp things as quickly as he did.[29]

Shoener was especially proud of one achievement because of its later effects. Earlier at both Spring and Chester he had helped consolidate dispatchers from several local offices into a main one. He wanted the same thing done in the sprawling Northwest territory. In forming a team to study the problem, Shoener plucked a trainmaster named Dennis Duffy from obscurity and promoted him. Duffy soon emerged as a key member of the team. Once up and running, the centralized Portland dispatching system reduced the number of dispatchers and made the operation much more efficient. It became the prototype for a later, more ambitious project, the Harriman Dispatching Center.[30]

During his stay in the Northwest, Shoener showed the UP hands a radically different style of management. Many of them did not appreciate it and left or had their jobs cut, but the operation became more efficient and economical, a rare combination. An old-line railroader in so many ways—Marchant called him "Old Testament"—Shoener understood that the industry was changing rapidly and that the old ways of doing things no longer sufficed. In that sense he showed the right stuff at the right time. He also became for many UP hands the emblem of the "Missouri Pacific mafia" that seemed to be taking over the company's management.[31]

In May 1986 Shoener was rewarded by being sent to Kansas City, the primary interchange point between the UP and MP systems. Kenefick and Flannery had decided to consolidate the combined railroad's six operating regions into three, with headquarters at Salt Lake City, Kansas City, and Spring, Texas. Ed May took charge of the Western Region, Shoener of the Central, and George Graham of the Southern. The number of operating divisions was reduced from fifteen to twelve, four in each region. Shoener presided over the busiest section in the entire system.[32]

On January 1, 1986, the use of separate names and "UP System" gave way to one name: the Union Pacific Railroad. The integration of the operating departments completed the MP's disappearance as a separate entity, but its presence lingered in the personnel who became part of UP and in many cases its leaders. Others besides Shoener were making an impression, but none occupied a more important or strategic position than Davidson. He had gone from being the top operating man in the MP to the number two guy in the combined railroad. It helped that he worked under an officer that was impossible to dislike, but much depended on how well he handled what some regarded as a demotion.[33]

Of all the officers Dick Davidson was the most deceptive. Tall, clean-cut, ruggedly handsome, he looked and sounded like the good ol' country boy he was. Although his managerial style could be cold and aloof, it was so sincere and simple, so utterly free of guile and cleverness, that people often underestimated the powerful intelligence behind it. The product of a hardscrabble childhood, Davidson had climbed the ladder of railroading in the most conventional way. On paper he was the most traditional of railroaders, yet he was something far more. Unlike most railroad men, Davidson did not recoil from change as if it were a snake ready to strike. Instead he embraced the possibilities it offered for the railroad and himself. Despite his roots in traditional railroading, he showed a remarkable capacity for growth throughout his career.

He was born on a small farm in Lyon County, Kansas, west of Topeka. His father died in an automobile accident when Dick was only six. His mother went to work as a nurse and somehow managed to keep the farm going. Dick and his older brother helped out at home and worked for local farmers. He played basketball in high school and earned a partial scholarship to Washburn University. In 1960 he went off to school while his brother stayed on the farm but had to find a job to pay for the rest of his expenses. He heard that the MP was hiring at Council Grove and that it paid well.[34]

"It was a wonderful learning experience working there," he said. "I loved the work. The pay was unbelievable. . . . It was just the best piece of luck I ever had because I made a good living while getting an education." After two years as a brakeman he was promoted to conductor. For two years he worked less and concentrated on school until his graduation in the winter of 1965. In April he seized an opportunity to go into MP's management training program.[35]

Davidson spent nine months in the program before being dispatched to Hollywood Yard in Shreveport as an assistant trainmaster. The name aroused visions of glamour, but the reality consisted of an old office building in a state of near collapse. Hollywood had some black workers, who were segregated from the whites; the bathrooms were still segregated as well. Davidson, who had never met a black person until he went to college, thought the arrangement was just wrong and eliminated the segregated bathrooms. It was a bold move and generated controversy, but within a short time the white workers came to accept their black colleagues.[36]

After six months in Shreveport Davidson went to Fort Worth as a trainmaster on the night shift. It proved to be a defining experience in his career. Built in the 1930s, the yard had a manual retarder for humping and retarder operators in the towers squeezing cars to slow their descent to the classification tracks. The work force lacked discipline, with problems ranging from drinking to phony injuries to stealing. It was also lily-white. Management decided the time had come to modernize the yard with a computer-controlled operation. To do that, the hump had to be removed. Davidson's boss foolishly said he could operate the yard without the hump while the modernization went forward, only to find trains backed up everywhere in short order. Nobody had ever flat-switched cars, and derailments piled up while they learned on the job.[37]

Davidson's boss collapsed with a heart attack—the first of several occasions when heart attacks opened the door to an unexpected promotion for him. At twenty-five he was made acting superintendent in charge of the modernization of what became Centennial Yard. "I didn't really even know what computers were at that time," he admitted, but John Lloyd had told him, "You really don't need to understand how those computers work. You just need to understand what they can do for you." Once Davidson saw what they could do, he became a convert.[38]

One experience impressed that lesson deeply on him. During a labor dispute some yardmen pulled off the classification cards nailed to the sides of cars, leaving Davidson with a yard full of cars and no clue as to their destination. He realized then that the guy with the nail gun had the most important job in the entire operation, and rejoiced when the YATS system rendered the nail guns obsolete. Jenks promoted Davidson to superintendent of the Fort Worth Terminal division.[39]

While overseeing the modernization, Davidson also did some cleaning out. Like Shreveport, the Fort Worth Yard was part of the old Texas & Pacific. Many old hands still resented being part of MP and referred privately to Davidson as that "MOP son of a bitch." They were, said Davidson, "a very close-knit group, and if you didn't have the ability to get along with them, they could really make your life miserable." He took the time to make friends with them, but he also had to weed out the drunks, thieves, and other bad apples. More than once while roaming the yard he found men in a drunken sleep at their posts and fired them on the spot. He also hired the yard's first two black workers. Some whites responded by scrawling ugly epithets on the walls, but grudgingly they accepted the blacks once they saw that they were good workers.[40]

At the age of twenty-nine Davidson had realized his fondest ambition. He had set a goal that if he did not reach superintendent by that age, he'd go back to school and become a lawyer. Despite the hard work, he could not have been happier. "From where I started," he said, "a superintendent was like God. . . . I just didn't dream that it could ever be possible to go beyond that." He thought of his brother still on the farm and could scarcely believe his own good luck. The old hands appreciated how hard he worked and helped him along. "One thing I had always tried to do," he added, "was be the very best I could be at whatever I was doing. I wanted to be the best brakeman and the best conductor."[41]

He loved being a superintendent but did not stay one for very long. Although Davidson did not yet realize it, his career had moved to the fast track. The year after Centennial Yard opened he was made superintendent of the Arkansas division, then went to Kansas City a few months later as assistant general manager. Before he could take hold, he was sent to the thirteen-week management development program at the Harvard Business School.[42]

Boston was an entirely new experience for a Kansas farm boy and another seminal learning opportunity. The participants were organized eight to a "can group," so named because they shared a bathroom. Davidson had a history degree from an obscure midwestern school; his classmates had MBAs or degrees in finance. The only other railroad man in his class happened to be Phil Jordan, the UP head of labor relations. Davidson looked and acted like the innocent abroad that he was, but he dug into the work and did well, driven as always by the twin demons of wanting to be the best and fear of failure.[43]

After completing the program Davidson returned to Kansas City briefly, then was sent in January 1974 to North Little Rock as general manager. He could scarcely believe the swiftness of his rise. "I never really felt that I was overly qualified for the job I was on," he said. "... About the time I got to the next level I thought, well, maybe I was getting the hang of the job I just had." Still, he was eager to embrace every new challenge. It was in this position that Davidson joined Shoener in untangling the Chicago mess.[44]

Then, late in 1975, Gessner summoned him to St. Louis as assistant vice president of operations. It was his first exposure to an administrative job, and for a time it made him crazy because nobody worked for or reported to him. But he learned the art of paperwork and dealt with every department—marketing, engineering, finance, information technology, and the other executives. Jenks took a personal interest in him and brought him to analysts' meetings in New York. Then Gessner had his first heart attack, and Jenks decided to create a less stressful position, executive vice president, for him. Davidson became VPO in October and senior vice president the following May.[45]

Life seemed good to Davidson. He was in over his head, a place he liked to be. He remained the top operating man through the merger and the transition from Gessner to Flannery in 1982. When Flannery moved to Omaha, Davidson became the ranking person in St. Louis and, by his own account, "the ombudsman for all those Missouri Pacific people that were worried about the merger... and what was going to happen to 'em."[46]

When time came to merge the operating departments, some UP people thought Davidson might have the edge for the top job because Flannery tended to favor MP officers and Davis had never met Flannery prior to the merger. However, Davidson did not like or get along with Flannery. He found him difficult to deal with and concluded that he had either grown lazy at WP or never had been much of a railroader in the first place. The only decision he could make was saying no; anything requiring a yes sent him scurrying first to Kenefick. He was also abusive to people, especially after a few drinks. Davidson thought that Flannery, being short, had a Napoleonic complex. "He'd pour a glassful of scotch in a water glass," he said, "and the more he drank, the bigger he got."[47]

Davidson regarded Flannery as little more than Kenefick's puppet. "In my opinion, he wasn't qualified to run the Missouri Pacific," he said flatly. "John clearly dominated things, and thank God he did. ... He'd get his instructions from John every day and then he'd go execute them, particularly after he moved here to Omaha." Other officers shared Davidson's disdain for Flannery. Rebensdorf called him "an absolute disaster. ... I don't think he did anything after the merger but smoke a big cigar." Another UP officer declared that "Flannery, on his best day, would have been an average division superintendent."[48]

Jim Dolan agreed that Flannery was in a "semi-retirement job" at UP but found him very knowledgeable, "one of the best transportation men I've seen." Other officers thought highly of Flannery. "He was a no-nonsense guy," said Davis. ". . . I think he was a smart man, and he treated me 100 percent." Jacobson liked him, and Marchant found him "a relatively easy guy to work for." Shoener, no stranger to controversy, praised Flannery for "pushing us to move the transportation product. I got along with him on the UP side. I thought he did a good job of stirring change over there. . . . I thought the world of him."[49]

The mixed reviews on Flannery were hardly surprising. Through a quirk of fate he had bounded to the presidency of two major railroads in a short time, and he was nearing retirement. Most officers figured that he served as Kenefick's surrogate, that Kenefick never really let go of the operating reins. If Flannery was a caretaker, the question was who would succeed Kenefick. Both Davis and Davidson had shown they had the right stuff to lead, but they were young and new at their positions. No one else in the ranks of either company seemed a likely candidate. To complicate matters, UPC was also undergoing changes at the top level. The final decision on who would lead the railroad depended on the outcome of that process.

12

The Operation

No railroad in America traversed a more varied or challenging landscape than the UP. Its trains braved the ferocious Wyoming winters and the stifling desert heat of Nevada, crossed the Rocky, Wasatch, and Blue mountains as well as the Continental Divide and the flatlands of the Great Plains. The addition of the MP and WP extended its reach to the Sierras, the Gulf Coast, and the barren steppes of West Texas. Temperatures in these regions ranged from 120° above to 40° below zero.

Along with the merger, the UP had to cope with three other profound forces: deregulation, a severe recession, and a wholesale transition in its own management. The company was still feeling its way through the new maze of marketing in a deregulated environment where, contrary to most predictions, prices tended to fall rather than increase. The recession intensified an already sharp competition for business and led UPC to rethink its overall strategy. The merger added one dimension of uncertainty and insecurity for workers, and looming changes in management after 1985 added still another.

The railroad's performance could be assessed through three very different measurements: internal operations, shareholder return, and customer satisfaction. Traditionally operating officers had always emphasized the first measurement. Little attention was paid to return on investment or customer satisfaction. Moving trains through harsh environments was a tough enough job, and pride came from doing it as effectively and efficiently as possible. "There's a natural tension in the railroad culture, at least the Union Pacific culture," said Schaefer, "where the operating department controlled the company and everybody else was viewed as being subordinate to the operating department. Whatever the operating guys wanted, that was fine." Jim Dolan saw the same pattern. "When I came here, it was still largely an old-fashioned railroad," he said. "Operating, do as you're told or go. Don't do anything without your boss's personal approval."[1]

The operating department showed its mettle in July 1971 when the United Transportation Union (UTU) struck the UP for eighteen days. By the second day supervisory crews had cleaned up the railroad and run sixty trains. Although the strike spread to other lines, the UP delivered and accepted freight from them. The experience encouraged the company to press for more changes in work rules.[2]

In 1979 David Morgan referred to the UP as that "glossy, fleet-footed, 9431-mile, 1.5 billion-dollars-a-year Overland Route of a railroad." That same year the UP posted an operating ratio of 83.1 compared to 85.1 for the MP, 88.6 for the KCS, 90.1 for the Frisco, 90.7 for the SF, 96.1 for the BN, and 97.7 for the SP. Still, many analysts cast a wary eye on the rail industry, viewing it as too many railroads with too much mileage chasing too little business.[3]

Within UP, however, John Rebensdorf saw a very different problem emerging. At a September 1979 board meeting he warned that "we are confronted with change . . . of a type that few of us on the railroad have previously encountered. . . . We are now seeing our line capacity strained to the limit by increasing traffic volumes in spite of the excellent condition in which our railroad has been maintained and our foresight in preserving double track or single track CTC on our main routes." The problem would worsen, he predicted, with an expanding traffic mix of high-speed expedited service and slower unit train movements. UP was in a unique position. While other roads were trying to shrink their mileage, it faced the opposite problem, "namely, *expanding* our plant capacity to efficiently handle current and future traffic levels."[4]

In the heavily traveled central corridor, the double track between Laramie and Rawlins handled fifty-nine trains a day and was projected to have seventy-nine by 1985. That between North Platte and Gibbon would increase from sixty-two trains a day in 1979 to ninety-five in 1985, while the single-track line between Gibbon and Topeka would soar from twenty-five to forty-eight trains a day. The factors creating congestion ranged from locomotive availability to a rise in slow orders to capacity constraints at terminals. The result was a slow but persistent degradation of service.[5]

Rebensdorf's presentation could not have come at a worse time. The next year witnessed the MP merger, the worst economic downturn since the 1930s, and the advent of deregulation. In February 1980 Kenefick created a priorities committee to examine all pending projects and determine which ones might be delayed to conserve funds. The object was to reduce costs but also to "ensure that no project that was crucial to Union Pacific's future efficiency was postponed." One project in particular could not be delayed because it held so much promise: Project Yellow.[6]

In July 1981 the ICC finally approved a plan granting CNW access to the Powder River Basin. BN continued to insist that it could handle all the business. However, the government and shippers, as well as the spirit of the Staggers Act, required competition in the region. The price tag for CNW's half of the joint line remained a bone of contention. BN demanded $95.5 million for the half interest; CNW offered $83 million provided BN agreed not to litigate CNW's right to serve the Powder River Basin.[7]

BN generated more animosity by distributing a letter with its dividend checks calling the CNW proposal "An abuse of federal aid for railroads." CNW responded by withdrawing its request for government funds and joining with UP to seek private financing. By the end of 1981 the two companies had obtained bank commitments for 75 percent of the estimated $460 million needed for the project. On July 15 they signed a formal agreement; three months later the ICC set $76.2 million as CNW's share for the joint line. Infuriated by the figure, the BN sought to overturn the ICC decision in court. On March 29, 1983, the court ruled in favor of CNW, and WRPI paid BN. The way was clear to go forward with the project.[8]

Project Yellow consisted of four segments. BN had to be paid $76.2 million for half ownership of its 103-mile line from Shawnee, Wyoming, to Coal Creek Junction, Wyoming. In addition, CNW had to improve 45 miles of its track between Shawnee and Crandall, Wyoming. From there a new 56-mile line had to be constructed to Joyce, Nebraska, the connection to UP. Finally, UP planned to upgrade its North Platte branch west of O'Fallons to the Wyoming border. In July 1982 the two companies signed an agreement with twelve banks to provide $345 million of the $460 million needed. UP contributed $96 million to the financial package with CNW providing $25 million. Ultimately the project cost only about $300 million, thanks to the recession that, as a CNW official observed, had "a lot of good contractors looking for work."[9]

After seven years of delay and uncertainty, crews started work in June 1983 on both the CNW upgrade and the new connector line. No one doubted the significance of the event. Western reserves held enough coal to feed America's insatiable energy appetite for centuries, and Powder River was the largest of them all. It was, said Jim Farrell, "overwhelmingly the single most important coal field in the western United States."[10]

The grading had hardly begun when the two railroads signed up their first major customer, Arkansas Power & Light Company. Contracts with utility companies in Wisconsin and Minnesota soon followed. The new line became the largest railroad construction project in nearly half a century. Its work included twenty-nine bridges and five sidings 2.5 miles long and capable of holding two unit trains. On July 12 the last track and switch went into the connector line at Joyce.[11]

At noon on August 16, 1984, with the thermometer hovering around 98°, more than three hundred officials, state and local dignitaries, workers, and well-wishers gathered near the Wyoming-Nebraska border to celebrate the first coal train on the new line. They cheered loudly as four locomotives hauling 110 cars rolled through a ceremonial barrier and lumbered down the new route. Everybody knew the Powder River project would be crucial to both UP and CNW but few imagined just how important it would become. When the agreement was first signed, UP estimated optimistically that it might haul as much as 25 million tons of coal annually from Powder River. Within a decade that figure became a source of much amusement.[12]

The quest for efficiency permeated every corner of operations. Fuel consumption became a prime target as the price of diesel fuel continued to soar, jumping from 56 cents a gallon in 1979 to 83 cents in 1980 alone. Through improved schedules and such measures as lower idling speeds, UP reduced fuel consumption per gross ton-mile by 3.2 percent during 1980. By 1986 the price of diesel fuel in the volatile petroleum market had retreated to 47.4 cents a gallon; however, everyone expected it to start upward again. The era of cheap fuel had passed.[13]

During the recession large numbers of engines and cars went into storage. In 1980 the company splurged for 230 new locomotives just in time for the falloff in traffic; it bought no new power for the next two years. Continual improvements in the technology raised the difficult question of whether it made more economic sense to retrieve locomotives from storage as business improved or acquire newer versions that performed more efficiently on less fuel. Late in 1984, for example, UP acquired sixty new SD50 locomotives from the Electro-Motive Division (EMD) of General Motors for $66.5 million. These 3,600-horsepower units did the work of ninety older units, used less fuel, were more reliable, and cost less to maintain.[14]

This purchase of locomotives revealed a newfound belief that it paid to upgrade the fleet continually rather than simply haul older units out of storage when business picked up. Kenefick admitted as much. "In prior years, we made up our programs based on traffic projections," he said. ". . . We knew how much horsepower we needed to meet certain traffic volumes, and we just bought enough power to stay ahead of demands. Now, we've been looking more at the total economics. We're looking at possible fuel savings and maintenance savings, and . . . even if we don't need additional horsepower it might make sense to upgrade the quality of the fleet."[15]

For more than a decade the staple model of the fleet had been the SD40 manufactured by EMD. Through the years UP had spread its orders between EMD and its major competitor, GE, to spur competition and innovation. In 1985 it continued that policy by ordering sixty new C36-7 locomotives from GE. This model generated 3,750 horsepower, making it the most powerful single-engine diesel yet built. Known popularly as the "Dash 7," it featured a number of innovations ranging from dynamic braking to a system controlling horsepower at all speeds. The following year UP ordered sixty 3,800-horsepower SD60 locomotives from EMD, the company's first units equipped with microprocessors.[16]

UP had always shown a willingness to experiment with new concepts and designs for power. During the age of steam it had commissioned the largest locomotives ever built, the legendary 4-8-8-4 "Big Boy," and acquired twenty-four of them during World War II. During the 1960s it did likewise with the diesel by investing in the largest units built, the twin-diesel Centennial. The first model generated 6,000 horsepower; a later version reached 6,600 horsepower. Although the Centennials performed well enough, they proved costly to maintain and encountered difficulties once they left UP track. Earlier the company had experimented with gas turbine units and even a coal-burning diesel engine. Neither proved successful or economical.[17]

For years the company even looked closely at electrifying part of the main line even though that technology had gone out of style thanks to the advent of the diesel. In 1940 Class I railroads had 2,811 miles of electrified track; by 1975 that figure had shrunk below 1,200 miles. During 1973–74 UP erected two test catenary systems as part of a five-year program to determine the cost-effectiveness, effects of weather, and other problems. It then commissioned studies on the feasibility of electrifying the line from North Platte to Salt Lake City and Pocatello. As late as 1981 the P&A department was still studying the feasibility question, but nothing came of the work.[18]

Rolling stock underwent a transformation similar to that of locomotives. Even as the ubiquitous 40-foot boxcar faded into the sunset, the UP continued to rely more than other roads on larger boxcars, many of them insulated. During the 1970s the surge in traffic led most railroads to scramble for enough equipment to meet peak demands. By 1974 the demand had grown so strong that Kenefick began placing his orders early to ensure delivery. At the same time, the company stepped up the construction of cars in its own shops. Between 1970 and 1977 it bought 13,024 cars from outside suppliers and built another 7,700.[19]

A more obvious trend was the growth in size and specialization of freight cars. The covered hopper, for example, served a variety of needs but often had to be tailored to fit each one. "Our studies clearly demonstrated that this car will do an excellent job of transporting soda ash," said market manager Jack Sunnygard, "a commodity which requires extremely careful handling." A fifteen-month survey of shippers and receivers revealed the need for a newly designed covered hopper for cement. The new version held 100 tons, compared to 70 for the older model, and could be loaded in half the time. A new piggyback model, the 4-Runner, unveiled in 1981, could handle four 45-foot trailers and pass through all the standard mainline tunnels while saving an estimated 9,200 gallons of fuel on two round-trips between Chicago and Los Angeles.[20]

As the type and shape of equipment evolved, so did the line itself. The growth of one-line service with its increase in run-through trains put added pressure on the infrastructure to support more trains with heavier loads moving at higher speeds. As doublestack trains grew longer and increased in number, they required longer sidings. Work went forward to extend twenty-five sidings between Los Angeles and Salt Lake City alone. Kenefick also continued to search for ways to straighten the line by eliminating choke points. Two of them were attacked with ambitious projects: the horseshoe at Crestline, Nevada, near the Utah border, and the notorious "Drawbar Alley" near Meacham, Oregon, in the Blue Mountains. Crestline required two different projects. The first eliminated a 4.2-mile horseshoe in the line that had ten curves with a maximum of 10°. In its place came a 3.2-mile track with only four curves and a maximum of 1°25'. A second project replaced a 4° curve with one of only 1°25'. Together the projects eliminated speed restrictions to save time and fuel at a cost of $8 million.[21]

Drawbar Alley posed a more formidable challenge. Its tight curves and steep grades pulled apart an average of six trains a year. The work was made even more difficult by the new line crossing the existing track seven times. Blasting, grading, and other work had to be scheduled around passing trains. Large as the project was, it produced valuable if not dramatic returns. The existing seven curves of 9° and 10° on a 2 percent grade were reduced to 6°, increasing the speed of trains from 20 to 30 miles per hour. Trainmen welcomed even that improvement.[22]

Bob Brown had one mile of the new Crestline track laid with concrete ties as part of an experiment to test their worth. Concrete ties had been invented a century earlier and used generally in Europe for more than thirty years but were slow to catch on in the United States. European railroads ran much lighter freight cars at slower speeds than American roads, along with high-density passenger trains. Amtrak used concrete ties in rebuilding the Northeast Corridor line for high speed, but no major American freight railroad had yet adopted them. In 1987 UP launched a five-year program of installing concrete ties on high-speed, heavily traveled corridors while conceding that the ties were still on trial for long-term results.[23]

The concrete ties looked nothing like their wood counterparts. They were six inches shorter than the nine-foot wood version, three inches wider, and weighed between 635 and 780 pounds compared to 180 to 200 pounds for the wood tie. The concrete version cost $40 to $50 each, twice as much as wood, but were expected to last up to fifty years compared to ten to fifteen years for wood. Moreover, they could be spaced more widely, requiring only 2,640 per mile of track compared to 3,000 for wood. They also provided a more rigid track structure, which helped reduce fuel costs.[24]

Choke points existed not only on the line but even more at terminals, where under congested conditions trains fell into a coma. One educated estimate of a freight car's average cycle found that 73 percent of its travel time was spent in terminals, including 39 percent in intermediate terminals. A mere 11 percent of its time went to actual train movement. Those numbers, observed *Railway Age*, "would send a motor carrier into gales of laughter, even as he carved chunk after chunk out of the railroads' traffic." Mergers reduced the number of intermediate terminals and created more run-through trains. New technologies like TCS, better blocking practices, improved equipment, and other innovations also reduced terminal times, but the sheer growth of business increased congestion.[25]

The Bailey Yard at North Platte had long been the heart of UP operations and performed under near ideal conditions. It did not have to contend with a large population center, industrial concentrations, or other railroads. It was, said Tom Watts, "a straight-forward but complex operation." Elsewhere the picture grew more complicated. The new Yermo Yard, located halfway between Los Angeles and Las Vegas, opened in 1981 and relieved congestion in both cities. Watts called it "the North Platte of the South Central District." The Pocatello Yard served as the gateway to and from the Northwest, while Hinkle, situated just south of Hermiston, Oregon, handled traffic moving to and from the Far Northwest terminals at Portland (where UP had two yards) and Seattle.[26]

Even the Bailey Yard got overwhelmed by the rush of business. Traffic increased 65 percent between 1968 and 1978, and most of it flowed through Bailey. The older west yard was clearly inadequate to the growing load. Rather than rehabilitate it, Kenefick asked the corporation for $40 million for a modern new hump yard to complement the east facility. Construction began in July 1978, and the new yard opened on April 15, 1980. It featured a fifty-track classification yard, a ten-track departure yard, a ten-track TOFC (trailer on flatcar) yard, an eight-track receiving yard, and a two-track run-through yard.[27]

The merger added several busy yards and potential choke points to the UP System. As a gateway St. Louis was second only to Chicago; the eleven lines reaching the city interchanged 23,000 freight cars daily. The MP operated terminals on both sides of the Mississippi River. It also operated two terminals in the Chicago area that were owned jointly with the Seaboard System: the Canal Street facility near downtown and a flat classification yard at Dolton just south of the city. Intermodal traffic dominated these yards. New Orleans and Houston handled a huge amount of chemical traffic; the MP ran three yards in New Orleans and the second-largest facility in Houston, the Settegast Yard. The Centennial Yard at Fort Worth served eleven grain elevators, an automobile plant, a large brewery, and an industrial warehousing complex, among other customers. Four main MP lines converged at North Little Rock, making it the second-largest terminal in the system even though it handled no interchange traffic. Between 1984 and 1986 it received a $13 million upgrade.[28]

After the merger, attention centered increasingly on Kansas City, where the two systems met. Neff Yard, the MP's largest terminal, occupied 220 acres of ground below Kansas City on the Missouri side of the river. The UP had three yards on the Kansas side of the river; one served eastbound traffic, one westbound, and the third took care of the busy local industrial district. Ten other roads interchanged traffic with the two systems at Kansas City, making it another nightmare hub for expediting trains. As the key connection between the two systems, the terminal had to be reorganized and streamlined for efficient operation.[29]

Like St. Louis, Kansas City had a Terminal Railway Company owned by the twelve roads to handle interchanges, but the business kept outgrowing its capacity. Altogether the twelve roads handled about 13,000 cars daily, 2,500 of them from the UP. Eight separate towers directed the flow of traffic; this arrangement gave way to one CTC tower that presided over 130 miles of track, 300 switches, and 450 signals. "Before I came, I always heard that Kansas City was difficult," said terminal superintendent Wayne Wright, "but you don't really appreciate the cooperation and coordination that have to take place before you come down here and experience it."[30]

Shortly after the merger, Davidson went to Kansas City to survey the scene. He got together with Ed May of the UP, who had been assigned to work MP territory just as Shoener had been sent in the opposite direction. They created a central command center and integrated the two workforces, keeping the best people regardless of which railroad furnished them.[31]

A major improvements program in 1983 helped but did not solve congestion problems. By 1985 the merger had thrust even more business on what had become the central hub of the combined systems. Every day an average of sixty-eight UP System trains alone passed through Kansas City. Along with being a major classification point, Kansas City was the frozen-food storage capital of the world, the hub of the winter wheat market, and the second-largest producer of motor vehicles in the nation. Its railroads served 1,300 industries.[32]

After careful study Davidson and May decided to keep all the existing yards but to streamline them. Both railroads had diesel shops, repair tracks, and other facilities; in most cases only one of each was needed. An evaluation team concluded that the UP diesel shop served the two roads better even though it was smaller. The MP shop was torn down, along with other duplicate facilities deemed unnecessary.[33]

One area of the Neff Yard needed a drastic overhaul. The Big Blue Interlocker had long been a logjam between UP trains and KCS operations. It was the point at which MP's east-west line intersected both a north-south line owned by KCS and another MP line leading south out of Neff that served as the switching lead for the yard's east end. Other roads used the line as well, leaving UP trains with long waits on sidings. In April 1985 UP began work on the Big Blue Hi-Line, a 1.5-mile project with a 1,372-foot bridge that would carry east-west trains over the KCS tracks as well as two MP north-south tracks and the narrow Big Blue River. The new line opened in January 1986, making UP the only road in Kansas City with an unobstructed, signalized route in and out of the city. Later that year work began on a significant upgrade of the Neff Yard itself.[34]

As the line improved, so did methods for handling the cargoes that crossed it. Computerization played a major role by enabling the railroad to track cars more precisely and plan more effectively which ones should go where at what time. Forecasting and planning became crucial to car utilization, which offered choice opportunities for cutting costs. The trick lay in converting commodity forecasts into car-type planning. "You are talking about a matrix that has included up to 170 major commodities and 150 car types," said Denny Robinson, who oversaw the work. The impact extended to equipment purchases as well; the more efficiently cars got used, the fewer had to be purchased. The cost of freight cars doubled between 1973 and 1978.[35]

The planners could anticipate shifts in commodity mixes and even the impact of deregulation, which, according to W. F. Sutton, the general director of car management, "forever changed the way we choose and use freight cars to meet customer requests for service." However, they were blindsided by the recession just as the merger increased the size of the car fleet from 66,835 in 1980 to 94,649 in 1985. To coordinate this larger pool of cars, the seventy-three-member freight car management team was centralized in Omaha in May 1985. The six commodity teams, grouped according to car types needed, worked directly with marketing and sales to give every marketing manager one particular contact for equipment supply.[36]

Finding more backhauls and reloads emerged as a key strategy in the new competitive environment. "Our choice of car types in head-haul service," said Sutton, "is now often determined by what cars will most likely attract a backhaul." If a shipment required only a 50-foot boxcar but a potential reload at the destination point needed a 60-foot car, the latter would be used. The commodity teams watched car-cycle patterns closely for reload or cost savings opportunities. Optimum utilization of available equipment became the great quest for the commodity managers.[37]

Every aspect of the operation grew more complex as the UP evolved from a linear to a network railroad. At every stage the technology grew more sophisticated and productive. In May 1983 Evans boasted that "we're running 40 percent more freight tonnage than we did 20 years ago—with half as many employees as we had then."[38]

That same year the UP System began testing new train scanners that brought a high degree of automation to detecting overheated journals, hot wheels, and dragging equipment. The scanners connected to a computer in the Omaha dispatching office that communicated directly with train crews. A year later UP began converting all of its maps to electronic files with new computer-aided drafting (CAD) equipment. The microwave system remained the backbone of the communication system, but in the early 1980s it faced an unexpected new challenger in the form of fiber-optics.[39]

Although few people yet realized it, fiber-optics were about to revolutionize communication. Alexander Graham Bell's original telephone utilized sound waves passing through copper cables, which became the standard for a century. However, Bell also theorized that sound could be transmitted by light. He managed to do this over a short distance but lacked both a reliable source of light and a conduit through which to pass it. Two later developments filled these gaps: the laser and the ability to manufacture pure glass fibers.

The result was a new form of communication that sent light waves instead of electrical impulses through strands of pure glass instead of copper wires. No thicker than a human hair, the fiber-optic strand was smaller, lighter, cheaper, and more versatile than copper wires. It did not conduct electricity, making it immune to electrical interference. A dozen bundles of twelve fibers each, a total of 144 fibers, could handle 96,000 simultaneous conversations at the speed of light within a cable no thicker than a man's index finger.[40]

As early as October 1978 UP tested fiber-optics in Colorado. Nothing came of it, and the UP did nothing more with fiber-optics until the early 1980s. By then the telecommunications industry was undergoing its own transformation and companies were seeking ways to put together national networks. One shortcut would be to lay cable along railroad rights-of-way, which traversed many states and had the obvious advantage of dealing with only one landowner. It did not take long for some of the players to approach UP.[41]

By chance John Jorgensen saw a letter from the general manager of the Kansas division noting that AT&T wanted rights to bury a fiber-optic cable along 50 miles of UP's right-of-way. The general manager told Jorgensen that he planned to let AT&T go ahead. "The use of our right-of-way is very strictly governed by the original land grant acts," Jorgensen reminded him.[42]

Jorgensen took the letter to Schaefer, who agreed that the land grant issue had to be explored. Schaefer had actually visited the issue in 1966–68 when McDonald asked him for a legal memo on whether the railroad could use its right-of-way to allow the laying of a coaxial cable. Several court cases had restricted the UP and other land grant railroads from using their rights-of-way for nonrailroad purposes. However, Schaefer noted that the UP's original charter was for the "Union Pacific Railroad & Telegraph Company," and that for years it had operated a public service common carrier telegraph company. The intent, he concluded, was for the UP to provide communication as well as transportation service. The coaxial cable merely amounted to a technological upgrade on the telegraph.[43]

Schaefer applied this same reasoning to Jorgensen's request. One of his lawyers, an expert on the land grant act, drafted an agreement flexible enough to deal with unanticipated situations that might arise in the field. In 1984 MCI offered UP $5,000 a mile to use the entire right-of-way for laying fiber-optic cable. Three other competitors, AT&T, LDX Net, and United Telecom Communications, soon followed with offers.[44]

By then Schaefer was exploring the question of whether the railroad should go into other businesses through UPC. An opportunity presented itself in the form of Sprint, the telecommunications offspring of SP, which invited UP to partner with it. SP had formed the Southern Pacific Communications Company (SPCC) in 1970 to provide communication services over its microwave network. It completed a coast-to-coast microwave system at great cost and launched Sprint as a private-line company. By 1981 SPCC was expanding rapidly but its immense capital needs weighed heavily on SP, already staggering under a sizable debt structure. The following year Ben Biaggini relieved the pressure by selling SPCC to General Telephone & Electronics. Sprint went hunting for a new partner, and UP was an obvious candidate.[45]

Schaefer concluded that the railroad had too little experience in commercial telecommunications to enter a business as capital intensive as the railroad itself. A better approach would be to license use of the right-of-way for a fee that included giving UP its own free bundles of fiber-optics for company use. In one operation UP would provide communication as a public service, expand its own communication capacity, and receive a nice pile of cash with virtually no expense of its own. Kenefick balked at the idea until Schaefer explained how much additional communication capacity would be acquired at no cost and how much licensing cash would flow directly to the bottom line.[46]

Late in June 1984 UP reached agreement with all four telecommunications companies for laying cable along 6,700 miles of the right-of-way. The companies received a perpetual underground easement with only limited access to the facilities. In return they paid $5,000 a mile and gave UP two thousand 64-kilobit digital circuits as well. Ultimately the deal extended to the rest of the system, giving UP about $65 million in found money along with a great new communication capability.[47]

By the end of 1985 UP had begun using fiber-optic communication between Dallas and Shreveport, but part of the line was leased. Not until March 1987 did the first call—from Omaha to St. Louis—go via an all-fiber-optic line controlled entirely by UP. By then the company had access to more than 4,000 miles of line installed by the communications companies along UP right-of-way. New connections between key cities opened for use in rapid succession. "It really was a historic moment in railroad communication," said one UP engineer. "... We were tempted to drop a golden spike onto a rail."[48]

Other innovations also improved operations. A new generation of hotbox detectors eliminated the need for dispatchers to read tapes manually. If the detector found no problems on a train, it cleared the next signal automatically. If a problem showed up, an alarm bell sounded, a red block went up, and a computer readout showed the dispatcher exactly where the problem was. Another technical marvel, the dynamometer car, served as a laboratory on wheels behind the locomotive of a work train. Using closed-circuit television, videotape, an oscillograph, and other sophisticated equipment, it measured and recorded nearly every aspect of locomotive and car performance from lubricant temperature to underframe stress. When a federal labor arbitrator ruled that cabooses were no longer necessary, UP bought ninety-five end-of-train monitors called Trainlinks, which cost $4,000 each compared to between $60,000 and $80,000 for a caboose.[49]

The vanishing caboose was but one symptom of a larger issue, the shrinking labor force. Here as elsewhere, efficiency and cost-effectiveness were the heart of the matter. The railroad unions were among the oldest and strongest in the nation. In 1940 the railroads had 1,026,956 union employees and turned in nearly 374 billion ton-miles. By 1980 the number of employees had dwindled to 459,410 while ton-miles increased to nearly 919 billion. The pattern was clear: Thanks to new technologies and other innovations, railroads were getting more ton-miles out of fewer and fewer employees.[50]

Work rules had long been the bane of the rail industry. The worst of them had been created in one era and rendered obsolete by advances in technology, but the unions clung leechlike to them. The most glaring examples were the fight to keep firemen after the advent of the diesel and the 100-mile workday even after new equipment made that figure meaningless in many cases. The caboose had become a similar relic, but one deeply ingrained in the public image of the railroad. In childhood the "choo-choo" train always had an engine up front and a little red caboose in the rear. Since olden days it had been the home of the conductor, who needed a place to do his paperwork, and the brakeman.[51]

The train was monitored from the caboose and its cupola, guarding against loss of air pressure in the brake system or a sudden uncoupling or disasters like ramming a car at a crossing. The advent of CTC took care of throwing switches, and computers eliminated the need for conductors. New electronic devices installed over the rear coupler performed the monitoring functions, which meant that on most trains the caboose itself was no longer needed. Contract negotiations in 1982 allowed cabooses to be eliminated on any class of service through local agreements. However, the price paid for union acquiescence was a 28.9 percent pay hike spread over thirty-nine months. Although a few states

· passed laws requiring railroads to keep cabooses, most railroads had shed them by the mid-1980s. It did not help UP that Nebraska was the last state to give up its restriction.[52]

The 1982 agreement also set up a neutral commission to recommend the most suitable kind of labor force that was equitable, safe, and able to compete with trucks. The commission highlighted another intractable work rule, the rigid wall between yard and road crews that created interminable delays in moving trains. Despite agreeing to take the commission's recommendations seriously, the unions rejected them categorically. Instead they demanded a 5 percent wage increase every six months, a cost-of-living adjustment, seven weeks of paid vacation, and restoration of cabooses. Grudgingly they consented to the final elimination of firemen. The final agreement lengthened the mileage-day to 108 miles and included a two-tier wage system with lower pay for new hires. But the unions extracted another 10.5 percent wage increase along with cost-of-living adjustments for the next forty-four months.[53]

Through decades of regulation a pattern had developed whereby the unions sought large wage increases and struck to get them; management ultimately acquiesced and then asked the ICC for rate increases to offset the cost. Under Staggers this formula no longer worked. Contrary to expectations, deregulation drove rates down instead of up, which meant wage hikes could not be passed along to customers. Productivity, cost control, marketing, and service became the key components to profitability, and every one of these elements ran smack into the work rules. Trucks could literally run circles around the railroad in all of these areas.[54]

Crew size became an obvious flash point in the quest for productivity. As early as 1963 the little Florida East Coast Railway pointed the way to the future. When its unions struck, management boldly fired the workers, hired replacements, and proceeded to operate as a nonunion railroad. Despite threats and acts of violence, it ran a lean, efficient operation and turned a marginal railroad into a prosperous one with two-man crews paid by the hour, no cabooses, and impressive service. Few railroads had conditions similar to the FEC, but the model was there for rail executives to study. In 1978 a much larger road, the N&W, performed extremely well when operated only by supervisory personnel during a strike. Through the inflation-bloated 1970s the unions routinely struck to get what they wanted, but that tactic was wearing thin by the 1980s.[55]

Even those union leaders who understood that the railroads were in the throes of massive changes struggled to find a course of action that both recognized the new facts of life and suited their union's members. They could not help but notice their shrinking membership rosters and the changing composition of the railroad workforce. Small wonder, then, that labor greeted every new wave of change with apprehension. In one important area, however, management and labor came together on the UP to craft an agreement that became a model for the industry.

Alcohol and drug abuse had become an increasingly important issue in the larger society as well as the railroad industry. Kenefick's pioneering 1972 employee assistance program handled a broad spectrum of personal problems ranging from compulsive gambling to marital conflicts to financial difficulties as well as substance abuse. By 1979 it boasted a recovery rate of 85 percent. However, alcohol and drugs remained a prime concern because of their obvious impact on safety.[56]

On November 1, 1980, UP signed an agreement with the Kansas City Local 1409 of UTU and the Brotherhood of Locomotive Engineers (BLE) of Salina, Kansas, to create what became known as the "Rule G Bypass." Under its provisions any employee removed from a position for alcohol or drug problems could avoid having the incident placed on his or her personnel record by agreeing to accept evaluation and counseling. The bypass was good only once in the employee's career. Co-workers had the right, indeed the obligation, to report anyone with a substance abuse problem without recrimination. Safety became the overriding concern. As crews grew smaller, faulty performance by any one member posed a greater danger to the others. "The agreement gives support to the worker," said Jim Dargon, president of Local 1409. "We don't say he's drunk or drugged. We simply say he is unsafe to work with."[57]

The bypass agreement proved successful, and other locals began joining the agreement. The Kansas City Local 1409 was the largest on the UP, with 530 members. Between 1981 and 1982 injuries in the Kansas City yard declined by 57 percent. In 1982 Jerry Davis launched a drug awareness program aimed at the operating department. The problem had grown serious in all industries; an estimated 4.4 percent of all American workers were classified as drug addicts. The unions agreed that the problem had to be confronted through cooperative efforts by management and labor. "Labor should be involved," stressed Willard Hirst, international vice president of the BLE. "We need peer intervention *early*—a total package."[58]

By July 1983 the bypass agreement had been accepted by 5,175 employees of the MP as well. A month later the ULU and BLE organized seminars on the subject. At the same time, eleven federal groups were studying the drug/alcohol problem within the industry. On the UP the two unions took the initiative in pushing the awareness and bypass programs aggressively. "I've put a man back to work seven times before we buried him," said Dan Collins of the UTU. "And it was alcohol that killed in his accident."[59]

Together with the unions, UP moved ahead with plans to launch in June 1984 what it called "Operation Red Block," a five-step prevention program. That April the issue drew national attention because of two grisly accidents on the BN that killed seven crewmen. Tests revealed that the engineer and fireman in one accident had been drinking prior to the collision in which both died. The engineer involved in the second accident admitted to drinking beer and smoking marijuana the day before the collision. While the FRA continued to debate whether to adopt the testing or bypass approach, the two unions and UP continued to implement Operation Red Block and pressed for it to be the model for federal regulation.[60]

The voluntary aspect of the approach, as well as its control by local officials, appealed to local chapters. "The local membership is beginning to understand that the program is something they can do," said Bill Hillebrandt, general manager of MP's eastern district. "... They can organize and run it the way they want to, and on their own terms." In January 1985 the FRA adopted the UP program and commissioned UP to produce generic promotional materials on the program for use by other railroads. "We have a program," said John Riley of the FRA, "that's going to touch the majority of the nation's rail workers." In May the Brotherhood of Railway Carmen (BRC) joined the UTU and BLE in the bypass agreement on the UP.[61]

On November 1, 1985, the FRA's new alcohol/drug regulations finally went into effect. Along with prohibiting on-duty use and impairment, they mandated pre-employment drug screening, post-accident testing, pre-accident testing based on "reasonable cause," and the establishment of a bypass policy by all railroads. Red Block, or some version of it, became a national policy. In this one arena at least, UP and the unions acted in concert to achieve a common goal. Impressive as this achievement was, it could not overcome the growing apprehension among the unions that their role in the relationship with management was shrinking.[62]

13

The Marketing Maze

For nearly a century railroads served as America's all-purpose carrier. They hauled almost anything to any place that tracks went with only the wagon, stagecoach, pipeline, and riverboat as competitors. Then came the automobile, truck, and airplane, which gradually swept away the short-haul traffic that once belonged to the railroads. Even then the railroads continued to dominate long-haul shipments until the 1950s, when the situation changed dramatically. Jet aircraft took away the long-haul passenger traffic as well as some freight. More important, construction of the interstate highway system, coupled with larger, more efficient trucks, blindsided the railroads with a lethal competitor for which they had no good answer.

Trucks offered shippers advantages that railroads could not provide. They could move goods door to door faster and often at a cheaper rate. They had far more flexible schedules and service. Although somewhat regulated, they did not have the rigid straitjacket of rules imposed by the ICC on railroads. Moreover, the large number of independent, owner-operated rigs sped merrily along outside of regulation. They traveled roads funded by the public while the railroads had to build and maintain their infrastructure. Trucks came in many sizes and lost no time in switching or snoozing in terminals. Once piggybacking began, they even hitched rides on trains when it suited them. They could pick and choose their cargoes and tailor rates on the spot to suit their needs.[1]

When railroads dominated overland transportation, they didn't have to market their product so much as deliver it. "The railroad industry was one of total operating dominance," said Tom Graves. "The railroads were basically operated for the railroads only, and the industry regarded its client as 'customer be damned.'" They did not have marketing departments or even use the term "marketing," let alone know what it meant.[2]

"You had . . . basically boxcar traffic," said Don Shum, one of UP's traffic managers. "Once you learned your trade as a salesman or manager you were fairly well able to respond to the customer's needs . . . because the customer wasn't changing, the railroad wasn't changing, the competition wasn't changing. The important attribute for a sales representative then was the ability to cultivate the customer. Charm was important." However, what the sales person couldn't guarantee was that anything promised the customer in terms of service or schedule would be honored or even noticed by the operations department.[3]

Because so much of its traffic funneled into West Coast ports, UP developed an early appreciation for Far Eastern business, especially from Japan. In 1966 the company opened its first office in Japan, and the following year it opened one in Taiwan. By 1971 it had representatives in nine Pacific Rim countries and an equal number of international trade departments in the United States. A new unit coal train to the West Coast began carrying coal bound for Japan in April 1969.[4]

The rising tide of Far Eastern imports into the United States got Kenefick's attention early. In 1972 the company joined with steamship lines and connecting railroads to offer "mini-bridge" tariffs for goods crossing the continent from West Coast ports to East Coast cities. In looking outward, the company developed a "profitability potential" yardstick for evaluating specific geographic areas and commodities. One growing segment of traffic consisted of automobiles and automobile parts destined for the West Coast. Special autorack trains moved from Omaha to Ogden in less than twenty-four hours, an improvement of eight hours over the normal operating schedule.[5]

Kenefick discovered that the flow of automobiles was increasing in the opposite direction as well. When Toyota's American business mushroomed, all the major roads sent their presidents to Japan to solicit it. Kenefick's marketing people advised him that the decision would be made not overseas but by the Toyota people in the United States. "They were right," said Kenefick. "We got the contract."[6]

The Toyota contract was a coup for UP. In 1977 the carmaker changed its port-of-entry from the Gulf Coast to Portland and shipped more than eighty thousand vehicles through there to midwestern distribution centers. Toyota proved a valuable customer, not only for the amount of business it provided but because its damage claims were less than a third of those from Ford or GM. Kenefick began making an annual fall trip to Japan. During one trip he persuaded Toyota to shift the business of its western plant from SP to UP.[7]

The threat posed by trucks became painfully obvious to Kenefick in several ways. Highway I-80 paralleled the UP through Wyoming, and on inspection trips he could observe the seemingly endless parade of semis moving down the road. When sugar beets were harvested in the fall, UP had to assemble extra crews, engines, and hoppers to carry them to the nearest sugar refinery. The business didn't make much money; the real profits lay in hauling the refined sugar, but the trucks scooped that business. "They came in and cut just under us enough that we had the honor of hauling the beets but not the profits," said Kenefick. "It was really just a hopeless sort of situation."[8]

The very sight of the trucks on I-80 infuriated Kenefick. "There are a lot of big fucking trucks over there that would have been pretty good if they had been on our tracks," he said. Through a consultant he learned that the cost of a double-bottom trailer going across Wyoming was not much higher than that of the railroad. The assumption had always been that trucks incurred much higher costs; this revelation did much to spur UP's interest in doublestack traffic.[9]

Trucks were not the only competitor. By 1984 the railroads' share of intercity ton-miles had dwindled to 36.1 percent. Trucks hauled 23.7 percent, barges 12.4 percent, and oil pipelines 24.4 percent. The river barge industry had 1,000 companies operating 7,000 towboats and nearly 32,000 barges. They moved more than 285 billion ton-miles of goods along 25,543 miles of navigable waterways that served 87 percent of the nation's cities. Like other modes they suffered from overcapacity and were willing to carry grain and other commodities even at a loss to help cash flow.[10]

The key to marketing strategy lay in long hauls and minimal time spent in terminals. Unit trains met these needs perfectly, and the UP hauled a number of commodities that could be served by them. Coal was the most obvious example of a cargo that could be carried over more than one railroad without changing locomotives or enduring terminal layovers. Others included iron ore, soda ash, mined phosphate, and fertilizer, much of which flowed from Idaho and Wyoming to West Coast ports. Grain was another prime candidate for unit trains, and a challenging one because of its seasonal schedule. During the early 1970s it was the largest single source of traffic for the UP; in 1972 it constituted more than 18 percent of all shipments.[11]

During the 1970s record harvests aggravated the usual crunch for cars. The shortage was intensified when the Soviet Union contracted for massive amounts of wheat, which had to be hauled by train to the West Coast for loading onto ships. To cope with what it called "two years' worth of bumper harvests in one" during 1973, UP assembled seven grain unit trains that shaved turnaround time to eleven days compared to eighteen days for single-car shipments. In 1975 UP began running one grain unit train a month to the West Coast; by 1979 it averaged three such trains a *day*. During those four years its corn and feed-grain traffic increased more than 85 times.[12]

During the early 1980s the trend reversed as American wheat exports declined 22 percent and grain elevators bulged with surplus wheat. Because the wheat-related industries had overexpanded in the 1970s, profit margins shriveled faster than markets. Global competition and government subsidies helped shrink American exports. UP marketers scrambled to rejuvenate domestic markets, offering customized services and special rates.[13]

The automobile business was relatively new but growing fast. Prior to the merger motor vehicles and parts brought in 6–8 percent of UP's freight revenue. MP did a larger business in the sector; as one trainman noted, "Service to the auto industry is our bread and butter at the Chicago gateway." When the two systems combined, the proportion of auto traffic jumped to 10.5 percent in 1983 and 13.3 percent in 1985. The surge in automobile business led UP to open two new facilities near Houston and Shreveport.[14]

Automobile traffic was another capital-intensive, low-margin operation. "Shipments of motor vehicles," said one UP manager, "are among the most competitive, time-sensitive traffic we handle." It also required careful handling to avoid claims for damage and vandalism. The carmakers complicated matters by insisting on different preferences for multi-level deck settings, tie-down equipment, and chain settings for automobiles in transit. As automobile sales soared during the 1980s, so did UP equipment orders. By 1984 its fleet exceeded 4,000 multi-level cars. During the next three years the company spent nearly $48 million for another 1,343 carriers.[15]

Grain, coal, soda ash, automobiles and parts, food products, and forest products remained staples of UP traffic. As early as the 1870s UP tried to encourage the production of trona, or soda ash, but not until the 1960s did it become a staple of the road's traffic. A key ingredient used in the manufacture of glass, detergents, and pharmaceuticals, soda ash existed in huge deposits at Green River, Wyoming. By the mid-1980s five mines were producing more than nine million tons a year. A growing international demand for American soda ash gave UP a long haul to West Coast ports for shipment overseas. UP assigned 3,500 cars to Green River for soda ash and ran many of them in unit trains.[16]

Coal had always been a major commodity for UP, but in 1980 exports of it began to increase sharply. Until then the road had moved only high-quality coal for export; in April the first trainload of American steam coal traveled over UP rails to the West Coast for shipment to Japan. By February 1981 the shipments had mushroomed to forty-two trainloads a month bound for Taiwan and Korea as well as Japan.[17]

The trend was clear. "Union Pacific appears to be moving toward becoming a bulk-commodity carrier," said Denny Robinson in February 1978, "centering on coal, soda ash, ash, and probably phosphate rock. Those areas, along with trailer-container traffic, are the ones which apparently will experience the greatest growth." Table 1 bears out this prediction.[18]

The new approach to marketing relied heavily on a team effort. Besides market managers and developers, the company also had equipment planners to match cars with customer needs, cost analysts, economic forecasters to spot trends nationally and regionally, and service planners. The new breed of sales people, known as traffic agents, had to know their territory and its industries.

Table 1   **Comparison of Freight Traffic Commodities (%)**

COMMODITY	1972	1982
Farm Products	18.1	16.9
Coal, Metallic Ores	16.4	31.3
Lumber, Wood Products, Furniture	12.5	6.2
Food Products	12.2	8.8
Chemicals and Allied Products	9.4	12.1
Nonmetallic Minerals	9.2	12.1
All Others	22.0	12.6
TOTALS	99.8	100

Source: *UP Report*, 1972, 4, and 1982, 47.

They were armed with a file of relevant information on every industry, shipper, and receiver in their territory. A firm profile was put together on every company that included its location, commodities shipped and received, origins of any raw materials used, and market destinations for its products.[19]

One grain company executive in Nebraska made clear what he expected from the traffic agent. "We expect him to keep us advised of rates being proposed in the future," he said. "We have leases with the railroad, some of them in his territory, that we expect him to handle for us. And any complaints or problems—he has to handle those, too." The same executive praised UP for improving its agents, observing that "they've really come a long way, compared with some of the other people that come in here from other railroads."[20]

The new approach involved not merely seeking out business from new customers but persuading industries to locate along the UP line. In 1978 the company lured 154 industries to build adjacent to the railroad, with projected revenues from them of more than $25 million. "You cannot overestimate the value of getting a large customer permanently on line," said one market manager. "You might be looking at 30 or 40 years worth of business." A satisfied customer might decide to place other facilities along the route, or a company in the same field might do the same if word of good service got out.[21]

However, the company still regarded anyone with a truckload or a pound of freight as a potential customer. "The type of management we had in the past was appropriate at that time," said Don Shum, "but not for today. The way we do things today may also seem terribly obsolete in 10 years." He was more right than he knew. Scarcely had UP embraced a more modern concept of marketing than the game underwent a sea change thanks to deregulation.[22]

One department was already exploring the impact of deregulation prior to the Staggers Act. Al Sloup's market and competitive research team focused not only on finding ways to help UP understand its own business better but also on what competitors were doing and how they were doing it. In 1979, on the eve of the Staggers Act, railroads were still fully regulated while motor carriers were 40–50 percent regulated and water carriers only about 18 percent regulated. Sloup's team had to keep tabs on what was going on in these rival fields.[23]

Not surprisingly, trucks got much of Sloup's attention. His research showed that 58,000 18-wheelers passed through North Platte every month, maybe 20 percent of them empties, the rest carrying loads worth about $1,200 each in freight revenue. That revenue, or at least a portion of it, became the railroad's target.[24]

The Staggers and the Motor Carrier acts of 1980 changed the ground rules for both modes of transport. Rate stability was the first casualty. Prior to deregulation nearly all rate changes for railroads were handled by the rate bureaus. A carrier had to give thirty days' notice of a change, and all changes received wide publicity. Under the new rules a change required only ten days and could be done with little or no publicity. Joint rates and gateway agreements were canceled; contract rates became the preferred instrument of the new order. The ICC retained power to regulate only rates where railroads had market dominance.[25]

Although the railroad remained a common carrier, it could set rates on its own and charge different customers different rates for the same service. The bounds of a rate would be determined by the market in the form of what competitors charged. This freedom bred fear and uncertainty. For all their drawbacks, regulated rates provided a protective cocoon of income for the carriers in which they need not worry about pricing to market. Giving railroads the power to make rates guaranteed that they would become far more volatile and unpredictable. "You can't stand behind tariffs anymore," said one market manager. "You have to react quickly." Another UP manager admitted that "we spend much more time now trying to find out what the other guy is doing. With rates now changing almost daily, we have to know what's going on so we can be competitive."[26]

Being able to set its own rates also gave the railroad the option to refuse business that didn't pay. "There was no more of this bullshit about the sugar and the sugar beets," said Kenefick. ". . . You could say, 'Look, buddy, unless you ship the sugar, don't look for us to haul the beets.'"[27]

Prior to passage of the Staggers Act the conventional wisdom was that rates would rise sharply once the regulatory restraints were loosened. Fate helped dissipate that fear in the form of the recession that fastened itself on the country shortly after the act became law and lasted into late 1983. By October 1981 UP had five hundred locomotives, nearly a third of the its fleet, and five thousand cars in storage. Carloadings dropped between 10 and 30 percent from 1980, depending on the commodity group. Fuel prices jumped sharply early in 1981, and the scramble for business grew more intense.[28]

With competition heating up on all sides and unfamiliarity with the new rules of the game, many railroads embraced long-term agreements as a way to secure guaranteed business. Some customers, especially power companies, demanded twenty-year contracts because they had similar deals to buy coal from a particular mine. Many of the contracts were negotiated during the recession, a buyer's market. Later these contracts became a burden, but at the time they seemed a godsend for weathering hard times. By 1985 contracts produced 42 percent of the railroad's revenues. Kenefick observed that of the first 1,500 contracts signed by UP, 1,499 were for lower rates than the previous tariff. "That is a success for deregulation," he said, but it also forced railroads to look more closely at their cost structure. "A cost-plus industry," he added, "is now a cost-cutting industry."[29]

The combination of Staggers and the recession intensified the search for new business and sources of profitability. Empties constituted a logical target. Day and night, strings of empty cars moved across the railroad. Finding backhaul business became more urgent than ever, but obstacles existed. Some car service directives mandated that their cars be returned empty even if a return cargo was available. Car hire charges pushed railroads to return cars empty rather than letting them sit idle. No information existed to identify empties across different railroads and coordinate their movement. Specialized cars were often not suitable for many kinds of backhaul freight.[30]

Even before deregulation UP looked in all directions for solutions. It formed joint agreements with Conrail and other roads to coordinate car management. Sales and marketing people searched for new opportunities. When a market manager learned that salt was moving east from Utah by truck, his team approached the shipper with a package of service, equipment, and special rates because empties returning east were available in the area. In another case a customer shipped all his product in assigned boxcars, which always meant return empties. UP offered him a series of refunds, depending on volume, destination, and type of car used, if he shipped on unassigned cars that were emptied in the East. The agreement gave the shipper lower rates while the railroad gained market share and more profits.[31]

During the past two decades UP had lost much of its fruit and perishables traffic to the trucks. Bolstered by improved reefers with mechanical refrigeration, the railroad worked hard to win back the business. In the fall of 1980 it advertised heavily that for a two-week period it would give fruit customers a $300 refund if they shipped by rail. The campaign produced 187 carloads of apples and pears compared to only 56 the year before, and revenues of $750,000 with potential refunds of $56,100. The fruit moved to thirty-one new consignees who had not used the railroad before.[32]

Food and food products remained staples of UP traffic. The lowly potato became a star on a railroad running through Idaho. By one estimate 80 percent of the potatoes consumed east of the Missouri River moved by rail, 70 percent of them on the UP. In 1978 it hauled more than 900,000 tons of french fries alone, which earned $31 million in revenue. Most of the potatoes were grown in eastern Idaho; from the western part of the state and eastern Oregon came another important crop, sweet Spanish onions. By 1981 the region was producing 27 percent of the nation's supply.[33]

UP's market development analysts determined that both the company and shippers would save money if the pricing on onions and some other fresh vegetables was changed from a 100-pound basis to a flat per-car rate. The latter would encourage shippers to load cars heavier and provide more efficient utilization of the UPFE reefers. After the switch was made in May 1979, the average load for onions jumped from 80,000 pounds to 100,000 pounds. Other fruits and vegetables, both fresh and canned, moved across the line in immense quantities along with large shipments of dairy products, livestock, and dog biscuits.[34]

Intermodal became one of the fastest-growing traffic segments during the 1970s and 1980s. Not until March 1981 did the ICC formally deregulate TOFC and container traffic. By then UP had long since built up an impressive intermodal business that reached a record high in 1976. Intermodal traffic was a fiercely competitive, low-margin business. Deregulation intensified the struggle among railroads and trucks. Rate adjustments came in a rush as companies scrambled to get and keep customers.[35]

A four-way deal signed in April 1981 joined UP, CNW, American President Lines (APL), and Transway International Corporation in a symbiotic arrangement to improve efficiency and reduce costs. APL steamships brought large numbers of containers to Seattle and Los Angeles for movement by rail to eastern and midwestern cities. Transway, a holding company for several freight forwarding firms, loaded the emptied APL containers with goods heading westward to San Francisco, Los Angeles, Seattle, Portland, and other points served by UP. The railroads provided guaranteed schedules and equipment availability in both directions. Eastbound trains ran straight through to Kearny, New Jersey, over UP, CNW, and Conrail trackage, cutting nearly two weeks off the all-water route through the Panama Canal.[36]

This pioneering arrangement could hardly have been more ideal. It became UP's largest single contract at a time when carloadings were sharply down. APL benefited from dealing with one railroad at all the ports for a major portion of its business, along with schedule and price stability at a time when rates fluctuated unpredictably and performance had to be negotiated. The APL agreement gave UP a solid base for its intermodal traffic that continued to grow. In September 1985 UP and APL signed a new ten-year contract under which APL would move major portions of its cargoes using its own equipment with UP locomotives, crews, trackage, and other services. By then APL trains were running doublestacks.[37]

Unlike most rival roads, UP encouraged APL and other shippers to own or lease the cars they used. APL worked with UP, CNW, and the Thrall Car Manufacturing Company of Chicago to develop a lightweight car strong enough to make doublestack loads cost-effective. Once they had a successful model, the doublestack business took off and UP got the lion's share of the business. In 1983–84 APL bought a fleet of sixty-five newly designed inter-modal cars that could handle doublestacks, thereby moving more cargo in less space.[38]

At first UP was dubious; it knew nothing about how such a train would ride, whether it would clear all structures on the line, or even how much horsepower it would require. Within a short time, however, the two companies agreed on a twenty-car high-speed train carrying 200 containers, twice the number of a con-ventional container train, with only a 30 percent increase in weight. The new service began in March 1984, ran from Los Angeles to Chicago in fifty-two hours, and proved to be a striking success. By 1986 UP was running twenty-two doublestack trains alone, most of them carrying 280 containers on twenty-eight cars.[39]

Although skeptics doubted that doublestacks had much growth potential, an executive for Sea-Land—a large steamship company that contracted with BN—retorted that "between the ocean carriers and the railroads the basic network is already in place. The big operators are going to make it work, and the bigger you get, the easier it is to make it work." He proved to be right. By 1986 twelve rail-roads and eleven steamship companies were involved in running thirty dou-blestack trains a week.[40]

Although a low-margin business, intermodal traffic required a large capital investment. Loading, docking, and parking facilities were installed or expanded in several cities, and $10 million went into another round of siding extensions at twenty-five sites along the line. These investments would not have been made if UP did not think the business would continue to grow and remain profitable. By 1986 intermodal accounted for 10.2 percent of all freight revenue, compared to 23.3 percent for soda ash and other chemicals, 18.3 percent for coal, 12.5 per-cent for automobiles and auto parts, and 10.7 percent for grain.[41]

In 1982 UP reorganized its marketing efforts into four broad product groups. One group consisted only of energy products, another of grain and grain prod-ucts. A third handled chemicals, forest products, and consumer goods, while the fourth dealt with automotive products, metals, food, and government traffic.

After the merger the company offered customers single-line service trains that saved them a full day to selected destinations.[42]

Other changes soon followed. In 1983 the railroad folded its rural agency operations into computer-equipped customer service centers at strategic locations. A toll-free phone line enabled customers to obtain any needed information. A year later sales offices were streamlined by reducing regional offices from sixteen to ten and closing twelve small agencies that could not provide a full range of services.[43]

The search for new business often involved the need to spend more money, which made cost-and-profit analysis even more imperative. Pressure also came from the new emphasis on price spawned by deregulation. "Shippers are buying price," said George Craig. ". . . The good ol' days are gone, and they are not going to come back." Kenefick agreed entirely. "In the days before deregulation," he said, "about the only thing the a railroad could sell was service and a smile. . . . Now service and a smile still count, but . . . the sweetest smile in the world won't count if your competitor is five cents under you."[44]

As Kenefick neared retirement, he commissioned several productivity studies undertaken first by Schaefer and Arthur D. Little consultants, and later by other consultants. In February 1985 he shared the results with UP employees and urged them to take the message to heart. Deregulation, he emphasized, had given UP both a challenge and an opportunity. "Today's competitive successes will determine whether tomorrow is bright or bleak," he said. "It's a whole new ballgame."[45]

14

The Studies

By the time his retirement loomed, Kenefick had become a legend in the company and the industry. Unlike many other executives, he had not slowed or coasted on his reputation as he grew older. Every weekend he arrived at the office for what he (and they) regarded as some of the best times to talk to his staff. On Saturdays he expected all the department heads to be there; Sundays were devoted mostly to the operating heads. The twelfth floor had an operations center that kept track of overall activity and communicated with the dispatchers at regional centers. Kenefick liked to light a fresh cigar, step into the center, nod or speak to a few people, and leave. "It had its effect," he said, smiling. "You could see some guy over on the telephone talking to the chief dispatcher in Pocatello, saying, 'Jesus Christ, you'll never guess who just walked in.' I think sometimes you've got to be a little bit of a ham."[1]

He remained a formidable and imperious presence. "I have never talked to all the employees," he said. "I never took a poll about any decisions that we made around here. If we closed down a shop, we closed it down." Davidson thought that Kenefick kept his officers on a tight leash so that they hesitated to do anything significant without clearing it with him first. "I honestly believe that Mr. Kenefick enjoyed making the decisions himself," he said. "And he made good ones."[2]

Kenefick had always been an anomaly in the industry—a career railroader from Princeton who realized that change was essential to the survival of railroads. He was, said Dennis Jacobson, "very eloquent about saying, If that's the way you've always been doing it, you've probably always been doing it wrong."[3]

He insisted on doing things the right way. After the merger Kenefick learned of a fire in Texas that burned down a small black Baptist church. Hearing that the fire might have been started by sparks from a locomotive, Kenefick called Joe McCartney, his public relations man, and told him he wanted UP to rebuild the church, which was in MP territory. McCartney called the local MP man and had to hammer the point home that Kenefick didn't want lawyers getting in the way of doing what he thought was right.[4]

"I would say the modern Union Pacific began with Kenefick," said John Marchant. ". . . We . . . started worrying about things other than intrigue and bullshit. And people started trying to have a real job to do rather than just show up and suit up." Dennis Duffy was impressed that Kenefick excelled not only at operations but also at marketing. "He was key in those major customers," he said. "He was the kind of guy that could go in there and make the sale, and he did."[5]

Kenefick was never one of the boys, but he had enough quirks to endear him to them. He looked to be the model of health even though he never exercised. Once he was approached with the request that the company open a fitness center. Kenefick explained that his idea of exercise was walking the dog from the driver's seat of his car while driving slowly down the street. "I actually saw him do it," said Paul Conley, "so he wasn't making it up."[6]

On more serious matters he exercised the kind of reasonable judgment that often eluded top managers. Jerry Davis recalled a Sunday morning story on the front page of the *Omaha World-Herald* about a UP official who had been killed during an apparent homosexual encounter. Kenefick had gone to mass and hadn't yet come to the office. Davis dreaded having to break the news to him; both of them knew the victim. When Kenefick arrived, Davis gulped and told him the story. Kenefick pondered the matter, then said, "Well, you know, Jerry, we probably have more of those homosexuals in our company than we realize. We'll get over this." That was the end of it; no posturing, no spin, no recriminations or polemics.[7]

In the strategic realm Kenefick saw one more opportunity for expansion. The Katy had floundered for decades, unable either to prosper amid its larger, stronger competitors or attract the right suitor to acquire it. After a long period of decline its fortunes improved when Reginald Whitman became its CEO in 1970. Whitman got control of expenses and reversed a long period of neglect. Between 1975 and 1980, thanks mostly to increased traffic from connecting lines, the Katy turned a profit but still lacked capital for improvements. By 1979 the road originated only 27 percent of its traffic, which made it vulnerable to the mergers taking place around it. For that reason it had long been assumed that one of the larger systems would absorb the Katy.[8]

The search for a suitor had been ongoing for many years. In 1967 a holding company, Katy Industries, was formed and began seeking a buyer as the railroad's losses mounted. Despite obtaining a $19 million USRA loan in 1975, the Katy remained a spinster. "The road frequently plays host to foreign-line office cars," observed a reporter, "but so far nobody publicly has asked for Miss Katy's hand in marriage." Few thought it could survive the impact of deregulation.[9]

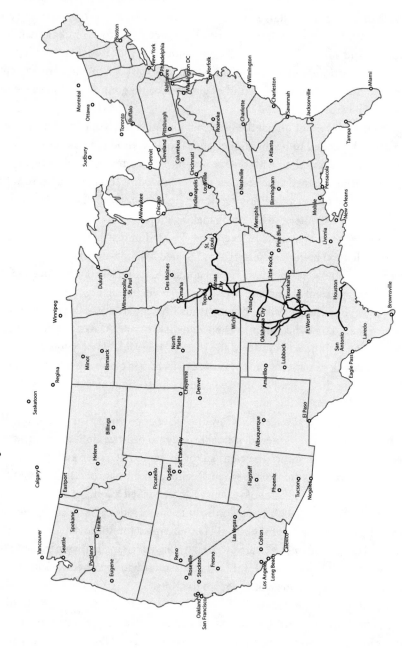

THE HOPEFUL BRIDE. The Katy on the eve of its acquisition by the Union Pacific.

On paper the Katy looked unappealing. By 1983 it had assets of $377 million and long-term debt of $206 million. Other roads owned a quarter of its 3,147 miles of track. A Katy official quipped that the road had two advantages: It owned the shortest route between Kansas and Texas, and it had the ability to survive past mismanagement. Kenefick liked the shorter, straighter route to the Gulf and had another reason for wanting the road: The Katy was an incorrigible rate cutter. However, it was in poor physical shape and would require a major overhaul.[10]

The UP planning people did their usual intensive analysis for what became known as "Project Wisconsin." On its 1,630-mile main line more than half the rail was 90-pound weight or less, and 17 percent of the line operated under slow orders. Some 36 percent of its locomotives and 73 percent of its freight cars were leased rather than owned, creating a major drag on operating income. Jim Patterson, who did the P&A report in August 1981, pronounced the Katy "basically insolvent with increasing deficits in both working capital and equity capital." Nevertheless, Kenefick was friendly with Whitman and struck an agreement with him. UPC raised only mild objections. "They thought it was a dumb thing to do," said Kenefick, ". . . but it wasn't so much that it was going to bust the balance sheet."[11]

After talking with Whitman, Kenefick assigned Rebensdorf to meet with Harold Gastler of the Katy to determine whether a merger would work. "It was kind of like counterintelligence," said Rebensdorf. "He had an assumed name and I had an assumed name." They met in Dallas motel rooms and concluded that a merger would benefit both roads. Since Katy Industries owned 98 percent of the railroad's stock, the transaction seemed an easy one.[12]

As the negotiations progressed, Gary Stuart, one of UPC's financial officers, identified two troubling forms of Katy debt: $51.7 million in subordinated income debentures and $73.4 million in non-interest-bearing certificates, both issued in 1958. BN was thought to own 40 percent of the income debentures, and no one knew what to make of the strange certificates. Stuart considered both dangerous. "If the income debentures and certificates were not retired prior to or as part of an acquisition," he warned, "the holders . . . could potentially frustrate consolidation of the M-K-T's operations into the UP System by asserting a claim on a disproportionate share of the gains resulting from the consolidation."[13]

In May1985 UPC announced that it had agreed to buy the Katy for $108 million. The stock market showed its disapproval of the price by knocking Katy stock down a third the next day. UP's lawyers were confident they could get past the parallel roads issue for several reasons. The two companies already shared six hundred miles of line through trackage agreements. More important, this was a different kind of parallel merger from that of SF and SP, which was then under ICC consideration. "The answer," said Dolan, ". . . was to play out the fact that the

Katy was basically going down. . . . We were preserving the Katy service, and that alone was a huge benefit, and I think that's what sold the case."[14]

Then a hitch developed, just as Stuart had feared. Once the merger was announced, BN decided not to sell its debentures but to see if their value increased. A financial covenant forbade paying any dividends on Katy common stock until all cumulative interest on the income debentures had been paid and at least 60 percent of the certificates had been retired. At first it appeared that the income debentures would pose the greater problem. Gradually, however, the mysterious certificates emerged as an annoying obstacle to the merger.[15]

In struggling through the Depression without going into bankruptcy, the Katy accumulated unpaid dividends on its preferred stock. During bankruptcy proceedings in 1958 it offset this obligation by issuing certificates valued at $110 per share. "Nobody knew certificates of what," said Kenefick. "It was sort of a vague claim on some of the earnings of the railroad." The uncertainty surrounding the certificates demanded their elimination prior to any merger. UP included in the merger agreement a stipulation that at least 60 percent of the certificates had to be redeemed. Since Katy Industries owned only 18 percent of them, it issued a tender offer for another 42 percent at $25 each. The certificates were selling for about $23. By August 1985, however, Katy Industries had acquired fewer than two-thirds of the required amount.[16]

One shrewd analyst, Glenn Cameron, galvanized the holders of the certificates. He had originally thought the certificates were worthless but changed his mind after the merger was announced. Every other Katy debt obligation had priority over the certificates, and the railroad was never going to earn enough money to start paying them off. In a merger, however, they would have to be dealt with somehow, possibly at face value. "Even though they represent no ownership," he said, "they represent future control of the entire Katy railroad." On that premise he acquired 49 percent of the outstanding certificates for himself and his clients.[17]

An impasse ensued. Late in August 1985 UP threatened to call the deal off; two months later it renewed the offer of $25 a certificate. Despite extended deadlines, few holders accepted. In November UP upped the ante to $33.50 without success. On January 13, 1986, it announced that the merger plan had been dropped and no new offer would be forthcoming. Cameron's clique found themselves in a quandary; without the merger their certificates were worthless. Late in April Katy Industries reported that the necessary certificates could be obtained for an additional $2 million and asked UP to put up half that amount. The board agreed to do so, and in early May the Katy announced a new offer of $39.75.[18]

The new offer finally brought in enough certificates to put the agreement into effect. In November UP formally submitted its merger application. Earlier that summer the ICC had stunned the industry by voting 4–1 to reject the SF-SP merger application. The ICC did not rush to judgment on the Katy application but finally approved it on May 19, 1988, and the deal was officially closed on August 12. Kenefick had the last laugh on those who thought UP paid too much for a run-down railroad. The Katy owned a lot of valuable real estate in Texas. Land sales in downtown Dallas and Houston alone more than paid for the deal. "It was a brilliant purchase," said Davidson. "We fixed it up and . . . made a good high-speed railroad out of it."[19]

By that time Kenefick had long since retired and the leadership in New York had undergone a sea change. UP entered yet another new era that would reshape the company.

The question of who would succeed Kenefick depended in large measure on who held the top post in New York. There, too, the succession issue had become controversial. Evans faced retirement in 1985 and was none too happy at the prospect. Cook, who was less than three years younger than Evans, expected to succeed him, but his tenure would be short. Evans loved being the face and voice of the company and especially the perks it brought—the company plane, the train trips, the splendid office on Park Avenue, and entertaining prominent guests. Everybody liked Evans; he enjoyed being treated like visiting royalty on a train excursion or elsewhere, and he remained the gracious, affable soul who was pleasant to everyone regardless of status.

For Evans every trip on the railroad became an event over which he presided with finesse. He was as impressive a host as he was a guest. His wife matched his sociability in a more regal manner. Rosemary Evans was an industrial heiress accustomed to having things her own way. Her whims and imperious style became legendary to the corporate and railroad staff who had to cater to them. "She believed that Union Pacific was her plaything," said Schaefer, "and abused the management and the use of company assets like the company plane." On one occasion a disgruntled employee wrote an anonymous letter to the UP board itemizing her abuses. The board showed its mettle by ignoring the complaint and seeking instead to expose the whistle-blower.[20]

During the early 1980s the corporate staff continued to expand despite the Reagan recession. Carl von Bernuth came aboard as assistant general counsel in March 1980 and succeeded Bill McDonald as general counsel in 1988 when the latter retired. In November 1981 Jim Otto, the controller, was made a vice president along with Ed Hill, who was in charge of financial administration. Chuck Eaton was elevated to senior vice president in charge of strategic planning, government affairs, and corporate relations. This amalgam, said Evans and Cook, was "necessitated by the continued growth and additional complexities of our several businesses coupled with the ever-expanding responsibilities of Messrs. Evans and Cook." By 1982 each of the three areas had its own vice president. Altogether UPC boasted three senior vice presidents and nine vice presidents.[21]

Evans had another addition in mind to relieve what he deemed the burden of duties at the top. In 1978 he had brought John Meyer of the Harvard Business School, a well-known authority on transportation, to the UP board. Deeply impressed by Meyer's ability, Evans persuaded the board in December 1981 to elect him to the newly created position of vice chairman of the board at a salary of $250,000 along with liberal stock options. Meyer's duties were vaguely defined as "assisting the Chairman and the President in the general management areas of the corporation and be[ing] responsible for the development of an economics staff."[22]

Evidently trying to position Meyer as his replacement, Evans persuaded the board a year later to give Meyer another title as chief administrative officer. Under the proposed arrangement, Meyer would coordinate all major corporate staff functions. The three senior vice presidents—McDonald, Surette, and Eaton—would report to him, as would two vice presidents. Cook would remain the chief operating officer with all four subsidiary presidents reporting to him. Harrington Drake, chairman of Dun & Bradstreet, praised the move. "There is a tremendous businessman hiding behind the academic robes," he wrote. ". . . There is also an intellect and integrity almost impossible to duplicate."[23]

Not every director shared Drake's enthusiasm. Oscar "Pat" Lawler, a retired Los Angeles banker, voted against creating the new position. Cook and Bill Smith, Champlin's CEO, missed the meeting but let Evans know they too opposed the move. The board in executive session approved the title but balked at the proposed new organization. Afterward Evans lobbied the directors hard to approve the new organization. As the January 1983 meeting approached, two new directors, Downing Jenks and Warren Shapleigh, joined the board as representatives of MP. Their first meeting looked to be a showdown on the issue of Meyer's authority.[24]

At the board meeting Evans startled the board with another surprise. He announced that Elbridge Gerry planned to resign as chairman of the executive committee. This was news to the directors, who later discovered it was news to Gerry as well. Several of the directors tried to divine what Evans was up to. One possibility came to mind. When the board imposed an age limit on directors, it had exempted the chairman of the executive committee. Although past sixty-five, Gerry could stay as long as the company wanted him. "We think what he [Evans] was planning," said Kenefick, "was, that then when he did retire, the chairman of the executive committee job would be open and [Evans] would take that, which wouldn't be the same as the chairman but he'd get a lot of the fringes."[25]

Two board members, Lawler and Lowell Miller, an Omaha banker, sent a telegram to Evans protesting the Gerry situation. Evans replied politely that he appreciated their views but had no intention of changing his mind. The next board meeting was scheduled for February 24. Miller told Kenefick that the Gerry matter would be on the agenda and that Gerry planned to attend the meeting. They hoped that the inside directors—those who worked for the company—would not have to be involved. But if they were, Miller wanted to know how Bill Smith would vote, as did another director, John Fery, the CEO of Boise Cascade. Kenefick asked Smith his views, then called Miller and said, "Tell Fery Mr. Smith says 'Whoopee,' which I take as an affirmative."[26]

Later Miller called Kenefick back and gave him a head count on who stood where. Evans had three close personal friends on the board who would support him. Kenefick briefed Jenks and Shapleigh and got their support. On the night before the meeting Minot Milliken, a textile manufacturer and director, hosted a dinner for the rebels. Lawler served as ringleader of the group.[27]

The meeting next morning proceeded through some routine matters before going into executive session, which excluded the inside directors. Evans was asked to leave the meeting while they discussed the Gerry situation. Kenefick and Smith sat waiting in a small anteroom for more than an hour while the session went on. Finally Gerry came out and said, "It's all over." Gerry remained chairman of the executive committee. Evans was called back into the meeting and told the board had decided to remove him as CEO. He could remain as board chairman, but Cook would be made CEO as well as president.[28]

Stunned as he was, Evans handled the news with aplomb. At lunch he was his usual affable self and only afterward told the senior officers of the board's actions. In the news release he said, "Bill Cook and I have worked closely together for fourteen years and I am confident he will provide splendid leadership in the years ahead. At the same time, by relinquishing the chief executive officer's position, I will be able to devote my primary attention to the major strategic opportunities available to this great company." No one elaborated on what those opportunities might be.[29]

The smoothness of the transition concealed any hint of the turmoil that had led to it. To the press Evans portrayed the change as one of his own choosing. A Fortune article on corporate successions described it as "carefully orchestrated." By retaining the chairmanship Evans also kept and even expanded his place in the broader corporate world, but he no longer had a role of any consequence in UPC policy. Meyer returned to Harvard on June 30 but remained on the board, where his expertise was welcomed.[30]

Increasingly Cook became the voice of the company. He lacked Evans's charm but was far more astute in the nitty-gritty details of corporate activity and had already made his approach clear. "You make sure you've got the right people in place," he said in an interview. "You evaluate their performance very objectively and coldly, and reward them if they do well and punish them if they don't. . . . You see that they have a challenging, aggressive program in place, evaluate their performance against those objectives, and then get out of the way and let them do the job."[31]

Cook intended to practice what he preached. In November 1984 he brought Schaefer to New York as senior vice president for planning and corporate development. The news release made clear what Cook had in mind. Schaefer would assume responsibility for "an expanded strategic planning function which will evaluate new business opportunities for Union Pacific Corporation and its four subsidiary companies." Cook was intent on increasing the return to shareholders, and Schaefer was at work on a plan to do that by striking out in a new direction.[32]

Return on investment had become a hot potato since the advent of the recession. With both the railroad and the other subsidiaries, especially Champlin, clamoring for more capital, UPC struggled to determine where the money would produce the best return. During 1983–84, while still in Omaha, Schaefer began what became known as the Productivity Studies because he suspected the railroad was underperforming financially. He wanted to better understand which types of capital reinvestment produced the highest returns for shareholders. No one had attempted this kind of analysis. Rebensdorf's group did one study, Arthur D. Little, Inc., another one.[33]

The results of this first study confirmed Schaefer's belief that the railroad had not achieved significant increases in productivity and was not earning an adequate return on invested capital. The Little report, submitted in October 1984, provided more detail. Since 1980 the UP System's tonnage had declined 20 percent to 1973 levels. Despite all efforts, little long-term improvement had been made in productivity. One obvious reason was labor costs, which had risen an average of 10 percent a year since 1973. The system's average hourly wage cost of $13.32 ranked third nationally behind coal miners and petroleum workers.[34]

Deregulation, enlarged rail systems, and the demise of rate bureaus had changed the game entirely. Once-uniform rates had been balkanized into contract rates that let railroads discriminate among shippers in response to specific competitive situations. All forms of surface transportation could no longer count on general market growth to increase revenues; instead they had to fight for improved market share. The growing intensity of this competition pressured the railroad to reduce costs and increase productivity.[35]

Meanwhile, favorable circumstances had enhanced the competitive position of motor carriers. In 1970 trucks owned 66 percent of total tonnage; by 1983 their share had expanded to 74 percent. Large companies used owner-operators as independent contractors, thereby reducing their capital investment and maximizing their flexibility. The Motor Carrier Act of 1980 stripped away a number of restrictions and did much to improve the productivity of trucks. Barges also hurt UP, which faced water competition over more of its mileage than any other railroad. During the 1970s inland waterway traffic grew faster than rail tonnage. Most river tonnage was bulk cargoes like grain and coal, the heart of UP's business. Between 1970 and 1981, for example, the amount of grain carried by barges increased 168 percent.[36]

The Little study confirmed UP's growing dependence on a few bulk commodities. In 1973 coal, grain, and soda ash comprised 32 percent of the road's total tonnage; by 1983 the figure had risen to 53 percent. The story was the same for MP. Coal, grain, and chemicals constituted 51 percent of all its tonnage in 1973 and 63 percent in 1983. The traffic base was shrinking even though the overall economy had expanded, and the trend looked to continue. The growth in coal tonnage helped compensate for declines in other commodities, thanks largely to the Clean Air Act of 1970 and the oil embargo of 1973 with its spike in oil prices. However, the Clean Air Act Amendments of 1977 put a crimp in this growth pattern by eliminating many of the advantages in using western low-sulfur coal, as did a sharp drop in the price of oil.[37]

Labor and capital posed special problems for UP. Improved financial performance depended in large part on reducing the unit cost of labor. Shrinking the overall size of the workforce and making it more flexible seemed more promising approaches. Reductions could be achieved through attrition, buyouts, and layoffs. Attrition seemed a limited possibility since nearly 56 percent of the union and more than 50 percent of the nonunion employees were under the age of forty and turnover averaged only about 6 percent in nonrecession years. Job buyouts looked more promising; however, if too many were made and a rush of business forced the rehiring of workers, the investment would be wasted. Layoffs were a last resort because of the stress they placed on everyone involved.[38]

The capital component of UP's current cost structure was twice as large as its labor component. Here, too, deregulation had changed the game radically. Railroad assets were largely inflexible and long-lived. UP's capital asset base had a weighted average life of thirty years, ranging from twenty years for locomotives to forty-one years for shops. Only a few assets like computers and communications had shorter life spans of five or six years.[39]

Under regulation, when the emphasis was on service rather than price, long-term assets were a competitive advantage because the best-maintained and -equipped railroad had the most capacity and could provide the best service. Stable rates offered assurance that investment in long-term facilities and equipment could eventually be recovered. When deregulation shifted the emphasis from service to price, it transformed long-lived assets into a liability. Rate instability magnified the risk of long-term investments, as did technological obsolescence in a competitive market where the latest new thing could give rivals an edge.[40]

Future capital productivity depended on finding ways to match capacity with demand. If projected market growth did not occur, UP would be saddled with excess operating capacity. One obvious way to avoid this was to reduce capital spending, which is always made in anticipation of specific market benefits. Another approach would be to externalize capital assets to outside parties like shippers, who in some cases provided their own cars.[41]

The Little analysis concluded that the money spent on capital investment during the past decade had been offset by declining income, increased labor costs, and the failure of anticipated traffic gains to materialize. Productivity would play an increasingly important role in the future as price and market-share competition kept pressure on UP to cut costs. New measurements for productivity had to be devised, along with specific goals for improving it in given areas.[42]

Schaefer found much to like in the reports. He had grown disenchanted with Kenefick's handling of the railroad, especially his policy of spending large sums to maintain and improve it. The outlays, he said later, "while beautifying it, yielded questionable returns." The studies also indicated that shareholders got better returns from buying out surplus labor than from funding rail projects because the labor "investment" returned its costs in less than a year. Not surprisingly, Kenefick dismissed many of the conclusions, and his relationship with Schaefer cooled. A few weeks later Schaefer was on his way to New York to take up his new post.[43]

On October 17 Kenefick and Schaefer presented their productivity findings and the railroad's strategic plan to the UPC staff in what was billed as a "good give and take session." Afterward the corporate officers posed four challenges to the railroad: develop a specific strategy for meeting truck competition; analyze the implications of the UP becoming a "predominately bulk railroad"; implement "aggressive productivity improvements" at all levels to be more cost-competitive; and develop integrated strategies for key market segments. Clearly Cook wanted the screws tightened on all these issues.[44]

One solution seemed as obvious to Schaefer as it was repugnant to Kenefick. "He came up with the theory that the way to get the railroad to perform better was to cut back on capital investment," said Rebensdorf, "that expenses had to be cut significantly, and that we should not be putting any more money into the railroad." Rebensdorf disagreed with this approach, but it found a receptive audience in Cook. Their agreement on these issues was one reason why Cook wanted Schaefer at UPC.[45]

Once in New York, Schaefer expanded the Productivity Studies to the other subsidiaries. For the next round, the Shareholder Value Study, he hired a Chicago firm that used a sophisticated model to measure shareholder impacts. Each subsidiary prepared case projections to aid "management decisions establishing the future direction of the Corporation, with the historical results being used to establish a context for the performance that can be expected from the existing businesses." The railroad did not fare well in these exercises.[46]

Schaefer's report to the board in March 1985 got its full attention. The railroad, he stressed, was not earning its cost of capital. Every dollar invested in it returned only fifty cents because of high costs and lack of productivity. "People knew that the railroad wasn't earning its cost of capital," he said later, "but that was a cold shower."[47]

The same pattern held true with Champlin, which in recent years had been battered by a slump in oil and gas prices. The refineries were not earning their cost of capital, and the millions poured into exploration had been poorly spent. As Schaefer went into more detail, Smith grew agitated and paced around the board table. One issue on the table was whether to invest $100 million in the Wilmington refinery. Schaefer opposed the investment because the company wasn't making any money on the refinery business. "It was the first time someone had countered [Smith] with a rational study," Schaefer said, "because in the past he'd stand up and pontificate, and everybody else sort of nodded." The land business, too, was not especially lucrative.[48]

Prior to 1979 the railroad had provided more than half of UPC's net earnings; between 1979 and 1982 that figure dropped to 38 percent. Some way had to be found to increase its productivity rather than simply keep pouring capital into it. Schaefer also thought the changing economy made railroading a less interesting business to be in. Some of the industries it served were stagnant and possibly dying. The rust belt was in bloom; the steel and automobile industries were losing ground to imports. "Either we should change the way we run the business," said Schaefer, "or we shouldn't be pouring a lot of capital into it."[49]

These views confirmed what Cook already suspected. On April 9, 1985, he wrote Kenefick, "The broad outline of this analysis is very clear. Since 1980 we have suffered a significant decline in the real earning power of most of our business units and based on our current projections that decline may well continue." In the railroad's case Cook wanted a clearer picture of what precipitated the "substantial decline in real ROI starting in 1982."[50]

Schaefer's analysis led logically to another line of reasoning. The railroad made plenty of money but swallowed most of it in capital investment. Would it make more sense to use the railroad as a cash cow and divert some of its earnings into other businesses with more promising futures? To explore other options a study team was put together in May 1985 to "identify specific diversification options which could reasonably be expected to increase shareholder value."[51]

This course, if pursued, would amount to a dramatic shift in strategy. Lovett's primary goal had been to protect existing company assets by putting them under managers that knew more about them. Under this arrangement the railroad always remained the primary business. The new approach contemplated acquiring other businesses that neither the railroad nor UPC had been in or knew much about. It would expand the role of the corporation. Conceived originally as a device to help the railroad develop its nonrail assets, it would become the headquarters for a conglomerate with the railroad as first among equals at best.

"When I joined the company in 1980," recalled Carl von Bernuth, "there was certainly the view that those nonrail assets had as bright or brighter future than the railroad. . . . If you were to . . . look at where the investment dollars went, whether they came from cash generated by the railroad or outside borrowings, and looked at where they went, you would see that certainly a tremendous amount was going to nonrail assets." Even though deregulation unleashed a new round of mergers that virtually compelled the corporation to put money into the MP-WP merger, this did not change Cook's doubts about the railroad's future. "Bill Cook's view," said von Bernuth, "was that the railroad industry was a cash cow but not one to invest in."[52]

A change in direction seemed possible because the leadership was undergoing changes at all levels. Frank Barnett, who remained a director after leaving office in 1977, contracted pneumonia in 1985 and died on April 4. Three months later Evans reached retirement age and left the chairmanship and the board. The board rewarded him with a lovely office at 375 Park Avenue that he still occupied as of 2009. L. B. Harbour Jr., the CEO of Upland, retired in 1985. Kenefick and Smith were due to retire in 1986 and Cook himself in 1987.[53]

In 1986 Gerry retired from the board after seventeen years of heading the executive committee. He was the last link to the Harriman family, if only by marriage, but the link remained in place when his son Elbridge "Ebby" Gerry Jr. replaced his father on the board. Ebby was also a partner at Brown Brothers Harriman, giving that firm a continuing presence in the company. Kenefick left the board that same year, as did Pat Lawler. In their place came two distinguished directors: Henry Kissinger, former secretary of state, and Bob Bauman, chairman of the Beecham Group. The old order was changing, and in ways no one could yet foresee.[54]

PART TWO

THE WALSH ERA, 1986–1991

15

The Succession Scramble

Cook's promotion to CEO did not represent a major shift because he belonged to the old guard, the second generation of leaders since the corporation was formed. Behind them stood a pack of young, ambitious, and aggressive men eager to replace them. Schaefer made no secret of his desire to run UPC one day. He was bright, knowledgeable, and the only man to have gone from the corporation to the railroad and back again. His diversification strategy offered a new direction for the company. "Barry believed that if he did this successfully, he had a very good shot to be the next CEO," said von Bernuth. But he was still young at forty-seven. Bill Surette, the CFO, thought he was being groomed for the top post, as did some others. At the railroad the obvious candidates for the top job were Davis and Davidson. The merger had also thrown into the mix the whole group of MP officers besides Davidson. One of them, White Matthews, had gone to UPC as treasurer. Matthews had been the treasurer at MP and aspired to become a CFO.[1]

In his own area of finance Cook had built a strong and talented staff, many of whom would be candidates for advancement. He had centralized the financial and audit functions to exert stronger controls over the subsidiaries. "The theory of the corporate audit staff," said Schaefer, "was to find irregularities but also to look at how operations can improve. These guys were basically in the feudal system of Union Pacific. They were viewed with instant hostility." Cook's predecessor, Reg Sutton, had done the same thing, but Sutton had come to New York from the railroad and knew its requirements well. He had left the audit function in Omaha; Cook moved it to New York. He longed to curb the railroad's independent ways; with Kenefick about to retire, Cook saw his opportunity.[2]

Kenefick had unwisely recommended Flannery as his successor, but Cook had grave doubts about him. He asked Schaefer's opinion and got a similar response. Schaefer suspected that Kenefick wanted Flannery so that he could continue to run the railroad from behind the throne. Whether this was the case or not, nearly everyone agreed that Flannery was not the man for the job.[3]

Although he lacked a strong leadership personality, Cook was determined to impose major changes on UP. The most obvious opportunity lay in the succession scramble. Early in 1986 Cook told Kenefick he planned to bring someone in from the outside to run UP. He warned Kenefick that the relationship between the corporation and the railroad would be different in the future, which Kenefick took to mean that New York would become more involved in the railroad's affairs. This would be easier to accomplish by bringing in not only an outsider but someone who was not even in the industry to run the railroad.[4]

At Cook's request Schaefer produced a list of potential candidates from other railroads, but none of them appealed to Cook. "There were some good CEOs," said Schaefer, "but there wasn't really a huge talent pool. . . . [We] went through every officer involved in the industry." Schaefer's list included Drew Lewis, who was also boosted by Jim Robinson of American Express, a board member. He and Lewis were friends; Robinson's wife had worked for Lewis when he was secretary of transportation during the Reagan administration. Cook agreed and claimed that he "had it in the back of my mind for a few years that he'd be the ideal guy."[5]

Lewis was receptive to the offer but insisted on a commitment that he would become CEO of the corporation when Cook retired in 1987. The board was concerned about Lewis's lack of experience with railroads and wanted him to spend time in Omaha. A plan was formulated in January that on April 1 Lewis would go to Omaha as chairman and CEO of the railroad. Kenefick would be promoted to vice chairman of UPC and tutor Lewis on the railroad until his own retirement at year's end. In the spring of 1987 Lewis would move up to president and chief operating officer of UPC; upon Cook's retirement in October, Lewis would succeed him as chairman and CEO.[6]

Lewis appeared to be an inspired choice. He had served as president of Simplex Wire and Cable Company, headed his own financial and management firm, and been a court-appointed trustee for the bankrupt Reading Railroad. Appointed secretary of transportation in 1981, he helped institute a program to repair the interstate highway system and laid the groundwork for the government's later decision to sell Conrail. In February 1983 Lewis became chairman of Warner Amex—a joint venture between Warner Communications and American Express, run by his friend Jim Robinson—which was plagued with severe financial losses. He reorganized the company and turned a profit by 1985.[7]

Lewis also knew his way around politics. He had run unsuccessfully for governor of Pennsylvania in 1974 and drawn 47 percent of the vote in a year when the party was tarnished by the Watergate scandal. He had been deputy chairman of the Republican National Committee and a national committeeman since 1976. These credentials looked impressive at a time when Republicans held power in Washington and several issues crucial to the railroads were still bouncing around in Congress. Lewis had friends on the Hill and in the agencies, talked their language, and knew the political game.

Although Lewis had no background in railroads, his stint in the Reagan administration had acquainted him with the transportation industries. He gained notoriety in 1981 when he urged Reagan to fire the air traffic controllers to break their strike. But he also earned a reputation for mixing with the Transportation Department's employees, learning their names, asking their views, and involving as many people as possible in decisions. "By the time Drew left," said a staff member, "2,000 people thought they were working directly for him."[8]

Small and trim, Lewis was a charming, genial man with a ready smile and an aggressive business style. He was also a tough negotiator and politically savvy—a crucial asset for the railroad. "He's a very efficient manager and well known on the political scene," said Cook, "which is increasingly important to any business today." Above all, Lewis was a political animal. Many people thought he was biding his time in the corporate world while looking for the next step in his political career. The company needed a leader skilled at politics for many reasons, not least the ongoing effort to roll back Staggers and reinstate some form of regulation.[9]

Lewis went to Omaha with his wife, Marilyn, in March. Pickets from the rail unions, mindful of his handling of the air controllers, greeted his arrival. On March 31 he and Kenefick held two "meet-and-greet" sessions with UP employees, Lewis to say hello and Kenefick to say good-bye. They each made short speeches that praised the employees as the backbone to the railroad's success. Lewis promised the audience they would not "see any radical changes in the direction of this company." On that reassuring note he took charge of the railroad next day, April Fool's Day.[10]

At Warner Amex Lewis earned plaudits for turning around a floundering company. Although he denied that this would be his role at UP, some analysts saw the railroad as an even greater challenge. "He has been hired to improve Union Pacific's lackluster earnings," said the *New York Times*, "and pare down its bloated cost structure—a task that may force him once again, into a showdown with organized labor." An analyst agreed that "the railroad has too much track and too many employees." Lewis did not deny the problem. "Survival of this railroad comes in being the lowest-cost competitor," he told an interviewer. "We're in a commodity business and it is no different from a 7-Eleven store or a shoeshine stand. There's got to be cash."[11]

The dilemma was clear. The railroad industry was, as the *Times* noted, "caught between having its costs set by the rules of one era and its revenues squeezed by the pressures of another." Competition kept driving rates lower, while the major cost factor, labor, had grown more powerful under regulation and kept costs high, leaving railroads little choice but to reduce their labor forces as fast as possible. Technology had enabled them to do that; during the past two years UP had shed nearly seven thousand employees, both union and nonunion, and looked to eliminate another six thousand. Observers eagerly awaited the first confrontation between Lewis and the union leaders, but Lewis demurred. "I have to show that I am here to preserve the company and jobs," he said, "and am not here to fire people helter-skelter to increase profits."[12]

But the labor dilemma was clearly on Lewis's mind. He asked Tom Watts, who had been made vice president of labor relations in the spring of 1984, "How in hell can we cut a couple of hundred million bucks out of our labor?" Watts and some of his staff had just started to search for ways to do something similar. Rebensdorf lent one of his men, a young accountant named Jim Young, to the project. They covered the windows of a large room so no one could see their work and bored into the details of every agreement looking for ways to make cuts. The result was a plan with a price tag of $400 million. Reluctantly they showed it to Lewis, who swore and asked what the return would be. Over a five-year period, Watts replied, almost a billion dollars. Lewis's expression brightened; he promised to see what he could do.[13]

Increasing both profits and return on investment lay at the heart of UPC's agenda. In 1984 the company began buying back its stock. By 1986, having purchased 10.4 million shares at a cost of $500 million, the corporation expanded the buyback program by another $750 million. The goal was to reduce the outstanding shares by about 20 percent to 100 million. During 1986 Cook took an even more drastic step. In June he announced a restructuring program at a write-off cost of $1.7 billion. Of that amount $600 million went to cover workforce reduction costs and consolidation of facilities, $577 million for a write-down on unproductive oil and gas properties, $305 million for a write-down on the newly expanded Corpus Christi refinery that had proved a bust, and $261 million to cover excess rail equipment, "probable future losses in a petrochemical venture," and other items.[14]

These moves made 1986 a forgettable year for earnings despite an impressive performance by the railroad. After the special charge of $1.7 billion, UPC reported a net loss of $460 million. Yet it increased the dividend from $1.80 to $1.85, thanks in part to the reduced number of shares. These moves landed Cook on the hot seat in financial circles. A May 1986 *Business Week* cover story on executive pay and performance ranked Cook ninth among the ten CEOs who gave their shareholders the least for the pay they drew.[15]

At both UPC and the railroad the pressure was growing to improve performance. However, Lewis had his own agenda. He had no intention of spending a year at the railroad. "He didn't spend a hell of a lot of time in Omaha," said von Bernuth, "and really had no particular interest in learning the details of Railroad 101." Kenefick, who was supposed to be Lewis's tutor, found himself without a student. "I don't think he spent one night a week in Omaha," he said. Schaefer thought his presence there was "an excuse to use the company plane to keep up his political involvements."[16]

Lewis made no secret of his desire to get on with his real work, which was to head up UPC. His impatience began to annoy Cook, who had enough tough issues on his hands. He informed Schaefer that Lewis would be coming to New York early as president of UPC, a position then vacant. Cook wanted Schaefer to return to Omaha, become president of the railroad, and be in line to succeed Lewis when he retired. To his surprise, Schaefer declined. "I had spent twelve years at the Railroad working on the major strategic issues facing the company and the industry," he said, "and saw little career value in going back to that. I wanted to broaden my experience base into nonrail businesses." Schaefer had personal reasons as well. He had just finished moving his family, including his parents, to Connecticut, and his teenaged daughter was struggling with the adjustment. Another round-trip move did not appeal to him.[17]

Schaefer did help with the selection process. Everyone agreed the new president had to come from the outside, and a headhunting firm was engaged to conduct a search. One name that surfaced was an executive vice president at Cummins Engine named Michael H. Walsh. He was young, aggressive, and had an impressive resume: degrees from Stanford and Yale Law School (where he was a classmate of von Bernuth), White House Fellow, and U.S. attorney for the Southern District of California before entering the corporate world.[18]

"He knew politics; he wasn't a virgin in the political sense," said Gary Schuster, who became one of Lewis's closest aides, "and Drew liked . . . the fact that he was a Democrat 'cause they could probably work both sides of the aisle." Walsh had made an impressive career shift from prosecutor to running a manufacturing operation. A *Fortune* article on "America's Most Wanted Managers" praised him as a "real leader, tough manager. Has incredible instincts and ability to read people." He was also the right age for the job. Lewis was fifty-four and Walsh only forty-three, making him young enough to be a potential heir apparent when Lewis retired.[19]

Convinced that he had found the right man and eager to move on to UPC, Lewis persuaded Cook and the board to hire Walsh and speed up the transition timetable. In September 1986 Walsh agreed to come aboard on November 1, at which time Lewis would go to New York as president and CEO. Under this arrangement the subsidiary heads would all report to Lewis, who along with the corporate staff reported to Cook. The new schedule put Lewis in New York six months ahead of the original plan.[20]

This arrangement thrust Cook deeper into the shade than even his quiet personality cared to endure. Lewis garnered most of the press and had already exerted his influence through the change in the transition timetable. The more Cook was around Lewis, the more he came to dislike him and resent his style.

Having set in motion the forces that he hoped would change UPC's direction, Cook longed to embed them in one major deal that could serve as his swan song. In May 1986 Schaefer obliged with a report summarizing the key findings and implications of the Productivity and Shareholder Value studies.[21]

The report's conclusions pointed clearly to a need for more diversification. The railroad's profit margin was declining, its large, inflexible asset base placed a heavy burden on its cost structure, and only 15 percent of its recent capital expenditures had "identifiable economic justification." Shareholder value could be enhanced either by improving performance or downsizing the asset base. The latter choice would reduce future capital needs and free up capital for more profitable uses.[22]

The railroad's future did not look promising from an investment point of view. The economy was becoming more service oriented, which meant reduced shipping volumes. UP could compete only by slashing costs and "making structural cost changes." Unfortunately, its long-lived assets kept it from responding quickly to changes in technology, shipper demands, and commodity or volume shifts. Boxcars, for example, became commercially obsolete before they wore out. Of the specialty cars, TOFC cars actually lost nearly 5 percent. The railroad's cost structure consisted of 49 percent capital, 27 percent material, and 24 percent labor, making capital the chief determinant of total productivity.[23]

These factors painted a grim picture of recent performance from an investment perspective. Between 1955 and 1972 the railroad's real rate of return equaled or exceeded the cost of capital in most years. Since 1972, however, its rate of return had dropped from 5 percent to about 1 percent. For UP alone the real ROI fell from 4.4 percent in 1981 to .2 percent in 1982 and had yet to recover much from that level. For its capital investments to earn a decent return, the railroad had to abandon the time-honored tradition of chasing business that did not pay its way. By that measure only soda ash and chemicals earned a ROI approaching the cost of capital.[24]

Historically the railroad comprised 70 percent of the corporation's total asset base. The other subsidiaries produced a ROI much closer to the real cost of capital—thus the need either to improve the railroad's ROI or downsize its asset base and put the capital where it would earn a more favorable return. Reducing the railroad's asset base would have a greater impact on shareholder value than increased earnings or reduced operating costs. This reasoning led Schaefer to look for investments with a better return. One in particular intrigued him: a less-than-truckload (LTL) trucking company named Overnite. Schaefer and Tom Boswell, a member of his staff, identified it as a good fit with UP, one that could "broaden UP's transportation footprint." They figured a price of about $650 million and took the proposal to Cook.[25]

The trucking business was both a new opportunity and an old problem for larger railroads. Several of them, including MP, had their own trucking subsidiaries to move freight between the railroad and its customers. In August 1982 UP created a subsidiary that brokered the hiring of trucks to move freight to and from some terminals. Five months later an ICC decision gave railroads greater freedom to enter the trucking business directly. With the country in a recession, however, the railroads already suffered from overcapacity. Kenefick saw no need to expand MP's trucking unit or go directly into the business.[26]

Schaefer and Cook were seeking acquisitions with a synergy to the railroad. Overnite seemed to fit that need. Its founder and owner, seventy-four-year old multimillionaire Harwood Cochrane, was a courtly but autocratic southern gentleman who had started out driving a horse-drawn milk wagon and grown his business into the fifth-largest trucking firm in the nation, with 10,400 employees and sales of $470 million in 1985. Overnite served thirty-four states, primarily in the East, and had no debt. Cochrane paid his nonunion workers wages and benefits totaling $16 an hour as opposed to $21 an hour on unionized lines, but he treated his employees well.[27]

Schaefer had Rebensdorf and his staff investigate whether to go after an LTL or truckload carrier. The former charged higher fees for smaller shipments, the latter a flat rate for an entire load. Rebensdorf concluded that the truckload carriers were dominated by owner-operators who worked on low margins compared to the higher margins on the LTL side. In addition, he noted, "the LTL side fit better into . . . the logistics or distribution chain." The fact that Overnite was nonunion also made it attractive, as did the possibility that Cochrane might stay on in charge of the business.[28]

This analysis fed into Schaefer's expanding vision of what UPC should do. He had come to view the railroad as providing wholesale transportation at a time when the money to be made was on the retail side—providing value-added services that commanded higher prices. These services included door-to-door delivery—hence the need for a trucking firm—as well as warehousing and assembling capacities wherein components could be brought to a location, put together, and the finished product shipped out. The buzzword for this approach was "kitting," and the combination of transportation, warehousing, and assembly services came together for Schaefer under the rubric of logistics.[29]

Although the proposal appealed to him, Cook hesitated because he knew Kenefick hated truckers. Schaefer understood the difficulty. "In order to do an acquisition," he said, "the problem was the railroad culture. The railroad culture dominated the transportation side, and it wasn't dynamic enough so you couldn't buy a small little ABC Company. You had to do something big enough but on the other hand not too big." Nor was the attitude confined to the railroad. Schaefer came to regard the heads of the subsidiaries as feudal barons presiding jealously over their fiefdoms.[30]

Once Lewis arrived in New York and his own exit date drew closer, Cook's thinking changed. It appeared that Conrail was going to be sold to private investors, and a rumor spread that Lewis wanted UP to acquire it and create a true transcontinental system. This possibility alarmed Cook, who had long opposed a transcontinental operation. Acquiring an eastern trucking company might provide synergy and also consume any funds available for another acquisition once Lewis assumed command. As Schaefer put it, "Cook decided that one way to sidetrack a Conrail deal was to lever up the UP balance sheet with a large acquisition."[31]

By the time Cook decided to do the Overnite deal, its stock had reached $31 a share, which hiked the price considerably. Cook didn't care; he wanted Overnite at whatever price. Despite reservations expressed by Schaefer and Boswell, he paid a whopping $43.25 a share, or $1.2 billion, for the company. "He gave away $100 million just sitting across the table," said a frustrated Schaefer. "He wanted to do something before he left. He was afraid Drew was going to do the Conrail deal." White Matthews was no less shocked. "We had a much lower number," he said, "and he [Cook] just went in and gave it away." Jim Dolan concluded that the exorbitant price was Cook's ego at work, that "Bill wanted to leave a big mark on the Union Pacific before he left."[32]

At a board meeting on July 31, 1986, Cook received approval to acquire 4.9 percent of Overnite's stock and negotiate for the remainder of it. Dolan and George Craig met with Cochrane in Washington to discuss ways to integrate the two companies. Not in the cards, Cochrane declared flatly. One problem lay in the fact that the railroad was union and the trucking company nonunion. "Really the only thing that justified Overnite was the merits of their own business," concluded Dolan, "and that didn't justify a billion two." Craig dutifully passed this information along to New York, where it evidently made no impression.[33]

A special board meeting was called on September 18 to approve the acquisition. Kenefick was in Omaha and scheduled to receive an award. He could not get to New York in time and attended by telephone, as did Spencer Eccles. Only two other directors were absent. For Gerry and the other new directors, it was the first controversial deal to come before them. Schaefer did a presentation entitled "A Strategic Vision for Union Pacific Transportation Services," then gave a detailed description of Overnite and its strategic fit with UP. A major reason for acquiring Overnite, he added, was its synergy with the railroad. Lewis opposed the deal but voted for it because, he said later, he was still new to the company. The only vote cast against the acquisition came from Downing Jenks.[34]

Cook had his legacy. He portrayed the acquisition as a perfect fit that would make UP a transcontinental surface transportation company. "In looking for growth of the transportation segment of our business," he said in a press release, "we decided we wanted a motor carrier with large scale, wide coverage, a customer service orientation, a market competitive cost structure, and a capacity to apply new technology. Overnite fits this bill." It would, he emphasized, "be a natural fit with our railroad subsidiaries." He and Cochrane agreed that, in Cook's words, "we expect this relationship . . . will create new business, new efficiencies and new forms of service." It represented, he insisted, "another important step in Union Pacific's evolution into a transportation company of the future."[35]

Analysts split over whether the deal was a good thing for UP. However, everyone agreed that Cook had made a bold move. In October 1986 the *Wall Street Transcript* bestowed an unintentionally ironic tribute on the management transition by naming Cook and Lewis jointly as the year's top CEOs in the rail industry. "Over the long haul," it concluded, "Cook and Lewis have significantly enhanced shareholder value and through the acquisition of Overnite have poised UP to capitalize on the emerging trends in this industry."[36]

The search continued for other business opportunities. Earlier Cook had decided to expand the company's real estate activity. A new subsidiary, Union Pacific Realty, was created in September 1986 and an experienced development executive, Arch Jacobson, was hired to run it. "The focus," said Gary Stuart, "was on finding businesses where we had a competitive advantage that complemented the railroad." Schaefer's studies identified hazardous waste as an area with excellent growth prospects and uncovered another, more modest acquisition that interested Cook and Lewis alike. United States Pollution Control, Inc. (USPCI), was a large Oklahoma City–based waste management company that dealt in hazardous waste sites. Lewis liked the idea because one of his sons had some hazardous waste interests in Pennsylvania.[37]

The possibilities for synergy looked promising. The business was growing along with the amount of waste. One method of handling hazardous materials was to ship them from urban areas like Los Angeles to remote regions like Utah. UP had both the railroad and political connections in all the western states where permits would be needed for incinerators and other facilities. In May 1987 UPC made a buyout bid for USPCI that was promptly rejected. After the stock market crashed in October, UPC returned with a tender of $25 a share; it too was rejected. By then UPC owned nearly 4 percent of USPCI's stock and was buying more.[38]

Schaefer's heightened interest in logistics extended to the technology for managing freight flows. The railroad already had a lead in this area thanks to TCS's car-scheduling program. It also had a pool of skilled computer and telecommunications people who could use their expertise to create similar and compatible systems for the other subsidiaries. The trick was finding the best way to leverage these assets. One possibility would be to spin them off into a separate company.[39]

As a first step UPC in 1987 acquired a 30 percent interest in Skyway Freight Systems, a "California-based transportation company which offers its customers one-stop, computerized logistics management." Skyway was attractive because it had developed a sophisticated software program and logistics system that enabled it to track and time-manage truck freight across the country. The system it developed resembled the one later used by both UPS and Federal Express. It also served as a potentially useful component for Schaefer's vision of a kitting operation.[40]

In May 1987 UP folded most of its IT operation into a new subsidiary called UP Technologies with Jim Shattuck as president and Merill Bryan as vice president. Lewis envisioned it providing services to all the corporation's subsidiaries as well as a broad commercial market. The move had another important advantage. After the merger, nearly all the MP programmers remained in St. Louis as a separate nonunion operation. When UP Technologies was created, the entire St. Louis staff became its personnel, thereby sidestepping the union issue[41]

The creation of UP Technologies enabled Schaefer to gain control of the IT function within UPC. He envisioned the new company as chiefly an in-house resource, serving all the subsidiaries and forging synergies between them. However, Lewis insisted the new subsidiary had to earn its keep by selling TCS and other programs to all comers. "We were really trying to get synergies between the operating units," said Bryan. ". . . Drew had a style that wasn't really that kind of style. He was more like a GE that just said, 'We have a whole bunch of companies and I'm going to hold all their feet to the fire and you're going to deliver your earnings.'" This disagreement joined a growing list of differences between Lewis and Schaefer.[42]

On October 1, 1987, Cook stepped down and Lewis took command of the corporation. He remained on the board until 1989 but did not enjoy a long retirement, dying in 1992 of prostate cancer. Near the end of his life he told a friend in the company he was sorry about the way things had turned out there—a reference to Lewis.[43]

In the annual report for 1987, Lewis acknowledged that "the Corporation is shifting from a very basic asset-oriented company concentrating on the Railroad and natural resource businesses to a Corporation determined to be on the leading edge of technology in delivering multi-modal transportation services, environmental services, creative oil and gas exploration programs and profitable real estate ventures." In particular he singled out USPCI as "the most exciting opportunity of 1987" in "a field with tremendous growth potential, a business with very little downside in terms of recession."[44]

As 1988 opened, UPC entered a new era under new leadership. The annual reports told the tale of the succession scramble. For years the lead letter to the stockholders had been signed by the trio of Evans, Cook, and Gerry. In 1982 John Meyer joined them in the group photograph. A year later he was gone, and in the 1985 report only Cook and Gerry remained. In 1986 Lewis took Gerry's place; a year later he occupied center stage by himself.[45]

16

The Whirlwind

Nobody at UP knew what to expect from Mike Walsh. He blew into Omaha like a whirlwind, swept through the company with irresistible force, left a deep imprint, and then moved on as abruptly as he arrived. Opinions varied widely on whether it was a cleansing or an ill wind, but no one doubted that it profoundly rearranged the UP landscape. Whatever else UP people said about Walsh, and the gamut of opinion was broad, nearly everyone agreed on one point. As Shoener put it, "Mike Walsh was a change agent. . . . He moved us quantum leaps ahead."[1]

The challenge could hardly have been more formidable. Walsh was an outsider stepping into an unfamiliar industry, trying to fill the shoes of a man widely regarded as the best operating leader in the business. He arrived at a time of transition within both UPC and the railroad under circumstances that boded ill for the latter's future. He did not know either Lewis or the executives he would be working with in Omaha. The railroad had one conspicuous loose end in Mike Flannery, who still occupied an office on the twelfth floor but had no clear role in the company. It was only natural for Omaha to view this brash young stranger with suspicion, especially given UPC's growing belief that the railroad swallowed too much capital for too little return. Was he going to be the corporation's hatchet man?

Challenges were nothing new to Walsh. All his life he had been a fighter and a winner. The harder the climb, the more he relished it. Born in 1942 in Binghamton, New York, he was the third of four children of a father whose own parents had migrated from Ireland to Butte, Montana, and eked out a hardscrabble existence working the mines. Somehow Walsh's father found his way to Binghamton, where he managed movie theaters. He lost that job when Walsh was ten, and the family headed west to Portland, Oregon.[2]

At Lincoln High School in Portland, Walsh made all-state as a running back in football and was elected president of the student body. Hoping to play professional football, he went to Stanford on an athletic scholarship only to have his dream crushed by a series of shoulder dislocations. During his junior year his father died of colon cancer. Despite these setbacks Walsh excelled at Stanford and was selected in 1965 for the first group of White House fellows. While in Washington he met and married Joan Royter, an assistant dean of foreign students at American University. The most interesting people he met in the capital seemed to have law degrees, so he decided to see if he could compete at that level. He graduated from Yale Law School in 1969 and took a job as a public defender in San Diego.[3]

"I represented people for three years who didn't have a nickel to their names and who were charged with doing the worst things imaginable," Walsh said later. "Do I understand the real world? The answer is, you better believe I do." He worked with John Gardner to help form Common Cause, the citizens' action group. In 1977 he was appointed U.S. attorney for the Southern District of California. Under his vigorous direction the conviction rate improved and the agenda broadened to more difficult cases such as white-collar crime.[4]

Everything about Walsh smacked of ambition, hard work, and success. At every level he became someone to be watched because of his ability and sheer animal energy. In San Diego he laid the foundation for a promising political career and seemed ready to climb the higher rungs of that ladder. Then, in 1980, Cummins Engine recruited him to be vice president of its international marketing operations. The offer marked a stunning shift in his career trajectory. Walsh had no corporate experience whatever. His stock was rising in California politics, he had a comfortable life, and his wife had a good job as a dean at UC–San Diego. While the money was better, he was asked to give all this up for unknown prospects in an unfamiliar industry with a company based in Columbus, Indiana.[5]

Yet he did just that, largely because the challenge appealed to him. At Cummins he worked under Henry B. Schacht, praised by *Business Week* as one of the nation's most highly regarded business executives. At thirty-seven Walsh plunged into the business world with his usual ferocious energy, and in four years he was an executive vice president and member of the Cummins board. Cummins was yet another company struggling to redefine itself amid the economic and global crosscurrents of the 1980s. A maker of diesel engines confronting formidable new competitors at home and abroad, it responded with a bold restructuring plan that focused on diversification of product line.[6]

In particular Cummins had to cope with the influx of high-quality engines sold at much cheaper prices by Japanese manufacturers such as Komatsu. A tour of Japanese diesel plants in March 1983 opened the eyes of four top Cummins executives to the advances made in quality by the Japanese. "I couldn't believe what I saw," said one of them. "Simply stated, they were doing things that we all said we couldn't do in terms of higher quality standards, lower costs, and involvement of people."[7]

Komatsu and other Japanese firms utilized the techniques of Total Quality Control to achieve their three essential goals of higher quality, lower cost, and faster delivery. In seeking to emulate this performance Cummins's top managers turned to the consulting firm of General Systems Company, Inc. (GSC), in Pittsfield, Massachusetts. Two brothers, Val and Don Feigenbaum, ran the company; Val had produced a thick book entitled *Total Quality Control* that became the manual for their work and, some said, an instant cure for insomnia. Walsh embraced the system and became a leading apostle within Cummins. The experience became a crucial lesson that proved useful when a new opportunity came calling in 1986.[8]

The offer from UP opened the door to another challenge. Walsh was ready to run a large company even if it involved another unfamiliar industry. Later he claimed that when the offer came, he looked up Nebraska and Omaha in the encyclopedia because he knew so little about them. To all these unknowns he brought the great advantage of having nothing to unlearn about the rail industry or its ways of doing things. Cook and Lewis made it clear that they wanted not merely changes in Omaha but a new mindset as to what their business was and how best to go about it. Put another way, the railroad's culture had to be rewired. Walsh was asked to do quickly what Kenefick had been trying to accomplish since the formation of the holding company.[9]

Important changes had taken place in Omaha even before Walsh's arrival. During 1983 Tom Graves was eased out as vice president of finance. Schaefer became vice president of both law and finance with Charley Eisele as his assistant. In New York Surette wanted his own man in Omaha to feed him financial data that was not filtered first through Kenefick, who had long manipulated it for his own purposes. Having been outfoxed so many times, Surette wanted someone who could brief him thoroughly before any meeting with Kenefick.[10]

The merger gave Surette the opening he needed. Kenefick put forward Rebensdorf for the finance job, but Surette vetoed the choice; he knew where Rebensdorf's loyalty lay. Instead UPC hired a headhunter, put Schaefer in charge of the search, and in May hired Richard A. Ames, the controller at Ford. Later that year Dolan arrived to oversee the law department. In July 1983 John Deasey had been replaced as controller by Gus Underhill, another GE veteran who had joined UP's P&A team in 1971.[11]

By the time Walsh arrived as chairman, the railroad had a president (Flannery) who was little more than a ghostly presence, two executive vice presidents, a senior vice president, and fifteen vice presidents. Walsh took office on October 15, 1986, two weeks ahead of schedule. That same day he transferred supervision of two departments from Flannery to Jerry Davis and changed the reporting lines of Davis, Guerdon Sines, and Tom Watts of labor relations and personnel from Flannery to himself. He had already taken Flannery's measure and concluded that he was "not a 'Mike Walsh' type of guy." For a few months Flannery kept his office, but he was not part of Walsh's senior staff and wasn't invited to staff meetings. He negotiated a sweetheart package for himself and retired back to California. Neither the railroad nor UPC noted his departure.[12]

During late October Walsh toured the system, talked with as many people as he could find, and studied everything but operations. "Walsh had a real intense personal interest in personnel matters, in culture," said Davidson. "He didn't have a real intense interest in operations." It bothered Davis that he couldn't get Walsh out on an inspection trip. "My problem with him was trying to explain to him a railroad operating problem," Davis admitted. "He didn't understand how our locomotives worked, how you switched cars, how you made up trains, how you blocked trains."[13]

The contrast with Kenefick produced mixed feelings. Walsh gave Davis and Davidson free rein to run operations so long as they didn't screw up. "He just wanted you to fix it if something went wrong," said Davidson. But Davis couldn't get him to see why money had to be spent on a project or new equipment. "Walsh would never go out on the railroad with you," he said. "You couldn't have those discussions with him. So when you'd come before him in budget time asking for $1.5 billion, he thought you were crazy."[14]

For a decade and a half Kenefick had worked to steer the sluggish UP organization in a new direction. Walsh brought to the task a fresh sense of urgency born partly of the times, partly of his mandate from UPC, and partly of his own ambitions. He respected Kenefick, who maintained an office in the building but stayed out of the way unless consulted, and often sought him out for advice. The two might have become close friends except for Walsh's lack of interest in the operations. Nor did it help that Walsh unblushingly sought the limelight as avidly as Kenefick avoided it.

Many officers who had come into their own under Kenefick also resented Walsh's approach. "I always felt like he didn't understand, or didn't give Kenefick the credit," said Dennis Jacobson. "He had the benefit of following a very, very good manager."[15]

Nor did Walsh endear himself with his basic message. In 1986 the railroad earned a record $385 million, a 20 percent increase over the previous year. Everyone felt great about the achievement until Walsh brushed the numbers aside and told them that earnings were the wrong measurement for performance. The key figure was return on assets, which remained anemic and would eventually prompt the corporation to invest its capital elsewhere. UP was not an earnings leader, he insisted; it was a turnaround candidate. Virtually all the new business since 1980 had been snatched by trucks despite the liberation given railroads by deregulation. The potential for taking back business was there, but only if the railroad changed its ways radically and quickly.[16]

Walsh wasted no time setting his agenda in motion. He told Davidson he was going to write a piece for *Info*, the company magazine, outlining his vision of what had to be done. On a trip to Houston Walsh sat scribbling furiously on a sheet of paper. When he had finished, he handed it to Davidson and asked his opinion. "I remember thinking—I didn't say it out loud," said Davidson, "What the hell is this all about? Are we going to teach school or run a railroad?"[17]

Walsh's "Message from the Chairman" appeared in the November 1986 issue as the first installment of a regular monthly feature. His tour had shown him UP was "a very fine company, staffed by a genuinely competent, capable and loyal work force." He acknowledged that the parade of recent changes had left everyone unsettled but accepting of the need for more innovations to meet the increased demands of a competitive marketplace. "We must continue to lead the process of change," he said, "or be left behind, as the world changes despite us."[18]

With this message Walsh launched his role as the Great Communicator. It was one he played tirelessly, superbly, and with great relish. He loved to speak and to write, and he was gifted at both. "He could write better than anybody," said White Matthews. "His messages to the organization . . . were awesome." Beth Whited, then a young auditor, found Walsh to be "incredibly compelling . . . knew what he was talking about, no nonsense." Gary Stuart marveled at how he "could communicate a clear message at a real high level to everyone." Walsh spent hours polishing his articles and speeches. He knew he had a tough sell to people skeptical of him and his motives.[19]

The monthly letter was not his only venue. While touring the system Walsh talked with every employee he could find, in groups or individually, in offices, on shop floors, over lunch or dinner. Their responses were enlightening: The company lacked a sense of direction. It was too big and bureaucratic and took forever to make decisions. The hierarchy was too rigid; too little responsibility got passed down to people actually doing the work, and the internal environment was plagued by too much office politics. Walsh also sounded out customers about the quality of UP service and got a very clear message. What they wanted above all else was consistency and a fast response when something went wrong. From these sessions Walsh concluded that the company's primary focus had to shift from internal concerns to customer service.[20]

On May 21, 1987, Walsh held the first of what he called town hall meetings in Omaha. During the next few weeks he traveled to eight other locations and held two sessions in each place. The meetings went far beyond the usual meet-and-greet. "We'd go to a place and invite all the people there," said John Marchant. ". . . And he would give them a speech and then he would take questions. And he'd go right at them toe to toe. He invited people to challenge him and he'd debate them. . . . It was quite a show."[21]

Handsome, athletic, quick on his feet, his dark eyes restless behind aviator glasses, Walsh thrived on give-and-take with the troops. By his own estimate he met with about ten thousand employees during this first round of town hall meetings. At every stop he rammed home the same message. Like it or not, the world was changing, the industry was changing, and so must UP. Deregulation had changed the game, and the recession had not only reduced business but knocked down prices so that the railroad had to haul more just to stay even. To earn the same revenues in 1987 as it had in 1986, for example, UP had to carry 6 percent more traffic, or 200,000 carloads. To stay alive, the railroad had to cut costs while improving service and quality. Surpluses were another problem. After the buildup of the 1970s, the recession left the railroad bloated with both equipment and people.[22]

In one meeting at the Elks lodge in North Platte, Walsh faced a sea of train crews and work hands clad in plaid shirts, cowboy boots, and hunting caps. To their demands for job guarantees he replied, "If I promise you a lifetime job, what is it worth if we're not competitive? It's worth a deck chair on the *Titanic*." Everywhere he insisted on less formality up the chain of command. Davis went so far as to fine subordinates a dollar every time they called him "Mister." At one meeting he collected nearly fifty dollars.[23]

Walsh's tough talk was tempered by his insistence that management listen more closely to the workforce. "We don't have a history of listening particularly well or carefully to people," he admitted. People within the company had to learn to talk more openly with each other across the barriers of rank, department, and station. A regulated environment did not encourage risk-taking, Walsh added, but deregulation demanded it and old-line employees had to adapt to the new game.[24]

In conveying this message Walsh did not spare his officers. He could be brutally frank with them. Once on the company plane he told some of them that one of the problems with railroad officers was that they didn't realize how far out of the game they were. It annoyed him that UP prided itself on being the best railroad in the country. So what? he said. Railway management was so far behind that bragging about being the best was damning yourself with faint praise. In general, he said, you're terrible managers. These harsh words coming from an outsider did not endear Walsh to proud railroad officers. "It just drove people crazy," said Marchant.[25]

Painful as the message was, many officers got the point. "We'd spent many years thinking of ourselves as the Union Pacific family," said Jack Koraleski. "And he was the person that came out and said no, we're not a family. . . . When you have a family and you have an uncle who's not performing, you don't kick him out of the family, but in a tough competitive market we needed to be the strongest team we can be and we've got to trim, we've got to shape up, we've got to cut players, and we got to be able to survive. Prove to the corporation that this in fact was a great place to invest money again."[26]

To reach the railroad's officers more directly, Walsh launched the first of what became annual Leadership Conferences in March 1987. He brought 170 top management people to Omaha for three days to set goals, discuss leadership, and find ways to create or improve it. "A good leader makes things happen," he said. "Leadership means managing and motivating others—a good leader picks good people and makes leaders out of them." He gave them room to operate and encouraged them to take risks and try new ideas. The process required "a steady, persistent, can-do commitment to continued improvement."[27]

The meeting was unlike anything they had done before. In the past, departments trotted out well-rehearsed dog-and-pony shows as an infomercial about how well the department was doing. Walsh would have none of it. Instead he called on managers out of the blue and peppered them with questions. "It's like you're back in school and making us think and making us change the way we looked at things," said Merill Bryan. But Walsh also listened. "People talked up—and people talked back," said one observer, who regarded it as a watershed moment in a culture long accustomed to taking orders. Walsh also did surveys at the conferences to elicit feedback.[28]

To reinforce his emphasis on performance, Walsh stunned the officers by eliminating the annual salary increases for about four thousand management people and replacing them with a bonus arrangement tied to the railroad's profitability. He wanted to encourage earning rewards rather than simply expecting them. The annual merit budget remained intact but was distributed differently. Half became dependent on the railroad's overall profitability targets; the other half went to the top third who did the best job of managing, leading, and changing. One percent was set aside to reward outstanding work with special promotions or awards.[29]

Walsh's attack on the old railroad culture required a delicate balancing act. Some officers cringed at the kinder, gentler approach to employees. Walsh invited even low-level workers to bring problems directly to him. In one case a brakeman, denied three days' bereavement pay, called Walsh's office directly and got the money. Jim Chubb, the supervisor of the Cheyenne freight yard, complained that this sort of end-run "undermined everyone." Railroad management had always been "kick ass and take names," he said. "The guys will argue with me more now because they know I can't completely express myself."[30]

Skeptical employees welcomed the town hall meetings but waited to see if anything concrete would come from them. They did not have long to wait. Walsh launched two crucial components of change: a new operating organization and the quality program. As an outsider he had no qualms about asking people why they did what they did the way they did it. From that process he extracted plans for overhauling every department on the railroad.

Despite all the changes made during the Kenefick years, UP still operated largely in the bureaucratic cocoon created during the regulated years. Walsh didn't blame Kenefick for the situation he inherited. "I'm not critical of the old Union Pacific," he said. "Most of the things we're changing are the natural product of the regulated era. . . . You tended to want a structure that kept things pretty stable." The railroad still had a formal chain of command in which communication slowly wound its way through the ranks or died of exhaustion in the attempt. Joe McCartney recalled press releases and other paperwork that passed through the hands of eight managers before reaching the president.[31]

Walsh wanted to shrink the layers through which everything passed. A few months before his arrival UP had consolidated fifteen road divisions into twelve and created the three new operating regions. It had also made buyout offers to all of its 5,600 managers, hoping to get acceptances from several hundred that were not needed. Since the operating department included about 85 percent of the company's 32,000 employees, it was the logical place to start the broader process of reorganization.[32]

Traditional operating organizations varied little among North American railroads. They were based on a geographical unit, the division, headed by a superintendent. On larger railroads two or more divisions might be combined into a region or district with a general manager in charge. A key issue had always been finding the most suitable number of people a superintendent could manage efficiently. If the number was too large, the superintendent could lose control; if too small, the result might be unnecessary layers of management and subsequent inefficiencies. Along with the geographical divisions, most operating departments were divided functionally into three areas: transportation (those responsible for train movements), engineering (those responsible for MOW), and mechanical (those responsible for maintaining locomotives and rolling stock.)[33]

This organization was of necessity military-like. Railroads had to manage large numbers of employees scattered across large geographical areas. As Davidson observed, "It tends to be hierarchical, rigid and status-oriented. It has lots of layers and is intended to create stability and predictability." Unlike workers in a typical manufacturing plant, people did not go to work in the same place at the same time to perform the same tasks. Strict organizational control was needed to operate so complex a business. The good employee was one who followed orders.[34]

Historically two forms of operating department organization had evolved, the departmental and the divisional. The former was a hierarchy that kept all reporting relationships rigidly within each department. Engineers at every level, for example, reported directly to their superior at the next level. The chief engineer had responsibility for the entire railroad. The divisional organization differed by separating the railroad into spheres, or divisions, each with its own virtually autonomous organization usually headed by a general manager. Under this arrangement the departmental officers reported to the division superintendent, who reported in turn to the general manager and through him to the vice president. The result was a more decentralized method of control that placed more responsibility on the local officers of each division.[35]

During its revival around the turn of the nineteenth century UP had used the divisional approach. Later it returned to the more traditional departmental system, which in many ways no longer fit the realities of modern railroading. The advent of computers and other new technologies offered promising avenues for centralizing many functions that had long been dispersed across the railroad. The elimination of whole armies of clerks and the closing of sales agencies had already demonstrated what might be done. The problem was discovering how far this quest for efficiency could be carried. Walsh determined to find the answer in every department beginning with operations.

The first Leadership Conference set the tone. Afterward Davis and Davidson told Walsh that any effort to reduce costs and improve customer service had to start with the operating department. Lacking a plan of his own, he told them to devise one that met the railroad's needs regardless of how far it departed from the existing structure. His only stipulation was that it had to shift the company's focus to the customer. To his delight Walsh got a plan that represented the most drastic change in the operations organization since the Harriman era. Walsh hailed it as "a sensible, practical and modern organization."[36]

The basic idea was already in the air when Walsh arrived. A McKinsey consultant had recommended that the company reduce its levels of organization. Davis and Davidson plucked Bill Hillebrandt from Rebensdorf's planning group and asked him to design a new organization. Hillebrandt had a bright and innovative mind; Stan McLaughlin referred to him as "one of the think tank people." Davis and Davidson liked what Hillebrandt came up with, and so did Walsh. The new plan claimed to reduce nine layers of management structure to three. In fact, it did no such thing because there weren't nine layers to reduce. "But we did take out a lot of positions," said Rebensdorf, "and we did expand the number of service units. We went from divisions to service units. We flattened the organization."[37]

The existing three regions each had a general manager with an assistant and four superintendents reporting to him. Each region also had a full-blown staff that mirrored Omaha's headquarters staff. Each superintendent had his own little bureaucracy as well. Every decision, large or small, had to climb the ladder—what Walsh and his staff called the nine layers of management—and that process could take forever. Customer requests often got lost or delayed in this maze of procedures. The new plan had two primary objectives: Every superintendent would know all the customers in his territory and would have authority to get things done.[38]

The new plan created a centralized organization in Omaha presiding over thirty decentralized superintendents who ran the day-to-day operations. In place of the traditional mechanical, engineering, and transportation departments five new groups were formed: Service Operations, Service Resources (which included dispatching and the mechanical shops), Engineering Services, Contractor Services, and Service Design. These groups reported directly to Davidson, who reported to Davis. Davidson also had a higher-level Service Support group staffed by Graham, May, and McDonough. Five other groups—Safety, Security, Purchasing, Administration, and Service Measurement—reported directly to Davis.[39]

Walsh unveiled this new plan at a leadership conference in July 1987. As he explained it, the new organization centralized key policy and support functions while decentralizing key operating and implementation responsibility. Three groups comprised the new matrix: senior management, the new centralized policy and support groups, and the decentralized implementation groups. Walsh called the thirty superintendents the "top guns" who "must make it happen on a day-to-day basis; they are the ones who must bend and not break when the heat is on."[40]

The superintendents would be independent but not unchecked. "We will not permit 30, or any, fiefdoms to develop," Walsh emphasized. No attempt was made to turn the units into profit centers. Everything depended on people learning to work together, communicate with each other, and dedicate themselves to common goals. "We are seeking to get away from the old 'cover your behind' way of operating," he said. ". . . *Cooperation, communication, working together to serve the customer*—these three concepts must be tattooed on the insides of each of our foreheads."[41]

Much depended on finding thirty superintendents capable of performing well independently. "I'm looking for self-starters," said Davis, "people who do not have to get direction daily, people who have the drive to get out and make decisions on their own." Omaha would not overrule them so long as they serviced customers well, met their budgets, and kept their labor relations in good shape.[42]

Hillebrandt oversaw the transition, which took place at a remarkable pace. Beginning on September 17, 1987, with two service units, the changeover proceeded at a rate of two to four service units a week. By December 5 all three regions and twelve former divisions had been replaced by the thirty service units. Each new unit underwent intensive two-and-a-half-day workshops on what was involved. "Some of our managers thought first that all we had done was put new titles on the same old jobs," said Hillebrandt. "They began to discover that in the new structure they are much more accountable than before. . . . They are also discovering that nobody is calling them to check every decision they make."[43]

Another innovation was already well under way before Walsh's arrival. Prior to the merger MP had begun creating customer service centers to centralize customer inquiries. The development of TCS made regional offices possible by providing the data needed to give customers complete information in a single telephone call. As TCS spread across the UP, local freight agencies gave way to regional CSC offices. Shippers gained direct access to the railroad for information instead of having it relayed through agencies. Davidson then advanced the idea of consolidating the regional offices into a National Customer Service Center (NCSC). In his view the service would be much better and the savings enormous if the center was done right. In 1986 UP had four thousand customer service clerks in 160 offices across the country.[44]

Such a center would be initially expensive and cost a lot of people their jobs. The current system assigned specific people to specific customers; this face-to-face contact would be sacrificed. "I misjudged the depth of that personal relationship," admitted Dennis Jacobson, who designed the system, but he argued that much of the existing contact took place over the telephone rather than in person. Pleased by Jacobson's plan, Davidson pushed hard for the project by emphasizing the large savings and improved service it promised. Drew Lewis bought the idea, and in May 1986 the board allocated $5 million for the project. The center would be located in St. Louis, absorb forty regional offices, feature one toll-free telephone number for the entire nation, and remain open 24/7.[45]

No other railroad had a system like it. Using data from TCS on special multi-session terminals that showed four files at once, the 600 employees at the NCSC had a new phone system that automatically shortened wait times to a matter of seconds. The system was designed to handle 20,000 calls daily once all forty regional centers had been phased into St. Louis by the end of 1987. Walsh applauded the center as a useful step toward better customer service.[46]

Train and crew dispatching also seemed ripe for consolidation. MP had introduced computer-assisted crew dispatching in August 1979 at Houston. The system handled some 750 train and switch engine assignments and more than three thousand calls to trainmen a day; by July 1983 it covered all eight Louisiana/Texas zones. Crews welcomed the change because it was more convenient and because, as a local UTU chairman observed, "the computer eliminates favoritism in crew assignments." After the merger the system spread to other parts of the combined roads.[47]

Train dispatching became increasingly centered around a cluster of CTC centers throughout the system. Thanks to TCS, MP had an edge in centralizing its dispatching. A state-of-the-art center opened in Spring, Texas, in 1981 to direct train operation throughout Texas and most of Louisiana. Another facility in North Little Rock, first opened in 1973, handled train movements in all of Arkansas and Illinois along with parts of Missouri. In 1984 UP opened a new complex in Salt Lake City to oversee Utah, Nevada, and southern California. Two major computer consoles with touch screens took care of switches and signal alignments for most of the territory. They were largely the brainchild of Emil Krause, the veteran signal engineer, who envisioned an automated, touch-control console in 1980 and oversaw its development before retiring in 1983. The new console reduced a dispatcher's hand movements from a hundred to four. An impressed division chief dispatcher called it "future world."[48]

As the technology improved, the centers extended their reach. In 1983 UP opened the first of six crew-dispatching centers that would ultimately cover the entire system. Building on the Spring model, the system dumped seniority rosters, basic labor agreements, and individual work histories into a computer and linked this database with automated telephone dialing systems and television monitors in crew locker rooms. The old log books went the way of the hand-written call board as the new system was gradually extended from one area to the next. By the end of 1984 two-thirds of all trainmen got their assignments from the new system.[49]

Art Shoener had been present at the creation of the new systems, thanks to his work in Spring. MP's southern region had three main dispatching offices at Fort Worth, Houston, and Palestine. Utilizing the latest technology, he had helped fold them into the new Spring facility along with two other outlying offices. After the merger, while in the Northwest, he formed a team of bright young men to design a new type of dispatching center at a cost of $6.7 million.[50]

When the new center opened in July 1986, it was unlike anything ever seen on a railroad. A giant 80' x 8' color display on a wall depicted the track and signals in all six dispatcher territories between Seattle and Granger, Wyoming. It pinpointed the location and assigned route of fifty to sixty UP trains operating on 1,530 miles of CTC trackage along with 2,000 miles of "dark" territory in the Northwest. Awed employees referred to it as the "Star Wars" room. Smaller monitors at every dispatcher's desk provided detailed views of all operations at 298 signal control points. Even more impressive, the CTC territory between Portland, Oregon, and Granger had autorouting capacity. After the dispatcher assigned an identity and priority to each new train, the computer took over and routed the train according to priority. "We've moved out of the dark ages," said one dispatcher.[51]

These developments took place before Walsh's arrival. The officer pushing hardest for the centralization of both customer service and dispatching had been Davidson, whose vision leaped ahead another step after the Portland facility opened. If dispatching could be consolidated into a few regional offices, why not into one major facility located in Omaha? He took the idea to Davis, who showed no enthusiasm for it. "I think he intuitively knew that Mr. Kenefick wouldn't like it," Davidson said, "and he didn't want to advance something that the boss didn't want."[52]

However, Davidson realized that while Kenefick would not go for the idea, Walsh surely would because of his desire to consolidate and cut costs across the board. From this thinking arose an internal struggle to gain approval for a centralized dispatching center in Omaha. Kenefick rejected it for several reasons. The security issue bothered him. If the computer system went down or was sabotaged or leveled by a tornado, the railroad would be paralyzed unless a complete backup system existed. He also worried about superintendents losing control over dispatchers in their territory.[53]

Shoener and Dennis Duffy had qualms as well. "Jesus, we don't want to do that," snapped Shoener. Other operating people disliked the idea of separating dispatchers from the regions they worked. But Walsh was not an operating guy, and he liked the concept. By late 1987 plans were under way to built a $50 million facility on the site of the old freight house where UP had been sold out of receivership in 1897.[54]

Shops became another target of force and facility reduction. The merger offered splendid opportunities to consolidate shop facilities but posed an awkward dilemma. The Omaha shops had been the mainstay of the UP since the 1900s. During the 1970s they had undergone extensive renovations at a cost of $19.4 million. This sprawling complex employed nearly 1,600 people and had a budget of $70.9 million in 1979. While the Omaha shops remained the crown jewel of UP facilities, the MP had its own special facility. Completed in June 1984 and named after Downing Jenks, the $40 million North Little Rock locomotive repair shop duplicated much of the work done at the Omaha shops.[55]

During the summer of 1988 Walsh decided to close the Omaha shops and transfer most of their work elsewhere. He left the happy task of making the announcement to Davis and went off to his place in Steamboat Springs, Colorado. For his pains Davis had the windows of his house shot out that same evening. Some 567 shopcraft employees were transferred elsewhere, 343 of them to North Little Rock, while another 120 accepted severance pay.[56]

"It wasn't fun to close the Omaha shops after more than a century," Walsh said later, "especially considering the impact on our people and the $24 million annual hit it represented to the economy of our headquarters city. But it was necessary and it was done." This phrase became another Walsh theme song: What was necessary would be done regardless of the pain it might inflict. Operating and marketing had been overhauled because "they were simply too big and too bureaucratic to get the job done." More changes would follow, and with them more pain.[57]

Contrary to much of the media reporting about UP, Walsh did not drag the railroad into the twentieth century. Kenefick had already done that. What Walsh did was force the railroad and its culture to face squarely the new realities of the industry that emerged in the wake of the recession, deregulation, mergers, and new technologies. Kenefick had been a strong leader who had freed the company from the shackles of tradition. He recognized the new world of railroad unfolding before his eyes and tried to communicate its nature to the troops. But he was still at heart an operating man committed to the dominance of operations and the need to pour large amounts of capital into sustaining the railroad. This approach aroused resentment among those who wanted UPC to lead and to diversify into areas more promising financially than the railroad.

Unlike most of his employees Walsh understood that this seemingly prosperous railroad was fighting for its life. At every stage he hammered home his themes of putting the customer first and finding ways to do more with less. Again and again he emphasized, "We're not in business to run trains. We're in business to meet customer needs." Too many of the company's measurements focused on the former and not on the latter. As Walsh reaffirmed, railroads had always been very good at gathering data but poor at interpreting it.[58]

To remedy that problem Walsh turned to past experience. What UP needed, he concluded, was an immersion in the same Total Quality System that had worked wonders for Cummins. He would bring the Feigenbaum brothers to Omaha and implement their program across the railroad.

The Quest for Quality

Walsh knew from experience the difficulty of applying the Total Quality System (TQS) to a traditional industry, and no industry was more traditional than the railroad. The key to acceptance would be finding the right people to buy into the program and take the lead in implementing it. TQS required not just a different mindset but a radically different way of doing things. It amounted to more than a set of buzzwords; it was an entirely new language for everyone involved.

The key elements in TQS for Walsh were its focus on customer service and doing things the right way the first time to reduce errors and failure costs. To get their importance across required more and better communication, which is why he devoted so much time and energy to that task. "Most organizations seem to operate on a 'need to know' basis," he said. "The problem is that most people need to know a great deal more than anybody tells them."[1]

To improve customer service Walsh looked first to the marketing and sales department. Pat Barrett had done a splendid job there, but he was on the verge of retirement. Walsh promoted him to an advisory position and brought in Fred Henderson, who at forty-six had spent twenty-one years with Xerox. Although Henderson was presently vice president of field operations for Xerox, an earlier item on his résumé especially appealed to Walsh: Henderson had served as vice president of quality for worldwide operations.[2]

Henderson was deemed a major catch. Two factors induced him to move to the UP: the new marketing challenges created by deregulation, and Walsh himself, who deeply impressed Henderson with his approach to the business and its emphasis on quality and customer service. Henderson wasted little time reorganizing his department in tandem with the restructuring of the operating department. Together they formed two teams responsible for the basic commodities carried by the railroad.[3]

When Henderson arrived in the spring of 1987, he found that most of the staff considered the UP to be one of the nation's very best-run railroads. He then talked with the UP's top two hundred customers and got quite another opinion:

"You guys are among the worst." Between 1980 and 1986 the transportation industry grew by $35 billion, but trucks got nearly all of it and Henderson wanted to know why. The railroad, he discovered, simply wasn't responsive to customer needs. Its processes, pricing, contracts, and communications were too cumbersome and chased potential customers away. A new approach was needed, and with it a new organization based on cross-functional teamwork between marketing and operating as well as other departments.[4]

In October 1987 Henderson launched a new approach based on four objectives: providing special attention to the two hundred customers who supplied 70 percent of revenue; streamlining the decision-making chain; strengthening the direct marketing operation; encouraging innovation to give bright, energetic workers a fast-track career path; and merging management responsibilities for intermodal and rail marketing. At present they competed with each other, which hurt pricing and confused customers.[5]

The revised marketing and sales organization had three basic levels. A cadre of forty-six highly trained national account managers were assigned to the road's two hundred largest customers. Another ninety account managers focused on forty-seven hundred medium to large accounts and reported directly to one of fourteen regional sales managers, while other account representatives handled small to medium-size accounts through telemarketing. "Our customers will see marketing decisions being made closer to them," Henderson promised. The team approach aimed to remove barriers and expedite service. The new marketing department evolved into eight commodity groups: autos, chemicals, food, forest products, grain, merchandise markets, metals, and minerals.[6]

During February and March the national account managers formed action teams with members from operating and other departments. The teams met with customers and drew up an action plan and measurement system to evaluate their effectiveness in meeting the customer's needs. One manager who had previously called on thirty-nine different grain customers now handled only eight, but those eight shipped products to 751 destinations. The object was to know the major shippers and their needs better in order to provide superior service.[7]

Bringing the TQS program to UP posed an intriguing challenge. The Feigenbaums had never worked with a service company like a railroad. Their teams had worked through Cummins plant by plant and practice by practice, concentrating on process flows. Efficiency, insisted Val Feigenbaum, consisted of 85 percent flow process and only 15 percent work content. Some Cummins managers found the approach too alien; others simply resented the intrusion into time-honored practices. One referred to the Feigenbaums as "the brothers Grim."[8]

However, Cummins was also a very traditional company that, like UP, recognized it had to adjust to a changing world. It had the same problem of silos and compartmentalized thinking despite all previous efforts to break down these barriers. The Feigenbaums showed Cummins how to improve quality, take out excess costs, and, above all, reduce failure costs by getting at the root causes of a given problem. This was exactly what Walsh wanted them to do at UP. In February 1987, only four months after arriving in Omaha, Walsh had Val Feigenbaum give a presentation to his senior officers. Val talked about ways to flatten the organization and break down the stovepipes between departments.[9]

Davidson was skeptical about the pitch. "We've had boatloads of industrial engineers working on this and people studying these issues for years," he said bluntly. "How in the hell are you two guys going to do that by yourselves?" "Well, kid," replied Val, "you got to trust me."[10]

Walsh then came up with an ingenious move. To ease resistance to the Feigenbaums, he put Davidson in charge of implementing their program on the railroad. It was a brilliant stroke for several reasons, not least of which was Davidson's talent for getting things done. Davidson was the most traditional of railroaders, as the men in the ranks well knew, but he was also thoughtful and had a capacity for growth. "Putting the guy who was a nonbeliever in it in charge of it was a very smart move," said Carl von Bernuth. "'Cause if you're going to make it work at the railroad, you've got to have the insiders believing in it.[11]

"This is the only way you can do it," Walsh said later. "If a new guy is perceived as coming in on a white horse and telling everybody what is wrong and how to fix it—before he even has time to understand—he'll fail. The key is to win the confidence of the key people who are there and get them in the boat rowing with you."[12]

Skepticism ran deep. TQS struck Rob Knight as another "flavor of the week." Joe McCartney took one look at the Feigenbaums' thick tome and offered to prepare an English translation. It didn't help that the brothers had roots in GE, the same company whose émigrés had become so prominent in UPC. Many people resented the notion that, in McCartney's words, "you could superimpose a General Electric–type efficiency network on the railroad." Walsh knew that Davidson had immense credibility in the ranks; if anybody could sell the program to them, it would be him.[13]

The assignment also solved a less obvious but equally important problem for Walsh: Davidson's lingering dissatisfaction at having to serve under Davis. The two men remained friends and handled their situation professionally, but Davidson resented having to go through Davis on issues where Davis was reluctant to push for a reform or change. Yet Davis's easy style let Davidson run the railroad without interference, and no one ever complained about Davis being hard to work for. "Jerry was a great guy, and we were personal friends," Davidson said; "his style just didn't suit my style."[14]

Nor did it suit Davidson's ambitions, which blossomed as his exposure to the higher ranks of management widened. Walsh astutely recognized this in Davidson and tapped into it. Putting him in charge of the quality program removed the tension between two capable officers, at least temporarily. It also gave Davidson another opportunity for personal growth, and Davidson was quick to respond.

Within a remarkably short time Davidson became a convert to the quality program. There was nothing false or forced about his born-again enthusiasm. "He saw the benefit of that right from the very beginning," said Koraleski. "... He really was able to understand the power of what the quality program could do for the productivity, service improvement, and the failure cost elimination." Once on board, Davidson recruited Charley Eisele and Chan Lewis as his helpers. Together they pulled talented people from every department to form quality teams that eventually numbered in the hundreds. The thinking was that every problem was at bottom a cross-functional one and required a team effort to diagnose and solve. The team members did double duty, working both on the team and in their regular jobs.[15]

By June 1987 the first phase of a five-phase process was under way. To employees Davidson and the GSC engineers defined quality as "what satisfies the customer." It meant doing the job right the first time and devising ways to measure performance so that it could be evaluated and improved. Customer satisfaction would also be measured, and accountability clarified within the company at every level. These goals would be achieved not through a one-time fix but through ongoing procedures and systems that required constant monitoring. "It's simply the way we're going to be running the business," said Davidson.[16]

Walsh stressed two key objectives. The first was integrating the operating and marketing departments to make the company more customer responsive. "This integration," he said, "requires an across-the-board discipline and focus on quality in everything we do." This meant better communication with employees at every level. "We must also involve our people considerably more in what we're doing," said Walsh. "We must treat them with basic respect . . . 'reach out' to them and address their real concerns. We must listen to their best ideas and we must respond. *We must do this because we cannot achieve our quality or our cost goals without their help.*"[17]

The goal amounted to nothing less than changing the way people went about every aspect of their work. "You got to remember," said Duffy, "all of us originally were rewarded and incentived and promoted based on the historical way of doing business, and that was not the way that we were going to do business."[18]

"It started with a very simple premise," said Koraleski. "When you start down a path, you're having a discussion and decide what is the problem you wanted to solve; what's the issue." From there the effort moved to finding the root causes of the problem and the best ways to solve them.[19]

GSC tried to impress on UP employees the operative principle that quality performance had to be *measured* in order to be managed. In examining the railroad thoroughly, the GSC engineers analyzed 279 "work elements" in terms of how well or poorly they were performed. The emphasis always was on failure costs—what it cost the company when something did not get done right the first time. To the astonishment of many officers, the failure costs on UP exceeded $600 million a year. In the current highly competitive marketplace, most future profits would likely come not from expanding business but from significant reductions in these costs. To accomplish that required getting at the root cause of each one.[20]

Finding the root cause of a given problem became the great quest. Even a skeptical Davis admitted that "if there's nothing more that I learned from the quality process . . . [it] was getting to the basis of the problem and understanding what the problem was all about." Operating people had never really done anything like that. "We get so tunnel vision on operating ratios and keeping costs down and running trains," added Davis, "without really looking at a problem and why it exists and getting down to the basis of it." Davidson agreed that "we didn't manage with data is what it amounted to. . . . It was almost like a miracle when we really started managing the company with accurate data and not based on just hunches or intuition but actually using the real data, the improvements we were able to make."[21]

The railroad had always focused on its own internal metrics to measure performance. "We really hadn't looked at the external metrics in terms of customer satisfaction and what our operation meant in terms of the customer," said Duffy. "We established—Dick did—[a] cost of quality system where we went in and we measured every critical aspect . . . so you knew every day what an hour delay of a boxcar meant, a terminal delay. . . . We put the dollars to that."[22]

For Davidson the concept of failure cost was nothing less than a revelation. It was fundamental to the Feigenbaums' system. "The basic message was," said McLaughlin, ". . . if you don't do things right the first time, it's a waste of money and you have to do it over." The object was to quantify the cost of not doing things right the first time and having to redo or undo them. "We found, much to our surprise," said Davidson, "that the cost of doing things wrong equated somewhere between 25 and 30 percent of our gross revenues. . . . So we started very carefully measuring our preventable failure cost."[23]

Two very different problems received early attention: billing errors and derailments. A close look at the billing process revealed that about 20 percent of bills turned out to be inaccurate. Some had the wrong address, others the wrong rate or misinformation. The team created a ranked list of the most egregious errors and developed methods to eliminate them. The result was a steady improvement in billing accuracy to 85 percent in 1987, 91 percent in 1988, and 94 percent in 1989.[24]

So too with derailments. No one had given much thought to the actual cost of derailments. The standard railroad response had always been to throw whatever resources were needed at the problem to clear the line as fast as possible. The quality team explored what caused derailments in the first place, then created a ranked list of the most frequent causes. Once finished, the team figured out ways to eliminate the top-ranked problem and then moved down the list. "Over time, over a five-year period," said Koraleski, "you could see that what was the number one root cause five years ago was no longer in the top five. And you had a different top five now, and you would work your way through a root cause analysis and a very structured approach at eliminating those failures."[25]

Within three years the cost of derailments dropped 28 percent. A similar approach was used to improve locomotive availability. In a twelve-month period between 1988 and 1989 this key measurement rose from 86 percent to 92 percent, which was the equivalent of adding 125 locomotives worth $1.3 million apiece to the fleet. This one achievement showed many UP employees the relationship between quality improvement and the capital budget. By 1990 the company had under way nearly fifty separate Quality System Procedures (QSPs). With them came more disciplined and systematic methods of dealing with problems. Between 1987 and 1990 they helped produce a 30 percent improvement in on-time service and a 23 percent reduction in safety incidents.[26]

Managing with data meant reporting every single accident, whether it caused damage or not, to get as accurate a list of causes as possible. The leading cause of derailments turned out to be broken wheels. Fixing the problem required changing the standards on wheels, which meant the UP had to go through the AAR. "That sounds a lot easier than it really was," said Davidson, "because every railroad had an opinion about things and they didn't have the data, or if they had it they wouldn't admit it, wouldn't admit to what was really going on. So we had to prove to people what was really happening out there, and we finally got the standards changed on wheels and bearings." At that point the number of derailments began to drop significantly.[27]

Engineering got the message as well. For McLaughlin the emphasis on quality dovetailed with the emphasis on safety, long a big-ticket item for the UP, as for other railroads, in both human and cost terms. "In the old days," said McLaughlin, "the culture was hell-bent-for-leather productivity; get the job done. Injuries was just a consequence . . . take your casualties, and that was wrong." It was also expensive, and growing ever more so as the number of employees and the cost of medical care soared. No one did more than Davis to ingrain safe practices in the railroad's culture. Duffy called him a "strong safety zealot," a label in which Davis took great pride.[28]

Although advances in technology as well as safety campaigns significantly reduced the number of fatalities and injuries, railroading remained a dangerous profession. A 1977 survey by the UP safety department revealed that 25 percent of all injuries in the transportation department came from getting on or off cars. In MOW unloading materials by hand led to 21 percent of all injuries, and use of hand tools caused another 17 percent. Other leading causes included stumbling or falling in places other than on cars or locomotives, foreign objects in eyes, and slack action accidents.[29]

The UP had an impressive historical legacy in the field of safety. In 1913 E. H. Harriman's widow, Mary, endowed the Harriman Safety Medal program to honor the railroad, department, and employee with outstanding safety records each year. The UP had won its share of Harriman Medals and launched a variety of programs to promote and enforce safety. Managers in the operations, mechanical, and engineering departments were instructed to take a personal approach to safety by setting realistic goals for improvement and taking positive steps to motivate employees in reaching them.[30]

After the merger Davis accelerated the emphasis on safety and accident prevention. Hammering home the theme "All injuries can be prevented," Davis enforced a written safety policy that required senior officers and their subordinates to conduct weekly "safety audits." Substance abuse emerged as one major root cause of accidents. The company created a twenty-four-minute film entitled "Too Dangerous to Work With" to underscore the dangers posed by fellow workers who had been drinking or using drugs. Competitions were established to see who could forge the best safety record over time, and awards were given to the winners.[31]

Apart from the human toll, accidents carried a large failure cost as well, thanks largely to the Federal Employers Liability Act (FELA). Passed in 1908 to protect a wide variety of workers, the act had become archaic in an age of no-fault workers' compensation. Under FELA an injured or ill employee could sue his or her employer for whatever amount a jury might award if it decided that the employer was at fault. Most industries had long since gone to a no-fault system that systematized awards, but the railroads were still saddled with FELA. In 1989 alone UP set aside $150 million just for potential personal injury and occupational illness claims.[32]

The whole FELA system rankled Walsh as not only expensive but unfair. One employee might win a multi-million-dollar settlement while another with the same injury got nothing. The real winners were the liability lawyers who feasted on such suits and promoted them vigorously. The process pitted employees against management at a time when Walsh was trying to bring them closer together. In his town meetings and monthly magazine message he denounced the system as obsolete, divisive, and a swallower of capital urgently needed elsewhere.[33]

The one time Walsh managed to get a congressional hearing on FELA, it turned into a disaster. "The unions brought in every person that they could find who had been in a train wreck or lost an arm or was in a wheelchair or lost an eye," said Mary McAuliffe, who later headed UP's Washington office. "... You were surrounded by injured union employees from railroads. It was horrible. ... The Republican members called us in afterwards and said, Don't you ever do this to us again." Despite Walsh's efforts, FELA remained doggedly in place while almost every other aspect of the railroad changed around it.[34]

As part of his reorganizing effort Walsh divided the claims and litigation department. Litigation remained with the law department, but claims moved to the operating department under a new title, casualty management. Along with investigating injury claims, the new department became more active with doctors, rehabilitation centers, and other facilities. The focus of the department, said its assistant vice president, Larry Prier, was "the issues of return to work and fair and responsive financial assistance." The amounts involved were hardly trivial. The UP spent $100 million on personal injuries in 1986 and $120 million the following year.[35]

On a smaller scale Walsh, himself a fitness fanatic, did what he could to promote good health as well as safety. He banned smoking, installed a fitness center in the headquarters building, and exhorted UP to shape up physically as well as organizationally. In Walsh's mind no issue existed in a vacuum. Safety, good health, and fitness all improved the quality of life, which in turn improved the quality of work. Here as elsewhere he led by example, working out every morning before coming to the office or going to the fitness center later in the day. Friday afternoons on the twelfth floor took on a radically different tone. Those senior officers still around were startled to hear rock music blaring down the hall from Walsh's office as he chilled out in a rare period of repose.[36]

As the number of quality teams multiplied, officers staggered under the extra workload. Some marketing people complained that they were on twenty-one different problem-solving teams, and that the effort consumed two-thirds of their time when they needed to be out dealing with customers. To those who grumbled and warned that company morale was slipping, Walsh repeated his mantra that the road to excellence was tough but necessary. "Morale built on excellence will be around a long time," he said. "Morale built on anything else won't last longer than a late snowfall."[37]

Whatever else Walsh did, he imprinted the concept of quality on the UP. For the next generation of managers it became a way of thinking and working. Davidson not only embraced the quality program personally but sold it to the generation of officers below him. "They took it to their heart," said Lou Anne Rinn. "It is in their soul. You can't talk to Dennis Duffy for more than fifteen minutes without something about getting to the root cause." Quality became not only a mantra but a method for the UP.[38]

As Walsh learned at Cummins, a quality program needed quality people to implement it. During his first months in office he took the measure of his senior personnel and did not shirk the tough task of weeding out those he found lacking. Chuck Dettmann, the vice president of transportation, did not meet Walsh's expectations and was demoted to assistant vice president of service design, where he did a good job. In realigning marketing and sales Walsh created a new position, vice president of customer service, and gave it to Ken Morrill, who had been an assistant vice president of market development. Late in 1987 the NCSC was shifted from operations to marketing and sales with Morrill in charge. "Ken was a career marketing manager and a smart guy," said Jacobson. "He was supportive and let us implement the plan as designed."[39]

The most serious personnel problem concerned Dick Ames, who had replaced Graves as vice president of finance. A bright, handsome man who knew his stuff, Ames inherited a difficult situation. Schaefer and Graves had gone head to head in seeking to take charge of the MP-WP merger. Both men had larger ambitions and saw the role as a great career booster. When Schaefer won out, Graves left the company and Schaefer assumed his position. However, Schaefer knew little about finance, and the merger posed some tricky and complex accounting issues. To help with these issues he recruited Eisele from the P&A group. Eisele helped Schaefer merge the law, finance, and accounting functions of the three roads and recruit a new vice president of finance so that Schaefer could move up to UPC.[40]

Surette and Schaefer considered Ames their man in Omaha and instructed him to change the way things were done there. At the same time, Schaefer made Rebensdorf assistant vice president of finance as a consolation prize. Putting Ames and Rebensdorf together proved disastrous. Ames wanted his own people and demanded loyalty to him alone, while Rebensdorf made no secret of his steadfast loyalty to Kenefick. Ames wished to reshape the department into one that resembled Ford's organization. "As a result," said Rebensdorf, "the UP finance group went from a culture of cooperation and teamwork to one of cutthroat competition and doing whatever was necessary to please Dick Ames."[41]

Some of the changes Ames made served the company well. He launched a more aggressive college recruiting program that looked beyond the Midwest. Like Schaefer, he was conscious of status and wanted more young MBAs from big-name schools, which meant bigger salaries than Rebensdorf paid to young hires from regional schools in UP territory. Eisele thought he introduced more disciplined budget and financial reporting and more sophisticated monthly financial projections. The problem was that no one liked working for him. Even people like Eisele and Koraleski, who managed to get on Ames's good side, found his management style unbearable. Eventually so did the people in other departments with whom he dealt.[42]

"I think Dick meant well," said Watts, "but I just think he couldn't get out of his own way. He just wanted things to be his way, and that was it." Rebensdorf was more blunt: "Dick Ames . . . was the type of person that it was difficult feeling comfortable around because you never knew whether he was going to pick your pocket or stab you in the back. . . . He liked to hear himself talk and he always believed that his point of view or ideas were better than anyone else's."[43]

This harsh condemnation coincided with judgments by other people who worked for Ames and found him utterly insensitive in his treatment of them. He would summon his staff to meetings and leave them sitting outside his office for an hour or more. Some meetings started at eight in the morning and dragged on until seven that evening. On one such occasion, with stomachs growling, they discussed arrangements for bringing the revenue accounting people from St. Louis for a Leadership Conference. Ames had officers ponder such crucial issues as whether the dinner seating should be assigned or unassigned, whether the tables should be round or square, and how many legs the tables should have. "We had to take the tax guy into the bathroom at about seven o'clock," recalled Koraleski, "and just kind of calm him down from wanting to just strangle Dick."[44]

When the dinner meeting finally took place, it turned out to be on Ames's birthday. The kitchen staff brought out a nice cake and ice cream and lit the candles. Before the eating could start, however, Ames insisted on saying a few words. Seventy-five minutes later, as he droned on, the long-dead candles and the cake went back to the kitchen with the melted ice cream. "We were all sitting there with our ears bleeding," said Koraleski.[45]

In one instance Ames's abuse of subordinates nearly changed the history of UP. His mind games drove one young officer to look for another job. Ames had been good to him in terms of salary, "but at a point it's not about money. It's about what kind of work environment you have." Finally the young officer received an offer from another large firm in Omaha. On the day he planned to resign, he learned that Ames was leaving the company. The officer, who decided to stay with UP, was Jim Young, the current CEO of the railroad.[46]

Koraleski thought he knew one source of Ames's problem. "He saw Finance as the 'auditor, scorekeeper, and budget police,'" he said. "His approach focused more on exposing people rather than working behind the scenes in a cooperative way to change their behavior." Finance ruled at Ford, but at UP operations still held sway, and Ames could not budge that reality. However, Koraleski credited Ames with building a strong centralized finance department, one that sent its people out to other areas of the company.[47]

Most of the finance staff tolerated Ames's behavior to protect their own careers. The lone maverick, as usual, was Rebensdorf, who was incapable of playing Ames's games. Unlike other staff members, he pushed back to the point of insubordination. "You needed to be totally subservient to Dick Ames in order to survive," he said, "and a yes man to all of his screwball ideas. This I simply could not do, and I ended up telling him what I thought."[48]

In his defiance Rebensdorf counted on and received support from Kenefick. Ames resented the fact that Kenefick, Davis, and others went directly to Rebensdorf when they wanted information. In the fall of 1985 he devised a plan to reduce Rebensdorf's role by splitting P&A into two groups: business planning and strategic planning under Eisele, who had become Ames's fair-haired boy, and cost and capital planning under Rebensdorf. Rebensdorf protested that the change made no sense and flatly refused to do it. A furious Ames went to Kenefick and said he wanted to fire Rebensdorf. If you fire Rebensdorf, Kenefick replied coldly, I'll fire you.[49]

Thwarted in this attempt, Ames waited for another opening. When Drew Lewis came to Omaha, Ames let him know that he thought Kenefick should go. This did not sit well with Lewis, who thought highly of Kenefick. A meeting took place with Lewis, Kenefick, Ames, and Rebensdorf at which Kenefick told Lewis pointedly that if he needed to know anything about the railroad, Rebensdorf was the guy to ask. For the rest of 1986 the tension between Ames and Rebensdorf remained unresolved.[50]

During the summer of 1986 Lewis sent Eisele to the Advanced Management Program at the Harvard Business School. While he was in Cambridge Ames came out to discuss what Eisele wanted to do once he returned. Ames wanted to remove strategic planning from finance and restore it to its old position as a direct report to the president. He also wanted to take it away from Rebensdorf. Eisele thought it should stay in Rebensdorf's hands. "John Rebensdorf was the smartest railroading guy I knew," Eisele said, "and had that capability to run a whole series of projects."[51]

Walsh inherited this long-simmering feud when he arrived in Omaha that fall. Aware that Walsh planned changes of all kinds, Ames tried again to get Rebensdorf fired. However, Davis and others, probably Kenefick, alerted Walsh to the conflict and suggested that he either dump Ames or move Rebensdorf to another position. It did not take Walsh long to recognize Rebensdorf's value to the company. In January 1987, only three months after his arrival, he promoted Rebensdorf to the newly created position of vice president of strategic planning. Eisele took over Rebensdorf's old job as head of the P&A group, which still reported to Ames.[52]

As for Ames, Walsh wanted to fire him a month after he came to UP. Watts persuaded him that it would look bad to fire a department head so soon after his arrival. However, Ames's fate was sealed by one of Walsh's communication techniques, the candid surveys run at the Leadership Conference. The reviews revealed the depth of dissatisfaction with Ames within the department along with an inventory of his faults.[53]

On a Friday afternoon in December 1988 Walsh summoned Koraleski to his office and told him Ames would be leaving and he, Walsh, wanted Koraleski to take his place. Koraleski was stunned. Nobody yet knew that Ames was leaving, and Koraleski expected Eisele to get the job if he did leave. Eisele harbored the same expectation and admitted it was "just an absolute shock to me." Later he asked Walsh why he had been passed over for the job. Walsh replied that Koraleski was the better manager, while Eisele's strength lay in strategy and planning.[54]

Info contained no notice of Ames's departure or Koraleski's promotion, a strange omission for a magazine that usually captured every major change in the ranks. A brief notice in the *Omaha World-Herald* and some trade journals recorded the event. For Eisele Walsh created a new position called "vice president management systems" and made him a direct report. More changes loomed as Walsh continued to tinker with UP's structure.[55]

In staking out his position as a change agent Walsh did not hesitate to put himself at risk. He was a big-stakes player, willing to get ahead of everyone else and try to drag them with him. "I always used to tell him," said Davidson, "'Goddamn, you're leading with your chin here. You're way out in front of where we actually are.'"[56]

The chin was a strong one, the ego even stronger. On one point everyone agreed: Walsh had a giant ego and an insatiable appetite for publicity. "He wasn't bashful," said Davidson; "he'd take credit." Marchant, who regarded Walsh as the greatest change agent and manager he ever knew, thought "he had an ego that would fill Yankee Stadium, and he was a shameless self-promoter. . . . We always said the most dangerous place to be was between Walsh and a TV camera." Walsh's middle initial, H., quipped McCartney, did not stand for Humble. Several officers assumed that his self-promotion and hunger for publicity were aimed at lining up his next job.[57]

Walsh got good press and lots of it, but one laudatory article soured his relationship with Kenefick. In December 1989 *Fortune* ran a piece praising Walsh as the man who turned around a sorry, floundering railroad. The writer, Andrew Kupfer, with a strange disregard for the facts, portrayed the UP of the Kenefick era as a moss-covered, inept enterprise whose "myopic managers . . . alienated shippers and watched in resignation as truckers captured more and more of the market for everything except commodity freight."[58]

The subhead for the article read, "Proud but hidebound, the UP was run for the managers, not the customers. Then Mike Walsh came along and taught this winded iron horse to compete." The "winded iron horse" phrase infuriated Kenefick and his officers. "It just set Kenefick off because he viewed that as an insult to his stewardship," said Rebensdorf, who understood that the phrase came from *Fortune* and not from Walsh. Others, such as Davidson, thought Walsh had coined the phrase and deeply resented the way the company was portrayed prior to Walsh's arrival.[59]

Although Walsh talked constantly of the need for changes, he didn't bad-mouth what had been there before. Rather he depicted the changes as necessary to cope with an environment constantly in flux that rendered old assumptions and methods obsolete. Nevertheless, some officers suspected that in interviews Walsh either fed favorable comparisons to reporters or didn't bother to contradict them when they were presented to him. The result was that Kenefick's value to Walsh diminished at a time when good counsel was urgently needed.

18

The Enigmatic Dynamo

Drew Lewis and Mike Walsh were running parallel tracks in New York and Omaha. They had to find the right people to impose a radical program of change onto a culture that resisted it. However, Walsh had to accomplish this with a workforce of more than thirty thousand people while Lewis had only to reshape the New York office.

Once in command, Lewis wasted little time sorting out the staff in New York. He had always been staunchly loyal to his friends and demanded that same devotion from those around him. "Loyalty," said White Matthews, "was *the* number one requirement." To handle his affairs he brought in two longtime assistants, Judy Swantak and Judy Waltos—the "two Judys," as the office staff called them. In September 1987 he hired Gary Schuster as vice president of corporate relations, a post that had been vacant since July 1986. A veteran newsman, Schuster had been White House correspondent for CBS and worked for the Reagan administration.[1]

Schuster and the two Judys became the staff members closest and most loyal to Lewis. Some referred to them as the palace guard. Swantak had worked for Lewis since her graduation from high school. "She had enormous power," said Dick Grove, the assistant secretary. "If you dealt with her and got along with her, and again, did her bidding, you were all right. But I'm sure she was disliked by many people." Matthews found her "tough as nails. Not particularly friendly." But she excelled at her job.[2]

Matthews had come to the corporation as treasurer, the same position he had held with MP and UP. During the two-year wait for the merger process to be approved he grew restless and looked for a CFO position, which was his ambition. UPC had people in all the financial positions, but the treasurer, Harry Shuttleworth, had a drinking problem. When he was finally let go, Matthews didn't want the job because it meant doing more of the same, but he took it and went to work under Surette.[3]

A pleasant man of owlish appearance glazed with southern charm and a soft Virginia accent, Matthews had a talent for finance that was exceeded only by his ambitions. He had no intention of remaining a treasurer forever; his smooth—some said slick—style barely concealed his desire to climb the corporate ladder. He was aggressive, driven, and very good at what he did. However, the men on the corporate rungs above him, Surette and Cook, were both finance guys. Matthews grew bored in a post that allowed little room for personal growth and started exploring the job market again.[4]

At first Lewis's arrival didn't change anything for Matthews. Even if Surette left or retired, Ed Hill or Jim Otto seemed next in line for his job. Some thought that Matthews ingratiated himself with Lewis and bad-mouthed Surette in the process. "White's a climber," said Schuster. "He was ambitious and a climber. . . . He would say of Surette, *geez*, and sort of shake his head and roll his eyes, and Drew wasn't necessarily happy with Surette either." The friction between Cook and Lewis had already begun, and Lewis took a dim view of those close to Cook, including Surette. In April 1987 Lewis heard that Matthews was looking for another place and advised him not to leave.[5]

Shortly before Lewis assumed command in October, he summoned Matthews and said, "Who do you want as your treasurer, as we're making you CFO tomorrow?" Matthews was flabbergasted. "Totally shocked," he said. "That was . . . the way Drew did things." Matthews chose Gary Stuart to replace him as treasurer and next day was named senior vice president of finance. Surette was allowed to take early retirement. In October another Cook man, Chuck Eaton, the vice president of external affairs, was replaced by Kip Hawley with the changed title of vice president of external relations. In January 1988 Schaefer was promoted to executive vice president, making him the number two man behind Lewis. To handle human resources Lewis brought in another old friend, Ursula Fairbairn, who had worked for Lewis in the U.S. Transportation Department. She became a formidable presence in the corporate office.[6]

Through this series of moves Lewis put together the staff he wanted. During 1986 Cook had revamped the leadership of the subsidiaries as well. Walsh took charge of the railroad, and Bill Adams, Champlin's vice chairman, replaced Bill Smith as chairman. Jim Wilson remained president of Rocky Mountain Energy, but Arch Jacobson arrived to head the new development subsidiary, Union Pacific Realty. Fresh blood was needed because UPC had suffered a down year in 1986. It earned $485 million compared to $501 million the previous year, but the special restructuring charge of $945 million transformed it into a loss of $480 million despite record earnings from the railroad and Rocky Mountain Energy. This performance put pressure on Lewis to deliver.[7]

To complete his inner circle Lewis made one more move. Early in 1988 UPC completed its acquisition of USPCI. Shortly afterward Lewis brought in an old friend and business associate, Jack Messman, to run the company. That Messman had no experience in the waste disposal business made no difference to

Lewis; he was fond of saying that a good MBA could do anything and didn't have to have experience in the industry. Messman had the one quality Lewis prized most: He was utterly loyal and quickly earned a reputation as Lewis's pet.[8]

Lewis wasted no time putting forth his agenda. In November 1987 he hosted a corporate conference at MP's unique castle and lodge in Selma, Missouri. The theme was "$150 a Share—How and When." All the subsidiary heads were to outline "their plans for the future given the $150 stock objective." The affair was a coming-out party for the new Lewis team, its theme aimed pointedly at increasing shareholder value via the stock price.[9]

The theme carried over to Lewis's first annual stockholders' meeting on April 15, 1988. His objective, Lewis stressed, was to shift a company with "a heavy asset orientation to one that will maximize the use of those assets." This would be done through aggressive use of advanced technologies to improve productivity and through equally aggressive marketing. The new businesses, trucking and environmental services, offered examples of this approach.[10]

All of this came straight out of the Barry Schaefer playbook, which Lewis wholeheartedly endorsed. However, he emphasized one other point in particular. "We have no doubt whatsoever that our primary responsibility is to our shareholders," he said. "That is something that I and everyone else on this dais today keeps uppermost in our minds. Our goal is to achieve a very substantial increase in shareholder value . . . within the next five years."[11]

UPC oversaw four basic businesses. First and foremost was transportation, which included the railroad, Overnite Trucking, Skyway Freight Systems, and UP Technologies. The second business was oil and gas, the third environmental services. "This is a business which we feel has very significant growth prospects," Lewis said of USPCI. "We plan to invest $200 to $600 million in this business over the next five years." The fourth business, UP Realty, reflected a change in strategy from merely trying to locate companies along the right-of-way to maximizing return on the landholdings through aggressive development.[12]

In this first encounter with the stockholders, Lewis gave a ringing endorsement to all four businesses. He defended Overnite as a "sound acquisition" and praised USPCI as a great entry into an industry that was expected to grow from $2.5 billion in 1987 to $10 billion or $12 billion by 1992. He expressed great confidence in the future of the oil and gas business but warned that "if certain assets do not meet our criteria, we intend to sell them." UP Realty had extended its reach beyond the railroad's territory to other parts of the country as well.[13]

Thus did Lewis deliver his vision of the future and his manifesto for performance. Some wondered how long he would stay on the job. He had never been one to linger long at any assignment, and many people thought he still harbored political ambitions.

To those who worked with him, Lewis remained a complex and often contradictory figure. A generous, warmhearted person with the charisma of a politician, he also had the cool, calculating instincts of a politico who knew when and how to charm. He was a strong, high-energy leader who lit up a room when he entered it. "He's like a little sprite," said Mary McAuliffe. "He's just got high energy, would just run all the time."[14]

Ebby Gerry viewed him as somewhat autocratic, yet others thought him democratic and willing to delegate. "He liked consensus," said Matthews, who admired Lewis's "amazing ability to get at the heart of the problem." Linda Waller, who served as Davidson's secretary, loved the way Lewis would do things for anybody in the office or see that people got help when needed. "It was almost like Camelot," she said, ". . . and he was king of Camelot and he took very good care of the people." But she thought him "a very complicated individual."[15]

Another side of Lewis emerged more slowly. "Drew was one tough, tough guy," said Rob Knight. "He had a way of staring you down. . . . deep blue eyes and he'd go after your jugular." No one wanted to get caught in the vise of his steely gaze. "Drew didn't want to be challenged," said Schuster. ". . . Right or wrong, he was right." Davidson, who towered over Lewis, had faced down any number of hard characters in his career, yet he admitted that Lewis was the only man who intimidated him. "We were all scared to death of him," Davidson said. "He had a temper," said Matthews. ". . . He could really climb on you."[16]

Schaefer thought Lewis set people against one another. One subordinate labeled him a "pathological liar"; another thought he held grudges. Lewis had a quick mind and a volatile, even manic style that unnerved some people. Knight recalled watching him bark different orders to three or four assistants while he talked to someone else on the phone. He loved a good argument and sometimes had trouble letting go of the topic until it was thrashed out to his satisfaction. Matthews recalled one debate that started on a ride to the airport and continued through the flight, during the ride to the hotel, in the company suite at the Waldorf, and at a shoeshine stand across the lap of a hapless stranger caught between them.[17]

Yet Lewis also showed genuine affection for the people who worked for him. Every year he held a Christmas party in the office for the staff and their families. He gave everyone a turkey and called each family into his office to thank them for their efforts and play with the children. "It sounds kind of corny, but it was cute," said Knight. ". . . I remember him actually crying in one of those sessions." Like Walsh, Lewis adored children. He had been an Eagle Scout as a boy and was pleased when Downing Jenks helped get him on the national board of the Boy Scouts.[18]

Lewis had a quirky side as well. Major decisions never cost him sleep, but little things bothered him. If he broke a shoelace, he had to stop and get a new one at once. When he played Monopoly, he liked to put a $500 bill in his back pocket in case of emergency. Once he got a suit back from the cleaner with the $500 bill tucked into a plastic bag; Lewis had left it in his rear pocket. Schuster attributed this need to put something aside for a rainy day to Lewis's Quaker heritage. "He wasn't cheap, but he was really frugal," said Schuster.[19]

The quixotic Lewis emerged clearly in one major decision that affected the entire office. Shortly after becoming CEO he walked through the office as he had done at the Transportation Department, talking with every employee and asking what they thought. Some people expressed concern that the company would leave New York when the lease on 345 Park expired. Afterward Lewis circulated a letter assuring people that the corporation would stay in New York. A few months later he dropped the bombshell that UPC was moving its headquarters out of New York.[20]

Renewal of the lease at 345 Park Avenue would double the rent, he stressed. After considering numerous other locations between Omaha and Washington, he had chosen Bethlehem, Pennsylvania. The board discussed the matter at length, then concluded that the selection of a new location was "a matter for decision by management and within the authority and responsibility of Mr. Lewis as the company's Chief Executive Officer."[21]

Why Bethlehem? The town was nowhere near the line of the railroad and had absolutely nothing to do with its history or business. Lewis offered a variety of reasons. It was situated between New York, the financial center, and Washington, the political center, making it easy for him to get to both places. The Allentown-Bethlehem-Easton airport offered excellent facilities for corporate aircraft at a savings of $500,000 for hangar space. Lewis obtained first-class office space from Bethlehem Steel in its Martin Tower at $14 per square foot compared to $50 at 345 Park, saving $2.5 million. Moreover, the quality of life there was great and the people hardworking.[22]

Although Lewis did not live in Bethlehem, the major (and unspoken) reason for the move was that it put corporate headquarters near his farm. The significance of that proximity did not emerge until later. He promised everyone in New York a job if they moved. "Drew's message to us," said Gary Stuart, "was . . . I want you to demonstrate your loyalty to the company . . . by relocating; otherwise, you're gone." The announcement devastated the office staff. "This was really destructive for everybody," said Stuart. "Nobody wanted to go to Bethlehem." For some the move posed no problem; others, however, struggled with family and financial issues.[23]

"Drew was determined to have the company move close to his farm," said Grove, "and how he ever sold that to the board of directors is beyond me. . . . Some director should have stood up and said, 'Drew, we're not going to put this company in your backyard.'" Schaefer had the same reaction. He had turned down the presidency of the railroad because he didn't want to move his family again; the prospect of going to Bethlehem infuriated him. "There was no reason to be down there," he said. ". . . Where's the goddamn board on this thing? . . . Why isn't anybody saying, 'This doesn't make any sense, Drew'?"[24]

Carl von Bernuth agreed that "the number one motivating factor was that Drew Lewis wanted to stay living in Pennsylvania, and that this was within a commute of his family farm." However, Bernuth saw nothing wrong with this reason. Schuster conceded that "there was a lot of grumbling on the way there, but once they were [in Bethlehem], the grumbling sort of quieted down."[25]

The move took place around Labor Day of 1988. The UP air force had already been bolstered to accommodate the new location. In May 1987 the same management that was pushing cost reduction on the subsidiaries traded in its Gulfstream II jet for a new $21.1 million Gulfstream IV model. During the summer of 1988 the board approved the purchase of a Sikorsky S76B helicopter for $4.76 million. "He wanted to have a helicopter because Jimmy Robinson had a helicopter," said Schaefer. As part of the move Lewis arranged country club memberships for the senior staff because he wanted them active in the community. He also provided them with new cars. They had to be Fords because Lewis was on the Ford board and because Bethlehem Steel allowed only American cars to park in the Martin Tower garage.[26]

If nothing else, the move reduced the corporate staff by about half. "Most of the regular employees, the clerks, the secretaries . . . they just didn't move," said von Bernuth. "They were ingrained there. Their families were there. Even though Bethlehem was only eighty miles, it's a world away." Lewis arranged a bus trip to Bethlehem for the senior staff. Afterward Bill McDonald asked pointedly, Where was the Chinese laundry? Where would he get his shirts properly laundered? An unrepentant New Yorker, McDonald was near enough retirement to resign. Von Bernuth replaced him as vice president and general counsel.[27]

McDonald was the first senior officer to reject the move. Schaefer followed at the end of 1988. "Drew, obviously, and Barry weren't going to work together no matter what," said von Bernuth. Rebensdorf, who was not at UPC, thought a major reason was that Schaefer was "unable to convince Lewis of the validity of his logistics vision." Marchant agreed that "Schaefer and Lewis had some major disagreements on philosophy, and that's why Schaefer left," but family issues played a role as well. Schaefer did not want to relocate his children and parents yet again.[28]

Stuart also sensed the friction between Schaefer and Lewis. "Barry wanted to be the CEO, and that didn't happen," he said, "so he's not likely going to want to work for the guy who did get it. Especially if he thinks he's brighter than that guy." Schaefer conceded that "I couldn't play the game. I couldn't suck up to

Lewis all the time." Matthews proved more adept at playing the game with Lewis, but he too struggled with the move.[29]

Schaefer went on to another career in finance. He grew embittered when he discovered that Lewis was blocking some firms in the industry from hiring him on the grounds that he had proprietary information. It was a sad conclusion to a distinguished career at UP. "I learned a lot in the railroad industry," Schaefer said later. "It was an exciting time. I had very good people. I had good bosses, not easy: Kenefick and McDonald. But they were very intelligent, honest people, and I was fortunate to work for them."[30]

The turnover in Bethlehem continued after the move. Two of Matthews's four vice presidents in the finance area, Ed Hill and Jim Otto, refused to move and left the company. Matthews filled the gaps by promoting Charlie Billingsley to vice president and controller and bringing in John E. Dowling from Warner Cable. John Halan was made vice president of human resources. Stuart was promoted to vice president as well as treasurer. Chuck Olsen, the longtime secretary, retired early in 1990. Dick Grove, who had served as assistant secretary for nearly forty years, hoped at last to get the top job. Instead Lewis promoted Judy Swantak to the position and also made her president of the Union Pacific Foundation. A disappointed Grove retired soon afterward. Judy Waltos, who had been promoted to executive administrative assistant in the summer of 1988, received a second position as director of aviation/travel services in March 1990. The new post put her in charge of the UP air force.[31]

While remaking the staff, Lewis also revamped the board and its procedures. The all-male board needed a woman director, and he recruited Judith Richards Hope, a senior partner at a law firm, in 1988. A year later Cook, Bill Grant, Downing Jenks, Morris Miller, and Minot Milliken all left the board. Their departure enabled Lewis to shape the board more to his liking—smaller, younger, and friendly to him. In 1989 the board shrank to seventeen with only two new members replacing the five who left. The newcomers were Thomas A. Reynolds Jr., chairman of Winston & Strawn, and Jimmy Robinson of American Express, Lewis's good friend who had gone off the board in 1985 and was returning. In 1990 two more stalwarts, John Fery and Hamilton Mitchell, departed, and only one new director was added. Claudine B. Malone, a management consultant, had the distinction of being the second woman and first black member of the board.[32]

Evans had given the board a broader geographical spread; Lewis made it a more diversified group but one largely in accord with his views. "One of the biggest raps on Drew," said Gerry, "was that he stacked the board with his friends." He cut the number of committees from seven to four and ran board meetings with a choreographer's precision. "Drew knew how to politic the board," said Schuster, "and so at meetings, when they came in, they were pretty much up to date. He'd send them a packet." Board meetings under Lewis's firm hand usually ran two hours or less.[33]

Like any good choreographer Lewis insisted on rehearsals, which took place on the Tuesday before Thursday's board meeting. "Everybody . . . would run through their spiel with the rest of us in the room," said Matthews. ". . . The joke in the company was 'If you can make it through Tuesday's presentation you're going to star on Thursday,' 'cause we'd beat him to death on Tuesday." After the presentations at the board meeting Lewis ran a tight Q&A session, partly because, Matthews observed, "he's got a relatively short attention span." Davidson, who came to Bethlehem later, agreed that "Drew would run an awfully tight board meeting. In fact, many times it'd only last about an hour and he . . . didn't want people asking a lot of questions and learn[ing] a lot about the business."[34]

This attitude reflected the impatience that had characterized Lewis's entire career. His constant urge was to get results and move on to the next piece of business. "No grass grew under him," observed Gerry. "Everyone knew about the sign in his office that read 'Lord give me Patience . . . and give it to me NOW.'"[35]

For the officers Lewis provided a special incentive plan. Approved in January 1988, the plan offered Lewis and thirty-nine top executives special bonuses totaling more than $17 million if the stock reached 100 and remained at that level for sixty days. During the winter and early spring of 1988 the stock hovered between 60 and 65 but the offer had its intended effect. "Within the finance function," admitted Stuart, "we started thinking of everything we do, What is this going to do to the price of the stock?"[36]

Predictably, Lewis gave special attention to the Washington office. He thought it poorly run when he first arrived at UPC and made its upgrade a priority. Hawley, who had worked for Lewis at the Transportation Department and knew Capitol Hill, cleaned house and brought in people more practiced in the fine art of lobbying. Under the new arrangement Schuster handled the media and Hawley took care of everything else. Lewis, said Schuster, "looked upon the Washington office as a cost center. It made money for us. . . . So what you did, or what you got through a committee, or what you got changed on railroad retirement, or what you got changed on fuel tax, or what you got changed through the ICC . . . there was a dollar number connected with that."[37]

Lewis also believed in contributing to both parties. "You can't buy votes," he said, "but you can gain access." During the Evans era UP was viewed as a Democratic railroad, but after Lewis's arrival it became very much a Republican company. What mattered most to Lewis, however, was that the Washington operation be professional and efficient. To spread this message around, he sometimes took young officers from UPC and the subsidiaries with him to meetings on the Hill so they could observe the process in action.[38]

Hawley instilled that sense of professionalism. A hyperactive go-getter, he worked furiously all day but insisted on going home to his family at night and so left activities like fund-raisers to staff members. Unhappy with some of the staff he inherited, Hawley persuaded Mary McAuliffe to join the office as his lieutenant and ultimate successor. At first she refused, telling him, "I can't tell my mom I work for railroads. You are the most pathetic lobbyists in the world. All you do is complain about your employees. . . . You are the laughingstock." But Hawley persisted, saying, "That's what we want to change." Finally McAuliffe agreed in 1989 to join UP and never regretted it.[39]

An energy-charged woman with a sharp mind, McAuliffe had impressive credentials. A native of Louisville, Kentucky, she graduated from Indiana University in 1968 and went to Washington to work first for a senator and then for the Consumer Product Safety Commission. "I hated it," she said. "It was so anti-business." She worked for Senators Lowell Weicker and Bob Packwood before moving to a lobbying firm. A savvy veteran of the Hill's politics and procedures, McAuliffe was the kind of consummate professional that Lewis wanted. She knew Lewis from his time in Transportation and thought highly of him. "Drew wanted to change the office," she said, "because Drew really respected and cared about what the government could do if they went overboard with regulation."[40]

Washington was familiar turf for Lewis, and one he loved. "Drew, I think, came in like twice a month and met with members on the Hill," said McAuliffe. "We just moved him around. And he was like a superstar. People loved him because he was a very popular transportation secretary. He'd bounce up and down the hall and . . . was like a wonderful asset to take anywhere. . . . He wanted to be the go-to guy in Washington for railroads."[41]

As these changes unfolded, the media focused on Lewis as the prime mover much as they did on Walsh. They portrayed UP as a fossil and credited Lewis with changes that had already occurred or were under way before his arrival. Even Bill Withuhn of the Smithsonian, a respected railroad authority and historian, hailed Lewis as "hauling the most tradition-bound company in the most tradition-bound industry into the future." The *Wall Street Journal* depicted UP as "notoriously hidebound even by railroad standards." *Forbes* praised Lewis for having "shaken that great business to its core. He has peeled off layers of management, chucked tradition and made his associates acutely aware that customers are not an incidental annoyance but the sole reason for being in business."[42]

Although Walsh was mentioned as Lewis's man in Omaha, *Forbes* directed its praise at the CEO for a "dramatic rise in productivity" and as the man who "scrapped the line's whiskered network of freight-forwarding agents and replaced

them with a single, centralized customer services office in St. Louis." His bold-
ness in moving the New York office, closing the Omaha shops, and slimming
down the energy subsidiary also drew kudos even though these actions outraged
veterans in both companies.[43]

These observations rankled Bill Cook as well as many other UP people.
"Drew Lewis is a very able guy, and he's done a good job," said Cook, "but the
way he goes about certain things gets a lot of people mad and doesn't accomplish a damn thing. . . . I can't recall many significant things [Lewis] initiated."
Lewis responded by saying, "I don't care who gets the credit. He can take it all."
But he did note pointedly that buying Overnite was a bad deal and cost the
company dearly. "They talked synergism with the railroad," he added, "and there
is none."[44]

Some analysts agreed with Cook and criticized Wall Street's tendency to
credit Lewis with UP's good moves and blame Cook for its shortcomings. "The
question," said Isabel Benham, a specialist in railroad securities, "is whether
Drew Lewis is truly the daring, forward-thinking executive we think, or a disappointment." Some analysts called for UPC to shed its natural resource assets entirely. Although some institutional stockholders urged it to ignore the demands
of short-term holders, the age of the quarterly bottom line was taking hold of
Wall Street.[45]

As expected, the unions took a dim view of Lewis's performance. Mindful
that pickets greeted his arrival in Omaha in April 1986, Lewis worked hard at
finding a conciliatory stance. Although a UP brakeman said flatly that Lewis
"was brought to UP because of his track record of getting rid of unions," others
admitted that he hadn't lived up to his reputation as a union buster. Still, the
policy of trimming the organization and cutting jobs bred fear in the ranks, and
no amount of conciliation could change that.[46]

Although Lewis and Walsh seemed to be following parallel courses, the differences between the corporation and the railroad continued to widen. There
had never been any love lost between them. The railroad culture tended to regard
UPC first as a nuisance and then, after Kenefick's departure, as a threat. Where
the corporation blanched at the railroad's voracious appetite for capital, the railroad heaped scorn on spending large sums for what it considered to be sideshow
companies.

"We in the field . . . always wanted to spend money on the railroad," said Dennis Duffy. "That's the way we had been brought up, and we always thought that
we could be . . . more successful than a damn old trucking company or a garbage
company." Brad King admitted that he "didn't ever understand what they did.
You look at the companies they bought and overpaid for, and that's all money
could have gone back into the railroad. . . . But we also kind of knew that they
were Ivy League people, not us."[47]

Gary Stuart thought the railroad never understood or appreciated the contribution of UPC. "We handled a number of functions that were not done at the operating company level," he said. "Capital allocation among all the operating companies, all the financing, all the insurance, investor relations, corporate legal matters, executive comp. But the operating companies looked at the holding company as a bunch of second-guessers and a cost center that provided little or no value to them." Small wonder that Schaefer referred to the subsidiary presidents as barons presiding over their fiefdoms and resisting any change that threatened their domains.[48]

When Lewis first arrived in Omaha, some people thought he might redress the balance in favor of the railroad. "He liked the . . . railroad's history," said Joe McCartney, "and he liked what the railroad was, what it meant to America." Rebensdorf saw promise in an early Lewis move seeking ways to trim UPC. "In fact, just the opposite happened," he said. "The corporation grew in power. The emphasis on earnings per share increased. More incentive plans were put in place that were driven by earnings per share and stock price. When Kenefick was here . . . we never even worried about stock price."[49]

Instead of relief, Lewis gave the railroad Walsh and more pressure to downsize, cut costs, perform more efficiently, and focus laser-like on customer service. No one knew how long either one of them would stay on the job. Walsh had a five-year contract, and those who knew him suspected that he was always looking for the next stop in his career. "I always felt that he was warming up with UP," said Dennis Jacobson, ". . . using the platform as a way to either become a politician and run for office, or whatever. . . . The sense was this was not a big enough pond to swim in."[50]

The job Walsh wanted most belonged to Lewis, and he was a logical candidate when Lewis left or retired. The age gap between them was a good fit in some ways but not in others. If Lewis stayed on until retirement, Walsh was not likely to wait that long.

Lewis's plans were far less transparent. Although he insisted that UPC was the last stop in his career, few believed him. "Most of his career has been a series of quick-fix turnarounds," observed Forbes. A former business associate observed that "Drew is a short-cycle guy, because he gets bored" but conceded that his stay at UPC "may be the longest he hasn't been bored." Some thought Lewis wanted to make another run for governor of Pennsylvania, and that was one reason for the move to Bethlehem. Though Lewis assured the staff that he planned to stay until he was sixty-five, he had also told them the company would remain in New York. "We thought," said Stuart, "that Drew had never stayed any place more than a couple of years."[51]

But Lewis did not go back into politics or leave UPC quickly. He stayed partly because he had created a situation there in which it was easier to deal with a problem that came increasingly to complicate his life. It was an old and familiar problem to both the corporation and the railroad, and to Lewis as well. He had managed to conceal it from most of his co-workers, and his palace guard protected him when needed. Indeed, it was a major reason behind the move to Bethlehem and its proximity to his farm. The question was how long he could keep it at bay even under the favorable circumstances he had created.

19

The Problem

On March 15, 1988, Mike Walsh sat down for a lengthy interview with John F. Kawa, a senior vice president at Dean Witter Reynolds. Walsh had been on the job for seventeen months. He had launched the revolution to retrofit the railroad to the new economic realities, and at least some of the dust had begun to settle. Shortly after joining UP he had committed the railroad to improving its net to $475 million in 1987 on what appeared to be flat or declining revenues. The road achieved a record net of $440 million. The operating ratio rose from 79.8 in 1986 to 81.4 largely because of higher fuel prices and personal injury charges. During the year the railroad had also adopted a mission statement to be "the safest, most customer responsive, highest quality, lowest cost, most financially successful, and best managed" in the nation.[1]

The interview gave Walsh yet another platform for his vision. He repeated his familiar litany about the importance of customer service, quality performance, and communication within the ranks. The reorganization of the operating department was necessary to bring the road into the modern business arena. He had imposed major cultural changes on the company in a short time, but most of the employees were adjusting to them. Those who resisted or faltered were not likely to have a future at UP anyway, especially as the ranks continued to thin. During 1987 the company had cut some three thousand people even though gross ton-miles increased 14 percent.[2]

On the labor front the UP, like all other railroads, still bore the burden of arbitrary work rules that undercut every attempt at efficiency and modernization. The endless fight to eliminate firemen offered a classic example. The 1964 agreement had been hedged to such a degree that in 1985 the UP still had 1,200 firemen on its roster with a total payroll of $60 million.[3]

The list of arbitraries seemed endless. If a train was delayed leaving its initial terminal or reaching its final terminal, each trainman got paid an extra twenty-five cents per minute, a charge that totaled $15 million a year. If a train stopped to pick up a locomotive en route, each crew member received an extra hour's pay (about $13) even though the stop usually took only a few minutes. Crews were paid full mileage for deadheading back from runs even though they did no work on the trip. Clerks had their own arbitraries. Dispatchers could not give train orders or clearances directly to crews but had to hand them off to clerks, who transmitted the orders. If the order went directly from dispatcher to crew, the clerk received an arbitrary of two to eight hours' pay.[4]

Not surprisingly, railroad workers earned more total compensation than any other industrial workers except coal miners. Between 1981 and 1984, a recession period, their wages rose 27 percent, compared to a mere 8 percent for the powerful Teamsters. "The plain fact is," said Tom Watts, "that over the last several years we have been forced to overprice ourselves, and we can't continue to do that." More recent labor agreements had made only modest inroads in whittling down arbitraries. In 1986 a train crew member's annual pay averaged about $52,000 including fringe benefits, while a unionized truck driver pulled in about $40,000 and a nonunion rig owner-operator about $32,000.[5]

Walsh's insistence that the company could no longer afford to pay so many people for work they didn't do had a solid basis in realities that the unions were loath to admit. To reverse this dismal trend, the company came up with an original approach.[6]

The Milwaukee Agreement, a forty-year pact, permitted train crews to be reduced only by attrition and imposed limitations on train lengths and work en route when reduced crews were used. A train could not use two-man crews, for example, if it had over seventy-one cars and did certain work such as switching en route. Nearly all UP trains were longer than seventy-one cars and did switching. Moreover, vacant positions rarely occurred in practice because anyone who was in service when the agreement was signed was eligible for them. If the position of second brakeman fell vacant, junior yard employees could opt into it; the job remained filled, and the company then had a vacant yard job to fill. For these and other reasons John Marchant called the agreements "largely smoke and mirrors."[7]

To skirt this obstacle, UP began negotiating agreements at the local level allowing it either to buy out trainmen or put them on a new contrivance called the reserve board. The first such pact became effective October 1, 1987, for UTU workers at the Memphis Union Terminal. Going on the reserve board gave an employee 70 percent of his base wage and benefits for doing no work at all. Selection was done by seniority. "If there were twenty second brakeman positions in a pool," said Marchant, "we'd establish twenty reserve board positions. And if twenty old heads went on the reserve board, then we'd blank all of those second brakeman jobs. It was quite a success." Other railroads did not appreciate their originality at first. Walsh told Watts and Marchant that three CEOs had called and wanted them fired.[8]

Critics who heaped ridicule on paying people not to work, and they were many, missed the point. "We were paying them 100 percent to come to work," said Marchant, "and their job's absolutely unnecessary." Those on the reserve board could work elsewhere or go to school and were on call if more workers were needed. In return the locals agreed to scrap the Milwaukee Agreement restrictions on crew size and eliminate the train-length and no-work-en-route restrictions for two-person train crews. "We reduce our personal injury exposure as well," said Walsh. "It's about a 40 percent, or maybe 50 percent, saving for the railroad." By 1987 nearly 50 percent of UP trains ran with two-person crews. The reserve board had about eight hundred members.[9]

The Memphis Agreement became the model for modern crew consist agreements. All later conductor-only agreements, on other railroads as well as the UP, contained similar reserve-board provisions. Much of the credit for the first version belonged to Mike Futhey, the UTU general chairman who negotiated and signed it. His foresight and credibility among his peers enabled other railroads to adopt similar agreements. Futhey maintained his high standing in the UTU; as of this writing he was the union's president.[10]

Despite Wall Street's fixation on short-term results, Walsh insisted that he focused on long-range prospects. One of his first moves at UP had been to form a small strategic-planning group that reported directly to him. "As much as I seem to pooh pooh strategic planning," he said, "I really fundamentally believe in it. I just think you have to be very modest about your ability to actually predict what's going to happen." Thinking long-term about what kind of company UP should be was crucial. "I don't see anything in any of my conversations with Drew that's inconsistent with this view, and I don't see any unwillingness on the part of the holding company to fund that vision."[11]

Working with Lewis, he added, was one of the reasons Walsh had come to UP. "Drew Lewis and I communicate in quick, simple terms," he added. "I agreed with him at the beginning of the year on certain key targets and objectives, and he gives me tremendous latitude and freedom as to how we organize and orchestrate things to achieve these objectives. That's true strategically as well as operationally. I don't have any expectation that it will change."[12]

But it was changing in ways that baffled Walsh. Lewis was becoming harder to talk to, and sometimes harder still to understand. "He could be on the phone with Drew," said Schuster, "and Drew would bark at him about something and he'd say, 'Okay, Drew, I'll get it fixed' . . . but he didn't like it 'cause some of it was, he thought, irrational." As their relationship grew more strained, Walsh turned increasingly to Schuster for an explanation or simply to vent.[13]

Lewis and Walsh were both high-energy men with enormous egos. There was no overt hostility between them, only a subtle but growing tension. Dolan thought that Walsh got on Lewis's nerves after a while. "Drew did not have the all-consuming passion for the job that Mike had," he said. On one business trip to New York Lewis and Walsh had adjoining rooms in the company's suite at the Waldorf. After dinner Lewis went to his room, turned off all his lights, and put a blanket under the door so that Walsh would not knock to come in and talk business.[14]

Nor did it help that Walsh got so much publicity and sought ever more, much as Lewis had when he first arrived in New York and began to upstage Cook. But there was something more that Walsh did not yet grasp. As it turned out, he was far from the only one who failed to see what the problem was.

Alcohol abuse haunted the history of UP as it did so many areas of American life. Railroaders had always been known as hard drinkers, but no one ever kept count of how many careers booze had destroyed along the way. Like many others, John Kenefick enjoyed his Jack Daniel's hour without letting it take over his life, but a surprising number of railroad men let alcohol dominate and sometimes ruin them. Their ranks included Drew Lewis.

Exactly how long alcohol had plagued Lewis's life remains unclear. He once told a confidant in passing that his father said he never knew a Lewis male who could handle his liquor. "It was in the genes," said the confidant. Whatever its roots, the problem apparently surfaced during the air controllers strike in 1981, when Lewis was under enormous pressure. "He was making the morning news show rounds every morning, sort of updating," said a friend. "And so he'd go to ABC, then over to CBS and to NBC and then back to the department. But he was drinking before every show. It was like a crutch." Schaefer heard on good authority that Lewis consumed a bottle of vodka a day during the strike.[15]

It was not an obvious problem when he came to UPC. Lewis was a sly drinker and for a time managed to control the habit so that it didn't interfere with his work. "You never saw him take a drink, ever," said Matthews. "I never remember him with a glass in his hand." Schuster, who had socialized with the Lewises before coming to UPC, wasn't aware of the problem until he went to work at the corporation. While in Omaha Lewis fooled Kenefick as well. "I don't think any of us knew about it at the time," said Kenefick. "I should have. My late first wife was an alcoholic, and she fooled me by sneaking the vodka all the time. Lewis used to run around with a glass of iced tea—iced tea, my ass—it was iced tea with a shot of vodka."[16]

"He was very sneaky," said Matthews. "He was a very good con artist, and most people bought it." Dick Davidson, who had no inkling of the problem for several years, agreed that "he was very clever . . . damn discreet about it." He was convinced the board knew nothing about the problem. Gary Stuart found it ironic that Lewis once identified an employee as someone with a drinking problem even though no one else in the office realized it.[17]

The iced tea, fed by a bottle of vodka kept in the toilet tank of his private bathroom, accompanied Lewis to board meetings. "It was a funny-looking iced tea," said Schuster. ". . . You knew he was drinking, 'cause you could smell it, and you could tell sometimes in the way he acted. Sometimes a little rowdy, sometimes he'd be angry. He wasn't an angry guy. Fun-loving guy . . . loved to tell jokes, but sometimes, if he'd been in his cups a little bit, he was tougher to deal with." Lewis came to the office early and started drinking early. "The old adage," said one staff member, "was that if you wanted to get anything done with him you had to get it done before noon."[18]

Despite the clues, discovery of the problem came slowly. The two Judys doubtless knew and did everything they could to shield him. Walsh did not understand what was going on; he was half a continent away. He didn't know why the phone calls to him always came so early in the morning. The problem remained under wraps, its root cause known only to a select few. Over time, however, it became a serious issue for the company and for Lewis.

In Omaha the whirlwind continued to swirl at a furious pace. Walsh seemed to be everywhere, crisscrossing the West to hold town meetings, do business, and attend fund-raisers, charity dinners, and the funeral of any employee killed in the line of duty—the latter to promote his emphasis on safety. Nor did he hesitate to carry his message to suppliers he felt were not performing up to his standards. Once he walked onto the floor of GE's locomotive works in Erie, Pennsylvania, to exhort the workers to improve the quality of their product. On another occasion he infuriated lower-level GE managers by complaining directly to John Welch about the poor quality of the locomotives being produced for UP.[19]

"Mike Walsh is far more visible than any other railroad chairman with employees and customers," said a vice president of Coors Brewing Company. While analysts continued to disagree over whether Walsh's approach would succeed, some shippers applauded UP's new responsiveness. When Cargill complained to Walsh that shipment delays were costing the company more than $1 million a year, a UP team visited the company within days. "We were astonished at how quickly they were willing to be in our office, on our turf, to resolve it," said a vice president.[20]

Performance was what analysts cared most about, and on that score Walsh delivered. Between 1987 and 1991 the railroad achieved record gross and net revenues nearly every year. It provided 69.8 percent of UPC's gross and 86.5 percent of its net income, compared to 43.7 percent of its gross and 56.7 percent of its net between 1980 and 1986. Far from being a fading enterprise, the railroad outperformed the other subsidiaries and remained a cash cow for UPC. During these two periods the railroad received almost the same proportion of UPC's total capital outlay: an average of $530 million, or 55.8 percent, for 1980–86 and $620 million, or 56.4 percent, for 1986–91.[21]

A closer look at earnings revealed 1988 to be an important turning point. Between 1984 and 1987 carloadings had increased but average revenue per car dropped because prices fell. In 1988, however, both carloads and revenue jumped 11 percent. "We have got to increase the amount of business we attract to the railroad," said Jack Koraleski. But he added, "The ability to increase our prices when necessary is equally important." Matthews considered pricing more important than volume. "They didn't price the business well," he argued. "They had volume strategies . . . the theory that maybe fifty cars pay for the train and the fifty-first is profit. But we weren't pricing it right, so we were hauling the volume and not making enough money to justify the capital."[22]

Matthews liked and admired Walsh but could never bring him around on the pricing issue. He made periodic trips to Omaha to discuss matters with Walsh and the finance people. Whenever Matthews raised the subject of pricing, however, Walsh put him off by saying he was focused on operations savings and would get to pricing later. After two futile meetings Matthews returned with Lewis at his elbow; still Walsh did not relent. "But on the expense side," Matthews conceded, "the guy was unbelievable. . . . He made the company a lot of money and ran it very well."[23]

The cost cutting instituted by Walsh showed clearly in the operating ratio, which averaged 80.7 between 1987 and 1991, compared to 83.4 during 1980–86. The ranks also thinned at an impressive rate, reaching 29,500 by 1990, compared to 37,600 in 1985. Fewer employees meant fewer benefit outlays and a reduced number of injury claims and FELA suits. The reduced ranks also enhanced efficiency. During the same 1985–90 period, the gross ton-miles handled by the UP increased 40 percent, from 262 billion to 366 billion, and the number per employee from 6.9 million to 12.4 million.[24]

The railroad's equipment improved in quality and performance if not in numbers, which fit Walsh's dictum of doing more with less. Between 1971 and 1979 new additions to the fleet averaged 104 locomotives and 2,923 cars a year. From 1980 to 1986 the numbers shrank to 80 locomotives and 944 cars, largely because of the recession and the MP-WP merger. Under Walsh the figures rose to 148 locomotives but only 706 cars per year. New technologies helped make locomotives more versatile, reliable, and fuel efficient. As cars grew more specialized, the UP leased rather than purchased rolling stock and increasingly used cars owned by shippers.[25]

Despite Walsh's success in cutting jobs at the railroad, the corporation's total number of employees continued to grow. In 1982, thanks largely to the recession, UPC reached a low of 27,950 workers. That figure shot up to 46,897 the following year when the MP and WP became part of the company. By 1986 the figure had been reduced to 39,476, only to jump back to 46,559 the next year thanks to the Katy and Overnite acquisitions. Other new subsidiaries such as USPCI helped push the ranks to a high of 48,323 in 1990. Altogether the number of employees averaged 47,471 between 1987 and 1991, compared to 38,522 during 1980–86.[26]

The MP-WP merger also broadened the base of stockholders in UPC from 68,047 to about 96,000 in 1982. Over the next decade, however, their ranks shrank every year but one (1990) to 65,092 in 1992, the lowest number of stock-holders in UPC since its creation in 1969. Why this occurred remains unclear. Between 1980 and 1991 earnings per share rose consistently except for the restructuring charge in 1986 and another special charge in 1991. The stock split two for one in 1977, 1980, and 1991, and the dividend increased from $1.45 per share in 1980 to $2.37 per share a decade later. Walsh's management did much to remove investor doubts about the viability of the railroad, but evidently the same was not true about the corporation's performance.[27]

For all the acquisitions and Lewis's talk of a diversified business empire, the railroad remained the dominant enterprise. In 1990 it represented $8.89 bil-lion, or 68 percent, of UPC's total assets of $13.1 billion. The next two largest enterprises, natural resources and trucking, had assets of $1.88 billion and $1.33 billion, or 25 percent of the total assets combined. The other subsidiaries totaled a paltry 7 percent. The early efforts to spread the asset base of the corpo-ration had succeeded somewhat until the MP-WP merger restored the primacy of the railroad. Like it or not, the very size of the railroad's assets required UPC to protect it.[28]

In June 1989 Walsh proudly unveiled his latest and most impressive showcase for progress: the centralized dispatching center in Omaha. Once the space-age Portland facility showed its mettle, the process gathered momentum. In July 1987 UP announced that it would close eight dispatching centers and consoli-date their functions in Omaha. The move eliminated 600 jobs, two-thirds of them managerial, in Kansas City, Salt Lake City, and Spring, Texas. Five months later the company began work on the new Omaha center. Despite his reserva-tions about wholly centralized dispatching, Art Shoener assumed the job of managing the project.[29]

No other major railroad had attempted to consolidate all its dispatching in one place. The design used the Portland facility as a model but on a greatly enlarged scale. Where Portland controlled 24 code lines in communication with 298 signal control points, the new Omaha system controlled about 150 code lines tied to more than 1,800 control points across 21,000 miles of track. Advances in technology made several improvements possible. The giant terri-tory display required 150 video projectors and associated rear-projection screens. It was flexible in that both the hardware and software could be updated with a minimum of expense and disruption.[30]

The final communication system routed 1,907 CTC control points, 223 hot-box detectors, 450 dispatcher radios, and 400 mobile telephone stations into the first railroad facility to be supported entirely by fiber-optics. Inside the center more than 500 telephones were tied into a Fujitsu electronic telephone switch for regular calls and automatic call distribution for crew and gang management. "By touching their color CRT screens," said John McKenzie, the communications manager, "dispatchers can access radios used in the field and talk to train crews. In addition, they receive telephone calls from their areas, as well as direct connections to yardmasters and foreign line dispatching centers."[31]

The new system replaced mountains of paper records with mountains of data stored on magnetic tapes. It also upgraded the handling of double-track territory, traffic planning, shared trackage, and corridor managing. To work the new system, 250 dispatchers underwent five days of special training, including half-day seminars on stress management and communication skills. As the $50 million project neared completion, the cutovers began on an orderly schedule to allow time for working out bugs.[32]

Portland was the first to convert since its dispatchers had experience with a system like the new one. On April 1, 1989, the first test run was made. Two months later five Portland dispatchers who had moved to Omaha took over running trains in Idaho, Oregon, and Washington. The plan was to add one new dispatcher a week until the roster was full. Every cutover required precise, military-like coordination between employees at the center and in field locations. "Never thought I'd be involved in a project like this," mused one thirty-two-year signal maintainer veteran. "It never occurred to me we might be a part of history, but I guess we are."[33]

The official opening ceremony took place on July 27 with Lewis, Walsh, Nebraska governor Kay Orr, and Omaha mayor P. J. Morgan presiding. By then thousands of visitors had toured the facility. The newly named Harriman Dispatching Center (HDC) was like nothing ever seen on a railroad. Housed in the shell of the oldest company building in Omaha on the site of the railroad's first depot, it was a striking blend of high technology and historic preservation. The interior contained a mixture of wooden and steel beams and whitewashed brick walls. At every turn could be found artifacts of the old railroad—clocks, telegraph equipment, signals, typewriters, a shovel from the Ames works—as if it were a museum.[34]

This impression changed radically inside the bunker, the room where the dispatchers actually worked. Two long, dark corridors extended the length of a football field, their walls entirely covered by two video screens fifteen feet high and three hundred feet long, tracking every movement of seven hundred trains a day across the nearly 22,000-mile UP system. In front of the wall stood a series of cubicles, each with a dispatcher watching several monitors showing his or her part of the road. The monitors replicated the big board for each sector. One displayed computer data on each train; others enabled the dispatcher to send instructions to the computer. As trains moved, they were handed off to the next dispatcher. Behind the dispatchers on an elevated tier sat supervisors in their own open cubicles with their own monitors, ready to assist in case of emergencies. Every station had a red light to signal an emergency in the sector.[35]

The atmosphere inside the bunker was quiet, cool, and professional—a medley of low hums and muffled voices. The bunker itself was built to survive any natural disaster and had an array of backup systems to sustain itself for up to a week. "Five hundred years from now," joked project manager Bill Ulrich, "someone may stumble upon the structure and wonder why it was built in the middle of the United States."

Completion of the HDC rendered it the dispatching counterpart of the NCSC. No one had pushed harder for these consolidations than Dick Davidson. Both projects enhanced his already impressive résumé, as did his handling of the quality program. Other railroads noticed his talent, as well as the fact that he still played second fiddle to Jerry Davis. The quality assignment had alleviated but not resolved that problem. Several railroads, including BN and CSX, made overtures to him. Davidson preferred CSX because it offered the greater challenge. He interviewed with the company and returned with an excellent offer to become president with a shot at the top job of chairman.[36]

It was an offer no ambitious railroad man could refuse. When Davidson told Walsh about it, Walsh fixed him with a stare and asked him to wait an hour. Davidson agreed and went about his business. When he returned, Walsh said, "Jerry Davis is going to CSX; you're going to be executive vice president." During that hour Walsh had called Lewis, who called John Snow, chairman of CSX. Snow said Davis was acceptable and could help his railroad.[37]

Davidson never knew whether Davis found out about this transaction. It happened that Davis was equally pleased about the surprise offer. "When I had the opportunity to go to CSX, something different, I jumped at it," he said later. "To be right honest, I was glad to get away from Mike Walsh." He liked and admired Walsh but considered him "very difficult to work with as far as an operating guy. . . . To be fair to the man, I'd worked for John Kenefick my whole career."[38]

Snow didn't know any more about operations than Walsh did, but he treated Davis well and gave him what he needed. The outcome was a win-win situation for both Davis and Davidson. Davis became president of CSX Rail Transport on July 23, 1989, and Davidson moved up to executive vice president. "Jerry Davis goes to the CSX with our thanks for many jobs, very well done, and with the affection and best wishes of everyone in the Union Pacific family," said Walsh.[39]

Davidson lost no time stepping into his new position. In 1989 the quality program entered its third year, which Davidson estimated as the halfway mark. The program had already yielded impressive results. The billing error rate had been cut in half, the percentage of on-time deliveries had increased, locomotive availability had improved from 85 percent to 91.5 percent, and the two power vendors, GE and EMD, put representatives on quality teams that focused on the most serious failure causes in the fleet.[40]

The earlier quality cost studies had provided powerful incentives for improvement. They showed the cost of preventing failures to be about $100 million, compared to a price tag of $500 million for failing to do things right the first time. "We drove out over $60 million of failure costs in 1988," said Davidson, "and it's our job to build on that improvement trend."[41]

Early in the program Davidson headed a team of sixteen top managers that spent months studying every management process. They began by grading themselves and learned two startling things: No one had clear responsibility for about 19 percent of their overall activities, and they had only a 44 percent proficiency in doing the things necessary to run a quality railroad. From this eye-opener evolved the first forty-five QSPs. Embracing every department, they tried to ensure that all major programs were planned, reviewed, and implemented right the first time. Each project had a program manager to oversee the process.[42]

While pushing the quality program Davidson also revisited the operating organization. The thirty service units and the slashing of nine layers of management to only three—one of Walsh's proudest and most frequent boasts—worked better on paper than in practice. "It's great to have thirty superintendents with authority to do their job," said Stan McLaughlin. "But the question is, do you have thirty good qualified individuals to be those superintendents, and frankly we didn't." McLaughlin divided the superintendents into three groups of about equal numbers. One consisted of well-qualified, able managers who did their jobs well. The second cared only about transportation and didn't want anything to do with engineering or the other departments. The third ran their districts as little fiefdoms and weren't qualified to manage with that level of responsibility.[43]

The thirty superintendents reported to Bill Hillebrandt. He had been instrumental in designing the system but was not a good leader for this diverse gang of thirty. Davidson shifted Hillebrandt to vice president of customer service and made Shoener vice president of field operations. Shoener reassigned ten of the superintendents, reduced the number of service units to twenty-four, and restored the position of general superintendent and appointed three of them, thereby adding back one layer of management. The twenty-four superintendents still reported directly to Shoener; the general superintendents were supposed to "assist service unit superintendents in their day-to-day operations and to assist other departments and senior operating management."[44]

Gradually the organization eased back toward some semblance of the old divisional type by restoring some layers of management. Even Davidson conceded that "we had the organization way too flat there for a little while." One middle manager complained that "we cut too deep below the superintendent level. They're constantly monitoring and changing our structure. And I've had five superintendents in five years."[45]

Having invested heavily in computer technology, UP continued to pour funds into upgrading its already advanced systems. TCS remained the heart of the operation, not only for moving trains but for making possible such innovations as NCSC and HDC. Between 1985 and 1988 the company invested $32.3 million in new equipment and peripherals alone. No one blinked at the outlay, so pervasive had the computer become. For example, UP paid about eighty thousand bills a month. When done by hand, invoices got filed in boxes or on microfilm, retrieval was slow, and vendors waited days or weeks for answers to their inquiries. Then came FileNet, a program and image processing system that automated the procedure and turned it into a showcase for other companies to emulate.[46]

TSC provided the railroad with total car control, among its many functions. By 1986 AAR and the Railway Association of Canada were at work on Advanced Train Control (ATC), which would use cutting-edge computer and telecommunications technology to control operation of the entire train. One approach involved burying transponders in the ballast next to a tie to communicate with computers on board locomotives; another relied on GPS satellites communicating to receivers along the route. UP chose to use transponders in the track.[47]

The system's potential excited Lewis, who saw in it a perfect example of what UPC ought to be doing with its combined expertise. In April 1986 UP set up a pilot system on 200 miles of track from the North Platte yard toward the western coal fields. Microprocessors had already proven they could function in a harsh environment, while satellite systems could not pinpoint trains accurately where double track was involved. That fall Lewis persuaded Cook to set up a new joint subsidiary to "develop and market ATCS and related products."[48]

No company yet possessed the expertise to produce ATC in a usable form. By March 1987 plans were underway to upgrade the North Platte subdivision test. UP hoped to install ATC on its entire system within five years; by September it had invested $3.4 million in the venture. In July 1988 it approved another $4.6 million to complete the full-scale test on the North Platte subdivision and begin limited testing on the Portland subdivision.[49]

Once perfected, ATC could provide real-time work orders and precise up-to-the-minute instructions for picking up and delivering freight cars. It was hailed as the ultimate link between the customer, the railroad, and the train crew. While work went forward, UP formed a Service Reliability Action Team to implement the work-order portion of the concept. The goal was to demolish the mistaken notion that the proper sequence of priorities was cost, quality, and delivery. In fact, everything started with delivery. The team drew its inspiration from the startling fact that the business accounting for nearly 75 percent of UP's profitability had the lowest service reliability record. This discovery guaranteed that service reliability became a major priority.[50]

By 1990 Walsh had his systems and personnel mostly in place. One major change occurred that summer when Guerdon Sines retired and was replaced by Jim Shattuck, who had been with Sines since their MP days. Merill Bryan replaced Shattuck as president of UP Technologies. In 1991 Walsh moved Shattuck to marketing and wanted Bryan to replace him as vice president of IT at the railroad. However, Lewis saw an opportunity to put a well-qualified woman in the position. The job went to Joyce M. Wrenn, who had held a similar post at American Airlines after stints at Bank of America and IBM.[51]

Walsh had turned in a strong performance, but he saw it only as a beginning. Phase I had been completed; the time had come for Phase II. At the annual Leadership/Planning Conference in October he declared that "the objective is to involve *all* Union Pacific people—top to bottom—in improving our service and delivering it to the customer." No matter how good a company got, the problems never stopped coming. The goal was to become not merely a great railroad but a world-class company.[52]

According to Val Feigenbaum, world-class companies had six characteristics. They never missed producing important business results regardless of external conditions. They stretched their goals to ambitious but realistic proportions, and made superior use of existing resources, especially human resources. They had sharp, competitive edges that enabled them to blindside the competition with innovative management. They sold their company as well as they sold their products and services. Finally, they gathered and analyzed data better than their competitors on the premise that when you measure right, you manage right.[53]

Walsh and his senior staff translated these principles into what they called the Business Objectives Matrix. A scorecard for the next three years, it listed ten key areas where the UP had to improve in order to attain world-class standing. It was to be the goal sought by their combined efforts. The quality improvement teams would spearhead the campaign. Five of them were created in 1990 as the pilot program. The results were so encouraging that Walsh planned to increase their number to 160 in 1991, with more coming in the next two years. This was the way to involve everyone in the company in the pursuit of quality and excellence.[54]

In typical fashion Walsh laid out an ambitious agenda for a company still struggling to absorb past changes. Some employees had been energized and rejuvenated by Walsh's exhortations and fresh approach; others were worn down by the unrelenting pressure. Much depended on how well the troops responded to Walsh's repeated calls to duty. Much depended, too, on Walsh's future plans. His five-year contract expired in 1991, and his success at UP had only enhanced his larger ambitions. His status, as well as the railroad's impressive performance, posed a peculiar problem for Lewis, who had already begun to rethink the original premises of UPC's business strategy.

20

The Unstable Chessboard

By 1980 seven major railroads dominated the industry: Conrail, CSX, and NS in the East and BN, SF, SP, and UP in the West. Around them lay a number of important Class I regional roads whose ultimate destiny remained in play. Their fate could do much to alter the balance of power, as could a merger between two or more of what became known as the Super Seven. After a shaky start Conrail had done so well that in March 1987, after a bitter fight in Congress, the government sold its shares to private investors in what was then the biggest single stock offering ever. The sale went well, and Conrail continued to do better than anyone expected.[1]

The merger movement unleashed by the Staggers Act gathered momentum as the number of players dwindled. The UP-MP-WP merger was followed by the liquidation of the RI and the Milwaukee and the BN acquisition of the Frisco. The Chessie and Seaboard merged into CSX; the N&W joined with the Southern to create the NS. As the 1980s proceeded the B&O absorbed the Western Maryland, the Chesapeake & Ohio absorbed the B&O, and CSX formally absorbed both the Seaboard System and the C&O.[2]

Every change of ownership altered the range of future possibilities for who might ally with or be absorbed by whom. Some of the mileage shed by larger systems found new life as born-again independent roads that might ultimately become threats to their original owners if acquired by another major system. The constant redrawing of the railroad map continued to result in a major loss of historic identity as railroads with long traditions vanished into the oblivion of merger or abandonment.[3]

For the SP the proposed merger with the SF promised salvation from two decades of unrelenting decline. It owned a long haul for more than half the traffic out of California and a huge amount of land in a separate entity, the Southern Pacific Land Company. However, by the early 1980s it had become a troubled road. Two major traffic resurgences, coal and grain, had mostly eluded it, and the company endured a series of poor management decisions. In an era of expanding traffic it lacked capacity and equipment. Instead it diversified into other businesses, buying an insurance company and forming a communications company that became Sprint. Too late it discovered that one capital-intensive business could hardly support another one, and in June 1983 it sold Sprint.[4]

Under Ben Biaggini SP's railroad decisions fared no better. Its eastbound traffic moved to East Texas on the Sunset Route, then north to Corsicana, Texas, and onto its Cotton Belt subsidiary. The route added 400 miles to traffic moving from California, making it noncompetitive. Shortening this haul lay behind Biaggini's eagerness to acquire the RI's Tucumcari line. He succeeded but then had to invest heavily in rehabilitating it. By borrowing heavily, SP managed to upgrade the Tucumcari line as far as Kansas City but not to St. Louis, its connection to CSX and Conrail. SP also had to spend $9.2 million for another RI segment to preserve its access to the Memphis gateway. All this work drained funds sorely needed for maintenance and equipment on the core system.

Then, in a stunning move, the ICC rejected the SP-SF merger in July 1986. The decision unsettled the entire strategic chessboard in the West. In 1983 the two railroads had been put into a holding company; the ICC ruling required it to sell one or both of the roads. In the complex corporate maneuvering that followed, Rob Krebs, who had become head of the holding company just before the ICC decision, tried to keep it independent from two factions seeking to acquire it.

While that struggle dragged on, another unexpected development occurred. In 1985 Philip Anschutz, a billionaire heir to his family's oil empire, bought the Denver & Rio Grande Western Railroad for $500 million. To suspicious observers he insisted that he was not a raider but wanted to be in the railroad business. Despite its reputation as a progressive, well-managed independent, the Rio Grande had fallen on tough times. However, it remained a sound property in good physical condition and with $200 million in cash. Then Anschutz, whom the *Denver Post* dismissed as a "railroad buff," struck again. In October 1987 he bought SP for $1 billion plus the assumption of $750 million in debt.[5]

The transaction astounded observers. The 2,248-mile Rio Grande acquired the 11,605-mile SP and all its problems. A holding company, Southern Pacific Rail Corporation, owned by the privately held Rio Grande Industries, took charge of both railroads. The following year SP Rail invested $395 million in upgrading the line and equipment. The transaction did not include SP's natural resources, which remained with the holding company (now called Santa Fe Pacific Corporation) along with the talented Krebs. The SF remained vulnerable as the smallest of the four major western roads. If Anschutz succeeded in rejuvenating his combined roads, competition in the West could become savage.

The middle of the continent remained a bundle of loose ends. The Soo Line acquired the mainline of the defunct Milwaukee between Chicago and the Twin

Cities, then spun off its own longer line between those cities to a private entity called Wisconsin Central Limited. The new owners were able railroad men who turned the Wisconsin Central into one of the era's success stories. The once powerful ICG belonged to a conglomerate, Illinois Central Industries, that regarded the railroad as little more than a tax shelter and let it deteriorate. It began to shed mileage, shrinking from 9,600 miles in 1972 to 4,772 miles in 1985. Five years later the 2,773-mile ICG amounted to little more than the original IC line from Chicago to New Orleans along with routes into St. Louis, Mobile, and Baton Rouge.[6]

Most of the companies formed around ICG spin-offs did well, at least for a time. In 1969 IC Industries (now the Whitman Corporation) spun off the ICG as the reborn IC Railroad. The KCS remained defiantly independent amid the merger mania. It owned the shortest and most direct route from Kansas City to New Orleans and belonged to yet another conglomerate, KCS Industries. Despite a period of bad management and legal woes, the KCS survived to become a solid performer.

Among the loose ends still operating as independent roads, none mattered more to UP than the CNW. Under Jim Wolfe it had risen from the near dead. Using 4R funds, Wolfe upgraded the key Chicago–Omaha line while shedding underperforming mileage. To fund the work he disposed of surplus real estate and sold the road's mammoth Chicago passenger station. In January 1984 work began on a dazzling thirty-nine-story showplace called the Northwestern Atrium Center that housed businesses as well as commuter passengers. It opened in April 1987.[7]

In 1983 Wolfe bought the RI line between Kansas City and the Twin Cities and pulled up his own company's inferior line between those points. Two years later he introduced the Total Quality Improvement System to CNW and vowed to "grow from both internal and external sources." In June 1985 the board created CNW Corporation as a vehicle for diversification. "We are a short-haul railroad and our densities are still among the lowest in the country," Wolfe admitted. "We need to look for ways to solve the structural difficulties." To that end CNW Corporation formed a new subsidiary, 400 Freight Services, and purchased Douglas Dynamics, a snowplow and log-splitter manufacturer.[8]

Despite Wolfe's best efforts, CNW continued to struggle during the mid-1980s. The combination of deregulation and recession undermined its most staple cargo, grain, and competition drove rates relentlessly downward even as overall business improved. "Our predicament is clear," said Wolfe. "Business is up, rates are down, yet we are restricted from eliminating unproductive costs." This last was a pointed barb at the intractability of labor costs. To survive, CNW had to execute the familiar formula of slashing costs, increasing and diversifying business, eliminating unproductive mileage, and improving prices. Unlike larger systems, however, it had fewer options for accomplishing these objectives.[9]

What kept CNW afloat more than anything else was its newfound coal traffic from Powder River. Prior to that bonanza the road did not serve a single western coal mine. During its first full year of operation in 1985, the new connection hauled enough coal to replace grain as CNW's leading revenue generator. Encouraged by the results, the company joined with BN in extending their line ten miles to reach three new mines. By 1988 WRPI had moved more than ten thousand trains carrying 115 million tons of coal and produced over half the company's pretax operating income. "Coal traffic," said Wolfe, "freed the North Western from being so dependent on the grain business and bridge traffic." But it could not solve the broader problems facing the road.[10]

UP executives followed these developments with a wary eye. Everyone agreed that CNW had become indispensable to UP; the issue was whether to insure ensure the connection through acquisition or rely on mutual need to sustain it. When Lewis arrived at the railroad in 1986, he ordered an acquisition analysis of CNW. The study recommended working to preserve the existing relationship. After inspection trips over two independent roads, the Chicago Central and the Iowa Interstate, Lewis ordered another paper to stimulate discussion over what strategy to follow.[11]

The mutual dependence of UP and CNW was obvious. UP required a reliable, service-oriented, and cost-efficient route between Chicago and the Nebraska gateway. Few options other than CNW remained on the shifting railway map. The two independents were longer and in poorer shape than CNW. However, CNW posed problems as well. Traffic over its noncore lines was marginally profitable at best, and it had debt totaling $687 million. The paper recommended that UP acquire up to a 5 percent interest in CNW, making it one of that company's largest stockholders. The timing was good for such a move; CNW stock had slipped from a high of $30 a share in March 1986 to around $20.[12]

That fall Lewis moved to UPC and Walsh took charge of the railroad. Amid his reforms Walsh did not lose sight of the CNW question. He and Lewis kept Kenefick in the loop because Kenefick was close to Wolfe and knew CNW well. Prior to a meeting in New York on March 10, Lewis asked Kenefick for his views. Kenefick replied that "the numbers suggest you could go either way." He and Rebensdorf thought UP should acquire CNW. The question was whether Lewis could look past the numbers to the broader issues involved.[13]

After the March 10 meeting again stressed the strategic importance of CNW, the two companies opened talks. A major disagreement quickly surfaced. CNW valued itself at $61 a share while UP calculated its value at $27. The spread between the two stock prices was widening, and in the eyes of officers at both companies so was the relationship between them. On July 13 Lewis asked for a memorandum summarizing the UP findings; Rebensdorf obliged with three documents evaluating CNW.[14]

Admitting that "CNW's problems won't go away simply because of a UP acquisition," Rebensdorf argued that other factors warranted a maximum price of $27 to $29 for CNW stock. The fact that a quarter of all UP loads and revenues involved CNW made the need for the connection obvious. "The key issue in a CNW acquisition," he stressed, "is whether UP needs to *own* a route between Chicago and Fremont/Council Bluffs. . . . The issue comes down to one of strategic need and balancing the potential financial risks of purchase against the risks of not controlling one's own destiny."[15]

Lewis asked Rebensdorf to expand the argument for a meeting on September 9. Rebensdorf responded with the strongest, most unqualified argument yet for going after CNW. He reckoned the company could pay as much as $33 a share. The reasons for acquiring CNW remained clear. As the shortest, fastest, highest-capacity route between Chicago and the Nebraska gateway, it provided a level of service no other connection could even remotely match. UP's two main competitors, BN and SF, already had single-line service from Chicago to the West Coast and were snatching business from UP. The possibility existed that some third party might buy the road.[16]

The arguments against acquiring CNW seemed compelling as well. UP already had a smooth and efficient relationship with it that would hardly be improved by single ownership. Acquisition would raise the hackles of other western railroads and spur them to counteractions. The ICC might impose conditions that would make the cure worse than the disease. Political repercussions could result in the states traversed by CNW. The financial community might balk at the price paid and downgrade UP's credit. CNW's vigorous campaign to reduce labor costs could be undermined if the unions thought a buyer with deep pockets loomed.[17]

At the September 9 meeting the railroad men formally recommended that CNW be acquired at a price in the low to mid-thirties. The timing for the meeting could not have been worse. Lewis was about to replace Cook as chairman and looked to broaden Cook's vision of a diversified empire. UPC had already acquired Overnite, had formed UP Technologies in May, was in the process of buying USPCI, and was trying to gain control of the Katy. The idea of swallowing another debt-heavy railroad held no appeal for Cook or Lewis. Despite the strong argument put forth by the railroad, the decision was made to take no action at the present time.[18]

Meanwhile, Wolfe struggled to keep CNW afloat. His attempt to introduce TQS to the railroad stumbled against resistance by workers who dismissed it as "happy horse shit." An attempt to restructure CNW's capitalization in 1988 flopped and was abandoned. The new policy of diversification faltered because the crushing debt burden of the railroad had to be lightened. To that end Wolfe sold off Douglas Dynamics in June 1988 and 1,035 miles of railroad in Wisconsin, Minnesota, and the Dakotas. The proceeds reduced the funded debt by $135 million in 1988 alone.[19]

Along with coal, intermodal traffic remained a bright spot for CNW. It too bound CNW and UP closer together. UP first experimented with piggyback service in 1954 between Los Angeles and Salt Lake City and expanded it so rapidly that it had trouble providing enough flatcars. In 1973 CNW suggested creating a dedicated, high-speed intermodal train across both lines that could cut twenty-four hours off the existing schedule. The growing eastbound traffic led UP to introduce its own train, known as "Super Van," from Los Angeles to Chicago over CNW.[20]

Gradually TOFC gave way to COFC (container on flatcar) as the preferred form of intermodal traffic. UP went into the container business during the 1960s and by 1969 was expanding its facilities in three major cities and buying more equipment. CNW began running COFC unit trains in 1977. The four-way pact in 1981 between UP, CNW, APL, and Transway International drew the two railroads even closer together. Three years later they began running doublestack container service between the West Coast and Chicago. Within a year CNW was averaging 1,500 doublestack units a week. To handle this growing surge of traffic, the road completed in November 1986 a new $36 million doublestack facility called Global One near Chicago.[21]

Wolfe also worked hard to rid CNW of archaic work rules. In the spring of 1985 he unveiled a manpower reduction program that cut the average number of employees by 15 percent in one year. The crew-size issue emerged as his pet project. In May 1987 CNW served notice on the UTU that it intended to alter the labor agreement. The talks that followed dragged on into 1988 with little progress. Wolfe was adamant that crews had to be reduced from four to two, with an estimated savings of $61 million.[22]

During 1988 UP's policy of watchful waiting received a severe jolt. By selling off Douglas Dynamics Wolfe committed the company to focusing anew on the railroad. His tough stance on labor led the UTU to reject mediation that spring. CNW followed suit, leading the National Mediation Board to withdraw its efforts and triggering a thirty-day cooling-off period. Two days before its end President Reagan created a Presidential Emergency Board (PEB) to study the dispute. Both sides agreed to maintain the status quo until August 3; on August 4 the UTU struck CNW. Four days later Jim Wolfe died of colon cancer, an illness he had concealed from his board and colleagues for several years.[23]

In his place came Robert W. Schmiege, an attorney who had done a brief stint with SP before rejoining CNW. Schmiege made clear his determination to continue the tough, no-nonsense management approach of his predecessors;

however, he had a smoother, less confrontational style. Where Wolfe could be imperious, Schmiege preferred consensus and was more open with employees and shippers alike. But Schmiege shared Wolfe's keen understanding of CNW's precarious position.[24]

Both CNW and UP had a very good year in 1988. Schmiege called it "one of the most eventful years in the history of the CNW Corporation." Pretax income soared to $43.4 million, compared to a $55,000 loss in 1987. Revenues grew 10.7 percent, WRPI's pretax income jumped more than 25 percent, grain loadings and steel loadings were the best since 1980, and automotive traffic rose 35.6 percent. The labor skies brightened as Congress imposed a settlement allowing CNW trains to run with three- instead of four-man crews beginning May 22, 1989. Rates ceased their downward spiral and climbed somewhat. Intermodal continued to flourish, straining the capacity of Global One. Plans were drawn for a second, larger facility, Global Two. More than $72 million went for improvements.[25]

In July 1988 UP revisited the question of what to do about CNW. Walsh, Rebensdorf, and Jim Dolan met with Bill McDonald and Ed Hill of UPC and Ted Tetzlaff of Jenner & Block, an attorney close to Walsh, to plot a course of action. Several parties seemed close to making offers for CNW. To counter these threats, they wanted UPC to fashion a buyout proposal for CNW in which the company held only a minority position. The deal had to be friendly and endorsed by CNW's management, and it needed support from labor. A full merger was not on the table; the object was to "avoid financial consolidation of CNW into UP." The most desirable way to accomplish this was as a partner in a leveraged buyout.[26]

A proposal was formulated and sent to Lewis, who liked the idea but did not want to pursue it "unless CNW was to find itself in a situation hostile to either itself or UP." In other words, noted a disappointed Rebensdorf, "we will put the proposal on the shelf for now." It did not gather dust for long. In November 1988 representatives of Japonica Partners, an investor group, met with Schmiege and his senior officers to discuss the "value gap" between CNW's stock price and its potential value.[27]

On March 13, 1989, Japonica disclosed that it had acquired 8.8 percent of CNW's stock and might seek control of the company. That same day it wrote Schmiege describing its role as a "proactive white knight and as a positive alternative to your current board members." Schmiege labeled the bid a hostile takeover by a "gang of corporate raiders." His fear was that Japonica would follow the current fad of buying a company and dismembering it to realize more from sale of the parts than it paid for the whole.[28]

Two days later another investor group, Blackstone Capital Partners, informed Schmiege of its desire to acquire CNW. Schmiege replied that the management had no interest in the proposal. However, on March 16 Japonica declared its intention to nominate eight directors for the CNW board. Early in April it began soliciting proxies from CNW stockholders, then offered to acquire all outstanding CNW shares at a price of $44. Schmiege and his senior managers huddled with a financial advisor and representatives from Donaldson, Lufkin & Jenrette (DLJ) to explore the possibility of a management-led buyout. On April 29 the CNW board appointed a special committee to consider the Japonica offer and alternatives. It hoped to find other, more friendly buyers.[29]

Clearly CNW was in play. On February 28 it had declared its first-ever dividend on the common stock, which Schmiege called "a milestone in the history of the company." A DLJ analyst admitted being "unable to unearth an investment vehicle in a related industry that has been examined and dissected in more different ways than has CNW Corp." After a detailed study the analyst concluded that it was worth $38 a share undiluted. "Unless there is total short-line freedom," he added, "it makes no sense to us for anyone to buy CNW as an *entity*." Yet less than two months later DLJ considered doing just that.[30]

These developments caught UP off guard. At the annual stockholders meeting on April 21, Lewis said flatly that "we have no plans whatsoever to acquire C&NW. We think the price is in excess of its value." But something had to be done. On May 3 Lewis and White Matthews met with Walsh to discuss options. Lewis complained that the railroad had not made clear to UPC the strategic importance of CNW, that it should have pursued purchase of the road when the price was lower, and that its negligence had created a situation where CNW's price had gone beyond economic reason.[31]

Walsh left the meeting steaming over these charges. "To put it mildly," he wrote in steely tones the next day, "we are concerned and dismayed over these statements." He shipped a packet of seven key documents with summaries to Bethlehem with his memo. "A close reading of these documents," he declared, "will demonstrate that the Railroad has been very clear on its position regarding CNW, on the strategic importance of CNW, and on our desire to obtain control of CNW."[32]

In particular Walsh reminded Lewis of the September 9, 1987, meeting at which the railroad made a formal recommendation to acquire CNW at a price in the low to mid-thirties. The incident became one more source of friction between Lewis and Walsh, but the point was made. On May 12 UP secured an option to buy the Iowa Interstate line as a pointed reminder that the company had other options if CNW fell into hostile hands. The 533-mile road consisted of the old RI line between Chicago and Omaha along with five branches. It was clearly inferior to CNW but could be made formidable with UP money behind it. UP, said Lewis, was "not going to be held hostage to a takeover."[33]

On May 25 Walsh briefed the UPC board on the importance of CNW as the company's best connection to Chicago. He reviewed the possible alternatives, including the Iowa Interstate, and concluded that none could match the value of CNW. A situation had arisen, he added, that would enable UP to acquire an interest in CNW, and it should be seized. The board approved investing up to $150 million in CNW and another $150 million if needed later for upgrading the line. At long last UP was prepared to act.[34]

Meanwhile, Schmiege searched desperately for ways to fend off the hostile bid. At a May 1 meeting Japonica demanded that the special committee enter a merger agreement within seventy-two hours. The committee stalled with requests for more information. During the next few days Schmiege's group agreed to partner with Blackstone and DLJ. The CNW annual meeting was scheduled for May 16; Japonica went public with its $44 offer four days before the meeting. The stockholders rejected Japonica's slate and elected all the directors recommended by CNW board. However, the Japonica offer still stood.[35]

The labor unions revived the idea of returning CNW to partial employee ownership, but Schmiege needed a friendly buyer with more muscle. Blackstone and DLJ appeared to be suitable partners. Blackstone at least knew something about railroads, having acquired USX's large railroad and shipping system in December 1988. "We've learned the railroad business and want to get deeper involved in the industry," said Blackstone's president. To gain more leverage, Blackstone approached UP on May 12 to join the partners.[36]

It was an invitation UP dared not refuse. After extensive negotiations UP agreed to buy $100 million of preferred stock on condition that CNW agree to invest enough capital to "maintain a high quality of service on the East-West main line." With these agreements in place, the special committee refused on May 23 to take a position on the Japonica offer. Instead it recommended that the company hold an auction with a deadline of June 2. The Blackstone coalition included not only DLJ and UP but Schmiege's own senior managers, who concluded that they had found the most suitable and profitable white knight. On June 2, 1989, the special committee received four bids, of which Blackstone's was the highest. After four more days of negotiation to improve the terms, the special committee recommended acceptance of the Blackstone bid, and the CNW board promptly approved it.[37]

The agreement turned CNW into a private company and provided $300 million for capital improvements. In November 1988 Walsh had complained that CNW was "undermaintaining and under-investing." Under the agreement $40 million would be spent in 1989 and another $115 million through 1992 to maintain and improve the Chicago–Fremont line. Moreover, UP's $100 million in CNW preferred shares was convertible after five years into 25 percent of the road's common stock.[38]

UP's relationship with CNW had been preserved but at a steep price and with a cumbersome organization. A holding company, Chicago and North Western Holdings Company, controlled another holding company, Chicago and North Western Acquisition Corporation, which controlled CNW Corporation, the parent of the railroad's Chicago and North Western Transportation Company. The deal saddled Holdings with more than $750 million in long-term debt, forcing the railroad into a new round of belt-tightening. Much depended on how well the railroad fared under the new arrangement. In securing the relationship UP put itself in a position where it could do nothing with its CNW stock for five years, and a lot could happen in that time.[39]

The vision of a transcontinental railroad has floated through railroad history at least since Jay Gould and Collis P. Huntington put forward plans for the One Big Railroad in 1888. George Gould, Jay's eldest son, tried to realize this vision during the 1900s. Although utterly unequal to the challenge, he built the WP as the western leg of his system. Some thought that E. H. Harriman aspired to create a line stretching from coast to coast, but he died before his plans became clear. Except for an occasional dreamer, the idea of such a system remained dormant until the merger mania of the late twentieth century revived it. With three major systems in the East and four in the West, a transcontinental system could be created with only one more merger.

The key question was whether any such merger made sense. During the summer of 1986 Lewis asked for a report comparing the three eastern roads as potential merger partners for UP. The report concluded that all three systems were important to UP. No single system covered all desirable markets, and each one had routes that were more efficient than the others.[40]

UP did not revisit the issue until January 1988, when P&A looked again at a potential merger with Conrail. Two months later the shifting chessboard prompted another analysis of the broader strategic picture. The Rio Grande was buying the SP, leaving the SF isolated and uncertain about its future. These events might lead to renewed efforts to forge a transcontinental line if one of the eastern systems decided to breach the traditional midcontinent dividing line. Moreover, intermodal traffic had become an important growth sector for UP, which prompted "reconsideration of transcontinental acquisitions as a possible strategy for improving traffic, service, and margins." The result was a lengthy paper in April that explored the subject in detail.[41]

Intended to be provocative rather than comprehensive, the paper declared, "Our transcontinental analysis and plans are subservient to our overall long term merchandise growth strategy." Merchandise (intermodal) traffic held the highest potential and most uncertainty for future growth because it offered the most promising avenue for the UP to escape the narrow confines of being a "coal and bulk" road. Bulk commodities tended to have short hauls, could be highly cyclical, grew slowly, and had a high proportion of transport cost in their delivered product value. The latter point gave shippers strong incentives to cut rates by any means possible. For these reasons merchandise traffic offered more potential for long-term growth.[42]

However, this growth potential was more volatile than that for bulk traffic because its origins lay outside UP's control. For most of its bulk traffic UP served as originator, while merchandise traffic in the form of container shipments originated elsewhere. Through its contracts with APC and other shipping firms UP had invested heavily in merchandise traffic. If it did represent the wave of the future, ownership of a transcontinental line would be a decided advantage. Doublestack service offered the perfect example. Begun only four years earlier, it had already emerged as "the most important innovation in the railroad industry since dieselization." The service had the potential to achieve 40 percent savings over conventional TOFC and involved longer hauls. The debate centered on whether UP should acquire a container ship company and get directly into the business or whether it should become an even more primary service provider by securing key connecting rail links.[43]

In 1987 UP interchanged almost equal amounts of traffic with Conrail and CSX, which exceeded that with NS by 53 percent. If, therefore, a transcontinental merger movement broke out, UP should look first to protect its Conrail and CSX interchanges. If UP took the initiative, the picture grew less clear. Each eastern system had its advantages and drawbacks; the choice might well come down to how important merchandise traffic became and which eastern system offered the best connection for it. On that basis alone Conrail seemed the most desirable partner. However, any such move would first require securing the CNW's Fremont–Chicago line. No transcontinental merger would be possible without it.[44]

Although internal discussions continued, the transcontinental issue lay dormant until the winter of 1989, when the rumor mill revived it. Early in February Schmiege alerted Walsh that Conrail and SF were talking merger. John Rebensdorf learned that SF had a major study under way to see whether the road fit best with Conrail, NS, CSX, or BN. "It would appear," he informed Walsh, "as if Santa Fe is shopping around for a potential buyer for the railroad and may have made this known to potential purchasers." Rebensdorf's counterpart at CSX confided that his company was looking at smaller roads and was desirous of establishing a transcontinental system with UP at the top of its list and BN at the bottom.[45]

At Rebensdorf's request an analyst queried two officers at Conrail, who said that what Conrail wanted was strategic alliances that did not require a change of ownership. Gerald Grinstein, BN's president, also dismissed the rumor and said his company intended to seek an acquisition that would get it into northern

California. SP offered a real possibility. "Anschutz is playing with house money," he said, and would sell off SP, possibly in pieces, once he got his own money out of the company. These insights convinced Rebensdorf even more that the best course for UP was to "initiate strategy partnerships or alliances with Conrail," and he told Walsh as much.[46]

At a meeting on February 10 Walsh, Rebensdorf, and others surveyed the chessboard. Several roads were in play, but the SF posed the biggest problem because of its value as a transcontinental connection. Of the eastern systems NS was looking, CSX waiting, and Conrail vulnerable. Did UP really want to be a transcontinental road? If so, should it be preemptive or reactive? Which eastern system made the best fit? Or was UP better off as a major regional carrier? No decisions emerged from the session. To complicate matters, two separate sources told Rebensdorf that NS had begun exploratory talks with BN about a merger.[47]

On March 7 Walsh, Kenefick, and Dolan met with Lewis and the corporate staff. Three hours of discussion produced more questions than answers. Everyone agreed the status quo was preferable but difficult to maintain because of SF's role as a wild card. They also believed the national rail system was winnowing down to a few dominant carriers, which left everyone jockeying for position. Management changes also clouded the picture. Anschutz at Rio Grande/SP was an aggressive expansionist; so was Samuel Zell of Chicago-based Itel, which owned 20 percent of both SF and American President Companies, the largest container lessor in the world and a prime UP customer. Grinstein of BN was amenable to expanding.[48]

UP had four basic options. It could watch and wait, seize the initiative, react by choosing a transcontinental partner after some other road had done so, or accept its role as a regional system even if the other western carriers all became part of transcontinental systems. Nearly everyone at UP preferred the status quo because choosing one eastern system as a partner offered fewer benefits than the ability to work with all three systems. If one had to be chosen, it was a close call between Conrail and CSX. Conrail offered the greatest potential but also the greatest risk. The legislation that privatized Conrail in 1987 also gave it three years of protection against a takeover. This provision would expire on April 1, 1990. Would NS or someone else make a run at Conrail then?[49]

Nor was this all. As Rebensdorf reminded the board in July, "A final factor contributing to instability is corporate restructuring in America. There is a lot of money out there looking to do deals and railroads are now an attractive target." Japonica might seek another railroad after its run at the CNW. Given Zell's large stake in both the SF and APC, he might try to move the latter's intermodal business from the UP to the SF. Nor could the CNW be forgotten; preserving that link remained more important than almost any other consideration.[50]

Late that fall UPC and the railroad undertook a new round of studies, now dubbed "Project Lincoln," on the three eastern systems based on two scenarios: each railroad remained independent or merged with UP. These efforts lasted into the winter, by which time changing conditions had lessened the pressure to merge. Anschutz and SP were beset with financial woes that removed them as a transcontinental threat. Zell too seemed to be concentrating on internal issues at both SF and APC. Conrail adopted a poison pill tactic to frustrate a takeover, and the stocks of all three eastern roads were trading at near record highs. "The numbers, even with somewhat aggressive assumptions," Walsh wrote Lewis, "don't play out, either on a stand-alone or a merged basis."[51]

These factors led Walsh to conclude that "we don't think that initiating a transcontinental merger at this point in time makes sense. . . . We don't see any reason to be first—and to take the 'heat'—since we believe UP is the preferred merger partner with all three eastern carriers. As well, we are not sure whether our preferred choice is Conrail or CSX."[52]

Although discussion of Project Lincoln continued, a stunning shift in financial conditions undercut the urgency of the issue. The junk bond market collapsed in the wake of Drexel Burnham Lambert's bankruptcy, making LBOs more difficult and driving raiders to cover. An air of conservatism, stressing equity over debt, crept over Wall Street. Conrail launched a $1.3 billion restructuring that reduced its cash holdings and increased its debt, making it less attractive as a takeover. Walsh talked to the heads of all three eastern systems, and none expressed any desire to initiate a transcontinental system. In the West Anschutz struggled with SP's weak performance and Zell looked to unload SF after first spinning off its oil and land companies. BN also underwent a financial restructuring and was more concerned with internal affairs than transcontinental expansion.[53]

Both Walsh and Lewis had worked actively to convince the industry and Wall Street that they had no interest in a transcontinental merger. The moment had passed. If it came again UP would stand ready, but neither the railroad nor its customers showed any enthusiasm for such a merger. However, the weak links in the industry remained the SF and the SP. Both had capable leaders who would not let their companies drift for very long.[54]

PART THREE

THE DAVIDSON ERA, 1992–2004

21

The Empire

By 1990 no one could doubt that UP had departed from many of its traditional ways. Every year Lewis acknowledged as much in the company's annual report. "At the Railroad," he said in 1988, "the cost-cutting, consolidation, work force reduction and reorganization programs of the past two years have brought about a complete transformation." A year later he declared that "the search for new efficiencies has become a way of life for Mike Walsh and the Railroad." In 1990 he boasted that "at Union Pacific Railroad we have achieved a cultural change of sweeping proportions.... Underlying this achievement is a total commitment to change."[1]

If, as Lewis noted, the railroad was on the right track, what about the corporation? During the late 1980s the UPC empire reached its apex. In the beginning it had sought only to separate out the nonrail assets to better manage and protect them. Under Cook and Lewis this intent was enlarged to the more ambitious goal of a diversified company in which the parts formed a synergistic whole and functioned smoothly together. The company turned into a transportation conglomerate that included energy, waste disposal, real estate, and technology components as well.

During Lewis's reign as emperor of UPC, its trajectory ran a bell-shaped curve that could be traced in the annual reports. In his first year Lewis radiated enthusiasm and optimism in laying down the direction he planned to take. He concluded his remarks by saying, over Schuster's strenuous objections, "Not only am I excited about the potential of our company, but I look upon this as a job that will be a lot of fun."[2]

A year later, in 1988, Lewis highlighted the parade of changes, including UPC's move to Bethlehem, the forthcoming consolidation of the regional offices of UP Resources into its Fort Worth headquarters, and the shift of UP Realty from Omaha to Dallas. Resources continued to be plagued by fluctuating energy prices, which prompted the corporation to get out of the refining business altogether. "By divesting itself of these downstream operations," Lewis explained, "Union Pacific Resources will be able to focus on its forte—exploration and development." UP Realty was "transforming itself into an integrated land and building development company," while USPCI had been strengthened and enlarged to realize its great promise.[3]

The optimism in Lewis's messages never faded, but privately his thinking had already begun to shift. In March 1989 he noted that UPC had been evaluating a range of alternatives for increasing shareholder value. Consultants had been hired to explore "spin-offs, sales and other restructuring of all U.P. subsidiaries in all imaginable combinations and permutations. . . . We are continuing to look at all options and have not ruled out any, recognizing that doing anything with the railroad is unlikely."[4]

Lewis was leaning toward four actions but had not yet committed to them: repurchasing $1–$2 billion worth of UP stock; selling off UP Realty; spinning off Resources or turning it into a joint venture; and divesting Overnite through an LBO. At the stockholders' meeting in April 1989 Lewis admitted that "we are currently looking at restructuring." In discussing the subsidiaries he said flatly, "We're in the railroad business, and in the railroad business to stay."[5]

Resources did well in its first year as a pure exploration, production, and minerals company. As for the still underperforming USPCI, Lewis noted that "Jack Messman has his new management team in place and working to fulfill the profit potential this business holds. . . . We remain fully committed to USPCI's success and expect marked bottom-line improvement in 1990."[6]

Arch Jacobson had done a terrific job in restructuring UP Realty. Lewis had hoped to develop properties and create a major real estate company, but access, environmental, zoning, and other issues complicated that objective. In December 1989 he sold off most of UP Realty's assets to a land development company. "The sale is part of our plan to realize the full potential of the corporation's assets," he explained, "and to focus our energies on our core businesses." In June UPC took another step in that direction by acquiring the $100 million worth of CNW preferred stock. It also bought back 13.3 million of its own shares, reducing its outstanding stock to about 100 million shares.[7]

Resources posed a thorny problem. "We have sold off the refineries," Lewis said. "We are out of a lot of the mines, which are very capital intensive, despite the fact we still have seven million acres of oil and natural resources, potential reserves on ground that we own either in fee or through mineral and oil rights." What bothered Lewis most was that "unfortunately our prices are determined by OPEC." The options remained open on Resources.[8]

During the early 1990s the subsidiaries continued to struggle. Overnite got a new CEO, Tom Boswell, and a new organization along regional lines in 1990. Despite a decent performance, it remained a leader in an industry with operating problems that seemed impossible to surmount. Two glaring weaknesses could never be overcome: The company had paid much too much for Overnite, and the highly touted synergies with the railroad never developed.[9]

Although Lewis never fully warmed to the Overnite acquisition, he tried hard to make it work. UPC pumped money into the company for expansion. In 1988 alone it received $56 million to buy 723 new tractors and 2,107 new trailers along with another $20 million for UP Technologies to upgrade its data processing capabilities. By 1991 Overnite had a network of 150 terminals serving every major metropolitan market in the contiguous 48 states. UP also introduced its quality program to Overnite.[10]

USPCI was another matter. Where Overnite had been Cook's legacy, USPCI was Lewis's deal. He believed ardently in the future of waste management and its synergy with the railroad. It owned major disposal sites in Utah and Oklahoma, both approved to accept Superfund waste, and a set of transfer stations. To realize its potential he had provided generous amounts of capital for expansion and development. Although the company continued to flounder, nothing could shake Lewis's faith in Messman.[11]

Other officers did not share his estimation of Messman. One described him as a person whose "values were on the edge and business judgment was poor." The normally circumspect Carl von Bernuth said bluntly that "he made mistake after mistake." Messman was notorious for demanding ever more capital for his company on the basis of extravagant projections of future growth. In one management meeting he stood up and said, in effect, I'm gold; give the money to me, not the railroad. To wheedle capital from the board he posited grand scenarios of future profits with no basis in fact. "I remember sitting in presentations that Jack and [his] people would do," said von Bernuth, "where projections showed rates of return which were frankly unbelievable."[12]

One such presentation resulted in a comeuppance for Messman. He brought in outside consultants for a major presentation that showed huge growth rates for the hazardous materials business. Dick Mahoney, the CEO of Monsanto Chemical, who had joined the board in 1991, listened with mounting impatience. When the consultants finished, he denounced their spiel as the craziest thing he had ever heard. I'm in the chemical business, he said; we produce hazardous waste. It's incredibly expensive to dispose of, and we're all seeking ways to eliminate or reduce it. This disposal business is not going to grow and make a lot of money; it's going to get smaller and smaller. Anyone who doesn't understand this fact simply doesn't know what he's talking about.[13]

After the meeting Mahoney lambasted the consultants for either not doing their homework or being dishonest. "And he turned out to be right," said von Bernuth. ". . . There was a feeling that Jack Messman . . . was making investments for the sake of expanding his empire." The most egregious of Messman's many mistakes at USPCI was the construction of a mammoth incinerator capable of handling 130,000 tons of waste a year at Clive, Utah. "Drew basically took some money from the railroad to give to USPCI to spend," said a disgruntled Jim Dolan. ". . . Cost twice as much as anyone ever thought. . . . That alone made USPCI an investment disaster."[14]

Projected to open in 1993, the $140 million incinerator still had not gone into service in September 1994. By then USPCI had done so poorly that a disillusioned Lewis saw little choice but to cut his losses. Having consistently boosted the company and its prospects, he finally admitted in 1994 that "for the past several years, USPCI had been a disappointment to Union Pacific." At a time when the trash business was booming, at least in the East, he sold USPCI to a Canadian firm for $225 million. UPC swallowed a loss of nearly $200 million on the transaction along with the money it had pumped into the company. "It was a huge write-off, a huge loss on the company," said Davidson.[15]

Gerry viewed the USPCI fiasco as an error in judgment by both Lewis and the board. "We were the largest shipper of hazardous waste," he said, "so that seemed like something that could be synergistic. It wasn't. Put on more liabilities and headaches than it did profitability." Later Lewis confessed that "without question, my worst decision was USPCI."[16]

Although USPCI joined UP Realty in the dustbin of empire, Lewis did not blame Messman. Instead he gave him what amounted to a promotion. In 1991, well before the sale, Messman moved to UP Resources as president and CEO beneath chairman Bill Adams. When Adams retired in 1993, Messman took charge of the company. The man whose job he took, Robert S. Jackson, had assumed he would one day move into the top job at Resources. Instead he found himself presiding over USPCI when it was cut loose from UP. "The guy . . . was given this dying, terrible, money-losing business as a sop," said von Bernuth. Loyalty, it seemed, mattered most to Lewis, just as the lack of loyalty enraged him.[17]

Nearly everyone who worked with Walsh agreed that he was tough and demanding. "A lot of people thought he was a slave driver," said John Marchant, who didn't share that view. "Some of the old guard at the railroad, they weren't used to being challenged like he challenged them. . . . When he had them in a meeting . . . the old prosecutor in him would come out and there would be cross examinations . . . very, very pointed, direct questions. He would lead the witness. He knew what he was doing. . . . He was very smart, and you just didn't bullshit him at all. And that made people very uncomfortable."[18]

Other officers, especially younger ones like Charley Eisele and Jack Koraleski, adored Walsh and what he brought to the railroad. The Walsh ego rubbed some people the wrong way, Koraleski conceded, and Walsh often didn't recognize it. "When you got crosswise with him," Koraleski added, "he would be very direct. You knew immediately what the issue was." But Walsh never carried a grudge.

Koraleski considered him "a great role model" and admired the way he developed young people. "He fundamentally believed that one of the greatest things that we had going for us was when we brought new people into the company," he said.[19]

To those with open minds Walsh became a superb educator. "He taught people important things," said Eisele, "but he taught them in ways that you would never forget . . . always found a way to make that indelible impression on you." Art Shoener became an eager student. "I learned a lot from him," he declared. ". . . The thing with Mike, you're either going to learn and change or you're going to find a job someplace else."[20]

The operating men got this message loud and clear from Walsh after a rash of derailments. They had grown accustomed to being left alone by him, but one Saturday morning—their special time and turf—Walsh summoned them to his office and reamed them out for losing touch with the quality program. Eisele happened to be there and was shocked at the outburst. "They saw a side of him they never saw before," he said. "I will guarantee you every single one of those guys came out of that meeting knowing exactly what the problem was. . . . I don't think he ever had another one of those meetings."[21]

Off duty Walsh left very different impressions on people. Dennis Jacobson thought he was not at all a people person. However, Gary Schuster described Walsh as a "fun guy. I remember I was at a party at his house. We put on Motown records and he was out dancing, he and his wife, Joan." Koraleski found him to be "wildly extroverted and enthusiastic, very talkative, very uninhibited . . . willing to have a good time even at his own expense. . . . He could talk to anybody about anything."[22]

On one occasion Dick Davidson saw a side of Walsh few people had ever experienced. The officers were at the NITL meeting at the Greenbrier, a large, rather stuffy gathering that featured more golf, eating, and drinking than business. UP had five or six tables, each one with five or six customers and two railroad officials. Walsh sat at one table with several important customers and UP marketing official John Sirois, who had a reputation for being a practical joker.[23]

At the end of the meal, they enjoyed an expensive after-dinner drink. Walsh, never much of a drinker, nevertheless ordered another round for the table. Sirois discovered that the supply had run out and filled the bottle with water as a joke. He poured a drink for Walsh, who took a sip and spit it out. Infuriated, he grabbed the bottle and emptied it on Sirois's head. "Sirois, in self-defense," said Davidson, "grabbed Mike and they fell on the floor right there in this stuffy goddamn resort in front of all the customers." Appalled at the sight of them rolling around the floor wrestling, Davidson hurried out of the room behind Fred Henderson.

They took refuge with some other railroad officers in a small waiting room trying to figure out what to do. "My God, we can never talk about this," Davidson concluded, "never admit that it happened, 'cause we wanted to protect Mike, and we thought, Well, Sirois's fired." Joan Walsh walked by on her way to her room, her face wreathed in a stern expression after giving her husband hell for his behavior. Sirois followed soon after, and behind him came Walsh, shuffling along with his head down. Sirois lay awake most of the night waiting for the phone call telling him he was fired, but it never came. Next morning everyone behaved as if nothing had happened.

While promoting the next phase of his transformation, Walsh remained active in the Omaha community. He and Joan had come to enjoy the city and believed strongly in civic spirit. Walsh helped raise $700,000 to benefit inner-city kids. In June 1990 he joined with Warren Buffett and Walter Scott to buy a 50 percent stake in the Triple-A Omaha Royals baseball team and keep them in the city. Rob Knight, himself a former center fielder, took charge of finances for the Royals. "It was," he said, "just something I did on the side."[24]

Shortly after the purchase some of Walsh's staff composed a parody memo to amuse the office. "The positions of pitcher and second baseman are consolidated," it read. "The position of shortstop is abolished. Ditto the right fielder, third baseman and catcher. The changes will minimize duplication of responsibilities, maximize profit potential, improve pace of play and heighten fan excitement."[25]

Walsh also looked beyond UP to the industry itself. It bothered him that every reform he instigated stopped at the terminus where traffic was handed off to other roads. It annoyed him even more that the industry's representative organization, the AAR, had grown stodgy and uncreative. The AAR had 720 employees and a budget of $80 million to lobby for the railroads, conduct research and development, and help railroads exchange information. Of that budget $55 million came from dues paid by the railroads—UP alone contributed $7.5 million—and the rest from data processing and research operations fees. A Boise Cascade official was not alone in complaining that "the AAR hasn't done enough to make the railroads a more efficient network."[26]

Walsh was appalled by the sleepy performance of the AAR and said as much. Despite being one of the youngest rail executives, he rounded up enough support to shake up the organization. A new position, chairman, was created to oversee longtime president William Dempsey, and Walsh won the job. He then endeared himself to the AAR staff by telling a reporter that he found the organization's political and public policy apparatus "moribund and unfocused," and that nothing happened at board meetings because the directors came to meetings ill prepared and concerned mostly about defending their own narrow interests.[27]

His supporters agreed with this assessment. Before Walsh's arrival, said David Hughes of the Bangor & Aroostook Railroad, "the AAR was overstaffed and underguided. . . . The board of directors . . . had gone to sleep for a decade. Walsh energized it." One issue in particular galled Walsh. UP's quality program had identified broken wheels as the chief cause of derailments. Walsh informed the

AAR of this finding and pushed for other roads to replace the type of wheels prone to failure, but his efforts made little progress. Once Walsh gained his new position, the AAR's director of rules and inspections allowed as how wheel replacement would be speeded up. Dempsey announced that he would retire at year's end.[28]

By 1991 Walsh had planted himself firmly atop the UP Railroad and become a force within the industry. He had imposed a sea change on the culture of the railroad and laid out an ambitious agenda for its continuation. Some railroaders grumbled at his style and complained about the pace of change, but no one could deny that the railroad was performing better. Then one day in August 1991 the whirlwind departed as quickly as he had come.

No one in Omaha saw it coming. "I don't think any of us had a clue," said Linda Waller. ". . . I mean, it just happened like within an instant." Stan McLaughlin had the same reaction: "He was here one day and basically gone the next." Walsh's own secretary was on vacation at the time and had to hurry back. Davidson was at a horse show in Tulsa with his daughter Elizabeth when he received a message from Lewis saying something big was up and ordering him back to Omaha immediately. Elizabeth asked whether he was being fired, and Davidson didn't have an answer.[29]

Once back, Davidson learned that Walsh had left the company. "Drew asked me to be president," said Davidson, "which I wasn't sure I wanted. I loved the operating department. I had done it for so long and was quite comfortable there. And I didn't think I'd like all the political and social and other things, but I told him I'd give it a whirl with the understanding I might ask for my old job back at some point." When Lewis told Gerry the news, he asked whether attempts were made to keep Walsh. "We tried," replied Lewis, "but we can't do it." Gerry called Walsh himself. Unable to budge him, he agreed that they had to go with Davidson.[30]

On August 8 the *New York Times* and *Wall Street Journal* reported that Walsh had been named chairman of Tenneco, a giant but troubled conglomerate based in Houston, and that Davidson would replace him at UP. Omaha and Bethlehem alike buzzed with speculation over why Walsh had left so abruptly. Everyone knew he had lofty ambitions. "Mike came to UP because it's a very visible company," said von Bernuth, who knew Walsh better than most. "He felt he could have a dramatic impact on the company. And he felt that it would be a staging ground, if not to be CEO of UP [then] to be CEO of another company. And he had a time period to do that. And then he had a time period after that to go into politics."[31]

Art Shoener and Brad King wondered whether Walsh had grown bored with the job once his changes started to take root. "He stayed two years too long," said King. ". . . I just didn't see the energy I saw the first three years." Eisele agreed that "he thought his job was done at UP. . . . Spent five years, he'd molded it. Got it thinking in a different way. He had produced a long string of record financials. What was left was stewardship and disciplined execution. Enter Dick Davidson." Tenneco was for Walsh the next rung on the ladder.[32]

Gary Schuster knew Walsh was frustrated. The phone calls from Lewis had grown more frequent and incomprehensible. There were also confrontations when Lewis and Matthews came out for the annual budget meetings or when Walsh went to Bethlehem for board presentations. Above all, the job Walsh wanted belonged to Lewis, who showed no inclination to leave. If Lewis stayed on until retirement, it meant for Walsh another five years of a relationship filled with mounting tensions and frustrations. He wasn't prepared to accept that wait, especially given the possibility that he might not be the chosen heir after all.[33]

Several officers were convinced that Lewis was grooming not Walsh but Messman as his successor. "It was obvious that Drew had designs on making Messman the chairman," said Davidson, "so I know that was one of the things that motivated Mike Walsh to leave . . . and Drew didn't like Walsh. . . . There is only room for so many egos in a company like that. Drew had a pretty substantial ego himself." Jim Dolan agreed that Walsh "was ready to leave the railroad. . . . Mike was a builder and a changer. I don't think he was a minder."[34]

All these considerations made Walsh receptive when headhunters came calling. As the negotiations with Tenneco proceeded, Lewis got wind of them through a friend on that company's board. When Lewis confronted him about the negotiations, Walsh made an uncharacteristic mistake: He denied that he was looking for a new job. Headhunters had come to him, he admitted, but he had put them off.[35]

Shortly after this conversation Walsh realized his mistake and called Lewis back to apologize, but it was too late. In Lewis's mind Walsh had been disloyal. "Drew was hot," said Matthews, "'cause loyalty . . . you're running out on me and then you lie to me." Lewis told Walsh he knew the job had been offered to him and said coldly that he ought to accept it. "That was really the end of the relationship," said Schuster. All Walsh said later was that Lewis was "supportive" of his decision to leave.[36]

Omaha received the news with mingled regret and relief. Many were sorry to see Walsh go but thought he had gone on to a bigger job. Davidson understood that for Walsh Tenneco was "a bird in the hand." Marchant thought there were "a lot of sighs of relief when he left," largely because "he demanded a lot and he just worked the shit out of people."[37]

Whatever their feelings about his departure, everyone agreed that Walsh had transformed UP in many important ways. Matthews told Walsh he was proud of him because the railroad industry had never been known for good management, and no one could remember when a major corporation had chosen a rail executive to be its CEO. At Tenneco Walsh got off to his usual fast start; ten days after taking office he cut the company's dividend in half. A short time later he cut eight thousand jobs and unveiled a $2 billion restructuring plan while leaving a trail of publicity in his wake. However, the revamping of Tenneco proved a tougher job than he anticipated, and fate played a cruel trick on him.[38]

On January 20, 1993, Walsh sent to a dozen of his former colleagues at UP, including Kenefick, copies of a news release he had written and distributed that day. It informed the public that he had been diagnosed with an inoperable brain tumor. He vowed to stay on the job and fight the affliction. For more than a year he did just that, garnering even more publicity for his courageous battle against long odds. However, in February 1994, he stepped down from his post at Tenneco to battle the cancerous tumor. Less than three months later, on May 6, he died at the age of fifty-one.[39]

The whirlwind was gone, leaving behind him an impressive legacy of accomplishment. Matthews, who had fought many a battle with Walsh over budgets, gave a terse but fitting epitaph for his career at UP. "A good guy," he said. "I mean, a really good guy. . . . What he did for the railroad was incredible."[40]

The empire depended heavily on the railroad, and the railroad had lost its leader. Whatever Lewis thought of Walsh, he understood how successful he had been in transforming the railroad and making money for UPC. Whether Davidson could do as much remained an open question. He was a fine operating man and widely respected, but he had never occupied the top position. At first glance observers tended to see what Davidson lacked in comparison to Walsh. He did not have the latter's charisma; nor was he a wordsmith or articulator of visions. He seemed slow and deliberate when measured against the perpetual motion machine that was Walsh. To their eyes he was a good ol' country boy who had climbed the ladder of success one careful rung at a time and found himself unexpectedly at the top. Not knowing him well, they underestimated him.

Lewis knew Davidson could run the railroad but did not know whether he could do anything more. "Dick Davidson has the experience and management capability to carry on," he said in what was hardly a ringing endorsement. Although the country had stumbled into yet another recession in 1990, Walsh had kept earnings up. Could Davidson do as much? The question added one more item to a growing list of uncertainties troubling Lewis. Few of the acquisitions had turned out well, and decisions had to be made about some of them.[41]

It pained Lewis to think in these terms because he had envisioned so much for UPC. Shortly after arriving he had complained that the company lacked entrepreneurship and needed to find small, related enterprises that would grow into cash cows. Several ventures were explored, including a telephone company utilizing fiber-optics. Lewis rejected that one but sank money into several others along with the creation of UP Technologies and acquisition of the 30 percent share of Skyway, which ballooned to full ownership in May 1993. Some of the ideas came from friends who showed up at his office with proposals for projects that might make it big.[42]

In this role Lewis acted as an in-house venture capitalist, investing company money in projects he hoped would strike it rich. Then one day he had a revelation that left a bad taste in his mouth. He walked into Matthews's office and said morosely, "You know, all the little stuff that I've put money into, it's not worth a wreck on the Union Pacific. You get me out of all of it. How much money do you think I've blown?" Matthews assured him the company had plenty of cash and told him not to worry about it, but Lewis insisted on a figure. "I said $50 to $75 million," recalled Matthews. "It was higher than that. . . . There was no sense in jumping on the boss and saying, Look how stupid you were."[43]

Increasingly it became clear to Lewis that the railroad remained the heart and soul of the corporation. "Over a short period of time," said von Bernuth, "he really rejected the invest-in-other-than-railroad businesses and became a believer in the railroad." It helped that Walsh had demonstrated to him the railroad's ongoing value and potential. Ironically, five months after Walsh's departure an article in *Forbes* gave Lewis full credit for the railroad's turnaround without even mentioning Walsh.[44]

Partners:
Drew Lewis (left) and
his loyal spokesman,
Gary Schuster (right).

The Founders 1:
Roland Harriman is
interviewed aboard a
train while Bob Lovett
(left) sits quietly.
Robert Millard of the
Omaha National Bank
sits next to Lovett; the
other gentlemen are
not identified.

The Founders 2:
Jim Evans (left) and
Frank Barnett enjoy a
lighter moment.

Generations: Three generations of UP leadership chat at the dedication of Kenefick Park in Omaha. From left: John Kenefick, Dick Davidson, and Jim Young.

Young Turks: Four key figures in the UP's revitalization. Clockwise from top left: Barry Schaefer, John Rebensdorf, Tom Graves, and John Jorgensen.

Merger Leaders:
Mike Flannery, John Kenefick, and
Jim Gessner pose in front of the ICC
building during the UP/MP/WP
merger hearings.

Friendly Rivals:
Dick Davidson and
Jerry Davis shake hands
in front of UP and MP
locomotives.

**Mr. Inside
and Mr. Outside:**
Bill Cook (left) and
Jim Evans (right)

Budding Star: Dick Davidson early in his career.

Whirlwind at Rest: Mike Walsh in a rare moment of repose.

Outside Leaders: Ron Burns (left) and Ike Evans both came to the UP from other industries.

Stranger in a Strange Land: John Kenefick casts a dubious eye on some computer and communications equipment.

Nerve Center: John Jorgensen leans on a stack of reel tapes in the UP computer facility. An IBM 370 computer is at right behind him. (Courtesy John Jorgensen)

New Technology: A modern Track Renewal Train at work.

The MP Mafia: Dick Davidson and Downing Jenks study a map during an "Old Timers" special trip in 1992. Art Shoener sits behind them. (Courtesy Stanley J. McLaughlin)

Studying the Line: Reg Whitman (left) of the Katy, Downing Jenks, Dick Davidson, and John Kenefick share thoughts on an "Old Timers" special train in 1994. (Courtesy Stan McLaughlin)

Meeting of the Minds: The Union Pacific and Missouri Pacific managers and boards pose for a picture taken sometime during the merger process. Front row (seated): W. M. Shapleigh, D. B. Jenks, J. H. Evans, W. S. Cook, E. T. Gerry, J. C. Kenefick, and W. T. Smith. Second row: J. M. Kemper, R. L. Terrell, O. T. Lawler, W. F. Surette, W. A. Gray, Jr., R. W. Roth, H. H. Friday, V. F. Taylor, Jr., and H. H. Celment. Third row: J. C. Wilson, W. J. McDonald, J. H. Bascom, L. B. Harbour, Jr., C. L. Eaton, and M. K. Milliken. Fourth row: P. K. Carlton, M. F. Miller, R. D. Simmons, E. V. Conway, R. G. Flannery, W. D. Grant, S. F. Eccles, and J. D. Robinson.

Team Kenefick:
The newly merged Kenefick senior staff in 1985. Clockwise from left: Jerry Davis, Dick Davidson, Jim Dolan, Dick Ames, George Craig, Pat Barrett, Kenefick, Mike Flannery, Herb Grau, Joe McCartney, Bill Bales, Guerdon Sines, and Tom Watts.

Team Walsh:
Mike Walsh's senior staff in 1991. Seated on desk from left: Jack Koraleski, Fred Henderson, Charley Eisele, and Joe Adams. Standing from left: Tom Watts, Harris Wagenseil, Jim Hildreth, Walsh, Dick Davidson, Art Shoener, Barry Shuman, Jim Dolan, and John Rebensdorf.

Team Davidson:
Dick Davidson's senior staff in 2004. Seated at table from left: Ike Evans, Davidson, Jim Young, and Barb Schaefer. Standing from left: Charley Eisele, John Marchant, Mike Hemmer, Rob Knight, Mary McAuliffe, Stan McLaughlin, Bob Turner, Merill Bryan, Joe Adams, Jack Koraleski, Joe O'Connor, Jim Dolan, Dennis Duffy, Carl von Bernuth, and Brad King.

The Money Men:
Four key figures
in UPC finance.
Clockwise from top
left: Elbridge T. Gerry
Sr., Reginald Sutton,
White Matthews, and
Bill Surette.

Age and Youth:
Two generations of key
UP officers. Above from
left: Bob Brown and
Guerdon Sines. Below
from left: Dennis Duffy
and Stan McLaughlin.

Insiders: Four prominent UP staff members: Clockwise from top left: John Marchant, Dennis Jacobson, Mike Hemmer, and Merrill Bryan

New and Improved:
The refurbished Centennial
Yard in Fort Worth.
Fittingly, it was renamed
after Dick Davidson in 2007.
Courtesy Mike Bates.

Yard on Wheels: The intermodal facility at Wilmer, Texas. Courtesy Mike Bates.

Grain Going to the Far East: UP trains deliver grain to elevators at Tacoma, Washington, for export to Pacific Rim countries. Courtesy of the Union Pacific Railroad.

The Start of Something Great: The first CNW train carrying coal from the Powder River Basin bursts through the celebratory banner in 1984.

Loading Up: A coal train takes on its load in the Powder River Basin.

High-wire Act: As part of upgrading the Western Pacific line, a track crew installs heavy-duty rail across the Keddie Wye trestle in Feather River Canyon. The track to the left is the Northern California Extension leading to Oregon; the one to the right is the main line to the east. Courtesy of Union Pacific Railroad.

Crossroads: The Bailey Yard in North Platte, Nebraska, remains the busiest railroad yard in the world.

The Old and the New: (Above) The CTC control center at Kansas City in 1968. (Below) The big board at the Harriman Dispatching Center in Omaha.

Awaiting the Call to Duty: Rows of stored UP locomotives wait for a summons to active service.

Indoor Work: A diesel shop hard at work. Photo by Bob Ervin, courtesy of Union Pacific.

Home Base: The Omaha yard and shops in their salad days. The Missouri River is just to the left of the scene.

Headquarters: The old Union Pacific office building in Omaha as seen from the construction site of the new one. It has since been demolished.

Nature's Wrath: (Above) A section of track is left hanging by flood waters in the Sacramento River Valley. (Below) Freight cars surrounded by flood waters. The flood in February 1986 caused more than $50 million in damage and washed out dozens of locations over a 200-mile stretch of the former Western Pacific line. (Courtesy Stan McLaughlin)

The Improbable Leader

Everyone agreed that Davidson was the logical choice to succeed Walsh as president and CEO of the railroad, yet in many ways he seemed the most improbable of leaders. No one doubted his credentials as an operating officer, and many at the railroad thought an operating guy was exactly what was needed after Walsh. However, he could not have been more different from Walsh or Lewis. He was neither smooth nor polished and had no experience beyond the operations arena. He loved being vice president of operations. "The days were always too short," he said later. "You never got as much done as you'd like to."[1]

Not only was Davidson happiest in operations, he believed strongly that "the success or failure of a railroad company is almost totally attributable to operations. Even the success of the marketing department. If you don't have a good transportation product to sell, they're not going to have any luck." But the transformation of the 1980s made the railroad less the unique industry it had always been and more like other businesses. New technologies reconfigured the face of railroads, brought more outsiders into the company, and caused the workforce to evolve and shrink at the same time. The old pattern of boys following their fathers into jobs on the railroad gradually fell away.

The changing world of finance also exerted a strong impact on the industry. Railroaders complained that the bean counters had far too much control over what was done. They were right, but things could hardly have been otherwise. Increasingly the railroads, like so many other corporations, found themselves beholden to Wall Street. As one of the most capital-intensive industries, the carriers had of necessity to plan for the long term. But Wall Street's idea of the long term was measured in quarters. The fact that UPC had charge of finances complicated the problem because nobody was more keenly aware of the bottom line's effect on investors than the corporate officers.

Kenefick had mastered the art of extracting capital from the corporation, and Walsh had also done well at it. Retired though he might be, Kenefick still had an office in the headquarters building and came in every day. Grateful for the privilege, he took care to stay out of everyone's business unless asked for his views. Walsh did not hesitate to bring Kenefick into discussions on issues that he knew well. Younger officers welcomed his presence and still revered him. Davidson had not known Kenefick as long as other UP officers, but he too admired him and did not hesitate to seek his advice.[2]

One key question about Davidson's leadership was whether he could deal with UPC as effectively as his predecessors had done. He hardly rivaled Walsh's ability as the Great Communicator, but he had a quality no one in Bethlehem yet appreciated: a remarkable capacity for growth. Behind his simple manner lay a shrewd, thoughtful mind and strong will. "Actually he doesn't look nearly as smart as he is," said Jim Dolan. "Dick is a very smart person." Lou Anne Rinn had the same impression. "He is very good at portraying himself as being just a simple farm boy, but he is really a very complex personality."[3]

Nor did Davidson give away much of himself, even to people close to him. "He doesn't say much, so you don't ever know where his mind is," said Mary McAuliffe. ". . . He keeps to himself a lot. Truthfully, you don't even know if he likes you or respects you or anything. . . . He's very unemotional in the way he deals with you."[4]

These qualities shone through from the beginning of his reign. Where Walsh blew into the corner office like a whirlwind, Davidson ambled into it, looked around, and settled in comfortably. In his first message to the employees he lavished praise on Walsh. "Beginning in 1986," he said, "Mike took a bunch of skeptics—I was head of the class—and showed us just how good we could be. . . . We are a much different company than when Mike arrived. His legacy, in my view, is a commitment to excellence from every UP employee." His own goal, Davidson assured them, was to continue down the path Walsh had marked.[5]

The focus would remain the same—on customer service, commitment to quality, and financial targets—and Walsh's insistence on collegiality would continue as well. "The first time I heard Mike use that word five years ago," he said wryly, "there was a stampede to the dictionary to look up what it meant." Now Davidson was a disciple of collegiality, but he added a new dimension to its meaning. "Collegial means everybody helps the new president—I can use all the help I can get from everybody who works on this railroad."[6]

By the time of the third bimonthly message, Davidson's column bore a new title: "Straight Talk." As 1991 drew to a close the number of quality improvement teams had grown from five in 1990 to 325, and Davidson wanted more. "Mike had started the quality process," said Jack Koraleski, "but Dick is the one that just basically relentlessly drove it through the company. Stayed with the program, kept us focused on streamlining the organization, taking the failure cost out, improving our work—all the things that we needed to survive." When Walsh first asked him to spearhead the quality program, Davidson thought it meant that he had been sidetracked in his rivalry with Davis. Then he realized how important the quality program was to Walsh. The program provided another unexpected benefit: It was, he declared later, "another damn great learning experience because that kind of turned me loose to get involved in every single facet of the operation of the railroad."[7]

Now the quality program was all his, and he intended to keep expanding it. A year earlier the company had launched "Project Cheyenne," described as "a management effectiveness and employee empowerment program." After rating the railroad's performance in 150 workplace activities that successful companies did well, the results were used to redesign UP management and work practices. The task added ten to fifteen QSPs to the forty-four already in use and constituted one aspect of the overall drive to turn UP into a world-class company. Davidson wanted it moved along; those who lacked enthusiasm soon ran up against another of their new leader's traits. "He's a hard charger," said Rob Knight, "holds people accountable, demands results."[8]

Rinn was right in seeing Davidson as a complex personality. He could be intimidating to the point where his reports hesitated to speak frankly to him. He did not get in people's faces the way Walsh did, but he had a way of making very clear what he wanted or expected. His cool, aloof manner made him more admired than loved, but he tempered it with a good sense of humor. Stan McLaughlin discovered this on one occasion when Davidson wanted to schedule a budget meeting for 7:00 A.M. on a Saturday. "Being a smart ass," said McLaughlin, "I said . . . we can have it at six o'clock if you want." Davidson said fine, six o'clock it is, and McLaughlin cursed himself for opening his mouth.

On Saturday morning McLaughlin got to the twelfth-floor conference room well before the meeting. When Davidson arrived shortly before six, he turned on the light and saw McLaughlin in his pajamas tucked into a sleeping bag and clutching a teddy bear. "There was silence for about twenty seconds," McLaughlin said, "and then he started to laugh. And he laughed and he laughed."[9]

Rob Knight, who worked closely with Davidson, thought he "had a stature and a leadership skill set that is probably second to none." Yet he displayed none of the airs or pretensions common to corporate leaders of that era. "Dick, of all the CEOs I worked under," said Dolan, "had the least ego. I never saw Dick's ego interfere with his judgment or his relationship with people, which is remarkable." Rinn thought "he was confident enough that he was not threatened by other people of talent and ability. . . . He really did understand that he would do best . . . if he had the strongest possible team." Rinn also admired Davidson's ability to laugh at himself.[10]

Walsh had a repertory of sayings that he liked to drop on the troops, so many of them that when he left his staff filled some posters with them. Davidson had his own collection, but his tended to be more folksy and sometimes unfathomable.

Walsh would say something like "We want to be more open-minded but not so open-minded that your brains fall out." Davidson would tell the staff that someone was busier than a one-legged guy in a butt-kicking contest. "He says, Well, we're as screwed up as Hogan's goat," said Koraleski. "And we're not sure who Hogan was, how screwed up Hogan's goat got, but he does that. Another one: He says, Well, we don't want to harelip the Pope. We all . . . think, Well, what the hell does that mean?"[11]

Other qualities endeared Davidson to his officers. He was adaptable and open to change, listened well, and knew how to delegate authority. A good manager, he observed, was "somebody that knows how to utilize teamwork and surrounds himself with good people and doesn't try to micromanage." One of his favorite techniques was to ask several different people the same question and compare the answers. "Davidson would learn as much as he could about the subject that he was asking [about]," said McLaughlin, "so if you gave him some bullshit answer, that was not a good thing." Jim Young was impressed at how hard Davidson worked to understand and manage with data. Beth Whited marveled at his "incredible mind for numbers."[12]

To the surprise of Whited and others, Davidson proved to be good with words as well as numbers. He was also forthright to a fault. "He would always cut right to the chase," said Whited. "There was never any flowery anything about Dick." Despite the occasional pain, Whited relished the learning experience. "I thought I was detail oriented before," she said, "but he took me to a whole new level." In this way Davidson became an educator, as Walsh had been, but few people beyond the recipients realized it.[13]

Business ethics also mattered greatly to Davidson. "Dick had a devotion to ethics as great as anyone I have ever, ever seen," said Dolan. "It was almost like a religion to him." He created at UP a two-part ethics program. The first educated employees to understand ethics and their importance. The second consisted of an Ethics Review Board that oversaw all complaints. Its task, said Dolan, who chaired it for several years, was to ensure that department heads policed their organizations for ethical violations large or small. A panel on conflicts of interest was created to see that violations were handled in a uniform manner throughout the company. "All that was Dick's doing," said Dolan. "And merely having that panel has an impact throughout the entire company."[14]

Dennis Duffy saw the same passion in Davidson. "Very ethical, just of the highest standards," he said, "and . . . taught me personally a lot about that, making sure that ethically we did the right thing, always taking the high road . . . always protecting the assets of the company fiercely. . . . He spent the company's money tighter than he'd spend his own money, if that's possible."[15]

Davidson's experience with the cash-strapped MP taught him to mind the budget process closely. "You break open Dick Davidson's head," said Jerry Davis, "a dollar sign would come out with a choo-choo train." Although he no longer had to scrimp for capital, Davidson knew he had to make a case to Bethlehem for what he needed and impressed this point on his financial people. He understood that in the new world of railroading operations, marketing, and finance had become equal partners, and that it was imperative for them to work together.[16]

Within a month of making Davidson president and CEO of the railroad, the board appointed him chairman as well. His staff underwent a shuffle. Art Shoener replaced Davidson as executive vice president of operations, putting that area in hands Davidson trusted. Koraleski was promoted to executive vice president of finance and information technologies, relieving Jim Shattuck of the latter field. Shattuck moved to vice president of marketing beneath Fred Henderson, who remained executive vice president of marketing and sales. Jim Young moved up to vice president of finance. Kip Hawley, who had been in charge of the Washington office, wanted to come to the railroad and was made vice president of transportation services.[17]

In 1991 Walsh had separated labor relations and personnel into two departments. Tom Watts kept labor relations while personnel, renamed human resources, went to Barry Schuman. When Schuman followed Walsh to Tenneco, Davidson made Charley Eisele vice president of human resources. "With these promotions," Davidson said, "I'm confident that we have in place a first-class team in every area of the railroad." He was more right than he knew. As of 2010 Duffy, Eisele, Koraleski, and Young remained the core of UP's management team.[18]

Shortly before Davidson's promotion the seemingly endless labor conflicts took an unexpected turn. During the 1980s the number of railroad employees shrank from 459,410 to 216,424, with more cuts on the way. The rail unions fought this attrition fiercely but could not escape the harsh truth that the work rules had long since ceased to fit the realities of modern railroads. Crew size remained the stickiest issue. Once it became a matter of local bargaining, the UP and other roads managed to get agreements for smaller crews in certain locations. However, the process was glacial and usually encountered stiff resistance. Discouraged, the carriers turned to buyouts and devices like the reserve board.[19]

After the existing national agreement expired in 1988, negotiations dragged on into 1990. By then rail workers had gone two years without a wage increase, and health care had come to cloud the picture. The question had been ducked in the past two rounds of negotiations and could no longer be avoided. The carriers wanted employees to pay half of all health plan increases imposed by insurance companies; the unions refused to accept any changes in cost. For a time the issue overshadowed the usual disputes over work rules and wages, making it ripe for a Presidential Emergency Board if one were convened.[20]

The Railway Labor Act of 1926 gave the president power to create ad hoc emergency boards to mediate disagreements as a device to postpone strikes for up to sixty days. The hope was that public opinion would pressure both sides to settle quickly. During the next half century an average of four boards a year were formed to handle disputes. After 1975 the number dropped to slightly over one a year. Most led to agreements, and no strike ensued from any of them. When negotiations for new national agreements commenced in June 1988, however, the unions served notice that they would not consider wages or work rules until the health care issue was resolved. Both sides agreed to dump the issue into the government's lap while talks proceeded on wages, crew size, and the separation of road and yard work.[21]

On May 3, 1990, President George H. W. Bush signed an order creating PEB 219 to investigate existing disputes between the carriers and unions. On July 12 the board produced some suggested guidelines for the health care issue and sent both sides back to the bargaining table. As the process dragged on, Richard I. Kilroy of the AFL-CIO predicted a rail strike by January 23, when Congress reconvened, because he did not see how the board could possibly come up with recommendations satisfactory to both sides.[22]

On January 15, 1991, PEB 219 issued a report that stunned the unions. It recommended annual wage hikes of 3 to 4 percent along with cost-of-living adjustments, half of which would be swallowed by employee contributions to health care. The existing mileage per day of 108, which the unions sought to roll back to the traditional 100 miles, was instead increased to 130. Even more important, crew size was to be decided locally with a provision for binding arbitration, and the hoary division between road and yard work was eliminated. Outraged at these findings, the unions prepared to strike.[23]

The PEB 219 provisions were due to go into effect at 12:01 A.M. on April 17. In desperation the unions called their strike, only to have Congress shut it down in less than twenty-four hours. The House passed the resolution by a crushing 400–5 margin; the Senate approved it without debate. A Congressional Special Board, charged with investigating disputed provisions in PEB 219, confirmed virtually all its recommendations. The union leadership felt the impact immediately. That summer the presidents of the Transportation Communications Union (TCU), BLE, and UTU were ousted from office. All three leaders were tough negotiators respected by management and congressional leaders alike, but in 1991 nothing could save them.[24]

PEB 219 proved to be a landmark in the history of railway labor relations. The railroads moved quickly to carry out its provisions. By November 26 UP had agreements in place for half its crew employees and awaited ratification from the other half. Several other roads had new contracts in place. With them came an end to the age of featherbedding.[25]

UP drew praise for its humane handling of the separations and relocations. One electrician who had lived in Omaha all his life faced the choice of moving to Little Rock or leaving the railroad. The company provided $15,000 for moving expenses and agreed to reimburse any difference between the sale price of his Omaha home and the purchase price of one in Little Rock. The company moved him and several others together so they would have co-workers they already knew, and threw a big bash after their arrival so they could meet new people in Little Rock. "I don't say this very often," admitted the BRC chairman. "The Union Pacific went the extra mile with me on seeing that our people got what they had coming to them . . . and gave some things that were not even in the agreement."[26]

"We tried to give everyone an opportunity to retrain," said Watts. "The aim was to keep the hard feelings down." The result was the opening of a new era of labor relations that fit nicely with the UP's desire for a more efficient railroad and more collegial workplace. But all was not peace and harmony. The railroad could still achieve more cost cuts through reductions and hope that traffic growth would enable it to call back many of the workers. Judging how large or small a workforce to keep on hand became one of many new fine lines that Davidson had to learn to walk. Moreover, the railroads and unions still did not have a general agreement, and union unhappiness with PEB 219 did not make negotiations any easier.[27]

The unions were free to strike if no settlement was reached by June 24, 1992. When that deadline arrived, the machinists' union called a selective strike against CSX. The major carriers responded at once with a carefully planned lockout that shut down nearly all freight traffic in the nation. Within two days a reluctant Congress passed legislation ending the strike, this time providing for binding arbitration if a settlement could not be reached. Some observers blamed the archaic Railway Labor Act for generating crises on a regular basis.[28]

A year earlier, when confronted by another strike threat, the leaders of the major railroads had agreed that a strike against one of them would be considered a strike against them all. However, that solidarity was weakening. On the evening of June 23 the rail executives met at the AAR to finalize plans for the lockout should a strike occur. No one yet knew what road would be hit. Lewis and Davidson represented UP, and Lewis disliked the plan. At the meeting he accused BN's Gerald Grinstein of stonewalling the labor talks.[29]

"Drew wanted to settle and I didn't," said Grinstein. He offered to remove himself from the negotiations but said BN would shut down if any carrier was struck. Lewis declared that UP would not join the lockout and walked out of the room, leaving Davidson to represent the company. John Snow of CSX managed to get Lewis back on board for the lockout. However, an unhappy Congress imposed binding arbitration to break out of a pattern that had compelled it to intervene fifteen times in eleven labor disputes since 1963.[30]

The national crisis eased, but for UP it amounted to little more than a breather. In April 1993 the UTU and TCU withdrew their members from all cooperative UP programs except Red Block, ADEPT, and Operation Lifesaver, the joint government-industry-labor educational program to reduce grade-crossing accidents. The union action hit hardest at Davidson's prized quality improvement teams, which had just been showcased in the 1992 annual report. "We can no longer accept a situation where UP makes record profits, gives out huge bonuses to top management, and then demands continual sacrifices and givebacks from our members," declared J. L. Quilty of the TCU. ". . . None of the productivity gains are shared with us."[31]

Sammy Rudel, the UTU general chairman, charged that the company's attitude had changed over time "from managing people and money to just managing money." UTU president G. Thomas DuBose asserted that "the decline took off with the current administration." An Omaha lawyer offered a different slant. "The committees serve a purpose of bridging the gap between management and employees," he observed. "Once you bridge that gap, the question becomes, 'Why do we need a union?'"[32]

Rail columnist Gus Welty praised Davidson and UP for creating "an openness with a communications system to match, that no other railroad can equal." Early in 1993 a satellite communications system went online with a capability of transmitting announcements across the entire system. Every quarter Davidson held meetings in which he answered questions from employees in the field; these too were broadcast. "People who work for a living want to know what's going on," Welty said, "and their paychecks don't come from the union."[33]

UP's newest communication tool was a private television network, Union Pacific Learning Information and Communication (UPLINC). The station went on air six months ahead of schedule because Davidson recognized its value and ordered the timetable accelerated. It enabled management to reach the entire system through fifty-three geographical places with 184 viewing locations. A two-way audio setup enabled feedback via phone-in questions. "This network," said the project manager, "has allowed us to do in two hours what used to take weeks of meetings and travel." It also expedited training in many sectors. Maintenance operations, for example, could train employees via the system instead of bringing them from eleven different locations.[34]

Unimpressed, DuBose declared that "the company-sponsored programs stand as a symbol of all that is wrong between the organization and the carrier." Evidently he had forgotten or chose to overlook the long-standing complaint of UP workers, verified repeatedly by surveys, that the company did not listen to or communicate with them. UP, DuBose charged, was "attempting usurpation of franchise or office belonging to UTU via company-sponsored programs and direct intervention . . . in the administration of union affairs." To these charges

Watts replied, "I know that it makes the union people very nervous, to break down 100-year-old working relationships. . . . We're just going to stay with it."[35]

The conflict revealed one more set of growing pains as both sides struggled to adjust to a workplace in which the old rules and practices grew outdated faster than ever before. Not surprisingly, the unions found it even harder than management to accept the emerging order of things, because it threatened their very existence.[36]

While this conflict played itself out, Davidson had also to fight an old and familiar enemy. During January and February 1993 record snowstorms in the Sierra Nevada mountains battered the railroad so severely that it was forced to utilize its rotary snowplow on the main line for the first time since the blizzard of 1949. Snow and rock slides, frozen switches, broken rails, and pull-aparts plagued the Northwest subdivisions, forcing the UP to "fleet" trains through the Feather River Canyon to avoid meetings. An employee on a hyrail preceded every train to scout for slides. Every yard took a hit from the snow and ice storms. Sub-zero temperatures and drifting snow slowed North Platte to a crawl and shut down the Powder River line three times. Icy conditions hampered crews traveling to their assignments or engineers trying to reach broken rails. Employee injuries spiked as the simplest tasks turned into ordeals.[37]

The severe weather finally relented after February, leading Davidson to hope that lost earnings might be recouped in the months ahead. However, the worst was yet to come. Beginning in June, rain poured down relentlessly across UP's entire Central and Southern regions, triggering what became known as the Great Floods of '93. On July 3 the Missouri River began pouring over its banks. A command post was set up at the HDC to monitor the spreading waters and juggle dispatching accordingly. As one subdivision went underwater, its traffic was shifted to another, only to see it shut down as well. When the Missouri emptied its waters into the Mississippi, that river began flooding subdivisions along its banks. Parts of the Chester subdivision were submerged beneath twenty-five feet of water.[38]

The UP, BN, SF, and NS bore the brunt of the flood. Altogether 783 miles of track went underwater at some time with nearly 100 miles of it washed away entirely. Some 2,877 trains were diverted over other railroads as companies scrambled to keep them moving. Hardest hit were lines in Missouri, Kansas, Nebraska, and Illinois, including the UP's main line from Council Bluffs to North Platte and from Kansas City to Gibbon, Nebraska. Cleanup crews slogged wearily from site to site once the waters began to recede. The line between Jefferson City and Kansas City remained closed for forty-seven days, that between Kansas City and Omaha for thirty-one days. Damage to the afflicted roads totaled $130 million.[39]

Davidson and McLaughlin surveyed the dismal scenes by helicopter. Davidson labeled it "the single-biggest natural disaster in the railroad's history." Altogether the UP had 1,694 miles of line damaged or out of service, costing it 40,000 carloads of business in July and August and $40 million in lost revenue. Another $30 million was needed to repair the damage. As usual, it took heroic efforts by the work crews to keep the railroad running. Whole squads of trackmen put in twelve-hour days with no time off for weeks. As a final blow, hard rains in October led the Mississippi River to breach already weakened levees and flood UP tracks again.[40]

The most costly work involved rebuilding signal systems drowned by the floods. Nevertheless, by autumn the UP was up and running except for the tracks along the Mississippi and struggling to handle a flood of traffic. Bailey Yard was swamped with cars. On September 30 the company set a system record of 97,787 cars loaded in a seven-day period; four days later the seven-day total hit 98,221 cars. By the year's end the system handled 4.6 million carloadings and kept its operating ratio at 79.1.[41]

It was a remarkable performance but a costly one in one unforeseen respect. "We never came out of those [floods] as the same company," said Brad King. "We got into so much more ad hoc decision-making and the company, I don't think, ever . . . got back into their disciplined operation. . . . They were five-hundred-year floods . . . and the water took forever to go down and you lost bridges, you lost things that you don't just throw some rock into and jack your track up on them. We lost routes for months."[42]

Despite these vicissitudes, the railroad continued to pile up impressive earnings. Between 1991 and 1994 its gross increased from $4.8 billion to $5.3 billion and its net from $639 million to $754 million. The operating ratio fell from 80.4 in 1991 to 77.9 in 1994, partly because of the personnel savings enabled by PEB 219. During that same period carloadings rose steadily from 4.3 million to nearly 5 million. The average length of haul rose steadily from 705 miles in 1991 to 731 miles in 1994. However, fluctuating prices lowered the average revenue per carloading from $1,064 to $1,045 and the average revenue per ton-mile from $2.28 to $2.15.

Although chemical traffic remained the largest earner, coal, intermodal, and automotive all reached record highs in 1994. Of the coal carried, the proportion from the Powder River Basin jumped from 69 percent to 77 percent. By 1994 the amount carried reached 131 million tons, a long way from the 25 million tons projected a decade earlier. Intermodal made the largest gains, going from 10.9 percent to 15.6 percent. Minerals and metals slipped somewhat, as did food products and forest products.[43]

By 1994 another expanding market, Mexico, produced $348 million in income in 1994, compared to $250 million in 1991. Just as the Clean Air Act of

1990 gave a powerful boost to Powder River coal, so did the North American Free Trade Agreement (NAFTA) of 1994 promise the same for the potent if problematic Mexican market.[44]

For more than a century Mexico had been a land of endless frustration for American railroads. During the early 1880s Jay Gould built the MP into a major system that included the Texas & Pacific, which reached El Paso and New Orleans. Gould also acquired a road from St. Louis to New Orleans and one extending from Longview to Laredo with a branch to Galveston. Together these roads enabled Gould to dominate traffic between St. Louis and eastern Texas. He also had access to Mexico at Laredo. In 1881 he secured a concession to build a road from Laredo to Mexico City, but the burden of his many projects led him to abandon it. Instead General William J. Palmer of the Rio Grande constructed a line to Mexico City.[45]

The Mexican market also intrigued E. H. Harriman. After rehabilitating UP and acquiring SP, he looked into extending the latter's line into Mexico. Earlier Collis P. Huntington had on behalf of SP leased the Sonora Railroad from Nogales on the Arizona-Mexico border to Guaymas on the Gulf of California. Huntington also bought large parcels of undeveloped coal land with a view of extending branches to them and mining coal for the energy-starved Southwest. Harriman took up this vision and acquired rights to lay track from Guaymas to Guadalajara as well as up the Yaqui River valley to a mineral region coveted by Huntington.[46]

Beginning in 1905, SP laid 800 miles of track in four years. Once completed to Guadalajara, SP owned the longest continuous line of railroad in the world, 3,750 miles of track stretching from Puget Sound to the Gulf of California. Then Harriman died in 1909, and three years later the federal government separated UP from SP. UP had no interest in or connection to Mexico for seventy years until its merger with MP. Prior to the merger UP's market in Mexico amounted to grain, beans, and soda ash handed off to the MP for movement through its Laredo gateway, which consisted of a single-track bridge across the Rio Grande River. Customs bureaucracy and official corruption led to congestion at the border, and cars rolling into Mexico returned very slowly if at all.[47]

Eight gateways dominated rail traffic between the United States and Mexico. The SF funneled mostly electronic equipment through San Diego. Calexico, the least developed gateway, belonged to the SP, along with Nogales, through which flowed mostly finished automobiles. El Paso got considerable traffic from the SP and SF and a pittance from the UP. Eagle Pass also belonged to the SP and handled a large traffic in automobiles and auto parts. The BN did not reach Mexico directly but handed off traffic at San Angelo to the South Orient, which touched the border at Presidio. Both the UP and SP used the Brownsville gateway, but the UP sent 65 percent of its cross-border traffic through Laredo, the most heavily used gateway.[48]

Deregulation in 1980 encouraged the flow of traffic southward but did not solve the problem of congestion and slow returns. However, the merger opened new possibilities. The UP had always been an east-west railroad, as were most other American roads. The MP was a north-south road, a basic link in the flow of traffic involving Canada, the United States, and Mexico. It exchanged traffic with Mexico at El Paso and Brownsville as well as Laredo. On exports MP locomotives pushed cars to the middle of the jointly owned Laredo bridge, where Ferrocariles Nacionales de México (FNM) picked them up. For imports the process was reversed. At Brownsville every exchange took place on the Mexican side of the border, while at El Paso everything was done on the Texas side.[49]

After a severe financial crisis in 1982 Mexico rebounded a year later to export more goods than it imported for the first time ever. Nearly 60 percent of Mexican exports went to the United States, while Mexico ranked fourth in importing American goods. Intermodal business picked up sharply as UP struck deals with more than forty Mexican motor carriers to provide ramp-to-door and door-to-ramp service. In October 1984 UP and FNM launched a new through service running two trains from Chicago to Mexico City in less than one hundred hours.[50]

Eager for economic growth, the Mexican government instituted policies to spur cross-border trade. In 1986 it joined the General Agreement on Tariffs and Trade (GATT) and authorized American as well as other foreign manufacturers to own and operate plants within the country. It also expanded an earlier policy that proved to be a roaring success. Mexicans called it "maquiladora" after a longtime practice in which farmers carted grain to millers for processing but kept ownership of it until the miller had finished. It allowed foreign companies to build fully owned manufacturing plants as "offshore" partners of the parent firm. Raw materials or components could then be imported from the United States and finished products returned there with duties being paid only on the value-added portion of their worth.[51]

Originally created in the 1960s, the maquiladora program mushroomed during the late 1980s. In 1970 a handful of companies employed about 20,000 people; by the end of 1988 an estimated 1,500 foreign companies boasted more than 400,000 workers. More than 16,000 of them toiled in seventy plants just across the river from Laredo, which emerged as the busiest rail crossing into Mexico between the Gulf of California and the Texas Gulf Coast. With encouragement from the Mexican government the Big Three American automakers, Ford, GM, and Chrysler, all built large production plants in Mexican cities, giving the automobile and auto parts traffic a huge boost. Congestion soon became a major issue in yards on both sides of the Rio Grande. Track had to be upgraded, more power added, and procedures streamlined.[52]

The more the Mexican market heated up, the more glaring became the problems plaguing it. The government-owned FNM struggled with lack of modern equipment, poor maintenance, and a bloated workforce. Where UP operated a 20,300-mile system with 29,000 employees, FNM had a whopping 82,000 workers on its 15,000-mile system. Every million tons moved required 100 UP employees compared to 1,700 for FNM. The border crossing remained a nightmare of red tape, corrupt officials, and congestion aggravated by bureaucratic impediments and increased surveillance for drugs.[53]

Even as railroads and manufacturers complained about delays, they rushed to expand their Mexican operations. By 1990 an estimated 85 percent of the five hundred largest American companies had investments in Mexico. No major railroad could ignore the growth potential offered by the Mexican market. In 1951 SP had sold its Nogales–Guadalajara line to the Mexican government, which folded most of it into FNM. Nearly half a century later, in March 1990, the company renewed its long-dormant interest in Mexico by launching a new container train from Los Angeles to Mexico City.[54]

By 1992 the Mexican boom was in full flower. Negotiations begun the previous year finally materialized in December 1993 as NAFTA. UP didn't wait for passage of the controversial bill. "We hope to double business in this marketplace in the next five years, then triple it in ten years," said Ken Morrill, vice president of sales, To reach this goal the company created thirty-four project groups utilizing 150 employees to explore every facet. The goal was to boost Mexican revenue by at least 15 percent a year.[55]

"The opportunity in Mexico," Davidson said, "is probably first or second in our list of opportunities for long-term growth, right in there with Powder River Basin coal." Double-digit growth had become almost routine. One reform, the Despacho Previo, expedited the customs clearance process at Laredo. FNM decided in 1991 to adopt UP's TCS system along with other communications and fiber-optics projects. It also leased thirty-five locomotives from UP. For its part UP opened a new 530-acre yard in Laredo in September 1990 and invested $25 million in a new 180-acre intermodal facility twelve miles north of Laredo.[56]

Once the TCS system was fully operational on FNM, it became possible to preblock trains going in both directions. UP created its first southbound preblocked train in 1984; three other trains were soon added, but northbound trains had to await full implementation of TCS on FNM trains. Negotiations also began on combined through rates that would lock in rates for six months, simplify currency conversions, and allow shippers to pay exclusively in the currency of their choice.[57]

While cultivating the Mexican market Davidson did not neglect his other top priority, the Powder River Basin. The competition with BN for customers kept rates down and led the company to lock up business even at low rates with long-term contracts. Although Powder River accounted for about 20 percent of all coal mined in the United States, it proved to be a tough business in which, as one observer noted, "capital investment is measured in billions of dollars and rates in tenth of cents."[58]

As the sheer quantity of coal moving out of Powder River grew, capacity and maintenance became ever more pressing issues. In 1991 UP launched a five-year $270 million program to upgrade the corridor from South Morrill to Kansas City. "It became obvious that we needed to accelerate our capital spending to keep up with growth up there," said Davidson. "We conjured up this vision, what we called Project Yellow Phase Two, invested $500 or $600 million over several years." When Lewis resisted spending so much money, Davidson asked Kenefick for help. Kenefick obliged by urging Lewis to see the necessity and the potential return on the investment.[59]

By 1993 nearly 110 unit trains of 110 cars each rumbled every day out of the Basin bound for more than fifty utilities in twenty-five different states. In November Davidson brought Art Shoener to Bethlehem to show the board where the greatest capacity restraints on the road were and what was needed to alleviate them.[60]

Despite their very different pasts, Mexico and the Powder River Basin represented two of UP's strongest hopes for future growth. That future in turn depended on two key factors: UP's improbable new leader and the continuing shakeout of the railroad industry. By 1994 Davidson had shown himself to be a steady hand, the ideal steward for Walsh's legacy, imposing the sound, conservative judgment of a railroad man on a company that some thought had come too far too fast. He had around him a familiar and seasoned staff that proved remarkably enduring with only a few exceptions. In 1991 Dennis Jacobson got into a dispute with his boss, Bill Hillebrandt, and left UP to join SP.[61]

It was a wrenching departure for Jacobson. He had invested nineteen years in the UP, and his wife seventeen years. But he did not like the way Hillebrandt treated field superintendents and managers. Walsh and Davidson came to a similar conclusion. After an internal review of his management style, Hillebrandt was demoted in July 1991 and then retired from the company in December 1992. Later Davidson told Jacobson he understood why he had left the company.[62]

The most surprising change came in April 1993 when Fred Henderson, one of Walsh's first outside hires, abruptly left. He had been considered a likely successor to Walsh, who once remarked to Rebensdorf that Henderson was presidential material. "It soon became apparent to me," said Rebensdorf, "and I think to everybody else in the organization, that this guy was not presidential material." Henderson, observed Davidson, "didn't tolerate pushback very well, and he really intimidated some people like Rebensdorf."[63]

Henderson carried this attitude up as well as down the organization. During a budget meeting with UPC officers he got into it with Lewis. The corporation proposed cutting money from Henderson's budget. Sitting across the table from Lewis, he said, You can't do that. "He says," recalled Gary Schuster, "'If you want this railroad to make money, we got to spend money to make money here. We got to entertain.'" As the exchange grew nastier, Walsh tried in vain to referee. "'They weren't you son-of-a-bitching to each other," said Schuster, "but you knew they were talking to each other and nobody else in the room. . . . Then the complicating factor is, it was in the morning and so you don't know what was in the iced tea."[64]

Lewis wasn't about to be challenged in the boardroom surrounded by his directors and railroad executives. "He was a banty rooster in that sense," said Schuster. "Right or wrong, he was right." Some, like Schuster, thought this might have sealed Henderson's doom with the company, but another issue proved to be decisive.[65]

Asked by a reporter why he was leaving, Henderson said that the reason was personal. He had reason to want it kept private. An internal audit uncovered irregularities in his expense account. It was relatively small stuff, the amounts incomprehensible for someone making Henderson's salary, but the malfeasance was clear. In giving Davidson the news White Matthews said, "If you want, I can get myself over this . . . if he's that valuable of an employee to you." However, Matthews added, "If you really want to save him, we're going to have to make an argument here."[66]

Davidson didn't take long to decide. Henderson had done some good work for the railroad. Jim Young thought he was responsible for modernizing the company's concept of marketing and sales. But Davidson had already demonstrated how much the issue of company ethics mattered to him. "I saw a lot of stuff going on that I didn't think was right," he said simply, "so we had to fix it." Henderson had to go regardless of his value to the company.[67]

Henderson's departure enabled Davidson to reorganize the entire marketing and sales operation. "I could never get through my mind what in the heck is the difference between marketing and sales," admitted Lou Anne Rinn. Henderson had shown her and others the difference. Marketing focused on the broader picture of the company's needs, and understanding in an objective, quantitative way the size of the market and the opportunities it offered. Sales went beyond mere selling to understanding customers, establishing relationships with them, and providing a liaison between marketing strategy and how a customer fit into it. Ideally it was a feedback loop, with the customer providing data on the service received.[68]

Davidson thought the two functions should be together. Two months after Henderson's departure he launched a series of changes that made clear he had become far more than a steward of the Walsh legacy. Marketing and sales were merged into one unit under Jim Shattuck, who had replaced Henderson.

Field-sales personnel were assigned to commodity groups, the number of which was cut from eight to five, including one that oversaw Mexican traffic. Davidson also shifted the service-design function from the operating department to marketing. The move, he said, would "place our equivalent of new product development under marketing and, at the same time, allow marketing to share responsibility for transportation expense."[69]

At the same time, a new "reengineering team" was created. Headed by Kip Hawley, who reported directly to Davidson, its mission was to find ways to boost productivity and quality of service. Within operations, transportation services and field operations were consolidated into a single unit headed by Bob Naro, who had been in charge of the NCSC. Chris Aadnesen became head of the HDC in place of Brad King, who was put in charge of risk management.[70]

The new organization put Davidson's stamp firmly on UP. He took pride in the solid earnings during his brief tenure despite a host of obstacles and anticipated even greater gains during the next few years. Neither he nor anyone else could have imagined the immense reconfigurations heading for UP and the industry during the middle 1990s.

23

The Bidding War

By 1994 Davidson had settled comfortably into his new job, and the railroad was flourishing. Earnings remained high, and morale seemed to be improving. He had kept in place the Business Objectives Matrix, developed soon after Walsh's arrival. The 1991 version listed a set of nine business objectives; by 1994 the reorganization had condensed the number to seven but the goal remained the same: to provide quantifiable targets against which progress could be measured in every category.[1]

Lewis seemed comfortable with Davidson at the helm, and Davidson was pleased at how smoothly their relationship went. "He called me about once a week on Monday to see how we were doing against our budget," he said, "and as long as we were doing fine, that was the last you ever heard of him." They still butted heads over capital budgeting and allocation. Like his predecessors, Davidson always wanted more than UPC was willing to give. He had learned well from Jenks and Kenefick that the most expensive course was to let a railroad run down and then have to build it back up again.[2]

No such comfort level existed at UPC. Although the 1993 annual report emphasized the theme of "seamless service," the company's affairs were far from seamless. USPCI was on its way out the door, but Skyway joined the company as a wholly owned subsidiary. In September 1991 Lewis decided on another restructuring plan that split the stock two for one and took an $870 million charge. Some $745 million of the charge applied to the railroad, mostly to cover severance and relocation expenses. The railroad also earmarked 7,100 miles of line for sale or abandonment. In explaining the moves to analysts Lewis called the railroad "a dinosaur not smart enough to fall down. The industry is changing. The dinosaur has learned how to dance."[3]

Lewis was even more blunt about some of the subsidiaries. Overnite, he declared, was "the best company in a lousy industry." USPCI he dismissed as "a lousy investment on my watch." This was not the usual language used by CEOs with analysts. Lewis's personal problem had grown worse and become apparent

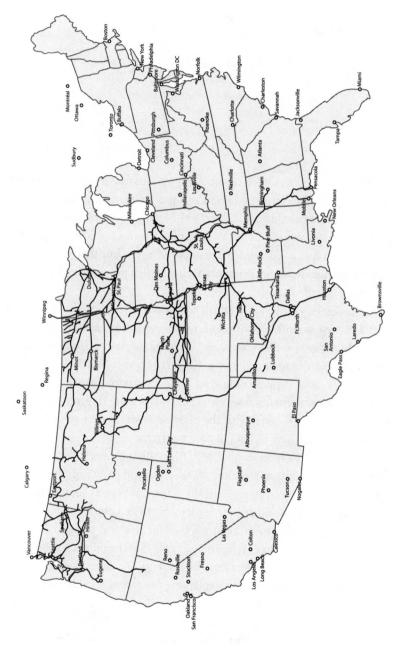

FORMIDABLE RIVAL. The Burlington Northern Railroad in 1995.

to more people within the company. "Everybody knew," said one staff member. "Everybody tiptoed around it." His staff and direct reports did what they could to protect him. Lewis asked Gary Schuster to attend AA meetings with him in New York but resumed drinking after returning to Bethlehem.[4]

Some board members knew as well. Robinson talked to Schuster about it. So evidently did Henry Kissinger; he and Robinson were on the American Express board with Lewis. Gerry was aware of the situation, and doubtless so were other directors who chose not to say anything about what was becoming an awkward dilemma. "He would lose perspective, I think, when he was drinking," said one member. "He could be tough, too, not only to reports but also to peers and to directors. You could always tell when he didn't like what you were saying. There were those beady eyes." "The whole office just played around it.," said White Matthews. ". . . But he was also pretty good about not tackling something when he wasn't okay."[5]

Although Lewis never admitted that alcohol interfered with his work, he agonized over his inability to control the drinking. Once he confided to a friend, "When you wake up at two in the morning, your thoughts go to what has to be done the next day. My thoughts go to planning how I'm going to sneak drinks all day." Nothing he did seem to help control the problem. His wife, Marilyn, did what she could to help. She would call Schuster and ask what was happening. "I finally told her," said Schuster, ". . . 'I'm in a tough position here, Marilyn. I don't want to lie to you, but I got to be loyal to him. . . . I know what you're dealing with, but I don't want to rat him out.'" After that conversation Marilyn stopped calling.[6]

The problem began to leak outside the company. Some people, reporters and others, already knew but kept their silence. Others began to notice the signs. Early in 1994 Lewis made a speech at the Union Club in Philadelphia. Schuster picked him up at the farm and drove him down to the city. When they arrived at the club, Lewis disappeared for a short time. Schuster knew what he was up to but had no way to stop it. The speech went poorly and made little sense; some people thought he was tipsy, and a reporter asked Schuster if Lewis had been drinking. "I don't know," Schuster replied. "I didn't see it."[7]

On the ride back to the farm Lewis took off his shoes, put his feet on the dashboard, and asked Schuster how the speech went. Schuster said bluntly that it stunk. "You can't drink and do this stuff," he said. Lewis slept most of the way home and never mentioned the subject again. The question of driving itself had become a sticky point. "I tried to get him in [chauffeured] cars all the time," said Matthews. "I couldn't get him to do it." Despite the liability of driving a company car after drinking, the warning went unheeded. A few weeks after the Union Club speech, Lewis got into a one-car accident that required eleven stitches on his head. At that he got off relatively easy, but 1994 proved to be a difficult year for him.[8]

Contrary to industry fears, the recession of 1990–92 did not hurt the railroads seriously, and earnings picked up sharply in 1993 despite the record floods. But no one expected the strategic chessboard to remain static. After their failed merger, SP under Anschutz struggled to regain its footing while SF undertook a bold reorganization and reorientation. In 1988 SF had incurred a whopping $3.7 billion debt to fend off a hostile takeover. By 1990 Krebs had whittled it down to $140 million, largely by selling off subsidiary businesses, including SP. He then downsized SF by selling off or abandoning more than 2,500 miles of the system.[9]

During these years BN had its own issues. It had come late to the diversification game, forming its holding company in 1981. The corporate headquarters moved from St. Paul to Seattle, while the railroad's main office relocated to Fort Worth. Morale plummeted as rail executives were let go and the railroad became a cash cow for other endeavors. Enmeshed in lawsuits, the company fought harsh battles with the unions and several states. Grinstein hired several executives from the outside. A series of bad decisions followed, and the operating ratio soared. A spate of articles heaped criticism on the company, leading Grinstein to complain, "Is all this BN bashing necessary?"[10]

Late in 1990 Grinstein became chairman as well as president and CEO of Burlington Northern, Inc. He shifted the focus back to the railroad and eased the tensions in labor relations, but the record of his administration remained uneven. In 1994 Grinstein turned sixty-two and focused on two objectives: finding his successor and pulling off a major deal to crown his accomplishments. A merger with SF would give him both the big deal and a worthy successor in the talented Krebs. Grinstein wanted an experienced railroader to succeed him, but Krebs was not his first choice. Instead he turned to Davidson.[11]

Early in the spring of 1994 Grinstein invited Davidson to become his successor. "You're probably not going to get the top job at the UP," he said, "and this would be a chance for you to have your own company." Davidson was noncommittal, but Grinstein persisted and even had former BN CEO Dick Grayson, who knew Davidson well, give him a call. "We were looking at Davidson as a heck of a guy," said BN director Daniel Evans. Apart from his ability as an operating executive, Davidson had been through a major merger and could steer BN and SF through that difficult process. He did not belong to either railroad and had no favorites or biases. The same could not be said of Krebs, whom BN executives feared would subordinate their people to his own.[12]

The problem was that BN could not have both Davidson and the merger. Davidson told Grinstein, "I'll do it if Drew tells me that I don't have a shot at the top job here because I would like to run my own company." Then he dropped the other shoe: "You can't go ahead with this SF merger if I come down there, because there is no way Krebs and I are going to work out together." Davidson had known Krebs since their days as young superintendents in Arkansas. While

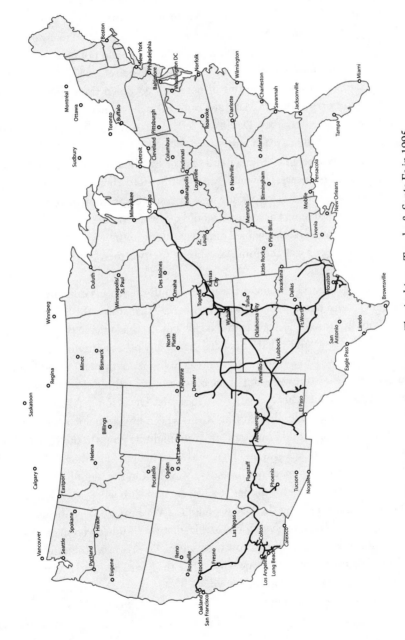

A MUCH-COVETED RAILROAD. The Atchison, Topeka & Santa Fe in 1995.

they liked each other, both men were far too ambitious to share the same stage when there was only one lead role. Grinstein agreed to put the merger talks on hold until Davidson talked to Lewis.[13]

Davidson went to Bethlehem the day before the regular board meeting in May and told Lewis, "I don't mean this to be a threat or hold you hostage or anything else. I'd like a chance to run my own company. If you really don't think I've got a shot here, I'd like to go run the BN." Lewis did not take the news well and asked for time to think it over. When Davidson returned later a glowering Lewis said, "You just get on out of here and go down there. After the board meeting tomorrow I'll take Matthews out to Omaha to make the announcement at the railroad." A shaken Davidson left to plan his move. He tried calling Grinstein but couldn't reach him.[14]

"Drew was such a fast thinker and reactor that he had a plan if Davidson did leave," said Ebby Gerry. He would send Matthews to Omaha to run the railroad. Like Grinstein, Lewis had to come up with a successor when he retired in 1996. Everyone in Bethlehem assumed it would be either Matthews or Jack Messman. Matthews's smooth style enabled him to get along with Lewis, but Messman was his pet. Matthews was the more capable of the two men but had never run an operating company.[15]

Before going to Bethlehem Davidson had discussed his dilemma with John Kenefick, who was appalled at what he heard. "That scared the living shit out of me, frankly," he said. "...Davidson was the only railroad man in the whole patch." He believed so strongly that a financial guy or any other nonrailroader would be disastrous for UP that he decided to break his own policy of nonintervention. "I don't care if they throw me out of the office and everything else," he said later. "I owed that much to this company, . . . to *not* let Davidson go. That would have been just terrible." He phoned Bob Roth, whom he had helped get on the UP board in 1972, and told him that Davidson might be going to the BN. Roth was as shocked as Kenefick and said he would see what could be done.[16]

The board was to meet on Thursday, May 26. On the night before meetings the directors gathered for dinner at a private golf club where they stayed. After dinner Roth brought up the Davidson issue. "We came to the conclusion," said Gerry, "... that Davidson was too valuable, that we couldn't let him go." Early the next morning they let Lewis know their views. Davidson was summoned to the board meeting without knowing why. While the board huddled in executive session, he fidgeted in the parking lot with Schuster, his normally placid face heavy with emotion over leaving UP.[17]

Finally the directors called Davidson in and informed him that Lewis had changed his mind and wanted Davidson to stay. In addition to being chairman and CEO of the railroad he would become president of UPC and a candidate for the top job. When Davidson agreed, Schuster tore up his original release and scribbled a new one. "L. White Matthews III, the former CFO, was named today as the . . . gone," he said later. "Next, put in another name."[18]

Matthews took the news badly, as might be expected. Davidson was relieved but had to tell Grinstein what had happened. Grinstein said he understood and appreciated being informed. "If I had got him that night [before]," mused Davidson, "I'da said, 'Here I come, Jerry.' I mean, it was a total flip-flop in about twelve hours. I was getting ready to pack up and go to Texas and then I was packing up and going to Pennsylvania."[19]

Although no one yet realized it, this decision set in motion a series of events that reshaped both UP and the industry during the next two years. What the outcome for both might have been if Davidson had gone to BN became a favorite plaything of speculation. On June 6 Lewis called Krebs to tell him of Davidson's decision. When Krebs returned the call next day, Lewis told him jokingly that he might want to apply for the BN position. Before long the humor drained entirely from that suggestion.[20]

Two immediate consequences flowed from the decision to keep Davidson. The first involved the creation of a succession procedure known in the company, often derisively, as the horse race. The second concerned the impact on BN. Grinstein resumed negotiations for the merger with SF, knowing that the price tag would be Krebs as his successor. It was hardly a bad choice given Krebs's strong reputation in the industry.

Keeping Davidson obliged Lewis to formulate a process for choosing his successor. The horse race amounted to a competition between Davidson, Matthews, and Messman. To most observers the playing field looked uneven, yet it had some intriguing wrinkles. Matthews was capable and politically astute and worked closely with Lewis every day, which could be an ordeal in itself. However, he had never run a company—he turned down an opportunity to take charge of Overnite—and some thought his ambition too obvious. Messman had run companies but not well. Although not in Bethlehem, he was closer to Lewis and put on a good front. That left Davidson, who didn't know Lewis well and had never worked closely with him.[21]

Fate had been kind to Davidson. At fifty-two he had been president of one major railroad, had been offered the presidency of two others, and had become a contender to succeed Lewis as head of UPC. Yet he scarcely believed his new opportunity. "I never really felt I was a contender for the job," he said later. "In fact, I would have bet anything that it would have been Messman."[22]

But he had an advantage overlooked by many observers. The BN offer, recalled Carl von Bernuth, "triggered the discussion about the future of UP and who should be the next CEO, and if Davidson was not the right person, then probably he should go because if somebody else was going to be the CEO,

Davidson wasn't going to stay." But the board made it clear that they wanted him to stay because he was the best man to run the railroad. "And because of that," said von Bernuth, "he's the best guy to be CEO when Drew goes, because it is a railroad. . . . He was the lead horse."[23]

All three men were put on the board to give them a broader taste of UPC's affairs and received golden handcuffs to keep them from leaving. To Matthews the race seemed interminable. "You were led to believe that it . . . was going to be settled in a year," he said, "but the race went on forever. I felt like I went out for the hundred-yard dash and I was running a marathon."[24]

The competition stretched out partly because of the second chain of consequences that flowed from the decision to keep Davidson. On June 30 BN and SF announced their intention to merge, with Grinstein as chairman and Krebs as president of the new company. Lewis held discussions with his staff and the board on how to respond. The usual scramble to gather data and formulate strategies began. Lewis scheduled a special board meeting by telephone for September 1.[25]

The board had undergone only a few changes since 1990, but they were significant. In 1991 it lost Edward L. Palmer but welcomed Dick Mahoney and William H. Gray III as new members. The second black director, Gray headed the United Negro College Fund and was an old friend of Lewis. A year later Henry Kissinger resigned because of a conflict of interest with another board on which he served. In his place came Richard B. Cheney, the CEO of Halliburton Company, who remained a director until other duties called him elsewhere in 2000. In 1993 Warren Shapleigh, the last remaining link to MP, retired. A year later the three candidates became directors.[26]

The BN-SF announcement muddled an already complicated chessboard. The proposed merger would leave SP in play. On July 19 KCS and IC declared their intention to merge, raising the possibility of another system in the making. In the East NS and Conrail were talking merger, and CSX was expected to respond. The moves revived talk about a possible transcontinental merger. Bill Withuhn, the Smithsonian's transportation curator, proclaimed that "we are entering the third and final great wave of railroad consolidation."[27]

During August Rebensdorf and the railroad's planners revived their transcontinental merger studies, calling it "probably the most important study we have done." A script cobbled together for the September 1 meeting outlined possible alternatives but had no clear recommendation. The board appointed a special committee with Gerry as chairman to assist Lewis in formulating a strategy. A corps of consultants was enlisted, including Arvid Roach from Covington & Burling and David DeNunzio from CS First Boston.[28]

John Rebensdorf already had material ready for them and was hastily putting more together. During the spring he had suggested to Davidson that UP go after SF. Once the special committee was in place, a small group from UPC and the railroad concluded that UP should offer a counter bid for SF. "We . . . were helped by the fact that their application, their operating plan, was extremely poor," said Rebensdorf.[29]

The impetus for a run at SF also came from Matthews, who said, "Why don't we do a hostile?" A hostile bid would bypass Krebs and his board by taking the offer directly to SF's stockholders. The industry hadn't seen one in years, but Matthews persisted. "Either we win it on our economics," he argued, "or if we lose it we cost our competitor a lot of money. What's wrong with that scenario?" Davidson and his senior staff liked the idea; so did Lewis and Gerry. Rebensdorf's crew went to work on "Project Blue."[30]

A key issue was whether to include a voting trust in the tender. The biggest risk in any merger offer was waiting for the ICC's decision. SF and SP had created a holding company only to see its work undone by an adverse ICC decision; SF stockholders did not care to endure that experience again. Putting the tendered stock in a voting trust removed it from control by UP and eliminated the risk of adverse consequences if the merger were disallowed. It transferred the risks of divestiture to UP and also deprived UP of control over SF for up to thirty-one months, the maximum time the ICC had to render a decision. BN did not include a voting trust in its offer.[31]

On September 19 Lewis reviewed for the special committee the options for acquiring SF, including the use of a voting trust, as well as alternatives such as going after SP. Davidson outlined the benefits of a merger with SF, calling it "an historic opportunity to substantially improve the Corporation's franchise." Matthews went through the finances involved, and von Bernuth explained the benefits and risks of a voting trust. Lewis interjected that the advantages of the transaction outweighed the risks of ICC approval and a voting trust. After the consultants weighed in with their views, the committee recommended that the acquisition be explored.[32]

At their regular meeting on September 28 Lewis urged the board not to use a voting trust. Why he decided to take the voting trust off the table remains unclear. After a spirited two-hour discussion the board instructed management to explore alternative means for proceeding with the bid. A week later, in a conference call, Lewis reviewed a proposal to acquire SF through several alternatives that did not include a voting trust. He let the discussion go barely half an hour before requesting a vote; he had a plane to catch. The proposal to pursue a merger agreement passed unanimously with only Dick Simmons abstaining.[33]

Lewis had a proposal ready that offered $18 in UP stock for each share of SF, about 35 percent above the BN offer. He called Krebs at SF headquarters in Schaumburg, a Chicago suburb, and insisted on seeing him later that afternoon. "The rationale for doing so," said Gary Stuart, "was to advise him that we were . . . going to be putting more money on the table than was proposed in the BN bid, and it was partly a courtesy." Lewis boarded the company plane along with Matthews, von Bernuth, and some others for the flight to Chicago; Davidson and Jim Dolan met them in Schaumburg.[34]

On the flight Lewis started drinking. Whether he had done so earlier is unclear. He liked to keep the company planes well stocked with small shooter bottles that he could sneak during trips and pocket a few for later use. Once at SF headquarters the others waited in the car while Lewis and Davidson went to see Krebs. Lewis insisted on doing the talking; the meeting went poorly, and Krebs rejected the offer out of hand. As Lewis was leaving he impulsively suggested that UP might consider a price of $20 a share and possibly a voting trust. On the way back to the airport he called Grinstein and said, "I just met with that _____. And I'd like to meet with you." Grinstein declined, and the UPC contingent returned to Bethlehem. Once back in Omaha, Davidson and Dolan told Rebens-dorf and a select few other staff people about Lewis's behavior.[35]

Later Krebs claimed that Lewis had soured the deal by making it contingent on ICC approval. "If he had paid what he offered the day he walked in my door," said Krebs, "he would have ended up owning the Santa Fe." That is hardly likely. In an interview Krebs listed several reasons why BN made a better fit for SF than UP did. The most compelling one was that the two roads amounted to an end-to-end merger, while UP presented more competitive problems that would complicate ICC approval. Throughout the fight Krebs and Grinstein reiterated this argument incessantly. However, Krebs discreetly omitted the most compelling personal rea-son. He had made it clear to Grinstein that any merger would happen only if he became Grinstein's successor. With Davidson ensconced at the UP, Krebs would have no clear role, let alone that of CEO, with the merged company.[36]

From this unpromising beginning events spiraled rapidly into confusion. After the October 5 meeting Lewis's attitude took a markedly different turn. The offer of that date was a friendly bid that UP wanted taken to the SF stockholders. Once Krebs and his board rejected the offer and refused to let their stockholders consider it as an alternative to the BN offer, the only alternative would be a hos-tile bid.[37]

Lewis let the offer go public and wrote Krebs expressing his disappointment at his refusal. The next day Krebs replied with a formal refusal; the offer would not be taken to the stockholders. He dismissed the last-minute offer of $20 a share and a voting trust as "inconsistent with UP's proposal and its press release." If UP made a clear offer on such a basis, the SF board would consider it. That same day UP filed suit in Delaware's Chancery Court—long the battleground of mergers—seeking to require SF to negotiate. One analyst labeled the fight "the equivalent of World War III in the railroad industry."[38]

Privately UP's officers and directors were shocked by the offhand change of terms made by Lewis without authorization. It became clear to the board that alcohol was taking a toll on his performance even though Lewis insisted otherwise. After agonizing over the question, several directors concluded that he could not remain involved in the negotiations. Robinson knew the problem better than any of the others; earlier that summer he had persuaded Lewis to tell Gerry about it. Both of them saw the problem escalating under the pressure of the SF clash. So far the issue had not gone public, but what if it did?[39]

The board decided that Lewis had to step down temporarily and enter a rehabilitation program. Afterward Gerry and Robinson went to inform Lewis. "It was a very emotional meeting," Gerry said later in his understated manner. It was also an ultimatum. Lewis resisted the idea until it became clear that his job was at stake if he refused. Marilyn Lewis helped persuade her husband that he should go. On October 24 Lewis quietly entered a treatment center. UPC hired a counselor to monitor him and keep the board informed on his progress. During his absence Davidson, Matthews, and Messman took charge along with Gerry. Matthews oversaw the SF operation.[40]

On October 28 Gerry outlined the arrangement at a special board meeting. A lengthy discussion ensued over the impact of Lewis's situation on UPC, its stockholders, management, customers, and other constituencies, especially the SF fight. From this exchange it became apparent that some directors remained uneasy about not only the SF bid but the primary role of the railroad itself in UPC. Lewis's departure, however temporary, brought these uncertainties to the forefront.[41]

The immediate question was how to present Lewis's absence. A draft news release dated October 28 said only that he had taken a short-term medical leave and was expected back in four to six weeks. However, it became clear that a cover-up was neither wise nor workable. Two days later UPC announced that Lewis had taken a medical leave to enter an alcohol treatment program. The response was low-key. The *Washington Post* praised UPC for being forthright about Lewis's problem.[42]

While this drama played itself out, the clash over SF heated up. Davidson pressed Krebs to present UP's offer to SF stockholders, but Krebs refused. SF set November 18 as the date for a special meeting to vote on the merger. On October 12 Krebs informed his stockholders that the board had rejected the UP offer and urged them to vote for the BN merger. UP countered the next day with a letter to SF stockholders soliciting proxies in opposition to the BN merger.[43]

On October 17 Krebs received a fourteen-page white paper on the merger prepared by Rebensdorf. As the exchanges escalated, *Traffic World* called it "the best soap opera to hit the railroad industry since the Penn Central merger and bankruptcy." Grinstein dismissed the hostile bid as "depression soup—all water and no beans." A reporter passed the remark along to Schuster. "If every word Jerry Grinstein used to disparage our offer was a dollar," Schuster replied, "he'd own the Santa Fe by now." Some analysts continued to doubt UP's sincerity even though a company spokesman assured them that "this is a very serious offer. We are not throwing a hand grenade at the Santa Fe/Burlington merger plan."[44]

The Delaware Chancery Court rejected the UP request to enjoin the BN-SF merger talks. Both companies ran full-page ads seeking proxies from SF stockholders. Matthews and others began making the rounds of institutional investors to explain why UP thought it could win ICC approval for a merger. Rebensdorf and others in Omaha courted shippers to the same end.[45]

Krebs had to fend off growing complaints about his handling of UP's bid. Some of his stockholders wanted a higher bid from BN despite Krebs's insistence that a UP merger would never win ICC approval. He had some large institutional holders to appease. Fidelity, the Boston mutual fund manager, controlled about 10 percent of SF's stock, and Alleghany Corporation had recently upped its holdings to about 6.4 percent, or 11.87 million shares. UP warned SF stockholders that its offer would be withdrawn if they approved the merger with BN.[46]

The failure to include a voting trust in the offer had come back to haunt UP. On October 28 it urged SF stockholders not to approve the merger. "Your vote AGAINST the Burlington Northern merger," it said, "will send a clear message to your Board that you want them to negotiate with Union Pacific." BN countered by raising its offer to $17 a share, topping the UP bid, which a decline in UP stock had lowered to $16.73. Grinstein declared that BN would not go any higher and would not offer a voting trust.[47]

Some SF stockholders remained unconvinced. Institutional investors held about 56 percent of SF's stock, arbitrageurs another 20 percent. Alleghany continued to oppose the merger, hoping for a better deal from UP. It also revealed plans to ask the ICC for permission to acquire as much as 15 percent of SF. At its meeting on October 28, the UP board debated whether or not to continue the hostile bid. Davidson laid out the long-term benefits and called SF the best merger partner for UP.[48]

"I tried to explain to the board," he said later, "that what would happen if the other guys got bigger and we stayed static . . . these guys were going to be so much bigger than us and they'd have more muscle than us and they'd just nibble us around the edges; and . . . we would not be able to stand up to them." The consultants spoke their piece and Matthews outlined alternatives, including a voting trust. This was no brisk, well-orchestrated board meeting of the sort Lewis liked; it began at 11:00 A.M. and did not adjourn until 5:15 that afternoon.[49]

Davidson remembered the division being so close that Gerry's vote carried the day. But the minutes recorded unanimous approval for a motion to continue the fight and increase UP's bid to $20 a share—ironically the same figure Lewis had blurted out to Krebs. Davidson conveyed this offer to Krebs that same afternoon. On November 1 he dispatched a letter to SF stockholders reminding them that an auction was on and urging them not to approve the merger. More full-page ads from both sides went into the *Wall Street Journal* and elsewhere seeking to sway stockholders. Unfazed, Krebs and his board rejected the new UP offer and refused a meeting to discuss it. "If UP makes a proposal at a fair price and with an adequate provision for a voting trust that would substantially eliminate the regulatory risk for SFP stockholders," he declared, "the Board would consider that proposal."[50]

There seemed no way around the voting trust issue. At a board meeting on November 5 Matthews put forward a proposal to acquire all of SF's shares, using a voting trust, at $17.50 a share with $10 paid in cash and $7.50 in UP stock. After nearly three hours the board decided to withhold a decision until November 8. The ICC was to hold a hearing then on UP's pending request to control CNW, and it might say something about the SF contest as well.[51]

The ICC hearing produced no insights, but the Alleghany Corporation offered to join with UP in a leveraged acquisition of SF. After Matthews opposed such a move, the board rejected the overture. In its final form the new UP bid was to acquire 57 percent of SF's stock for $17.50 per share in cash, and then accept the remainder at the time of merger for the same price. The earlier offer of $20 a share without a voting trust was left on the table as an alternative to SF stockholders. Davidson sent the offer to Krebs, who had on October 30 muddied his own position by disclosing that he had also held merger talks with SP.[52]

The new UP offer surprised everyone. The president of a mutual fund that owned 7 million shares of SF hailed it as "far superior" to BN's bid. Although BN denounced the new bid, Krebs saw he had no choice but to consider it. Still he refused to discuss the proposal with UP, prompting Davidson to write a sharp letter of complaint. Feeling the press of time, Krebs had the SF board postpone the November 18 meeting to December 2.[53]

The stakes of the contest were high. Whoever won SF would emerge as the largest rail system in the West and trigger another redrawing of the railroad map. The *Wall Street Journal* called it "the bitterest rail-industry battle" since Robert Young's celebrated proxy fight for the New York Central in 1954. "This is like Europe before World War I," said one rail executive. "Nobody trusts anybody anymore. Today's ally can be tomorrow's enemy." Some rail executives saw egos involved as well. Grinstein wanted to leave the nation's largest rail system as his legacy, Krebs wanted to run that largest system, and Davidson, caught up in the three-man horse race, wanted to show Lewis and the board that he could perform on a larger stage.[54]

On November 28 the ICC approved UP's use of a voting trust, laying that issue to rest. Krebs postponed the special stockholders' meeting again to December 16. He still urged stockholders not to tender shares to UP but said he would meet with UP to consider its offer. Analysts observed that if the special meeting had taken place, the stockholders would almost certainly have voted down the BN merger. The SF board also put a poison pill provision in place to ensure that no takeover could occur without its approval. Nevertheless, some analysts conceded that the ICC ruling meant that UP would win unless BN increased its offer.[55]

During the last week of November Lewis returned from rehabilitation and took charge of the contest. "He is chomping at the bit," said Matthews. "He can't wait to get back in the business. He loves a fight." Documents sent to the treatment center had kept him informed of events. Lewis fended off a threat by the California attorney general to oppose the merger and chided Krebs for continuing to dodge a meeting despite his public statement to the contrary. It was painfully clear that Krebs was interested only in the BN merger. His latest argument was that UP's cash offer would be taxable, while BN provided a tax-free transaction.[56]

UP continued to assert that an auction was in progress. Krebs disputed this notion vigorously, arguing that SF was not for sale but rather in the midst of a merger. Many analysts thought the UP bid stronger because stockholders would get their money sooner. Davidson insisted that acquiring SF would position UP as "the strongest railroad in the West, in the U. S., and maybe in the world." On December 4 SF representatives finally met with their UP counterparts to share financial information. SF again postponed its stockholders' meeting, this time to January 27.[57]

Having insisted for weeks that it would not raise its bid, BN on December 18 did exactly that, sweetening the pot to $20.40 a share, or $3.85 billion in all. In addition, the two roads unveiled a stock purchase scheme intended to lock up their merger with a joint tender offer. This plan clearly trumped UP's offer, and Lewis cried foul.[58]

Two days after SF's announcement, the ICC dismissed the BN's appeal and upheld UP's voting trust. The news came as small consolation. While Bethlehem pondered its next move, Rebensdorf did his own analysis. He and Matthews had agreed from the start that any hostile bid had to have a walk-away point—a price where the acquisition made no sense financially. BN's latest move had shoved the price very near that point, and everyone realized that Krebs and SF were doing everything possible to prevent a transaction with UP. Without telling Davidson, Rebensdorf and Dale Salzman closeted themselves in the twelfth-floor conference room over the Christmas holidays and tried to figure out the best possible response.[59]

Rebensdorf assumed that UP had made its highest bid and would not raise it. Matthews had pounded this point home. If SF went to BN, the obvious recourse was to acquire SP. Two major drawbacks loomed: The two systems had considerable overlap and SP was in poor shape. After digging into the issues, however, Rebensdorf and Salzman concluded that the competitive issues weren't as severe as they originally thought.[60]

After the holidays Rebensdorf broached the subject with Davidson. "It's a lousy railroad," Davidson replied. "It's in bad condition; it's just going to be a big drain." But Davidson was willing to listen, and Rebensdorf persuaded him that he didn't have a choice. "It's in lousy condition," Rebensdorf agreed, "but there is a franchise opportunity there. It fills in the gaps in our franchise, and if we don't do it, the BN–Santa Fe is going to sit out there and just pick us off." As usual Rebensdorf backed his argument with sheets of data. Davidson agreed to pitch the idea to UPC.[61]

While Davidson and Rebensdorf laid their plans, Bethlehem continued the bidding war. After BN and SF commenced their joint tender offer, the special meeting to approve the merger was postponed yet again, this time to February 7. On January 17 Lewis sent Krebs a new offer of $18.50 per share in cash for *all* of SF's outstanding stock. The new bid was simpler and offered SF stockholders the chance to get their money faster than BN's tender allowed. UP also asked the Delaware Chancery Court for a speedy ruling on a suit to invalidate SF's poison pill provision. As the duel of full-page ads resumed in earnest, the *Wall Street Journal* labeled the contest "too close to call."[62]

On January 22 Krebs informed Lewis that his board had rejected the latest offer in favor of the BN merger. BN agreed to buy another 10 million shares of SF stock under certain conditions. Alleghany declared its willingness to increase its holdings of SF to 15 percent. Four days later Lewis recommended that the company not increase its offer, and the board concurred. On January 30 the Chancery Court denied the request for a speedy hearing. A day later Lewis informed Krebs and Grinstein that UP was terminating its offer and congratulated them on their success. Grinstein responded with a handwritten note thanking Lewis for his "gracious and appreciated" letter. Krebs wrote his thanks as well, adding that "I know that Union Pacific will continue to be a formidable competitor."[63]

BN and SF proceeded with their merger, and Krebs ultimately got the top job he coveted. However, BN paid a steep price for its victory. As Matthews had hoped, the bidding war spiraled the price of SF from $2.7 billion to $4 billion, leaving SF holders thrilled and BN with a heavy debt burden. "Thank God for Union Pacific," said one SF shareholder. Around Schaumburg the new favorite joke was "Four billion dollars is a lot to pay for Rob Krebs." UP agreed not to oppose the merger in exchange for some modest trackage rights over an SF branch line. "We felt we shouldn't ask for things that we had criticized other carriers demanding in other merger cases," said UP spokesman John Bromley.[64]

Despite the loss of SF, UP had other opportunities to consider. Along one of the walls on the twelfth floor of UP headquarters could be found a row of pictures depicting the roads acquired by UP over the years. The Santa Fe would not be joining this gallery, but ample room remained for one or two other candidates. Far from concluding matters, the BN-SF merger opened yet another upheaval in the rail industry.[65]

24

The Shaking Out

The BN-SF merger triggered yet another shaking out of the rail industry that ultimately boiled the so-called Super Seven Class I railroads down to the Final Four—two in the West and two in the East. Formally created in September 1995, the Burlington Northern Santa Fe became the nation's largest system. However, the UP was already at work to reclaim that title. Nor was the shaking-out confined to the railroads. During 1995 the regulatory system underwent a dramatic change as well.

Even before the SF bidding war UP took up a major piece of unfinished business. The five-year restriction on converting its CNW preferred shares into common stock was due to expire in 1994. During those years UP wrestled with the question of how best to maintain the close connection between them. Bob Schmiege continued the policy of shrinking the CNW and slashing costs. By 1993 he had pared it down to 4,300 miles, about 40 percent of its 1972 size. Yard control centers were shut down, shops closed, and some rolling stock sold.[1]

Schmiege also centralized dispatching and customer service in Chicago. Global Two, the second doublestack facility, opened in November 1992. However, the smaller lines around him continued to draw business from CNW. Schmiege could make little headway against the crushing debt burden of $750 million imposed by the leveraged buyout of 1989, which consisted mostly of high-yield bank loans and junk bonds. Despite all Schmiege's efforts, CNW ran in the red during 1990 and barely eked out a profit in 1991. Its future remained in doubt.[2]

The only hope lay in recapitalizing CNW and dumping as much of the debt load as possible. Falling interest rates and a soaring stock market late in 1991 gave Schmiege a window of opportunity. During the winter of 1992 he sold 23 percent of Holdings—CNW's parent company—stock and used the proceeds to pay off debt. As part of the restructuring deal, UP agreed to exchange its $100 million in preferred stock for a like amount of nonvoting common stock of Holdings and to buy another $28 million of the stock, giving it a 24.3 percent

THE CHICAGO CONNECTION. The Chicago and North Western Railroad in 1994.

interest in CNW. To acquire the CNW preferred, UP had created a new subsidiary, UP Rail. It also gained a seat on the Holdings board. However, the deal had of necessity been put together in haste, ahead of ICC approval, which left the arrangements in a limbo of uncertainty.[3]

In 1990 the ICC had exempted the CNW buyout deal from regulation and approved the UP's haulage and trackage rights. However, it also ruled that nothing in the agreement gave UP control over CNW. To gain a voice in CNW's management UP had to persuade the ICC to allow conversion of its shares from nonvoting to voting status. In August 1992 UP announced its intention to do so even though it could do nothing with the shares until 1994. In effect the company sought ICC approval for common control well in advance of being able to exert it, so that when the time came, UP would be free to move as circumstances dictated.[4]

Davidson gave four reasons for this unusual move. The first and most obvious was to enable UP to vote its stock. The second was to allow UP and CNW to integrate their operating and marketing coordination without wondering constantly whether they had overstepped the vague boundary defining common control. Third, UP wanted a free hand to buy more Holdings stock if needed. Finally, the two companies wished to be free to merge if later conditions warranted such a move. "I want to stress that UP has no intention at present to take this course," Davidson told the ICC, "and it is our understanding that CNW management prefers for CNW to remain independent."[5]

Late in 1992 Blackstone and DJL decided to sell 2 million shares each of their Holdings stock. UP paid $39 million for all of Blackstone's shares and bought another 182,000 shares in the open market. By year's end UP owned 29.5 percent of Holdings, while Blackstone held 28.8 percent, DLJ 5.1 percent, the CNW management 4.2 percent, and the public 32.5 percent. Schmiege insisted that "UP does *not* control CNW" but admitted that "the dynamic of the marketplace is pushing CNW and UP toward closer and closer cooperation."[6]

The issue grew more urgent in June 1993 when both Blackstone and DLJ decided to sell all their remaining Holdings stock—a total of 14.3 million shares. UP bought 500,000 shares, rounding its total to 30 percent of the stock. In the process it gained two more seats on the Holdings board and termination of the original provision that it could do nothing with the stock until 1994. On September 28 the ICC held that voting this stock and having three board seats would in effect give UP control of CNW and asked all sides for additional evidence on that basis. Davidson maintained that UP would keep its share of Holdings stock below 50 percent, and that it occupied only three of nine board seats. Schmiege repeated the argument that "UP and CNW are natural end-to-end partners. We need each other in order to succeed."

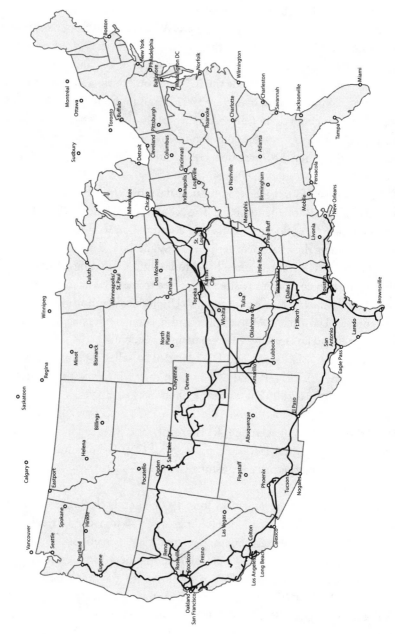

TOGETHER AGAIN.   The Southern Pacific Railroad in 1996 on the eve of its acquisition by the Union Pacific.

While awaiting the ICC decision, Rebensdorf dissected the pros and cons of a full consolidation. One draft analysis, completed in November 1993, urged full consolidation as a market-driven necessity. "CNW has a survivor mentality, independent pride and a brinkmanship attitude," it noted. "Despite sincere and continuous efforts, a true partnership is absent." CNW also committed fewer resources of all kinds to the interline partnership. "Service is viewed narrowly," said the analysis, "and UP often has to make up for CNW shortfalls." The CNW management was regarded as hierarchical with little effort at cross-functional communication or information sharing. All these cultural factors seriously restricted CNW's ability to respond to competitive challenges. The obvious solution was full consolidation.[7]

In July 1994 UP reassessed its position on acquiring CNW. The stock was widely scattered. Some fifty institutions held nearly 60 percent of it; UP had 29.1 percent, individual holders 9.3 percent, and 703 institutions 1.6 percent. Then the SF bidding war intervened and took priority. In mid-December the ICC finally granted authority for UP to control CNW. Davidson was eager to acquire CNW even though the company kept denying it in public.[8]

When the UPC board met on February 23 to discuss the railroad's strategic options, the SF bidding war had ended, and the issue became one of response. Although several options were reviewed, primary attention went to a merger with CNW. The traffic interchanged between UP and CNW amounted to 35 percent of the former's and 68 percent of the latter's business. Two key commodities, coal and intermodal, accounted for 88 percent of this traffic, reinforcing the belief that the two roads were indispensable to each other. Jack Koraleski and others looked into what positions could be found or created within UP for key CNW personnel.[9]

At long last, after years of delay, UP was ready to move. On March 7 Lewis and Davidson met with Schmiege and told him that UP would soon present an offer. He assured Schmiege that his people would have a place in the new organization, and that "you have my word and Dick's that we'll try to do the right thing." He mentioned a range of $32 to $34 a share for stock then selling in the low twenties.[10]

Schmiege needed little convincing. He convened his board on March 9 to discuss a possible offer from UP. During the meeting Lewis called to make an offer of $34 a share. The board asked Schmiege to negotiate a higher price if possible. When Lewis upped the price to $35, the board accepted without hesitation. On March 10 word of the deal went public. The price for the outstanding 70 percent of CNW stock was put at $1.1 billion. "No one should underestimate Union Pacific's desire to think big," said one analyst. By April 25 UP had acquired 99.47 percent of the outstanding CNW stock. In June the proud CNW disappeared from the railroad scene, the last of the storied Granger road flags to fall.[11]

For two decades the once mighty SP had been losing money, prestige, and significance in the railroad world. For five years during the failed SF merger it had dangled in limbo, falling behind other western roads in every category. When Phil Anschutz bought the railroad in 1988, no one knew what to make of the deal. To most people he was an oilman who dabbled in railroads after acquiring the Rio Grande. Few people expected him to stay with them, especially since he had invested so little of his own money. Anschutz bought the Rio Grande for $500 million, only $90 million of it in cash; he borrowed the rest, paid it off in eighteen months, and owned the road free and clear. For his leveraged buyout of SP he put up no cash at all but pieced together the more than $1 billion price tag from various banks as well as assuming $780 million in SP debt.[12]

Although Anschutz insisted he was in the railroad business to stay, few believed him. A short, athletic man who shunned interviews and avoided publicity, he was reclusive but a tough bargainer. "If you're across the table in negotiations," said banker David Schulte, "he'll wear you down, he'll frustrate you, because he comes back and back, tireless and tenacious. . . . He's a talented guy, a very rich guy, and he's used to having his way." In a rare interview Anschutz admitted that transforming SP was much harder than he had suspected but that he would succeed in bringing it around. "I've tried to be involved," he said. "I've tried to learn. I'm not a sideline sitter."[13]

One rail officer observed that while Anschutz had done financial due diligence on SP, he failed to do a "heart and soul due diligence. He could value the assets but was unable to determine how poor morale was and how badly the management had deteriorated." Nor did he know what wretched shape the railroad was in physically. These lessons he had to learn the hard way. Contrary to the belief of naysayers, Anschutz did not abandon SP, but neither did he effect a quick turnaround. Hayes Watkins of CSX once told him that it was difficult to change the culture of any company in less than five years. "I thought I could do it in 18 months," Anschutz admitted later. "I was wrong."[14]

The SP's problems spread out in every direction like tentacles that never stopped growing. Its traffic base was shaky, its locomotives old and outmoded, and much of its rolling stock, especially the lumber cars that carried one of its most important commodities, in deplorable shape. The roadbed needed massive infusions of capital after years of neglect, as did many of the facilities. In competing with its more efficient rivals, SP either lost business to them or acquired it at rates that were too low.[15]

The one bright spot remained SP's extensive landholdings, valued at anywhere from $600 million to $2 billion. From the first Anschutz viewed these holdings as a cash cow that would allow him to pay down the road's enormous debt load and make improvements on the line. In 1989 alone land sales fetched more than $350 million. To his dismay, however, a large chunk of the proceeds from land sales went to offset operational losses. In 1990, for example, land sales totaled $98 million, of which $66 million went to offset losses. Vice chairman Bob Starzel put on a brave front. "Even if company forecasts for profitable rail operations next year don't pan out," he said, "Southern Pacific could support its railroad with proceeds from real estate sales for years."[16]

To make matters worse, the poor shape of the road led to a string of costly derailments and accidents. In May 1990 a runaway freight train plowed into a row of homes, demolishing seven of them and killing four people in West San Bernardino. Thirteen days later, earthmoving equipment clearing away the debris ruptured a pipeline, causing a blast that killed two more people and destroyed or damaged twenty-one more homes. The National Transportation Safety Board blamed the accidents on glaring mismanagement. Through the fall of 1990 a string of accidents racked up more casualties and spills. Contamination issues also became a nightmare for the company.[17]

The worst was yet to come. In July 1991 an SP tanker car derailed and spilled 13,000 gallons of pesticide into the upper Sacramento River. While nearby residents fled the noxious fumes, the poison flowed downstream, wiping out all life in a 40-mile stretch of the river before flowing into Lake Shasta, the state's largest reservoir. Two weeks later a broken axle derailed another SP train near the Ventura County border and dumped several 55-gallon drums filled with hydrazine onto Highway 101, closing the road and forcing the evacuation of three hundred people to avoid the spreading cloud of noxious gas. In the public relations disaster that followed, one paper used the headline "Once-mighty Southern Pacific is just a shell of its former self." Representative Barbara Boxer unveiled government records showing that SP locomotives had more than an 80 percent failure rate in federal inspections, and charged the company with skimping on maintenance to save money.[18]

Against this backdrop of bad news Anschutz struggled to reshape SP. He shifted the road's day-to-day operations from president Mike Mohan to vice chairman William J. Holtman, a Rio Grande veteran. An intense, old-school operating man, Holtman had worked wonders at the Rio Grande but soon found that its lessons did not apply to the much larger SP system. As one reporter observed, Holtman went about changing the SP "with the finesse of Rambo, destroying lines of authority all over the railroad and even putting himself at cross purposes with his chairman." Named executive vice president in November 1991, he had by then alienated nearly every career officer on the SP. One of them described Holtman as bringing "a 1500-mile mentality to a 15,000-mile railroad."[19]

In May 1990 Anschutz brought in Don Orris, who had three weeks earlier abruptly resigned as president of American President Domestic Company, to revamp SP's marketing operation. One shipper who praised the move said of SP,

"They have no long-term focus. They are constantly starting and stopping plans. Orris should set up a major program and stick to it." Anschutz also hired Kent Sterett, an expert in quality programs, to instill that approach in the railroad. Tom Matthews came over from Eastern Air Lines to replace a vice president that the unions despised. Dennis Jacobson left UP to become vice president of customer service for SP.[20]

Gradually Anschutz improved his staff by replacing the old guard, yet the impression persisted that he didn't know enough about railroads to run such a complex enterprise. "Phil tends to listen to people from the outside who sound as if they know the problems but have never absorbed the details of our operation," said one operating department veteran. "He himself doesn't know what to look for." A marketing official agreed with this observation. "Phil is a visionary," he said. "But as far as managing the property is concerned, he has relied on other people, and has had a real difficult time."[21]

In May 1990 Anschutz outraged many people in the Bay Area with plans to sell SP's historic headquarters in San Francisco and move his operation to Denver. The Customer Service Center moved to Denver, but San Francisco kept the headquarters building. Anschutz tried to buy the Soo Line's route between Kansas City and Chicago but settled for a trackage agreement with the BN that finally gave the SP access to Chicago. His sale of 5 percent of his rail holdings to Japan's largest shipping company in October 1990 reinforced the image of SP as a railroad struggling to stay solvent.[22]

Despite these efforts SP remained afloat chiefly by its land sales. By August 1991 the company had reaped more than a billion dollars from property and trackage rights deals, but the railroad continued to lose money and the real estate market had turned sour. Operations remained a problem largely because of Holtman's determination to keep the Rio Grande distinct from the SP. Service plans broke down, budget controls went awry, crew starts mushroomed, and shippers grew furious. Between Tucson and El Paso, for example, forty to forty-five trains were dispatched daily to carry the same volume hauled earlier by thirty to thirty-two trains.[23]

Although progress had been made, it was clear by 1992 that much more was needed if SP was to survive. Already Krebs was sounding both UP and BN about the possibility of dividing up SP. In November 1991 Anschutz gave a presentation, later distributed to all employees, emphasizing that 1992 would be the year of decision as to whether the company would survive.[24]

"We need some major changes, some major success stories," he declared. ". . . We can't live with indecision and bureaucratic delays in this company. . . . I intend to demand results." The quality program would receive added emphasis. He expected leaders to lead and everyone to do their job to the utmost. If you can't do this, he emphasized, "get out of the company before you are forced out. . . .

I don't have, the leadership of this company doesn't have, and you shouldn't have, the patience any longer to put up with a lot of whining, complaints, and general grousing."[25]

Anschutz defined his own role as providing "the right environment, the right people, the right leadership, the right goals, the right strategic objectives," but not to make the major operating decisions. SP could no longer afford "the expense or the luxury of operating as if we were separate railroads.... The names of the Cotton Belt and Rio Grande are going to have to disappear." He demanded more teamwork and better communication. "The real gut issue," he concluded, "... is simply this—*will this company survive?*"[26]

To resolve the management tangle in operations, Anschutz in March 1992 hired Glenn P. Michael, formerly of CSX, as vice president of transportation field operations. On June 29 he was made VPO, and Holtman retired at year's end. Together Michael and Orris rethought existing schedules route by route over the system.[27]

The new Transportation Service Center, which coordinated train movement and network operational plans, joined the Customer Service Center in Denver, centralizing both functions in that city. The Burnham shops in Denver got a major overhaul to concentrate locomotive repair work there. During April SP consolidated three regions and twenty-one divisions into a single fifteen-state network divided into five areas. It also launched a four-year plan to rehabilitate more than 20,000 cars. As promised, the Rio Grande and Cotton Belt were absorbed. To showcase the "new SP" to customers, a special train featuring two new GP60 locomotives and eight rebuilt cars traveled to twenty cities in eleven states.[28]

The "new SP" featured not only an emphasis on quality but town hall meetings hosted by senior managers. "We expect 1992 to be a break-even year," said Orris, "with the next four bringing us into the black numbers. We still have a good deal of rebuilding to do before everything falls into place." In a rare interview Anschutz admitted that "our service during the last four months has been awful," largely because of problems caused by moving all the dispatchers to Denver. But progress was being made. "I know our service is coming back dramatically," he said. "What we are headed for is a railroad that operates on time."[29]

After a slow start Anschutz had infused the company with fresh management, modernized attitudes, and a fighting spirit. But earnings continued to languish. SP had lost $35.8 million in 1990 and $78.9 million in 1991; in 1992, the promised year of decision, it lost another $28.5 million. The record floods of 1993 blasted hopes for a rebound that year, causing a loss of $40 million in the third quarter alone. The old pattern of making ends meet by selling off real estate persisted in spite of all efforts to wean the railroad away from it. Problems continued to mount, especially in operations. On March 11 Orris wrote bluntly, "We're

losing business in the tens of millions of dollars at this point. Our service is absolutely terrible."[30]

During 1993 Anschutz poured what capital he could muster into roadway
maintenance, buying and leasing new or refurbished equipment, and disposing
of old locomotives and cars. As the losses mounted, however, he concluded that
more drastic action was needed. "This railroad is going to learn to get by on less,"
he told an interviewer in May, ". . . and we're going to learn to like it that way."
That same month Anschutz decided to take the company public with a $550
million stock offering that he hoped would bring $20 a share and wipe out nearly
all the remaining debt from his purchase of the road. The offering would put
only about 25 percent of the stock in public hands, leaving Anschutz firmly in
control.[31]

Columnist Allan Sloan ridiculed the offering as "yet another sign that mad-
ness has infected the IPO market." If successful, he noted, "Anschutz will have
turned an investment of less than $90 million into more than $1.4 billion of
stock in less than 10 years. Which is probably the biggest single profit ever made
in the history of U.S. railroading." He blasted SP as a company "loaded to the
eyeballs with debt . . ., losing hundreds of million of dollars annually on its railroad business," and covering its losses "by selling an average of $350 million of
real estate a year."[32]

In July a dose of reality induced SP to lower its IPO price to a range of $13–15
for the August listing. As one analyst quipped, "It was DOA at $20." Anschutz
sprang another surprise by naming Edward L. Moyers president and CEO of SP
Rail Corporation and chairman and CEO of its railroad subsidiaries. In December 1992 Moyers had abruptly retired as head of the IC only months after sign-
ing a four-year contract with the road. Mohan promptly resigned.[33]

Anschutz had a special reason for bringing in Moyers. Apart from his reputation as a railroader, he had a good relationship with the analysts, and the company was going public. Shippers applauded the move. "You could write a book
about the service problems with the SP," said one of them. Analysts wondered
whether Moyers, who was sixty-four and had recently undergone heart surgery,
had the health and stamina to do the job. The challenges facing him included
solving the acute shortage of locomotives, matching them with a more reliable
supply of freight cars, improving on-time performance, turning increased volume into sustained profitability, trimming down SP's still bloated bureaucracy,
and finding better ways to counter its aggressive competitors who had been
doing these things for years.[34]

Since Moyers had a reputation for cutting costs, everyone knew what was
coming. On August 10 SP sold 30 million shares of common stock for $13.50 a
share and another $375 million worth of senior secured notes, returning the
company to public ownership for the first time since 1983. Less than a month

later SP announced plans to cut 4,000 employees from its workforce of 22,000, twice the number originally planned. Moyers wanted 500 of the company's more than 2,500 management people trimmed. The five operating regions were reduced to two.[35]

Moyers brought in more fresh faces from the outside and promised that signs of a turnaround would appear within six months. When an interviewer observed that the SP was known for having "the worst customer service, the least reliable service, the most unpredictable service in the railroad business," he cringed but did not deny the charge. He admitted that "SP has a history of going to one area and fixing that, and then other things fall apart."[36]

Through the rest of 1993 and 1994 Moyers pushed his cost-cutting campaign. He thinned the ranks of vice presidents from twenty-six to twenty, slashed the budget for outside consultants from $14 million to $1.5 million a year, and reduced travel budgets. Anschutz approved the moves.[37]

In one controversial move Moyers outsourced SP's information systems work to an IBM subsidiary in hopes of saving $10 million annually. As the mainframes were cut over to IBM's system in Boulder, Colorado, forty-five SP employees lost their jobs. The company also announced that it would negotiate its own labor contracts rather than accept national settlements. The board approved an ambitious $106.3 million rail, tie, and ballast improvement program for 1994. To bolster its depleted power fleet, SP leased 100 locomotives from GE, bought 50 more from EMD, and acquired 133 remanufactured engines from Morrison Knudsen.[38]

The sale of land and unwanted branch lines continued, and more funds went into improving the power and car supply. In October 1994 another $40.8 million was allocated to double-tracking 53.7 miles of line on the Sunset Route between Tucson and El Paso. For all his reputation as a cost cutter, Moyers realized that service could not be improved without spending money. Yet so desperate was SP that it obtained rail for the Sunset Route double track by pulling up one of its two lines over Donner Summit and from spots in Nevada.[39]

Early in 1995 Moyers's fragile health worsened and he retired. In February Anschutz replaced him with Jerry Davis, who came over from the CSX. Davis wanted one last chance to run his own railroad and regarded the opportunity as a last contract before his own retirement. His reputation as a competent and popular executive made him welcome at SP.[40]

For nearly six years Anschutz had struggled with limited success to turn SP around. Some of that time had been wasted and costly, his tuition for learning how different running a large system was compared to the smaller Rio Grande. His acquisition of SP for little or none of his own money was a masterful stroke but also the source of his most intractable problem. To operate successfully SP needed massive infusions of capital that could not be raised easily while the company staggered under its crushing burden of debt from the acquisition.

In taking over SP Anschutz had reinstated the company's venerable sunset emblem. It seemed a fitting symbol for a railroad that looked to be heading into its sunset. There was, however, one option that would both reward Anschutz handsomely and provide the capital SP needed. To that end he called Drew Lewis to see whether UP would be interested in buying SP.[41]

During the summer of 1994 senior executives of UP and SP discussed the possibility of a merger. The talks proceeded far enough to produce a confidentiality agreement in September but broke off a few weeks later when UP decided instead to make its run at SF. Once that campaign ended, talks between UP and SP resumed in February 1995. UP had long coveted a southern route, which BN now had, and it needed a stronger presence throughout California. In many respects SP represented a better fit for UP than SF, but it was in much worse physical shape.[42]

In February 1995 Davidson and Rebensdorf went to Bethlehem to persuade Lewis, Matthews, and von Bernuth that UP had to go after SP to remain competitive. Lewis was dubious but let the analysis go forward. At the February board meeting Matthews briefed the directors on the complexity of the competitive issues. Davidson followed with an overview not of SP but of the situation in Mexico, where the government was considering the privatization of its national railway. The board agreed that all options should be pursued.[43]

Word was out that SP was on the block. Anschutz and Bob Starzel put together a road show to show the eastern roads as possible merger partners, but UP remained uppermost in their thinking. In March Lewis, Davidson, and Rebensdorf flew to St. Louis to meet with Anschutz and Starzel, who arrived with a bundle of rolled-up maps under his arm. SP made its pitch, and they agreed to continue discussions. Matthews, von Bernuth, and David DeNunzio of CS First Boston took up the negotiations with Anschutz. On April 8 UP's lawyers gave SP a draft agreement but no negotiations over it occurred. A week later the discussions terminated.[44]

Nearly all the talking had taken place between senior officers and lawyers from both roads. "It was hired guns talking to hired guns," said Schuster. Lewis and Anschutz did not know each other well and were not particularly fond of each other. But Anschutz wanted to get out from under the financial burden of SP, and Lewis wanted the merger as a capstone for his UPC career. Like it or not, they needed each other.[45]

After some preliminary meetings Lewis, Davidson, and their officers met the SP contingent on July 17 at the Kansas City airport. Anschutz and Lewis excelled at this kind of tough bargaining. With the two sides still far apart, Lewis took

Anschutz into a private room and hammered out a preliminary agreement in which UP would acquire up to 25 percent of SP's stock for cash at $25 a share, then offer cash or UP stock for the remainder following ICC approval of the merger. Anschutz held 31.8 percent of the outstanding SP stock; his ally Morgan Stanley owned another 8.5 percent. Both agreed to support a merger if the terms could be agreed upon.[46]

Several disparate issues were coming together for Lewis. The broader vision he had cherished for UPC had flamed out. He had already bought CNW; acquiring SP as well would confirm the railroad's position as the overwhelmingly dominant subsidiary in the corporation. In that case there seemed no choice but to anoint Davidson as Lewis's successor because he knew how to run the railroad. This decision would frustrate Matthews and disappoint Messman. If Davidson moved up to UPC, Lewis wanted someone from outside the railroad to take his place at its head. He put headhunters in motion to find the right man.

At a special telephone meeting of the board on July 21 Lewis laid out the proposal and discussed a possible role for Anschutz at UPC. Davidson, Matthews, von Bernuth, and the consultants offered their assessments. When they finished, the directors asked more questions and discussed the matter until Lewis wrapped the meeting up with a projected timetable for the offer. The board agreed that discussions should continue. The entire process took only forty-five minutes.[47]

On July 26, the day before its regular monthly meeting, Lewis presided over an executive session of the board at the Four Seasons restaurant in New York. Virgil Conway, chair of the Compensation, Benefits, and Nominating Committee, recommended that Davidson receive the additional office of chief operating officer of UPC and that Ronald J. Burns, president of Enron, succeed him as president and CEO of the railroad. Bringing Davidson to Bethlehem would send a clear signal that the horse race was finally over. No one knew much about Burns, but the directors approved the motion. Lewis then unveiled his plan to spin off Resources to the stockholders, giving Messman his own company to run.[48]

Next morning, in executive session, Lewis described his meetings with Anschutz and what role he might play at UPC. A new board would be formed for UP Resources once it was spun off after an initial public offering (IPO). Matthews reviewed the financial implications of an IPO, and Messman followed with his usual glowing account of the company's possibilities. After some discussion the board approved an IPO for up to 17.25 percent of Resources' stock. UPC kept the remaining shares for a later spin-off in order to make it tax free.[49]

With that business concluded, Lewis launched into the SP negotiations. A merger, explained Davidson, would make UP more competitive, increase capacity, strengthen intermodal capabilities, and provide greater access to Mexico.

Asked about the SP's physical condition, he described the capital investment needed to upgrade its equipment and facilities. When one director asked about possible objections from other roads, Arvid Roach of Covington & Burling outlined the likely position of other roads, shippers, and constituencies. The directors agreed that negotiations should continue.[50]

On August 2 senior officers from both roads reviewed progress of the negotiations. The exchange ratio remained a major sticking point until agreement was reached on .4065 shares of UP for each share of SP for the 75 percent of stock acquired after ICC approval. During a special conference-call meeting the UPC board approved a complex set of terms to acquire SP for an estimated $3.9 billion. The initial step would be the tender offer for 25 percent of SP's shares. The SP board approved the terms that same day.[51]

During the next month UP disarmed BN's expected strong opposition to the merger with an agreement giving that road trackage rights over about 3,800 miles of UP lines. BN also agreed to buy some 335 miles of UP track outright and grant UP trackage rights over 350 miles of BN lines. The deal gave BN rights to run from Denver to Salt Lake City and northern California as well as between Houston and Memphis. In effect the agreement replaced SP with BN as a competitor for the petrochemical, Mexican, and northern California business. "Customers should be well pleased with this agreement," said Davidson, but some still complained that the merger was being rammed down their throats.[52]

UP struck the agreement for SP even as it continued to digest the CNW acquisition. The same September board meeting that approved the agreement with BN also approved the absorption of the Holdings company. Together the new additions would thrust UP past BNSF as the nation's largest system. No one knew how long it would take to win ICC approval for the SP merger, especially given the fact that the future existence of the ICC itself was on the table in Congress.

25

The Sorting Out

The fall of 1995 proved to be one of the busiest and most fateful seasons in UP history. The merger required yet another mountain of paperwork and time expended in dealing with those who objected to it. Hearings commenced on the fate of the ICC and what would replace it. UP took a keen interest in the outcome because the SP merger would be the first order of business for whatever entity resulted. Although the CNW merger was completed, absorbing the road inflicted a bad case of indigestion on UP. The railroad had a new president who was not a railroader, and the corporation had a new heir apparent who was not warmly received in Bethlehem. Much remained to be sorted out during the months following the merger's announcement.

The UP-SP merger announcement sparked renewed debate over whether too much power was being concentrated in too few hands throughout the industry. Conrail wanted a key part of the SP line, while both CSX and NS wanted all or part of Conrail. Labor protested expected job losses. The NITL, which represented major shippers, denounced the merger as stifling competition. The Justice Department agreed. Both sides readied their lobbyists for the fight. "When you have a merger of this type," shrugged Lewis, "everyone wants to see how they can benefit."[1]

Mergers took on a radically different character in an age when Wall Street called the tune and demanded instant gratification. The standard justifications for most mergers were the synergies and economies to be gained from the combination. The synergies arose from operating once separate roads as one system, the economies from eliminating duplicate personnel and facilities. Less obvious were the problems posed, such as the blending of different corporate cultures, operating standards, computer systems, and maintenance practices. In any merger differences greatly outnumbered similarities, and as rail systems grew larger, their joining became vastly more complicated.

The CNW merger, said Davidson, "was really going well, much smoother than I had hoped." His optimism was grounded in personal observation; during May he spent four days going over the CNW system. Some 200 to 250 of CNW's nonunion employees at its Chicago headquarters were offered transfers to Omaha; the rest accepted buyouts. Altogether nearly 500 managers from both UP and CNW took severance packages, which amounted to $64 million in savings over the next eighteen years. By July 1 the formal acquisition process was completed. Ron Burns came aboard in Omaha on August 1, and shortly afterward Davidson left for Bethlehem.[2]

In some ways the CNW deal was more an acquisition than a merger. It was a true end-to-end combination with only a few common points to merge. "We integrated the system," said Tom Watts, "but the survivors were all Union Pacific people." This pattern suited UP managers, who were eager to impose what they deemed their superior methods and procedures on the system.[3]

The trouble began as fall approached. A record grain harvest increased shipments 30 percent on the CNW. Already shy of adequate power, the road staggered under the loads thrust on it. Delays and disruptions backed service up through Chicago, Kansas City, and other major gateways, stalling shipments to eastern roads as well. By November the problem had escalated into a major crisis. "It has been about the ugliest operational situation I have seen since I have been around railroads," said one grain shipper. New locomotives scheduled for delivery did not arrive on time, compounding the shortage. The loss of so many experienced CNW managers also crippled efforts to ease the spiraling congestion.[4]

The timing could not have been worse. Davidson, the experienced railroad man, had just gone to Bethlehem, leaving Burns, whose strength was marketing, in command. As grain trains gridlocked on the Iowa lines, Burns decided not to seek Davidson's advice. The last thing he wanted to do was run to Davidson for advice on the first major problem confronting him. Instead he wrote an open letter to customers on November 6 apologizing for their "unprecedented problems with service. . . . With power already tight and line capacity strained, we knew that implementation of C&NW would be a challenge. Indeed, the learning curve on the cutover has been steep. As a result, service has deteriorated to levels never before seen on UP."[5]

It was a courageous act, and it cost Burns dearly. "Writing a letter of apology like that was not something that was typically done on the railroad," said Stan McLaughlin. Merill Bryan added, "Especially you don't do it without telling the guys back East." Davidson saw another problem. "It wasn't the apology," he said. "That kind of put us in a legal position that was indefensible. And then he wrote a subsequent letter that said, 'We've got things fixed and you're never going to have problems again.' . . . You can't say things are fixed and that you're never going to have problems again."[6]

The letter pleased some critics but infuriated most UP officers. The proud UP culture was not one that apologized, and UP's officers had said the merger was going smoothly. Even worse, the letter appeared only a few weeks before the SP merger application, a time when UP was arguing that the integration of SP into UP would be seamless. "There's never a good time to give bad service," noted the president of a connecting regional road, "but one of the worst times is when you have to get major shipper support for a major merger application." Burns got a chilly reception when he explained the situation to the board on November 30, the very day the merger application was filed.[7]

To ease the congestion, UP leased 137 locomotives, hired two hundred new crew employees, brought back a key CNW manager, and devised a new operating plan. "It was like taking chemotherapy," said Dennis Duffy. "You're going to fix the patient, and you really have to just hold your nose and get through it." By Thanksgiving UP had twenty to twenty-five grain trains still backed up. "We took that holiday weekend and cleaned them all up," said Duffy. But it took several more weeks to restore normal service. Analysts blamed UP for cutting CNW personnel too quickly and too deeply. Several UP officers, including Davidson, agreed they had gone too fast in combining the roads.[8]

A major reason was the bottom-line mentality of the 1990s. "We wanted to produce savings," said Marchant, "and show Wall Street how good we were and how quickly we could produce these savings." Eisele agreed that "there was a tremendous amount of pressure, not only to get those savings in place fast but actually to get them in place at levels that exceeded expectations." Those expectations came not only from the financial community but also from UPC; the railroad, after all, was the driver of its stock price.[9]

Overconfidence also soured the process. What some critics called UP arrogance was in part a belief that history would repeat itself. "They underestimated the difficulties of managing the North Western network," said Rebensdorf. "... You took people from the UP ... [and] sent them over to run the North Western, and they ran it like they tried to run the UP." Eisele conceded that UP had underestimated "the complexity and our ability to do this simply because of the gold standard we had set in past mergers." The MP experience had gone so smoothly that UP officers assumed the same would hold true with CNW.[10]

Installing the TCS computer system on the CNW inevitably caused integration problems, as did new routing opportunities created by the merger. Davidson admitted that the loss of senior CNW managers hurt operations but insisted that "to think that we wholesale got rid of all the senior management is wrong. There was a lot of them I tried to keep, but that damn golden parachute they had in place was just too attractive for them."[11]

By year's end the CNW traffic congestion problem had eased, but it left a bitter aftertaste. Davidson and other officers still seethed over the November 6 letter; in their eyes Burns had fumbled the ball on his first carry. Others saw the CNW service problem as a warning for what might happen if UP took over the much larger and more complicated SP. Burns guaranteed that "there won't be a repeat of service problems in the future, with or without the Southern Pacific."[12]

Since the Staggers Act the ICC had become, in Richard Saunders's words, "a hateful place." It had less and less to do, and much of what it did was badly done. Its peak of more than 2,400 employees in the early 1960s had dwindled to fewer than 300 with only five commissioners, who bickered with each other so intensely that they sometimes refused even to meet in the same room. Republican congressmen were eager to eliminate it; one called it "the dinosaur that wouldn't die." In his January 1995 State of the Union message President Bill Clinton called for eliminating a hundred unneeded programs and mentioned the ICC as one example. A month later Congress reduced the committee's funding from $50 million to $40 million and introduced bills to get rid of it entirely.[13]

The Justice Department and DOT both wanted oversight of rail mergers transferred to them. Justice viewed mergers as an antitrust issue, DOT as one of transportation policy. At Justice staff lawyers would handle the cases as they did all other business mergers; DOT would have to create a new body—a Surface Transportation Board (STB)—to deal with cases. Clinton, like Reagan before him, favored a move to Justice, but Congress leaned toward DOT. Critics charged that a new board amounted to a trimmer version of the ICC under a new name.[14]

The debate went mattered greatly to UP because the SP merger harbored a number of antitrust issues. A new body at DOT would be a far more friendly forum for the hearings. Lewis still had considerable clout among congressional Republicans. When the House considered a bill to eliminate the ICC late in 1995, Lewis made his influence felt. He mounted an intensive lobbying campaign that included Mary McAuliffe, Ann Eppard, who had been the top aide for Representative Bud Shuster of Pennsylvania for many years, and two major lobbying firms. Lewis's longtime friendship with Shuster proved crucial; Shuster had steered the ICC bill through the House. Anschutz contributed his troops from SP, prompting an NITL official to complain, "They're blanketing the Hill."[15]

On November 9 the House Rules Committee took up an amendment to the bill that would give authority over rail mergers to Justice. Lewis surprised everyone by taking a seat in the hearings room to follow the proceedings. Through days of hearings and deliberations Lewis worked the phones, buttonholed Speaker Newt Gingrich and other key representatives, and wrote letters. His efforts paid off; the amendment was defeated and jurisdiction over mergers went to DOT.[16]

That Lewis devoted hours to attending obscure committee meetings showed how important he thought it was to keep the merger away from Justice. The House obliged by passing the ICC bill 417–8 on November 14. A tougher fight ensued in the Senate, but two weeks later it passed. When Bob Dole stunned everyone by raising an objection, Lewis tracked him down by phone and got his good friend to relent as a favor. The act included a provision for the creation of a Surface Transportation Board. A union lobbyist opposing the merger called it "a Drew Lewis memorial law."[17]

Clinton then threatened a veto because the bill gave the STB no power to protect labor. Provisions were hastily added and a new bill rushed through on December 21 and 22. Congress was about to adjourn for the holidays, but McAuliffe rallied her troops to get the bill passed first. She told both Lewis and Davidson they had to be present for the final House vote on the twenty-second.[18]

The need for Lewis's presence posed a problem. After learning of the Senate's final approval on December 21, Lewis celebrated with a few drinks and climbed into his white Ford Explorer. Driving south on route 563 in Pennsylvania, he swerved erratically into the northbound lane and then veered back into his own lane. A state trooper pulled him over and measured his blood alcohol content at .15. Although his DUI arrest and night in jail went largely unnoticed by media outside the local newspaper, word of it got to Washington.[19]

Despite this embarrassment, Lewis joined Davidson for the final House vote. After the bill passed, Bud Shuster hurried off the House floor to hug and high-five Lewis. Clinton signed the bill a week later, and the ICC became extinct. On January 1 a *Wall Street Journal* headline read, "U. S. Agency, Once Powerful, Dead at 108."[20]

However, word of Lewis's arrest reached the UP's directors. Since his first rehabilitation stint Gerry had given the board regular reports on his recovery program. The DUI incident forced the board to consider whether Lewis should be fired or allowed to finish out his final year in office. At a meeting on January 24, 1996, it was decided to increase the assistance given Lewis and allow him to complete his term as chairman and CEO. However, he was to focus entirely on the SP merger and "assuring an orderly management succession." The board affirmed Davidson as Lewis's successor and ordered all operating department except Resources and Finance to report to Davidson.[21]

This arrangement allowed Lewis to keep his job while easing Davidson into the position. Apart from wanting to give Lewis every consideration, the board sensed that his talents, however flawed, would be needed in the fight to get the merger approved.

Bethlehem did not welcome Davidson with open arms. It was, after all, the board and not Lewis who insisted that he go there. Most of the corporate staff expected

Matthews to win the horse race. The senior executive among the candidates, he had endeared himself to the board personally and with his lucid presentations, and he had cultivated a good relationship with Wall Street. Some said he managed better up than down, but he seemed far superior to Messman. Davidson was an unknown quantity to most of them.[22]

The locals had good reason to favor Matthews or Messman over Davidson. "They were all afraid that the corporation was going to leave Pennsylvania," said Linda Waller, "because there wasn't really any reason for it to be there except that Mr. Lewis wanted it there." Some clung to the hope that the race had not really ended.[23]

When Davidson arrived in Bethlehem, Lewis told him to leave the railroad to Burns; he was there to learn the other side of the business. "I hated to let go of the railroad," Davidson admitted, "'cause I was nervous as hell about a nonrailroad guy coming in and running it." The CNW service congestion did nothing to ease his mind, but here was another of the challenges on which Davidson thrived. "I was very interested in learning the trucking business and about this Skyway Company," he said. He also had to come to grips with government relations, investor relations, and community involvement as well as the finer points of corporate governance, finance, and structure. Thus began the next chapter in the education of Dick Davidson.[24]

He had much to learn. To the suave, urbane easterners he still resembled the country boy come to the city. Davidson knew as much. "I was still an operating guy," he said, "and had to smooth off a lot of edges as far as the social and political and marketing side of things." Lewis didn't like Davidson's table manners or the way he dressed and ordered an aide to "turn him into a CEO." Tactfully the aide took Davidson shopping for new shoes and new suits from a Philadelphia tailor.[25]

Appearance posed a curious problem for Davidson. He always made a strong impression in person, where his straightforward manner soon won people over, but he did not photograph well. Unlike Lewis, who nearly always wore a smile in pictures, Davidson usually wore a sober, almost grim expression that with his small, partially closed eyes created the image of a man who wanted to sell you a used car. His smile looked pained, forced. Yet in person, although somewhat aloof, he loved a good story and laughter came easily to him. Unlike corporate executives, operating men did not live in a world governed by images, and Davidson had to master that distinction.

Rob Knight understood this adjustment better than most. A fellow Kansan, he was almost alone in welcoming Davidson to Bethlehem. "He makes a physical presence obviously that people can't help but notice and respect," he said, ". . . but they weren't going to cut him any slack."[26]

Waller, who accompanied Davidson to Bethlehem as his secretary, described the experience as "going into the lion's den." On the surface it seemed "almost like Camelot." Lewis was king and provided for his subjects in generous fashion. An excess of staff took care of everyone's personal needs down to oil changes, leaving them free to work. When Lewis and Judy Waltos heard that Waller was about to marry a company pilot who worked out of Omaha, they moved him to Bethlehem and switched one of their pilots to Omaha.[27]

Office relationships were another matter. Waller was resented because she was loyal to Davidson. Judy Waltos treated her well, but Judy Swantak proved especially difficult. Waller regarded her as "a very volatile person. She just wasn't the nicest person in the world, and so most of her staff was scared of her. But again, she could turn around and be really nice. . . . She could be very good to her staff, and then the next minute she was screaming about something."[28]

Waller struggled to get even basic information from Swantak on such things as where Davidson needed to be when, and relied instead on friendlier staff below Judy. These people were hardworking but worried about their future. The Bethlehem economy was depressed, and few locals were likely to get as good a job if UPC left the city. The tenor of office politics hit home to Waller early one morning when Lewis summoned her to a meeting. The two Judys were there along with an assistant. Matthews usually worked out in the morning and joined the meeting on speakerphone. Unaware that Waller was there, he began putting Davidson down in a number of ways. Lewis squirmed in his chair and finally told Matthews they'd discuss the matter later.[29]

"White sort of ran the roost," said Knight. "Not just within the finance function but I'd say all of Bethlehem." The relationship between Davidson and Matthews was complicated. They had known each other for many years, dating back to their MP days. Both had strong personalities, excelled at their jobs, and demanded results from those who worked for them. They were also very competitive but worked in different spheres until the horse race turned them into rivals. Its outcome left Matthews embittered because, in Knight's words, he "desperately wanted that position."[30]

Matthews freely admitted as much; what ambitious executive does not long to be CEO? He did not dislike Davidson, who had taught him the rail business. Davidson was "nice and polite," said Matthews, "but he's pretty tough down under, and he'll do whatever he needs to." He thought Davidson lacked vision and told his staff as much. Although his ambition to become a CEO did not diminish, Matthews couldn't leave the company because of the golden handcuffs agreement. He tried therefore to help Davidson while continuing to feel underappreciated. Davidson didn't trust Matthews, largely because of his thwarted ambition. "I thought he was pretty aggressive about wanting to further his own career," said Davidson, "and I didn't think it would bother him to step on somebody else to do that." Their relationship remained coolly professional.[31]

Amid these internal tensions Davidson kept his focus on the business at hand. "I really did enjoy some of the other things more than I would have ever dreamed," he admitted, "the political things and dealing with the financial community and marketing things." Increasingly he became a public face of UP, something that most operating people had always shunned. "We encourage our operating guys to stay anonymous," said Davidson, "so they can focus on operations and not get caught up in all the other things that can distract you."[32]

So much was new to him at this level, but he approached it with the same work ethic he had displayed at every stage of his career. He watched, listened, absorbed, and moved on to the next challenge. He was at Lewis's elbow through the hearings to eliminate the ICC and followed him around the Hill to learn the political game. He joined Lewis and Matthews on their rounds of meetings with analysts, investors, bankers, and other key financial people. He studied the other subsidiaries, paying especially close attention to Overnite because the trucking business was new to him.[33]

The vaunted synergies with the railroad had never materialized; Davidson wanted to know why not. He realized that an LTL trucking operation was "very much like a railroad with your terminals being like a big rail yard and filling your trucks up, which is equivalent of filling trains up to go to destinations and that sort of thing." Overnite's struggle to turn a profit was plagued by its running battle with the Teamsters, who wanted to unionize the company. After Harwood Cochrane's retirement in 1990 Tom Boswell had run Overnite. The fight with the Teamsters intensified. When Boswell quit in January 1995 Lewis put Jim Douglas in his place. Like Boswell, Douglas had a background in finance, not trucking.[34]

The key to Overnite's problems, Davidson concluded, was lack of proper leadership. Boswell and Douglas were good men, but they were not truckers. He mentioned this to Lewis, who replied that Douglas was an MBA, and an MBA could do anything. This was one of Lewis's favorite conceits. Davidson thought otherwise and went hunting for an experienced trucking executive. He found one in Leo Suggs, head of a Yellow Freight subsidiary. Suggs had gone into trucking at the age of fourteen and continued even while in college. He made an immediate impact on the business and its employees.[35]

The irony of the situation could not have escaped Davidson. Hiring Suggs put Overnite in the hands of an experienced trucker shortly after Lewis had placed the railroad under the command of someone with no railroad experience whatsoever. He had hired Burns over Davidson's objections because he was determined to put another outsider in charge.[36]

Davidson had lobbied hard for Art Shoener, but Lewis didn't want operating men at the head of both UPC and the railroad. Shoener was deeply disappointed. Earlier he had been offered the presidency of the IC but stayed at the UP on the belief that he was next in line for the top job. Lewis had done the same thing with Walsh, who had acquitted himself splendidly. Evidently Lewis hoped that Burns could have a similar impact on the railroad.[37]

Nearly everybody liked Ron Burns. He had the highest recommendations and a strong endorsement from a headhunter. Tall, handsome, intelligent, articulate, and personable, he fit the profile for someone in marketing. "He was kind of a hand-gripping, back-slapping, wide-smiling kind of guy," said Eisele, "and he played to that strength because he played golf." Burns played golf very well, and it was his passion. A native of Omaha, he had spent all but the past decade of his life in the city. His mandate from Lewis was to change not only the railroad's culture but its marketing approach as well.[38]

The Omaha officers knew little about Burns or why he was chosen. In his first message to the employees, whom he called "teammates," he promised to spend his first months "doing far more listening than talking," but already he saw a need to "streamline, simplify and focus on those drivers and issues that count most in the long-run." A believer in informality as a way of breaking down barriers, he asked everyone to call him Ron and urged other managers to follow suit.[39]

The time for listening rather than talking proved to be short. Burns had already made up his mind about some key issues, and the annual Leadership Conference, scheduled for November 8–9, was the ideal forum for introducing a new approach. The conference had a sports motif to highlight the emphasis on teamwork and included a pep talk from Tommy Lasorda, manager of the Los Angeles Dodgers. As always the conference blended serious issues with generous doses of boosterism, but the 1995 edition contained two other distinctive elements as well. It marked the debut of a new president of the railroad, and it took place against the backdrop of the service congestion crisis on the CNW.[40]

The opening day occurred only two days after Burns had written his infamous apologetic letter. During the next six weeks Burns kept constantly on the move. He spent a week in the field, "learning, listening and sharing perceptions and our vision for the future," and applauded the drive to clear up the worst of the congestion over Thanksgiving weekend. On November 30 the SP merger application, all fourteen volumes and more than eight thousand pages of it, was formally submitted. Four days later Burns sent another letter to UP customers updating them on the steps taken to relieve the congestion.[41]

In Omaha Burns imposed a more informal, people-friendly style on the organization. Walsh had introduced casual Fridays to company headquarters; Burns extended it to the entire week and led the parade by wearing jeans to the office. He had the UP Museum, long a fixture on the first floor of the headquarters building, ripped out in favor of an employees' cafeteria and closed the executive dining room on the twelfth floor.[42]

Nearly all the senior staff agreed that Burns was a gracious man with superb people skills. He relied heavily on the senior staff except on one issue that for him was crucial. To foster better communication and harmony within the leadership team, he brought in a consulting firm he had used at Enron. The firm held a series of off-site meetings devoted to vision, values, and leadership traits. Merill Bryan, then at UP Technologies, dismissed it as "touchy, feely" stuff. The sessions alienated the operating staff, which was still scrambling to clean up the CNW congestion mess. Eisele referred to it as "Nero fiddling while Rome burned" from "a novice who had probably just recently learned how to spell railroad."[43]

Tom Watts was even more blunt. "We have a 150-year-old culture and he'd been there a week and . . . felt we should change our culture. So he brought in this raft of people that had these séance kind of meetings for everyone, which was total disaster." Brad King had a similar reaction. "He brought that green dragon and sunshine group on," he said, "which, with a bunch of railroaders doing group hugs, that didn't work." Duffy agreed that "it just did not fit our culture. . . . He tried to impose a leadership style on an operating company. This company was steeped in a style that likes to get things accomplished quickly. . . . I'm not sure he knew where the levers are that had to be pulled to move this company forward. Just thought you could do it with leadership."[44]

Nearly everything Burns did seemed to antagonize the operations people, and they were the ones he needed most to convert and on whom he most depended. The heart of the matter was simple: Burns knew nothing about operations and showed little interest in learning much about it. "I don't remember a trip he ever made on the railroad," said Duffy. Davidson was more blunt. "He wouldn't have known a good operating guy if he'd bit him in the ass," he said. "I offered to take him out on trips a number of times," said Shoener, ". . . and Ron was always busy." Marchant never saw in Burns the intensity he found in Walsh.[45]

In his eagerness to revamp the railroad's culture Burns did not hesitate to trample on sacred cows. One of them was the long-standing tradition of the Saturday meeting. He did not like working on weekends—some said it was because it cut into his golfing time—and so rarely held Saturday meetings. On one occasion Davidson came to town and wanted to go over some things with everyone on a Saturday morning. At 8:00 A.M. sharp everybody assembled except Burns, who strolled in ten or fifteen minutes late wearing blue jeans. This did not sit well with Davidson.[46]

Burns thought Shoener had too much power on the railroad and tried to curb his reach by putting the Harriman Center and service design under Duffy. "That put me in a precarious position," said Duffy, "but at the end of the day I really didn't care because I knew Shoener; I could work with Shoener. That was Burns's way of mitigating the overwhelming influence around him."[47]

Duffy was not alone in seeing the irony of a president trying to mitigate the influence of operations on an operating company, but that was precisely the point behind Burns's move. Throughout their history operations had dominated railroads. In the modern era the holy grail of railway management had become a seamless integration of operations and marketing. Walsh, whose lack of interest in operations rivaled that of Burns, had worked tirelessly to hammer home the message that railroads existed not to run from point A to point B but to get enough business to justify that journey. The two functions were in fact inseparable. Without marketing, operations had nothing to deliver; without operations, marketing had no way to deliver it.

Lewis saw in Burns a perfect complement to Davidson's strength in operations. In an ideal setting the two might form a strong team, but the setting was far from ideal. Davidson was in Bethlehem distracted by his new duties and under orders not to interfere with the railroad. Burns arrived in Omaha at a time when a strong hand was needed in operations because one merger was under way and another even more complicated one was on the table.[48]

"There were two problems," Eisele said of the CNW traffic snarl. "One, he [Davidson] wasn't here, and two, Burns didn't talk to him. . . . And so you didn't have Dick's attention and you didn't have Ron talking to Dick." Davidson had impressed on the senior staff the importance of loyalty to their boss. "A lot of people were advising Ron at the time," said Eisele, ". . . 'You got to talk to Dick. You got to keep him in the loop.' . . . Ron just wasn't hearing it."[49]

When the message fell on deaf ears, the inevitable backbiting began. "You heard a lot of bad-mouthing of him as just being kind of fluffy and a golfer," said Marchant. Amid this growing tension and the uproar over Burns's letters it was easy to forget that he had not caused the CNW foul-up. Jim Young was not alone in placing the blame squarely on the shoulders of UP itself. "We underestimated, in my mind, the condition the railroad was in," he said, "the culture and the capacity, and in many ways we said it's UP's way."[50]

Rebensdorf saw the same pattern. "We are the big UP," he said. "We know how to run a railroad. This is the North Western; we're just going to swallow them up. You know, the North Western was a little more complicated than anybody in Omaha thought it was. They underestimated the difficulties of managing the North Western's network." The CNW experience, especially when compared with the MP version, offered UP an invaluable classroom for the merger process. The question was how well UP absorbed its lessons just before plunging into a merger that dwarfed this earlier experience.[51]

26

The Changing of the Guard

The first major piece of business for the new Surface Transportation Board, or "Surf Board," as it became popularly known, was the UP-SP merger. The size of the two roads ensured that it would be a complicated process. Although BNSF had been appeased with trackage rights, other roads wanted a piece of SP as a condition for not opposing the merger. IC offered to buy the trackage from Memphis to Dallas, Houston, and Brownsville, Texas, and from New Orleans to Houston. Conrail put in a bid for about 3,000 miles of SP route. UP rebuffed both offers. KCS also coveted key SP routes in Texas. Offered some trackage rights instead, Mike Haverty of KCS declined and said he would continue to oppose the merger, especially in Texas.[1]

Texas seemed a logical battlefield since eight other states had already endorsed the merger. The merger would give UP control of all the gateways to Mexico except for El Paso, where BNSF had access. Haverty craved entry into the lucrative Mexican market and wanted SP's entire line from St. Louis to Houston along with a 160-mile stretch from Houston to Corpus Christi. To that end he lent support to a coalition of Texas shippers, farmers, and politicos who lined up against the merger. They were joined by the NITL, which threatened to fight the merger unless UP agreed to sell some SP Texas mileage.[2]

In March the Texas Railroad Commission (TRC) voted 3–0 to oppose key provisions of the merger. An association of two hundred plastics shippers complained that the combination would "eliminate any real competition in the Gulf Coast region." Davidson brushed aside these charges. "The overwhelming preponderance of public opinion is in support of this merger," he declared. "It is just that the naysayers have been extraordinarily vocal." Bob Starzel of SP insisted that "the Texas scheme would butcher the merger. It would return rail transportation to the financially weak and service-deficient Balkanized state that prevailed prior to deregulation."[3]

UP's strategy was to highlight SP's precarious financial condition and deteriorating service. Its application listed $1.3 billion worth of planned new construction and upgrades of existing lines and facilities once the merger was approved. The largest projects would double-track another 100 miles of SP's Sunset Route and improve its Golden State Route between Topeka and El Paso. UP would impose its own right-of-way standards on the entire SP system, "ensuring that SP lines are maintained to high standards for future decades." Shippers might fear less competition after the merger, but they already knew and despised SP's poor service.[4]

For the lawyers the merger became an all-consuming task. "Almost the day it was announced we were ready to go," said Jim Dolan, who headed the in-house team. "From that day forward, probably wasn't much I did that was not merger driven." California and Texas were the key states. Texas proved to be a lost cause but California trumped it when the state's Public Utilities Commission threw its support behind the merger. Dolan won its members over by giving the state a five-year oversight period, which had not been done before.[5]

To handle regulatory issues UP relied again on the Washington firm of Covington & Burling, where Arvid Roach had emerged as the guru of UP rail mergers. He worked closely with Mike Hemmer, another Covington lawyer, whose love affair with railroads began at eighteen when he began training for a job as a yard clerk in Oklahoma City. Roach became involved in the diversion studies showing how much and what traffic a merged company would take from other roads. "I think Arvid personally changed the way regulators and other parties look at the competitive effects of a railroad merger," said Hemmer. Roach saw that the mere loss of traffic by a connecting railroad didn't necessarily mean a drop in competition. "Arvid was the first to drive the process by looking all the way down to the shipper-by-shipper level," Hemmer added.[6]

The STB members liked Roach's work because it enabled them to separate the real competitive issues from the self-serving arguments of roads seeking to get something out of the merger. Roach and Hemmer relished the challenges posed by the merger's complexities. "We also all had the sense," said Hemmer, "that we were putting back together again something that the government had broken a long, long time ago." The weak link lay in the southeastern sector, which had several parallel lines and real loss of competition. UP attacked this problem with deals providing competition to show the STB that nothing had been lost. This strategy led to the trackage deal with BNSF. Its very strength helped blunt criticism over lost competition.[7]

By spring the lines had been clearly drawn. UP had the support of twenty states, all the major Pacific Coast ports, most of the Gulf ports, some 1,200 customers, and most of the unions. Opponents of the merger included the NITL, the Society of the Plastics Industry, the TRC, four state attorneys general, Conrail, and KCS. Both KCS and Conrail clung to the hope of getting SP trackage as a condition of the merger. In mid-April Justice joined the opposition on anti-competitive grounds; two months later DOT and the Department of Agriculture also weighed in against the merger unless it included some divestitures of track.[8]

However, the ultimate decision rested with the STB. Davidson accused Conrail and KCS of trying to "cherry-pick" the merger and declined their offers once they were formally made. He understood Conrail's desire to acquire western mileage; it was trying to resist takeover efforts by CSX and NS. KCS he found more objectionable. It was a comparatively small system trying to strong-arm its way to a much larger one.[9]

Justice argued that the claim for efficiencies was overstated, that rates would rise, and that the argument that SP needed the merger to survive was unfounded. Bob Starzel retorted that "SP needs $1 billion of capital expenditures above its normal capital spending over the next four years if it is even to hope to remain competitive in the West. Its operating results make it unlikely that it will be able to obtain that capital." As a result, SP would have to shrink its services. The alternative to the merger, he added tersely, would be "a market dominated by one mega-carrier, a smaller competitor, and a financially weak third-tier Southern Pacific struggling to compete."[10]

John W. Barriger, a legendary executive who had headed several roads, called it "the most natural merger in American railroading." As a *Wall Street Journal* writer noted, the interchange problem still plagued American railroads. "It still takes the Norfolk Southern and the Santa Fe longer to move a boxcar between their two Kansas City yards than it does to haul it to Los Angeles," he wrote, adding that "the average railcar still sits idle for 21 hours out of 24." The obvious solution was creating more one-line service.[11]

On July 3, 1996, the STB approved the $5.4 billion merger by a 3–0 vote subject to certain conditions. Dolan and the other lawyers had chosen the correct strategy. The board accepted the argument that SP could not survive without the merger, and so did most of the unions. "Normally we oppose mergers," said a lobbyist for the UTU. ". . . We recognized that the Southern Pacific could not continue to sell real estate to operate."[12]

After chairwoman Linda Morgan cast the final vote, Davidson flashed a thumbs-up gesture to a beaming Drew Lewis. A *New York Times* editorial condemned the merger as "a colossal blunder by the fledgling Surface Transportation Board in its first major merger decision." It warned that "Union Pacific must redeem its own management reputation after it bungled the much-smaller $1.1 billion takeover last fall" of CNW. No one wanted a repeat of that embarrassment.[13]

The return of UPC to its roots in transportation took another major step in September 1996 when the company completed its spinoff of Resources by distributing the remaining 83 percent of its stock to UP stockholders. Two directors, Claudia Malone and Larry Jones, chose to move to the new UP Resources Company board; Jack Messman also left the UPC board. The transaction left the corporation with only four subsidiaries: the railroad, Overnite, Skyway, and UP Technologies. It also fulfilled Lewis's desire to give Messman his own company to run.[14]

The spin-off did not please everyone. It outraged Matthews that the railroad was giving away a major piece of its heritage, the land grant. "It was the railroad's natural birthright," he said later, "and it could have provided much-needed capital." Instead of handing it over to the new company, Matthews thought, the railroad should keep it and lease out the mineral rights on a five-year basis. "I called Dick to help me sell this point to Drew," he said, "and Dick would not help me."[15]

The land grant went to the new company, which soon floundered under Messman's management. In July 1999 Messman left Resources after miring the company deeply in debt. Nine months later Anadarko Petroleum acquired UP Resources, including the land grant. Matthews was furious. "The birthright of the Union Pacific is at Anadarko for so cheap you can't believe it," he said. "We gave it away and it could have been a source of cash for the railroad for next hundred years."[16]

The SP merger unleashed a flurry of changes at UP, many of them unexpected. In the September/October issue of *Info*, Ron Burns introduced a new format for his column in which he answered questions dealing with "current employee issues and concerns" and promised more of the same. The issue became a collector's item because a month later Burns was gone from the railroad.[17]

"There were no speeches, no testimonial dinners, no historic locomotives pushed into a park bearing his name," wrote a journalist. "Just a terse press release dated November 6 stating 'Ronald J. Burns has resigned.'" Coincidentally, the date was exactly a year after Burns's letter apologizing publicly for the CNW service delays. "He had detractors from the day he arrived," said a UP executive who asked to remain anonymous. "He was a change agent at a company that doesn't want to change."[18]

Hardly anything had gone right for Burns at UP. Davidson had not wanted him in the first place and never felt comfortable with him. "It seemed like everything he did just infuriated Davidson," said John Marchant. Especially did Burns's lack of interest in operations annoy Davidson. Burns "was like a politician," said Art Shoener. "He'd go out and get some photo ops with the tie gang or the rail gangs or fly in, walk around the yard with the superintendent, and leave."[19]

Burns's inability to relate to Davidson ultimately proved his undoing, along with a series of unfortunate incidents. After arriving in Omaha he moved into Fair Acres, an older but elite neighborhood. Kenefick lived there, as did other business people. Burns bought one of the largest houses in the neighborhood and tore it down to make room for a bigger one. He bought all his clothes from a custom outfitting firm. In August, having dropped twenty-five pounds, he needed his pants altered. As always he had the tailor come to his office. In an article on custom services for people who could afford them, the *Omaha World-Herald* featured a photograph of Burns being fitted. Evidently he thought the image portrayed an executive too busy to leave the office, but the others got a very different impression.[20]

Golf ultimately undermined his credibility. Burns was a scratch golfer, a useful skill for someone in marketing but anathema to the operating department. As Dennis Jacobson observed, "Davidson thought golf was a four-letter word." Burns couldn't resist playing whenever an opportunity arose. A retired friend told Kenefick he had seen a sight at the Omaha Country Club he had never witnessed in forty years: the president of UP showing up at 1:00 P.M. on a Wednesday looking for a game.[21]

One incident in particular may have been the death knell for Burns at UP. Davidson was flying in for a major staff meeting scheduled for a Monday morning. On Sunday afternoon Burns asked one of his senior staff, who was a decent golfer, what he was doing on Monday. Giving my presentation at the meeting, he replied. Well, said Burns, my wife is sponsoring a charity golf benefit tomorrow morning, and I need a partner.[22]

"I was in a tough spot," said the staff member afterward. "I knew it was the wrong thing to do, but I didn't know what to do." The boss wanted him to play golf, so reluctantly he skipped the meeting and went to the golf course. When word got back to Davidson, he was livid. He didn't blame the staff member because he understood the dilemma Burns had foisted on him. Davidson brought his list of complaints to Lewis and said flatly: I can't work with this guy. Lewis, by then only two months from retirement, saw little choice but to agree.[23]

A few days later Lewis and Davidson flew to Omaha with Rob Knight, who then headed human resources at UPC. They checked into the Red Lion Hotel under assumed names, not wanting anyone to know that they were in town. A surprised Burns was summoned to meet them. He walked the block and a half from UP headquarters to the Red Lion and was told he no longer had a job. Knight mopped up the details of a severance package. UP was generous as usual, and Burns left the hotel well off but unemployed.[24]

Davidson did not have to look far for a replacement. The man he wanted was already waiting in the wings and willing to accept another twist in his own career. When the next issue of *Info* appeared, the president's column featured the smiling face of Jerry Davis. He was thrilled to get the offer and had no problem working for the man who had once worked for him. His longtime rivalry with Davidson had bruised but not broken their relationship.[25]

Lewis's original plan to retire Davis with a handsome pension while Burns presided over the merging of the two systems made no sense to Davidson. Davis was a railroad lifer who knew both systems firsthand. "This is nuts," Davidson told Kenefick, who agreed entirely and wrote Ebby Gerry to that effect. "The next thing I know," said Kenefick, "the phone rings and I've got a conference call with Davidson, Gerry, and Lewis. Gerry says, 'Drew,' he said, 'I've got a letter here from John with a copy to Dick saying we ought to put Davis in as president.' Well, that motion carried." Afterward Lewis called Kenefick back and said, "You and I got to talk more often."[26]

Lewis offered no resistance because he was a lame duck. On November 4 he turned sixty-five, the mandatory retirement age. The board let him remain until the year's end to collect his bonus, then sent him off with a lavish resolution of praise and an even more lavish compensation package featuring a performance award of $4 million and a five-year consulting arrangement with an annual retainer of $750,000.[27]

However, Lewis refused a retirement party. "I've been on a lot of boards where CEOs leave," he said. ". . . It's the hardest damn thing to get them out the door. . . . I've always advised the incoming CEO and the outgoing CEO to just cut it. It's not yours anymore. . . . I got to live by what I've been advising." And he did. Lewis walked out the door and never came back.[28]

On January 1, 1997, Dick Davidson took complete charge of UPC. Rung by rung the improbable leader had made it all the way to the top. Five years later he was inducted into the Horatio Alger Association of Distinguished Americans. For Davidson there could have been no more fitting tribute.[29]

He wasted little time putting his own stamp on the company. During his first three months at UPC Davidson had quietly formulated his agenda. He wanted the company out of Bethlehem, its air force sharply reduced, and the staff downsized to fit the corporation's dwindling role. He also wanted to emphasize a program in corporate ethics. The remaining subsidiaries would be disposed of as soon as practicable, reconfiguring UP back to what he called a "pure railroad." Expenses were to be cut and waste eliminated from UPC, much of it in the form of duplication with the railroad.[30]

On February 27, less than two months after becoming CEO, Davidson put most of his agenda before the board and won approval to go forward. Three weeks later he announced that UPC would leave Bethlehem as soon as a new home was chosen, and that its staff would be pared from 120 to 45. He created a new Corporate Governance and Nominating Committee with a mission to "ensure board independence and promote excellence in governance" by periodically reviewing virtually all board activities.[31]

Lewis preferred a large board of seventeen or eighteen members, which made it hard to generate meaningful discussions. This approach annoyed directors who wanted a more active role. Davidson reduced the board from sixteen in 1996 to eleven in 2004. He opened meetings up to more discussion, letting them go as long as the members wished to talk. "He started to pay more attention and talk to directors," said Carl von Bernuth, ". . . and he knew they were now more empowered because he didn't have the, let's say the board charisma, the stature, that Drew had." However, Davidson had something that Lewis lacked: intimate knowledge of the railroad. He could and did answer questions fully and welcomed whatever comments the directors had to make.[32]

One new director surprised everyone. Contrary to predictions, Phil Anschutz did not take the money and run but became vice chairman of the board and a member of the executive committee. "He was terrific, actually," said Davidson. "He would challenge you on spending money and capital and things like that to make sure you knew what you doing, and that the expenditures were justified." At first the directors were suspicious of Anschutz. He got off to a rocky start on an inspection trip through the Northwest. Gerry recalled Anschutz "telling us everything that was wrong with the railroad. Most of it was true, but it wasn't what we wanted to hear." However, they soon realized that Anschutz liked the railroad business, knew a lot about it, and was an asset to the company.[33]

During his apprenticeship in Bethlehem Davidson did not hesitate to ask people about what worked and what could be improved. Rob Knight was more forthright than most in offering his views, especially on downsizing UPC. Davidson put Knight in charge of the project after he became CEO. The number of employees at UPC shrank from nearly 120 to between 40 and 50. Knight even recommended that his own position as head of human resources be consolidated back to the railroad. A surprised Davidson agreed to make Barbara W. Schaefer head of human resources for both the railroad and UPC. Appalled by the expense of the corporate air force, he got board approval to sell three planes and the helicopter, replacing them with one smaller plane.[34]

The search for a new home boiled quickly down to Dallas and St. Louis. Omaha was eliminated because it was thought that Davidson and the railroad president should not be in the same place. St. Louis had its MP roots, but UP had more employees in Texas than in any other state. Dallas lobbied hard to get the UP corporate headquarters. Governor George W. Bush even invited Davidson and Knight to lunch to give them a hard sell of Texas. Davidson was more impressed by the depressed state of the downtown real estate market, which enabled him to lease the top floor of the Bank One Building at a bargain price.[35]

The move took place in July 1997. Gary Schuster, von Bernuth, and a reluctant Matthews went to Dallas, but Judy Swantak took a severance package and left the company. At lower levels the rate of attrition was high because of the downsizing as well as the move. As Davidson whittled down the corporation, he had only three subsidiaries remaining: Overnite, Skyway, and UP Technologies.

Leo Suggs was doing a splendid job managing Overnite and dealing with the Teamsters' efforts to unionize the company. Davidson wasted no time dealing with the other two companies.[36]

Incorporated in 1977, Skyway billed itself as the freight delivery system of the future, combining air freight and trucking service with an advanced real-time tracking system called Skynet. This use of advanced technology to coordinate transportation modes had especially intrigued Barry Schaefer, who urged the board to partner with or acquire Skyway. The deal was closed in November 1987, but the high hopes for it never materialized.[37]

Synergy was the buzzword of the era in UPC, but no one ever figured out how Skyway fit into this vision. It had been a pioneer in many respects, but other companies began catching up and introducing innovations of their own. Through 1988 Schaefer struggled to realize his logistical vision; then he left UPC, and his vision vanished into corporate limbo. UPC completed its acquisition of Skyway in 1993, but Lewis had no clear plan or role for it.[38]

In October 1994 Skyway needed $4.1 million to upgrade its core business information systems. Davidson concluded that Skyway couldn't survive precisely because it depended so heavily on advanced technology. "The guys that sold that company to us dressed that pig up so we'd pay maximum price for it," he said. He began hunting for a buyer in the spring of 1997, but the transaction was not completed until November 1998.[39]

UP Technologies posed a different problem. Originally created as an independent entity to get around union issues in the IT sector, it evolved into an important part of Schaefer's vision for a transportation company with its components interlocked by a common logistics system. To that end he wanted it to focus entirely on internal development, but Lewis insisted that the company earn its keep like any other subsidiary. For the railroad this created a peculiar situation in which it no longer directly controlled all its IT technology.[40]

UP Tech's dual mandate to provide the railroad with systems enabling it to maintain a competitive advantage in the industry and to create information systems for customers proved to be a tall order. By the summer of 1988 the in-house function emerged as primary to any commercial sales. The railroad remained its biggest "customer," with thirty-three projects employing 150 people.[41]

After Schaefer's departure in 1988 the logistics mission lacked a driving advocate. Inevitably conflicts developed between the railroad's own IT department and UP Tech. When Joyce Wrenn took over IT at the railroad in March 1992, she wanted a clear separation of roles in which UP Tech focused on the commercial business and her department handled the internal programs. This did not square with Tech's mission of providing integrated programs for all the subsidiaries.[42]

Davidson viewed UP Tech as important but too bloated. He asked Merill Bryan to develop a plan for streamlining the company and moving it back to

Omaha. The process could not be rushed, however, because Tech was engaged in one overriding project among others: It had to orchestrate SP's cutover to UP's current version of TCS. This proved to be more difficult than anyone suspected.[43]

Another major project for Tech involved installing TCS on FNM, Mexico's northeast rail system, which lacked any computerized communications and tracking system. Earnings from Mexican traffic jumped 20 percent in 1994, went flat the following year, and then soared nearly 25 percent in 1996. UP continued to expand its modern intermodal facility twelve miles north of Laredo and joined with a Mexican construction company to improve FNM lines.[44]

Like Powder River, the Mexican market seemed capable of almost nonstop growth, especially after the passage of NAFTA. However, it involved a host of other complications such as delays at the border, FNM's relative inefficiencies, and changes in Mexico's government. Deeply in debt and under pressure from the United States and other creditors to cut spending and reduce debt, Mexico began selling off some of its government-owned enterprises. In 1995 it looked to privatize the railroad system.[45]

When Mexico put FNM on the auction block in 1996, UP joined with Grupo ICA, the construction company, to prepare a bid for the best component of FNM, which ran from Mexico City through Monterrey to Nuevo Laredo at the border. The UP partnership bid $527 million and fully expected to win the fifty-year concession for 2,400 miles of railway. However, it did not reckon with Mike Haverty's ambition to elevate KCS into a major system.[46]

After the UP-SP merger was announced, Haverty had asked UP for concessions in return for not opposing the merger. "KCS could have done a deal with us," said John Rebensdorf, "but Haverty overreached. . . . He wasn't interested in trackage rights; he wanted to acquire these things, and we weren't about to do that. So he didn't get the deal, and he was really put out by that." UP's decision to do a trackage deal with BNSF instead of KCS derived in part from a conviction that it would help get the merger approved. Rebensdorf, Dolan, Roach, and Hemmer agreed that UP's case would be improved by having a strong rather than a weak competitor. Some Texas shippers made it clear they would support an agreement only with BNSF.[47]

Thwarted in this quest, Haverty took another, bolder tack. In September 1996 KCS bought the Texas Mexican Railway, which ran between Laredo and the port of Corpus Christi. That same month, in approving the UP-SP merger, the STB imposed two conditions UP did not like: One granted the Tex Mex trackage rights between Corpus Christi, Houston, and Beaumont, enabling KCS to reach Laredo from its terminus at Beaumont. Three months later KCS acquired a former Gulf Mobile & Ohio line between Kansas City and St. Louis.

These acquisitions gave Haverty the connections he needed to make a run at FNM. Joining forces with Mexico's largest steamship line, the parent company of KCS entered a bid of $1.4 billion.[48]

The size of this bid, nearly three times that of UP's partnership, staggered observers. A rail company with 2,900 miles of track and $500 million in revenue had far outbid one with more than 30,000 miles of track and $9.5 billion in rail revenue. "Essentially," Rebensdorf told a reporter, "they are paying a third of what we paid for the Southern Pacific for a tenth of the revenue." Haverty insisted the road was worth the price.[49]

Stung by this loss, Davidson vowed to get a piece of Mexico's second busiest railroad, the 4,052-mile Pacific-North Railway, Ferrocarril Mexicano (FXE), when it went on the auction block in June 1997. The northwest line connected Mexico City with the border at Ciudad Juárez in Chihuahua and Mexicali in Baja California. This time the partnership included Grupo México, a mining company, as well as UP and ICA. As the only bidder it won the road easily for $527 million. Although UP owned only a 13 percent share of the road, it talked of diverting as much as 70 percent of the traffic going through Laredo to the northwest line.[50]

Before UP could even lay plans, however, a situation arose that plunged it into one of the gravest crises of its long history.

The Nightmare

The arrival of Jerry Davis put UP in a unique position. For the first time experienced railroad men headed both the corporation and the railroad. In Shoener they had one of the best operating officers in the nation. With Davidson moving quickly to strip away the remaining subsidiaries, the future looked bright. Earnings in 1996, boosted by a full year's contribution from CNW and three months' worth from SP, set new records of nearly $8.8 billion operating revenues and $1.53 billion operating income.[1]

Everyone understood the stakes involved in making the merger go as smoothly as possible. Success would improve operations, impress both Wall Street and Washington, silence critics, and inspire confidence in Davidson, who was fresh on the job and eager to do well. Everything looked to be in place for a banner year in which the newly combined UP-SP system would dazzle the industry with its strength and efficiency. Instead the year dissolved into a nightmare in which anything that could go wrong did go wrong.[2]

The troubles began with the weather. Beginning on December 29, 1996, a series of storms blasted the West Coast and wreaked havoc with both the UP and the BNSF. Mudslides closed UP's main line along the Columbia River for two days. Heavy rains and melting snow caused floods that led to twenty-nine deaths and forced 125,000 people from their homes. The SP's Shasta, East Valley, Donner Pass, and San Joaquin Valley lines were all shut down. Along UP's Feather River Canyon route, slides riddled 100 miles of track with gaping washouts. A month passed before engineers could even get in to assess the damage. Blizzards raked the northern Plains in January. Most of UP's lines except Feather River had reopened by January 22, when yet another storm hit the Sierras.[3]

The elements were an old and familiar enemy for railroaders. They knew the drills and spent considerable time preparing for them. Accidents too were an inevitable part of railroading. For decades UP had waged a relentless safety campaign. Both Davidson and Davis had made it a priority in their careers. Every year the railroad held a Safety Leadership Conference to emphasize the theme "Safety Is My Responsibility," a slogan introduced in 1994. The message seemed to be getting across; during the first nine months of 1996, incidents dropped 28 percent.[4]

Then the accidents began and kept coming—a dozen by October on the UP alone. On June 22 two freight trains collided near Devine, Texas, killing two crew members and two stowaways. Two days later a switchman died after being run over by a rail car in Brooklyn Yard south of Portland. On July 2 a UP freight train loaded with hazardous materials plowed into a passenger train near a small Kansas town, killing a crew member and forcing an evacuation. The clincher came on August 20 when a UP train rolled off a siding and crashed head-on into another freight train, killing two engineers. The crew had set the hand brake on the locomotive they were driving but not on the other three engines. Late in October the company endured its eighteenth derailment of the year.[5]

Altogether the transportation department suffered eleven fatalities in 1997, the highest number in fourteen years. Davis was beside himself; the events of these months seemed to mock everything he had done. Critics denounced the UP on all sides. The unions blamed two-man crews; others said crews were overworked and fatigued because mergers had eliminated so many jobs. Still others questioned the consolidation of dispatchers into centralized headquarters, causing them to lose close touch with large areas.[6]

In August the FRA launched a seventeen-day review of UP safety procedures, sending 60 inspectors across the system. A weeklong inspection in June had found at least one error in 80 percent of the dispatches examined and resulted in a directive calling for new procedures. The BLE threatened to strike the UP to protest safety concerns, especially excessive hours by crews. Jolene Molitoris, the FRA's head, expressed concern that the safety shortcomings were merger related.[7]

The FRA report concluded that there had been "a fundamental breakdown in basic railroad operating procedures and practices essential to a safe operation." Among other things it found heavy workload stress and fatigue among dispatchers, unfamiliarity with their territory among some dispatching supervisors, employees not trained on handling new equipment, crews ordered to move trains despite defective equipment they had reported to supervisors, and "widespread evidence of employees being harassed and intimidated to cover unfamiliar territory, to not report defects, and to not report injuries." Of the locomotives inspected 57 percent had defects, and some key shop personnel were inexperienced in locomotive repair. The FRA demanded "vast improvement" during the next six months.[8]

These findings deeply embarrassed Davis and Davidson. Davis promised full compliance with the FRA recommendations. "I recognize that we must refocus every UP employee's attention on safety," he said. "Let there be no doubt that this company's commitment to safety improvement is serious and comes straight from the top."[9]

As a first step Davis hired 1,500 new employees, many of them train and engine people. All training procedures for train, engine, yard, and dispatching employees went under the microscope, and a new position, director of testing, was created for the HDC. Fatigue management received new emphasis. Bob Naro was named vice president of safety and risk management, reporting directly to Davis. Finally, Davis instituted a safety hotline that went directly to his office. Opened on September 8, it fielded 370 calls the first two weeks.[10]

The UP-SP merger became official on September 11, 1996. The combined system covered about 31,000 miles through 24 states and ran 2,000 trains a day with 6,400 locomotives and 142,000 freight cars. In its application the company anticipated saving between $500 million and $750 million from the merger, including the elimination of 3,390 mostly administrative jobs. The next step was drawing up careful plans and forming teams to implement the merger. "There's probably been more intense and thoughtful planning for this merger," said Davidson, "than any merger in the history of North America." Two past experiences shaped their thinking: the smooth integration of the MP and the botched absorption of the CNW.[11]

Both those transactions involved end-to-end mergers with few meeting points. The SP paralleled the UP far more than the MP had; it was also in much worse physical shape. UP's management never found out just how poor its condition was because their lawyers admonished them that the SP-SF merger had been torpedoed by just such actions. "We were so focused on avoiding the mistakes of SF-SP so that no one could argue that there was premature control of SP," said John Rebensdorf. "We were told that we should avoid any trips, any inspection trips over the railroad."[12]

Shoener formed between seventy-five and a hundred teams to identify all the issues that had to be addressed. "We started going out and looking at the SP property," he said, "and Conley pitched a tizzy with Davidson and everybody and said you guys cannot go out and look ahead of time because that'll look like the Santa Fe/SP thing, like you have already bought the company. . . . In retrospect that was a terrible mistake."[13]

"We were very cautious because of the Santa Fe–SP thing," said Dennis Duffy. "We were warned, we were cajoled, we were threatened not to screw this merger up. . . . So we were very, very cautious, and we made damn sure that we didn't do that. Some of our guys knew stuff about the SP. We . . . didn't get to spend a lot of time understanding the real intricacies and the physical nature of the structure. That was a challenge."[14]

Of all the issues confronting the merger teams, two loomed largest: computer integration and labor agreements. Combining computer systems grew more difficult with each merger because the systems had grown larger and more sophisticated. Having subcontracted its computer operation to IBM, SP had virtually no in-house capacity of its own.[15]

The plan was to replace SP's TOPS system with TCS. A debate arose over whether to do it in phases or attempt to convert it all at once. As Duffy put it, "Do we go at this thing with the big bang theory or do we parcel it out?" UP converted the CNW all at once, but it was a smaller, less complex road. Duffy thought the big bang approach for the SP unwise. However, the phased approach had its own perils, most notably the frontier points where trains crossed from one system to the other. Nevertheless, it was decided to implement the cutover in four phases.[16]

Having worked for SP, Merill Bryan knew it treated the former Rio Grande and Cotton Belt lines as separate roads. They were mostly end-to-end frontiers and could be cut over fairly easily compared to Texas and California, which had the large Englewood and West Colton yards to reprogram. The crew management system also had to be changed over to get everyone on one payroll. "It's a massive undertaking," said Bryan, "the largest ever in the railroad industry."[17]

Integrating the labor agreements was crucial because UP was eager to implement a new operating procedure, the "hub-and-spoke" plan. Once in place it would radically change the way trains and trainmen worked. Instead of having assigned routes, trains could be sent in several directions from a "hub" such as Houston or Salt Lake City. Existing labor agreements permitted crews to operate only on one line in and out of major rail centers. Instead of being confined to these assigned routes, crews would man trains moving along any of the spokes connected to the hub and return home. The concept promised greater flexibility for customers and gave crews a permanent home base, adding stability to their lives.[18]

UP also wanted to implement another major change, directional running. In places where the system had parallel lines between key terminuses, each one could serve as a thoroughfare on which trains ran only in one direction. UP had already done this on a limited basis, using former MP and Katy routes as one-way corridors south of Kansas City. Directional running could expand capacity, raise train speeds, eliminate hundreds of train meetings, reduce fuel consumption, greatly increase efficiency, and improve service reliability. It amounted to creating a double track without having to construct one.[19]

The concept extended to yards as well. In Houston UP had Settegast Yard and SP had Englewood. Arkansas had two major electronic yards, in North Little Rock (UP) and Pine Bluff (SP). Prior to the merger all four yards handled cars and trains bound in all directions. With directional running in place, North Little

Rock could block all northbound and Pine Bluff southbound traffic. So too with the Houston yards: Englewood could specialize in westbound traffic, Settegast in eastbound.[20]

For these changes to happen, new labor agreements had to be negotiated. Crews had to learn new routes and in many cases accept some loss of seniority. Blending UP and SP personnel was a complicated process. After the reshuffling of seniority, someone who had been working 8:00 A.M. to 5:00 P.M. with weekends off might find himself assigned to a midnight to 8:00 A.M. shift with Wednesday and Thursday off. "Those deals have to be all negotiated on a territory-by-territory basis," said Davidson, "and it's a quite painful, contentious issue."[21]

The plan was to move the computer cutovers and labor agreements forward together. However, both proved to be far more complicated and time-consuming than anyone imagined. UP was venturing into unknown territory. The complexity of putting the systems together was unprecedented. UP was taking a giant step in its transition from a linear to a network railroad.[22]

A network railroad was far more complex to operate than a linear one. With a network, said Duffy, "You have alternative routes; connectivity is a big deal. . . . Something that happens in one part of the network can severely influence other parts of the network. We didn't have to worry about that when we were a linear railroad." Duffy tried to convince Davidson that they had to make changes, learn how to manage a network. "And he kind of gave me that look," recalled Duffy, "like *What in the hell are you talking about?*"[23]

He was about to find out the hard way.

Despite the stormy weather, optimism remained high as 1997 opened. The merger seemed to be moving along well. Leadership teams were in place for all departments, marketing and sales had begun consolidating, and several unions had signed agreements. UP sent a hundred locomotives to help relieve the power shortage on SP, along with eighty-five volunteer engineers and conductors. Davis spoke of "great progress blending the two companies." Davidson echoed the sentiment and added, "I pledged to our customers that we would not allow a lapse in service during implementation, and we will do whatever it takes to keep that promise."[24]

Plans for upgrading track and facilities moved along. In February the board approved more than $30 million to expand the Livonia, Louisiana, yard, which was to assume a major role in handling chemical traffic. More than $750 million was earmarked for upgrading SP's Sunset Route, the infamous Tucumcari route between El Paso and Kansas City, and UP's line between Topeka and Denver. Another $718 million went to buying new power and freight cars. The largest single project involved rebuilding SP's Roseville, California, yard at a cost of more than $148 million.[25]

At the annual Leadership Conference in March Davis said, "I'm so delighted with the way things are going that I expect to go back before the board of directors next January and report that the merger is 75 percent complete." Davidson added that he wanted to see the merger "well over halfway home" by year's end and the operating ratio lowered from 83.5 to 81.[26]

Gradually new working arrangements fell into place. SP dispatchers in Denver moved to the HDC in Omaha. A group of twenty-four SP locomotive managers, who had moved to Denver only five years earlier, made the pilgrimage to Omaha during the winter. Teams in both Omaha and Denver coordinated office space, computer equipment, and the necessary software. The computer gear was shipped out by plane on March 22 and put back online the following day. The data stream was so continuous that one shop manager didn't know a move had taken place.[27]

Overnight on May 1 the first phase of the TCS cutover, embracing the former Rio Grande, was completed. On that same date the rules and special instructions of the two systems were consolidated. Extensive reviews of personnel had led to the most qualified candidates being chosen in departments and severance packages offered to five hundred UP and SP nonunion employees.[28]

Early that summer, however, things began to unravel. The string of fatal accidents roused critics and damaged UP's credibility. More congestion than usual piled up at the Mexican border as Transportación Ferroviaria Mexicana (TFM, a successor to FNM) began operating under new management. A more ominous service slowdown occurred around the Houston area, the heart of the UP's lucrative chemicals and plastics traffic. Beginning in July an unexpected surge of this business poured onto UP. "Everybody started billing out on the UP," said Charley Eisele. ". . . Volumes were going up dramatically and quickly even before we had a chance to make the physical connections."[29]

The timing could not have been worse. SP was already short of locomotives and crews despite the loaners from UP. As a the merger concession UP had sold to BNSF a key part of SP's Sunset Route between Iowa Junction just west of Lafayette, Louisiana, and New Orleans. Beginning in April, the BNSF shut this line down for eight to ten hours every day to upgrade it. The move severely clogged UP-SP operations. "We had dozens of trains we needed to be running," said Davidson, "and so it backed us up to hell and half of Georgia." UP could not divert trains off the line because it did not yet have labor agreements in place allowing SP crews to use other routes, and alternative routes lacked capacity to handle more trains. If that were not enough, the crucial connection linking SP's Englewood Yard to UP's Settegast Yard had not yet been approved or installed.[30]

Spring floods washed out part of the Sunset Route west of San Antonio. In July Hurricane Danny devastated CSX tracks and bridges northeast of New Orleans, forcing UP connecting trains to detour via Memphis. Derailments at the Englewood Yard compounded difficulties, as did the glacial pace of labor negotiations for hub-and-spoke operations and directional running. Even where agreements had been ratified, crews were still being qualified to run over unfamiliar territory.[31]

These problems lay beyond UP's control, but others did not. The yard situation at Houston proved to be the catalyst for an emerging crisis. On an average day Englewood's ninety-six tracks handled eleven hundred cars and a hundred trains, but the definition of average was changing rapidly. For years it had operated on a shoestring, always short of personnel and power. "Some nights during the summers in the past," said Shoener, "they just shut the yard down. Nobody to hump cars, nobody to run the trains." At its best Englewood was kept going by workers who knew how to improvise to keep traffic flowing. It was in atrocious condition, another victim of deferred maintenance, its performance often interrupted by derailments. Veteran railroaders still shuddered at the gridlock there in 1979.[32]

"Southern Pacific learned in 1979," said writer Fred W. Frailey, "that when Englewood tilts, you may as well hang an 'Out of Business' sign at its entrance." Whenever possible trains were made up to go around rather than through Englewood. Most of the chemical cars were processed in two small satellite yards, Strang and Dayton. SP also resorted to block-swapping among trains to sort them out on the road rather than in the terminals. These jerry-built techniques appalled UP, which never understood the culture of a railroad that had been running on fumes for years. UP's method was to process cars in big, efficient yards that spewed out trains bound for single destinations. "If your yard begins to choke waiting for those solid trains to accumulate," noted Frailey, "you simply quit your sniveling . . . and do the job by brute force." Some called this pride in doing whatever needed to be done; others saw it as UP arrogance.[33]

"The real limitations were in the Strang/Bayport area and in the Dayton/Baytown area," said Rollin Bredenberg, who left SP in 1993. ". . . Every gathering job on . . . Strang had crew members who knew exactly what their role was and the consequences for the network if their assignment did not make it back into Strang on time. . . . If all the cars had not departed Strang by noon you had a bad day and were positioning yourself to have an even worse one."[34]

Strang received empties and humped them for the various industries on the Bayport Loop. Locals operating out of Strang brought loads back to be humped for four outbound trains. UP decided to eliminate all outbound humping at Strang and consolidate it at Englewood. It seemed a good plan, but a local practice unknown to UP torpedoed it. Local crews habitually moved cars from one local plant to another without reporting the moves. These shifts ended up at Englewood as well.[35]

Almost overnight congestion built up at Englewood. Some SP employees tried to warn general manager Charlie Malone that disaster loomed; Malone insisted that both an extensive study of car flows through the three yards and the men running Englewood and Strang assured him the change would work. It did not; within a few weeks outbound humping was moved back to Strang and Dayton. But by then it was too late.[36]

Even as Davis declared that the merger was "on track in virtually every area," Houston became the epicenter for an escalating gridlock. "Exit to the south gone," said Eisele, "Mexican privatization. . . . Exit to the east gone, courtesy of our friends at BN. Exit to the north gone, derailments and washouts. Exit to the west gone. Loss of institutional knowledge and huge buildups in volumes of business. . . . We probably could have swallowed . . . maybe even four of those . . . but all five, same time, same state."[37]

The chemical business exacerbated the problem. Key shippers in an area between Houston, San Antonio, and Fort Worth were allowed to store cars fully loaded with plastic pellets. One small yard near Houston was devoted to this "storage in transit." The surge overwhelmed it and sent the overflow into other already crowded yards. Englewood was already overloaded, and Settegast soon approached capacity. "Shippers started changing routings," said Shoener, ". . . routed it over the UP instead of the SP side, and so we [were] just buried with more business. Instead of getting maybe 100 cars a shift . . . all of a sudden the UP side's getting 200 and 300 cars. . . . You don't have engines to run the trains." Some shippers complained that they had to curtail production.[38]

The congestion had a domino effect. Trains missed their schedules and had to be recrewed. "All the trains are moving slower," said Marchant, "so it's like a traffic jam. And then the sidings get full and . . . your locomotives are out of position because they're not cycling properly." Terminals clogged as dwell time increased, slowing train movement even more. Crews ended up out of position, making it difficult to match them to train locations.[39]

Computer glitches compounded the traffic snarls. By August 1, when the phase two cutover occurred on the Cotton Belt, the congestion in Texas was well under way. "We'd get cars that were supposed to go to Houston that . . . were taken up to St. Louis to just park for space," said Merill Bryan. "The operating people were not following a plan. They were just doing whatever they could to expedite the movement of any train to get some room so they could make some moves."[40]

The TOPS and TCS systems still did not speak to each other in the largest and most important regions, California and Texas. At frontier points cars got misread or ignored altogether when crossing from one system to the other. "A car would show as an empty going to the SP on the UP system," said Jacobson. "It would come over as a load going off. The computer would say no, that's an empty and send it back. And then it would say no, it's a load, send it back, and you'd have these ping-pong cars that you can't explain to a customer. . . . It's a

60-foot boxcar or 60-foot covered hopper and it's been going for six or seven loops like this."[41]

Tech people tried desperately to create programs for finding ping-pong cars on the first rather than the eighth failure. Some cars got completely lost, forcing the railroad to tell an outraged customer that it had no idea where his shipment was. On one occasion an officer received a call saying that if he could not find certain cars in the next twenty-four hours the water supply of Los Angeles would have to be shut down. The cars carried chlorine to purify the city's water. Some shippers went out on the line and located their cars only to learn that the railroad still couldn't move them to their destination. The media had a field day with the congestion.[42]

Some chemical shipments contained stabilizers that lasted for up to three months, but they sometimes sat in storage before being put into trains. When these fell into the computer twilight zone, the marketing people worried about what would happen if the cargoes grew unstable. How in the hell are we going to find them, they asked? Don't worry, came the answer; they'll find you.[43]

Many of the lost cars were attached to trains piling up in the Houston yards and on sidings along the line. Sometimes locomotives were needed; more often crews were lacking because they were not in the right place at the right time. As the delays grew longer, customer protests grew louder and more incessant. Officials of the NITL missed no opportunity to bash the railroad for its performance.[44]

Shoener, who had always prided himself on being able to solve any problem, was at his wits' end. "I had a few tricks in my bag," he said, "and we used every one of them. . . . It got to where the faster you ran, the worse you got."[45]

His first response, which Davidson favored, was to do what UP had always done: overwhelm the problem with resources. He threw as many trains as possible into Houston to clean up the excess car inventory. But this tactic backfired. "Things soon spiraled out of control," said John Rebensdorf. "We did not have the crew base to move the trains, and even if we did, we had no place to move them to." Houston turned into a giant bowl of molasses, trapping everything that entered its sticky grip.[46]

At first neither Davidson nor Davis realized how bad the situation was. In his usual style Davis concerned himself with external issues and the safety campaign, leaving operations in Shoener's capable hands. Davidson had a full plate of activities after becoming CEO but kept an eye on operations. "I stayed tuned into it," he said, ". . . but I wanted the other people pretty much to make the decisions."[47]

Shoener was old-school, the product of a culture that never showed weakness or admitted defeat. Above all, he didn't want to disappoint Davidson, who'd always had complete faith in him. As trains stacked up, he assured Davidson that things were under control. Neither did he let Davis know how grim the situation was. Jim Dolan likened Shoener to the hero in the epic poem *Song of Roland*, in which pride kept Roland from sounding his horn for help in the heat of battle until it was too late. "That was Art's problem," said Dolan. "... He wouldn't sound the horn that would have brought the troops in."[48]

Brad King saw Shoener acting like a "trainmaster of the whole system. Well, let's switch this train here; give me a list of that train; let's do this here and do that here. The ad hoc-ing began." He thought the problem traced back to the 1993 floods. In fighting that disaster the company lost and never regained its disciplined approach to solving problems. "And then what you have," he said, "is . . . a lot of people running and gunning."[49]

Duffy agreed but saw another, deeper problem, one that had escaped Davidson as well. "Here's Art," he said, "very proud guy, very forceful personality, and he's able to trainmaster himself out of almost anything up to this point. This point, this is a network issue. . . . We were a linear railroad prior to the SP merger . . . very simple. . . . We were starting to become a very sophisticated network, and the SP just put us out of the stratosphere."[50]

Davidson had just completed moving UPC to Dallas and was on the road a lot that summer. Although many assumed he still ran the railroad by proxy through Davis—much as Kenefick had done through Flannery—he gave Davis and Shoener room to do their jobs. By August, however, the congestion and flood of customer complaints had grown too severe to ignore. Gary Schuster told Davidson he was not getting a straight story from Omaha. "I thought that Shoener was pulling the wool over his eyes," he said. He urged Davidson to go to Omaha. "If you're there," he said, "they can't fool you."[51]

Davidson had already grown skeptical of Shoener's repeated assurances that the congestion crisis was under control. "We could actually see the trains parked right out the Dallas office window," said Linda Waller, who also fielded the rising tide of calls from unhappy customers. Davidson listened to the morning reports and went to Omaha for the weekly Monday morning meetings. He also followed his practice of going around his direct reports to informants in the field—in this case Duffy and King. Everything he heard told him the crisis was getting worse rather than better.[52]

The gravity of the situation landed full force on Davidson the Friday before Labor Day when he faced a crowd of three hundred angry customers demanding to know why the railroad's service was so fouled up. He had asked Davis if he wanted to come to this meeting. "Shit no," said Davis, "those goddamn customers are mad." Nothing better illustrated the difference between them. Unlike Davis, who hated conflict, Davidson realized he had to face the customers in person.[53]

The shippers climbed all over him, bemoaning losses that ran into the millions, pointing to the string of fatal accidents and derailments, and demanding to know when service would be restored. A contrite Davidson did the very thing in person that Ron Burns had been denounced for doing by letter: He admitted the service had been screwed up, apologized, and promised to fix it. "He got up there and ate crow," said a NITL official. "You can't just run and hide," Davidson said. "You've got to be the public face."[54]

Afterward Davidson went to Omaha and summoned the senior railroad officers. Yes, there were problems, they admitted, and listed the steps they had taken. The approaching Labor Day weekend should give them enough slack in demand to work off the congestion. But instead of improving over the weekend the situation grew worse. "My employees had been working hard and they were tired," said Davidson, "and a lot of them took the holiday off." One 7-mile stretch outside Houston held five UP trains of 100 or more cars backed up nose to tail. It soon became clear that the crisis would not yield to traditional solutions.[55]

"The computer systems just were crashing and . . . we were running the railroad with continual conference calls and yellow tablets," said Marchant. "You couldn't rely on the computer system. And Davidson thought, justifiably so, I guess, that it was because we weren't doing it quickly enough."[56]

A depressed Davidson summoned what he called a "come-to-Jesus" meeting and demanded answers. "Our inventory has gone from about 210,000 cars on line to about 250 or 255,000 cars," he said. "We've got to drain off this inventory to get things running again." He told Shoener and Jim Shattuck to bring all their people in from the field offices and find a solution. "I don't care about the budget," Davidson added. "There is no budget. You have to do whatever it takes to get this inventory off."[57]

All weekend long Shoener, Rebensdorf, Duffy, and Dolan discussed with King, the regional vice presidents, and others how to solve the crisis. "That was Art Shoener at his finest," said Dolan, "because he didn't run it. He gave his people encouragement, let the ideas flow without any discouragement into full discussion, and they came up with a plan that was pretty good." Shoener admitted that "I don't have the answer this time."[58]

The recovery plan that emerged was far-ranging. Fewer trains would be run, and many would be rerouted away from Houston and central Texas. Some trains would be suspended temporarily, notably UP's intermodal unit between Texas and Chicago. Other yards on and off the UP line would be rented to help ease the load. More crew members would be hired and retirees summoned back, but this would take time. Locomotives would be bought, leased, and borrowed, including even some from Conrail and Amtrak.[59]

The recovery plan became part of a quarterly report required by the STB. News of these steps stunned the industry, especially the surrender of UP traffic to rival roads. "Most railroad guys would rather sell their mothers than give up a carload of traffic to another carrier," said UP spokesman John Bromley. "If that doesn't show that the railroad is serious about fixing this, I don't know what else would."[60]

For Shoener the meeting turned out to be a swan song to his UP career. The style that had served him so well in the past proved his undoing this time. Painful as the decision was, Davidson concluded that Shoener had to go. "Dick was hurt and furious that Art didn't bring this in its full importance to his attention," said Dolan. ". . . He felt Art was too old-school railroad in his management techniques." To Davidson's surprise, complaints about Shoener surfaced even in Washington, where Mary McAuliffe reported that the STB people were getting them.[61]

Reluctantly Davidson summoned Shoener to the conference room on September 25. When Shoener walked in he saw Davidson, Davis, Dolan, and Barb Schaefer at the table. Schaefer's presence told him what was coming; she had responsibility for severance packages. We're making some changes, Davidson said. King would replace Shoener as executive VPO, and Jeff Koch, a former CNW officer, would take King's place as vice president of transportation. Davidson wanted to keep Shoener but had no place for someone of his high rank, so an exit package was created for him.[62]

Dennis Jacobson, who liked and admired Shoener, was not alone in regarding him as "a casualty of the service problem. I don't necessarily think he was the cause of it." Rebensdorf thought the real problem lay within UP itself: "It was our arrogance in thinking that we could take the Southern Pacific and run it like we run the Union Pacific." Some SP supervisors described the merger as a takeover with a "shut up and do as you're told" style of management.[63]

Shoener left UP convinced that King had set him up, but King had a very different take. "I never wanted to be vice president of operations," he said, "because I didn't want the lifestyle it demanded, that Dick wanted." But the job was now his, and the hours became endless. To coordinate the recovery effort a war room, staffed by eight employees on a twenty-four-hour basis, was set up at the HDC. "Inventory reduction is the goal," King said. The goal was to move 45,000 cars off UP tracks to reduce the inventory to about 310,000 cars, the maximum number the system could handle efficiently.[64]

As October opened the congestion worsened, thanks in part to another surge of business. Record crops of corn, wheat, and soybeans clamored for more cars. Holiday shipments hit the line along with record imports from Asia. By October 17 no fewer than thirty-six trains sat idle on former SP lines in Texas. The crisis at Englewood had begun to ease, but the congestion had only been pushed to West Colton, where trains piled up between there and the Arizona border as well as from Yuma to Tucson.[65]

That fall the directors got their first real insight into what was going on. They began an inspection trip in St. Louis; by the time they reached Little Rock the magnitude of the crisis had become apparent. "The number of trains we passed that were on the sidings as we went by, we just couldn't believe," said Ebby Gerry. "And the answer was they're just getting out of the way of the directors' train. Baloney. They couldn't move."[66]

The media climbed all over UP for both the service foul-ups and the string of fatal accidents. "The biggest railroad merger in history," wrote Dan Machalaba of the *Wall Street Journal*, "is fast becoming one of the industry's biggest debacles." Too many cars continued to bounce back and forth along the line or simply vanish. A carload of rice shipped in August still had not been found in October. A shipment of plastic pellets took fifty-one days to reach Fort Worth from Houston, leading one company official to grumble, "A covered wagon could have gotten it there quicker."[67]

The comedy (or tragedy) of errors seemed unending. A shipment of 15,000 gallons of liquid argon, arriving twenty-one days late, lost 90 percent of its content through evaporation. One grain shipper watched his own freight car roll past his office in opposite directions and said morosely, "It's like watching volleyball." A car carrying 120,000 pounds of carbon soot toured the line for more than a month, stopping fourteen times in Arkansas and Louisiana without going anywhere near its destination outside Nashville. "It's like a lost puppy looking for its home," said the shipper.[68]

As the media paraded these and other horror stories, a more ominous pattern emerged. The gridlock around Houston began to affect service in more distant terminals. For the first time UP confronted an unpleasant characteristic of a network system: trouble in one place, if not contained quickly, could infect other areas as well. At the busy Los Angeles/Long Beach harbor complex three thousand containers awaited freight cars. Many of them carried merchandise for the coming holiday season, prompting howls of outrage from shippers and merchants alike. The car shortage reached Coos Bay, Oregon, where Georgia-Pacific had to barge products to southern California after rail service fell three weeks behind.[69]

The gridlock threatened to put a major dent not only in the railroad's earnings but in the economy itself. Chemical producers, who supplied raw materials for everything from toys to tires, were reducing or shutting down production and taking huge losses that would soon spread to the companies they supplied. Some turned to trucks, which hiked their shipping costs. Others demanded reparations and threatened suit to recover their losses or talked of asking the STB to let other railroads take over UP's clogged lines temporarily.[70]

Infuriated customers demanded action from the STB. Already the FRA had castigated UP for its breakdown in safety practices. On October 27 the STB held a twelve-hour emergency hearing. Thus far Davidson had refused to give a date by when the crisis would be contained. At the hearing, however, he said, "I will be terribly disappointed if this isn't back to normal by Thanksgiving or very shortly thereafter. That's my goal." Much later he noted with a thin smile that he was smart not to have said Thanksgiving of what year.[71]

After testifying, Davidson sat unflinching for hours while more than thirty major customers and shipping organizations cursed and condemned the rotten service they were getting. Some demanded that the government open UP's tracks to competing railroads; others realized there was little the government could do and argued that UP should be given more time. One interested spectator sat attentively through the entire proceeding three rows behind Davidson but never spoke to him. Rob Krebs knew what the UP was going through because the BNSF had struggled mightily with many of the same issues in its merger. On the stand he surprised Davidson by saying, "Dick has pledged every resource the Union Pacific has to straighten this out. They ought to have a chance."[72]

Already BNSF had increased its business by 10 percent, the same amount lost by UP. A week before the hearing Krebs had told his marketing people that they had "the chance of a lifetime" to boost market share. Linda Morgan, chair of the STB, was on the hot seat as well. The UP-SP merger had been the board's first major decision, and she had pushed for its approval. She recognized that no practical alternative existed. If the board opened UP tracks to other roads, it could clog them even more. The UTU's legislative director helped by opposing any takeover of UP operations by other railroads on safety grounds. The board agreed to give UP more time and scheduled another hearing for December 3. However, it also opened 119 miles of UP and 24 miles of BNSF track to KCS's Tex Mex subsidiary, giving it access to Houston, on a temporary basis.[73]

There was another ripple effect to the issue. Nearly everyone seemed intent on blaming the crisis on the merger. In April 1997 CSX and NS, after a long and bitter struggle, reached agreement to acquire Conrail jointly. Their formal application came before the STB on June 23. CSX and NS hoped for a quick decision given the past approval of the UP-SP merger. However, the service meltdown sank that hope and raised doubts as to whether approval would even be forthcoming. The STB postponed a ruling until June 1998.[74]

November brought more problems. The huge soybean, corn, and wheat harvests, lacking enough hoppers, overflowed silos and had to be stored on the ground. The container ports in southern California groaned under a traffic increase of 13 percent and at one point had sixteen freighters anchored because they could not unload their cargoes. The Department of Defense curtailed its shipments on the UP because of the delays. An economist at North Texas University estimated that the delays had cost the state's businesses $762 million and could reach $1.3 billion.[75]

Just when many managers had left their posts to crew trains in Texas, a fierce blizzard smacked the "Red X," UP's lines between Council Bluffs and Cheyenne on one axis and Kansas City and the Powder River Basin on the other, with Bailey Yard at its center. Together they accounted for 40 percent of all crew calls on the entire system. For thirty-six hours hardly anything moved in Nebraska; the situation reached a point where UP declared a "stand-down" at North Platte. Incoming trains were held back for a day while the yard classified and cleaned out thousands of accumulated cars. Coal trains stalled on the Powder River line were also moved, along with grain trains that had stacked up. Not until December 1 did operations return to anything resembling normal.[76]

A pattern developed in which UP toiled furiously through the week to clean out yards only to slip backward on weekends when exhausted crews declined work calls. On Thanksgiving UP shut down entirely to give its crews a much needed holiday, then offered them a $300 bonus to work that weekend. Earlier in the month Davidson had gone on the company's closed-circuit TV network to implore the crews to "stick with us over the weekends. . . . The last thing we want to have happen to this company is to have the STB carve it up and give it to people like the BN Santa Fe and the Kansas City Southern."[77]

Abuse became a way of life for UP personnel at all levels. Marketing people dreaded hearing the phone ring because they knew what was coming. In Dallas Linda Waller felt the brunt in and out of the office. Apart from fielding the phone calls that poured in for Davidson, she had a neighbor who worked for an oil company knock on her door demanding to know what UP was going to do about people being laid off at his company because of the crisis. "I got so I wouldn't wear my UP jacket anymore because I was always getting harassed in the store," she said.[78]

Wearily Duffy, Jacobson, and other officers made the rounds to share the flagellation. "One rep would go to General Motors every week and give them an update," said Jacobson. "I've never been treated as bad as I was treated by those General Motors people." The pressure came from all sides—not just shippers but federal and state officials, investors, analysts, and the board as well. "You had weekly calls with the board," said Jim Young. "At one point it was weekly calls with shareholders who were looking for blood. . . . It was brutal." For Young the experience became a study in leadership. "He could have easily sent some other people," he said of Davidson. ". . . When it was time to have the customer meetings in Houston . . . he was the guy in front and he took it, took the hits."[79]

McAuliffe marveled at Davidson's performance in Washington. "He would say I've come to apologize about where we are and . . . what we're trying to do about it," she said. ". . . You just couldn't be mad at somebody like that. And it was such an odd behavior for a CEO because most CEOs don't apologize. He said, The buck stops here and I'm responsible." When he said this to John McCain, who chaired the Senate Commerce Committee, McCain told him not to worry but just go back and run the railroad.[80]

At one point Davidson told the board he was willing to step aside if they wanted someone else to solve the crisis. "We decided all along that we were going to stick with him," said Gerry, "and that was one of the best decisions we ever made. A lot of companies would have said okay, he's got to go 'cause he's the one at the top when these problems occurred. We never would have gotten out of them if we hadn't stuck with him."[81]

Waller thought the board refused to let him go because "they knew they couldn't find anyone else to fix the problems and were smart enough to realize that." Phil Anschutz emerged as one of Davidson's strongest supporters. He knew more about railroads than most of the other directors and told Gerry, "You've got to stick with this guy." Dick Cheney explained to a reporter, "If we were to look around the country for a guy to deal with the crisis, Dick was the guy. There wasn't anyone with his credentials and knowledge."[82]

As the crisis grew worse, Davidson spent more time in Omaha. Every Monday morning he, Waller, and the senior officers flew to Omaha for an 8:00 A.M. staff meeting and stayed until Friday afternoon. Saturdays would be spent in the Dallas office catching up on the week's mail and phone calls. Finally someone urged him to move UPC to Omaha and combine the operations.[83]

Davidson hesitated for several reasons. Having just relocated the staff to Dallas, he was reluctant to make them move again. Moreover, Texas was second only to California in terms of UP's assets and number of employees. Political capital would be lost, and leaving in the midst of the service crisis could be seen as turning tail. Davidson still wanted physical separation between himself as UPC CEO and the railroad president, yet all this paled before his need to take hold of the railroad firsthand. "If this goddamn thing is going to fail," he told the operating officers, "I'm going to be right there with it because I'm not going to stand idly by and see this thing going south."[84]

Davidson told Waller they would be moving to Omaha right away and the rest of the senior staff would follow later. Many of them, including Davidson, had just bought houses and had to put them back on the market. Although most of the senior officers migrated to Omaha, the Dallas office remained open until the following summer.[85]

The move posed a delicate problem in that it put Davidson, Davis, and King all in the same place. "Jerry," Davidson told him, "I know it'll be painful for you, but I'm going to start having these people reporting directly to me. I am the guy where the buck stops." Davis surrendered his office to Davidson and moved into another one, saying, "He did the right thing. . . . Dick brought it back to Omaha, and that's where it belonged." It was also where Davidson belonged. The operating man was back doing what he loved best: running the railroad.[86]

To the employees Davidson delivered a defiant, upbeat message reaffirming that the merger was still on track despite all the service problems and carping.

He also tried to demolish some of the myths spread by the railroad's critics. In particular he refuted the endlessly repeated charge that UP got into trouble because it let go thousands of seasoned SP employees. "Of SP's 950 field transportation managers," he wrote, "only 12—a dozen—did not receive positions on the Union Pacific. Some others left for jobs elsewhere or simply declined to relocate. But there was no massive layoff of train crews or SP transportation managers."[87]

Others confirmed Davidson's assertion. "I do not believe that UP dumped SP talent," said Rollin Bredenberg. ". . . Most of the people who had actually been leading the company through the tough times had decided to leave during the Anschutz years." But Bredenberg also thought UP "did miss some opportunities to avoid traps. . . . This was especially true in the Houston area and in California."[88]

At the STB hearing on December 3 shippers repeated their complaints. Davidson asked the board to lift its expiring order allowing the Tex Mex temporary access to UP tracks. "We are hearing from users of the system that the situation is not resolved," said Linda Morgan in extending the order another three months to March 15.[89]

"For sheer size and catastrophic consequences," wrote Fred Frailey, "nothing since the presidency of Woodrow Wilson matches the mother of all coagulations that settled in on industry giant Union Pacific during the second half of 1997." For proud, experienced railroaders it had become their ultimate nightmare, and it was far from over.[90]

28

The Road to Redemption

For UP the darkness before the dawn proved to be polar in length. Instead of days or weeks it persisted for months, exhausting everyone and wearing down even the most dogged of optimists. "We were at war," said Jim Dolan in language uncharacteristic of lawyers. "We had our foxholes dug and were fighting the war on a lot of fronts," echoed Dennis Jacobson. As the conflict dragged on, there came a moment in March 1998 when Dennis Duffy, normally the most upbeat of persons, learned that some five hundred trains were being held and thought, "My God . . . we're not going to get out of this." The fear lingered for about five minutes before he murmured, "Oh Jesus, okay. We just have to keep going here."[1]

Outsiders labeled the crisis a service meltdown, but that was the wrong image. It was rather a perfect storm that had engulfed the company and showed few signs of letting up. Already it had cost UP market share in every sector of its business. Jim Shattuck estimated the lost revenues for the first half of 1998 alone at $400 million.[2]

Houston, the most difficult and complex terminal in the nation, continued to plague operations. On December 1, 1997, phase three of the TCS cutover, involving the eastern half of the SP, including Texas, was completed, and the inevitable pain of absorbing a new system followed. Part of the problem lay in the rush to get Texas converted to the new system. Originally the phase three cutover had been scheduled for February 1, 1998, but the Houston mess led to urgent demands that it be moved forward and that crew management be implemented at the same time.[3]

All SP traffic in Texas was still in the TOPS system but not in TCS. With shippers demanding to know what was being done to fix everything, the TCS and crew implementation cutovers for the Houston area took place on the same date, November 1. The result was turmoil that left many trains without crews to man them. SP also used reporting codes from four other railroads it had acquired, which had to be designated in routings. These and other complications made the usual learning curve even steeper. The cutover and its fixes continued through December.[4]

By the year's end six hub-and-spoke agreements had been signed, setting the stage for directional running. On February 1 the first trains began running northbound on UP lines and southbound on SP lines between Dexter Junction, Missouri, and the Houston area. By April 1 directional running was in place, but Davidson postponed the phase four TCS cutover of western SP lines from May 1 to July 1.[5]

Every element of the recovery plan took time—the computer cutovers, the labor agreements for hub-and-spoke, the training for directional running, the upgrading of SP lines and facilities. UP's managers understood this, and so did the unions, whose people worked hard to clear the congestion. "The unions stuck with us," said John Marchant, "UTU particularly. They're the most powerful politically, and they stuck with us." Davidson praised the workforce as "the best railroaders in the world." The system's safety record improved dramatically despite the pressure and long hours imposed by the crisis.[6]

However, outside constituencies showed no patience for either delays or explanations. Shippers wanted their problems fixed and their missing cars located and delivered *now*. The STB and FRA wanted tangible results ASAP; the former required a weekly letter from Davidson outlining what progress had been made. Investors and analysts demanded immediate evidence that the crisis was not seriously damaging UP's finances and earnings. On that point they were doomed to disappointment. Earnings crumbled, and the company bled cash in its frantic efforts to solve the crisis.

Earnings actually rose 33 percent to $216 million during the second quarter of 1997 and 24 percent to $240 million in the third quarter even though Davidson estimated that the congestion cost the company $80–$85 million. By the fourth quarter the impact had hit full force; the company lost $152 million. Davidson called the disastrous figures a "one-time event."[7]

White Matthews saw what was coming. The company's cash flow was flowing all in one direction—out the door. "You buy your locomotives and you place orders early in the year," he said, "so you're spending your cash flow at the beginning of the year that you're going to develop during the course of the year ... and the service crisis hits. We're not making money but we've spent it." In February he asked Gary Stuart to think about the possibility of bankruptcy. Stuart agreed it was a possibility.[8]

Matthews concluded that the only solution lay in finding a way to raise cash by selling equity. He explained the situation to the management team and was voted down 8–2 with the only positive votes coming from Stuart and himself. "Guys, if we do not fix this," Matthews pleaded, "we are out of money."[9]

Stuart understood the dilemma. "Our labor costs go up; our fuel costs go up; our car rental costs go up. All the costs are going up. Revenues are going down. Customers are pissed off. Our workforce is pissed off. Our investors are pissed off because our share price is going down, so we have a real tough time with everybody." After a strenuous debate Davidson let Matthews take the issue to a board meeting.[10]

When Matthews got up to present his plan, Judy Hope asked, "Why are you recommending that the dividend be cut in half? Why wouldn't you totally eliminate the dividend?" Her reaction told Matthews that the directors understood the need for immediate and drastic action. They approved the plan without blinking. Matthews was adamant that any offering had to be equity; otherwise the company would have to sell some form of junk bonds at exorbitant interest rates. But equity would be difficult to peddle with the company's reputation scarred by the crisis, especially since news of the offering and dividend cut would hit Wall Street like a bomb. Nevertheless, UP forecast a first-quarter loss, cut its dividend in half, and announced plans for a new issue of securities to relieve its cash crunch.[11]

The credit agencies had dropped UP's debt from BBB to BBB–, which all but closed the company's access to the commercial paper market. Matthews and Stuart went to CS First Boston, which had already helped UP raise $500 million through long-term bond financing in January. Together with Dick Bott, First Boston's vice chairman, they came up with an ingenious security called a trust preferred issue. The usual preferred stock was not tax deductible; by using a trust the bankers turned their version into a tax-deductible investment. It remained junior to the company's bonds but carried a higher rate of interest and could later be converted into common stock. "It's a very good security," said Bott. "You get paid to wait."[12]

Hoping to raise $1 billion, Davidson and Matthews managed to sell $1.5 billion, which bought enough time for UP to revitalize its cash flow. "No one in the company would have thought to do that," said Carl von Bernuth. ". . . I think he deserves an awful lot of credit."[13]

For his pains Matthews got hammered by Wall Street. For months the investor relations people had been telling the Street that everything was fine. "They got diluted in their stock," he said. "Their dividend cut in half. . . . It was a hit, a huge hit, and I took a huge personal hit 'cause I had a pretty good reputation of shooting straight to the Street. And I shot it straight here but way too late. They didn't see it coming. Quite frankly, I didn't see it coming until I convinced myself that we could go bankrupt. So we did it. I took a huge professional hit but don't care because quite frankly we had to save the company."[14]

But Matthews damaged his own reputation within the company by threatening to resign if he were not promoted to vice chairman of UPC. "He put a gun to our head," said one director. ". . . We were trying to raise money through the preferred stock offering, and he wanted to have a title that would help his résumé so he could get a job as a CEO." Without a promotion, Davidson thought, Matthews "really didn't feel comfortable staying with the company and putting his heart in raising the cash. . . . That was not the way to do things."[15]

"My reputation was going down on Wall Street," countered Matthews. ". . . If I'm going to stay, I got to get more authority." Everyone knew he was looking to become a CEO elsewhere. "He was undermining Dick, and they were never going to get along," said a director. "It was too bad 'cause they would have made a hell of a team." Matthews was willing to leave if he got the right exit package. The board obliged with a generous three-year package, and Matthews left the company in June. That same month UP stock sank to 44½, its lowest figure since 1994. "I don't think," said one fund manager, "you could find an analyst who will give management a high ranking on performance or credibility."[16]

The security sale eased the company's cash flow problem, but Houston remained the worst obstacle, a 200-mile maze of tracks that Davidson called "the toughest nut for us to crack." One problem was the inability of the rail infrastructure to keep up with the rapid growth of business in the region. "They have built more factories, refineries and a lot more freeways there," observed a UTU official, "but they haven't built any new railroads." Merely substituting one railroad for another would do nothing to solve the problem and might make it worse.[17]

BNSF and KCS waited expectantly in hopes that the STB would award them prime chunks of Texas and Louisiana trackage. In February Rob Krebs told Davidson that he would ask the STB to divest the eastern end of SP. He threatened to come out against UP unless it capitulated to his demand for ownership rights between Houston and New Orleans and access to more customers. According to Hemmer, who was intimately involved, Davidson regarded Krebs's demand as "outright bribery if not thievery."[18]

UP had no intention of surrendering trackage crucial to its chemical, plastics, and Mexican business, but it had to find some way to keep BNSF's support and give the STB something to show it was dealing with the crisis. Hemmer pushed strongly for a dispatching protocol that he called "an incremental improvement, not a breakthrough. Directional running was the breakthrough." It became part of a deal reached by Davidson and Krebs that helped resolve the Houston muddle.[19]

BNSF returned to UP a half interest in the 194-mile Louisiana line from Iowa Junction to Avondale it had acquired as a result of the UP-SP merger. In exchange UP sold BNSF a half interest in its 148-mile line from Iowa Junction to Houston. The two companies would share the entire road and dispatch it jointly so that neither one would get priority. The deal gave BNSF access to a hundred or so shippers formerly exclusive to UP; they were Krebs's real target.[20]

The agreement, announced February 13, prompted the STB to reject demands that UP sell its Houston area lines to a neutral operator, which infuriated Mike Haverty. KCS and Tex Mex were invited to participate in the new joint dispatching center but declined. Throughout the crisis Haverty had been poised like a vulture looking to gobble up any pieces of UP he could snatch. Thwarted in this hope, he accused Davidson and Krebs of "getting together and carving up Texas."[21]

Other reactions to the deal were mixed. Predictably, the chairman of the TRC, a good nineteenth-century regulator, opposed the idea, grumbling that "I feel like there's been a sale and Texas has been sold and didn't even get a notice of sale." Transportation consultant Robert Banks compared it to "Coke and Pepsi sharing the same bottling plant." The STB extended its oversight of the crisis from March 15 to August 2 but rejected a request to transfer some yards and track to Tex Mex. "Adding carriers to an already congested and inadequate infrastructure is not going to improve service," said Linda Morgan.[22]

El Niño–driven storms produced more washouts in California during February, shutting down the Santa Barbara sub for two weeks. During February the number of cars online rose to 345,220, while the average speed of trains dropped to 12.7 miles per hour compared to 18.8 a year earlier. In March a fierce blizzard wracked the Midwest, forcing the Powder River mines to close and temporarily shutting down the North Platte sub. A jam-up on KCS's TFM line backed up trains all the way to Kansas City, forcing UP on March 28 to embargo certain traffic until the line cleared. The partial embargo at Laredo lasted until April 22.[23]

In a *Fortune* article an unnamed former UP executive blamed Davidson for the road's problems. The STB too endured a hail of criticism. "Government is not in the business of running the railroads," retorted Linda Morgan, "and so our job in addressing mergers is not to micromanage every detail of how the railroads should integrate their systems."[24]

Davidson and others had long insisted that the real problem was the lack of sufficient capacity in the Houston area and elsewhere. The solution could only be massive investment by the railroads. UP had already pledged to spend nearly $1 billion to improve and maintain its lines in 1998. During 1997 the company had also hired 3,500 new employees. In another mea culpa to the STB, Davidson said he was "acutely embarrassed, and our company is embarrassed, at the time it has taken to recover from our congestion crisis."[25]

Since the STB itself was coming up for reauthorization, shippers mounted an intense campaign to have it abolished. Despite data showing that since 1981 average freight rates had dropped 56 percent while railroad efficiency had risen 171 percent, shippers insisted that the consolidating rail industry was hiking rates and providing poor service. They demanded more competition and a simpler process to challenge rates. In response the STB gave the railroads and shippers more time to agree on rule changes that would allow railroads to share one another's tracks and yards in situations where one company dominated the market but stopped short of any more stringent action.[26]

Davidson again opposed any efforts to restore competition through shared track. "Just cramming more people into already congested facilities would create additional problems," he insisted. Conceding that railroads charged higher rates to captive customers, he defended the practice as necessary to enable competition elsewhere and provide adequate return on investment to make improvements. This debate echoed in many ways the long and bitter dispute over through versus local rates a century earlier. A few years later it would expand into a dialogue over pricing.[27]

UP took another earnings hit for the first quarter of 1998, posting a $62 million loss, but in April the skies finally began to clear. "Over the last two to three weeks," said an analyst, "we've seen probably the most dramatic improvement" in clearing up the congestion. Having already been burned several times, Davidson expressed cautious optimism that the worst was past.[28]

The solution to the congestion proved to be exactly what Davidson, Duffy, and others at UP insisted had to be done: complete the merger plan. Capacity increased once the bugs were worked out of both directional running and the computer integration. Phase four of the computer integration was completed on July 1, putting both UP and SP entirely on the same system for the first time. The joint dispatching center at Spring opened for business on March 15 and became what Duffy called a "spectacular success." In February 1999 UP and BNSF agreed to set up joint dispatching centers covering southern California and Kansas City.[29]

By May it had become clear that capacity and congestion problems were hardly confined to UP. All the major roads suffered similar rounds of service delays and customer complaints. "It's getting to the point where you can't count on them," said an NITL official. The reason for lagging performance had become clear long before it was grudgingly accepted by shippers: the sustained growth of the American economy that produced a 30 percent increase in demand for rail service during the decade. "This industry was in a state of decline for decades," said an NS vice president. "Not in our wildest dreams could we have expected this kind of growth." The sale of Conrail to CSX and NS, approved by the STB in June 1998, led to a year of confusion and congestion before service at both surviving roads began running smoothly.[30]

The absorption of Conrail left four major roads dominating the industry: UP, BNSF, CSX, and NS. All four agreed on the need for heightened capital spending to relieve the capacity problem. Together they projected expenditures of $7 billion in 1998 for improvements and upgrades to their systems. UP announced plans to spend $2.4 billion, more than half of it for projects in Louisiana and Texas alone.[31]

In 1996 the company unveiled Project Yellow III, a five-year project to increase capacity in the strained Powder River Basin. It included $116 million for work on a 108-mile third main line between North Platte and Gibbon, Nebraska, as well as double-tracking other coal-heavy lines. Another $79 million went to ongoing work on modernizing the Roseville Yard and $33 million to complete the $64 million new Memphis intermodal facility. The funds raised by the new equity issue made this work possible.[32]

For the second quarter of 1998 UP swallowed a loss of sixty-four cents a share. On July 31 the STB lifted its emergency order issued nine months earlier but allowed shippers to use BNSF and Tex Mex in the Houston area for forty-five more days. The decision marked the end of a nightmare that for a time seemed endless. When delays arose in August at Long Beach and Los Angeles, the problem was simply too much business pouring into overworked ports. By then the company was ready to launch a new round of changes that put it solidly on the road to redemption.[33]

The service crisis was for Davidson "one of the darkest periods in my life." He had worn a hair shirt through a prolonged and humiliating failure in the first year of his leadership. Bloodied but unbowed, he took all the abuse heaped on him without losing his poise, dignity, or belief that the railroad would eventually pull out of its miseries. Where others might have hidden behind excuses or spokespeople, Davidson personally took on all comers and criticism. The merger implementation plan had been a good one, he insisted, "but we came out of the starting gate well and fell on our face. We didn't execute."[34]

Everyone had his or her own notion of what had gone wrong. Rebensdorf, Shoener, and others agreed that UP had underestimated the complexity of the integration. Koraleski and Marchant thought the company had gone too fast in getting it done. Koraleski, Rebensdorf, and Young saw UP as too arrogant, too sure of its ability to pull off so complicated a task.[35]

Davidson believed that somehow the railroad had gotten away from its commitment to quality. The railroad's culture was changing in a way that fed a growing disconnect between management and the employees. Shoener's failure to recognize this change had been a major reason for letting him go. Returning to Omaha gave Davidson a much clearer sense of what had been happening during his absence. Like King and Duffy, he saw how much ad hoc decision-making had crept into operations.[36]

Simple demographics promised more changes in the culture. Large numbers of employees were approaching retirement age; by one estimate the UP would be hiring four thousand new workers a year for the next decade in what amounted to a generational shift in the ranks. Davis grasped the implications of this change. In April 1998 he stressed that "people today don't have the same attitudes that I and others of my generation had when we went to work for UP. Today, many people don't want to work seven days a week on uncertain schedules, or spend long periods away from home, just to have a job."[37]

Unlike their parents, the younger generation had no memories of economic hard times and weren't desperate for a job. However, one aspect of the railroad had not changed; it remained a 24/7 operation and needed workers willing to accept its demands. The challenge was reconciling its needs with the changed expectations of workers. Although cultural changes could improve the lifestyles of railroad employees, nothing could alter the fundamentals of railroading that made stiff demands on them. "Railroaders are special," said Davis. "They meet challenges and handle situations that most people never have to handle, and probably *couldn't* handle."[38]

Davidson recognized this and showed his appreciation for the yeoman service turned in during the crisis by giving every employee two hundred stock options. To relieve exhausted crews in the field, he had asked for volunteers from the general office building to go out and help. Hundreds of those qualified to run locomotives stepped forward. "They packed big suitcases," he said, "and were gone from their families for weeks at a time." Retirees also came forward to help in the field, and Davidson tapped former officers for advice. The unions let management crews run trains without protest.[39]

Davidson also realized how right Duffy had been in trying to impress on him the complexity of a network railroad and the need to understand its intricacies. In the spring of 1998 he asked Duffy to head a task force to determine what the newly merged system should look like. The team concluded that neither a quick fix nor incremental changes would work; what was needed was nothing less than a transformation. The ultimate goal was ambitious: an organization capable of running local systems while also being optimized to the network. By August Duffy's team had come up with plans for a revamped organization that fit this need.[40]

UP was about to undergo yet another reconfiguration, one that reversed previous trends. For the past thirty years it had moved to consolidate and centralize as many functions as possible. Through mergers the company had greatly increased in size to become one of only four giant systems left standing in the United States. The computer and other technologies had made this process of consolidation and centralization possible, but the complexities of an enlarged network taxed the capacities of the most sophisticated machines.

The SP merger pushed UP over the edge of its ability to assimilate. It revived one of the oldest debates within railway management: departmental versus divisional as the most suitable organization. E. H. Harriman's ambitious and largely successful attempt to run both UP and SP kept the railroads separate but consolidated the finance, accounting, law, and traffic departments. Harriman became president of both companies, but each road had its own vice president of operations. A director of operations and maintenance, headquartered off both lines in Chicago, supervised the vice presidents and oversaw major capital programs, equipment pooling, the creation of common standards, and other items of shared interest. Most rail executives dismissed this arrangement as bizarre, but it worked well until the federal government split the two systems.[41]

During the twentieth century change rolled unceasingly through every department. Each merger brought difficult, often painful adjustments in personnel and procedures. Each new generation of technology required steep learning curves and changed habits. Each new generation of workers brought with them different attitudes, mindsets, and expectations. Every shift in the traffic mix imposed different needs for cars, power, and service. Each new CEO or president was eager to impose his own stamp on the company and its culture.

As the pace of change quickened, so did the need for rapid response to it. Employees might trivialize the process as the fad du jour, but the problem was real and the need urgent. The traditional railroad organization, like fine Victorian furniture, had been built to endure, but the context in which it operated underwent so many profound changes that no arrangement could last for very long. UP management recognized that the time had come for yet another shift in organization. Earlier the answer had been consolidation and centralization; the new context seemed to demand a retreat from those goals.

"Centralization vs. decentralization is the classic argument within the rail industry," observed Duffy. The SP merger and service crisis had cast serious doubts on the policy of centralization. The railroad needed a clear change of direction that combined some recently neglected values in a striking new framework. Duffy put the need bluntly. "If we don't change," he said, "we'll be a dinosaur and lucky to be alive." However, any change had to reckon with the polyglot culture of a company that embodied so many mergers.[42]

Duffy and his team evaluated every process and function to find the optimum system for meeting company objectives, and searched for the proper balance between centralized and decentralized activities. Out of this effort emerged a novel plan. It would be Davidson's legacy to the company, a reconfiguration worthy of those created by Kenefick and Walsh before him. To emphasize its importance he called the new program the Transformation.[43]

It consisted of three main parts. The first imposed a new decentralized structure on the railroad. The second created a new department, network design and integration (NDI), charged with combining the work of operations and marketing in a new way. The third, which Davidson called the centerpiece, was a leadership and culture component that sought to revitalize the company's sense of mission.[44]

The new structure appeared first. Davis, doing what he did best, had gone into the field and talked to employees in every service unit. The cry he heard repeatedly was for the company to move more decision-making authority out of Omaha. Employees wanted more latitude to make decisions based on local conditions that they knew better than did Omaha. "We're a detail business," observed King, "but it was too much detail at the wrong level."[45]

Duffy's plan divided the organization into three regions with a vice president in charge of each one. Steve Barkley, based in Houston, took charge of the Southern Region, Mike Kelly (Omaha) of the Northern Region, and Jeff Verhaal (Roseville) of the Western Region. The dispatchers remained at the HDC but were realigned to fit the new regional configuration. "We learned this is such a large company," said Davidson, "that we could not manage it from a single center in Omaha." BNSF and CSX had already come to that conclusion; after spending millions to create network operations centers, they began pushing managers back into the field.[46]

First announced in August 1998, the new structure contained twenty-two operating units headed by superintendents. Support functions such as engineering and mechanical were also decentralized and reported to the regional head to enable quicker responses to local operating needs. "They have all the resources they need to make the right customer-service decisions in a very timely fashion," said Davidson. The key to the arrangement lay in giving the regions considerable authority and responsibility while requiring them to work within a centralized plan.[47]

During the 1980s Davidson had led the charge to centralize functions. This approach had served the railroad well for a decade, but the CNW and SP mergers doubled the size of the company and made it unwieldy. The new regions each presided over 10,000 to 13,000 miles of road, making them about the same size as the former UP, SP, and MP systems. This "coincidence," as Davidson called it, harkened back to Kenefick's decision to run the UP and the MP as separate railroads until they could be gradually integrated. The key factor then and later was what he called "span of control—how many individuals one supervisor could supervise efficiently."[48]

The new structure marked the first step in a major overhaul. The second step, unveiled a week or so later, created the new NDI department. As a separate but equal partner of operations and marketing, it was charged with closing the historic disconnect between them. "We have assumed too often," said Davidson, "that the product was there when capacity, whether measured as people, equipment, track or facilities, was not. . . . NDI will design the process to assure that commitments match delivery capacity and that our transportation network is effective and efficient."[49]

Drawn largely from the existing customer service planning and delivery department, NDI brought together in a single organization the responsibility for decisions relating to railroad services, the creation of plans to deliver those services, and the allocation of resources to support their execution. "Think of it this way," said Davidson. "NDI will develop the game plan, Marketing will win the business and Operating will execute the plan."[50]

"We went to more of a fully integrated regional aspect," said Duffy, "where we gave these guys every resource they needed to run their business. On the other hand, we overlaid it with a network management. . . . We didn't allow them to establish fiefdoms out there." Then Davidson added a surprise twist: He offered Duffy the chance to run the whole operation. "I'm thinking, Jesus, I'm not sure," said Duffy, "but you can't turn down an opportunity to be a key player at Union Pacific."[51]

King had grown disenchanted since replacing Shoener. He and Davidson disagreed over how to run the railroad, and King's position was not helped by having to report to two former operating men, Davidson and Davis. On one occasion he observed pointedly that the road could have only one VPO. When Davidson proposed that he take over the new NDI department, King welcomed the change. Duffy moved up to VPO.[52]

NDI's task was to develop two-year rolling business plans organized around three product groups headed by vice presidents who reported directly to King. The three departments were to be separate but equal. "One of the criticisms in our business going way back is that operating and marketing did their own things, and 'never the twain shall meet,'" said spokesman John Bromley. "This is really a full-press effort to resolve that traditional conflict."[53]

The third component of the Transformation aimed to improve every aspect of employee relations through changes in the railroad's culture, much as Walsh had tried to do a decade earlier. It sought to instill the company's vision, values, and behavior into all fifty-three thousand employees while also dealing specifically with basic needs like employee fatigue, work schedules, pay systems, staffing levels, and enhanced training.[54]

Despite vigorous past efforts at changing the culture, vestiges of the old-style management still clung leechlike to the company. Jolene Molitoris of the FRA had charged that "their culture was dysfunctional and characterized by noncommunication. They were separated from each other in a way that almost guaranteed problems." Some employees attributed the problem to Davidson's personal style. A review by his senior managers described him as cold, brusque, demanding, slow to praise, impatient for results, intimidating, and resistant to innovation. Davidson accepted the criticism well, saying, "It's like an alcoholic. To get better, you have to admit your weakness." In urging a hundred field officers to change their style, he shared his personal review with them.[55]

A key element of this effort involved revitalization of the quality program. "Continuous improvement, teamwork, managing with data and customer satisfaction," said Davidson; "if we just remember those four Quality principles, we're going to be a winner." Failure costs had risen 8 percent since the two mergers. Teamwork had gone slack, customer satisfaction had vanished, and everything needed improving. Train performance slid to 36 percent from the low sixties. Failure costs, estimated at $200 million, especially galled Davidson and offered a clear opportunity for improvement if the company could get back to the basics of the quality program.[56]

The new organization took effect on September 1. Two weeks later Davidson stunned both the railroad and outside observers with yet another change. Davis was bumped up to vice chairman of UPC prior to retiring in six months. In his place as president of the railroad Davidson introduced Ivor "Ike" Evans, who was then senior vice president at Emerson Electric Company in St. Louis.[57]

Davis remained popular both inside and outside the railroad to the end of his tenure. Columnist Don Phillips described him as "Teflon and believability." In dealing with the safety and other issues, said Phillips, "the feeling that he engenders is that he has not a single insincere bone in his body." "Among our employees," said Davidson, "he probably is the most well-respected senior leader I've seen." Duffy declared that "today's safe railroad environment owes its very existence to Jerry and his 'radical' ideas." As a tribute the company named its new yard in Roseville after him.[58]

Evans spent his first two weeks at UP on the road with Davis, visiting all but two of the service units along with shops, major yards, the HDC, NCSC, and a host of other facilities. Davis introduced Evans to all twenty-two superintendents, the AAR board, the STB board, and the FRA's Jolene Molitoris. Through this process Evans got a feel for the railroad that Burns never had. He enjoyed Davis's company and found him "very insightful about the railroad." He also thought Davis was tired and eager to retire[59]

The new approach to organization involved assessing actual traffic against what was possible. "We had capacity to sell, and we told Marketing and Sales to bring on the volume to create gross revenue," said King. "Well, we brought it on until it created bottlenecks. As we went through the CNW and SP mergers, we began to approach too many of our problems as episodic instead of systemic. . . . We weren't doing the same thing at the same time every day. In the early '90s, for example, we used to revise our transportation plan three to four times a year for season reasons. Now there are hundreds of changes weekly. There's no consistency, and that's lengthened our transit times."[60]

This tendency to emphasize volume above all else had long characterized railroads. Trains moved whether filled or not, and they had a long tradition of scratching for whatever business they could get to keep it out of a competitor's hands. Often marketing did not know (or care) whether operating could handle the traffic it solicited in a timely manner or at all. Little attention was paid to the fact that the business acquired might be very low margin or not even profitable.

The emergence of capacity restraints intensified this problem. Service deteriorated, and situations arose where low-margin business pushed aside traffic with higher margins. The service crisis gave UP a golden opportunity to throw off low-margin business to other railroads, but even then old habits died hard. In one meeting some of the finance people wanted to suggest leaving some low-margin traffic to BNSF to free UP for better-paying business. Before they could even speak, however, it was announced proudly that UP had just scooped some of BNSF's intermodal traffic by offering a lower rate.[61]

In announcing the new structure, the company hinted that it was studying what sorts of traffic produced the best results and whether to charge more for shipments moving through crowded corridors at peak seasons. Davidson added hastily that the object was not to chase customers away. "Rationing the business really isn't the main underpinning of what we're getting at here," he said.[62]

Bromley offered a more revealing comment. "We've certainly learned the hard way that the days of seemingly unlimited capacity are behind us," he said, "and before we sign a contract we'd better be careful. That's a sea change in our thinking. We can't be all things to all people." The problem was that UP was already locked into many long-term contracts. Even with a newborn emphasis on pricing it had to find ways to solve or at least mitigate the capacity problem. The business kept coming, and Davidson said his primary goal was to recover the 10 percent of traffic lost during the crisis.[63]

To ease capacity crunch on the Powder River lines, UP bought back a 107-mile line in northeastern Kansas that it had sold in 1990. The line could relieve pressure on the Red X by serving as an alternative route between the Midwest and Wyoming, especially for returning coal empties. UP also decided to rebuild the old Kansas Pacific line to handle eastbound Colorado and Utah coal. Having decided earlier to abandon the Tennessee Pass line in Colorado, one of the steepest and costliest to operate in the country, UP found it useful during the capacity crisis and postponed its demise.[64]

In December the STB formally declared the crisis ended and rejected yet another attempt to force the UP to share its tracks in the Houston area. The board also noted that the service failures had been caused not by the SP merger but by an "operational crisis that has now been solved." A Dow Chemical official grumbled, "It's obvious we are getting nowhere with the STB. The next step will have to be Congress." Ahead loomed a fight over reregulation that had loomed since passage of the Staggers Act.[65]

History hung over the UP as it did over every railroad. Many of the problems facing Davidson echoed those confronted by Walsh a decade earlier: the growing pains induced by mergers, the decline in quality, the disconnect between marketing and operations, changes wrought by new technologies; the roller coaster of employee morale, the need to delegate responsibility, and the lack of communication within the ranks. The struggle to free itself of the shackles of the past proved more difficult than anyone suspected.

As 1999 opened, however, UP had reason to celebrate. It had survived the service crisis and lived to fight another day. Davidson had kept his post and brought in a new leader to preside over the Transformation. "We went to hell, looked the devil in the eye, and came back," said Davidson. "It has been a profound experience. We have all made a blood-oath commitment that we're going to learn from the desperate situation we were in and come out of it a far better railroad."[66]

The road to redemption, like another well-known artery, was paved with good intentions. The question that intrigued some and worried others was where it would lead and how successful the company would be in staying on it.

29

The Lessons Learned

The hiring of Ike Evans puzzled many railroaders. He was an outsider, the third in a dozen years. However, Lewis had picked Walsh and Burns; Evans was the first to be chosen by Davidson, a hard-core railroad man. Davidson did not explain either his selection or the process, which had been a deliberate one.

No inside officer fit the needs of the moment. The two most obvious candidates, Duffy and King, had just taken new positions and were not yet considered by Davidson to be ready. The board encouraged Davidson to go outside but left the choice to him. A search was launched using a headhunter who identified several potential candidates at Emerson Electric. Headquartered in St. Louis, Emerson presided over more than seventy subsidiaries with an impressive management team headed by Chuck Knight, one of the nation's most talented CEOs.[1]

Evans had no plans to leave Emerson even though he was not to be Knight's chosen successor. Still, he agreed to meet Davidson at the St. Louis club. The two men hit it off well from the start. Davidson liked the fact that Evans had sales and marketing as well as operating experience in industry. "He thought the sales and marketing process was broken at Union Pacific," said Evans. Schuster was even more blunt. "Dick was not a marketer," he said. "... So he wanted somebody who would beat up on the marketing department."[2]

Evans had another quality that Davidson sought. "Ike was hired not only because of his ability," said Ebby Gerry, "but also he was the same age as Dick.... He recognized he was never going to be CEO." This mattered to Davidson because he had already identified someone he thought would be the best person to follow him.[3]

Evans's résumé was impeccable. His father had spent his entire career with the Pennsylvania Railroad and moved his family twenty-three times in twenty-seven years. Born in York, Pennsylvania, Evans went to high school in Indianapolis and then to Kansas State on a baseball scholarship—a bond he shared with Rob Knight. He graduated in 1965 with a degree in engineering and took a job with General Motors. During the next twenty-one years he moved seven times to jobs with increasing manufacturing responsibilities.[4]

He grew restless at GM because he wanted more responsibility. After a brief stint with Blackstone Corporation he went to Emerson and became one of six executives who ran major business segments and reported directly to Knight. Evans oversaw one-sixth of a $12 billion company that enjoyed a string of consecutive earnings and dividend growth for more than forty years under a CEO who had a unique but highly successful style. "The company was not for everybody," said Evans. "His style was confrontational, and you knew he was going to challenge you to ensure you had thought through your strategy."[5]

The confrontational style worked brilliantly at Emerson because it never became personal and soon weeded out those unable to handle it. Evans spent ten years absorbing the process and determined to introduce the Emerson style and discipline to UP.[6]

Manufacturing and railroading overlapped in three significant areas: safety, quality, and customer service. In his first "Message from the President" Evans vowed total commitment to the Transformation as well as to safety and open communication with the employees. "I'll always be willing to listen," he said. "I'll also be open and up front with everyone." But, he added, "what I care most about are results." He listed three priorities for the coming months: increased revenues and improved customer service; reduced failure costs; and improved training programs. These were not new goals, but Evans determined to give them fresh urgency.[7]

To accomplish these goals Evans launched in 1999 a ten-year growth plan based on the Transformation. To grow revenues and eliminate failure costs, the company had to sell to its strengths, broaden its customer interactions, and not try to be all things to all shippers. Choices had to be made to avoid making promises that could not be fulfilled. The quality program had to be reinvigorated to drive out failure costs through "a relentless, day-to-day focus on doing things right the first time."[8]

Evans came to UP at an opportune time. For all their grumbling, many if not most customers wanted to come back to UP. Trucks were for them a poor alternative because of their higher costs. If the game plan could be executed and the lingering bad taste of the service crisis finally laid to rest, the future looked bright.

Analysts expected UP to rebound in 1999, and it did not disappoint. The railroad set new records in gross revenue of nearly $9.9 billion, operating income of $1.8 billion, and carloads of 8.6 million. For the first time all six business groups—energy, intermodal, industrial products, agricultural products, chemicals, and automotive—posted earnings above $1 billion thanks to a surging economy and improved performance. Energy shipments, mostly coal, led the charge with a 22 percent share of all traffic. The operating ratio fell to 82.1, compared to the horrendous 95.4 of 1998, and the recrew rate dropped 47 percent. Cost of quality declined from 21 percent to 14 percent of revenue.[9]

This dramatic improvement confirmed Davidson's belief that the growing pains of the merger were past. By 1999 the computers were finally integrated, directional running was working magnificently, and all but one of the hub-and-spoke labor agreements were completed. The modernized Davis Yard at Roseville, the third main line between Gibbon and North Platte, and a new inspection facility at Laredo all went into service during the year.[10]

A pleased Davidson itemized the progress made on every goal of the Transformation and gave special emphasis to changing the railroad's culture by "uniting our employees under a common vision and a common set of values. While perhaps the most difficult to quantify, we believe this culture change will result in the most positive and far-reaching impact of all." In November 1998 the corporation finally shed Skyway. Earlier that year it also tried to divest Overnite through an IPO but withdrew the offering when it attracted little interest. However, even Overnite had record gross earnings in 1999 despite a Teamsters strike.[11]

One area of activity underwent rapid expansion. Although Davidson was no more computer literate than Kenefick had been, he viewed e-commerce as something ideally suited for rail service. Already customers could obtain prices, provide shipping instructions, and track shipments. Hits on the company Web site soared from 239,000 in January 1998 to 5.76 million in 2002. During those same years, calls to the NCSC declined 40 percent. The new century brought even better results despite a slowdown of the economy during the fourth quarter and a sharp rise in fuel prices. Once past the Y2K scare, the railroad again racked up record gross revenues of nearly $10.3 billion, operating income of $1.9 billion, and 8.9 million carloads. It had also begun to outperform the other major systems.[12]

The new structure seemed to be working well. In the Western Region Jeff Verhaal organized roving strike teams of repairmen to handle emergencies faster, saying, "We couldn't wait for Omaha to do it." Steve Barkley helped untangle Houston by devising a way to move cars through a loop that kept single tracks open on a regular basis. The new setup cut twenty-four hours from many shipments and kept more than four hundred cars out of the Houston yards every day. Sidings were clear, car inventories down, and train speeds up. Traveling along the new triple track between North Platte and Gibbon while two freight trains rumbled along on both sides of him, Davidson chortled, "This is how it's supposed to work. . . . It's phenomenal."[13]

New services helped win back lost customers and woo new ones. In April 2000 UP created Express Lane, which in conjunction with CSX hauled fresh and frozen fruits and vegetables from the West Coast to New York City in eight days and Boston in nine. On the I-5 corridor the Cascade Connection between Seattle and Los Angeles featured day-of-the-week pricing northbound to manage capacity but offered incentive pricing southbound to fill trains and attract new customers. To accommodate DaimlerChrysler's need for shipping vehicles of different sizes, UP worked with Thrall Car Manufacturing to develop the new Q2 autorack. The new car helped UP win all of Chrysler's auto business west of the Mississippi River.[14]

Express Lane signaled a determined effort by the UP and other railroads to recapture some of the produce business long since lost to trucks. During the 1970s Sunkist had filled 25,000 cars with fruit; by 1999 the figure had shrunk to 200 cars. Although the railroads' overall share of the perishable market remained small, Express Lane gave it a significant boost. By January 2001 its business had increased 40 percent. UP extended its service farther to the Northwest.[15]

Davidson predicted that Express Lane would remove 75,000 truckloads from the highways. During 2001 it moved 35,000 carloads, the equivalent of 105,000 trucks. Where trucks charged about $4,000 a load to move the fruit to the East, an Express Lane carload cost $6,000 for the equivalent of three truckloads with a $200 rebate for late arrival. UP and CSX ran more than twenty joint trains through five gateways and exchanged more than 2,000 carloads a day. Express Lane became a significant part of that business.[16]

On-time performance for Express Lane exceeded 90 percent. Another new service, Blue Streak, joined with NS to offer five-day intermodal service from Los Angeles to Atlanta with three levels of service on a sliding price scale. Blue Streak ran at 99 percent on-time performance and was virtually sold out, with most customers booking at the highest price level. To improve service from the Northwest, UP had in 2000 launched its 5-7-9 service along the I-5 corridor, moving goods into northern California in five days, southern California in seven, and Arizona in nine.[17]

Mexico and Canada also got increased attention. Once UP lifted its embargo on southbound shipments through Laredo in April 1998, the surge of traffic resumed in earnest. A year later UP opened its new $1.5 million inspection center at Port Laredo to expedite passage of trains that often stood for three hours on the International Bridge. The inspection process moved from the bridge to the new facility, speeding it up and allowing southbound trains to cross the bridge in minutes. Early in 2000 the company launched an automated manifest system (AMS) that collected car information in advance and compiled it into an electronic manifest for Customs; by 2002 it was in place.[18]

Traffic increased 12 percent in 1999 and 20 percent in 2000, most of it automobiles, auto parts, intermodal, and grain. Every day 7,300 trucks and more than 800 loaded rail cars crossed the three international road bridges and one rail bridge. The installation of CTC between San Antonio and Laredo cut transit time from nine hours to four and a half, easing the strain on the bridge. Improved performance by the reorganized TFM also helped speed up train movements on the other side of the border.[19]

Laredo was hardly the only gateway thriving on the surge in border trade. The five other towns reached by UP—El Paso, Eagle Pass, Calexico, Nogales, and Brownsville—also enjoyed significant upswings in business. Of the five crossings, only Brownsville interchanged traffic with TFM; the others all connected with FXE. In February 1999, when Grupo México, UP's partner in FXE, ran into financial problems, UP bought another 13 percent interest in the railroad, doubling its share. In 2002 revenues from Mexican traffic totaled $873 million.[20]

To the north the Canadian connection, revitalized by NAFTA, took on added importance thanks to an alliance between UP and CP. The two roads met at Eastport, Idaho, and interchanged mostly potash mined in Canada. Besides an increase in the potash business that strained capacity, two other developments stirred UP and CP interest in promoting a new route. In 1998 the Canadian National acquired the IC, giving it a north-south route from Canada to the Gulf. Then, in December 1999, BNSF and CN stunned the industry by announcing their intention to merge. Should the merger be approved, UP might have no choice but to ally with CP and choose either CSX or NS as a merger partner. The result would leave North America with just two major railroads.[21]

UP, CSX, NS, and CP joined forces to oppose the deal as too soon after the last round of mergers. "If the proposal proceeds," warned John Snow of CSX, "it greatly increases the odds that we will prematurely trigger the endgame of the railroad industry into two big transcontinental systems." David Goode of NS agreed that "we need a period to concentrate on service improvements without the distraction of another major merger." Davidson shared these views but said only that UP would evaluate its options and not necessarily seek another merger even if BNSF-CN was approved. Shippers also rose in protest. "The rail shippers are still waiting for the railroads to deliver on the better service promised by the earlier mergers," growled Edward Emmett of NITL.[22]

Politically the timing could not have been worse, given the service problems arising from both the UP-SP merger and the acquisition of Conrail by CSX and NS. The STB came up with a unique solution in the form of a fifteen-month moratorium on all railroad mergers to give the "already fragile" industry time to solve its existing difficulties and for the board to devise new merger guidelines. "Carriers whose management should be focused on fixing their service problems," said the board, "would instead be fixated on finding merger partners, defending their proposals and responding . . . to other carriers' proposals." Already rail stock prices had taken a hit, complicating their efforts to raise capital for improvements.[23]

BNSF and CN took the STB to court, challenging its authority to issue such a moratorium. When the Court of Appeals voted 2–1 to uphold the STB in July, UP's Bromley hailed the decision as "a significant step to restore stability to the rail industry. Mainly we just wanted the board to revisit the way mergers are reviewed." Rob Krebs and Paul Tellier of CN walked away from the merger. Instead a new approach was emerging that Davidson and others considered far superior to the mega-mergers.[24]

The idea was to form alliances with other major roads instead of trying to buy them. This approach resembled one tried unsuccessfully in the nineteenth century that stressed cooperation over competition. The context had changed radically in 125 years, however, and alliances made far more sense in an age dominated by a few giant systems. Agreements to create run-through trains paved the way for more ambitious alliances to forge single-line service. Thus was born the "Pacific CanAm Corridor" route put together by UP and CP. "We are two railroads thinking of ourselves as one," said Jack Koraleski, who was now vice president of marketing and sales. "We looked at all the advantages a merger might present, then applied them to an alliance."[25]

Davidson and Evans extended the approach to other railroads, especially after turnovers in leadership brought in CEOs more amenable to it. Tellier left CN and was followed by Hunter Harrison; John Snow at CSX gave way to Mike Ward. "Most of the new chairmen, they didn't want to merge," said Linda Waller. "They just wanted to work together.... We would have scheduled alliance meetings with the CSX, NS, and with Canadian National." Davidson regarded UP's relationship with the Mexican roads, TFM and FXE, as alliances as well. Apart from improving transit times and expanding market reach, the alliances helped bring the industry closer together while easing the pressure to create transcontinental systems.[26]

Improved efficiency and service also depended on continual upgrades of locomotives and rolling stock. By the early 1960s it had become apparent that the DC generator was fast approaching its upper limits. As horsepower increased on locomotives, the generator required ever more space within an already cramped car body. Every hike in the power level increased the maintenance problems caused by the inherent features of DC motors such as brushes and commutators. The obvious solution was to replace the DC generator with an alternator. AC motors had transformed productivity in factories since early in the twentieth century, but the adaptation of AC technology to the type of traction motor required by locomotives proved extremely difficult.[27]

On several occasions since 1950 UP had explored the possibility of running locomotives with natural gas. By the 1990s improved technology, soaring diesel fuel prices, and environmental concerns led UP to join with GE in another project to develop an engine that ran on liquefied natural gas. The tests of three different versions began in 1994 and were scheduled to run until 1996. By then, however, the AC motor had finally come of age. The key element proved to be a device known as a thyristor that could be turned on and off without the extra circuitry required by earlier versions. The new thyristor system converted DC to AC power in a smaller, lighter, more efficient unit, making it suitable for locomotives. As early as March 1993 a *Wall Street Journal* headline proclaimed, "DC Locomotives Near End of the Line After 50-Year Run on U.S. Railroads."[28]

The announcement was premature and only partially accurate. AC power for locomotives was clearly superior for most uses, but no sizable railroad could simply replace its fleet in one gulp. Every new technology or upgrade rendered older models less useful and more inefficient. The UP had been the first road to install computers in its locomotive cabs and to accept the wide "safety-cab" design. One striking example of changes could be found in the 9480, a specially equipped model with GE's Integrated Function Computer that was the first to contain an electronic ISC display screen and EPIC 3102 electronic brake control systems. The first GE unit with AH traction motors, it also pioneered electronic fuel injection. "We and GE consider it a rolling test bed," said Bromley, "and more changes are planned."[29]

The UP fleet was a menagerie of types and sizes thrown together by purchases over the years and further diversified by every merger. It hauled many different kinds of trains over many different types of terrain. Cost efficiency demanded that it be standardized as much as possible to reduce maintenance and parts inventories, but different routes required different locomotives. Given the wide variety of units acquired through mergers, it made sense to reduce the fleet by replacing them with fewer but more powerful and versatile models. However, the cost would be enormous.

Between 1992 and 1995 UP bought only 282 locomotives. During 1996–99 it purchased 959 units, and during the next four years another 1,746. The pattern of these acquisitions derived partly from the SP merger and service crisis and partly from the desire to standardize, upgrade, and make the fleet more efficient. In 1994 UP had agreed to buy at least 248 4,500-horsepower AC locomotives from GE and EMD over a four-year period. A key provision in the agreements specified that the units be convertible to 6,000 horsepower when the technology became available.[30]

The orders signaled UP's keen interest in 6,000-horsepower locomotives. It showed little interest in 5,000- or even 5,500-horsepower units, on the premise that the larger AC locomotives offered the best bargain for UP's high-speed, heavy-tonnage trains traveling long distances. Simulation tests showed that a doublestack train from Chicago to Oakland powered by two 6,000-horsepower AC locomotives in place of three 4,000-horsepower units saved 1,700 gallons of fuel and 40 minutes running time in each direction. The potential existed, concluded the company, to save an average of 65,000 gallons of fuel a year.[31]

AC traction motors appealed to railroads because they were tougher, more powerful, easier to control, less vulnerable to bad weather, required less maintenance, and allowed big jumps in horsepower. They also proved valuable in reviving another long-standing but not yet realized innovation: distributed power (DP). As part of its program UP retired older 3,000-horsepower units ahead of their normal schedule and stopped rebuilding older locomotives. The service crisis disrupted these aims for a time as UP scrounged locomotives from every source.[32]

Every locomotive purchased by UP between 1994 and late 1998 featured AC traction motors. Then, in October 1999, the company startled the industry by agreeing to lease from EMD 1,000 units at a cost of more than $2 billion over a four-year period. All the units were to be DC-traction SD70s of 4,000 horsepower to replace 1,500 older, less efficient locomotives on a two-for-three basis. UP went back to DC units for use primarily on manifest trains that did not warrant more expensive AC power. Once arrived, they would reduce the fleet's overall age by five years and slash the number of different locomotive models in service from thirty-three to eighteen. They were also expected to lower fuel and maintenance costs while improving reliability and productivity. "We were faced with significant maintenance and overhaul costs if we hadn't done something to reduce the average age of the fleet," said Bromley.[33]

The enormous order in no way suggested a retreat from the use of AC locomotives. In the summer of 1998 UP received the first full 6,000-horsepower locomotives from EMD and put them to work on soda ash unit trains between Green River and Chicago. By December it had in service 1,145 AC-traction locomotives of all sizes, three times the number of BNSF or CSX and 16 percent of its total fleet.[34]

During 1999 GE's C60AC models began arriving. The new machines weighed the same as a Dash 9 locomotive and had the same number of cylinders but produced two-and-a-half times the high-speed tractive effort of SD40-2 units. They also contained nearly two dozen microprocessors controlling various parts. "We accelerated quickly to the speed limit," said one pleased engineer. "It handles like we have only a 25-car train instead of 89 cars." The engine climbed hills and braked going downhill more easily as well, though it produced a rougher ride.[35]

UP also viewed distributed power as a key to improving efficiency, especially for longer trains. A new control system, the GE Harris Locotrol III, enabled engineers to operate by remote control from the front cab several units spaced in the middle and rear of the train. The lead unit contained the controls and all brakes as well as status and alarm indicators. DP minimized in-train forces, reduced pull-aparts, improved train handling, allowed greater use of track capacity, and cut slack action, and with it the amount of lading damage. It permitted the operation of trains with length and volume right up to the capacity of available sidings, which meant fewer trains and helper units.[36]

UP employed DP first in the Blue Mountain region, then on the coal route from the Powder River Basin to Texas. It was tested over SP's Donner Pass route as well. By mid-1998 nearly 1,000 of UP's 7,100 locomotives had been equipped with DP technology, including a third of the Powder River coal trains. The number of cars hauled on coal trains increased from 115 to 137. One of UP's largest coal customers, Ameren of St. Louis, agreed to use DP technology on all trains cycling through its power plant in Labadie, Missouri. The move gave Ameren eight extra coal loads per unit train while saving three hours of locomotive moves within the plant; it reduced mainline blocking as well.[37]

Rolling stock underwent a similar pattern of change in types, numbers, and ownership. Railroads demanded more specialized cars, bought fewer of them, and owned fewer of them. In 1977 railroads owned 1.3 million cars, 80 percent of the total fleet; by 2002 their share shrank to only 610,000 cars, or 47 percent of the fleet. The rest belonged to shippers or leasing companies that emerged as the most significant factor in a shift to short-term leases, a transaction that kept the equipment cost off the company books by making it an expense rather than a liability, thus enhancing borrowing power. Short-term leases gave railroads more flexibility by not tying them down to fifteen- to twenty-year commitments on equipment at a time when the traffic mix was growing increasingly volatile. It also freed up capital.[38]

The types of cars needed also shifted over time. In 1977 railroads owned 450,000 boxcars, making them king of the road. By 2002 their number had dwindled to 138,000, while covered hoppers rose from 236,000 to 385,000 and became the new most popular car. The weight limit for freight cars rose from 263,000 to 286,000 pounds, rendering some older cars uneconomical even though they remained in good mechanical condition. The difference enabled the larger covered hopper to carry 112 instead of 100 tons of corn.[39]

In its quest for more business UP did not hesitate to experiment with car types for particular traffic. In 1987 it spent $6.7 million to test market 175 RoadRailer vans on the highly competitive Chicago-Dallas corridor. Built by Thrall, the Mark V RoadRailer units went into service that fall. Three years later UP unveiled a new enclosed auto carrier of its own design: the Secured Modular Automotive Rail Transport (SMART) car. Using a spine car rather than a standard flatcar as its base, the SMART car reduced tare weight by as much as 10 percent.[40]

UP also worked with Thrall and the automobile manufacturers to fit equipment to their specific needs. When Chrysler wanted a rail car capable of hauling automobiles, vans, minivans, and trucks at the same time, UP, Thrall, and Trailer

Train cooperated in providing a fleet of 122 new tri-level autorack cars for that purpose. UP also spent $6.5 million to lease 100 bi-level autoracks for the GM national pool. Automobiles mattered greatly to UP because by 2001 it carried 80 percent of all new vehicles transported in the western United States and 30 percent of all auto parts.[41]

By 2003, as Table 2 shows, UP possessed the largest fleet of freight cars in the industry.

Altogether UP's freight car fleet totaled 140,399, compared to 96,779 for BNSF, 108,304 for CSX, and 115,087 for NS. However, these figures paled before the number of cars owned privately by shippers or leasing companies, which totaled 728,485 in 2003. The privately owned fleet included 260,034 covered hoppers and 264,401 tank cars alone; the major railroads, including Mexico's, owned only 701 tank cars. Privately owned cars comprised 53 percent of the total American fleet; major railroads owned 37 percent of the remainder, and smaller roads the other 10 percent. This distribution differs radically from that of a few decades earlier and reveals the extent to which railroads had moved to leasing and encouraging shippers to own their cars.[42]

By 2001 the transformation seemed complete. Even critics conceded that the service crisis was a thing of the past. "Union Pacific is back," proclaimed Fred Frailey. "Welcome to the biggest, baddest railroad in the world." The old SP Golden State Route from El Paso to Kansas City was being rebuilt and put under CTC. The former Texas & Pacific line from Fort Worth to El Paso was undergoing its biggest facelift in half a century, and traffic hummed over the new triple track between North Platte and Gibbon. The long-neglected but now rejuvenated Kansas Pacific line between Topeka and Denver carried a parade of coal trains heading east. CTC and high-speed crossovers would soon enable the old

Table 2   **Union Pacific Freight Cars 2003**

TYPE	NUMBER	RANK	LEADER	NUMBER
Covered hopper	39,787	1	—	—
Open-top hopper	20,966	3	NS	24,077
Gondola	17,555	3	NS	38,278
Box	20,107	3	CN	26,888
Flat	31,455	1	—	—
Refrigerated	10,379	1	—	—
Tank	150	4	BNSF	549

Source: Trains, January 2004, 61.

CNW to run in both directions on both its tracks between Chicago and the Missouri River.[43]

Directional running, claimed the UP, avoided about 60,000 meets between trains every year. "And in Houston itself," said Frailey, "it's hard to believe the events of 1997 ever occurred." Davidson's alliances with eastern roads were working well and quelled further talk of transcontinental mergers. "We don't see another round of consolidation," said Dolan. "We think it would be a horrible mistake."[44]

One analyst declared that UP "is showing signs that management will take the company to a whole new level, possibly to a place not witnessed by any other major U.S. railroad." Davidson could not have been more pleased. "Even though our history is grand and stretches back 140 years," he said, "I like to think that we are just four years old." The lessons of 1997 had been learned and applied. The new century looked to be promising if the lessons remained alive within the institutional memory.[45]

30

The Clash of Styles

Outside presidents always posed a problem for UP officers. They came to the company from an entirely different culture and brought with them strange ways and concepts. Flannery had been a railroad man, but he served largely as a caretaker. Walsh succeeded in selling many of his ideas to the railroad, while Burns failed utterly to do so. Although many of Walsh's reforms endured, so did the attitudes and problems that confronted him when he arrived in Omaha.

Although UP's culture had evolved in many respects, it retained a strong flavor of its unique style. Like the cultures of many other corporations, it was caught in an ongoing transition complicated by having to meld the differing styles of so many merger partners. The service crisis with its avalanche of bad publicity also left its humbling imprint on the company. "This was a situation none of us had ever seen before," said Duffy.[1]

Ike Evans brought a managerial style that had thrived at Emerson Electric but was alien to UP and most other railroads. He arrived in Omaha just as the Transformation was launched. One of its key elements involved significant changes in the corporate culture; Evans added another complication to that ongoing process.

Evans liked what he saw in Omaha. "I was impressed with the people," he said. "They worked hard, and there was an intellectual capacity far greater than I expected. . . . We had some people that could think about things, and you could sit down and have the discussions that were really important to the company."[2]

The lingering hierarchical tradition bothered Evans. "At Emerson," he observed, "if a lower-level guy had the information, that's where you would go." The trick was never to undercut one's boss in the process. "You never make a decision with that guy," he added. "You're just going to him to get the information." He didn't know that Kenefick, Walsh, and Davidson all had their own way of doing just that, but Kenefick believed railroads needed a hierarchical management because of the environment in which they operated.[3]

The hierarchy imposed discipline, order, and, hopefully, employee pride in a job well done, but it could be rigid to the point of ossification, which discouraged initiative in the ranks. Officers could be overbearing, demanding complete obedience and punishing anyone who acted without first getting an okay from his superior. It stifled communication as well; few people were willing to stick their necks out and get lambasted for their pains. It also reinforced the seniority system that valued longevity over merit and experience over talent. Through the years UP's hierarchy had been more rigid than most despite efforts by Walsh and others to loosen its grip. The Transformation was only the latest attempt to free the railroads from its worst features.

Evans confronted a paradox that undermined his best intentions. He hoped to improve communication by introducing the Emerson style of managerial dialogue. Chuck Knight presided over frank, even brutal discussions and debates that usually got heated without getting personal. The fireworks were intended to illuminate any problems that might exist and force managers to clarify their thinking by defending what they were doing and how they were doing it. As Evans conceded, it was a style that took getting used to and was not for everybody. At UP it resembled the hierarchical tradition of strong-willed presidents who intimidated their staffs.

"Railroad people like to be comfortable," said Evans. "The organization was somewhat dysfunctional in its civility." His forceful personality came on strong in meetings. He challenged people, got in their faces, pushed them and wanted them to push back. A few did so, but most were taken aback and, unfamiliar with the Emerson style, regarded him as argumentative and overbearing. "He was an intimidating guy," said Rob Knight, "not unlike . . . Dick. They had that similarity, and I saw people quiver when he walked in the room. And those same people, I think, were sometimes afraid to tell it like it is. And he needed to hear that 'like it is' before he made a decision."[4]

Evans sometimes stifled the very response he was trying to elicit. At the Monday morning meetings some thirty or thirty-five people including senior staff, department heads, and others heard presentations and discussed whatever issues were on the floor. While presiding over these sessions, Evans tended to jump to conclusions, interrupt speakers, dismiss their points as inane, and ream them out. Some recipients took the attacks personally and vowed never again to make themselves a target. One junior officer, after absorbing such an onslaught, muttered, "That's the last time I'll ever put a creative idea on the table for this company."[5]

To many targets and bystanders alike, the attacks seemed arbitrary and brutal. Others, however, sensed what Evans was trying to do and responded to it. Beth Whited, who first worked with Evans in January 1999, liked what she saw. "He wants somebody who's going to stand up and tell him what they think," she said. What others regarded as abrasive, Whited saw as "more test, test, test. I think he enjoyed throwing the fight on the table, wanted you to fight back. . . . Some people figured it out sooner than others. Some people never really figured out that he wanted you to argue with him."[6]

Marchant got along with Evans yet considered him "a tyrant and a bully. . . . Whereas Walsh was sharp, questioning, and more cerebral . . . with Evans I mean it was just four-letter words and yelling and screaming. . . . You had to stand up to him. You couldn't lie to him. That was one thing you never wanted to do is lie to him." One of UP's biggest problems, Evans told Marchant, was its civility. "Well," replied Marchant, "you've gone a long way to solving that problem, I think."[7]

Others found Evans to be mercurial. "Ike was a guy that could explode like a rocket in two minutes," said Jim Young, but added, ". . . I respect the man tremendously. He helped me a lot learning different things." Koraleski agreed that "Ike had a short fuse and there were days when it was just best to avoid him. . . . He's also a pretty reflective guy, and after he cooled down he'd laugh at himself and how upset he was and talk about why he was mad when we were alone together. He was just one of those high-strung, highly competitive guys who always wanted to win."[8]

Evans's style grated on Duffy and led to some memorable clashes between them. "You had to be very, very careful about standing your ground," Duffy said, "and if you got intimidated easily or if you got bullied, you were going to get more of it . . . and so you just had to stay right in there."[9]

Apart from his personal style, most UP officers respected Evans and his approach to work. He was intense, hardworking, bristling with energy, a quick study, very data driven. Even Duffy appreciated that, unlike Walsh and Burns, Evans took an interest in operations and went on inspection trips to learn the railroad. "He was very much focused on quality," he said, "and very much focused on the marketing aspects."[10]

The key to taking firm hold of UP, Evans thought, was grasping the fundamentals of how it worked as a complex network. "He's a very process-oriented guy," said Whited, "and . . . he felt like if he could understand the basic processes, he could understand whatever the thing was." Evans saw at once that UP, once merged with SP, posed an unprecedented complexity. "There's no model," he said, "and we're totally dependent upon experience. Less experience in some cases would have been better. The railroad industry . . . sometimes confuses industry knowledge with competency. There's a difference. Industry knowledge would be having that same experience fifteen times as opposed to having fifteen different experiences."[11]

The capacity issue lay at the heart of the matter. At one of his first staff meetings Evans asked what the UP's capacity was. A senior member replied that it couldn't be determined. The answer astonished Evans, who did not yet understand how difficult a problem it was to figure capacity with all the variables involved. He grappled with the capacity issue and its close relationship to capital needs. Emerson had, in his words, "a disdain for capital" and spent about $300 million a year. At UP he discovered that "sorting out where we were going to spend our capital was really a tough process." The company was praised for its $1.8 billion capital program, but his first budget review produced needs that totaled an astounding $4.8 billion. "What we didn't understand at the time," he said, "was how much work it was going to take to fix the Southern Pacific."[12]

It was easy to forget that the railroad had a new president, a new organization, a new VPO—and Davidson. Speculation arose about the extent to which Davidson actually ran the railroad. "Dick needed someone to take the day-to-day responsibility off of him," said Dolan, "and Ike was a very good manager in doing that." Still, many people thought that Davidson loomed like a ghostly presence over both Evans and Duffy. He listened to every morning report and phoned Duffy and other officers when he had a question. "I did not try to manage the operation on a day-to-day basis," he said, but he went to the Monday morning meetings and did not hesitate to offer his thoughts.[13]

"You know Dick Davidson," said a resigned Duffy. "He's never going to let loose of this railroad. . . . There isn't a day that hardly goes by that I don't talk to him about the operations of this company." Davis thought it fortunate for Evans that he had Davidson to consult, but it didn't make life easy for Duffy. "I wanted the other people pretty much to make the decisions," insisted Davidson, but the other people always knew who was looking over their shoulder.[14]

Some UP people thought Evans merely fronted for Davidson much as Flannery had for Kenefick, that he wanted to please the boss and implement what Davidson wanted done. Marchant noticed Davidson's tendency to "operate best when he's not the bad guy but he has a manager who does that for him." Others shared that view. "An element of Dick's management style," said Rebensdorf, "was always to have someone else carry out and take the heat for any tough decisions or calls."[15]

However, Ebby Gerry thought Evans had a blank check from Davidson to do whatever was needed. Evans denied vehemently that he was merely a puppet for Davidson. "Dick was tired," he said. ". . . He was ready to have someone come in and run the railroad. He let me run the railroad. Now what he still continued to keep his fingers on was the operating side." Evans agreed that "Dick always wanted to have somebody to be the bad guy. I played a little bit of that role. We both understood our roles."[16]

Davidson and Evans occupied offices on opposite sides of the twelfth floor. A staff joke was that the floor tilted back and forth depending on which one of them was doing what. They shared a host of values and worked together harmoniously. Since both of them arrived at the office early, they liked to talk during those early hours. "Those conversations were the basis of the relationship between the two of us," said Evans, "because we were both at an age where you said, We don't care. All we want to do is make this a good company."[17]

The good times continued to roll for UP even though the economy went into a nosedive that began even before the 9/11 disaster and accelerated thereafter. Not even the soaring price of oil halted the steady improvement in UP performance. In the first quarter of 2000 UP paid $100 million more for fuel than it had during the same period a year earlier. For four consecutive years UP delivered steadily increasing returns despite the turgid economy. The gains in volume were not huge—around 1 percent a year—but as Davidson liked to say, it was better than a sharp stick in the eye.[18]

Despite the economic recession UP achieved a third consecutive record performance in 2001. The railroad grossed nearly $10.4 billion in earnings and an operating income of $2.07 billion while hauling 8.9 million carloads. The operating ratio fell to 80.7 and the stock rose 30 percent during two years when the S&P 500 declined 22 percent and the NASDAQ Composite Index 52 percent. Here at last was the performance Davidson had hoped for when he first took command.[19]

In June 2001 the company announced plans to build a much larger headquarters building directly across Dodge Street from the old one at an estimated cost of $260 million. The following spring UP celebrated its regained reputation by launching its first major advertising campaign since the 1980s. Using the theme "UP: Building America," television ads featuring actor Sam Elliott's resonant voice appeared on four major networks in thirty-two markets before migrating to print media.[20]

The campaign to make a better company reached its apex in 2002. Revenues reached nearly $12.5 billion and net income more than $1.3 billion. UP stock rose 5 percent during a year when the Dow fell 17 percent and the S&P dropped 23 percent. The operating ratio dropped to 79.8, the first time it fell below 80 since the merger. Traffic continued to pour onto the railroad in record volumes despite the sluggish economy. The drive to reduce failure costs produced savings of $133 million. Failure costs as a percentage of revenue declined from 15.3 percent in 1999 to 11.3 percent in 2002.[21]

Davidson and Evans savored these results and promised even better ones. "We don't need a robust economy to be successful," said Evans. The company that had become a national joke during the service crisis now drew praise for its remarkable comeback. To improve these results, Evans homed in on two main goals: enhancing revenue and cutting costs. He saw three ways to improve revenues: know the railroad's business and capabilities; sell to its strengths; and broaden its interaction with customers. BNSF still had 3 percent of UP's combined pre-merger business, and Evans wanted it back. But even more he wanted to slice into the immense highway traffic.[22]

Evans focused first on revenues because he knew marketing better than operations and because Davidson wanted marketing shaken up. Davidson, said Schuster, "would tell you it used to tickle him to sit in on a meeting when Ike just beat the hell out of the coal guys and the auto guys and the grain guys and the ag product guys. . . . It was entertainment for Dick, but the guys didn't like it."[23]

Unimpressed with traditional railroad methods of analyzing revenue plans and results, Evans introduced a process called "market, price, and penetration." The basic concept was simple, the execution much less so. Revenues (market) grew or contracted because the customers' markets grew or shrank. How much of those markets the railroad gained depended on core price increases (price) and how much it scooped up of someone else's share (penetration) of the business, whether trucks, barges, or other railroads.[24]

"There were very rigorous reviews," Whited said. ". . . This market, price, penetration gets you to a strategy. He was trying to drive that thought process." It proved to be a lasting legacy, but it came hard to UP. "I think the mechanics of it were difficult for people to grasp onto," said Whited, ". . . It's a totally different mindset."[25]

At his first budget review with the sales and marketing staff Evans was told they anticipated growing 6 percent even though they had managed only 2.2 percent the previous year. "Well, how in the hell are you going to grow 6 percent?" he asked. ". . . What's the plan?" He found there was none. "Our guys didn't understand their markets," he said. "They didn't understand the factors that drove our customers' growth rates. They were selling services. . . . On one train we had fifteen different rates for the same boxcar for the same customer and we didn't know it. Because we didn't have any records."[26]

"We didn't market," he concluded. "We didn't say, Okay, here's a market that requires this service. We went out and said, We'll do this for you and here's your price . . . At one point in time we had 217 different boxcar configurations. Now think about the operational complexity of getting that boxcar with that door at that dock the right way all the time. . . . It was an impossible task. . . . My vision was that we would sell products that were based on demand."[27]

However, selling products on that basis meant knowing the nature of the markets and the railroad's ability to meet their needs. Evans found UP unsure of both. Davidson agreed to let him bring in a McKinsey consultant who had done similar work at Emerson. From this effort Evans concluded that part of the problem was the new NDI department headed by Brad King.[28]

The Transformation projected NDI as the interface between operations and sales and marketing. Evans considered it a mistake to give the responsibility to "staffers as opposed to operations or sales and marketing. . . . You want guys who are going to own it." Inevitably he clashed with King, who left the company in 2004. "I dismantled Network Design," said Evans, "and I was disappointed I couldn't get the operating guys to do it." He concluded that the regional vice presidents lacked the intellectual capacity to take it over and searched outside for someone who could get marketing and sales to function as business leaders.[29]

The results pleased Evans. "We proved that we could recruit good people from outside the industry," he said, "and that they could be successful in this culture." Davidson liked what he saw because, Evans thought, "they brought a different dimension. They brought accountability." Some within the company took a less favorable view. "It took him less than eighteen months to completely gut the NDI-led business process," said Rebensdorf, "and assume the role of chief business planner for the company."[30]

The dismantling began at the top. Shattuck was ready to retire, and Davidson wanted someone who could impose financial discipline on marketing. In March 1999 he offered the job to Koraleski, who had spent twenty-seven years in finance. Evans regarded Koraleski as a bright guy who got the message about going after the truck traffic. He was also flexible enough to adapt to the new order and was not invested in the old system. Under Koraleski marketing launched a series of new services aimed at eating into the trucking market share.[31]

Davidson and Evans also believed in the power of technology to raise revenues and lower costs. "Technology is *pervasive* throughout our company," Merill Bryan told a meeting of security analysts, "and is vital to the railroad's day-to-day operation. You'd be hard pressed to find any task that doesn't rely on technology in one form or another for its success." By 2000 the railroad owned 20,000 miles of backbone microwave and had 30,000 miles of carrier-owned fiber-optic along its right-of-way. It also had 1,500 radio tower sites, 1,200 microwave towers, 172 telephone exchanges, some 3,000 trackside devices, and a skilled support workforce. This extensive network and broadband capability might be extended to other uses as well.[32]

More than a decade earlier Lewis had pushed to make UP Technologies a profit center rather than a mere provider of IT to the railroad. To a limited extent it had done that until the strategy of UPC as the home to a stable of businesses came unraveled. Although every nonrail company except Overnite had been divested, the idea of UP's technology as a marketable asset still intrigued some directors. In 1999, with the dot-com craze in full flower, a few directors encouraged the rail officers to find ways of leveraging the railroad's technology assets. This would not be another stab at diversification, it was said, but rather an extension strategy to gain new revenues.[33]

To keep this effort from being a distraction to the railroad, a separate company called Fenix was formed in June 2000. Wholly owned by UP, it hired Osmo Hautanen, the recent CEO of Formus Communications in Denver, to head the company. Fenix became a holding company with four subsidiaries: Transentric, which absorbed UP Technologies; Nexterna, which absorbed AMCI, another UP subsidiary that marketed onboard communications systems to railroads, trucking companies, and fleet operators; Timera, which absorbed yet another existing subsidiary, PS Technology, home of the crew-scheduling software; and Ekanet, a new company formed to market UP's excess communications capacity.[34]

Davidson saw an opportunity not only to broaden the market for UP's proprietary software but also to utilize the microwave towers that had been superseded by the fiber-optic system. "The Norfolk Southern, as an example, has the same similar situation in the East," he said, "so we were working together with them to see if there isn't some way we could bring high-speed internet communications to rural America." Hautanen described Fenix as "an incubator company designed to expand and develop UP's technology businesses beyond the railroad industry."[35]

These high hopes were quickly dashed. UP's annual report in 2000 trumpeted the creation of Fenix and its possibilities, and included Hautanen in the group photograph of CEOs along with Davidson, Evans, and Leo Suggs of Overnite. A year later the annual report contained not a single mention of Fenix. The railroad discovered that other, more experienced companies were already doing the same things. "The field was crowded," said Davidson. ". . . We got in the game a little late and . . . it never did really amount to much."[36]

UP moved quickly to cut its losses. "We did not wait for the bubble to burst," said Charley Eisele. "We pretty much saw the handwriting on the wall, so we moved quickly to unwind Fenix and . . . move the three former railroad subsidiaries back into UP." The core technology subsidiaries returned safely to the railroad. Hautanen and the entire staff except one individual were let go.[37]

Fenix became Davidson's only foray into a nonrail activity. "I think he got sucked up by the euphoria over the telecommunications and information technology," said Rebensdorf. ". . . To his credit, he knew when to cut the losses." The experience was an old lesson relearned the hard way. He had pursued an opportunity that went against the grain of his desire to make the company strictly a railroad. Unfortunately, he then returned to an old and time-honored instinct that got him into much greater trouble by overriding another crucial lesson that had just been learned.

The parade of good earnings from 1999 through 2003 put constant pressure on UP to keep raising the bar. Even as the officers expressed satisfaction at the record performance of each quarter, they pondered how it could be matched or exceeded the next. The standard response was to keep boosting revenues while finding ways to shave costs. Through these years Davidson and Evans kept repeating the mantra of innovative growth, reliable customer service, and cost cutting. With the economy sluggish and fuel costs soaring, it made sense to

Davidson to run as lean an operation as possible. This had always been his style, and he saw no reason to change.

Evans got the message and carried it out with unusual zeal. It fit his re-emphasis on the quality program and campaign to drive down failure costs. It also reflected his desire to get everyone to do things in what he considered the right way. He liked to stress the importance of working smart over working hard.[38]

To that end Evans introduced the Six Sigma concept to the railroad. It was a process for eliminating failure as measured by six standard deviations. "Intelligent Solutions" became a slogan for improving quality while reducing costs. Many people struggled to grasp and apply the concepts, and Evans had little patience for their slowness. Throughout this process he viewed his role as that of educator. "If you want people to change," he said, "negative reinforcement does not work."[39]

Some staff members resented Evans's tendency to second-guess them or go behind their back for information. "He believed he knew more than anyone else, could make better decisions than his direct reports or subordinates," said Rebensdorf, "and fancied himself as a top negotiator and deal maker. . . . Ike always wanted to make the decision, which made him a poor delegator, and he was constantly second-guessing you. . . . He was quick to make judgments based on his intuition."[40]

Evans's proclivity for making deals especially bothered his officers. "He liked to make deals," said Duffy, "and had a hard time walking away from a bad deal." Evans hated to lose business. Rather than let it go, he would intervene personally to cut a deal for a long-term contract at a price point his people thought much too low. Many thought the automotive contracts he negotiated were money losers. "He was intense and he wanted to win," said Young. "He was a guy that when it came to, do I want this contract and the customer's kind of jerking me around right now, I want the contract."[41]

Duffy cringed at one long-term locomotive maintenance contract with GE. "We didn't think it was a good deal," he said, "and we had positioned the deal to say no to this. We were the only railroad that did not have a maintenance contract with GE for good reason, 'cause GE has a tendency to leverage you to the hilt . . . but they had made a pitch to Ike, and 'we,' meaning Ike, made the deal with them, and to this day we're still living with it."[42]

Although the cultural clash between Evans and his troops eased somewhat over time, it was never fully resolved. In 2002 Mike Hemmer came to UP as vice president of law to replace Dolan and von Bernuth, both of whom were nearing retirement, and found to his surprise that he reported to Evans rather than Davidson. A bright, energetic lawyer with a passion for railroads, Hemmer was no stranger to UP. As a partner in Covington & Burling he had done work for the company since the late 1970s and knew the culture well. While Evans treated him well personally, Hemmer noticed cynicism and demoralization about his leadership style among the senior staff and elsewhere. Evans liked Hemmer because he stood his ground and spoke his mind. He told Hemmer to fight, not settle, lawsuits. "I want people to know," said Evans, "if they're going to sue us, they're going to be in a dogfight."[43]

Like Davidson, Evans wanted UP to do well and be his legacy. He also longed to be CEO of the company, if only for a short time. His hope was that something might be done in the way of succession to fulfill his wish. "Clearly Ike had his eye on Dick's seat," said Young. "But you know, Dick also was . . . thinking about retiring earlier than he did."[44]

"I thought there was an understanding between Dick and myself," said Evans. The plan as Evans saw it was that Davidson would retire early and give Evans some time as CEO. Before anything could happen, however, a situation partly of his own making brought all of Evans's fighting instincts to the surface and threatened his own future.[45]

The Lessons Relearned

Like Walsh before him, Davidson badly wanted UP to win the Malcolm Baldrige National Quality Award, which had eluded it for years. Although the application process leeched an ungodly number of hours away from many employees, he thought the effort worth it. Davidson had come close to earning the honor in 1994. Winning the award would confirm that UP had truly come back from the service crisis. Evans pushed the process hard. In both 2001 and 2002 UP was named a finalist but failed to win. The reason in both cases, thought Hemmer, was that the Baldrige examiners learned that employees still harbored deep resentments toward management, and that communication between them was still poor despite all the efforts to improve it. The examiners had cited the same problem in 1994.[1]

The tumult and dislocation wrought by constant change remained a hard barrier to surmount even in the best of times, and it was fortified by another ongoing goal—cost cutting. Although business continued to grow despite the lingering recession, it grew more difficult every quarter to match the previous one.[2]

In 2003 UP seemed to be in splendid shape. That year it paid off the $1.5 billion in convertible preferred securities (CPS) issued to get through the service crisis. In November Davidson reached a cherished goal when the company finally sold off the last of its subsidiaries. "We became a 'pure' railroad again with the completion of the Overnite initial public offering," he told the stockholders. "Overnite is a great company with a terrific management team, but it shared few synergies with the Railroad." The company took a big loss on the sale but used the cash to pay off the last $500 million of the CPS issue, which reduced future interest payments by $71 million. Earnings fell somewhat during the first half of the year but still outshone those of other railroads.[3]

To cope with the stagnant economy, Davidson and Evans looked for more cuts. Evans pinched pennies as tightly as Davidson—thus his mantras to work smarter, not harder, and figure out how to do more with what you have rather than ask for more. "We went back to where we felt strong," said Marchant.

"Started cutting. Proved ourselves capable of dealing with the recession and . . . did it the old-fashioned way by just cutting and cutting." This attitude rippled through the entire organization. "From senior management down to the region," said Rebensdorf, "people were cutting back on projected crew requirements so that, for example, what started out as a requirement to hire four hundred people ended up being actual hiring of only one hundred people."[4]

By 2003 the urge to cut had become all-consuming. Evans decreed that no one could be hired without his personal approval. "It stopped the hiring," said Marchant, "and it sent a clear message that you're not going to be hiring." The process of getting approval became so arduous that most department heads didn't bother trying. Budgets became a source of tortuous sessions where Evans hammered away at the presenter. "He had these horrible budget meetings," said Marchant, "and he'd make people cry and then he'd laugh about it."[5]

Evans knew how to run a tight ship and had done a good job of it since 1999. "We were getting better in everything—safety, service, value, all of them," said Duffy, "and we wanted to get better and better, and . . . we were playing it very close to the vest." Evans pushed marketing to get more business and intervened personally in deals partly because he wanted more volume. Davidson approved because it fed the bottom line and he wanted to please the board with good results. The board in turn demanded ever better figures, as did Wall Street. "Dick tried to satisfy the board a little too hard," said Dolan, "didn't say, No, we can't meet those numbers. . . . We took on more business than we were capable of handling."[6]

This desire to keep the good times rolling posed a serious dilemma for Davidson and Evans. "We did a lot of work on cost and returns," said Jim Young, "but we also had an attitude of . . . more volume is better. It drives unit costs down. We'll deal with the issues later on." But the issues were already arriving, especially capacity, density, and personnel. "That mentality of very tight cost control," said Duffy, ". . . really left you vulnerable and particularly when you were close to the capacity curve anyway." Rebensdorf agreed that "we brought in business in the early part of this century that in retrospect we shouldn't have gone after. . . . So we started overloading our railroad."[7]

"I think culturally we thought, God, we'll never see the day when we fill the railroad up," said Rob Knight. ". . . So the concept of putting volume caps on commercial agreements so that somebody couldn't just flood you with volume and you have no say, was just foreign." Commercial agreements then in place rewarded shippers with lower rates for more volume and bound UP to handle every car thrown at it. The railroad could not refuse cars or raise its price on an extra surge of them. "The crux of the issue," said Knight, "was, we never envisioned that we'd fill up the railroad."[8]

Running lean also meant having fewer crews available, which posed a delicate balancing act. It meant pushing the available crews hard with only a thin reserve behind them. "We had very little surge capacity," said Young. "You could see it when you had a derailment that your recovery time was much, much more elongated. . . . You had no recovery capability if you had a problem with crews or weather or a computer system and you got behind the curve." It also created manpower problems, especially on weekends and holidays. Evans wanted operations to run the crew boards at high-mileage levels, but exhausted crews needed time off.[9]

Another issue complicated the crew question. By the end of 2002 large numbers of crewmen would reach 30/60—the company's shorthand for thirty years of service and sixty years of age—making them eligible to retire. The problem was compounded that year by a change in the federal retirement law allowing employees with thirty years' service to retire with full benefits at sixty instead of sixty-two. No one knew how many of UP's engineers and conductors would actually leave, but the best guess was that it would be a large number.[10]

That fall a team headed by Tom Haley, one of Rebensdorf's direct reports, made a startling discovery while updating the quarterly revenue and carload forecasts. Apart from the potential loss of crews, the figures indicated that many more of them would be needed to handle a projected upsurge in business, and that hiring should begin at once because it took time to qualify new hires. In the old days UP could simply reach down in the ranks and promote people who already had railroad experience and needed only a modicum of training. But those ranks had been emptied by personnel cuts; new hires had to come mostly from outside, and they had to learn railroading from scratch.[11]

"When I was a brakeman," said Davidson, "I broke in and went to work in a week. Now it takes six months to train somebody to be a brakeman conductor and a year to get somebody ready to be an engineer." Haley's team warned that a serious shortage of crews could occur if the hiring process did not begin immediately. Rebensdorf seconded this conclusion. But hiring and training new people would impact earnings. In the discussion that followed, one general manager offered some dubious projections that showed he would not need to hire new crews. Without digging deeper into the assumptions behind this claim, Davidson and Evans seized on it as a rationale to put off hiring.[12]

The issue surfaced again at a meeting late in 2002. By then it had become clear that the attrition from retirement would be much greater than expected, and it was coming at a time when crew boards were already at the high end of the monthly mileage per person. Yet Evans again rejected the forecast and recommendation for hiring new crews. Davidson offered the opinion that the gap could be filled partly by cutting back on guarantee and protection pay and by utilizing people more productively.[13]

"Both Ike and Dick were told the specific locations where we needed to hire crews in order to meet the projected increases in traffic in 2003," said Rebensdorf. "Ike, in particular, challenged and ultimately disparaged the assumptions that led to the crew forecast. . . . The decision not to hire additional crews came directly . . . from Ike Evans."[14]

Although no one yet realized it, a crucial turning point had been reached. The dilemma facing Davidson and Evans was simple: No one knew when the recession would end and traffic pick up. "Economists were saying over and over and over again, the economy is going to start getting stronger," said Hemmer, "but it didn't happen. And they'd say it again and it didn't happen." Davidson grew skeptical of the predictions. "We had been in a recession for three years," he said, "and the government kept saying the second half of the year is going to be stronger, and we just didn't believe it."[15]

"The prognosticators had said that the economy was going to turn around every year," said Duffy, ". . . but three years, four years in a row it never happened, and so we said, Well, this is probably going to be just like every other year. . . . Bit us in the ass, big time." Given this pattern, standing pat on crews seemed to make sense. In March 2003 UP actually announced a plan to eliminate another thousand jobs through attrition and layoffs to cut costs by as much as 20 percent.[16]

The timing could not have been worse. The attrition rate from retirements soared beyond expectations, reducing ranks already stretched thin. Then the long-predicted surge of business arrived with a vengeance, catching by surprise a UP ill equipped to handle the rush. Volume during the first quarter of 2003 rose slightly, then dipped slightly the second quarter. "So we're sitting there saying, Yeah, there's no way we're going to gear up in the second half," said Koraleski. ". . . Suddenly in September of 2003 somebody lit the fire. Six of our businesses just heated up enormously."[17]

The scale and suddenness of the rush overwhelmed the operating department. "The whole economy turned around," said Duffy. ". . . Money was cheap; building products just went crazy; that I-5 just accelerated in terms of the lumber, so it was across the board that it came on us. . . . And then the organic growth from the existing customers, they all took off . . . and volume just went nuts." Duffy called his people together and said, "Look, guys, this is a turning point. We're seeing things here that we have not seen before."[18]

He did not yet know how right he was. They were witnessing the harbinger of a new era in American railroad history. Throughout its history, except for abnormal periods like wartime, the industry had suffered from excess capacity. For nearly a century it had undergone a painful downsizing to correct the overbuilding that created the problem. Railroads had been merged and mileage abandoned to forge a smaller, leaner, more efficient network. Ironically, the ordeal succeeded only too well. By 2003 the railroads had not only shed their excess capacity but arrived at a historic moment when they were starting to run out of capacity.

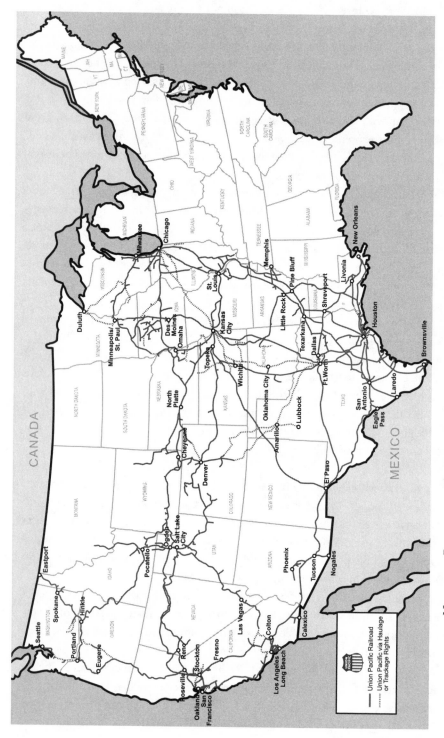

NETWORK RAILROAD. The Union Pacific Railroad in 2004 after all its mergers and acquisitions.

For most of the past century the rail system had been shrinking even as the traffic pouring onto it grew. For many years it absorbed more business thanks to technological and other innovations that expanded capacity without adding more track. But the expanding American economy and the rise of a global economy thrust an even greater burden on the rail system. The time had come to rethink how railroads did their business in this new global environment.

This tsunami of business brutally exposed the underlying weaknesses of UP's cost-cutting strategy. In their dogged attempts to meet shrinking budgets, the regional vice presidents had cut training expenses. No one had done this more vigorously than Jeff Verhaal in the Western Region, where the storm of traffic hit hardest. The region became the flash point for what UP dreaded most: a new service crisis.[19]

As the Sunset Route in particular grew more congested, it aroused institutional memories of the recent nightmare. The circumstances differed sharply. No merger was involved, no unaligned computers, unmade labor agreements, or unfamiliarity with routes. The core problem was elemental: too much business and too few crews to run trains. Too late Davidson and Evans realized their mistake and scrambled to correct it. "We started hiring like hell," said Duffy. UP went after a thousand new hires that fall and a few months later said it would seek another four thousand workers. But any newcomers would not be ready to crew trains for six months to a year, and relief was needed at once.[20]

Evans set up 7:00 A.M. meetings to monitor the situation and exchange ideas. Marchant scrambled to find ways of getting enough crews to get through the next few months. To keep the Los Angeles Basin fluid he arranged with the UTU to let UP use reduced crews on a temporary basis, only to have locals reject the deal because of lingering resentments over the merger.[21]

Frustrated, Marchant devised a new scheme he called "officer borrow-outs." The UP system had over a hundred officers with trainman seniority. While retaining their current positions, they reported to L.A. as newly hired trainmen, joined the UTU, which winked at the arrangement because it knew the railroad was in danger of another gridlock, and manned trains. "So they were still officers back in Little Rock or Chicago or wherever they came from," said Marchant, "and still getting full officer pay and benefits, and then they got paid as trainmen, too."[22]

This clever maneuver continued for the duration of the crisis. However, as the volume of business increased, many more bodies were needed than could be culled from the ranks. As 2003 drew to a close, the crew and congestion problems threatened to get much worse. In the annual report Davidson downplayed the looming crisis, saying almost in passing that "shortages of train crews and locomotives limited our growth potential and impacted both operating costs and service as volumes increased in the second half of the year."[23]

To outward eyes the railroad seemed to be doing well. Third-quarter earnings for 2003 slumped because of higher fuel costs and what the company discreetly called "operational challenges." A Wall Street analyst warned that "the first challenge for the major railroads will be to correct the service glitches that appear to have affected the North American system." Davidson expressed gratification that the economy was picking up but remained cautious as to whether the recovery was genuine.[24]

Fourth-quarter earnings soared 6 percent to a record $2.8 billion, with intermodal jumping 13 percent and industrial products 9 percent. The results would have been even better, admitted Davidson, except for "operating inefficiencies and freight delays . . . caused by a shortage of train crews and other resources." Still he questioned whether the recovery was real. He had no immediate answer for the crew shortages other than a blitzkrieg of hiring, but he did have in mind some management changes at the top.[25]

The board underwent significant changes in the new century. Bob Bauman retired in 2000 and was replaced by two newcomers, Archie W. Dunham, the CEO of Conoco, and Steven R. Rogel, the CEO of Weyerhaeuser. A year later Virgil Conway and Dick Simmons left, while Ernesto Zedillo Ponce de León, former president of Mexico, joined; his presence attested to the growing importance of the Mexican connection. During 2004 Ebby Gerry and Dick Mahoney reached the retirement age and stepped down. Gerry's departure was especially poignant; apart from his considerable ability, he represented the last direct link to the Harriman family. Mike McConnell, the managing partner of Brown Brothers Harriman, replaced Gerry and preserved UP's longtime connection to that firm.[26]

Important changes also took place at the railroad. Although Davidson was not scheduled to retire until 2007, he did not wait to tackle the question of succession. Mindful of the clumsy horse race that preceded his appointment, he wanted a clean transition. Evans assumed that Davidson would retire as CEO a year early, remain as chairman of the board, and give Evans that time as CEO. He did not know that Davidson had much earlier decided whom he wanted to follow him. "I had identified Jim Young as a potential replacement for me even before I became president of the company," he said.[27]

Davidson had first met Young in 1986 when he moved from St. Louis to Omaha after the MP merger. He saw quickly that Young was bright and tough. "He had courage and integrity," said Davidson, "and didn't mind pushing back if he thought he was right. . . . When I got in a position where I could, I started guiding his career. . . . He never disappointed me. He was smart and worked hard and had integrity, had guts. Just the kind of guy you want."[28]

Young knew nothing of this even though Davidson went out of his way to get him in the loop with activities not normally associated with his job. He orchestrated Young's rise to CFO and was pleased at his performance at every level. During the summer of 2003, as the congestion problem was heating up, Davidson walked into Young's office one day and said, "Jim, I'm thinking about making some changes, making you president at some point in time."[29]

Young was flabbergasted. "That wasn't some discussion we had years earlier," he said later. "That was months." The board had to be convinced that Young was capable of running the company; making him president of the railroad earlier than planned, especially in the midst of a growing service crisis, would enable him to show what he could do.[30]

Promoting Young early undercut any possibility of putting Evans in as CEO even for a short time. Ike won't like this, Davidson told the board, but he's a player and he will play. "Give the guy credit," said a disappointed Evans. "He knew me better than I knew myself because I played." The news went public at the end of January, and Young assumed the presidency a month later. Evans was bumped up to vice chairman of UPC, and Knight replaced Young as CFO.[31]

An even greater surge of business hit the railroad during the first quarter of 2004. Davidson had undergone a trial by fire upon taking office, and Young was about to get his own version. Davidson formed a committee consisting of himself, Evans, Young, Duffy, Koraleski, and Knight to oversee the crisis. As sidings began filling up with trains, especially in southern California and the Southwest, and customer complaints soared, everyone dreaded a replay of 1997–98. "My first year as president," said Young, "I spent about half of my time with my customers and about 40 percent in front of employees, and I will tell you it was brutal. I'd go out for a week and I had customers really very mad, one-sided conversations, guys that lost their jobs. We had employees mad. Their spouses were mad. . . . I'd think, We're in serious trouble here."[32]

But he didn't stop. Back out he went, over and over, taking Duffy or Koraleski with him, to listen, reassure, explain, and promise that he would be back to check on whether things had improved. "We were melted down in Phoenix," Young said. "We were in severe gridlock, and what we had to do is, customers that could truck we were walking away from." For Young and the other officers it became another painful learning experience. "In this business customers have long memories," he said. "They really do. . . . We were the best marketing arm for the Burlington Northern Railroad in '03, '04, '05."[33]

A spike in incoming Asian traffic aggravated congestion in the Los Angeles Basin. By late March 2004 the number of freight cars on the system had increased from 302,711 in first-quarter 2003 to 325,634, and their average dwell time at West Colton, the major yard for southern California, had jumped from 30.8 hours a year earlier to 52.5. Average train speed fell from 24.8 to 21.4 during that same period. This was no small item; every decline of one mile per hour required 250 extra locomotives, 5,000 more freight cars, and 180 extra employees to make up the decrease in efficiency. A survey of freight customers showed the UP next to last among the seven major railroads.[34]

A service crisis on the UP was no small matter. By 2004 railroads were handling 40 percent of the nation's freight traffic, and the UP hauled a third of that amount, or about $300 billion in raw materials and finished goods a year. "With trucking companies and other railroads also squeezed for space," wrote one analyst, "Union Pacific has become a major business constraint that could create shortages for retailers and higher prices for customers." As a stopgap the company asked some customers in the most congested areas to shift to trucks, reduce their shipments, and take other measures to curb the number of crews needed.[35]

By May the congestion had backed up into Houston and the Northwest even as it eased somewhat in the Southwest. The Overland Route remained fluid until March 26, when a coal train derailed twenty-two cars and forced UP to reroute coal traffic over the Marysville sub. Still the traffic kept coming. The Sunset Route struggled to handle forty-one trains a day, compared to thirty-three trains in 2001. Problems in the Davis Yard and design flaws in the clogged West Colton Yard aggravated attempts to ease the congestion. The much vaunted high-speed service installed on several routes compounded the problem by forcing slower trains onto sidings while they passed. Reluctantly the UP stopped running its prized fast UPS intermodal train from southern California to the Southeast.[36]

Everyone at UP knew the crisis would ease once the new crews were ready to be deployed, but that took time. In June the company announced it would add another eight hundred new hires, running the total to five thousand. Traffic for the first twenty-three weeks of 2004 climbed 4.2 percent over the previous year, with the peak shipping season yet to come. Although the entire rail network groaned under the strain, one writer labeled UP "a poster child of sorts for the industry's current service and capacity problems." Along with bringing in new hires, Davidson increased the locomotive and freight car fleet with accelerated deliveries, purchases, and leases.[37]

By July the Sunset Route struggled with as many as fifty trains a day. The old nightmare loomed again of trains grinding to a halt because their crews had reached the federally mandated limit of twelve hours' work. Crews needed for other trains had to be sent to pick up stopped trains, move them onto sidings, and later move them out again. One ill-starred Los Angeles–Memphis train hauling a hundred cars packed with Toyotas, electronics, and other cargo waited three days for a locomotive, then was broken in half to avoid blocking a grade crossing before being shunted onto a branch. When trains finally got power, they often sat waiting for other trains to pass, wasting precious crew hours. Customer complaints escalated; one lumber dealer in Tempe, Arizona, waited a month for orders that normally reached him in ten days.[38]

"We couldn't take trains out of terminals," said Rebensdorf. "Last thing you want is not to be able to move a train out of the terminal because it just backs up the terminal, which means trains can't get in, which starts backing up your line of road, and the vicious cycle starts."[39]

While awaiting the arrival of freshly trained crews, UP tried to shift business onto other railroads, trucks, or anything that would take it. BNSF hesitated because it feared getting clogged in the same manner; it too tried to limit volume with selective price increases. Trucking capacity was so strained that its customers were shifting to the railroads. As the peak traffic season arrived, Koraleski marveled at the figures accumulating on his desk. Seven-day carloadings for August set a record for the twelfth consecutive month; on September 15 UP set a new all-time record for seven-day carloadings of 192,000.[40]

UP began deploying its fresh recruits and resorted to an allocation system to protect terminals from overload. It consolidated select automobile and chemical trains and regulated the volume of some agricultural products. Fewer cars made the system more fluid, improved car cycle time, increased network velocity, and reduced congestion on sidings. Customers helped by increasing train length, loading and unloading their cars on weekends, and working with UP to shrink their car inventories.[41]

The service crisis of 2004 did not end abruptly but ebbed gradually like a tide going out. Unlike the tide, it did not return but left in its wake a host of lessons relearned along with insights on how the industry seemed to have entered a new era. "We're seeing a sea change in demand for rail transportation," said Davidson late that summer. "From Staggers forward until the last year or so, we were living out of the cupboard. We had more people and assets than we needed. Now, all of a sudden, that's gone. We have more demand than supply. We're running like hell to try to keep up with volume, and our business is growing. We've had ten months of record volume. The gratifying part is the strength of the economy and the huge demand for our service. But the fact that we've disappointed a number of our customers puts a little cold water on our euphoria. The lack of resources and qualified personnel has offset strong revenues, and we haven't put the results on the bottom line."[42]

The numbers bore him out. Operating revenues in 2004 increased from $11.6 billion in 2003 to $12.2 billion, but operating income fell from $2.13 billion to $1.3 billion, and net income shrank from $1.6 billion to $604 million. The operating ratio soared from 81.5 to 89.4, while the return on equity dropped from 13.8 percent to 4.8 percent. The stock plummeted from nearly 70 in January to 56 in May. For the service crisis Davidson offered a disarmingly simple explanation. "It was a very straightforward problem," he said. "We just hadn't geared up for a big growth in business. . . . And so when business just zoomed, why, we weren't ready."[43]

The most obvious lesson to be learned was that running lean by cutting costs in every direction was no longer a viable strategy. While no railroad could entirely escape dancing to Wall Street's tune, neither could it afford to focus on the next quarter's bottom line at the expense of broader needs. Economy had been drilled into the bones of rail executives and it was a worthwhile goal, but in the new era it had to be balanced by keeping resources at a level that matched the amount of traffic even if such measures cost money.

Nearly everyone sensed that the age of excess capacity had ended even if they did not fully understand what that meant for the future. "We started understanding that you only can get so many trains across a track," said Dennis Jacobson. "You can only get so many cars through a terminal." Carl von Bernuth believed that "the theory of the railroads for so long was that there were no limits to capacity. At a modest cost you add signals, add another line, but that's not true anymore." Long after he retired, Kenefick continued to preach the centrality of capacity.[44]

Rob Ritchie of CP argued that lack of capacity—both at present and for projected growth—posed the biggest problem facing railroads. "On too many railroads, at too many places," he said, "we have to make do with terminals that are too small for today's trains and long stretches of congested track with inadequate capacity." Federal policy since the Transportation Act of 1920 had done much to drive the downsizing of the American rail system. "Everybody recognized that there were too many miles of track out there and not enough business," said Hemmer. ". . . Deregulation underscored the need for it. It created such a premium on eliminating excess cost [because] you could compete for the first time on the basis of efficiency."[45]

Deregulation drove railroads to look for every way to purge inefficiencies from their operations. It encouraged roads to merge not only to economize but to pare away excess track. By restoring price competition, deregulation also spurred the creation of single-line service and the desire of railroads for long-term contracts to guarantee traffic. It became clear very early that rail competition lowered rates, which pushed railroads to compensate by acquiring as much volume as possible. The goal of every major railroad was to haul as much stuff as possible at the lowest winning rate with the best service. These were laudable but contradictory ambitions. No amount of volume could swell the bottom line if prices went too low, but it could choke the railroad's capacity and thereby hike costs through inefficiencies.

From long experience most railroaders shared Knight's belief that they could never fill up the railroad with traffic. As shippers did the unthinkable by filling them up, the UP and other roads found themselves burdened with more business than they could handle efficiently. The result was deteriorating service hauling cargoes under contracts that did not pay and kept better-paying business off the road for lack of capacity. Like Gresham's law concerning money, bad business drove out good business.

In the new era of railroading a crucial lesson emerged: Price mattered more than volume. It was a gospel Matthews had preached twenty years earlier. Walsh never converted to it, and Matthews thought Davidson never did either. Matthews conceded that it was difficult to raise prices but insisted that the rewards were great. The railroad would need fewer locomotives and other equipment, endure less wear and tear on the infrastructure, and, best of all, keep the network much more fluid.[46]

To do that, however, required a seismic shift in attitudes and conventional wisdom. Railroads had always been dominated by operations people who believed fervently in volume. The railroad was, after all, a high-fixed-cost business; the cost to maintain its infrastructure continued regardless of the volume thrown over it, so it was only natural to think in terms of moving as much traffic across it as possible. Ironically, even marketing innovations like the high-speed UPS train and similar specials backfired by helping to congest the system. "Intermodal is the most time-sensitive business," said Evans. "It's our fastest trains, so you set stuff aside. So you use your capacity for this and it's your least profitable business." Some of the worst early contracts belonged to intermodal and did not expire for years.[47]

"We came to the conclusion," said Evans, "that . . . we should have been charging our industrial customers a hell of a lot more than we were." He cited the example of a scrap dealer in Fort Worth who gave UP two cars of business and called to complain that the railroad kept raising its price. "My response," said Evans, "was, We switch your two cars on our main line every other day, and every time I do that I shut down our main line. Why don't you go to truck? I really don't want your business." But Evans conceded that this could be a dangerous path because the consequences cascaded.

Suppose a customer in Phoenix, where business was booming, had a siding for two cars and decided he wanted five cars. "So where do we put those other three cars?" asked Evans. "And if this customer is typical of other customers, where do we put all these cars? Our yard is backed up so we take them out and park them on the main line, and pretty soon we're congested. I'm not a truck. I can't take a back road, so you lock yourself up. We keep raising prices to these guys, and all of a sudden they're complaining to John McCain, who's on the Senate Transportation Committee, UP is running me out of business. . . . The economic impact to Phoenix is now an issue, and McCain threatens to do something about it. . . . Everything the rails do at some point ends up involving the federal or a state government."[48]

Pricing held the key to changing the historic pattern in which volume reigned supreme. For the first time, said Evans, railroads had pricing power. He moved to push prices up, to get price points on existing business. He also wanted to get free of older contracts that bound the railroad to lower prices. "We inherited some horrendous contracts," he declared. Yet during the recession years he too had succumbed to the siren's call of volume by insisting on some horrendous contracts of his own.[49]

An era of full capacity required a railroad to be more selective about the business it solicited and walk away from anything that didn't pay or the railroad couldn't deliver. As CFO Young fully supported the effort to raise prices and be more selective. As president he carried the effort even further. "We're good at pricing," he said in October 2008. "In fact, I will lose a $200 million, $300 million a year contract if I can't get the pricing up. . . . I have contracts today that I'm losing money on, cash cost every carload I handle." This approach required a different and often painful mindset for marketing and sales people. "Raising prices is not easy," said Young. "You're testing relationships that were built up over many, many years."[50]

Above all, the service crisis of 2004 impressed on Young the importance of never getting caught short of resources. Honoring this lesson meant resisting the temptation in tough times of cutting everywhere possible until business picked up. "Our volume's down," he said when the next recession hit. "It'd be very cost-efficient [to make cuts] . . . and I've said we're not going to do that. . . . I've got a thousand surplus locomotives right now. A thousand employees furloughed." This approach dovetailed with that of focusing only on business that paid, which put a premium on good service. To deliver that service, the railroad had to be well resourced and keep its network fluid. Like a utility, it had to be prepared to meet not just ordinary but peak demand.[51]

Duffy put the transition into a new era another way. "The thing that changed in May of '03," he said, "is that we came from a cost-control, low-return industry to a major growth industry, which to me is just accelerating. It's exhilarating. . . . I have the utmost confidence that it's going to be probably the best time in this industry."[52]

If Duffy was right, the rail industry had in less than forty years gone from the worst of times to the best of times. No one in 1969 could even remotely have foreseen what was to come. "I can recall in the 1970s when I was working on the Penn Central bankruptcy," said Hemmer, "sitting in a bar with members of the board of trustees late at night, speculating about whether there would be a railroad industry in 2000. We had serious doubts about that. . . . Government regulation was too severe, labor conditions were intolerable. We were being required to operate services that didn't make any sense, we couldn't price to market, and many of us believed that the railroad industry would die."[53]

But it didn't die. Instead it reconfigured itself to become a strong and thriving industry. UP played a crucial if not dominant role in that process. No one believed that the service crisis of 2004, embarrassing as it was, amounted to anything more than a blip in its continuing reconfiguration into the world's largest and most complex railroad. It had the most storied past of any surviving American railroad, yet its focus remained firmly fixed on the future. The central question remained, as it had always been, What would the next railroad be?

Epilogue

The Next Railroad

In 1969 UP was a bridge railroad with 9,473 miles of track, essentially the same railroad that emerged from the split with SP in 1912. By 2004 it had grown into a sprawling network with 32,616 miles of track that handled one-third of all American rail traffic. During that thirty-five years it had evolved from an independent railroad to the dominant subsidiary of a holding company and back to a pure railroad. In the process it absorbed five major railroads and became one of only four major American rail systems. On a landscape littered with the fallen flags of so many former railroads, UP remained the only major system still bearing its original name.

A railroader of 1969 would hardly have recognized what railroads had become or how they operated. Excessive government regulation was gone, along with passenger traffic, the caboose, manual signals, hundreds of depots, the telegraph, thousands of miles of track, mountains of paperwork, and armies of employees who performed tasks by hand. In their place had come computers, new types of locomotives and rolling stock, fiber-optic communication systems, centralized dispatching and customer service, automatic signals, electronic devices of all kinds, track-laying machines, the Internet, and a host of other technologies that performed tasks quicker, cheaper, and more precisely.

A vast portion of the changes in what railroads did and how they did it stemmed directly from new machines and techniques. During the 1950s the steam locomotive gave way to the diesel; forty years later the DC diesel locomotive yielded to its AC counterpart. Freight cars took on new configurations, many of them evolved from traditional forms. The venerable reefers of the 1960s, for example, were refurbished and given new features such as remote monitoring capability. The fabulous Track Renewal Train could lay 2 to 3 miles of 141-pound welded rail a day on concrete ties.[1]

One technology alone, the computer, changed the way railroads did virtually everything. No aspect of operations went untouched by its influence. Computers could be found not only in offices but in locomotive cabs, trackside, and in the hands of employees on the move. Communication throughout the UP system became instantaneous and incessant. "The stunning progress of the cellular phenomenon," observed a report, "has spurred unprecedented interest and rapid evolutionary growth in wireless technology." A flood of new products—cell phones, PDAs, satellite-based networks—generated demand for smaller, lighter, and better integrated devices with increased capability.[2]

Evolving generations of computers also enabled complex terminal operations like those at North Platte, the busiest stretch of road in the world. Altogether UP's network handled about 300,000 cars, 1,500 trains, and 6,000 to 8,000 locomotives every day. On the Powder River line an endless parade of coal trains crawled along like enormous black caterpillars while speedier intermodal trains flowed across the other side of the Big Red X. Everything converged at North Platte, which received a fourth mainline track to handle the load. Work also went steadily forward on double-tracking the Sunset Route. By the end of 2008 about 65 percent of the route had been completed.[3]

The next railroad would run on technologies still being perfected or not yet even conceived. Positive Train Control had been under development for more than a decade, distributive power had already arrived along with the AC locomotive, and RCL (switching by remote control) and a variety of new technologies to improve service and efficiency were being tested. Since the days of E. H. Harriman UP had been a laboratory for experimenting with new devices, and it would remain so.[4]

As always, the future posed problems and pitfalls as well as prospects. The long-standing concerted effort, especially by shippers, to get Congress to reregulate the railroads continued with undiminished energy. Not all railroads shared UP's prosperity, and some analysts still doubted their future. The overall system continued to shrink as railroads shed more track. "There is still a lot of track being sold off, abandoned," said Hemmer. Some organizations like OnTrackAmerica directed their efforts to finding new ways for moving more traffic from the highways to the rails.[5]

"The investment community," said Hemmer, "is banking on the future. It's banking on our ability to take advantage of this new balance . . . between capacity and demand. . . . And if we fail, they'll pull their money, and . . . start looking for other places to invest." The endless campaign to earn cost of capital depended greatly on the outcome of the fight to reregulate the railroads. "The biggest single question we face," declared Hemmer, "is whether the government . . . or local interests prevent us from earning an adequate return on investment. And if so, we will decline again."[6]

During 2004 UP entered a new era in quite another fashion by moving into its beautiful new nineteen-story office building. Located directly across Dodge

Street from the old headquarters, the building enabled the company to concentrate in one place workers that had been scattered across seven locations in Omaha and St. Louis. It contained 1.1 million square feet of space organized around an atrium that extended through its entire nineteen floors. For top management the old twelfth floor became instead the nineteenth floor. Among other amenities the new facility featured a workout gym and one of the best company cafeterias found anywhere.[7]

Davidson enjoyed his new quarters only until the end of 2006, when he stepped down according to his plan in what was probably the smoothest transition in the company's history. Asked to name his most important accomplishment, he said, "It's having a strong management team in place to run the company." Evans retired after a year as vice chairman, and in January 2007 Young assumed the position of CEO and chairman as well as president with Duffy and Koraleski as his chief lieutenants. Besides being a close-knit team, they were remarkable in being truly a "homeboy" leadership. Both Young and Koraleski were Omaha natives; Duffy hailed from Sioux City across the river. All three men attended the University of Nebraska at Omaha (UNO).[8]

For the first time in its modern history UP had a local management team, raised in the area and graduates of the same university. Young came from a working-class family; his father drove a truck, and he lost his mother at an early age. He worked full-time while he attended UNO full-time, did not graduate until he was twenty-six, and spent fifteen years paying off student loans. Duffy was the second of eight children in a staunch Irish Catholic family and got his education in parochial schools. Koraleski was to the manner born in that his father was in finance. He followed his father into finance and got an MBA as well from UNO.[9]

Besides their local roots, all three leaders had worked under and been trained by Rebensdorf in his P&A group. "If I leave a legacy to this company," said Rebensdorf, "... it's that I can look back and say ... three of the top people in the company came through planning and analysis." All three men remain deeply grateful for what they learned from that experience.[10]

Before leaving UP Davidson was honored with a series of dinners and celebrations across the system. "When Dick Davidson retired," joked Young, "I gave at least seven speeches, and I told Dick, I'm not doing any more." The triumphal procession came to an abrupt and amusing end. On the day after his retirement Davidson came to UP headquarters only to discover that his card key had already been canceled and he couldn't get in.[11]

Young felt fortunate to be UP's leader, despite his rugged introduction to the office. "I think I was handed kind of the keys to the Cadillac," he said. "If you think about what you had to do to get the company put together, it was very tough. It was consolidating companies with different cultures, taking jobs out, dealing with unions." Having inherited the fruits of that long process, Young intends to use them wisely. "I was handed a great opportunity," he said, "and I always believe through crisis good things can happen."[12]

So far the next railroad has thrived under its new management and engineered a remarkable turnaround. From 2005 onward service improved steadily to record levels even as the company achieved record low operating ratios. Despite the crash of 2008 and its aftermath, UP's earnings and service remained strong. Investment in the infrastructure and capacity expansion continued as well. Even with reduced traffic the railroad set new records in safety, service, and financial performance. Still the question lingered as to whether UP absorbed the lessons of the past well enough to maintain its outstanding performance. Young has vowed that it will.

ABBREVIATIONS

Source Abbreviations

BW	*Business Week*
CSM	*Christian Science Monitor*
JC	*Journal of Commerce*
JCK	Material furnished by John C. Kenefick
JHR	Material furnished by John H. Rebensdorf
JLJ	Material furnished by John L. Jorgensen
JRD	Material furnished by Jerry R. Davis
MR	*Modern Railroads*
NYT	*New York Times*
OWH	*Omaha World-Herald*
RA	*Railway Age*
SJM	Material furnished by Stanley J. McLaughlin
TW	*Traffic World*
UPM	Union Pacific Museum
UPR	Union Pacific Records
WP	*Washington Post*
WSJ	*Wall Street Journal*

Text Abbreviations

AAR	Association of American Railroads
AMS	Automated manifest system
APC	American President Companies
APL	American President Lines
ATC	Advanced Train Control
BLE	Brotherhood of Locomotive Engineers
BN	Burlington Northern Railroad
BNSF	Burlington Northern Santa Fe Railroad
BRAC	Brotherhood of Railway and Airline Clerks
BRC	Brotherhood of Railway Carmen
C&EI	Chicago & Eastern Illinois Railroad
CAD	Computer-aided drafting
COFC	Container on flatcar
COIN	Complete Operating Information System

CN	Canadian National Railroad
CNW	Chicago & North Western Railroad
CP	Canadian Pacific Railroad
CPS	Convertible preferred securities
CRI	Cambridge Research Institute
CSC	Customer Service Center
CSPD	Customer Service Planning and Delivery Group
CTC	Centralized Train Control
DLJ	Donaldson, Lufkin & Jenrette
DOT	Department of Transportation
DP	Distributed power
EC	Executive committee
EDP	Electronic Data Processing
EDPM	Electronic Data Processing Machines Committee
EMD	Electro-Motive Division (General Motors)
FELA	Federal Employers Liability Act
FNCB	First National Bank of New York
FNM	Ferrocariles Nacionales de México
FRA	Federal Railroad Administration
FXE	Ferrocarril Mexicano
GATT	General Agreement on Tarrifs and Trade
GE	General Electric Company
GSC	General Systems Company
HDC	Harriman Dispatching Center
IC	Illinois Central Railroad
ICC	Interstate Commerce Commission
ICG	Illinois Central Gulf Railroad
IPO	Initial public offering
IT	Information technologies
ILWU	International Longshoremen's and Warehousemen's Union
KCS	Kansas City Southern
LBO	Leveraged buyout
LCL	Less than carload
LINCS	Logistics Information Control Systems
LTL	Less than truckload
MIS	Management Information Services
MOW	Maintenance of Way
MP	Missouri Pacific Railroad
MRFC	Mississippi River Fuel Corporation
NAFTA	North American Free Trade Agreement
NCSC	National Customer Service Center
NDI	Network design and integration
NITL	National Industrial Transportation League
NS	Norfolk Southern Railroad
N&W	Norfolk & Western Railroad
NYC	New York Central Railroad
P&A	Planning and analysis
PEB	Presidential Emergency Board
PFE	Pacific Fruit Express
QSPs	Quality System Procedures
QTAM	Queued Telecommunications Access Method
RI	Chicago, Rock Island & Pacific Railroad
ROI	Return on investment

SF	Atchison, Topeka & Santa Fe Railroad
SFSP	Santa Fe Southern Pacific
SP	Southern Pacific Railroad
SPCC	Southern Pacific Communications Company
STB	Surface Transportation Board
TCS	Transportation Control System
TCU	Transportation Communications Union
TFM	Transportación Ferroviaria Mexicana
TIS	Terminal Information System
TOFC	Trailer on flatcar
TOPS	Transportation Operating System
TQS	Total Quality System
TRC	Texas Railroad Commission
UNO	University of Nebraska Omaha
UP	Union Pacific Railroad
UPC	Union Pacific Corporation
UPFE	Union Pacific Fruit Express
USPCI	United States Pollution Control, Inc.
USRA	United States Railway Association
UTU	United Transportation Union
VPO	Vice president of operations
WRPI	Western Railroad Properties, Inc.
YATS	Yard and Terminal Subsystem

NOTES

Introduction

1. Maury Klein, *Unfinished Business: The Railroad in American Life* (Hanover, N.H., 1994), 30.

Prologue

1. The place where the rails met, often called Promontory Point, is actually Promontory Summit. The Point is located twenty-two miles to the south at the extreme southern end of the Promontory Range. The Summit occupies a plateau midway across the Promontory Mountains and nearly even with the north end of the Great Salt Lake. See *Ogden Standard-Examiner*, February 16, 1968.
2. The detailed story of this earlier history can be found in Maury Klein, *Union Pacific: The Birth, 1862–1893* (New York, 1987) and *Union Pacific: The Rebirth, 1894–1969* (New York, 1989).
3. *Ogden Standard-Examiner*, January 27, 1967.
4. W. G. Burden to R. M. Sutton, April 9, 1965, UPM.
5. C. R. Rockwell to W. R. Moore, February 25, 1966, UPM. In the end the replica locomotives were found elsewhere. No. 119, an old Virginia & Truckee engine, was borrowed from MGM Studios, while the Jupiter was borrowed from the West Coast chapter of the Railroad and Locomotive Historical Society. See *Trains*, July 1969, 15.
6. Al Krieg to W. R. Moore, November 8, 1966, UPM; C. H. Mertens to E. H. Bailey, November 17, 1966, UPM; *Provo Herald*, May 12, 1968; *OWH*, October 20, 1968, and January 16, 1969; *Railway Employees Journal*, January 1969, 5; C. R. Rockwell to E. C. Schafer, March 6, 1969, UPM. Rockwell's memo includes the schedule for the museum train's tour. The schedule can also be found in *Info*, March 1969, 1. *Info* was the employees' magazine.
7. *OWH*, January 16, 1969; "Golden Spike Centennial Highlights 1969," UPM, 1. For the Centennial Expo train's schedule, see C. R. Rockwell to E. C. Schafer, March 6, 1969, UPM.
8. *Railroad Employes* [sic] *Journal*, January 1969; *OWH*, January 16, 1969.
9. "What's Happening? A Calendar of Events," UPM.
10. *NYT*, May 11, 1969; *RA*, May 19, 1969, 12–14, 40; *Trains*, July 1969, 12–15; Union Pacific Golden Spike Centennial Press Kit, UPM. The description that follows is taken from these same sources. The fifth excursion train was an hourly special run from Salt Lake City over a short stretch of track by members of the Promontory Chapter of the National Railway Historical Society.
11. Pictures of the new visitors' center are in *Info*, May 1969, 5. For pictures of the ceremony, see *Info*, June 1969, 1.

12. Klein, *UP: The Birth*, 220–23; *RA*, May 19, 1969, 40; *Trains*, July 1969, 8.
13. *Trains*, July 1969, 8, 10.
14. *RA*, May 19, 1969, 40.
15. Ibid.
16. *1869–1969 Union Pacific Centennial: Report to Shippers*, passim. A copy of this brochure is in UPM.
17. Steven W. Usselman, *Regulating Railroad Innovation: Business, Technology, and Politics in America, 1840–1920* (New York, 2002), 142.
18. The verse comes from stanza 15 of Arnold's *Stanzas from The Grande Chartreuse* (1855).

Chapter 1

1. Maury Klein, *The Genesis of Industrial America, 1870–1920* (New York, 2007), 64–65.
2. Ibid., 66–67.
3. U.S. Bureau of the Census, *Historical Statistics of the United States: Colonial Times to 1970* (Washington, 1975), 2:728. The mileage figure pertains only to mainline track and does not include yards and sidings.
4. This discussion is drawn largely from Klein, *Unfinished Business*, 122–34, which has more detail.
5. Quoted in ibid., 126.
6. Quoted in ibid., 127.
7. Ari Hoogenboom and Olive Hoogenboom, *A History of the ICC: From Panacea to Palliative* (New York, 1976), 105.
8. Quoted in I. L. Sharfman, *The Interstate Commerce Commission: A Study in Administrative Law and Procedure* (New York, 1931–37), 3A:432–33, 461.
9. Richard Saunders Jr., *Merging Lines: American Railroads, 1900–1970* (DeKalb, Ill., 2001), 75–76.
10. Quoted in Klein, *Unfinished Business*, 131.
11. Richard Saunders Jr., *Main Lines: Rebirth of the North American Railroads, 1970–2002* (DeKalb, Ill., 2003), 35–36.
12. The figures are taken from Saunders, *Merging Lines*, 121, 151.
13. Ibid., 123.
14. Ibid., 130–34.
15. Saunders, *Main Lines*, 41.
16. Ibid., 5.
17. Ibid., 15–16.
18. Ibid., 5, 18.
19. Ibid., 30–31, 65.
20. Ibid., 31–32, 65.
21. For a full if uneven portrait of Brosnan, see Charles O. Mogret, *Brosnan: The Railroads' Messiah*, 2 vols. (New York, 1996).
22. Ibid. 1:164, 355, 207–8.
23. Ibid.; Saunders, *Merging Lines*, 291.
24. Mogret, *Brosnan* 1:212–13, 250, 278–79, 389–96; Saunders, *Merging Lines*, 291.
25. Mogret, *Brosnan* 1:425–31; Saunders, *Merging Lines*, 293–94.
26. Mogret, *Brosnan* 1:483–85, 512; Saunders, *Merging Lines*, 294.
27. Mogret, *Brosnan* 1:356–58, 397, 447–48, 2:90; Saunders, *Merging Lines*, 292.
28. Mogret, *Brosnan* 1:323, 445–46. Mogret errs in saying that the Southern was the first railroad to use computers. The UP, among others, began computerizing as early as 1954. See Klein, *UP: The Rebirth*, 507–9.
29. Mogret, *Brosnan* 2:54, 86, 89–91.
30. Ibid. 1:512; Saunders, *Merging Lines*, 294–95.
31. Mogret, *Brosnan* 1:581, 2:112; Saunders, *Merging Lines*, 295–96.

32. Mogret, *Brosnan* 1:594–97; Saunders, *Merging Lines*, 296–97; *Time*, August 9, 1963, 16.
33. Mogret, *Brosnan* 1:579.
34. Ibid. 1:475–76; Saunders, *Merging Lines*, 292.
35. Mogret, *Brosnan* 1: 548, 2: 202–3, 628.
36. Ibid. 2: 336–37.
37. Saunders, *Merging Lines*, 209–28; Klein, *UP: The Rebirth*, 516.
38. Saunders, *Merging Lines*, 157–206.
39. Ibid., 277–84, 300–47.

Chapter 2

1. Klein, *UP: The Rebirth*, 459–61; interview with Frank Barnett, October 19, 1981, 9–10.
2. Figures taken from *Union Pacific Corporation Annual Report*, 1969, 1, 19, hereafter cited as *UP Report*.
3. Klein, *UP: The Rebirth*, 533.
4. Ibid., 532–35; interview with Tom Watts, July 22, 2009, 7; interview with John Marchant, May 27, 2008, 9.
5. Klein, *UP: The Rebirth*, 475–76.
6. Interview with Dick Grove, January 20, 2008, 25–26.
7. Klein, *UP: The Rebirth*, 470. The following paragraphs are drawn from this source.
8. Interview with John L. Jorgensen, July 15, 2007, 39–40.
9. Klein, *UP: The Rebirth*, 471; Grove interview, 25–26.
10. Klein, *UP: The Rebirth*, 471–72.
11. More detail on these transitions can be found in ibid.
12. Ibid. For a good sense of Roland Harriman, see his autobiography, *I Reminisce* (Garden City, N.Y., 1975).
13. Klein, *UP: The Rebirth*, 434–36; interview with Reginald Sutton, February 15, 1982, 72.
14. Klein, *UP: The Rebirth*, 473; Sutton interview, 69; Barnett interview, 6, 12; interview with James H. Evans, October 20, 1987, 18, hereafter cited as Evans1 interview; interview with Elbridge T. Gerry, October 20, 1981, 54.
15. Klein, *UP: The Rebirth*, 473–74; Evans1 interview, 18–19; Sutton interview, 67–68.
16. Klein, *UP: The Rebirth*, 474; Evans1 interview, 19; interview with Robert A. Lovett, September 8, 1981, 1.
17. Klein, *UP: The Rebirth*, 474; Evans1 interview, 19; Gerry interview, 44–46.
18. Klein, *UP: The Rebirth*, 475.
19. Telephone interview with Robert A. Lovett, June 13, 1982, 4; Bruce J. Relyea to Jack Rudarmel, December 28, 1971, UPR.
20. Lovett to A. E. Stoddard, August 8, 1960, UPR; interview with C. Barry Schaefer, August 30, 2006, 17–18; Klein, *UP: The Rebirth*, 476.
21. Klein, *UP: The Rebirth*, 476–77; Barnett interview, 8–9.
22. Sutton interview, 14–15; Barnett interview, 15; Barnett to Lovett, July 19, 1962, and December 8, 1964, UPR.
23. Klein, *UP: The Rebirth*, 477–79; Gerry interview, 12–16; Harriman and Lovett to Osborne and A. G. Ritter, January 1, 1965, UPR; Harriman and Lovett to John W. Godfrey, December 14, 1965, UPR.
24. Klein, *UP: The Rebirth*, 479; Gerry interview, 13.
25. Klein, *UP: The Rebirth*, 514–15.
26. Ibid., 515–16; Barnett to Lovett, July 19, 1962, UPR.
27. Klein, *UP: The Rebirth*, 516. The Ogden gateway case dragged on until 1968, when the Supreme Court upheld an order nullifying the 1923 provision. The complicated transcontinental cases were ultimately decided against the western lines and settled by a series of compromises.

28. Unless otherwise indicated, the merger story is drawn from ibid., 517–31, which provides more detail.

29. See ibid., 514–31.

30. Bailey to Harriman and Lovett, July 13, 1966, UPR; Lovett to Bailey, July 19, 1966, UPR; Klein, *UP: The Rebirth*, 534–45.

31. Evans1 interview, 1.

32. Sutton interview, 17–18.

33. Barnett interview, 10–11; Evans1 interview, 2.

34. Gerry interview, 33–41; Evans1 interview, 22–23.

35. CRI, "Report to Frank E. Barnett," July 15, 1970, 1, UPR; Simon to Barnett, July 25, 1967, UPR. For the basic contract between UP and CRI, see Simon to Barnett, June 21 and August 12, 1968, UPR.

36. Simon to Bailey, August 11, 1967, UPR; Bailey to Barnett, September 2 and December 21, 1967, UPR; Frederick V. Fortmiller to Barnett, January 3 and June 14, 1968, UPR.

37. L. M. Schneider to J. L. Heskett and S. Cunningham, January 27, 1968, UPR; CRI to Bailey, December 1, 1967, UPR.

38. CRI internal memo on "Transportation Division Organization Planning," March 8, 1968, UPR; J. L. Heskett and S. M. Cunningham to Barnett, March 21, 1968, UPR.

39. Barnett to Bailey, March 14, 1968, UPR.

40. Bailey to K. I. Jones et al., March 14, 1968, UPR; Bailey to Barnett, May 3, 1968, UPR.

41. Bailey to Barnett, May 3, 1968, UPR.

42. Simon to Bailey, May 9, August 22, and August 30, 1968, UPR; Learned memorandum, July 25, 1968, UPR. Emphasis is in the original.

43. Interviews with John C. Kenefick, June 15–17, 2004, 30–31. This series of interviews with Kenefick is combined in one typescript.

44. Ibid., 80.

45. Ibid.

46. Ibid., 31; Barnett interview, 33–34.

47. Kenefick interview, 81.

48. Barnett interview, 35–37; Evans1 interview, 24; second interview with James H. Evans, September 13, 2006, 12–13, hereafter cited as Evans2.

49. Evans1 interview, 13; Gerry interview, 1, 35, 39.

50. Gerry interview, 34; Evans interview1, 12; James Evans to Simon, April 18, 1969, UPR; Frank Barnett to Courtney C. Brown, April 19, 1969, UPR; Barnett memorandum, May 28, 1969, UPR; *NYT*, March 20, 1983; UP news release, September 29, 1975, UPR.

51. Gerry interview, 1, 35; Barnett interview, 37–38; Schaefer interview, 6, 9; Evans to UP Compensation Committee, September 27, 1968, UPR.

52. Barnett memorandum, November 15, 1968, 1–2, UPR. Barnett penciled on the memorandum, "Read 11/15/68 to CEO's."

53. Ibid., 5–15. Emphasis is in the original.

54. *RA*, February 10, 1969, 9, and May 10, 1969, 95; *WSJ*, January 31, 1969; *NYT*, January 31, 1969; *Info*, July 1969, 1, 5. Details on the process of transferring the nonrail assets to the new corporation can be found in James N. Land Jr. to Frank Barnett, May 11, 1971, UPR.

55. E. Roland Harriman et al. to members of the UP organization, January 30, 1969, UPR; McDonald memorandum to Evans and Gerry, June 20, 1969, UPR; *WSJ*, June 18, 1969; Barry Schaefer e-mail, December 2, 2008; "Notice of Special Meeting of Stockholders," June 1, 1971, UPR.

Chapter 3

1. *BW*, November 14, 1970, 68.

2. Ibid., March 11, 1972, 56, 58; *RA*, August 18, 1969, 14–16.

3. *RA*, August 18, 1969, 25.

4. *TW*, April 12, 1971, 70, and May 28, 1973, 7; *RA*, March 31, 1975, 5.

5. Saunders, *Main Lines*, 54–60.

6. Ibid., 61–88; *TW*, May 7, 1973, 7. For samples of the ongoing debate, see *TW*, March 12, 1973, 15–17, March 19, 1973, 17–20, April 2, 1973, 65–67, April 16, 1973, 20–32, April 23, 1973, 69–71, April 30, 1973, 17–20, May 7, 1973, 17, 24, May 14, 1973, 17–18, and May 28, 1973, 28–33, 39, 75.

7. Saunders, *Main Lines*, 87–93; *RA*, January 14, 1974, 38–40; *MR*, January 1975, 51; *Trains*, March 1974, 7–8.

8. *UP Report*, 1969, 2–3, 9; *Info*, September 1969, 1.

9. *UP Report*, 1969, 3, 10–13; *RA*, January 27, 1969, 7, February 3, 1969, 34, April 7, 1969, 7, September 1, 1969, 11, September 8, 1969, 7, September 29, 1969, November 17, 1969, 60, January 19, 1970, 100, January 26, 1970, 42, and March 29, 1971.

10. Kenefick interview, 6.

11. *UP Report*, 1974, 14.

12. *MR*, May 1969, 56.

13. Kenefick interview, 4.

14. *UP Report*, 1974, 3.

15. *MR*, May 1969, 53.

16. Ibid., 53, 90–92, 96–98; UP news release, July 14, 1976, UPR.

17. *MR*, 84–85.

18. Ibid., 84–86.

19. Unless otherwise indicated, this section is drawn from Klein, *UP: The Rebirth*, 503–10.

20. Ibid., 54; Jorgensen interview, 5; *MR*, May 1969, 78; Union Pacific Railroad, *Management Information Services and Communications* (Omaha, 1980), 3. I am grateful to John Jorgensen for providing me a copy of this booklet.

21. Interview with Stanley J. How, February 17, 1982, 55–56; Sutton interview, 28.

22. Sutton interview, 74–75.

23. Jorgensen interview, 7–8, 10.

24. Ibid., 1–2; UP news release, September 16, 1975, UPR.

25. Jorgensen interview, 3, 6.

26. Dennis Jacobson e-mail, February 10, 2009.

27. Jorgensen e-mail, September 30, 2008; UP news release, December 3, 1975, UPR.

28. Ibid.

29. *MR*, May 1969, 78–80.

30. Ibid., May 1969, 80.

31. *Info*, October 1969, 3.

32. UP Railroad, *Management Information Services and Communications*, passim; *RA*, December 27, 1971, 30; UP news release, September 16, 1975, UPR.

33. *MR*, May 1969, 86; UP news release, March 4, 1976, UPR.

34. *MR*, 103–4.

35. Jorgensen interview, 44.

36. CRI, "Report to Frank Barnett," July 15, 1970, 3, UPR.

37. Ibid., 5–16.

38. Ibid., 16–18.

39. This section is drawn from Kenefick interview, 117–30.

40. Ibid., 85. This profile of Perlman is drawn from *Trains*, March 2002, 38–45.

41. Unless otherwise indicated, this section is drawn from Kenefick interview, 131–36.

42. Ibid., 1.

43. Ibid., 145.

44. Klein, *UP: The Rebirth*, 543.

45. Ibid., 544; *TW*, September 7, 1970, 27, October 11, 1971, 39.

46. Barnett memorandum to file, August 25, 1970, UPR; Barnett notice, August 27, 1970, UPR; Edd Bailey to Frank Barnett, October 14, 1971, UPR.

47. *WSJ*, December 30, 1971; *North Platte Telegraph*, December 30, 1971; Evans1 interview, 35–36; *WSJ*, December 31, 1971; UP board minutes, July 27, 1972, UPR; Paul Haney to Keith Blackledge, October 17, 1986, letter in possession of Keith Blackledge. I am grateful to Mr. Blackledge for sharing his materials on the scandal with me.
48. Interview with John P. Deasey, July 24, 2009, 13–14, 26–28.
49. Kenefick interview, 98; interview with John Rebensdorf, May 24, 2006, 6–7.

Chapter 4

1. Barnett interview, 34; Evans1 interview, 33.
2. Marchant interview, 8–9; Klein, *UP: The Rebirth*, 463.
3. Kenefick interview, 15–16, 81–82; Klein, *UP: The Rebirth*, 464.
4. Kenefick interview, 127, 129; interview with Jerry Davis, August 5, 2006, 58–59; Marchant interview, 10.
5. Kenefick interview, 15, 84–85.
6. Ibid., 83–84.
7. Ibid., 13; interview with Stan McLaughlin, August 24, 2006, 11. According to McLaughlin, a section gang covered 8 or 10 miles of track. A roadmaster typically oversaw 100 miles of mainline track and as much as 250 miles on single-track, light-density road.
8. Davis interview, 8–9.
9. Kenefick interview, 13, 187; interview with Paul Conley, July 17, 2007, 23.
10. Interview with Dennis Duffy, May 27, 2006, 8–9; Jorgensen interview, 32, 47–48; McLaughlin interview, 21; interview with Richard K. Davidson, May 9, 2007, 61, hereafter cited as Davidson5.
11. Interview with Dennis Jacobson, August 23, 2006, 14–15.
12. Davis interview, 13.
13. Duffy interview, 9–10.
14. Ibid., 5–6.
15. Jorgensen interview, 47–48.
16. Ibid., 17; Marchant interview, 17; Duffy interview, 10; Jacobson interview, 20.
17. Jorgensen interview, 17; Jacobson interview, 15–16; McLaughlin interview, 19–20; interview with Dick Peterson, August 25, 2006, 19–20.
18. Jorgensen interview, 17.
19. Ibid., 9, 16–17, 31.
20. Ibid., 16; John Rebensdorf e-mail, May 22, 2009.
21. *RA*, December 27, 1971, 23; Jorgensen e-mail, February 7, 2009; Jorgensen interview, 31.
22. Jorgensen interview, 31–32.
23. Ibid., 33.
24. Kenefick interview, 180; Duffy interview, 6, 8.
25. Davis interview, 9, 11.
26. Rebensdorf interview, 3, 5.
27. *Info*, October 1969, 8, September 1970, 12; *UP Report*, 1971, 5; Deasey interview, 6–7, 10.
28. *Info*, October 1972, 14; Deasey interview, 15, 40–41; UP news release, August 1, 1972, UPR; Jorgensen interview, 49; Peterson interview, 2.
29. Schaefer interview, 4–5.
30. Ibid., 1–6.
31. Ibid., 64–65; *Info*, April 1972, 15.
32. Schaefer interview, 65–66.
33. Ibid.; UP news release, March 4, 1977, UPR; Marchant interview, 16; Watts interview, 77; interview with Lou Anne Rinn, July 14, 2007, 9–11.
34. Marchant interview, 19–20; Watts interview, 76; Rinn interview, 9–10.
35. Marchant interview, 21–23; Watts interview, 76; interview with Gary Stuart, May 20, 2008, 8.

36. Conley interview, 16–17.
37. Schaefer interview, 38.
38. *UP Report,* 1972, 21.
39. Ibid.; *Info,* November 1972, 6–7, March 1973, 5.
40. Klein, *UP: The Rebirth,* 467; Kenefick interview, 58, 195. Rule G contained three provisions: 1) The use of alcohol or drugs while on duty was prohibited. 2) Being under the influence of alcohol or drugs while on duty or on company property was prohibited. 3) The use or possession of alcohol while on duty or on company property was prohibited. See *Info,* November 1981, 14–15.
41. Kenefick interview, 195–96; *Info,* November 1972, 5, April 1975, 14–15; *UP Report,* 1972, 21.
42. Rebensdorf interview, 1–2.
43. Ibid., 2–3.
44. Ibid., 4–6; Jorgensen e-mail, November 16, 2008; Deasey interview, 9.
45. Rebensdorf interview, 7–9.
46. Ibid., 9–10; UP news release, February 23, 1977, UPR; Jorgensen e-mail, November 16, 2008.
47. Interview with Jack Koraleski, May 25, 2006, 16–17; interview with James Young, October 30, 2008, 5.
48. Ibid., 2–3.
49. *RA,* December 27, 1971, 22; *Info,* November 1974, 6–9, and August 1979, 18–21.
50. *RA,* December 27, 1971, 23.
51. Marchant interview, 11.
52. Ibid., 11–12.
53. Ibid., 8.
54. Davis interview, 15.

Chapter 5

1. Figures are taken from *www.1970sflashback.com.* Stagflation refers to a rise in both the rate of inflation and that of unemployment. Prevailing economic theory held that a rise in one should result in a decline in the other.
2. Daniel Yergin, *The Prize: The Epic Quest for Oil, Money, and Power* (New York, 1991), 588–634.
3. *UP Report,* 1974, 7, 1977, 5, and 1980, 8; Saunders, *Main Lines,* 183.
4. Unless otherwise indicated, all figures are calculated from data in *UP Reports.*
5. *UP Report,* 1980, 8; UP news release, July 14, 1976, UPR.
6. *Info,* May 1976, 5, June 1976, 8–11, May 1977, 20–21, and November 1977, 16–17; UP news release, May 3, 1976, UPR.
7. *Info,* August/September 1976, 6–11; *Bailey Yard* (n.p., n.d.), 14–15. The UP published this pamphlet.
8. *Bailey Yard,* 15; Bailey to Lovett, May 24, 1966, UPR; *RA,* September 1, 1969, 7, May 10, 1971, 20, and July 26, 1971, 31.
9. *Info,* August 1978, 6–9, and May 1979, 24–25.
10. Ibid., November 1973, 12–14, and January 1974, 16–18; *RA,* July 27, 1970, 47–48, October 11, 1971, 15, and December 27, 1971, 60; *TW,* May 10, 1971, 20, January 29, 1973, 12, and May 21, 1973, 31; *Market Outlook,* July 26, 1971, 50.
11. *RA,* December 7, 1971, 22, June 12, 1972, 8, May 28, 1973, 48, October 8, 1973, and June 30, 1975, 65; *Trains,* February 1976, 11.
12. *MR,* January 1978, *RA,* December 1983, 42; *Progressive Railroading,* March 1976, 1. The latter is a five-page pamphlet published by UP; it has no page numbers.
13. *Progressive Railroading,* March 1976, 1.
14. *RA,* June 11, 1973, 38.

15. Ibid., 39; *Progressive Railroading,* March 1976, 1–2; *RA,* December 1983.
16. UP news release, May 20, 1975, UPR.
17. *RA,* December 1983; Stan McLaughlin e-mail, February 3, 2008. I am grateful to Stan for helping me to understand the work performed by the Engineering Department.
18. *RA,* June 11, 1973, 39; *MR,* January 1978, 40.
19. *RA,* June 11, 1973, 39–40.
20. Ibid., December. 1983.
21. Ibid., June 11, 1973, 40–41; *Progressive Railroading,* 2–3.
22. *Progressive Railroading,* 3; *MR,* January 1978, 41; *RA,* May 10, 1971, 36–37; UP news release, May 6, 1983.
23. *Progressive Railroading,* 3–4.
24. *MR,* January 1978, 40.
25. Ibid., 39; *RA,* June 11, 1973, 41; *Trains,* August 1979, 11.
26. Saunders, *Main Lines,* 105–8.
27. Ibid., 108; H. Roger Grant, *The North Western: A History of the Chicago & North Western Railway System* (DeKalb, Ill., 1996), 215–19.
28. *BW,* May 24, 1976, 56.
29. Saunders, *Main Lines,* 108–10.
30. Ibid., 110–11.
31. Ibid., 112–18.
32. Ibid., 122–23.
33. Ibid., 124–26.
34. Ibid., 126–27.
35. Ibid., 128, 141.
36. Ibid., 141–43.
37. *BW,* May 24, 1976, 56.
38. Saunders, *Main Lines,* 143; *RA,* January 10, 1972, 17; Kenefick to Barnett, September 7, 1975, UPR; William J. McDonald to Barnett et al., November 23, 1976, UPR.
39. *RA,* February 3, 1969, 11, October 20, 1969, 12, and November 17, 1969, 7, April 13, 1970, 12, July 27, 1970, 14, and December 14, 1970, 14; *TW,* February 28, 1970, 39, May 2, 1970, 72–73, February 22, 1971, 15, and April 3, 1972, 50–51; Saunders, *Main Lines,* 19.
40. *RA,* April 10, 1972, 18, September 10, 1973, 10, and October 28, 1974, 8; *TW,* February 19, 1973, 14, and March 19, 1973, 22.
41. Henry Crown to Barnett, April 10 and April 27, 1973, UPR; Barnett to Crown, April 20, 1973, UPR; Bruce Relyea to Barnett, June 7, 1973, UPR; William M. Gibbons to Barnett, May 2, 1975, UPR; Barnett to Gibbons, June 12, 1975, UPR; Barnett to Kenefick, July 9, 1973, UPR.
42. *RA,* January 13, 1975, 8; *Trains,* February 1975, 3–4.
43. *UP Report,* 1975, 9; *Trains,* July 1975, 21.
44. Saunders, *Main Lines,* 145–87.
45. Rebensdorf e-mail, October 17, 2008; Jorgensen interview, 56–57.
46. Rebensdorf e-mail, October 17, 2008; Rebensdorf interview, 9–10; Jorgensen e-mail, November 16, 2008; Fox to G. H. Baker et al., January 3, 1972, UPR.
47. Rebensdorf interview, 9–11.
48. Koraleski interview, 9–10; Rebensdorf e-mail, October 17, 2008.
49. Koraleski interview, 11.
50. Ibid., 6.
51. Rebensdorf interview, 7, 10–11.

Chapter 6

1. These holdings are detailed in "Present Value of Non-Transportation Assets of Union Pacific Railroad Company," May 18, 1976, 1–24, UPR.

2. *UP Report,* 1969, 2, and 1972, 2.

3. John C. Kenefick, "Union Pacific Corporation: 1969–1999," 5, JRD. The cash management policy of the UPC is detailed in William F. Surette to Kenneth H. Tuggle, March 31, 1975, UPR. Unlike many holding companies, UPC did not allocate overhead or administrative expenses to each subsidiary. Instead it deducted these expenses from the combined net earnings of the companies.

4. UP EC minutes, September 25, 1969; UP news release, October 9, 1969, UPR; Edd H. Bailey to Kenefick et al., May 8, 1970, UPR; Surette to Barnett, August 2, 1974, UPR; Deasey interview, 30.

5. Deasey interview, 12, 31.

6. Kenefick, "Union Pacific Corporation," 5–6; Cook to Barnett, July 30, 1971, UPR; Kenefick to Barnett, October 1, 1971, UPR.

7. Memorandum from John Rebensdorf, March 26, 2009.

8. Evans to Kenefick, R.S. Plummer, J.C. Wilson, and J.W. Godfrey, July 29, 1974, UPR; Surette to Barnett, September 6, 1974, UPR; Barnett to Kenefick, September 6, 1974, UPR.

9. Barnett to Kenefick, September 6, 1974, February 5, July 3, and November 18, 1975, UPR; Kenefick to Barnett, November 19, 1974, February 12, June 5, and October 24, 1975, UPR; Surette to Barnett, May 14, June 13, and November 17, 1975, UPR;

10. Kenefick interview, 9–10.

11. Ibid., 10.

12. Ibid., 34–35; Kenefick, "Union Pacific Corporation," 6; UP news release, December 11, 1975, UPR.

13. UP news release, December 11, 1975, UPR.

14. *UP Report,* 1973, 2–3, 10–13.

15. Ibid., 1974, 12–13, 1975, 2, 11–12, and 1976, 2, 9–13.

16. Surette to Barnett, December 20, 1976, UPR; "Union Pacific Corporation: Summary of 1978 Plans and Objectives," 1–11, UPR.

17. Evans2 interview, 13; UP news release, October 26, 1973, UPR; McDonald to Barnett and Evans, December 13, 1973, UPR.

18. Barnett to Bailey, August 21, 1974, UPR; Charles N. Olsen to Barnett, August 23, 1974, UPR; George S. Moore to Barnett, September 3, 1974, UPR; Schaefer interview, 17, 32; Evans2 interview, 14, 16–17; Grove interview, 24–25; *UP Report,* 1978, 2; UP board minutes, May 26, 1977, UPR; *Info,* August 1977, 5. Barnett lived until 1985, Lovett until 1986.

19. *UP Report,* 1978, 2, 28, 1979, 40.

20. Interview with Carl von Bernuth, March 28, 2007, 6; Kenefick interview, 37; Schaefer interview, 21.

21. Evans2 interview, 1–13; résumé of James H. Evans, December 17, 1979. I am grateful to Jim Evans for providing me a copy of this résumé.

22. Evans2 interview, 14; Schaefer interview, 21–22; UP news release, September 25, 1975, UPR. A file of speeches by Evans can be found in UPR.

23. Kenefick interview, 3; Jorgensen interview, 59; Cook résumé, UPR; "William S. Cook," UPR; Barnett to Courtney C. Brown, April 17, 1969, UPR.

24. Schaefer interview, 31–32; Cook résumé, UPR.

25. Kenefick interview, 10.

26. *UP Report,* 1978, 2, 4, 10, 20.

27. Ibid., 1979, 4, 6, 12; "Presentation to Security Analysts," 2.

28. *UP Report,* 1979, 4; *Trains,* November 1979, 15.

29. Don L. Hofsommer, *The Southern Pacific, 1901–1985* (College Station, Tex., 1986), 261, 281.

30. A brief but informative history of the Utah gateway can be found in "Merger Planning Study 1976," October 1976, 2: 3–45, UPR. Hereafter the volumes of this study will be cited as Project XYZ, which was its more familiar name.

31. Quoted in ibid., 20.
32. Quoted in ibid., 35. The text of the conditions can be found in ibid., 44–45.
33. Ibid., 58, 60; Kenefick to Barnett, October 9, 1971, UPR; Hofsommer, *SP*, 286.
34. Klein, *UP: The Rebirth*, 358–59, 499; Hofsommer, *SP*, 286–87; UP news release, April 24 and August 25, 1978, UPR.
35. Project XYZ, 3:22.
36. Ibid., 3:22, 25; Kenefick to Barnett, July 11, 1975, UPR.
37. Kenefick to Barnett, October 16, 1974, UPR.
38. Rebensdorf e-mail, November 17, 2008; Rebensdorf interview, 12–13.

Chapter 7

1. Kenefick interview, 24; Hofsommer, *SP*, 279–80; Schaefer interview, 11.
2. The account of this episode is drawn from Rebensdorf interview, 13–15, and Schaefer interview, 10–12. John Kenefick confirmed the Palm Springs meeting in my interviews and other conversations with him.
3. "A Preliminary Review of a Possible Merger of Union Pacific Corporation and Southern Pacific Company," March 5, 1976, 1–19. The quotations are found on pages 3, 4, and 19. The document is not paginated in whole but rather by sections; I have supplied my own page numbers. I am grateful to John Rebensdorf for furnishing me a copy of this report.
4. *Info*, November/December 1993, 15.
5. Schaefer interview, 11–12; Rebensdorf interview, 15.
6. Rebensdorf e-mail, December 2, 2008; Schaefer e-mail, November 15, 2008. The Project XYZ volumes are in UPR.
7. Project XYZ, "Union Pacific and Other Western Roads," March 19, 1976, 10:1–2.
8. Evans presentation to the UP board, undated but January 1980, 2, UPR.
9. *WSJ*, July 7, 1967; Grant, *North Western*, 219–22.
10. Kenefick interview, 25–26; Rebensdorf interview, 11.
11. Grant, *North Western*, 222, 224; Kenefick interview, 26–27; *NYT*, October 21, 1976; Olsen to Barnett et al., October 20, 1976, UPR; *Annual Report of the Chicago and North Western Transportation Company*, 1976, 2, hereafter cited as *CNW Report*.
12. Rebensdorf interview, 14, 16; *BW*, May 24, 1976, 56.
13. *Trains*, July 1976, 8.
14. Barnett to Evans et al., July 9, 1976, UPR; McDonald to Graves, September 28, 1976, UPR; Schaefer e-mail, November 15, 2008.
15. Saunders, *Main Lines*, 145; Kenefick to Barnett, January 12, 1977, UPR.
16. Kenefick interview, 45.
17. Project XYZ, Summary, November 1976, 1:2–5.
18. Ibid., 1:15, 26.
19. Project XYZ, "Utah Gateway Study: Revised Report," October 1976, 2:121–43.
20. Project XYZ, "UP-CNW: Final Report," October 1976, 3:1–8; *CNW Report*, 1976, 3.
21. Project XYZ, "UP-MP-CNW: Final Report," October 1976, 3:1–3, 10.
22. Ibid., 3:8, 21–40.
23. Project XYZ, "UP-Frisco: Final Report," October 1976, 5:15–25; Project XYZ, "Route Analysis: Major Western Service Corridors," December 10, 1976, 10:5–88.
24. Rebensdorf to Kenefick, January 7, 1977, UPR; McDonald memorandum to files, January 14, 1977, UPR.
25. Kenefick to Barnett, January 12, 1977, UPR.
26. Ibid.
27. Ibid.; Kenefick to Biaggini, January 1, 1977, UPR; Biaggini to Kenefick, January 10, 1977, UPR.
28. Biaggini to Kenefick, January 10, 1977, UPR; Kenefick to Barnett, January 12, 1977, UPR.
29. McDonald memorandum, January 14, 1977. Unless otherwise indicated, the account of this meeting is drawn from this source.

30. Surette to McDonald et al., March 25, 1977, UPR; Ed Hill, "Memorandum of Strategic Decision Regarding C&NW Acquisition," March 25, 1977, 1–7, UPR.

31. Barry Schaefer, "Comments on Memorandum Prepared for Project XYZ—Phase II," April 15, 1977, 1–6, UPR; Schaefer to McDonald, April 20, 1977, UPR; McDonald to Schaefer, April 25, 1977, UPR; Schaefer to Kenefick, May 2, 1977, UPR.

32. Kenefick board presentation, January 1980, 5, UPR; H. Craig Miner, *The Rebirth of the Missouri Pacific, 1956–1983* (College Station, Tex., 1983), 216; Cook memorandums, June 2 and June 9, 1978, UPR. This account of the merger talks is drawn largely from the Cook memorandums. For the complex MP recapitalization story, see Miner, 82–154.

33. Rebensdorf to Schaefer, June 27, 1977, UPR; Schaefer to Kenefick, September 14, 1977, UPR; W. P. Higgins to W. P. Barrett, October 4, 1977, UPR; *WSJ*, December 20, 1977; Rebensdorf interview, 14.

34. John McPhee, "Coal Train—1," *New Yorker*, October 3, 2005, 76.

35. Grant, *North Western*, 226.

36. Ibid.

37. Ibid., 227–28; *CNW Report*, 1976, 3; *Trains*, February 1974, 10.

38. Kenefick to Barnett, October 12, 1972, and May 17, 1976, UPR.

39. Grant, *North Western*, 277; Rebensdorf interview, 17–18; Kenefick to Provo, September 29, 1976, UPR; John C. Kenefick, "Union Pacific Railroad Organization: 1968–1986," March 24, 2006, 3. I am grateful to John Kenefick for furnishing me a copy of this memorandum. Grant's account is taken from a Kenefick letter dated August 11, 1995. Menk's derisive reference is not necessarily racial but more likely referred to the fact that UP's locomotives were painted yellow. Rebensdorf thought the name "Project Yellow" came from Gene Lewis, who recalled that the German invasion of the Lowland countries in World War I was called Plan Gelbe (Project Yellow). His view is confirmed in *Info*, November 1980, 26.

40. Grant, *North Western*, 228; *CNW Report*, 1977, 3; Evans to Robert E. Brooker, October 5 and October 21, 1976, UPR; Brooker to Evans, October 15, 1976, UPR; Rebensdorf to Schaefer, May 13, 1977, UPR.

41. Union Pacific Railroad, "Merger Planning Study," April 1978, 7.

42. Ibid., 7–9 contains the list of conclusions.

43. *Info*, December 1978, 22–23; UP news release, December 4, 1978, UPR; *UP Report*, 1978, 6; *CNW Report*, 1978, 3; *Trains*, February 1979, 18.

44. *Trains*, September 1978, 11; *JC*, November 6, 1978; Schaefer to Kenefick, October 3, 1978, UPR.

45. Schaefer, "Project XYZ: Summary of Proposed Presentation," 2. This document is attached to the October 3 memorandum listed in the previous note.

46. Ibid., 3–5.

47. Ibid., 6–8.

48. Ibid., 10.

49. Ibid., 8–11.

50. *NYT*, November 12, 1978.

51. Ibid.

52. *Trains*, January 1979, 9–11; *Forbes*, March 5, 1979, 43.

53. *Forbes*, March 5, 1979, 43.

54. Ibid., 44, 47, 48.

55. Ibid., 47.

56. Ibid., 43, 48.

Chapter 8

1. Andras R. Petery, "Progress Report: Union Pacific," July 1979, 2, 3, 8, 21, UPR.

2. Ibid., 8, 12, 15, 19, 21.

3. Ibid., 25–27.

4. Rebensdorf e-mail, December 23, 2008.

5. UP news release, August 1, 1977, UPR; Rebensdorf e-mails, December 2 and December 23, 2008; *Info*, October 1972, 14, and August 1977, 6.

6. Interview with Charles Eisele, May 23, 2006, 2–5, 11–12.

7. Hillman to all concerned about the Milwaukee Road and its future, August 3, 1978, UPR; Kenefick to R. L. Richmond et al., August 3, 1978, UPR; Saunders, *Main Lines*, 167–68; Milwaukee news release, December 4, 1979, UPR; J. D. Patterson to G. F. Call et al., January 8, 1980, UPR; *Info*, October 1979, 4–5, April 1980, 2, May 1980, 2, July 1980, 12–13, September 1980, 2, and November 1980, 2; Strategic Planning Group, "Project M," December 18, 1978, UPR; Schaefer to Kenefick, January 6, 1978, UPR; *JC*, August 4, 1978; *WSJ*, August 4, 1978; Kenefick to Hillman, July 31 and December 28, 1978, UPR; Kenefick to Cook, December 29, 1978, UPR; J. D. Patterson to H. T. Clark, February 5, 1979, UPR.

8. Kenefick to Evans, March 30, 1979, UPM. The full report, including details on the dialogue sessions and evaluation reports, is available in thick binders at UPM.

9. Kenefick to Evans, March 30, 1979, UPM; Graves to Dialogue Session Participants, March 9, 1979, UPM.

10. Union Pacific Railroad, "Long Range Plan," March 1979, 4–14, UPM. For the eleven objectives, see ibid., 50–82.

11. Ibid., 1, 14–23.

12. Ibid., 24–26.

13. Ibid., 26–30, 35.

14. Ibid., 37–39.

15. Ibid., 37.

16. *JC*, August 27, 1979; Grant, *North Western*, 229.

17. Evans to Kenefick, October 18, 1979, UPR.

18. Schaefer e-mail, December 12, 2008.

19. Eisele interview, 13; interview with Linda Waller, May 8, 2007, 4.

20. Rebensdorf e-mail, December 2, 2008; Eisele interview, 12–13; Deasey interview, 46.

21. Graves to Kenefick, November 2, 1979, UPR.

22. *WSJ*, April 26 and July 31, 1979; *CNW Report*, 1979, 3; *Trains*, July 1979, 18.

23. Rebensdorf to Graves, December 17, 1979, UPR; Miner, *Missouri Pacific*, 122.

24. Charles L. Eaton to Cook, November 11, 1979, UPR; *Info*, November 1979, 5. For a brief history of the project, see *Info*, November 1980, 22–26.

25. Ibid; *BW*, July 14, 1980, 66.

26. Schaefer interview, 13; interview with Richard K. Davidson, May 23, 2006, 39, hereafter cited as Davidson1.

27. Saunders, *Main Lines*, 146–51; Kenefick interview, 46–47; Kenefick e-mail, December 26, 2008; Rebensdorf e-mail, December 26, 2008.

28. John C. Kenefick, "Union Pacific Operating Crisis, 1997–1998," 3, JRD.

29. Kenefick interview, 46.

30. Kenefick interview, 47; Rebensdorf interview, 16–17; Rebensdorf e-mail, December 23, 2008; *BW*, July 14, 1980, 67; *Info*, November/December 1993, 16. No copy of the famous memo has been found.

31. Kenefick interview, 47; MP EC minutes, January 3, 1980, UPR; "Agreement in Principle," January 8, 1980, UPR; MP board minutes, January 8, 1980, UPR; Miner, *Missouri Pacific*, 218, 220; *Mo-Pac News*, February 1980, 1. Under the agreement a share of MP common would be converted into .550 shares of UP common and 275 shares of a new convertible preferred stock.

32. Evans presentation to the board, January 1980, 7–9, UPR.

33. Kenefick presentation to the board, January 1980, 1–6, UPR.

34. Evans presentation to the board, January 1980, summary, 1, UPR; Miner, *Missouri Pacific*, 218, 220; *Mo-Pac News*, February 1980, 1; UP news release, January 21, 1980, UPR.

35. Deasey interview, 41–42.
36. Rebensdorf interview, 17; Kenefick, "Union Pacific Railroad Organization," 4; Conley interview, 40; *Info*, November/December 1993, 17.
37. Hofsommer, *SP*, 283, 297; *RA*, July 14, 1980, 3.
38. Hofsommer, *SP*, 297–301; Miner, *Missouri Pacific*, 223.
39. Schaefer to Kenefick, February 1, 1980, UPR.
40. Ibid.
41. Graves statement before the ICC, Finance Dockets nos. 28934 and 29066, March 10, 1980, 2–10, UPR.
42. Ibid.; "Project Yellow: A Market Opportunity for Union Pacific," June 1980, "Executive Overview," first page (no page numbers), UPR; *Trains*, June 1980, 16; Surette to Evans, June 13, 1980, UPR; *NYT*, September 29, 1980; Grant, *North Western*, 229; *CNW Report*, 1979, 2; *Info*, March 1980, 21.
43. *BW*, May 15, 1971, 55, June 19, 1971, 45, June 26, 1971, 24, and September 11, 1971, 53; Saunders, *Main Lines*, 173–74. The quotations are from the June 26 issue.
44. Saunders, *Main Lines*, 175.
45. Ibid., 176–77.
46. Ibid., 178–79, 183–84.
47. Ibid., 186–87.
48. *NYT*, September 29, 1980.
49. Saunders, *Main Lines*, 187–88; *Mo-Pac News*, December 1980, 1.
50. *BW*, November 3, 1980, 116, 121.
51. Ibid., 121–22.
52. Ibid.
53. Kenefick memorandum to file, November 24, 1980, UPR; Evans to Russell R. Rogers, January 14, 1981, UPR; *WSJ*, January 13, 1981; R. E. Duffy, "The Coal Line Connector Route Proposal: An Abuse of Federal Aid for Railroads," n.d., UPR. The latter is a letter distributed by the BN to its stockholders along with their dividend checks.
54. Saunders, *Main Lines*, 189.

Chapter 9

1. Union Pacific Corporation et al., "Application," ICC Financial Docket no. 30000, September 15, 1980, 1: 37–38; *Info*, February 1983, 7.
2. "Union Pacific–Missouri Pacific–Western Pacific Mergers: Summary Fact Sheet," n.d., 1, 10, UPR; Cook board presentation, n.d., 6–7, UPR.
3. *NYT*, September 16, 1980, January 1 and March 4, 1981; *BW*, March 9, 1981, 61; *Washington Star*, March 4, 1981; *Salt Lake City Deseret News*, March 11/12, 1981; Miner, *Missouri Pacific*, 221–22.
4. Miner, *Missouri Pacific*, 224–25, 228. As the notes suggest, I have relied heavily on Miner's excellent history in the writing of this chapter.
5. Conley interview, 34; Watts interview, 76.
6. Schaefer interview, 15–16; *NYT*, July 23, September 14, and September 27, 1982; *BW*, September 27, 1982, 29; *RA*, September 27, 1982, 15–16.
7. *NYT*, September 14, 1982.
8. *NYT*, December 10 and December 11, 1982; *WSJ*, May 23, 1984.
9. *RA*, December 27, 1971, 5, 52; *Trains*, March 2002, 40.
10. For background, see Maury Klein, *The Life and Legend of E. H. Harriman* (Chapel Hill, 2000), 321–24, 418–19.
11. *Info*, February 1983, 11; Ralph W. Hidy, Muriel E. Hidy, Roy V. Scott, and Don L. Hofsommer, *The Great Northern Railway* (Boston, 1988), 184–87.
12. *Info*, November/December 1993, 16–17.
13. *RA*, July 1983, 43–44. For a detailed description of the WP line, see *Info*, February 1983, 7–10.

14. For more detail, see Maury Klein, *The Life and Legend of Jay Gould* (Baltimore, 1986), 137–264; Klein, *UP: The Birth*, 306–417.
15. Klein, *Gould*, 242, 264–69.
16. Ibid., 486; Miner, *Missouri Pacific*, 1–10, 82–83.
17. Ibid., 33–41.
18. Ibid., 41–42, 56–57.
19. Ibid., 42–46.
20. Ibid., 46–47.
21. Ibid., xix, 49; Davidson1 interview, 60.
22. Miner, *Missouri Pacific*, 48–50.
23. Ibid., 50–51.
24. Ibid., 51–53, 175.
25. Davidson1 interview, 60.
26. Miner, *Missouri Pacific*, 51–81; *Trains*, May 1988, 33–34.
27. Miner, *Missouri Pacific*, 82–86.
28. Ibid., 82–136.
29. Ibid., 121, 137–54; *Mo-Pac News*, October 1971, 1, June 1972, 1.
30. Miner, *Missouri Pacific*, 210.
31. Ibid., 210–11; Davidson1 interview, 61; interview with Dick Davidson, May 7, 2007, 61, hereafter cited as Davidson2.
32. Miner, *Missouri Pacific*, 163, 211–12.
33. Davidson2 interview, 61–63.
34. Ibid.; Miner, *Missouri Pacific*, 213–15.
35. Miner, *Missouri Pacific*, 216; interview with Brad King, July 16, 2007, 2.
36. *Mo-Pac News*, September 1972, 6, February 1974, 6, September 1975, 3, and September 1976, 1.
37. Ibid., May 1978, 1; Davidson2 interview, 56.
38. *Mo-Pac News*, September 1972, 6, April 1974, 3, September 1976, 1, May 1978, 1, and June 1979, 1.
39. Jorgensen interview, 25; Davidson1 interview, 7–8; Davidson2 interview, 58.
40. *Mo-Pac News*, April 1974, 3; Miner, *Missouri Pacific*, 181–82.
41. Miner, *Missouri Pacific*, 184–86.
42. Ibid., 180, 187.
43. Ibid., 188–89.
44. Ibid.
45. Ibid., 189–90; interview with Merill Bryan, November 19, 2008, 18–19.
46. Miner, *Missouri Pacific*, 190–91; Bryan interview, 19.
47. Bryan interview, 20.
48. *Port of Houston Magazine*, September 1967, 11; *Mo-Pac News*, June 1977, 1.
49. Miner, *Missouri Pacific*, 191–92; Bryan interview, 13; interview with Dick Davidson, May 8, 2007, 31, hereafter cited as Davidson3.
50. Miner, *Missouri Pacific*, 196.
51. Ibid., 193.
52. *Mo-Pac News*, December 1970, 1; Bryan interview, 21.
53. Davidson1 interview, 63.
54. *Mo-Pac News*, November 1971, 1, December 1972, 1, January 1974, 3–4.
55. Ibid., August 1973, 1; Miner, *Missouri Pacific*, 196–97.
56. *Mo-Pac News*, January 1974, 3–10, and September 1975, 1; Miner, *Missouri Pacific*, 198–99.
57. *Mo-Pac News*, January 1974, 8; Miner, *Missouri Pacific*, 198–99.
58. Jacobson e-mail, February 6, 2009.
59. Miner, *Missouri Pacific*, 199–200.
60. *Mo-Pac News*, January 1974, 10.

61. Miner, *Missouri Pacific*, 200–1.

62. Bryan interview, 21.

63. Miner, *Missouri Pacific*, 201–2.

64. Ibid., 155–58; *Mo-Pac News*, March 1971, 1.

65. *Mo-Pac News*, August 1972, 1, and September 1972, 4–5.

66. Ibid., September 1971, 6, October 1971, 6, November 1973, 3, and October/November 1974, 6–7; Miner, *Missouri Pacific*, 160–61.

67. *Mo-Pac News*, March 1974, 1, 4, 5, 8, May/June 1974, 2, June 1978, 1, June 1980, 1, and May 1981, 1.

68. Ibid., November 1981, 1–2; Miner, *Missouri Pacific*, 172–75, 209.

Chapter 10

1. See, for example, *Info*, June 1984, 6–11.

2. *UP Report*, 1982, 5.

3. Ibid.

4. *BW*, July 14, 1980, 70.

5. Kenefick interview, 48, 106; *Mo-Pac News*, June/July 1982, 1; interview with L. White Matthews III, April 30, 2008, 64–65, hereafter cited as Matthews2.

6. Interview with Dick Davidson, May 8, 2007, 64–65, hereafter cited as Davidson4; Matthews2 interview, 61; Davidson1 interview, 17.

7. Davidson4 interview, 65–66; interview with James Dolan, August 25, 2006, 25; UP news release, November 7, 1983, UPR.

8. Kenefick interview, 52.

9. Ibid., 50–51, 107; *UP Report*, 1982, 6; *Mo-Pac News*, February 1983, 1; Kenefick to Flannery, May 2, 1983, UPR; *BW*, January 17, 1983, 44.

10. Kenefick interview, 51, 107; *Trains*, November 1984, 44; *Info*, March 1984, 10–11; UP news release, May 31, 1984, UPR. The UP used the yellow for maximum visibility on its first streamliners in 1934 as a safety factor. Its color scheme was one of the oldest, if not the oldest, among American railroads.

11. Davis interview, 24–25.

12. Ibid., 25; Dolan interview, 47.

13. Davidson3 interview, 4–6.

14. King interview, 4; Jacobson interview, 49; Matthews2 interview, 63.

15. Davidson 3 interview, 1, 5; Kenefick, "Union Pacific Railroad Organization," 3.

16. Jacobson interview, 11; Deasey interview, 16.

17. Davis interview, 24; *Info*, March 1984, 9–11; Eisele interview, 22.

18. Eisele interview, 25–26; Kenefick presentation, May 31, 1984, 2, UPR.

19. Eisele interview, 25; Dolan interview, 1–3.

20. Jorgensen interview, 26; UP news release, December 21, 1978, UPR; *Info*, January 1979, 25; Surette to Cook, January 11, 1982, UPR.

21. Bryan interview, 26.

22. *Info*, March 1983, 13; Jorgensen interview, 26; Jorgensen e-mail, February 5, 2009; UP news release, April 28, 1983, UPR.

23. Bryan interview, 25, 29; *Info*, April/May 1983, 26, and June 1983, 25; Jorgensen e-mail, February 7, 2009.

24. *Info*, August 1983, 13–15; UP news release, April 7, 1983, UPR.

25. Bryan interview, 38–39; *Info*, September 1983, 4.

26. Jacobson e-mail, February 6, 2009; Jorgensen e-mail, February 5, 2009. I am grateful to Dennis Jacobson and Merill Bryan for helping me understand the TCS system, and to John Jorgensen for helping me grasp the COIN system.

27. Jacobson e-mail, February 6, 2009; Bryan e-mail, February 14, 2009.

28. Guerdon S. Sines, "The Computer: A New World for Railroads," *Progressive Railroading*, December 1986, 26; Jorgensen e-mails, July 21, 2007, and February 5, 2009; "Management Information Services and Communications," 19; Jacobson e-mail, February 10, 2009.

29. Jacobson interview, 11.

30. Jacobson e-mail, February 11, 2009; Bryan interview, 13, 15.

31. Jorgensen interview, 28; Jorgensen e-mail, February 7, 2009; Jorgensen to Kenefick, March 10, 2004, JLJ.

32. Jacobson e-mail, February 10, 2009; Sines, "The Computer: A New World for Railroads," 26; Bryan e-mail, February 14, 2009; King interview, 40–41.

33. *Info*, March 1984, 12–15; Bryan interview, 38.

34. Bryan interview, 39–40; *Info*, February 1985, 4, April 1985, 10–11, and January 1986, 14–15.

35. Jacobson e-mail, February 10, 2009.

36. Bryan interview, 33–34; Jorgensen interview, 28–29; Jorgensen e-mail, February 7, 2009; Bryan, February 14, 2009; *RA*, April 1984, 36; Kenefick presentation, May 31, 1984, 4, UPR.

37. Jorgensen e-mail, February 7, 2009.

38. Deasey interview, 21, 34.

39. Jorgensen interview, 35; Jorgensen to Kenefick, March 10, 2004.

40. *Info*, March 1983, 21–23, June 1983, 22–23, and October 1984, 4; interview with Joe McCartney, May 25, 2006, 55; Watts interview, 53–54.

41. Kenefick to Cook, November 19, 1985, UPR.

42. Kenefick interview, 9, 191.

43. Marchant interview, 41; McLaughlin interview, 16–17; UP news release, June 19, 1980, November 15, 1983, UPR.

44. McLaughlin interview, 17–18; *Info*, August 1985, 19; January 1986, 21; UP news release, August 10, 1983, UPR.

45. King interview, 7; McLaughlin interview, 1, 18–19.

46. McLaughlin interview, 18; *Info*, June 1983, 23; Kenefick to Cook, November 19, 1985, UPR.

47. Kenefick to Cook, November 19, 1985; UP news release, November 21, 1985, UPR; *Info*, December 1985, 5, January 1986, 4.

48. Davidson1 interview, 35; Davidson2 interview, 37; Davidson3 interview, 12; Rebensdorf interview, 55; Davis interview, 22.

49. Watts interview, 17–18, 20; King interview, 8; UP news release, February 4, 1983, UPR.

50. Davis interview, 1–4, 63; *Info*, July 1974, 30, December 1978, 24, and January 1981, 3; UP news releases, June 18, 1976, February 22, 1978, December 11, 1978, and December 12, 1980, UPR.

51. Jacobson interview, 17–18; Davis interview, 63.

52. Jacobson interview, 18; Davis interview, 63; interview with Art Shoener, November 18, 2008, 91.

53. Davis interview, 24; Marchant interview, 41–42.

54. Marchant interview, 42, 60.

Chapter 11

1. Shoener interview, 38–39.

2. *RA*, April 1984, 36.

3. Shoener interview, 39–40, 45; *Trains*, November 1984, 47.

4. Shoener interview, 41–45; King interview, 32; Davidson3 interview, 1.

5. Shoener interview, 46–47.

6. Ibid., 42–43, 48–49.

7. King interview, 5–6.

8. Shoener interview, 1–3.
9. Ibid., 4–11.
10. Ibid., 15; Davis interview, 41; Marchant interview, 61; Duffy interview, 12.
11. Shoener interview, 7–11.
12. Ibid., 14, 19–21; Davidson1 interview, 11; Davidson2 interview, 57.
13. Davidson1 interview, 7, 12; Davidson2 interview, 57–58.
14. Shoener interview, 11–14; *Info*, November 1984, 7. The *Info* article includes a brief history of the Houston Belt & Terminal.
15. Shoener interview, 11–14.
16. Ibid., 14–16.
17. Ibid., 14–18, 21–22; Shoener e-mail, May 18, 2009.
18. Shoener itnerview, 22–25.
19. Ibid., 26–27; *Info*, November 1984, 6–9.
20. Shoener interview, 26–32; Shoener e-mail, February 8, 2009.
21. Davidson3 interview, 2.
22. Shoener interview, 51–52.
23. Ibid., 53.
24. Ibid., 53–55.
25. Ibid., 55; McLaughlin interview, 42–43.
26. Marchant interview, 61–63; McLaughlin interview, 43; Shoener interview, 56–57; Davis interview, 41.
27. McLaughlin interview, 43–46.
28. Shoener interview, 57–58; UP news release, November 30, 1984, UPR; *Info*, July 1984, 10–11, December 1984, 18–19, and February 1985, 18–19.
29. Davis interview, 41.
30. Shoener interview, 58–61; Shoener e-mail, February 8, 2009; Duffy interview, 2.
31. Marchant interview, 62.
32. *Info*, May 1986, 5.
33. Ibid., January 1986, 4.
34. Davidson1 interview, 1–2.
35. Ibid., 2–3.
36. Davidson4 interview, 49, 51.
37. Davidson1 interview, 4, 6.
38. Ibid., 4; Davidson2 interview, 8–9.
39. Davidson1 interview, 5–6; Davidson2 interview, 9; *Mo-Pac News*, September 1971, 6, October 1971, 6, and February 1974, 6.
40. Davidson1 interview, 4–5; Davidson2 interview, 50–51; Davidson4 interview, 49.
41. Davidson1 interview, 8; Davidson2 interview, 58–59.
42. Davidson4 interview, 21–22; Davidson1 interview, 9.
43. Davidson1 interview, 9–10.
44. Ibid., 10–12; Davidson2 interview, 59; *Mo-Pac News*, February 1974, 6.
45. Davidson1 interview, 13–14; *Mo-Pac News*, September 1976, 1, and June 1977, 1.
46. Davidson1 interview, 15.
47. Davidson3 interview, 13–14.
48. Ibid., 13; Davidson1 interview, 33; Rebensdorf interview, 57–58; interviewee's name withheld by request.
49. Dolan interview, 13; Davis interview, 20; Jacobson interview, 20; Marchant interview, 28; Shoener interview, 63–64.

Chapter 12

1. Schaefer interview, 5; Dolan interview, 47.
2. *RA*, December 27, 1971, 24, and July 12, 1972, 16.

3. *Trains,* April 1979, 3, 7.
4. Rebensdorf board presentation manuscript, September 26, 1979, UPR, 1–3.
5. Ibid., 4–20.
6. *UP Report,* 1980, 8.
7. *NYT,* July 25, 1981; *CNW Report,* 1981, 2; Evans to Russell R. Rogers, January 14, 1981, UPR; *WSJ,* January 13, 1981; McDonald to Evans and Cook, October 25, 1982, UPR; Kenefick to Schaefer, February 4, 1982, UPR.
8. McDonald to Evans and Cook, October 25, 1982, UPR; UPC news release, December 15, 1981, and July 15, 1982, UPR; *WSJ,* December 16, 1981; *JC,* December 16, 1981; *CNW Report,* 1981, 2, and 1982, 7; Grant, *Northwestern,* 229; *NYT,* January 17, 1981; *Info,* June 1981, 2–3, September 1981, 3, November 1981, 4, January 1982, 4–5, September 1982, 7, December 1982, 4–5, and April/May 1983, 3–4; Russell R. Rogers to Evans, January 5, 1981, UPR. The BN letter is an attachment to the Rogers letter.
9. *WSJ,* December 16, 1981; *NYT,* July 16, 1982, and July 5, 1983.
10. *Info,* August 1983, 20–22; *CNW Report,* 1983, 2.
11. *Info,* August 1983, 5, September 1983, 20–21, October 1983, 3, December 1983, 18–19, February 1984, 5, March 1984, 16–18, June 1984, 15–16, August 1984, 3, and September 1984, 19–21; UP news release, January 18, February 2, and March 21, 1984, UPR.
12. *Info,* September 1984, 19–21; *RA,* September 1984, 32; *UP Report,* 1978, 6; *CNW Report,* 1984, 2; UP news release, August 16, 1984, UPR; Kenefick presentation, May 31, 1984, 8, UPR.
13. *UP Report,* 1980, 8, and 1986, 47.
14. Ibid., 1980, 8; Surette to Evans, December 11, 1981, UPR; *Info,* May 1984, 3, January 1985, 11; *RA,* June 1984, 12; Kenefick presentation, May 31, 1984, 6, UPR; UP news release, May 10, 1984, UPR.
15. *RA,* April 1984, 37.
16. Ibid., May 1985, 16, June 1985, 4, December 1985, 19, and January 1986, 14.
17. J. Parker Lamb, *Evolution of the American Diesel Locomotive* (Bloomington, Ind., 2007), 125–29; Klein, *UP: The Rebirth,* 497; *Info,* September 1980, 13; *Trains,* January 1969, 16, May 1969, 18, April 1971, 10, and April 1978, 12; *RA,* May 10, 1969, 11, and December 27, 1971, 61. The two giant locomotives, the Big Boy and the Centennial, can be seen side by side at Kenefick Park in Omaha.
18. *Info,* August 1974, 6–7; *Trains,* November 1975, 38; Union Pacific Railroad Planning & Analysis, "Electrification: An Update," March 1980, and "1981 Electrification Study."
19. *RA,* January 20, 1969, 27–31, January 19, 1970, 71–72, January 25, 1971, 84, January 31, 1972, 88, January 29, 1973, 84, January 28, 1974, 95, May 13, 1974, 8, January 27, 1975, 82, January 26, 1976, 66, 95, October 11, 1976, 8, 49, and January 31, 1977, 76; *Trains,* April 1969, 4.
20. *Info,* April 1978, 18–19, October 1981, 3, November 1981, 16–17, and April 1984, 16–17; *RA,* March 8, 1982, 32–33, and April 1984, 12.
21. Kenefick to Cook, September 14, 1981, UPR; Surette to Evans, September 17, 1981, UPR; *Info,* November 1981, 2, August 1982, 19, and June 1986, 10–11; *RA,* August 9, 1982, 20, 22; UP news release, October 21, 1981, UPR.
22. *Info,* July 1982, 6–9; *UP Report,* 1981, 8–9, and 1982, 13.
23. *Info,* August 1982, 16–18, October 1982, 3, and November 1987, 18–19; *UP Report,* 1982, 13; *RA,* September 27, 1982, 12.
24. *Info,* November 1987, 18–19.
25. *RA,* May 1986, 32.
26. *Info,* April/May 1983, 9–11.
27. Ibid., August/September 1976, 6–11, November 1977, 10–11, August 1978, 6–9, May 1979, 24–26, July 1979, 4, May 1980, 22–23, and January 1982, 5; UP news release, April 12, 1979, UPR.
28. *Info,* April/May 1963, 11–13, and March 1986, 6–7.

29. Ibid., April/May 1983, 9, 11.
30. Ibid., October 1979, 6–11.
31. Ibid., March 1983, 29; Davidson3 interview, 2–3.
32. UP news release, May 20, 1983, UPR; *Info*, January 1985, 6–9.
33. Davidson3 interview, 3–4; *Info*, November 1983, 16–17; Surette to Cook, December 11, 1985, UPR.
34. *Info*, June 1985, 8–10, February 1986, 16, and June 1986, 16–17; *RA*, September 1984, 36; UP news release, July 30, 1984, and January 15, 1986, UPR.
35. *Info*, February 1978, 10–13.
36. Ibid., December 1985, 8–9; *UP Report*, 1980, 43, and 1985, 43.
37. *Info*, December 1985, 8–9.
38. *WP*, May 27, 1983.
39. *Info*, July 1984, 18–20; *RA*, July 1983, 25, and March 1984, 30.
40. *Info*, December 1978, 15, and March 1986, 10.
41. Ibid., December 1978, 15; Jorgensen e-mail 1, April 14, 2009.
42. Jorgensen interview, 62–63.
43. Jorgensen e-mail 1, April 14, 2009; Schaefer e-mail, April 14, 2009.
44. Schaefer e-mail, April 14, 2009; Jorgensen e-mail 2, April 14, 2009.
45. Hofsommer, *SP*, 278–79, 317.
46. Jorgensen e-mails 1 and 2, April 14, 2009; Schaefer e-mail, April 14, 2009; Jorgensen interview, 64.
47. Jorgensen interview, 65; Jorgensen e-mails 1 and 2, April 14, 2009; Schaefer e-mail, April 14, 2009; *NYT*, June 30 and July 3, 1984; *WSJ*, July 2, 1984; *Info*, August 1984, 4, and October 1984, 6–9.
48. *Info*, May 1987, 10–11, and August/September 1987, 12–15.
49. *RA*, October 1984, 28, December1984, 12, and December 1985, 30; *Info*, February 1985, 5; *UP Report*, 1972, 4; UP news release, October 11, 1984, UPR.
50. The figures are taken from Saunders, *Main Lines*, 212.
51. Ibid., 212, 214.
52. Ibid., 212–13.
53. Ibid., 314–15.
54. Ibid., 311; *RA*, February 1984, 78.
55. Saunders, *Main Lines*, 133–37.
56. *Info*, June 1979, 24–25.
57. Ibid., October 1980, 3, November 1981, 14–15.
58. Ibid., August 1982, 3, December 1982, 18–19, and September 1983, 3–4.
59. Ibid., July 1983, 3–4, October 1983, 10–13, and May 1984, 7.
60. Ibid., May 1984, 6–9; *NYT*, May 21, 1984; *RA*, July 1984, 20; Deasey interview, 38–39. The May issue of *Info* provides details on the five-step program.
61. *Info*, July 1984, 10–11, December 1984, 18–19, and June 1985, 4; *RA*, January 1985, 21.
62. *Info*, November 1985, 20–21.

Chapter 13

1. *Info*, September 1978, 8.
2. Ibid., 7.
3. Ibid.
4. *RA*, April 21, 1969, March 8, 1971, November 8, 1971, 18, and December 27, 1971, 28; Barnett to Bailey, March 7, 1967, UPR; *TW*, March 14, 1970, 23, and October 23, 1972, 31.
5. *UP Report*, 1972, 6–7.
6. Kenefick interview, 150–51.
7. Ibid., 151–52; *UP Report*, 1976, 5; *Info*, June 1982, 6–9.

8. Kenefick interview, 166.
9. Ibid., 66–67.
10. *Info*, September 1984, 8–9.
11. *UP Report*, 1972, 4, 1974, 7–8.
12. Ibid., 1979, 6; *Trains*, June 1973, 4; UP news release, March 29, 1978, UPR.
13. *Info*, July 1985, 6–9.
14. Ibid., September 1983, 14, 16, July 1984, 16–17; *UP Report*, 1980, 43, 1984, 43, and 1985, 43; UP news release, May 29, 1984, and October 21, 1985, UPR.
15. *Info*, September 1983, 14–17, and July 1984, 15–17; Surette to Cook, November 19, 1985, UPR; UP news release, January 22, 1986, UPR; UP board minutes, October 30, 1986, UPR.
16. *Info*, June 1986, 12–15. For the company's early experience with soda ash, see Klein, *UP: The Birth*, 335, 519–21.
17. UP news release, July 3 and July 7, 1980, and March 27, 1981, UPR.
18. *Trains*, July 1978, 13.
19. *Info*, September 1978, 8–9, and August 1980, 10–12.
20. Ibid., August 1980, 12–13.
21. Ibid., December 1978, 6–11, and July 1985, 14–17.
22. Ibid., September 1978, 9.
23. Ibid., January 1979, 10–11.
24. Ibid., 12–13.
25. Ibid., March 1982, 12; Hemmer e-mail, May 14, 2010.
26. *Info*, March 1982, 13, and September 1984, 13; Rinn interview, 21.
27. Kenefick interview, 169.
28. *Info*, October 1981, 17; *UP Report*, 1981, 7, 1982, 11, and 1983, 8.
29. *Info*, June 1985, 14; Kenefick presentation, May 31, 1984, UPR; *RA*, March 1985, 15; *UP Report*, 1985, 7; Rinn interview, 24.
30. *Info*, September 1979, 18–21.
31. Ibid., March 1982, 11–12.
32. Ibid., February 1981, 10–13, and February 1986, 10–11.
33. Ibid., March 1979, 7, November 1979, 21, and June 1981, 8–9.
34. Ibid., November 1979, 21, June 1981, 9, and December 1982, 21.
35. Ibid., December 1979, 22–25, May 1981, 2, March 1982, 13, May 1982, 6–8, and July/August 1982, 18–22.
36. Ibid., May 1981, 4–9; *RA*, May 1986, 36.
37. *Info*, May 1981, 8; *WSJ*, September 12, 1985; *RA*, October 1985, 13, and May 1986, 38–39.
38. *Info*, February 1986, 7–9.
39. Ibid., June 1984, 12–13, February 1986, 7–9; UP news release, April 24, 1986, UPR. For background on the doublestacks, see Saunders, *Main Line*, 206–11.
40. *Info*, February 1986, 7–9; UP news release, April 24, 1986, UPR; *RA*, May 1986, 36.
41. *RA*, March 1986, 14; *Info*, October 1983, 9; and June 1986, 10–11; *UP Report*, 1986, 47.
42. UP news release, January 21, 1982, and February 17, 1983, UPR.
43. Ibid., August 19, August 26, October 19, 1983, and January 20, 1984, UPR.
44. *Info*, June 1985, 13, and May 1986, 11.
45. Ibid., February 1985, 6–9.

Chapter 14

1. Kenefick interview, 103; Peterson interview, 25.
2. Kenefick interview, 97; Davidson3 interview, 9–10.
3. Jacobson interview, 10.
4. McCartney interview, 29–30.
5. Marchant interview, 37; Jacobson interview, 10; Duffy interview, 23.

6. Conley interview, 44–45.

7. Davis interview, 7.

8. "Missouri-Kansas-Texas Lines," n.d., 1, 4, 6, 9–10, UPR; J. R. Osman to John H. Lloyd, July 28, 1971, UPR; "Project Wisconsin," n.d., 2–3, UPR.

9. Barnett memorandum for file, May 22, 1963, UPR; *WSJ*, September 11, 1967, and May 15, 1970; *Trains*, December 1975, 10. For the earlier history of the Katy, see V. V. Masterson, *The Katy Railroad and the Last Frontier* (Norman, 1952).

10. *Trains*, December 1975, 10; *WSJ*, February 8, 1985; Kenefick interview, 166, 173; interview with J. Michael Hemmer, May 22, 2006, 17, 34.

11. Isabel H. Benham to Matthews, May 27, 1981, UPR; James W. Otto to Matthews and Stuart, October 18, 1983, UPR; James Patterson, "Katy Railroad and Subsidiaries," August 7, 1981, 1–8, UPR; First Boston Corporation, "Comparison of Selected Railroads," August 10 and August 11, 1981, UPR; First Boston Corporation, "Alternative Approaches to the M-K-T Debt," August 17, 1981, UPR; Kenefick interview, 172–74.

12. Rebensdorf interview, 18–19.

13. Stuart to Surette, January 12, 1984, UPR.

14. UP EC minutes, May 22, 1985, UPR; *WSJ*, February 8, May 23, and May 24, 1985; *Info*, June 1985, 6–7; *RA*, June 1985, 23; *Annual Report of the Missouri-Kansas-Texas System*, 1984, 1; Dolan interview, 4; Hemmer interview, 34–35.

15. Matthews to Surette, June 25, 1985, UPR; "Missouri-Kansas-Texas Railroad Company," undated, 6, UPR.

16. Kenefick interview, 173; *WSJ*, August 6, 1985.

17. *Barron's*, January 20, 1986.

18. *TW*, January 20, 1986, 11, and May 12, 1986, 4; UP board minutes, April 24, 1986, UPR; *NYT*, August 22, 1985, January 14 and June 6, 1986; *RA*, September 1985, 31, December 1985, 32, February 1986, 13, and June 1986, 13; *WSJ*, October 21, November 1 and November 18, 1985, January 14 and June 6, 1986; UPC news release, January 13 and June 5, 1986, UPR.

19. *RA*, January 1987, 19, and October 1987, 25; J. M. Krier to Davis, November 5, 1987, UPR; W. G. Barr memorandum to file, January 22, 1987, UPR; *WSJ*, May 17 and August 15, 1988; Paul Conley Jr. to R. B. Schoultz, November 30, 1988, UPR; Davidson1 interview, 37; UPC news release, November 14, 1986, UPR.

20. Schaefer interview, 22; Jorgensen interview, 60; *Forbes*, November 14, 1988, 182.

21. McDonald to Evans and Cook, March 18, 1980, UPR; UPC news release, November 19, 1981, UPR; Corporate Office Bulletin from Evans and Cook, September 25, 1980, UPR; *UP Report*, 1982, 53.

22. UPC news release, November 19, 1981, UPR; Kenefick interview, 158.

23. Corporate Office Bulletin from Evans, November 18, 1982, UPR; UPC board minutes, November 18, 1982, UPR; Drake to Evans, December 13, 1982, UPR.

24. UPC board minutes, November 18, 1982; UP news release, January 27, 1983, UPR; Kenefick interview, 158–59. A corporate office bulletin, dated November 18, 1982, and signed by Evans, UPR, states that Meyer would have the proposed duties.

25. Kenefick interview, 159, 163.

26. Ibid., 160.

27. Ibid., 161.

28. Ibid. The gist of this episode is verified in *Forbes*, November 14, 1988, 182.

29. Kenefick interview, 161–62; UPC news release, February 24, 1983, UPR; *NYT*, February 25, 1983; *WSJ*, February 25, 1983; *UP Report*, 1982, 9.

30. *Fortune*, May 2, 1983, 61; *UP Report*, 1983, 5; *Hermes*, Winter 1983, copy in UPR; UP news release, June 30, 1983, UPR.

31. *NYT*, March 20, 1983; Cook to Employees, June 30, 1983, UPR.

32. *OWH*, November 1, 1984; UP news release, October 25 and October 29, 1984, UPR; Cook to Eaton et al., October 29, 1984, UPR.

33. Hill to McDonald, March 2, 1981, UPR; Schaefer e-mail, March 15, 2009.
34. Arthur D. Little, Inc., "Productivity Study Project Management Report," October 1984, I-2–5, UPR. The report is paginated not consecutively but by individual sections labeled with Roman numerals.
35. Ibid., II-4–6.
36. Ibid., IV-1–4, 22–26.
37. Ibid., V-1–17.
38. Ibid., VI-1–11, 14.
39. Ibid., VII-1–3.
40. Ibid., VII-4.
41. Ibid., VII-5–13.
42. Ibid., VIII-1–6.
43. Schaefer e-mail, March 15, 2009; Rebensdorf e-mail, May 22, 2009; "Presentation to Union Pacific Management: Union Pacific System Productivity Study Project," October 1984, 1–61, UPR.
44. Eaton to Cook, October 11, 1984, UPR.
45. Rebensdorf interview, 19–20; von Bernuth interview, 11.
46. Schaefer e-mail, March 15, 2009; "Union Pacific Railroad: Evaluation of Business and Financial Performance: Review of Recent Strategic Studies," May 1986, 1, UPM, hereafter cited as "Review of Recent Strategic Studies"; Robert C. Shaw to James W. Otto, February 13, 1985, UPR; CMA Executive Briefing, March 14, 1985, UPR; Shareholder Value Project: Comments on March 14, 1985 Agenda, UPR.
47. Schaefer interview, 36; Schaefer e-mail, March 15, 2009.
48. Schaefer interview, 37.
49. Ibid.; Stuart interview, 8–9. The figures are calculated from data in *UP Reports*.
50. Cook to Kenefick, April 9, 1985, UPR.
51. "Review of Recent Strategic Studies," 6.
52. Von Bernuth interview, 11.
53. Chuck Olsen to Cook, March 29, 1985, UPR; *NYT*, April 5, 1985; *JC*, April 5, 1985; Evans to E. J. Faulkner, June 21, 1985, UPR; UP board minutes, June 27, 1985, UPR; Kenefick interview, 54; *UP Report*, 1985, 5.
54. *UP Report*, 1987, 4.

Chapter 15

1. Schaefer interview, 25, 32, 34–35, 49, 70; von Bernuth interview, 11; interview with L. White Matthews, III, April 29, 2008, 18, hereafter cited as Matthews1.
2. Schaefer interview, 32, 56; Rebensdorf interview, 60; Schaefer e-mail, February 3, 2009.
3. Kenefick interview, 52–54, 93–94; Watts interview, 14–15; Schaefer e-mail, March 11, 2009.
4. Kenefick, "Union Pacific Corporation: 1969–1999," 8.
5. Schaefer interview, 34–35; Schaefer e-mail, March 11, 2009; Jorgensen interview, 38; Olsen to Cook, February 26, 1985; *NYT*, January 31, 1986.
6. *NYT*, January 31, 1986; *Info*, February 1986, 3; Schaefer interview, 35; Schaefer e-mail, March 11, 2009.
7. *UPDATE*, April 1986, 1, UPR. This was a management newsletter published by UPC.
8. *Fortune*, January 5, 1987, 82.
9. Ibid.; *NYT*, January 31, 1986; *Info*, April 1986, 6.
10. *Info*, April 1986, 6–8; Kenefick interview, 87; *WSJ*, January 18, 1989; interview with Gary Schuster, March 6, 2008, 18, hereafter cited as Schuster2.
11. *NYT*, July 10, 1986.
12. Ibid.
13. Watts interview, 22–25.

14. *UP Report*, 1984, 4, 1985, 4, and 1986, 3–4; *WSJ*, June 12, 1986; *NYT*, June 12, 1986; *Info*, July 1986, 14; UP news release, June 11, 1986, UPR.

15. *UP Report*, 1986, 1; *BW*, May 5, 1986, 49, 51.

16. Von Bernuth interview, 13; Kenefick interview, 87; Schaefer e-mail, March 11, 2009; Koraleski interview, 19.

17. Schaefer interview, 35, 38; Rebensdorf interview, 56; Schaefer e-mail, March 11, 2009.

18. Interview with Gary Schuster, March 5, 2008, 33, hereafter cited as Schuster1; Evans2 interview, 17; von Bernuth interview, 13; *OWH*, September 25, 1986.

19. Schuster1 interview, 33; *Fortune*, February 3, 1986, 24.

20. *OWH*, September 25, 1986; UPC news release, September 25, 1986, UPR; *Info*, October 1986, 3; UPC board minutes, September 25, 1986, UPR.

21. Dolan interview, 48.

22. "Review of Recent Strategic Studies," 3–4, 7. For the preliminary versions, see "1985 Strategic Review: Part One," January 30, 1986, and "Strategic Analysis: Transportation Services: Part Two," March 1986, both in UPR.

23. Ibid., 9, 18, 29.

24. Ibid., 25–28.

25. Ibid., 30–33; Schaefer interview, 45.

26. *NYT*, February 5, 1983.

27. *Fortune*, January 5, 1986.

28. Rebensdorf interview, 20; Jorgensen interview, 58.

29. Rebensdorf e-mail, May 22, 2009.

30. Schaefer interview, 45.

31. Ibid., 45–46; Matthews2 interview, 3; *RA*, October 1986, 33; Schaefer e-mail, March 10, 2009.

32. Schaefer interview, 46; Schaefer e-mail, March 10, 2009; Matthews2 interview, 3; Dolan interview, 48; *WSJ*, September 19, 1986; *RA*, October 1986, 33; *BW*, October 6, 1986, 38; *Info*, October 1986, 5.

33. UP board minutes, July 31, 1986, UPR; Dolan interview, 48–49.

34. Cook to Lewis, October 2, 1986, UPR; Kenefick interview, 7–8; von Bernuth interview, 14; interview with Elbridge T. Gerry Jr., September 6, 2006, 5–6, hereafter cited as GerryJr. interview; Davidson1 interview, 44; Rebensdorf interview, 20; UP board minutes, September 18, 1986, UPR. The minutes include an attendance sheet noting that Kenefick and Eccles attended by telephone. They also registered Jenks's vote against the motion to approve.

35. UP news release, September 18, 1986, UPR; Cook to John B. Fery, October 2, 1986, UPR; *JC*, October 17, 1986; *RA*, February 1987, 26; *Info*, October 1986, 5.

36. *Wall Street Transcript*, October 13, 1986.

37. *RA*, September 1986, 25; Stuart interview, 9; Schaefer e-mail, March 10, 2009.

38. *WSJ*, May 28, June 9, and December 7, 1987; UP EC minutes, May 19, 1987, UPR; UP board minutes, May 28, 1987, UPR.

39. Schaefer e-mail, March 10, 2009.

40. *UP Report*, 1987, 2; Schaefer e-mail, March 10, 2009; Rebensdorf e-mail, May 22, 2009.

41. *UP Report*, 1987, 2; Bryan interview, 44–47, 50; Sines to Employees, May 28, 1987, UPR; UPC news release, May 28, 1987, UPR; *St. Louis Post Dispatch*, May 29, 1987; *JC*, June 3, 1987.

42. Bryan interview, 50–51; Rebensdorf e-mail, May 22, 2009.

43. William S. Cook death certificate, July 30, 1992, UPR; interviewee's name withheld by request.

44. *UP Report*, 1987, 2–3.

45. Ibid.; UPC board minutes, September 24, 1987, UPR; UP board minutes, September 24, 1987, UPR.

Chapter 16

1. Shoener interview, 72.
2. *Info*, July 1987, 12; *BW*, September 20, 1993; *NYT*, May 7, 1994; UP news release, September 25, 1986, UPR.
3. *BW*, September 20, 1993; *NYT*, May 7, 1994; UP news release, September 25, 1986, UPR; *Info*, July 1987, 12; *OWH*, October 13, 1988.
4. *BW*, September 20, 1993; *NYT*, May 7, 1994; *Info*, July 1987, 12; UP news release, September 25, 1986, UPR.
5. *BW*, September 20, 1993.
6. *OWH*, November 20, 1988; Jeffrey L. Cruikshank and David B. Sicilia, *The Engine That Could: Seventy-Five Years of Values-Driven Change at Cummins Engine Company* (Cambridge, Mass., 1997), 331–77.
7. Cruikshank and Sicilia, *Engine That Could*, 379–99; *OWH*, November 20, 1988.
8. Cruikshank and Sicilia, *Engine That Could*, 395–412, 452.
9. *OWH*, October 13, 1988.
10. Schaefer e-mail, May 22, 2009; UP news release, May 31, 1983, UPR.
11. Rebensdorf e-mail, March 26, 2009; Schaefer e-mail, May 22, 2009; UP news release, May 31, 1984, UPR; *Info*, June 1984, 3.
12. *UP Report*, 1986, 53; UP news release, October 15, 1986, UPR; Rebensdorf e-mail, March 25, 2009; Kenefick interview, 54, 93.
13. Davidson4 interview, 28–29; Davis interview, 28.
14. Davidson4 interview, 29; Davis interview, 29.
15. Jacobson interview, 12.
16. *Fortune*, December 18, 1989, 134; *UP Report*, 1986, 6; "Chapter One: Foundation for the Future, 1986–1990," n.d., 7, UPM, hereafter cited as "Chapter One." These documents emanated from Walsh. As Marchant explained, "What he'd laid out for Union Pacific . . . almost like writing a book, chapter one, chapter . . . I think we were on chapter four when he left. He actually named them chapters." Marchant interview, 56.
17. Davidson5 interview, 12; "Chapter One," 10.
18. *Info*, November 1986, insert opposite p. 2.
19. Matthews2 interview, 13; Whited interview, 31; Knight interview, 41; Stuart interview, 45; Davidson1 interview, 30–31; Rinn interview, 42.
20. "Chapter One," 8–9; Eisele interview, 38.
21. *Info*, July 1987, 8; Watts interview, 35–37; Marchant interview, 37–38; Rebensdorf interview, 51.
22. *Info*, July 1987, 3, 8, and May 1988, 2, 5.
23. *WSJ*, January 18, 1989.
24. *Info*, May 1987, 14.
25. Marchant interview, 39–40.
26. Koraleski interview, 27.
27. *Info*, March/April 1987, 2–3. Walsh intended the Leadership Conference to be a semiannual event, and two meetings were held in 1987. After that, the meetings were held annually.
28. Bryan interview, 86; "Chapter One," 11; Eisele interview, 38.
29. *UP Report*, 1988, 5; John F. Kawa, "An Interview on March 15, 1988, with Michael H. Walsh," 10–11, UPM, hereafter cited as "Interview with Walsh." Kawa was senior vice president at Dean Witter Reynolds.
30. *WSJ*, January 18, 1989.
31. *OWH*, November 20, 1988.
32. Ibid.; UP news release, April 29, 1986, UPR; *WSJ*, May 1, 1986.
33. Unless otherwise indicated, this discussion is drawn from John C. Kenefick, "Railroad Operating Organization," April 7, 1998, 1–5. I am grateful to John Kenefick for providing me with a copy.
34. "Chapter One," 12.

35. See the discussion in Chandler, *Visible Hand*, 176–85.

36. Michael H. Walsh, "Remarks, Operating Department Leadership/Reorganization Meeting," July 15, 1987, 3–5, UPR, hereafter cited as "Remarks"; *Info*, August/September 1987, 2; "Chapter One," 12.

37. Rebensdorf interview, 53–54; McLaughlin interview, 39.

38. "Chapter One," 13.

39. *RA*, August 1967, 25; "Union Pacific Railroad Operating Department Organizational Structure, Fall 1967," UPR.

40. Walsh, "Remarks," 5–6.

41. Ibid., 6, 8–11. Emphasis is in the original.

42. *Info*, August/September 1987, 7; "Chapter One," 14.

43. *Info*, January 1988, 8.

44. Davidson2 interview, 6; Davidson3 interview, 7; "Chapter One," 17.

45. Jacobson interview, 33–35; UP board minutes, May 29, 1986, UPR; Union Pacific Railroad Post-Completion Comparison Report, n.d., UPR; UP news release, July 1 and July 9, 1986, UPR; *RA*, August 1986, 24.

46. *Info*, January 1987, 8–11, February 1987, 3, 6. Although the NCSC opened in 1986, the last regional service office did not close until August 1990. See *JC*, August 30, 1990.

47. *Info*, January 1984, 22–24.

48. Ibid., May 1984, 20–23.

49. Ibid., June 1984, 20–21.

50. Shoener interview, 58–61; Duffy interview, 63; Shoener e-mail, February 8, 2009; Surette to Cook, June 28, 1985, UPR.

51. *Info*, October 1986, 8–10; *RA*, March 1988, 56–59.

52. Davidson3 interview, 9; Rebensdorf interview, 54.

53. Kenefick interview, 88–89.

54. Duffy interview, 62–63; *Info*, February 1988, 5; King interview, 12, 16.

55. "Omaha Shops," September 26, 1979, 1, 59, UPR; *Mo-Pac News*, November 1981, 1–2; *RA*, February 22, 1982, 17–23; *Info*, August 1972, 12–13, June 1974, 6–9, November 1976, 10–13, January 1983, 8, December 1983, 20–21, June 1984, 3, and August 1984, 19–21.

56. *Info*, August 1984, 19–20, and November 1988, 5; Davis interview, 32.

57. *OWH*, October 20, 1988.

58. *Info*, May 1987, 17, and July 1987, 16–17.

Chapter 17

1. *Info*, May 1987, 13.

2. *Info*, March/April 1987, 6; UP board minutes, February 26, 1987, UPR; UP news release, March 2, 1987, UPR; Barrett to UP board, September 22, 1987, UPR.

3. *Info*, October 1987, 14–15.

4. "Chapter One," 19.

5. Ibid., 20.

6. Ibid.; *Info*, October 1987, 15.

7. *Info*, March 1988, 12–15.

8. Cruikshank and Sicilia, *The Engine That Could*, 405–6.

9. Davidson1 interview, 18–19; Davidson3 interview, 18.

10. Davidson3 interview, 18.

11. Von Bernuth interview, 28–29.

12. Kawa, "Interview with Walsh," 7.

13. Interview with Rob Knight, July 17, 2007, 41–42; Davidson3 interview, 19; Cruikshank and Sicilia, *The Engine That Could*, 403; McCartney interview, 18.

14. Davidson1 interview, 22.

15. Davidson3 interview, 18, 24–26; Koraleski interview, 24, 28.

16. *Info,* June 1987, 12–15.
17. Walsh, "Remarks," 17–20.
18. Duffy interview, 18.
19. Koraleski interview, 23.
20. "Chapter One," 15.
21. Davis interview, 27; Davidson3 interview, 21, 23.
22. Duffy interview, 21.
23. McLaughlin interview, 27; Davidson3 interview, 28.
24. Davidson3 interview, 20, 29–30; "Chapter One," 15.
25. Davidson3 interview, 20–21; Koraleski interview, 24.
26. "Chapter One," 5, 15–16.
27. Davidson3 interview, 20–21.
28. McLaughlin interview, 28, 70; Duffy interview, 14.
29. *Info,* July 1977, 5.
30. Ibid., February 1981, 22–25; Klein, *UP: The Rebirth,* 369–70, 511–13; Julius Kruttschnitt to Robert S. Lovett, May 6, 1912, UPR.
31. Duffy interview, 14; McLaughlin interview, 27–28; *Info,* January 1983, 17–19, February 1983, 1–13, August 1983, 26–28, and November 1983, 10–11.
32. *Info,* October 1989, 2.
33. Ibid., 2–3.
34. Interview with Mary McAuliffe, September 17, 2009, 90.
35. *Info,* June 1988, 6–11.
36. Eisele interview, 47; Waller interview, 9–10; Koraleski interview, 22; *Fortune,* December 18, 1989, 133; *OWH,* November 20, 1988.
37. *Info,* July/August 1988, 2–3; Peterson interview, 24.
38. Rinn interview, 30.
39. Walsh to Lewis, August 24 and October 1, 1987, UPR; Cook to Virgil Conway et al., September 16, 1987, UPR; UP Railroad board minutes, September 24, 1987, UPR; Chuck Olsen to Walsh, October 29, 1987, UPR; *Info,* May 1989, 6–9; Jacobson e-mail, September 9, 2009.
40. Eisele interview 20, 24–26; Rebensdorf e-mails, May 18 and May 22, 2009.
41. Rebensdoff e-mail, May 22, 2009.
42. Ibid.; Eisele interview, 29; Koraleski interview, 33–34.
43. Watts interview, 69; Rebensdorf e-mail, May 22, 2009.
44. Eisele interview, 27; Koraleski interview, 36; Watts interview, 70.
45. Koraleski interview, 36.
46. Young interview, 54–55.
47. Koraleski e-mail, June 16, 2009.
48. Rebensdorf e-mail, May 22, 2009.
49. Ibid.
50. Ibid.
51. Eisele interview, 36.
52. Ibid., 38; Rebensdorf e-mail, May 22, 2009; UP board minutes, January 29, 1987, UPR.
53. Watts interview, 42–43.
54. Koraleski interview, 37–38; Eisele interview, 40–41.
55. Eisele interview, 41; Koraleski e-mail, June 18, 2009.
56. Davidson1 interview, 21.
57. Ibid., 21, 30; Marchant interview, 33; Jacobson interview, 25; Matthews2 interview, 12, 15; Schuster1 interview, 37; Stuart interview, 46; McCartney interview, 16–17; von Bernuth interview, 25; Schaefer interview, 51.
58. Bryan interview, 86; Kenefick interview, 88; *Fortune,* December 18, 1989, 133–34, 138, 142, 146.
59. *Fortune,* December 18, 1989, 133; Rebensdorf interview, 52; Davidson4 interview, 28; Jacobson interview, 12, 25; Peterson interview, 21–22.

Chapter 18

1. UPC board minutes, September 24, 1987, and January 28, 1988, UPR; UPC nominating committee file, September 24, 1987, UPR; Matthews1 interview, 40; Schuster1 interview, 1–7.

2. Schuster1 interview, 7–8, 14; Grove interview, 9–11; Matthews1 interview, 59.

3. Matthews1 interview, 16–18.

4. Ibid., 23–26; Davidson 2 interview, 39; Knight interview, 31, 34; Schuster 2 interview, 3; Stuart interview, 18; Waller interview, 24.

5. Matthews1 interview, 28–29; Schuster2 interview, 3; Schaefer interview, 49–50; Stuart interview, 13.

6. Matthews1 interview, 29–30; UPC board minutes, September 24, November 19, 1987, and January 28, 1988, UPR; UPC news release, January 28, 1988, UPR; UPC nominating committee file, September 24, 1987, UPR; Schuster1 interview, 16; Knight interview, 6–7.

7. *UP Report*, 1986, 4–5.

8. Ibid., 1988, 2; Cook to UPC board, June 3, 1987, UPR; UPC board minutes, November 19, 1987, January 28 and November 17, 1988, UPR; *WSJ*, January 11, 1988; Davidson1 interview, 48; Schuster1 interview, 14.

9. Drew Lewis to W. L. Adams et al., September 11, 1987, UPR.

10. "Remarks by Drew Lewis," Annual Meeting, Salt Lake City, April 15, 1988, 1–2, UPR.

11. Ibid., 2.

12. Ibid., 3–4.

13. Ibid., 5–7.

14. McAuliffe interview, 42.

15. Gerry Jr. interview, 16; Grove interview, 8–9; Stuart interview, 26, 38; Knight interview, 20–21; Schuster1 interview, 9–11; von Bernuth interview, 15, 17–18; Matthews1 interview, 39; Waller interview, 20.

16. Knight interview, 22–23; Schuster1 interview, 42; Davidson1 interview, 53; Matthews1 interview, 42; Matthews 2 interview, 1.

17. Schaefer interview, 39–41; Knight interview, 23; Matthews1 interview, 40–42; von Bernuth interview, 17–18; Source withheld by request.

18. Knight interview, 22; Schuster2 interview, 30.

19. Schuster1 interview, 9–11.

20. Stuart interview, 38.

21. UPC board minutes, February 25, 1988, UPR.

22. Ibid.; Stuart interview, 51.

23. Stuart interview, 48; von Bernuth interview, 18; UPC board minutes, April 28, 1988, UPR.

24. Grove interview, 18; Schaefer interview, 48.

25. Von Bernuth interview, 18; Schuster1 interview, 13.

26. Surette to Cook, May 18, 1987, UPR; UPC board minutes, May 28, 1987, April 28 and July 28, 1988, UPR; "Report of Matters Approved or Assented to by the Executive Office during Period May 25 through July 25, 1988 Under Authority of the Management Policy Statement," UPR; Schuster1 interview, 13; Schaefer interview, 41, 48; Grove interview, 19.

27. Schuster1 interview, 51–52.

28. Von Bernuth interview, 19; UPC board minutes, July 28, 1988, and January 26, 1989, UPR; Rebensdorf e-mail, May 22, 2009; Marchant interview, 54.

29. Stuart interview, 47–48; Schaefer interview, 41, 50; Matthews1 interview, 34, 38; Grove interview, 16.

30. Schaefer interview, 43–44, 49; Lewis to Schaefer, December 30, 1988, UPR; Schaefer to UPC board, January 3, 1989, UPR; UPC board minutes, January 26 and February 23, 1989, UPR; Chuck Olsen to Lewis, January 6, 1989, UPR.

31. Matthews1 interview, 33–35; UPC board minutes, May 26, October 27, and November 17, 1988, and January 25, 1990, UPR; Matthews office bulletin, December 11, 1989, UPR;

Union Pacific Foundation trustees minutes, January 25, 1990, UPR; Lewis office bulletin, March 14, 1990, UPR; Grove interview, 27, 35–36.

32. UPC board minutes, November 19, 1987, and February 23, 1989, UPR; *UP Report*, 1987, 54–55, 1988, 46–47, 1989, 46–47, and 1990, 46–47. The board actually shrank to sixteen members but then added one member in July 1989. See UPC board minutes, July 27, 1989.

33. Grove interview, 19–20; Gerry Jr. interview, 23; Schuster2 interview, 11–12.

34. Schuster2 interview, 14; Matthews1 interview, 52–53; Davidson4 interview, 39.

35. Gerry Jr. interview, 4; *WSJ*, January 18, 1989.

36. UPC board minutes, January 28, 1988, UPR; *Forbes*, November 14, 1988, 190; Stuart interview, 37; Kawa, "Interview with Walsh," 10. On the day of the interview UP stock stood at 62.

37. Schuster2 interview, 27–28.

38. *Richmond Times-Dispatch*, October 14, 1988; Young interview, 12.

39. McAuliffe interview, 6–7.

40. Ibid., 1–4, 11.

41. Ibid., 16, 42–43.

42. *WSJ*, January 18, 1989; *Forbes*, November 14, 1988, 182.

43. *Forbes*, November 14, 1988, 182, 184, 188.

44. *WSJ*, January 18, 1989.

45. Ibid.

46. Ibid.

47. Duffy interview, 27; King interview, 32, 34.

48. Stuart interview, 64.

49. McCartney interview, 49; Rebensdorf interview, 37–38.

50. Jacobson interview, 29.

51. *Forbes*, November 14, 1988, 190; *WSJ*, January 18, 1989; Stuart interview, 40–41.

Chapter 19

1. Walsh, "Remarks," 12–13; *UP Report*, 1987, 7.

2. Kawa, "Interview with Walsh," 5–6, 24–25, 32.

3. Interview with Tom Watts in **UP**DATE, April 1986, 6.

4. Ibid., 6–7.

5. Ibid., 4–5, 7.

6. Ibid., 7.

7. Kawa, "Interview with Walsh," 29; Marchant interview, 44–45. The agreement got its name from the fact that it originated with the Milwaukee road.

8. Kawa, "Interview with Walsh," 29–30; Marchant interview, 45; Marchant e-mail, May 16, 2008; *UP Report*, 1991, 8; Watts interview, 27–28.

9. Marchant interview, 45–46; Kawa, "Interview with Walsh," 29, 39–42.

10. Marchant e-mail, May 16, 2008.

11. Kawa, "Interview with Walsh," 38, 43.

12. Ibid., 5, 12.

13. Schuster1 interview, 35, 42–43.

14. *WSJ*, January 18, 1989; Matthews2 interview, 14–15; Dolan interview, 23.

15. Source withheld by request; Schaefer interview, 39; Matthews1 interview, 51; McAuliffe interview, 47; Stuart interview, 43.

16. Matthews1 interview, 45; Schuster1 interview, 21; McAuliffe interview, 44; Kenefick interview, 58; Watts interview, 33–34.

17. Matthews1 interview, 44–45; Davidson2 interview, 31; Stuart interview, 33–34; Shoener interview, 70.

18. Schuster1 interview, 18; Schaefer interview, 40; Matthews1 interview, 57; McAuliffe interview, 51; Source withheld by request.

19. *WSJ*, May 25, 1989.
20. Ibid.
21. All figures are calculated from data found in the company's annual reports for the relevant years.
22. *Info*, January/February 1989, 10; Matthews1 interview, 66–67.
23. Matthews1 interview, 65–66; Matthews 2 interview, 13.
24. *UP Report*, 1990, 5.
25. Ibid. All figures are taken from company annual reports for the relevant years.
26. The figures include the railroad and all subsidiaries. They indicate the average number of employees for each year.
27. Ibid.
28. *UP Report*, 1990, 31. All figures are rounded.
29. *NYT*, July 21, 1987; *RA*, December 1987, 42, and March 1988, 57; *Info*, January/February 1989, 12; Matthews to Lewis, January 14, 1988, UPR; UP Railroad board minutes, January 28, 1988, UPR.
30. *RA*, December 1987, 42, and March 1988, 57, 59.
31. *Info*, September 1989, 9–17; *BW*, September 23, 1991 (Fujitsu ad). The *Info* article on the new center is a special report with no page numbers, and is inserted between the page numbers given here.
32. *Info*, January/February 1989, 12–15, and April 1989, 11.
33. Ibid., April 1989, 12–13, June 1989, 4–5, July/August 1989, 5, and September 1989, insert.
34. Ibid., September 1989, insert. Some details are drawn from my visit to the HDC.
35. Ibid.; *UP Report*, 1989, 10, 13.
36. Source withheld by request.
37. Ibid.
38. Davis interview, 6, 30.
39. *Info*, June 1989, 4.
40. Ibid., March 1989, 6–21.
41. Ibid., 9–10.
42. Ibid., 10, 15.
43. McLaughlin interview, 39–40.
44. Ibid., 40–42; *Info*, September 1989, 23.
45. Davidson3 interview, 16; Jacobson interview, 9; *Fortune*, December 18, 1987, 146.
46. Surette to Cook, December 11, 1985, and January 6, 1986, UPR; *RA*, March 1987, 14; Matthews to Lewis, March 4, 1988, UPR; "Chapter One," 18.
47. *RA*, January 1986, 39–40, January 1987, 43, and March 1987, 23.
48. Ibid., January 1987, 43; Lewis to Cook, October 23, 1986, UPR.
49. Lewis to Cook, October 23, 1987, UPR; *RA*, March 1987, 23, and June 1987, 39; UP board minutes, September 24, 1987, UPR; Matthews to Lewis, July 26, 1988, UPR.
50. "Chapter One," 22.
51. UP board minutes, July 26, 1990, UPR; Bryan interview, 56–57; *Info*, March/April 1994, 8. Bryan remained president of UP Technologies.
52. Quotation inside cover of "Chapter Two: Involvement and Growth 1991–1993," UPM, hereafter cited as "Chapter Two."
53. "Chapter Two," 2–3.
54. Ibid., 4–8.

Chapter 20

1. Saunders, *Main Lines*, 220, 233–40.
2. Ibid., 221.
3. Ibid., 187, 281.
4. These paragraphs are drawn from ibid., 249–75. See also *NYT*, November 20, 1982.

5. *Trains,* November 1988, 3–7.
6. These paragraphs are drawn from Saunders, *Main Lines,* 276–96.
7. Ibid., 282–83; Grant, *North Western,* 243–45.
8. Saunders, *Main Lines,* 294; CNW Report, 1983, 2–3, 1984, 2–4, and 1985, 2; Grant, *North Western,* 234–38.
9. *CNW Report,* 1984, 2, and 1987, 3.
10. Ibid., 1985, 2, 1986, 2, 1987, 3, and 1988, 3, 6–7; Grant, *North Western,* 226.
11. Walsh to Lewis, May 4, 1989, UPR; John Rebensdorf, "Acquisition Analysis: CNW Corporation," July 3, 1986, JHR.
12. R. A. Ames to Lewis, September 16, 1986, JHR; "Chicago and North Western Transportation Company," September 15, 1986, 2–10, JHR.
13. Kenefick to Lewis, February 17, 1987, JHR.
14. "Chicago and North Western," March 19, 1987, 1–2, JHR; Walsh to Lewis, May 4, 1989, JHR; "Chicago and North Western," July 13, 1987, JHR; Rebensdorf to Lewis, July 17, 1987, JHR.
15. Rebensdorf to Lewis, July 17, 1987, JHR; "Chicago and Northwestern Summary," July 17, 1987, 1–2, JHR.
16. "Chicago and North Western," September 8, 1987, 1–12, JHR.
17. Ibid., 5–7; Schaefer e-mail, August 11, 2009.
18. Walsh to Lewis, May 4, 1989, JHR.
19. Grant, *North Western,* 243; CNW Report, 1986, 3, 1988, 2–3; *CNW Report to Stockholders, First Quarter 1988,* 4, UPR.
20. Klein, *UP: The Rebirth,* 499, 513; Grant, *North Western,* 239; *Info,* June 1976, 18. An *Info* article claims that the UP first used piggyback service in August 1953 between California and Nevada. See *Info,* September 1972, 6.
21. *UP Report,* 1969, 6; *Info,* March 1970, 4–6, and May 1981, 7; Grant, *North Western,* 239; *CNW Report,* 1985, 11, 1986, 2, 1988, 13, and 1992, 9.
22. *CNW Report,* 1985, 3; *CNW First Quarter Report,* 1988, 3; *RA,* June 1987, 13; Grant, *North Western,* 242.
23. *CNW First Quarter Report,* 1988, 3; *CNW Report,* 1988, 3–4; Saunders, *Main Lines,* 295; Grant, *North Western,* 247.
24. Saunders, *Main Lines,* 294–95; Grant, *North Western,* 247.
25. *CNW Report,* 1988, 2–4, 9–16.
26. "Chicago and North Western Meeting Summary," July 11, 1988, 1–2 and attachments, JHR.
27. Rebensdorf to Walsh with attachments, August 5, 1988, JHR; *NYT,* June 7, 1989; *Trains,* August 1989, 7; CNW Corporation to Its Stockholders, October 5, 1989, 31, UPR, hereafter cited as CNW Letter.
28. CNW Letter, 31; Grant, *North Western,* 248–49.
29. CNW Letter, 31–32; CNW news release, April 6, 1989, UPR.
30. CNW news release, February 28, 1989, UPR; Donaldson, Lufkin & Jenrette Research Bulletin, "CNW Corporation," March 2, 1989, 1–2, UPR.
31. Ibid.
32. "Questions and Answers," UPC Annual Meeting, April 21, 1989, 30, hereafter cited as "Questions and Answers"; Walsh to Lewis and Matthews, May 4, 1989, JHR.
33. Walsh to Lewis and Matthews, May 4, 1989, JHR; UPC news release, May 12, 1989, UPR; *WSJ,* May 15, 1989; Grant, *North Western,* 248.
34. UPC board minutes, May 25, 1989, UPR.
35. CNW letter, 32–33.
36. Ibid., 33; Grant, *North Western,* 249; *WSJ,* June 5 and June 7, 1989; *NYT,* June 7, 1989; *Trains,* August 1989, 7.
37. CNW Letter, 33–36.
38. *WSJ,* June 7, 1989; *Trains,* August 1989, 7; *UP Report,* 1989, 3.

39. Grant, *North Western*, 249–50.
40. Saunders, *Main Lines*, 233–40; J. M. Ostrow to W. P. Barrett et al., February 11, 1985, UPR; Rebensdorf to Ames, April 23, 1986, UPR; Ames to Lewis, August 11, 1986, UPR; "Assessment of Union Pacific's Transcontinental Merger Options," August 11, 1986, UPR.
41. "Conrail," January 26, 1988, UPR; "Future Railroad Industry Structure and Potential for Transcontinental Mergers," March 15, 1988, UPR.
42. "Transcontinental Railroads: Initial Discussion Paper," April 4, 1988, 2–6, 43, UPR. This copy is stamped "draft." As with many of these documents, there is no indication as to who wrote the paper.
43. Ibid., 6–10.
44. Ibid., 22–32, 37.
45. Walsh to Rebensdorf, February 7, 1989, UPR; Rebensdorf to CSX file, February 9, 1989, UPR; Rebensdorf to Walsh, February 9, 1989, UPR.
46. Rebensdorf to Walsh, February 10, 1989, UPR.
47. Rebensdorf to Tetzlaff with attachment, February 15, 1989, UPR; Rebensdorf to Walsh, February 22 and February 27, 1989, UPR; Jim Dolan to Walsh, February 23, 1989, UPR; Dick Peterson to Rebensdorf, February 27, 1989, UPR.
48. Rebensdorf to Bill McDonald et al. with attachment, March 2, 1989, UPR; Itinerary for John Rebensdorf et al., March 6/7, 1989, UPR; "Discussion Points," March 7, 1989, UPR.
49. Dolan to Mike Walsh et al., June 20, 1989, UPR; Rebensdorf to Walsh, June 27, 1989, UPR; Bob Gallamore to Dolan et al., June 27, 1989, UPR; "Personal and Confidential Issues from TC Meeting," June 28, 1989, UPR; "Transcontinental Merger Strategy Issues," undated, UPR; "Business Group Leader Meeting: Issues Raised," July 24, 1989, UPR; "Business Group Leader Meeting: Results of Meeting," July 24, 1989, UPR.
50. "Summary, Conclusions, Recommendations, Observations," undated, UPR; "What Has Changed Since 1986," undated, UPR; Rebensdorf presentation, UPC board of directors meeting, July 27, 1989, 3–6, UPR; Rebensdorf to Walsh, September 20, 1989, UPR.
51. Dale W. Salzman to Bill Hillebrandt et al., December 6, 1989, UPR; Rebensdorf to Walsh, January 8, 1990, UPR; "Eastern Railroad Profiles and Potential Fit with UP," January 22, 1990, UPR; "Project Lincoln: Conclusions to Date," January 23, 1990, UPR; "Project Lincoln: Corporate Culture and Management Issues," January 23, 1990, UPR; "Lincoln Outline for Review with Lewis," undated, UPR; Walsh to Lewis with attachment, February 14, 1990, UPR.
52. Walsh to Lewis with attachment, February 14, 1990, UPR; Rebensdorf to Matthews, February 20, 1990, UPR.
53. *TW*, September 9, 1991, 27; "Project Lincoln: Presentation to Board of Directors Meeting," May 8, 1990, 2–4, UPR. This document, labeled "draft," does not have Walsh's name, but the content makes clear that it was drafted for him to use.
54. "Project Lincoln: Presentation to Board of Directors Meeting," 4–7.

Chapter 21

1. *UP Report*, 1988, 2, 1989, 2, and 1990, 1.
2. Ibid., 1987, 2–3.
3. Ibid., 1988, 2–3; Surette to Cook, May 26, 1987, UPR; Matthews to Lewis, July 26, 1988, UPR; UPC board minutes, July 28 and September 27, 1988, UPR; UPC EC minutes, September 2, 1988, UPR.
4. Lewis to Robinson, March 8, 1989, UPR.
5. Ibid.; "Questions and Answers," 27.
6. UPC board minutes, October 26, 1989, UPR.
7. Ibid.; *UP Report*, 1989, 2–3.
8. *UP Report*, 1989, 28–29.

9. Ibid., 1990, 17; Schaefer interview, 46.

10. *UP Report*, 1987, 19, 1988, 8, 1989, 8, 1990, 17, and 1991, 3, 16; Matthews to Lewis, April 5, 1988, UPR; Knight interview, 41; UPC board minutes, January 25, 1990, UPR.

11. *UP Report*, 1987, 23, 1988, 9, 1989, 9, 1990, 21, and 1991, 20; von Bernuth interview, 14.

12. Source withheld by request; Matthews 2 interview, 7, 54; von Bernuth interview, 52.

13. Slightly differing versions of this meeting are in Davidson1 interview, 45, Davidson2 interview, 28, and von Bernuth interview, 52–53. Davidson called it "a great speech."

14. Von Bernuth interview, 52; Dolan interview, 49; *UP Report*, 1991, 20, 1992, 10, and 1993, 20.

15. *NYT*, November 1, 1994; *Trains*, April 1995, 21; Davidson1 interview, 46; *Outside*, September 1993.

16. Gerry Jr. interview, 12; *Info*, September/October 1996, 10.

17. *UP Report*, 1990, 48, 1991, 48, 1992, 52, and 1993, 48; von Bernuth interview, 53.

18. Matthews 2 interview, 12; Marchant interview, 57–58.

19. Koraleski interview, 20–22.

20. Eisele interview, 46; Shoener interview, 73.

21. Eisele interview, 45–46.

22. Koraleski interview, 21; Jacobson interview, 25; Schuster1 interview, 36–37.

23. This episode is taken from Davidson5 interview, 57–60.

24. *WSJ*, October 5, 1989, and August 8, 1991; *Topeka Capital-Journal*, September 21, 1991; Knight interview, 19–20.

25. *WSJ*, August 8, 1991.

26. Ibid., August 12, 1991; *OWH*, December 18, 1990.

27. *WSJ*, December 18, 1990, and August 12, 1991; *RA*, September 1991, 15.

28. *WSJ*, August 12, 1991; *RA*, September 1991, 15.

29. Waller interview, 11–12; McLaughlin interview, 28; McCartney interview, 19; *Info*, July/August 1991, 2.

30. Davidson 4 interview, 24; Gerry Jr. interview, 20–21.

31. *NYT*, August 8, 1991; *WSJ*, August 8 and August 9, 1991; *Info*, July/August 1991, 6; von Bernuth interview, 26; Waller interview, 8; McCartney interview, 17; Schaefer interview, 51.

32. Jacobson interview, 30; Shoener interview, 73; King interview, 29–30; Eisele interview, 47.

33. Schuster1 interview, 40–42; Matthews 2 interview, 14; Davidson 4 interview, 30; Rebensdorf interview, 51.

34. Davidson1 interview, 24; Dolan interview, 23; Koraleski interview, 22.

35. Schuster1 interview, 43–44; Matthews 2 interview, 16.

36. Schuster1 interview, 43–44; Matthews 2 interview, 16–17; *Fortune*, September 9, 1991, 185.

37. Davidson 4 interview, 32–33; Dolan interview, 22–23; Marchant interview, 57–58.

38. *WSJ*, September 12, 1991, and September 8, 1992; Matthews 2 interview, 12; *NYT*, September 15, 1991, and January 6, 1992; *BW*, November 25, 1991, 174–79; *Fortune*, November 18, 1991, 153–54.

39. Walsh to Joe Adams et al., January 20, 1993, UPR; *WSJ*, January 21 and January 22, 1993, and February 25, 1994; *Fortune*, February 22, 1993, 76–77, and December 13, 1993, 82–84, 88, 90; *BW*, September 20, 1993, 55–57, 60–62, 64; *OWH*, November 2, 1993; *NYT*, May 7, 1994; Drew Lewis to R. Baker et al., May 9, 1994, UPR.

40. Matthews 2 interview, 11.

41. *Info*, July/August 1991, 6.

42. *UP Report*, 1993, 3; Matthews2 interview, 9.

43. Matthews 2 interview, 9.

44. Von Bernuth interview, 13; *Forbes*, January 6, 1992, 173.

Chapter 22

1. Davidson1 interview, 51.
2. Kenefick interview, 190; McLaughlin interview, 22.
3. Dolan interview, 26; Rinn interview, 44; Conley interview, 23; Koraleski interview, 28, 30; Stuart interview, 54; Whited interview, 28.
4. McAuliffe interview, 33.
5. *Info*, July/August 1991, 2.
6. Ibid., 21.
7. Ibid., November/December 1991, 2; Koraleski interview, 28–29; Knight interview, 42; Davidson1 interview, 19.
8. *Info*, October 1990, 10–11; Koraleski interview, 28–29; Knight interview, 36.
9. Koraleski interview, 31; Young interview, 24; Knight interview, 37–38; Watts interview, 50; McLaughlin interview, 32–33; Rinn interview, 46–47.
10. Knight interview, 35; Koraleski interview, 31; Dolan interview, 26; Rinn interview, 45.
11. Koraleski interview, 31–32.
12. Rinn interview, 45–48; Dolan interview, 43; Schuster1 interview, 69; Davidson 4 interview, 19; McLaughlin interview, 34; Young interview, 23; Whited interview, 28.
13. Whited interview, 28.
14. Dolan interview, 27–28.
15. Ibid., 29; Duffy interview, 15.
16. Davis interview, 26.
17. *Info*, September/October 1991, 4; *UP Report*, 1990, 48, 1991, 48; Koraleski e-mail, August 27, 2009; McAuliffe interview, 7.
18. *Info*, July/August 1988, 6–11, and September/October 1991, 4; Koraleski e-mail, August 27, 2009; Eisele interview, 49–50.
19. Saunders, *Main Lines*, 212–16.
20. *JC*, March 26, 1990; *TW*, July 23, 1990, 17–18.
21. Saunders, *Main Lines*, 217; *JC*, March 26, 1990; *TW*, July 23, 1990, 17–18.
22. *TW*, July 23, 1990, 17–18; *JC*, November 19, 1990.
23. *NYT*, April 18, 1991; Saunders, *Main Lines*, 217–18.
24. *NYT*, April 18 and April 19, 1991; Saunders, *Main Lines*, 218; *TW*, July 29, 1991, 8–10, and September 2, 1991, 7–10; *JC*, September 11, 1991; *WSJ*, September 17, 1991.
25. *TW*, September 9, 1991, 39, 41, and December 2,1991, 31; *JC*, September 25, September 28, and December 18, 1991; *WSJ*, November 27, 1991.
26. *NYT*, October 13, 1991.
27. Ibid.
28. *JC*, June 18 and June 25, 1992; *WSJ*, June 29, 1992.
29. *JC*, July 2/3, 1992.
30. Lawrence H. Kaufman, *Leaders Count: The Story of the BNSF* (Austin, Tex., 2005), 290.
31. *TW*, April 5, 1993, 23, 26.
32. Ibid.; *OWH*, April 4, 1993.
33. *JC*, April 18, 1993.
34. *Info*, March/April 1993, 16–19.
35. *RA*, June 1993, 12.
36. Ibid.
37. *Info*, March/April 1993, 14–15.
38. Ibid., July/August 1993, 26–27; *UPDATE*, October 1993, 1–3.
39. *Info*, July/August 1993, 26–27, and September/October 1993, 7.
40. McLaughlin e-mail, September 1, 2006; **UPDATE**, October 1993, 1–3; *Info*, September/October 1993, 7; *UP Report*, 1993, 14; UPC board minutes, September 30, 1993, UPR.
41. **UPDATE**, October 1993, 3; *NYT*, October 6, 1993; *UP Report*, 1993, 14.
42. King interview, 14, 26, 37.

43. All data are taken from *Union Pacific Transportation Companies: Financial and Operating Statistics*, for 1991, 1993, and 1994, hereafter cited as *UP Transportation Companies*. This publication resembled the annual report but was limited to detailed data on the railroad and Overnite. The 1994 version was retitled *Union Pacific Railroad and Overnite Transportation*. The figures as given have been adjusted to fit changes in commodity categories between 1991 and 1994.

44. All data are taken from *UP Reports* for 1991–94, and from *UP Transportation Companies*, 1994, 22.

45. Klein, *Gould*, 269–75, 305–6.

46. Klein, *Harriman*, 264.

47. Ibid., 264–65; *Info*, December 1980, 4–9.

48. *Trains*, January 1993, 50–52.

49. *Info*, June 1983, 11–13.

50. Ibid., January 1985, 18–20; *RA*, June 1985, 43, 49–50.

51. *Info*, August/September 1987, 16–17, and July/August 1989, 7.

52. Ibid., July/August 1989, 7–10; *Trains*, January 1993, 48.

53. *Info*, May/June 1992, 23; *Intermodal Age*, January/February 1990; *TW*, February 5, 1990, 33–34.

54. *JC*, March 13 and April 17, 1990; *Trains*, January 1993, 49; SP news release, September 12, 1990, UPR.

55. *Info*, May/June 1992, 16–24, and September/October 1992, 4.

56. Ibid.; Shoener e-mail, February 8, 2009; *RA*, April 1992, 47–48, and October 1992, 82–83; *UP Report*, 1990, 8.

57. Shoener e-mail, February 8, 2009; *Info*, May/June 1992, 22–23.

58. *RA*, May 1985, 28, March 1986, 27, and April 1986, 22; *WSJ*, January 3, 1986.

59. *Trains*, June 1991, 16; Davidson1 interview, 56.

60. *UP Report*, 1991, 5, and 1993, 14; *TW*, November 15, 1993, 25–26; UPC board minutes, November 18, 1993, UPR.

61. Jacobson interview, 8.

62. Jacobson e-mail, September 9, 2009.

63. *OWH*, April 20, 1993; Rebensdorf interview, 55–56; Davidson3 interview, 24.

64. Schuster1 interview, 40–42.

65. Ibid., 42.

66. *OWH*, April 20, 1993; Matthews2 interview, 58; Watts interview, 68.

67. Young interview, 40; Davidson4 interview, 44–45.

68. Rinn interview, 33.

69. *OWH*, June 13, 1993; *TW*, June 14, 1993, 37.

70. Ibid.

Chapter 23

1. *UP Transportation Companies*, 1991, 2–3, 1992, 3, and 1994, 4–5.

2. Davidson1 interview, 55–56.

3. *UP Report* 1993, 1–12; *JC*, September 5, 1991; *TW*, September 9, 1991.

4. *TW*, September 9, 1991, 28; Schuster1 interview, 22; Matthews1 interview, 47; Schaefer interview, 40; Waller interview, 30; Source withheld by request.

5. Sources withheld by request; Matthews1 interview, 43–44; Knight interview, 24.

6. Source withheld by request; Schuster1, interview, 25–26.

7. Schuster1 interview, 26–27; *Fortune*, March 6, 1995, 176.

8. Schuster1 interview, 27; Matthews1 interview, 46; *Fortune*, March 6, 1995, 176.

9. *Chicago Tribune*, January 12, 1990; *Topeka Capital-Journal*, July 15 and July 20, 1990; *JC*, October 24, 1990.

10. Saunders, *Main Lines*, 249–56; *JC*, October 16, 1990; *Kansas City Star*, October 9, 1991; *Pacific Rail News*, April 1992, 5; Kaufman, *Leaders Count*, 264–70.

11. *JC*, October 16, 1990.
12. Davidson1 interview, 27–28; Kaufman, *Leaders Count*, 296–97.
13. Davidson1 interview, 28, 36.
14. Ibid., 28; Davidson2 interview, 38.
15. Gerry Jr. interview, 18.
16. Kenefick interview, 94, 97, 188; Davidson1 interview, 29.
17. Gerry Jr. interview, 18–19; Davidson1 interview, 28; Schuster1 interview, 54; Schuster 2 interview, 16–17; UPC board minutes, May 26, 1994, UPR.
18. Schuster1 interview, 54; Schuster2 interview, 15–16.
19. Schuster2 interview, 17; Davidson1 interview, 29.
20. Corporate Control Alert, "Blood on the Tracks," March 1995, 1, UPR. This document has no other identification, hereafter cited as "Blood on the Tracks."
21. Schuster1 interview, 53.
22. Davidson1 interview, 27.
23. Von Bernuth interview, 32–34.
24. Gerry Jr. interview, 17; Matthews 2 interview, 28, 32–33; UPC board minutes, May 26, 1994, UPR.
25. *WSJ*, June 2, 1994; *WP*, July 1, 1994.
26. Von Bernuth to Lewis, April 8, 1991, UPR; Lewis to Kissinger, April 8, 1991, UPR; Palmer to Lewis, April 18, 1991, UPR; UPC board minutes, April 18, 1991, UPR; Kissinger to Lewis, October 3, 1991, and October 15, 1992, UPR; Edwin S. Rothschild to Janet D. Stelger, April 2, 1992, UPR; Lewis to Robert P. Bauman, October 19, 1992, UPR; *Info*, November/December 1995, 15.
27. *OWH*, August 7, 1994; *WSJ*, August 11, 1994.
28. "Project 'T,'" August 8, 1994, 1, UPR; "Action Items—Board Conference Call—9/1/94," UPR; "Proposed Script, Board of Directors Meeting, September 1, 1994," August 30, 1994, UPR; UPC board minutes, September 1, 1994, UPR; Lewis to Board, September 19, 1994, UPR.
29. Rebensdorf interview, 25, 27.
30. Matthews2, interview, 19; Matthews e-mails, September 14 and September 16, 2009.
31. "Information sent to Board for 9/28/94 meeting," September 18, 1994, UPR.
32. Lewis to board of directors, September 19, 1994, UPR; UPC minutes of the special committee, September 19, 1994, UPR.
33. UPC board minutes, September 28 and October 5, 1994, UPR.
34. Lewis to Krebs, October 5, 1994, UPR; Stuart interview, 31; Matthews e-mail, September 16, 2009.
35. Two sources withheld by request; Dolan interview, 14–15; *Fortune*, March 6, 1995, 176; Krebs to Lewis, October 6, 1994, UPR; "Blood on the Tracks," 1; Kaufman, *Leaders Count*, 303. The blank space is in the Kaufman original.
36. Kaufman, *Leaders Count*, 301–3.
37. "Blood on the Tracks," 1.
38. Lewis to Krebs, October 5, 1994, UPR; UPC press release, October 5 and October 6, 1994, UPR; Krebs to Lewis, October 6, 1994, UPR; *WSJ*, October 6, 1994; *WP*, October 6, 1994; *TW*, October 17, 1994, 10.
39. Source withheld by request; *WP*, November 3, 1994.
40. Gerry Jr. interview, 9; Two sources withheld by request; *Fortune*, March 6, 1995, 176; *WSJ*, October 31, 1994; *WP*, November 3, 1994; UPC news release draft, October 28, 1994, UPR; *BW*, November 14, 1994, 100.
41. UPC board special meeting minutes, October 28, 1994, UPR.
42. UPC news release draft, October 28, 1994; UPC news release, October 30 and October 31, 1994; *WSJ*, October 31, 1994; *NYT*, October 31, 1994; *WP*, November 3, 1994.
43. Duffy interview, 31; *NYT*, October 7 and October 12–14, 1994; *WSJ*, October 7, October 12, and October 14, 1994; Lewis to Krebs, October 11 and October 12, 1994, UPR; Krebs

to Lewis, October 11, 1994, UPR; UPC news release, October 11 and October 12, 1994; Krebs to SF stockholders, October 12, 1994, UPR; "Special Meeting of Stockholders of Santa Fe Pacific Corporation: Proxy Statement of Union Pacific Corporation," undated, UPR.

44. Lewis to Krebs, October 17, 1994, UPR; John Rebensdorf, "Memorandum re: UP/Santa Fe Merger," October 17, 1994, 4, UPR; *TW*, October 17, 1994, 9–12; Schuster2 interview, 26; *CSM*, October 17, 1994.

45. *WSJ*, October 19 and October 26, 1994; *NYT*, October 19, 1994; Kidder, Peabody release, October 20, 1994, UPR.

46. *TW*, October 24, 1994, 28–29; *WSJ*, October 25, 1994.

47. Lewis to SF stockholders, October 28, 1994, UPR; Krebs to SF stockholders, October 28, 1994, UPR; *WSJ*, October 28, 1994; *NYT*, October 28, 1994; Brown Brothers Harriman release, October 28, 1994, UPR. The change in offer values occurred because the offers were made in terms of exchanging shares. BN, for example, increased its offer from 0.27 to 0.34 shares of BN stock for each share of SF. Changes in the market value of each stock obviously affected the value of the offer.

48. Davidson to Krebs, October 30, 1994, UPR; *RA*, November 1994, 17; UPC news release, October 30, 1994; UPC board minutes, October 28, 1994, UPR.

49. Davidson2 interview, 26; UPC board minutes, October 28, 1994, UPR.

50. Davidson to Krebs, November 1, 1994, UPR; Davidson to SF stockholders, November 1, 1994, UPR; UPC news release, November 1, 1994, UPR; *WSJ*, November1 and November 3, 1994; Krebs to Davidson, November 2, 1994, UPR; *JC*, November 2, 1994; *Ft. Worth Star-Telegram*, November 2, 994; *NYT*, November 3, 1994; Krebs to SF stockholders, November 3, 1994, UPR.

51. UPC board minutes, November 5, 1994, UPR.

52. Ibid., November 8, 1994, UPR; *NYT*, November 7, 1994; *TW*, November 7, 1994, 8; Davidson to Krebs, November 8, 1994, UPR; UPC news releases, November 8 and November 9, 1994, UPR.

53. *WSJ*, November 9, November 10, November 14, and November 15, 1994; UPC board minutes, November 17, 1994, UPR; UPC news release, November 10 and November 14, 1994, UPR; *NYT*, November 10–12 and November 15, 1994; Davidson to Krebs, November 13, 1994, UPR; John J. Burns to Krebs, November 14, 1994, UPR; Krebs to SF stockholders, November 14 and November 15, 1994, UPR; *BW*, November 14, 1994, 100; *TW*, November 14, 1994, 13; *CSM*, November 15, 1994.

54. *WSJ*, November 22, 1994.

55. Ibid., November 29 and November 30, 1994; *NYT*, November 23, November 29, and November 30, 1994; Davidson to Krebs, November 28, 1994, UPR; UPC news release, November 28, 1994, UPR; *TW*, November 28, 1994, 10; Krebs to SF stockholders, November 29, 1994, UPR; Santa Fe Pacific Corporation news release, November 29, 1994, UPR; *JC*, November 30, 1994.

56. Matthews2 interview, 20; UPC board minutes, November 29, 1994, UPR; Daniel E. Lundgren to Lewis, November 29, 1994, UPR; "Conversation with Governor Wilson," November 30, 1994, UPR; Lewis to Roderick E. Walson, December 1, 1994, UPR; *TW*, December 5, 1994, UPR; Lewis to Krebs, December 6, 1994, UPR; Lundgren to Lewis, December 6, 1994, UPR; "Blood on the Tracks," 3–4.

57. UPC news release, December 7, 1994, UPR; *WSJ*, December 8, 1994; *NYT*, December 8, 1994; *BW*, December 12, 1994, 50.

58. UPC board minutes, December 13 and December 20, 1994, UPR; Santa Fe Pacific news release, December 18, 1994, UPR; *TW*, December 19, 1994, 33–34; *WSJ*, December 19, 1994; *NYT*, December 19, 1994; Lewis to Krebs, December 20, 1994, UPR.

59. UPC news release, December 20, 1994, UPR; *NYT*, December 23, 1994; Carl von Bernuth to Drew Lewis et al., December 20, 1994, UPR; Rebensdorf interview, 27–28; Rebensdorf e-mail, September 20, 2009.

60. Rebensdorf interview, 28; Matthews2 interview, 21.

61. Rebensdorf interview, 28.

62. *WSJ*, December 27, 1994, and January 16–20, 1995; *JC*, December 27, 1994; Krebs to SF stockholders, January 13, 1995, UPR; UPC board minutes, January 17, 1995, UPR; Lewis to Krebs, January 17, 1995, UPR; Krebs to Lewis, January 17, 1995, UPR; UPC news release, January 17 and January 18, 1995, UPR; *NYT*, January 18 and January 19, 1995.

63. Krebs to Lewis, January 22 and January 31, 1995, UPR; *WSJ*, January 23–27, January 30, January 31, and February 1, 1995; Santa Fe Pacific news release, January 24, 1995, UPR; *NYT*, January 24 and January 25, 1995; UPC news release, January 26, January 27, and January 31, 1995, UPR; *TW*, January 30, 1995, 9; Lewis to Krebs, January 31, 1995, UPR; Lewis to Grinstein, January 31, 1995, UPR; Grinstein to Lewis, January 31, 1995, UPR; UPC board minutes, January 26, 1995, UPR; von Bernuth to UP board, February 1, 1995, UPR.

64. *WSJ*, February 2, February 3, February 6, February 8, March 10, and March 30, 1995; *OWH*, February 5, 1995; *NYT*, February 8, 1995; *BW*, February 13, 1995; *TW*, February 13, 1995, 20–21; *RA*, May 1995, 63.

65. *WSJ*, December 8, 1994.

Chapter 24

1. Grant, *North Western*, 229–30; *Trains*, April 1994, 42.

2. *Trains*, November 1992, 8, and April 1994, 41–42.

3. *CNW Report*, 1992, 1; *JC*, November 7, 1990; *TW*, August 6, 1990, 52; *Trains*, February 1991, 18B, April 1992, 18, and November 1992, 8–9; *WSJ*, January 27, 1992; Testimony of Richard K. Davidson, *ICC Finance Docket 32133*, January 29, 1993, 1:313–15; Testimony of Robert W. Schmiege, *Docket 32133*, January 29, 1993, 1:327–29. The UP's preferred shares in CNW carried a dividend rate of 13 percent payable in additional preferred stock for the first five years and in cash thereafter.

4. Schmiege testimony 1:328; *ICC Finance Docket 32133* 1:4–5.

5. Davidson testimony 1:316–20.

6. *ICC Finance Docket 32133* 1:6–9; Davidson testimony 1:315–20; Schmiege testimony 1:328–31; UPC board minutes, November 19, 1992, UPR.

7. *TW*, May 24, 1993, 20, and June 28, 1993, 13; *Docket 32133*, Supplement, 14–16, 20–22.

8. J. M. Butler to Steven V. Wilkinson, June 13, 1994, UPR; "CNW Acquisition: Commentary," July 15, 1994, UPR; "CNW Shareholders," September 30, 1994, UPR; *WSJ*, December 14, 1994; "RKD Talking Points on CNW," January 13, 1995, UPR; Rebensdorf e-mail, September 28, 2009.

9. "Agenda: Railroad Strategic Options," February 2, 1995, UPR; Joe O'Connor to Distribution, February 3, 1995, UPR; UPC board minutes, February 23, 1995, UPR; "Iowa Interstate as an Option to CNW for Union Pacific between Chicago and Omaha," February 13, 1995, UPR; O'Connor to Lewis, February 11, 1995, UPR; O'Connor to Rebensdorf, February 13, 1995, UPR; Koraleski to Rebensdorf, February 15, 1995, UPR; "Board Book Material," February 23, 1995, UPR; R. B. Peterson to Mike Boone, February 24, 1995, UPR.

10. CNW board minutes, March 9, 1995, UPR; *Trains*, June 1995, 19; "Highly Confidential" document, undated but clearly March 1995, UPR. The latter document's internal language suggests that it was prepared for Lewis's conversation with Schmiege.

11. *WSJ*, March 13, April 17, April 26, and June 26, 1995; CNW board minutes, March 16, 1995, UPR; J. Tomlinson Hill to CNW board, March 9 and March 16, 1995, UPR; *NYT*, March 8 and March 11, 1995.

12. *WSJ*, June 8, 1990; *Forbes*, May 28, 1990, 39–40, and February 3, 1992, 86.

13. *Forbes*, May 28, 1990, 39, and February 3, 1992, 87; *JC*, August 26, 1992.

14. *JC*, August 25, 1992, and May 17, 1993.

15. Ibid., August 25, 1992; *WSJ*, June 8, 1990.

16. *WSJ*, June 8, 1990; *Real Estate Week* (western edition), March 5, 1990.

17. *Houston Chronicle*, January 12, 1990; *Riverside Press Enterprise*, May 12, 1990; *Los Angeles Times*, June 25, September 10, and September 11, 1990; *Sacramento Bee*, June 29, 1990; *Shreveport Times*, July 12, 1990; *Sacramento News & Review*, September 20, 1990; *Arizona Daily Star*, September 28, 1990, and July 23, 1991; *Hutchinson (Kansas) News*, October 20, 1990; *Inland Valley Daily Bulletin*, November 28, 1990; *Guymon (Oklahoma) Daily Herald*, December 6, 1990.

18. *Albuquerque Journal*, July 21, 1991; *San Diego Evening Tribune*, July 22, 1991; *Los Angeles Times*, July 24, July 25, and August 1, 1991; *Salem Capital Press*, July 26, 1991; *Santa Barbara News-Press*, July 30, 1991; SP news release, July 31, 1991, UPR; *Carpinteria Herald*, July 31, 1991; *San Jose Mercury News*, August 1 and August 4, 1991; *Petaluma Argus-Courier*, August 1, 1991; *San Francisco Chronicle*, August 3, 1991; *Camarillo Daily News*, August 6, 1991; *San Francisco Examiner*, August 8, 1991.

19. *JC*, February 5, 1990; *TW*, June 4, 1990, 8, 10–11; *Forbes*, May 28, 1990, 39; *Trains*, September 1993.

20. *JC*, May 21, 1990, and March 11, 1992; *San Francisco Chronicle*, May 22, 1990; *TW*, May 28, 1990, 8, 10–11; SP news release, November 26, 1990, UPR.

21. *Trains*, September 1993.

22. *San Francisco Chronicle*, May 16, June 4, July 23, and October 2, 1990; SP news release, August 1, 1990, UPR; *Kansas City Star*, August 2, 1990; *Trains*, October 1990 and December 1990, 18; *Rocky Mountain News*, October 4, 1990, and August 27, 1991; *Denver Post*, October 7, 1990, and September 20, 1991; *San Francisco Business Times*, September 13, 1991; *WSJ*, June 8, 1990.

23. *Los Angeles Daily News*, October 13, 1990; *Orange County Register*, October 13, 1990; *JC*, October 16 and October 19, 1990, and January 29, 1992; *TW*, October 22, 1990; *San Jose Mercury News*, August 4, 1991; *Trains*, September 1993.

24. SP Update, November 20, 1991, 1, and February 5, 1992, 1, UPR; *San Francisco Chronicle*, November 11, 1991; *Forbes*, February 3, 1992, 86.

25. SP Update, February 5, 1992, 1–2, UPR.

26. Ibid., 3–6. Emphasis is in original.

27. SP news release, March 2, April 24, June 24, and July 7, 1992, UPR; *JC*, March 11, 1992; *Trains*, September 1993; Davis interview, 33.

28. SP news release, March 20 and April 24, 1992, UPR; *Pacific Shipper*, May 18, 1992, 27; *Denver Post*, May 21, 1992; *Rocky Mountain News*, May 14, 1992; *Distribution*, July 1, 1992, 42.

29. SP Update, April 7, 1992, UPR; *Pacific Shipper*, June 29, 1992; *JC*, August 26, 1992.

30. *JC*, September 3, 1993; *TW*, January 25, 1993, 30–32; *WSJ*, October 26, 1993.

31. SP board minutes, January 27, April 2, May 26, July 1, and August 27, 1993, UPR; *RA*, May 1993; *JC*, May 17, 1993; *TW*, May 24, 1993, 20.

32. *WP*, June 8, 1993.

33. *JC*, July 20, July 23, and July 26, 1993; SP board minutes, September 29, 1993, UPR; *TW*, September 13, 1993.

34. Davis interview, 36; *JC*, September 3, 1993.

35. *JC*, September 3, September 15, and October 5, 1993; *TW*, September 13, 1993.

36. *JC*, September 3, 1993; SP board minutes, September 29, 1993, UPR; *TW*, October 18, 1993, 21–26.

37. *WSJ*, October 25, 1993.

38. *JC*, November 2, November 9, and November 24, 1993; SP board minutes, December 20, 1993, and January 27 and March 1, 1994; Henry Chidgey to John Herbots, October 27, 1993, UPR.

39. SP board minutes, March 1, April 14, June 28, August 25, October 13, November 7, December 13, and December 27, 1994, and April 27, May 30, and June 29, 1995, UPR; Hemmer e-mail, May 14, 2010.

40. Telephone conversation with Jerry Davis, October 12, 2009.

41. Rebensdorf interview, 29.

42. Union Pacific Corporation, Form S-4 filing with the Securities and Exchange Commission, December 1, 1995, 24, 28, UPR, hereafter cited as Form S-4.

43. Ibid., 29; UPC board minutes, February 23, 1995, UPR.

44. Rebensdorf interview, 29; Rebensdorf e-mail, October 5, 2009; Form S-4, 24.

45. Schuster1 interview, 67.

46. Form S-4, 24–25.

47. Ibid.; Rebensdorf interview, 29; UPC board minutes, July 21, 1995, UPR; Rebensdorf e-mail, October 5, 2009.

48. UPC board minutes, July 26, 1995, UPR.

49. Ibid., July 27, 1995, UPR; von Bernuth interview, 54. As von Bernuth explained it, the corporation had to spin off at least 80 percent of the stock to the shareholders to make the transaction tax free.

50. UPC board minutes, July 27, 1995, UPR.

51. Form S-4, 25–26; UPC board minutes, July 21, 1995, UPR; *RA*, September 1995, 20.

52. UPC board minutes, September 28, 1995, UPR; *WSJ*, September 27, 1995; *WP*, September 27, 1995; *NYT*, September 27, 1995; SP board minutes, November 8, 1995, UPR. The SP board ratified the agreement on November 8.

Chapter 25

1. *WP*, October 21, 1995.

2. *WSJ*, April 20, April 26, June 26, and July 3, 1995; *NYT*, April 20, 1995; *RA*, July 1995, 9; *Trains*, June 1995, 20, August 1995, 21, and October 1995, 21; *UP Report*, 1995, 7.

3. Watts interview, 57.

4. *RA*, December 1995, 20; *Trains*, February 1996, 17–18; *WSJ*, November 30, 1995; Davidson1 interview, 41–42; Duffy interview, 30.

5. *RA*, December 1995, 20; *Trains*, February 1996, 18; Eisele interview, 60.

6. McLaughlin interview, 38; Bryan interview, 89; Davidson1 interview, 78.

7. *RA*, December 1995, 20; *Trains*, February 1996, 18, and March 1996, 18; *WSJ*, November 30, 1995; Eisele interview, 55; Form S-4, 39; UPC board minutes, November 30, 1995.

8. *Trains*, February, 1996, 18; Duffy interview, 3; *WSJ*, November 30, 1995; Jacobson interview, 39; Davidson1 interview, 42–43; Eisele interview, 52, 56.

9. Marchant interview, 66, 69; Eisele interview, 52, 56–57.

10. Rebensdorf interview, 35; Eisele interview, 56–57; Marchant interview, 67.

11. Davidson1 interview, 42–43.

12. *WSJ*, November 30, 1995.

13. Saunders, *Main Lines*, 308–10.

14. Ibid., 308–9.

15. *WSJ*, November 27, 1995.

16. Ibid.; *BW*, July 1, 1996, 52; Saunders, *Main Lines*, 309–10.

17. *WSJ*, November 27, 1995; Saunders, *Main Lines*, 310; Davidson1 interview, 52; Hemmer e-mail, May 14, 2010.

18. McAuliffe interview, 29–31.

19. Ibid., 31, 54; *Allentown Morning Call*, January 1, 1996; *BW*, July 1, 1996, 52.

20. *WSJ*, November 27, 1995, and January 1, 1996; *WP*, December 8, 1995; Saunders, *Main Lines*, 311–12.

21. UPC board minutes, January 26 and November 30, 1995, and January 24, 1996, UPR; Gerry Jr. interview, 11.

22. Knight interview, 26–27; Waller interview, 24; Davidson2 interview, 39, Schuster1 interview, 4; Stuart interview, 21.

23. Waller interview, 25; Knight interview, 27–28.
24. Davidson1 interview, 50–51; Davidson2 interview, 14, 17–18.
25. Davidson1 interview, 25; Source withheld by request.
26. Knight interview, 30.
27. Waller interview, 20–23.
28. Ibid., 19, 21.
29. Ibid., 23, 25–27.
30. Knight interview, 31–33.
31. Matthews 2 interview, 32–33; Davidson 2 interview, 38–39; Davidson 4 interview, 33–34; Source withheld by request.
32. Davidson1 interview, 26.
33. Davidson 2 interview, 18–19.
34. Davidson1 interview, 47; Davidson 2 interview, 19; *UP Report*, 1994, 3, 15.
35. Davidson1 interview, 47; Davidson 2 interview, 19; *UP Report*, 1996, 2–3.
36. Jacobson interview, 38
37. Shoener interview, 74; Shoener e-mail, October 28, 2009; Schuster1 interview, 46–47; Waller interview, 44.
38. Davidson1 interview, 49; Eisele interview, 59; *Info*, July/August 1995, 2, and September/October 1995, 2.
39. Duffy interview, 58; *Info*, September/October 1995, 2.
40. *Info*, November/December 1995, cover, 11.
41. Ibid., 2–3.
42. Eisele interview, 59; Knight interview, 43–44; Watts interview, 61; Bryan interview, 88; McLaughlin interview, 36–37; Marchant interview, 90–91; Dolan interview, 29.
43. Eisele interview, 56–57, 60; Marchant interview, 89–91; McLaughlin interview, 35; Conley interview, 26; Young interview, 31; Dolan interview, 29–30; Duffy interview, 59–60; Bryan interview, 88.
44. Watts interview, 60; King interview, 44–45; Duffy interview, 59–60; Waller interview, 44–45.
45. Duffy interview, 59–60; Davidson4 interview, 27; Shoener interview, 76; Marchant interview, 89–91; Dolan interview, 30.
46. Eisele interview, 59–60.
47. Duffy interview, 59, 61.
48. Shoener interview, 77; Waller interview, 44; Knight interview, 43, 45; Marchant interview, 89; Schuster1 interview, 47.
49. Eisele interview, 55–56.
50. Marchant interview, 89; Young interview, 30–31.
51. Rebensdorf interview, 34–35.

Chapter 26

1. *WSJ*, November 16, 1995; *Trains*, January 1996, 22; Davidson to Haverty, September 5, 1995, UPR.
2. *WSJ*, January 17 and March 22, 1996; *NYT*, March 22, 1996.
3. *NYT*, February 3 and March 27, 1996; *RA*, February 1996, 21, and March 1996, 28; *WSJ*, March 27, 1996.
4. Dolan interview, 32; *RA*, December 1995, 46, and March 1996, 41–42.
5. Dolan interview, 31–33; *WSJ*, March 29, 1996.
6. Hemmer interview, 1, 18–19.
7. Ibid., 20–21.
8. *RA*, April 1996, 20–21; *WSJ*, April 1, April 15, and June 4, 1996; *NYT*, April 16 and June 4, 1996.
9. *WSJ*, April 5, 1996; *NYT*, June 10 and June 12, 1996; Source withheld by request.

10. *WSJ*, April 23, May 20, and June 4, 1996; *NYT*, June 4, 1996; *RA*, May 1996, 18, and June 1996, 26.
11. *NYT*, June 4 and June 28, 1996; *WSJ*, June 18, 1996.
12. *WSJ*, July 1, 1996; *NYT*, July 4, 1996.
13. *NYT*, July 5 and July 8, 1996; *RA*, August 1996, 33–34.
14. UPC board minutes, November 30, 1995, UPR; *UP Report*, 1995, 2, 39, and 1996, 2, 25.
15. UPC board minutes, July 25, 1996, UPR; Matthews2 interview, 49–52.
16. Matthews 2 interview, 51–52; *Los Angeles Times*, June 24, 1997; *Fortune*, December 27, 1997; *CNNMoney*, November 22, 1998, and April 3, 2000.
17. *Info*, September/October 1996, 2–3.
18. *NYT*, November 7, 1996; *RailNews*, January 1987, 88.
19. Marchant interview, 89–91; Shoener interview, 76.
20. Kenefick interview, 95–96; Schuster1 interview, 48; Marchant interview, 92; Watts interview, 60; *OWH*, August 7, 1996.
21. Jacobson interview, 39; Kenefick interview, 95; Dolan interview, 30.
22. Source withheld by request.
23. Ibid.; Schuster1 interview, 47–49.
24. Knight interview, 52–53; *RailNews*, January 1997, 88.
25. *Info*, November/December 1996, 2–3; Davis interview, 35–37, 60; *RailNews*, January 1998, 88.
26. Kenefick interview, 57–58, 100; Davidson1 interview, 50.
27. Schuster1 interview, 66–67; UPC board minutes, November 27, 1996, UPR.
28. Schuster1 interview, 67–68.
29. Davidson 2 interview, 60.
30. Davidson 5 interview, 66.
31. UPC board minutes, February 27, 1997, UPR; *NYT*, March 19, 1997; Schuster2 interview, 12.
32. Schuster2 interview, 12; von Bernuth interview, 35; Davidson 4 interview, 37.
33. Davidson5 interview, 2; Gerry Jr. interview, 28.
34. Knight interview, 1–6, 11–13; Stuart interview, 65–66; Waller interview, 31–32; *Info*, March/April 1997, 4; UPC board minutes, April 24, 1997, UPR.
35. Waller interview; 32; UPC board minutes, February 27, 1997, UPR; Knight interview, 13–14; Eisele interview, 62–63; *NYT*, April 23, 199; Davidson5 interview, 64–66.
36. Knight interview, 15; *Info*, March/April 1997, 4; Davidson1 interview, 68; Davidson5 interview, 67.
37. Schaefer to James Watson and Robert Baker, October 15, 1986, and January 27, 1987, UPR; Lew W. Huff to Schaefer, October 26, 1986, UPR; Schaefer presentation to UPC board, October 26, 1987, UPR; Skyway, "Backgrounder," September 1987, 1–2, UPR.
38. Schaefer to Watson, November 16, 1987, and May 27, 1988, UPR; Lewis to Skyway Freight Systems, November 16, 1987, UPR; Schaefer to T. W. Boswell and J. M. Bielenberg, November 17, 1987, UPR; Boswell to Watson and Baker, November 17, 1987, UPR; Baker to Boswell, November 18, 1987, UPR; UPC board minutes, November 19, 1987, UPR; "Skyway—In the Union Pacific Family," May 7, 1992, UPR; *WSJ*, May 13, 1993; UPC board minutes, May 27, 1993, UPR.
39. Matthews to Lewis, October 5, 1994, UPR; Davidson1 interview, 46; Davidson2 interview, 34; UPC board minutes, April 24 and May 29, 1997, UPR; *UP Report*, 1996, 3, 1997, 19, and 1998, 16.
40. Bryan interview, 51–55. See also chapter 15.
41. "Union Pacific Technologies 1987 Long Range Plan," n.d., 1–2, UPR; Surette to Cook, July 27, 1987, UPR; "LINCS," April 19, 1988, 1–4, UPR; "Business Plan Outline," April 20, 1988, UPR; Strategic Planning and Corporate Development Department, "Strategic Use of Information Technology," July 28, 1988, 1–18, UPR.

42. Bryan interview, 57.
43. Ibid.; Davidson2 interview, 34–35.
44. *UP Report*, 1994, 7, 1995, 2, and 1996, 11; *Laredo Morning Times*, January 24, 1993; *RA*, April 1993, 39–42, and October 1994, M23–28; *OWH*, November 18, 1993; *JC*, December 17, 1993; *Info*, July/August 1993, 12–15; *WSJ*, February 9, 1995; *Trains*, May 1995, 21.
45. *NYT*, June 2, 1995.
46. *Trains*, March 1996, 22; *WSJ*, July 12 and December 9, 1996; UPC board minutes, November 20 and November 27, 1996, UPR.
47. Rebensdorf interview, 30–32; Hemmer e-mail, May 14, 2010; Davidson to Haverty, September 5, 1995, UPR.
48. Saunders, *Main Lines*, 316–17. The other unfavorable condition gave BNSF access to any new industry located on lines where it was granted trackage rights.
49. *JC*, December 9, 1996; *WSJ*, December 9, 1996; Gary Stuart to Davidson, December 9, 1996, UPR; *TW*, December 16, 1996, 8–10.
50. *WSJ*, April 30 and June 20, 1997; *NYT*, June 28, 1997; *RA*, August 1997, 24; *Trains*, September 1997, 23; UPC board minutes, January 30, 1997, UPR.

Chapter 27

1. *UP Report*, 1996, 22–23.
2. Ibid., 2; *RailNews*, June 1998, 78; *Info*, March/April 1997, 10.
3. *Trains*, April 1997, 24–29; *Info*, January/February 1997, 16–17, and March/April 1997, 14–15.
4. *Info*, November/December 1996, 16–20, and January/February 1997, 19, 21.
5. *WP*, August 22, August 24, August 27, and October 29, 1997; *WSJ*, July 3, July 27, August 27, and October 30, 1997; *NYT*, August 31, 1997; *Info*, July/August 1997, 5; *RailNews*, January 1998, 27.
6. "Union Pacific Railroad: FRA Reportable Rates, Employee Injuries and Fatalities as Reported at Year End 1982–2001," February 22, 2002, SJM; *WSJ*, July 3, 1997; Duffy interview, 14; *Info*, September/October 1997, 2, 9.
7. *WSJ*, August 27, 1997; *WP*, August 27, 1997; *NYT*, August 31, 1997; *RailNews*, September 1987, 10–11.
8. *WSJ*, September 11, 1997; *NYT*, September 11, 1997; *RA*, October 1997, 17.
9. *RA*, October 1997, 17.
10. *Info*, September/October 1997, 2, 9.
11. *WSJ*, December 1, 1995; Form S-4, 39; Duffy interview, 35, 40; *Info*, September/October 1996, 11.
12. Rebensdorf interview, 40.
13. Davidson1 interview, 66; Shoener interview, 78–79.
14. Duffy interview, 35–36.
15. Davidson1 interview, 66.
16. Duffy interview, 36–37; Koraleski interview, 49.
17. Bryan interview, 63–66.
18. *Info*, September/October 1997, 10–11; *UP Report*, 1997, 10; Rebensdorf e-mail, November 9, 2009.
19. *Info*, May/June 1998, 14–18; *RA*, June 1996, 53.
20. Davidson1 interview, 71.
21. Ibid., 67; *Info*, May/June 1998, 15.
22. Davidson1 interview, 69–70; *Info*, September/October 1996, 22, 24.
23. Duffy interview, 42, 62.
24. *Info*, January/February 1997, 2, 5; *Trains*, January 1997, 20; *RA*, March 1997, 23.
25. UP Railroad board minutes, February 27 and May 29, 1997, UPR; *RA*, March 1997, 23. Although the boards of the corporation and railroad met at the same time, separate minutes

were kept for each meeting. They record the boards as meeting at the same time in the same place with the same directors but transacting different business.

26. *Info*, March/April 1997, 10–12.
27. Ibid., May/June 1997, 8–9; *RailNews*, April 1997, 90.
28. *Info*, May/June 1997, 5, 25; UPC board minutes, April 24 and May 29, 1997, UPR; *RA*, June 1997, 20.
29. *WSJ*, August 29, 1997; Eisele interview, 66.
30. Eisele interview, 66; Hemmer e-mails, November 8 and November 13, 2009; Rebensdorf e-mail, November 18, 2009; Davidson1 interview, 68. The UP retained trackage rights over the 200-mile section sold to BNSF.
31. *Trains*, January 1998, 27–28.
32. Jacobson interview, 48–49; *Info*, March/April 1997, 18; Shoener interview, 79; Rebensdorf e-mail, November 18, 2009.
33. *Trains*, January 1998, 29; Jacobson interview, 49; Hemmer e-mail, November 8, 2009.
34. Rollin D. Bredenberg e-mail, May 16, 2010.
35. Rebensdorf e-mail, November 18, 2009.
36. *Trains*, January 1998, 29–30.
37. *Info*, July/August 1997, 5; Eisele interview, 67.
38. *Info*, July/August 1997, 5; *Trains*, January 1998, 28; Jacobson interview, 49; Shoener interview, 81; *WSJ*, August 29, 1997.
39. Marchant interview, 87–88.
40. *Info*, July/August 1998, 22; Bryan interview, 68.
41. Jacobson interview, 42; *RailNews*, October 1997, 67.
42. Jacobson interview, 53; *RailNews*, December 1997, 78; Source withheld by request.
43. Marchant interview, 73; *NYT*, November 3, 1997.
44. *WSJ*, August 29, 1997.
45. Shoener interview, 82.
46. *Trains*, January 1998, 30; Rebensdorf e-mail, November 18, 2009.
47. Davidson 4 interview, 1–2.
48. Dolan interview, 35; Knight interview, 39–40.
49. King interview, 25–26.
50. Duffy interview, 42–43.
51. Schuster1 interview, 70; von Bernuth interview, 37.
52. Rebensdorf e-mail, November 18, 2009; Davidson4 interview, 1; Waller interview, 33.
53. *BW*, October 6, 1997, 110; Source withheld by request.
54. *BW*, October 6, 1997, 110; Davidson1 interview, 77.
55. Davidson1 interview, 69; *RailNews*, September 29, 1997, 28–29, and October 1997, 66; *Info*, November/December 1997, 6; *WSJ*, August 29 and October 2, 1997.
56. Marchant interview, 72.
57. Davidson1 interview, 69, 77; Dolan interview, 36.
58. Rebensdorf e-mail, November 18, 2009; Dolan interview, 36; Shoener interview, 84; *WSJ*, September 29, 1997; *CNNMoney*, September 29 and October 1, 1997; *NYT*, September 30 and October 1, 1997;
59. Rebensdorf e-mail, November 18, 2009; *WP*, October 2, 1997; *Trains*, January 1998, 30–31; *RailNews*, December 1997, 8–9. For a timetable of steps taken, see *Info*, September/October 1997, 8.
60. *RailNews*, December 1997, 10. The reports to the STB were required as a condition of the SP merger.
61. Dolan interview, 41; Source withheld by request; McAulliffe interview, 59.
62. Shoener interview, 90; *RailNews*, December 1997, 8.
63. Jacobson interview, 66; Rebensdorf interview, 42; Bredenberg e-mail, May 16, 2010.
64. Shoener interview, 85; King interview, 20–21; *RailNews*, December 1997, 8.
65. *BW*, November 24, 1997, 40; *Trains*, January 1998, 26, 30–31.

66. Gerry Jr. interview, 38.
67. *WSJ*, October 2, October 8, and October 13, 1997; *WP*, October 2, 1997; *NYT*, October 2 and November 3, 1997; *BW*, October 6, 1997, 110–11.
68. *WSJ*, October 13, 1997.
69. Ibid., October 2 and October 8, 1997.
70. Ibid., October 8, October 10, October 17, and October 21, 1997; *NYT*, October 21, 1997.
71. *BW*, October 6, 1997, 111; *WP*, October 28, 1997; *RA*, November 1997, 8; *Trains*, January 1998, 32.
72. *Trains*, January 1998, 32.
73. Ibid., 32–33; *NYT*, October 26 and November 1, 1977; *WSJ*, October 27 and November 3, 1997; *WP*, October 28, 1997; *RailNews*, November 1997, 72–73; *RA*, November 1997, 8.
74. Saunders, *Main Lines*, 322–28.
75. *WSJ*, November 6, 1997; *CSM*, November 5, 1997; *NYT*, November 28, 1997.
76. *Trains*, February 1998, 25; *WSJ*, November 18, 1997.
77. *Trains*, February 1998, 24–26.
78. Waller interview, 36.
79. Jacobson interview, 55; Waller interview, 34–35; Young interview, 48–49; Knight interview, 36.
80. McAuliffe interview, 55–57.
81. Knight interview, 37; Davidson2 interview, 44–45; Davidson4 interview, 36; Gerry Jr. interview, 22.
82. Waller interview, 65–66; Gerry Jr. interview, 22; *WSJ*, August 25, 1999.
83. Waller interview, 34–35; von Bernuth interview, 37.
84. Davidson1 interview, 76; von Bernuth interview, 37–38.
85. Waller interview, 35; von Bernuth interview, 38; Eisele interview, 71–72.
86. Davidson1 interview, 76; Davis interview, 39.
87. *Info*, November/December 1997, 6.
88. Bredenberg e-mail, May 16, 2010.
89. *WSJ*, December 4, 1997; *NYT*, December 4 and December 5, 1997; *RA*, February 1998, 16.
90. *Trains*, January 1998, 26.

Chapter 28

1. Dolan interview, 40; Jacobson interview, 56; Duffy interview, 38.
2. *Info*, July/August 1998, 7.
3. Ibid., November/December 1997, 4, and July/August 1998, 20–21; Marchant interview, 75; Bryan interview, 68.
4. Bryan interview, 68–69; *Industry Week*, October 5, 1998, 33–35.
5. *Industry Week*, October 5, 1998, 70; *Info*, November/December 1997, 4–5, and April/May 1998, 6; *RailNews*, April 1998, 9, 23; Hemmer e-mail, May 14, 2010.
6. Marchant interview, 74; *Info*, November/December 1997, 6.
7. *WSJ*, July 18 and October 23, 1997, and January 6 and January 23, 1998.
8. Matthews 2 interview, 35.
9. Ibid.
10. Ibid., 36; Stuart interview, 79.
11. Matthews 2 interview, 36–38; *WSJ*, February 27, 1998.
12. Stuart interview, 82–84; *Treasury & Risk Management*, January/February 1999, 38. The UP called the issue "convertible preferred securities." For a detailed description of them, see *UP Report*, 2000, 45.
13. Matthews 2 interview, 37–38; von Bernuth interview, 20–21; *RailNews*, July 1998, 32.
14. Matthews 2 interview, 36–37.
15. Source withheld by request; Davidson 4 interview, 35.

16. Source withheld by request; Davidson 4 interview, 35–36; Waller interview, 41–42; *BW*, June 15, 1998, 53.

17. *WSJ*, February 10, 1998; *NYT*, February 14, 1998.

18. *WSJ*, February 9, 1998; *CNN Money*, February 9, 1998; Hemmer e-mail, May 14, 2010.

19. Hemmer e-mail, May 14, 2010.

20. *NYT*, February 14, 1998; *WSJ*, February 17, 1998; *BW*, February 23, 1998, 47; *RA*, March 1998, 20.

21. *RailNews*, May 1998, 9.

22. *NYT*, February 14, 1998; *WSJ*, February 17 and 27, 1998; *Trains*, March 1998, 16–17, 76; *BW*, March 2, 1998, 46.

23. *Info*, January/February 1998, 4, March/April 1998, 5, and May/June 1998, 12; *WSJ*, March 12, 1998; *NYT*, March 26 and April 10, 1998; *RailNews*, May 1998, 9.

24. *Fortune*, March 30, 1998, 99, 102; *RA*, April 1998, 24.

25. *RA*, April 1998, 24; *RailNews*, April 1998, 23; *WP*, April 1, 1998.

26. *WSJ*, April 2 and April 20, 1998; *CSM*, April 7, 1998; *WP*, April 17, 1998.

27. *NYT*, April 21, 1998.

28. *CNNMoney*, April 23, 1998; *Trains*, April 1998, 21; *WSJ*, April 24, 1998; *RA*, May 1998, 23.

29. *Trains*, May 1998, 24; *NYT*, July 7, 1998; *RailNews*, July 1998, 23; telephone interview with Mike Hemmer, December 20, 2009; *Info*, March/April 1998, 4, and January/February 1999, 12–16.

30. *WSJ*, May 29, 1998; Saunders, *Main Lines*, 340–45.

31. *WSJ*, April 30, 1998; *RA*, June 1998, 34–35, 70.

32. *RA*, June 1998, 34–35, 70; *Info*, January/February 1998, 8–12.

33. *NYT*, July 7 and August 1, 1998; *WSJ*, July 7, July 24, July 28, August 3, and August 19, 1998; *CNNMoney*, July 23 and August 14, 1998; *RA*, August 1998, 27.

34. Davidson1 interview, 73, 75; Davidson2 interview, 44–45; *Info*, September/December 1998, 8.

35. Rebensdorf interview, 35–36, 40–42; Koraleski interview, 48–49; Marchant interview, 71–72; Young interview, 31–33; Peterson interview, 40.

36. McAuliffe interview, 59; Bryan interview, 79.

37. *Info*, March/April 1998, 2.

38. Ibid. Emphasis is in the original.

39. *Info*, May/June 1998, 8–9; *UP Report*, 1998, 46; Davidson1 interview, 73; Davidson5 interview, 48–49.

40. Duffy interview, 48–49; Davidson5 interview, 37–39; *Info*, September/December 1998, 18.

41. Kenefick, "Railroad Operating Organization," 4. For more detail on Harriman's organization, see Klein, *UP: The Rebirth*, 129–42.

42. *WSJ*, August 25, 1999; *RA*, August 2000, 47–49.

43. *RA*, August 2000, 49.

44. *Info*, May/June 1998, 2, and September/December 1998, 7, 10.

45. Ibid., September/December 1998, 12; Schuster1 interview, 82–83; *WSJ*, August 25, 1999.

46. *NYT*, August 20 and August 21, 1998, and March 7, 1999; *CNNMoney*, August 20, 1998; *RA*, September 1998, 22.

47. *Info*, September/December 1998, 9, 11.

48. Ibid., 8; Kenefick, "Railroad Operating Organization," 1.

49. *JC*, September 14, 1998; *PR Newswire*, August 31, 1998; *RA*, October 1998, 22.

50. *PR Newswire*, August 31, 1998.

51. Duffy interview, 48.

52. King interview, 21.

53. *PR Newswire*, August 31, 1998; *JC*, September 14, 1998.

54. *Info*, September/December 1998, 15.

55. *WSJ*, August 25, 1999.

56. *Info*, September/December 1998, 10, 16.
57. *WSJ*, September 16, 1998; *NYT*, September 16, 1998; *RA*, October 1998, 22; Gerry Jr. interview, 34; Schuster1 interview, 76–77.
58. *Trains*, June 1998, 14–15; *Info*, January/February 1999, 18–19, and May/June 1999, 12–13.
59. Davis interview, 47; "Memo to file," undated, JRD; interview with Ike Evans, June 11, 2008, 7–8, 77–78, hereafter cited as IEvans interview.
60. *Info*, September/December 1998, 16.
61. Matthews1 interview, 68–70; Source withheld by request.
62. *NYT*, September 1, 1998.
63. Ibid.
64. Ibid., August 20, 1998; *Trains*, July 1997, 88–89; *Info*, September/December 1998, 17; *RailNews*, October 1997, 23, November 1997, 27, December 1997, 76–77, and June 1998, 32; *RA*, September 1998, 24.
65. *NYT*, December 22, 1998; *RailNews*, March 1999, 9, 21.
66. *NYT*, March 7, 1999.

Chapter 29

1. IEvans interview, 18–19; Schuster1 interview, 78. For Emerson's story, see Charles F. Knight with Davis Dyer, *Performance Without Compromise: How Emerson Consistently Achieves Winning Results* (Boston, 2005).
2. IEvans interview, 22; Schuster1 interview, 78; Young interview, 39.
3. Knight interview, 48–49; Schuster1 interview, 81; Gerry Jr. interview, 35; Davidson2 interview, 1–2.
4. IEvans interview, 1–3, 18, 23.
5. Ibid., 7–14.
6. Ibid., 15–16.
7. *Info*, September/December 1998, 2.
8. Ibid., January/February 1999, 2–3.
9. *UP Report*, 1999, 1–2, 20, 54; *CNNMoney*, April 23 and October 21, 1999; *BW*, May 10, 1999, 122; *WSJ*, July 12, October 22, and December 20, 1999; *RA*, January 2000, 6.
10. *UP Report*, 1999, 1, 4; *Info*, January/February 1999, 12–16, May/June 1999, 12–13, and Fall 1999, 8–9; *RailNews*, August 1999, 66–67; *Trains*, March 2000, 18, 20.
11. *UP Report*, 1999, 2, 14–15, 54; *WSJ*, May 21 and November 6, 1998, October 26, 1999; *NYT*, November 6, 1998; *CNNMoney*, May 21, 1998, September 23, September 24, and October 25, 1999; *BW*, July 20, 1998, 40; Stuart interview, 87–88.
12. *UP Report*, 1999, 4, 2000, 54, and 2002, 8; *Info*, January/February 1999, 7; *CNNMoney*, April 20, 2000; *WSJ*, April 21, July 28, and October 20, 2000; *RW*, August 2000, 20, and February 2001, 1, 16.
13. *WSJ*, August 25, 1999.
14. *UP Report*, 2000, 9; *RA*, July 2000, 18, and February 2002, 40.
15. *RA*, January 2001, 53–55, and February 2002, 40; *WSJ*, November 6, 2000; *UP Report*, 2001, 7.
16. *RA*, May 2002, 29–31; *Trains*, November 2002, 14.
17. *UP Report*, 2001, 3, 7–16.
18. Ibid., 2002, 6; *Info*, March/April 1999, 2, and Fall 1999, 6–9; *RailNews*, July 1998, 32–33; *RA*, February 2001, 41.
19. *RA*, February 2001, 40–41; *Info*, Fall 1999, 4–9.
20. *Info*, Fall 1999, 8, and Winter 2000–2001, 8–13; *WSJ*, February 4, 1999; *UP Report*, 2002, 12; *RA*, March 1999, 6, February 2001, 40–41, and June 2002, 32–33.
21. *WSJ*, December 20, 1999; *CNNMoney*, December 20, 1999; *NYT*, December 21, 1999; *Trains*, April 2000, 12–13.

22. *Trains*, April 2000, 12–13; *CNNMoney*, January 20, 2000; *WSJ*, March 7, 2000; *NYT*, December 21, 1999.

23. *Trains*, May 1998, 15; *WSJ*, March 20, 2000.

24. *CNNMoney*, July 14, 2000; *RA*, July 2000, 47; *WP*, July 15, 2000.

25. *Info*, Spring 2000, 17–21; *RA*, October 2001, 31–33.

26. Waller interview, 48–50; *UP Report*, 2000, 11, and 2002, 10; *RA*, November 2001, 18, and December 2001, 6; *WSJ*, October 16, 2001; *Info*, March/April 1999, 2.

27. Lamb, *Evolution of the American Diesel Locomotive*, 138. For the evolution of AC motors, see Maury Klein, *The Power Makers* (New York, 2008), passim.

28. *Forbes*, February 19, 1990, 30; *JC*, May 29, 1992, and November 15, 1993; *Trains*, June 1992, 16; *RA*, December 1993, 43–44, and March 1994, 44–45; *NYT*, January 15, 1994; *WSJ*, March 25, 1993.

29. *WSJ*, June 8, 1992; *Trains*, November 1995, 55–56.

30. *RA*, April 1994, 22; *NYT*, May 14, 1994; *WSJ*, May 16, 1994; *Trains*, June 1994, 18, and October 1994, 18. Figures for the acquisitions are all taken from *UP Reports*.

31. *RA*, March 1994, 44–45, and April 1995, 20.

32. Ibid., April 1995, 20; *NYT*, May 14, 1994; *Trains*, November 1995, 61, January 1996, 29, and February 1998, 23; *RailNews*, January 1998, 42.

33. *NYT*, October 7, 1999; *RA*, November 1999, 20, and January 2000, 12.

34. *RA*, July 1997, 33–38; *RailNews*, January 1998, 40, and September 1998, 33; *Trains*, September 1998, 18.

35. *Info*, Fall 1999, 16–18.

36. *RA*, March 1996, 63; *Trains*, August 1997, 43.

37. *RA*, March 1996, 63, and April 1996, 33–34; *Trains*, April 1996, 23, August 1997, 43, and October 1998, 20; *RailNews*, December 1998, 77, and April 1999, 69.

38. *Trains*, January 2004, 59–61.

39. Ibid.

40. Surette to Cook, July 2, 1987, UPR; Charles Olsen to Walsh, July 9, 1987, UPR; *RA*, October 1987, 31, and April 1990, 32–35.

41. *RA*, February 1991, 16, and July 2000, 18; *JC*, January 27, 1992; Matthews to Lewis, December 12, 1993, UPR; *Info*, Fall 2001, 20–21.

42. *Trains*, January 2004, 61, 63.

43. Ibid., March 2001, 38–39.

44. Ibid., 40; *RA*, October 2002, 27.

45. *RA*, October 2002, 26.

Chapter 30

1. Duffy interview, 41.

2. IEvans interview, 31, 82–83; Rinn interview, 52; Hemmer telephone interview, December 20, 2009.

3. IEvans interview, 83; Kenefick, "Draft Memorandum," 2.

4. IEvans interview, 55; Knight interview, 46; Jacobson interview, 65.

5. Hemmer telephone interview, December 20, 2009.

6. Whited interview, 15–16, 18–19.

7. Marchant interview, 79, 82–84.

8. Young interview, 37–38; Waller interview, 50–51; Hemmer telephone interview, December 20, 2009; Koraleski e-mail, December 28, 2009.

9. Marchant interview, 83; Duffy interview, 53; IEvans interview, 55.

10. Duffy e-mail, December 18, 2009; Knight interview, 45; Davis interview, 50; Dolan interview, 43; Waller interview, 47.

11. Whited interview, 17; IEvans interview, 29.

12. IEvans interview, 16, 27–28.

13. Dolan interview, 43; Rinn interview, 51; Davidson4 interview, 1; Hemmer telephone interview, December 20, 2009.

14. Duffy interview, 17; Waller interview, 54; Davis interview, 51; Davidson4 interview, 1.

15. Marchant interview, 81; Rebensdorf e-mail, December 22, 2009.

16. IEvans interview, 33–34, 65–66; Gerry Jr. interview, 36; Conley interview, 31.

17. Hemmer telephone interview, December 20, 2009; IEvans interview, 34–35.

18. *UP Report*, Spring 2000, 2; Koraleski e-mail, December 28, 2009.

19. *UP Report*, 2001, 2, 22; *CNNMoney*, April 26, July 19, and October 29, 2001, and January 24, 2002;.*RA*, August 2001, 16, November 2001, 19, and February 2002, 9; *WSJ*, October 19, 2001, and January 25, 2002.

20. *RA*, July 2001, 20, and May 2002, 15; *UP Report*, 2001, 53.

21. *UP Report*, 2002, 1–14; *RA*, May 2002, 16, August 2002, 12, September 2002, 26, November 2002, 12, and February 2003, 13; *CNNMoney*, April 25, July 18 and October 24, 2002; *WP*, July 19, 2002; *WSJ*, October 25, 2002, and January 23, 2003.

22. *RA*, October 2002, 26; *WSJ*, January 23, 2003; *Info*, January/February 1999, 3, and Fall 1999, 3; Whited interview, 20.

23. Schuster1 interview, 78–79; Koraleski interview, 3–4.

24. Koraleski e-mail, December 28, 2009.

25. Whited interview, 20–21.

26. IEvans interview, 50.

27. Ibid., 50–51.

28. Ibid., 56.

29. Ibid., 57.

30. Ibid., 57–58; Rebensdorf e-mails, December 22, 2009, and June 2, 2010.

31. Koraleski e-mail, December 28, 2009; Davidson5 interview, 7; *Info*, Fall 2000, 4–5; Koraleski interview, 3–4, 54–56.

32. Bryan speech to UP board, January 27, 2000, 10; Bryan presentation to Security Analysts, November 15, 2001, 6. Emphasis is in the original. I am grateful to Merill Bryan for providing me with copies of these documents.

33. Eisele e-mail, October 29, 2009.

34. Ibid.; *WSJ*, June 14, 2000; *UP Report*, 2000, 4, 16–17; Davidson5 interview, 37–38; *Info*, Summer 2000, 2.

35. Davidson5 intervew, 38; *WSJ*, June 14, 2000.

36. *UP Report*, 2000, 1, 4, 16–17; Davidson5 interview, 38–39.

37. Eisele e-mails, October 29 and December 24, 2009; Rebensdorf interview, 64–66.

38. IEvans interview, 32, 72.

39. Ibid., 32, 59, 71; Hemmer telephone interview, December 20, 2009; *UP Report*, 2000, 13.

40. Rebensdorf e-mail, December 22, 2009; Duffy interview, 52; Hemmer telephone interview, December 20, 2009.

41. Duffy interview, 51–52; Jacobson interview, 65; Young interview, 38; Source withheld by request.

42. Duffy interview, 51; Source withheld by request.

43. Hemmer interview, 2; Hemmer telephone interview, December 20, 2009; IEvans interview, 73. Von Bernuth retired May 31, 2004; Dolan retired the next day after serving as vice chairman of the railroad.

44. Young interview, 49.

45. IEvans interview, 69.

Chapter 31

1. Hemmer telephone interview, December 20, 2009; *UP Report*, 2001, 4, and 2002, 2; Saunders, *Main Lines*, 307.

2. *UP Report*, 2001, 4.

3. Ibid., 2003, 2, 51; *WP*, August 5, 2003; *WSJ*, March 25 and July 25, 2003; *RA*, May 2003, 14, 17, and September 2003, 16.

4. Marchant interview, 79; *UP Report*, 2000, 51; *CNNMoney*, December 27, 2000; *RA*, January 2001, 20; Rebensdorf e-mail, December 30, 2009.

5. Marchant interview, 80, 84; Hemmer telephone interview, December 20, 2009; Rebensdorf e-mail, December 30, 2009.

6. Duffy interview, 54; Dolan interview, 26; Hemmer telephone interview, December 20, 2009.

7. Young interview, 35; Rebensdorf interview, 48.

8. Knight interview, 50–51.

9. Young interview, 33–34; Marchant interview, 87; Rebensdorf e-mail, December 30, 2009.

10. *WSJ*, May 5, 2004.

11. Duffy interview, 54–55; Hemmer telephone interview, December 20, 2009.

12. Davidson2 interview, 42; Duffy interview, 56; Jacobson interview, 60, Rebensdorf interview, 46; Hemmer telephone interview, December 20, 2009.

13. Rebensdorf e-mails, December 30, 2009, and January 2, 2010. Guarantee pay guaranteed workers a certain number of miles per month whether they worked that many or not. Protection amounted to the same thing—payment whether work was performed or not. Both types were usually embedded in agreements. UP inherited a number of high levels of guarantee pay from SP agreements.

14. Rebensdorf e-mail, December 22, 2009.

15. Hemmer interview, 26; Davidson2 interview, 42.

16. Duffy interview, 54; Hemmer interview, 26–27; Koraleski interview, 56; *RA*, April 2003, 6.

17. Koraleski interview, 56.

18. Duffy interview, 55.

19. Rebensdorf e-mail, December 30, 2009; Hemmer telephone interview, December 20, 2009.

20. Duffy interview, 55; *CSM*, October 27, 2003; *RA*, November 2003, 6.

21. Marchant interview, 84.

22. Ibid., 84–85.

23. *UP Report*, 2003, 2–3.

24. *RA*, November 2003, 18, and December 2003, 25.

25. Ibid., February 2004, 11, and March 2004, 16; *WSJ*, January 22, 2004.

26. Ibid.

27. Davidson2 interview, 1.

28. Ibid., 1–2.

29. Young interview, 42–43.

30. Ibid., 43–44.

31. IEvans interview, 69; *NYT*, January 31, 2004.

32. Young e-mail, January 1, 2010; Young interview, 46.

33. Young interview, 16, 46, 50–52.

34. *NYT*, March 31, 2004; *Trains*, June 2004, 13.

35. *WSJ*, April 1, May 5, and July 22, 2004; *RA*, May 2004, 4; *Trains*, June 2004, 12.

36. *NYT*, March 31, 2004; *TW*, May 24, 2004, 1; *Trains*, June, 2004 12–13; IEvans interview, 47.

37. *NYT*, June 18, 2004; *RA*, July 2004, 31–34.

38. *WSJ*, July 22, 2004.

39. Rebensdorf interview, 47.

40. *Trains*, August 2004, 10–11; *WSJ*, August 10, 2004; *RA*, October 2004, 11.

41. *RA*, September 2004, 4, and December 2004, 4.

42. Ibid., September 2004, 4, 37.

43. *UP Report*, 2004, inside cover; *RA*, April 2004, 17, August 2004, 12, and November 2004, 13; *NYT*, April 30, 2004; *BW*, May 31, 2004; Davidson2 interview, 42.

44. Jacobson interview, 60; von Bernuth interview, 47; Duffy interview, 6.
45. *RA*, May 2004, 4; Hemmer interview, 21–22.
46. Matthews1 interview, 68–71; Matthews2 interview, 13–14, 39–40.
47. IEvans interview, 47–48.
48. Ibid., 53.
49. Ibid., 44–48.
50. Young interview, 36, 38, 41.
51. Ibid., 53.
52. Duffy interview, 58.
53. Hemmer interview, 25–26.

Epilogue

1. *WSJ*, March 25, 1993; *RA*, September 2004; conversation with Dennis Duffy, October 30, 2008.
2. "Corporate Disaster Recovery Financial Program," November 17, 1993, UPR; UP Technologies board minutes, November 17, 1993, and July 12, 1994, UPR; UP Technologies, "Wireless Communications Research Study," December 1994, 2–4, UPR.
3. Duffy conversation, October 30, 2008; Young interview, 52.
4. Duffy conversation, October 30, 2008.
5. Hemmer interview, 28.
6. Ibid., 29–30.
7. *RA*, July 20, 2001; *WSJ*, January 14, 2004.
8. Davidson 2 interview, 41.
9. Young interview, 1–2; Duffy interview, 1; Koraleski interview, 1–2.
10. Rebensdorf interview, 69; Young interview, 5; Koraleski interview, 16; Duffy interview, 3.
11. Brenda Mainwaring e-mail, January 4, 2010.
12. Young interview, 57–58.

INDEX

Note: Page numbers in *italics* indicate maps.